National Accounting Handbook

for Practical Compilation

Professional Edition

- This handbook reflects the major methodological revisions introduced in the 2025 System of National Accounts (2025 SNA). Some numerical examples are based on data compiled under the 2008 SNA framework; however, this does not affect the conceptual interpretation or practical application of those examples.
- All proceeds (royalties) from this publication will be donated to programs supporting young adults preparing for independent living.

ISBN 979-11-990821-0-6 (print)
ISBN 979-11-990821-1-3 (PDF)

First published in 2026 by National Accounts Institute

Table of Contents

Preface xviii

Chapter 1. Structure of National Accounts 1

1.1 Introduction 1

1.2 Coverage of the System of National Accounts 4

1.3 The Compilation procedure of the sequence of economic accounts 7

Chapter 2. Understanding basic concepts of national accounts 10

2.1 The production boundary 10

2.2 Product Balances 11

2.3 Types of taxes and subsidies 15

2.3.1 Types of taxes 15

2.3.1.1 Taxes on products 16

2.3.1.2 Gross or net recording of value added tax 21

2.3.1.3 Special types of taxes 22

2.3.2 Types of subsidies 23

2.4 Types of prices applied in the SNA 23

2.4.1 Basic price 24

2.4.2 Producer's price 25

2.4.3 Purchaser's price 25

2.5 Product balance reflecting the types of prices 28

2.5.1 The goods and services account, gross value-added, and GDP 30

2.5.2 Components of gross value-added 32

2.6 Residence and GDP 33

2.7 Establishments and industries, institutional units and institutional sectors 34

2.7.1 Establishments and industries 35

2.7.2 Institutional units and institutional sectors 36

2.8 Types, valuation and use of output 38

2.8.1 Definition of output 38

2.8.2 Types and valuation of output 39

2.8.3 Use of output 41

Chapter 3. Supply and use tables: their functions and structure 45

3.1 Functions of supply and use tables 45

3.2 Structure of supply and use tables 46

3.2.1 Structure of the supply table 47

3.2.2 Structure of the use table 48

3.3 The structure of supply and use tables incorporating price types 50

3.4 Valuation basis for each component in supply and use tables 54

3.4.1 Valuation of components in the supply table 54

3.4.2 Valuation of components in the use table 55

Chapter 4. Components of the supply table 57

4.1 Output 57

4.1.1 Market output 58

4.1.2 Non-market output 64

4.1.3 Output for own final use 67

4.1.4 Estimation methods of output by industries 69

4.2 Imports 71

4.3 Distribution margin and transport margin 75

4.3.1 Distribution margins 76

4.3.1.1 Definition of distribution margin 76

4.3.1.2 Allocation of distribution margins 77

4.3.2 Transport margins 79

4.3.2.1 Definition of the transport margin 79

4.3.2.2 Allocation of the transport margin 82

4.4 Taxes on products and subsidies on products 83

4.4.1 Types of taxes on products 84

4.4.2 Types of subsidies on products 85

4.5 Adjustment of ownership transfer costs 86

4.6 Example of the supply table 86

Chapter 5. Components of the use table 88

5.1 Intermediate consumption 88

5.1.1 Types of intermediate consumption 89

5.1.2 Valuation of intermediate consumption 89

5.1.3 Estimation of intermediate consumption 90

5.2 Final consumption expenditure 91

5.2.1 Household final consumption expenditure 92

5.2.1.1 Methods for estimating household final consumption expenditure 93

5.2.1.2 Actual final consumption of households 94

5.2.1.3 COICOP Classification of households' expenditure 95

5.2.2 Final consumption expenditure of general government 96

5.2.2.1 Estimation method of government's final consumption expenditure 97

5.2.2.2 Individual consumption versus collective consumption of general government 97

5.2.2.3 COFOG classification of government expenditure 98

5.2.3 Final consumption expenditure of NPISHs 99

5.2.3.1 COPNI classification of NPISHs' expenditure 100

5.3 Gross capital formation 101

5.3.1 Gross fixed capital formation 101

5.3.2 Changes in inventories 106

5.3.2.1 Types of inventories 106

5.3.2.2 Valuation of changes in inventories 108

5.3.2.3 Estimation method of changes in inventories 110

5.3.3 Acquisitions less disposals of valuables 110

5.3.3.1 Valuation and accounting for acquisitions less disposals of valuables 110

5.4 Exports 111

5.5 Gross value added 112

5.5.1 Remuneration of employees 112

5.5.2 Other taxes on production and other subsidies on production 114

5.5.3 Operating surplus and mixed income 115

5.5.4 Depreciation 117

5.5.5 Depletion of natural resources 117

5.6 Example of the use table 118

Chapter 6. Practical compilation of the supply and use tables 120

6.1 Selection of the classification systems 120

6.2 Collection of source data 121

6.3 Balancing procedure for the supply and use tables 125

6.3.1 Procedure for the column adjustment 126

6.3.2 Procedure for the row adjustment 128

6.3.3 Balancing the data for columns and rows 128

6.4 Compilation of supply and use tables for the benchmark year 129

6.4.1 Estimation of output 130

6.4.2 Estimation of imports and exports 134

6.4.2.1 Estimation of imports and exports of goods 134

6.4.2.2 Estimation of imports and exports of services 134

6.4.3 Estimation of intermediate consumption 136

6.4.4 Estimation of final consumption expenditure 140

6.4.5 Estimation of gross fixed capital formation 143

6.4.5.1 Estimation of buildings and structures 143

6.4.5.2 Estimation of machinery and equipment 144

6.4.5.3 Estimation of cultivated assets as gross fixed capital formation 146

6.4.5.4 Estimation of intellectual property products 146

6.4.6 Estimation of changes in inventories 148

6.5 Compilation of supply and use tables for non-benchmark years 149

6.6 Compilation of supply and use tables by the product flow method 152

6.6.1 Estimation of expenditure-side GDP items by the product flow method....152
6.6.1.1 Selection of the product classification....153
6.6.1.2 Estimation methods by the expenditure item....154
6.7 Compilation of the use table at basic prices....158
6.7.1 Extraction of distribution margins....161
6.7.2 Extraction of transport margins....163
6.7.3 Extraction of taxes less subsidies on products....164
6.7.4 Derivation of the use table at basic prices....166
6.7.5 Separation of the imports use table and domestic use table....167
6.8 Calculation of GDP using the use table....174
Chapter 7. Classification of industry and institutional sector....176
7.1 Establishment as a production unit, and industry....177
7.2 Institutional unit and institutional sector....178
7.3 Classification of domestic institutional sectors....179
7.3.1 Corporation....179
7.3.2 General government....181
7.3.3 Non-profit institution....181
7.3.4 Unincorporated enterprise and quasi-corporation....183
7.3.5 Household....184
7.3.6 Scope and classification of public sector....186
7.4 Correspondence between institutional sectors and industries....187
7.5 Procedure for classifying the data of production unit into that of institutional sector....189
7.6 Cross-classification by industry and institutional sector....191
Chapter 8. Basic concepts of the sequence of economic accounts....194
8.1 Some basic concepts for the sequence of economic accounts....194
8.1.1 Flows and stocks....194
8.1.2 The accrual basis of recording....195
8.1.3 Double entry versus quadruple entry accounting....196

8.1.4 Netting, consolidation, and "net" concepts 199

8.2 Characteristics of the sequence of economic accounts 200

8.3 Statistical data sources of the sequence of economic accounts 208

Chapter 9. Current accounts 210

9.1 The production account 210

9.2 Income accounts 212

9.2.1 Earned income accounts 212

9.2.1.1 The generation of earned income account 212

9.2.1.2 The allocation of earned income account 214

9.2.1.2.1 Components of earned income 215

9.2.1.2.2 Property income 218

9.2.2 Transfer income accounts 225

9.2.2.1 The income transfers other than transfers in kind account 225

9.2.2.1.1 Current transfers versus capital transfers 227

9.2.2.2 The social transfers in kind account 229

9.2.2.2.1 Social transfers in kind 230

9.2.3 Use of income accounts 232

9.2.3.1 The use of disposable income account 232

9.2.3.2 The use of adjusted disposable income account 234

9.3 Supplementary explanations on income accounts 236

9.3.1 The concepts of income in the SNA 236

9.3.1.1 Accounting treatment of property income 237

9.3.1.2 Transfer income in the balance of payments 239

9.3.1.3 Social transfers in kind 239

9.3.1.4 Entrepreneurial income 240

9.3.1.5 Income on equity, distributable income of corporations, and retained earnings 240

9.3.2 Life insurance and non-life insurance 242

9.3.3 Social insurance schemes 244

9.3.4 Imputation and rearrangement of transactions......248

9.3.4.1 Rerouting transactions......249

9.3.4.2 Partitioning transactions......257

9.3.5 Social contributions and social benefits......258

9.3.5.1 Social contributions......258

9.3.5.2 Social benefits......261

9.3.5.3 Distinction between social benefits and social transfers in kind......263

9.3.6 Accounting treatment by insurance types (Comprehensive summary)......264

9.3.6.1 Accounting treatment of non-life insurance......264

9.3.6.2 Accounting treatment of life insurance......265

9.3.6.3 Accounting treatment of social contributions and social benefits in social security schemes......266

9.3.6.4 Accounting treatment of social transfers in kind by social security schemes......267

9.3.6.5 Accounting treatment of employment-related pension......269

Chapter 10. Accumulation accounts (I)......272

10.1 The capital account......273

10.1.1 Classification of non-financial assets......273

10.1.2 Compilation of the capital account......276

10.1.3 Components of the capital account......278

10.1.3.1 Gross fixed capital formation......278

10.1.3.2 Costs of ownership transfers......280

10.1.3.3 Changes in inventories......281

10.1.3.4 Acquisitions less disposals of valuables......282

10.1.3.5 Depreciation......284

10.1.3.6 Non-produced assets......285

10.1.3.7 Depletion......291

10.1.3.8 Capital transfers......293

Annex to 10.1: Representation of the sequence of economic accounts in a matrix form......295

10.2 The financial account....297

10.2.1 Classification of financial assets....297

10.2.2 Compilation of the financial account....298

10.2.3 Components of the financial account....301

10.2.3.1 Items related to other current accounts....306

Chapter 11. Accumulation accounts (II) and balance sheets....311

11.1 The other changes in the volume of assets and liabilities account....311

11.1.1 Main items and structure of the account....311

11.1.2 Examples of accounting treatment for main items in the account....313

11.2 The revaluation account....316

11.2.1 Measurement of nominal holding gains and losses....317

11.2.1.1 Measurement of nominal holding gains and losses on non-financial assets....318

11.2.1.2 Measurement of nominal holding gains and losses on financial assets....320

11.2.2 Measurement of neutral holding gains/losses and real holding gains/ losses....322

11.3 The balance sheet....323

11.3.1 Compilation of balance sheets....324

11.3.2 Valuation of balance sheet items....327

11.3.2.1 General valuation methods for balance sheets....328

11.3.2.2 Valuation of produced non-financial assets....329

11.3.2.3 Valuation of non-produced non-financial assets....329

11.3.2.4 Valuation of financial assets and liabilities....330

11.3.2.5 Valuation of net worth....331

Chapter 12. The government account and the NPISHs account....333

12.1 The government account....333

12.1.1 Data sources for the government account....334

12.1.2 Revenue and expenditure of the government....334

12.1.3 Government's output, balance of earned income, disposable income....338

12.1.4 Government's final consumption expenditure and actual final consumption....340

12.1.5 Government's capital account and financial account 344

12.2 The NPISHs' account 345

12.2.1 Revenue and expenditure of NPISHs 346

12.2.2 NPISHs' output, final consumption expenditure and actual final consumption 346

12.2.3 The case of NPISHs that produce both non-market and market output 348

Chapter 13. International accounts and the rest of the world account 349

13.1 Framework of international accounts 349

13.2 Accounting principles of international accounts 350

13.3 Compilation of international accounts 352

13.3.1 Compilation of balance of payments 353

13.3.1.1 Types of external transactions in the balance of payments 353

13.3.1.2 Example of compiling the balance of payments 354

13.3.2 Imports and exports of goods in the balance of payments 358

13.3.2.1 Classification of the imports and exports of goods 358

13.3.2.2 Deriving the total value of goods in the BOP using customs data 361

Annex to 13.3.2: Merchanting, Goods sent abroad for processing, and Factoryless goods producers 363

13.3.3 Imports and exports of services in the balance of payments 374

13.3.3.1 Classification of imports and exports of services 374

13.3.3.2 Example of compiling the imports and exports of services 377

13.3.4 Derivation of the freight and insurance services in the BOP 378

Annex to 13.3.4: Treatments of imports/exports of the freight and insurance in the BOP and the supply and use tables 381

13.3.5 Treatment of interest and FISIM in the balance of payments 385

13.3.6 Compilation of the international investment position 386

13.4 Compilation of the rest of the world accounts 387

13.4.1 Compilation of the current account, capital account and financial account in the ROW accounts 388

13.4.2 Conversion from the integrated IIP to the rest of the world accounts 390

Chapter 14. Derivation of output for special industries (Supplement to Chapter 4) 391

14.1 Agriculture, forestry and livestock industry..391

14.1.1 Estimation of agricultural output..391

14.1.2 Estimation of livestock output..394

14.1.3 Estimation of forestry output..396

14.2 Wholesale and retail distribution..397

14.3 Financial and insurance services..401

14.3.1 Central bank..403

14.3.2 FISIM..404

14.3.2.1 Selection of reference rates and calculation of FISIM..407

14.3.2.2 Accounting treatment of FISIM..410

14.3.2.3 Accounting treatment of FISIM in external transactions..411

14.3.2.4 Example of recording FISIM in the supply and use tables..412

14.3.2.5 Example of recording FISIM by institutional sector in the sequence of economic accounts..413

14.3.3 Insurance industry..416

14.3.3.1 Nature of different types of insurance..417

14.3.3.2 Output of non-life insurance and reinsurance..418

14.3.3.3 Output of life insurance and annuities..423

14.3.3.4 Output of the social security pensions and employment-related social insurance pensions..427

14.3.4 Standardized guarantee schemes..429

14.4 Dwelling services industry..431

14.4.1 Methods for measuring dwelling services..432

14.4.2 Accounting treatment of dwelling services in the SNA..432

14.5 Paid domestic services..434

14.6 Research and development (R&D)..435

14.6.1 Nature and valuation of research and development..435

14.6.2 Recording of research and development expenditure in the SNA..437

14.6.2.1 R&D expenditure of the corporations sector....437

14.6.2.2 R&D expenditure of non-market producers (government and NPISHs)....438

14.6.3 Derivation of output and gross fixed capital formation for R&D....439

14.7 Computer software, data and databases....443

14.7.1 Computer software....443

14.7.1.1 Output of computer software....444

14.7.1.2 Measuring gross fixed capital formation of computer software....445

14.7.1.3 Presentation of computer software in the supply and use tables....446

14.7.2 Data and databases....447

14.8 Mineral exploration and evaluation....450

14.9 Military equipment....451

14.10 Head offices and ancillary activities....453

14.11 Travel agency services....455

14.12 Digital products....457

14.12.1 Categories of digital products and national accounts treatment....458

14.12.2 Output of free platform....459

14.12.3 Output of free software....460

Chapter 15. Calculation of output and value-added using business financial statements...462

15.1 Calculation of output, intermediate consumption, and value added for non-financial corporations....464

15.2 Calculation of output, intermediate consumption, and value added for financial corporations....469

Chapter 16. Basic concepts for the compilation of volume and real indicators....471

16.1 Current prices and constant prices....471

16.1.1 Distinction between volume terms and real terms....472

16.1.2 Conversion of values at current prices into volume or real measures....473

16.2 Concepts of index numbers and their application in the SNA....475

16.2.1 Basic understanding of index numbers....475

16.2.1.1 Value index, volume index and price index....475

16.2.1.2 Concept and calculation of modified indices....478

16.2.2 Two-period comparison indices....481

16.2.2.1 Characteristics of Laspeyres and Paasche indices....481

16.2.2.2 Example of constructing modified Laspeyres and Paasche indices....483

16.2.2.3 Superlative indices....485

16.2.3 Practical example of index compilation....486

16.2.4 Chain indices....488

16.2.4.1 Characteristics and features of chain indices....488

16.2.4.2 Practical compilation of chain volume indices....491

16.3 The measurement of prices and the treatment of quality changes....497

16.3.1 Methods of measuring individual product prices for price indices....497

16.3.1.1 Matched-model approach....497

16.3.1.2 Hedonic approach....498

16.3.1.3 Production cost approach....500

16.3.1.4 Model pricing versus specification pricing approach....501

16.3.2 Treatment of quality changes....502

16.3.2.1 The distinction between volume and quantity....502

16.3.2.2 Preferred price indices for the measurement of volumes....504

Chapter 17. Compilation of volume measures in the SNA....505

17.1 Volume measurement in the national accounts....506

17.1.1 Volume measurement of GDP from the production side....506

17.1.1.1 Deflation of output....509

17.1.1.2 Deflation of intermediate consumption....512

17.1.2 Volume measurement of GDP from the expenditure side....513

17.1.2.1 Deflation of final consumption expenditure....513

17.1.2.2 Deflation of gross capital formation....515

17.1.2.3 Deflation of exports and imports....517

17.1.3 Volume measurement of GDP from the income side....518

17.1.3.1 Deflation of remuneration of employees....519

17.1.3.2 Deflation of taxes less subsidies on production....519

17.1.3.3 Deflation of operating surplus and mixed income....520

17.1.4 Deflation using the chain index method....520

17.2 Compilation of the supply and use tables in volume terms....521

17.2.1 Price indices used to compile the supply and use tables in volume terms....521

17.2.2 Compilation of the supply and use tables in volume terms....525

Chapter 18. Derivation of aggregate measures of real income....529

18.1 Derivation of real income aggregates from the production side of GDP in volume terms....529

18.2 Derivation of real income aggregates from the expenditure side of real GDP....533

18.3 Derivation of real income aggregates by the chain index approach....535

18.3.1 Data required to derive real income aggregates using chain index techniques....535

18.3.2 Calculation of real income aggregates on the production side using chain index techniques....535

18.3.3 Calculation of real income aggregates on the expenditure side using chain index techniques....537

18.3.4 Example of deriving GDP in volume terms and real income aggregates using chain index techniques....537

18.4 Calculation of the GDP deflator, GDP growth rate, and sectoral contributions to the GDP growth....540

Chapter 19. Major compilation techniques for quarterly national accounts....542

19.1 Benchmarking: Resolving inconsistencies between quarterly and annual data....543

19.2 Compilation of quarterly chain indices....547

19.2.1 Annual overlap technique....547

19.2.2 One-quarter overlap technique....551

19.2.3 Over-the-year technique....553

19.3 Calculation of quarter-to-quarter growth rates using seasonally adjusted data....556

19.3.1 Method for removing seasonality....556

19.3.2 Year-to-year growth rates versus quarter-to-quarter growth rates....560

19.3.3 Measurement of calendar effects 561

19.3.4 Adjustment of outliers 562

19.3.5 Procedures of seasonal adjustment 562

19.3.6 Methodology of seasonal adjustment using a model-based approach 563

19.3.6.1 Decomposition of the original series 563

19.3.6.2 Indirect and direct seasonal adjustment 569

19.3.6.3 Consistency between annual totals of original unadjusted series and seasonally-adjusted data 571

19.3.6.4 Use of software packages for seasonal adjustment 572

Chapter 20. Measurement of capital stock, depreciation, and capital services 574

20.1 Overview of the OECD approach to measuring capital stock 574

20.1.1 Procedure for measuring capital stock and depreciation 575

20.1.2 Retirement function, age-efficiency function, and age-price function 576

20.1.2.1 Retirement function 576

20.1.2.2 Age-efficiency function and age-price function 578

20.2 Derivation of the age-price function 580

20.2.1 Declining-balance method and straight-line method 580

20.2.2 Straight-line method combined with a retirement function 581

20.2.3 Present value of efficiency method 584

20.2.3.1 Efficiency function of a single asset 585

20.2.3.2 Age-efficiency function for a cohort of assets 588

20.2.3.3 Age-price function under the present value of efficiency method 589

20.3 Estimation of gross capital stock, productive capital stock, and net capital stock 593

20.3.1 Estimation of gross capital stock 593

20.3.2 Estimation of productive capital stock and costs of capital services 595

20.3.2.1 Productive capital stock 595

20.3.2.2 Capital services 596

20.3.3 Estimation of net capital stock 597

20.3.4 Comparison of gross, productive, and net capital stock 600

20.4 Derivation of depreciation 600

20.5 Summary of methods for measuring capital stocks and depreciation 602

Chapter 21. Transformation of the supply and use tables into input-output tables 604

21.1 Introduction 604

21.2 Converting supply and use tables to input-output tables 606

21.2.1 Principles for constructing transformation tables 607

21.2.1.1 Transformation to a product-by-product input-output table 607

21.2.1.2 Transformation to an industry by industry input-output table 609

21.2.1.3 Clarifying the terminology of the input-output table 610

21.2.2 Examples of constructing transformation tables 611

21.2.2.1 Constructing product-by-product IOTs 611

21.2.2.2 Constructing industry-by-industry IOTs 614

21.3 Practical procedures for deriving input-output tables 616

21.3.1 Compilation of product-by-product IOTs under the product technology assumption 616

21.3.2 Compilation of product-by-product IOTs under the industry technology assumption 620

21.3.3 Compilation of industry-by-industry IOTs under the fixed industry sales structure assumption 621

21.3.4 Compilation of industry-by-industry IOTs under the fixed product sales structure assumption 623

21.3.5 Handling negative cell entries in the input-output table under the product technology assumption 624

21.3.5.1 Almon method 625

21.3.5.2 Hybrid (or mixed) technology assumption method 626

21.3.5.3 Manual adjustments 629

21.3.6 Pre-adjustments required for transforming SUTs into IOTs 630

21.4 Examples of deriving input-output tables from supply and use tables 633

21.4.1 Derivation of a product-by-product IOT under the product technology assumption 634

21.4.2 Derivation of a product-by-product IOT under the industry technology assumption 635

21.4.3 Derivation of an industry-by-industry IOT under the fixed industry sales structure.............636

21.4.4 Derivation of an industry-by-industry IOT under the fixed product sales structure.............637

Annex to Chapter 21: Matrix formulas for transforming SUTs into IOTs under the technology and sales structure assumptions (quoted from the 1968 SNA).............638

Chapter 22. Interpretation and application of the input-output table.............644

22.1 Basic concepts of the input-output table.............644

22.1.1 Presentation of imports in the input-output table.............645

22.1.2 Basic structure of the input-output table.............646

22.1.3 Input coefficients versus output coefficients.............649

22.1.4 Intermediate input ratio and intermediate use ratio.............651

22.1.5 The Leontief matrix and the Leontief inverse.............651

22.1.6 Requirements.............652

22.1.7 Ghosh inverse.............655

22.2 Applications of input-output analysis.............655

22.2.1 Derivation and interpretation of the total requirements table.............656

22.2.2 Types of total requirements table.............660

22.2.2.1 Derivation of total requirements table in an IOT with a net-exports column.............661

22.2.2.2 Derivation of total requirements table from the IOT that separates domestic output and imports.............662

22.2.3 Impact analyses based on the quantity model.............663

22.2.3.1 Total effects on economic variables by changes in final use for domestic output.............666

22.2.3.2 Effects generated by the production activity of a specific industry.............674

22.2.3.3 Summary of impact analyses in the quantity model.............680

22.2.4 Measurement of forward and backward linkages using inverse matrices.............681

22.2.5 Impact analyses based on the price model.............682

22.2.5.1 Methodology for impact analyses on the price side.............682

22.2.5.2 Examples of impact analysis in terms of prices.............686

22.2.5.3 Summary of impact analyses by the price model.............693

22.3 Assumptions and limitations of the input-output analysis.............694

22.4 Updating intermediate input coefficients in the input-output table 694

22.4.1 Principle of the RAS method 695

22.4.2 Use of RAS software 700

22.5 Aggregation to a higher-level classification using a conversion matrix 701

References....704

Index....707

About the Author.... 717

Preface

National accounts provide a systematic framework for measuring the economic activities of a national economy in accordance with internationally recognized accounting standards. While corporate accounting records economic activities at the level of individual enterprises, national accounts measure economic activities at the level of the entire national economy. Because national accounts are grounded in well-defined concepts and rigorous methodological principles, it is possible to establish standardized compilation procedures and develop manuals to guide their practical implementation. At the same time, national accounts must faithfully reflect evolving economic realities by applying accounting measurement techniques that are conceptually sound and internationally comparable. National accounts compilers must therefore continuously monitor changes in economic structures and incorporate appropriate measurement methods into their compilation practices. The periodic revisions of the System of National Accounts (SNA) reflect these ongoing efforts to ensure that the framework remains relevant in a changing economic environment.

The process of compiling national accounts can be likened to constructing a building based on a complex architectural blueprint. A well-constructed building requires both high-quality foundational materials and advanced construction techniques. Similarly, the compilation of national accounts requires reliable statistical inputs as well as robust and well-designed compilation methodologies. Neither element can be neglected. While statistical source data provide the essential foundation, the methodologies used to transform those data into a coherent accounting system are equally critical. This book focuses on providing the methodological techniques necessary to construct a complete and internally consistent system of national accounts.

National accounts manuals typically explain both individual components and the overall accounting framework simultaneously. This approach, while comprehensive, can make it difficult for beginners to fully grasp the structure and compilation process. Because these manuals often assume prior familiarity with technical terminology and concepts, it may be challenging for new practitioners to understand the framework in a step-by-step manner. In practice, a comprehensive understanding of national accounts can only be achieved through repeated learning and hands-on experience. This book seeks to address this challenge by presenting national accounts compilation methods from the perspective of a compiler actively constructing the accounting system, rather than from that of an external observer. The methodological framework is explained systematically, and numerous examples based on both hypothetical and actual statistical data are provided to illustrate key concepts. In addition, relevant methodological guidance from international manuals is cited where appropriate.

In technical and applied disciplines such as national accounting, visualization plays a crucial role in facilitating understanding. Experience has shown that diagrams, accounting frameworks, and numerical examples provide the most effective means of conveying complex concepts. From the learner's perspective, working through numerical examples and visual representations enables a more precise and intuitive understanding than relying solely on descriptive explanations. Accordingly, this book places strong emphasis on the use of diagrams, structured accounting presentations, and numerical illustrations to enhance clarity and comprehension.

This book reflects more than two decades of the author's professional experience and research in national accounts. The decision to undertake this work was motivated in part by encouragement from colleagues and mentors, including Yeon-Ok Yoon, former Director General of Statistics Korea, whose support played an important role in bringing this project to completion. The work began in the spring of 2013 and has since evolved into its present form through continued refinement and practical experience.

The primary objective of this book is to provide practical guidance for beginners and intermediate-level practitioners engaged in the compilation of national accounts. The chapters are organized to introduce fundamental concepts in the early sections, followed by more advanced and specialized topics. While certain concepts are revisited in different contexts, this is intended to reinforce understanding within the broader accounting framework. Particular emphasis is placed on explaining GDP-related transactions using the framework of the supply and use tables, and national income-related transactions using the sequence of economic accounts. In addition, the book highlights the methodological developments introduced in the 2025 SNA, enabling readers to understand both the conceptual changes and their practical implications.

The structure of this book consists of six main parts. Chapters 1 and 2 introduce the fundamental concepts necessary for understanding national accounts. Chapters 3–6 and 14–15 provide detailed explanations of the structure, components, and compilation methods of the supply and use tables, which serve as the central framework for national accounts compilation. Chapters 7–13 explain the sequence of economic accounts, which represent the complete accounting system for measuring economic activities and their outcomes. Chapters 16–18 address the compilation of price indices and the estimation of volume and real measures, which are essential for measuring real economic growth by removing the effects of price changes. Chapters 19 and 20 discuss the compilation of quarterly national accounts and methods for estimating capital stock. Finally, Chapters 21 and 22 explain the transformation of supply and use tables into input-output tables and demonstrate how input-output techniques can be used to analyze economic impacts. Considerable effort has been devoted to presenting practical compilation techniques based on the author's professional experience. It is hoped that this book will serve as a useful reference for national accounts compilers, supporting both the development of compilation skills and the implementation of internationally recommended standards, including those introduced in the 2025 SNA.

Lastly, the author would like to express his sincere gratitude to the many individuals and institutions whose support, guidance, and encouragement made the preparation of this book possible. In particular, the author is deeply grateful to the staff of the Ministry of Data and Statistics in Korea (formerly Statistics Korea), including former Commissioner **In-sil Lee** and former deputy Commissioner Yeon-Ok Choi, who provided valuable opportunities for research and discussion on national accounts and encouraged me to undertake this work. The author also wishes to express his profound appreciation to **Barbara Fraumeni**, former Chief Economist of the U.S. Bureau of Economic Analysis (BEA), who broadened his perspective on national accounts by providing him with an invaluable opportunity during his time at the BEA (May 2001–April 2002). The author is equally grateful to **Paul Schreyer**, **François Lequiller**, and **Denis Ward** of the OECD Statistics Directorate, whose guidance and collaboration during the author's secondment to the OECD (September 2003–August 2006) provided a deeper understanding of international standards and methodologies in national accounts and strengthened the author's global perspective on statistical compilation.

The author would also like to acknowledge with sincere appreciation **U Kyin Htay** and **Ramesh Kolli**, with whom he worked closely as a consultant to the Asian Development Bank (May 2017–October 2018) in supporting the development and compilation of Myanmar's national accounts. Their collaboration provided valuable experience in applying international standards within a developing country context. The author is deeply indebted to colleagues at the Economic Statistics Department of **the Bank of Korea**, whose professional environment provided the foundation for developing practical expertise in national accounts compilation. The author also expresses his sincere appreciation to Professor **Jörg Beutel** for his valuable guidance and insights into input-output analysis and its application in economic measurement.

Special thanks are extended to **Andrew Sharpe**, Executive Director of the International

Association for Research in Income and Wealth (IARIW), whose encouragement and advice provided important support during the preparation and publication of this book. Finally, the author expresses his heartfelt gratitude to his family for their unwavering support, patience, and encouragement throughout the many years required to complete this work.

January 2026

Yong-Gil CHO

Chapter 1. Structure of National Accounts

1.1 Introduction

In a paper published in early 2000 by the Bureau of Economic Analysis (BEA), the institution responsible for compiling national income statistics in the United States, GDP and the related national income accounts were described as one of the greatest inventions of the 20th century[1]. The paper explained that just as satellites in space observe the Earth's weather conditions, the state of a national economy can be monitored using the economic aggregate called GDP.

In practice, these indicators are widely used by policymakers, economists, entrepreneurs, and other economic entities to assess whether a nation's economy is in a state of boom or recession and to determine if measures for economic stimulus are necessary. In this sense, compiling the national accounts, which encompass these indicators, is a vital task that consolidates all underlying economic data to derive a comprehensive measure of a nation's economic performance. This process can be considered a sophisticated methodology that processes and integrates individual economic data and statistics as components to construct a holistic view of the economy. If compared to architecture, it is akin to constructing a building by combining numerous raw materials and various technologies into a unified structure.

The figures in the national accounts provide economic policymakers with the most comprehensive and objective indicators of the aggregate outcomes and resource stocks of a national economy. While most economic indicators show only a fraction or one dimension of the economy, the indicators in the national accounts serve as a comprehensive measure. The business cycle indicator, which is a means to measure fluctuations of the national economy as a whole, is derived by weighting and synthesizing heterogeneous economic variables, but the most reasonable way to identify business cycles is to measure fluctuations in real GDP, a key statistic of the national accounts. Rather than artificially weighting heterogeneous economic indicators, measuring national production and income indicators converted into a uniform monetary scale enhances objectivity in identifying economic situation.

Historically, the origin of national accounts can be traced to the early 20th century, when the

---

[1] Landefeld Steven (2000 Jan.), One of the Greatest Inventions of the 20th Century. (Survey of Current Business).

growing economic role of governments highlighted the need for measuring macroeconomic aggregates. As governments increasingly focused on formulating macroeconomic policies and assessing the availability of national resources in times of emergency, the demand for reliable economic aggregate measurements emerged. In response to these historical demands, the national accounts evolved into the most comprehensive and essential indicators for measuring a nation's overall economic performance and analyzing business cycles.

In the national accounts, a unified measure for capturing economic phenomena is monetary units, which allows for aggregation and integration of diverse economic data. For instance, measuring industrial activities such as the production of goods or the construction of railroads and roads using their respective unique units of measurement would make it difficult to derive a consolidated result. However, by converting these activities into a common measure - monetary terms - an objective and integrated measurement becomes feasible.

Since the national accounting is a technique that comprehensively measures the economic activities over a specific period of time based on specialized accounting standards, the compilation process requires a high level of technical expertise in the compilation process. National account compilers need at least several years of relevant work experience and statistical processing skills, and additionally, they must be familiar with the following areas of specialized knowledge in advance.

Prior understanding of accounting concepts

National Accounting, as a tool for measuring economic activities, are based on a distinct accounting framework. This framework extends the measurement scope from the economic activities at the enterprise level to those at the national level. Despite the broader scope and the introduction of various concepts and application rules grounded more deeply in economic theory, national accounting can be largely be considered an extension of business accounting. For example, the adoption of different price types (basic price, producer's price, and purchaser's price), the treatment of value-added tax (VAT), and the inclusion of ancillary costs in the calculation of purchaser's price reflect the characteristics of business accounting and follow, in practice, the bookkeeping conventions of business and tax accounting[2]. Furthermore, the quadruple-entry used

[2] For example, the acquisition cost of goods for inventories such as materials and supplies purchased by an enterprise are recorded as the total amount paid at the time of purchase, including freight and insurance charges. Similarly, fixed assets purchased by an enterprise are recorded at the total amount paid, including all associated costs (i.e. costs of ownership transfer) at the time of purchase.

in national accounts is an expanded application of the double-entry bookkeeping principles fundamental to corporate accounting. Similarly, the financial statements prepared by enterprises (e.g., income statement, statement of changes in equity, and balance sheet) are implemented in national accounts as the sequence of economic accounts (current accounts, accumulation accounts, and balance sheets).

Key balancing items in national accounts, such as GDP, GNI, and savings, are derived from the principle that values of both debt and credit sides in the account must be equal. Additionally, the accrual basis, which is universally applied in the SNA with respect to timing of recording transactions, is a direct adoption of the accounting principles employed in business accounting. Furthermore, the 2008 SNA incorporates trends reflecting the International Financial Reporting Standards (IFRS), which serve as a common accounting standard across countries.

Prior understanding of economic concepts

National accounts define production, expenditure, and income distribution at the national level from a macroeconomic perspective to comprehensively assess a nation's economic performance. Based on these definitions, national accounts depict the flow of supply and use of goods and services at the national level using the "product balance" identity. The **System of National Accounts (SNA)**, co-published by the United Nations and four other international organizations (European Commission, International Monetary Fund, Organization for Economic Co-operation and Development, and World Bank), provides definitions for the scope of production, consumption, investment, and income as applied to the product balance identity and explains in detail the specific methods for their measurement.

Unlike traditional business accounting, national accounts incorporate economic concepts to measure economic activities, introducing distinctions in their approach. For instance, fixed assets and inventories are valued using the Perpetual Inventory Method (PIM) to exclude holding gains and losses on assets and treat them separately. This method differs from traditional business accounting practices. Additionally, the measurement of depreciation (consumption of fixed capital) is based on valuing fixed assets at the present value of future rental income. These measurement approaches, grounded in economic concepts, fundamentally differ from the traditional business accounting method, which relies on acquisition costs as the basis for valuation. The 2025 SNA measures capital services, in the same manner as labour services, from the perspective of factor inputs, thereby enabling the compilation of analytical indicators such as capital productivity and capital intensity. This approach clarifies the role of capital as a factor of production and strengthens the economic basis for analyzing the production structure.

Prerequisites for understanding national accounts

For those who are new to the national accounts, having a prior understanding of a few basic concepts can be helpful in comprehending the content of this book and gaining a clearer understanding of the overall structure of the national accounts. The key terms are summarized as follows:

- **Understanding basic economics concepts**: Product balance identity, production, products, economically significant prices, output, expenditures (intermediate consumption, final consumption, gross fixed capital formation, changes in inventories, depreciation).
- **Understanding accounting system**: T-type account representation, types of prices used in product valuation (basic price, producer price, purchaser's price), value-added tax system, structure of government finance (taxes and subsidies system), accounting principles (e.g., accrual basis), and imputed transactions (imputation).
- **Understanding indices**: Basic theory of price indices, reference year (base year, 100), weight base year, current prices, constant prices.
- **Basic units for statistical data collection**: Distinction between establishments and institutional units.
- **Basic calculation method of matrix in input-output tables**: Inverse matrix, transpose matrix, unit matrix, unit vector, etc.

These terms will be partially explained in Chapter 2 and further elaborated in more detail in the relevant sections of each chapter.

1.2 Coverage of the System of National Accounts

According to the 2025 System of National Accounts (2025 SNA), a manual established by the United Nations and other international organizations (hereafter, unless otherwise stated, "the SNA" refers to the 2025 SNA), the system of national accounts consists of the **integrated framework** which constitutes its core, and a set of **thematic and extended accounts** (formerly referred to as satellite accounts). Within the integrated framework, the SNA sequence of economic accounts must be compiled. To construct this sequence of economic accounts, a set of bridging or supplementary tables are prepared, including the supply and use tables and input-output tables, the accounts in volume terms, labour market tables, capital stock and capital services tables (introduced in the 2025

SNA), as well as other various supporting tables. The overarching objective of the system of national accounts is to compile the sequence of economic accounts, through which the key aggregate indicators of national accounts, such as GDP, GNI and a wide range of other macroeconomic indicators are derived. In particular, the supply and use tables constitute the most essential supplementary tables for compiling the sequence of economic accounts, presenting the supply and use of goods and services within the national economy in a matrix format. These tables serve as a bridge linking basic data sources to the sequence of economic accounts. Furthermore, the accounts in volume terms provide information on real income measures from the volume perspective, thereby supplying indispensable inputs for economic monitoring and macroeconomic policy formulation. This handbook places substantial emphasis on the sequence of economic accounts, as well as on the compilation methods of the supply and use tables, the volume-term (or real-term) national accounts and capital stocks, which must be prepared in advance for the sequence of economic accounts to be constructed.

Figure 1.1 Coverage of the system of national accounts

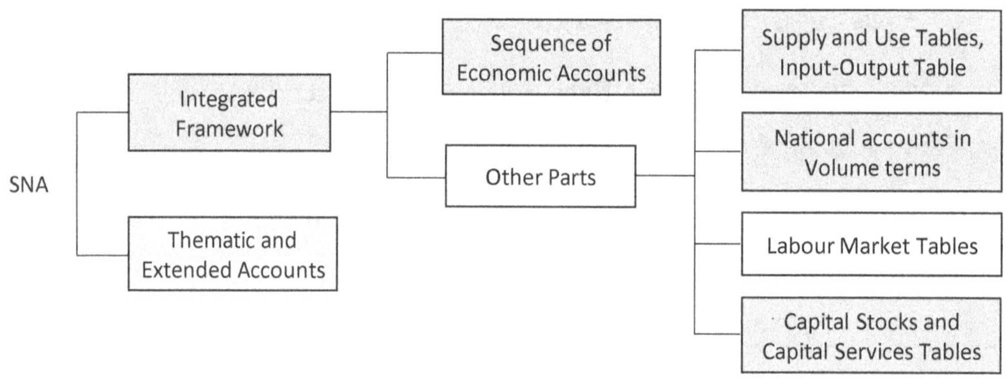

The sequence of economic accounts is a set of T-form accounts of production, income distribution, expenditure, capital accumulation, financial transactions, other economic activities and balance of assets and liabilities in a national economy over a period of time. These accounts are presented by economic entities which are collectively referred to as **institutional sectors** in the SNA (i.e., corporations, government, households, non-profit institutions serving households, and the rest of the world sector). The sequence of economic accounts can be regarded as an expansion of the financial statements of economic entities, such as corporations, to the national level.

The diagram below (Figure 1.2) illustrates the structure of the sequence of economic accounts. These accounts are composed of the **current accounts** (the production account, the generation of earned income account, the allocation of earned income account, the income transfers account, the use of income accounts), **accumulation accounts** (the capital account, the financial account, the other changes in assets and liabilities account), and **balance sheets**. In each account of the sequence of economic accounts, a **balancing item** is derived as the difference between the totals on the left-hand and right-hand sides. These balancing items include GDP, operating surplus, GNI, GNDI, saving, and net worth.

Figure 1.2 Summary of the Sequence of economic accounts

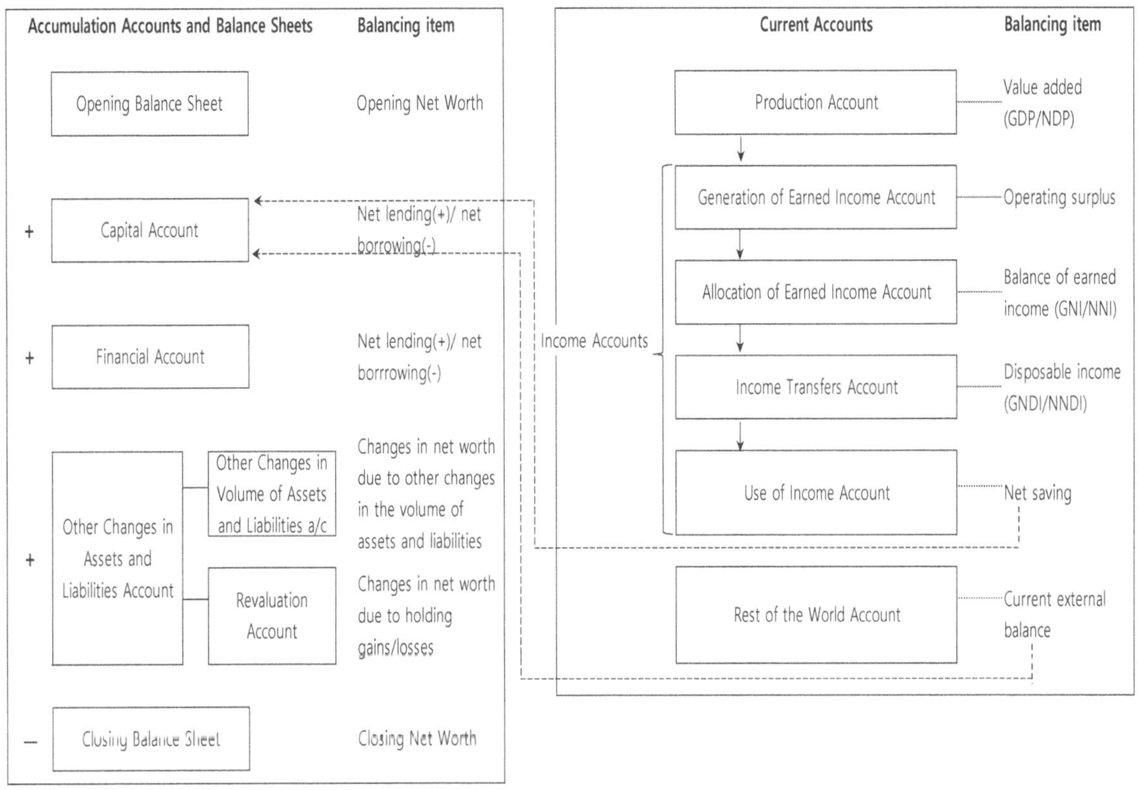

Other parts of the integrated framework include not only the supply and use tables but also the tables in volume terms, labour market tables, and the capital stocks and capital services tables. The **accounts in volume terms** refer to a set of accounts and supplementary tables that remove the effects of price changes from current national accounts data and measure economic activities in volume (or real) terms. The purpose of compiling these accounts is to measure real growth, to make meaningful comparisons of economic size across different periods at a constant price level or purchasing power, and enable productivity analysis based solely on quantitative changes. While fixed-weight methods were used in the past, the internationally recommended standard is now the chain index method.

The **labour market tables** are introduced in the SNA as a systematic means of capturing labour input within the integrated framework. They present not only quantitative measures such as the number of employed persons and hours worked, but also qualitative attributes of labour, including sex, age, educational attainment, and skill level. By linking the structure of labour income and industry-level labour productivity, these tables serve as essential data for analyzing national-economy productivity, assessing income distribution, and formulating employment policies. A core recommendation of the 2025 SNA is to use "hours worked" as the principal indicator of labour input.

The **capital stocks and capital services tables** present, in monetary terms, the stock of capital and the capital services that this stock contributes to the production process. These tables systematically record capital inputs by industry and by asset type, and are designed to link directly with the production account and productivity analysis by capturing the productive contribution provided by fixed assets.

Thematic and extended accounts are compiled when there is a need to modify the concepts or methodologies of the existing integrated framework. **Thematic accounts** provide additional information on specific subject areas without diverging significantly from the core concepts of the integrated framework. Examples include tourism accounts, R&D accounts, and agriculture accounts, in which existing classification schemes are refined or modified and the account structure is flexibly adapted accordingly. **Extended accounts** introduce new conceptual frameworks and classifications that go beyond, or replace, those of the existing national accounts system. Examples include human capital accounts, environmental accounts, and unpaid household services accounts, each of which is designed and compiled under a new conceptual structure. Thematic and extended accounts are used to explain economic phenomena that cannot be fully captured within the current accounting framework and to reflect the additional dimensions of well-being and sustainability emphasized in the 2025 SNA.

1.3 The Compilation procedure of the sequence of economic accounts

To compile the sequence of economic accounts which are the core accounts of the SNA, the following statistical compilation procedures must be followed. First, raw data is collected from economic census, various surveys, or administrative records. Based on these data and statistics, the supply and use tables are then compiled. The raw data includes all survey information collected by national accounts compilation agencies from economic entities. In recent years, various administrative records gathered by government agencies for public administration purposes have become indispensable. Examples include databases from the National Tax Service, Customs Service, and Financial Supervisory Service, as well as government budgets and settlement reports. These sources play a crucial role in enhancing the accuracy and precision of national accounts.

Supply and use tables serve as basic statistical tables not only for the production account and the generation of earned income account, which form the starting points of the sequence of economic accounts, but also for the compilation of the capital account. These tables represent the total supply and use of goods and services in an economy in a matrix format. The rows are broken by products, while the columns are detailed by domestic industries and imports/exports sectors. Input-output table is constructed by transforming the rows and columns of the supply and use tables into an industry-by-industry or product-by-product format. As the input-output table is a symmetric matrix with identical rows and columns, it enables various economic impact analyses using the linear algebra technique.

The sequence of economic accounts systematically organizes the results of all economic activities within a national economy into a series of accounts, categorized by institutional sectors (such as corporations, households, government, and non-profit institutions serving households). Therefore, to compile the sequence of economic accounts based on the supply and use tables, it is necessary to convert industry-specific production and expenditure data from the supply and use tables into data categorized by institutional sectors. This process involves reclassifying the industry-specific data from the supply and use tables, such as output, intermediate consumption, and value-added, into institutional sector data, making it suitable for use in the production account and the generation of earned income account in the sequence of economic accounts. This task is referred to as the compilation of the **cross-classification table by industry and by sector** (CCIS). Once the cross-classification table by industry and by sector is completed, the data from the supply and use tables can be effectively utilized to compile the production account and the generation of earned income account in the sequence of economic accounts, ensuring a seamless and accurate process.

Figure 1.3 Procedure for compiling the sequence of economic accounts

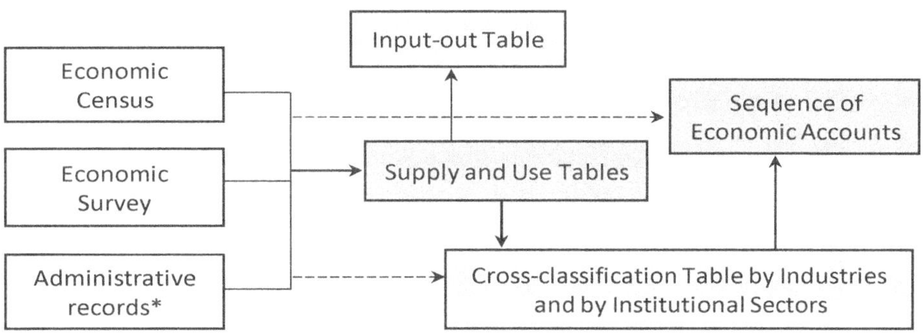

* Administrative records: Government budget and settlement statements, National tax service, Customs service, Public procurement agency, Financial supervisory agency data

This book focuses exclusively on the compilation processes of the supply and use tables, the cross-classification table by industry and institutional sector, and the sequence of economic accounts, excluding the raw data sources such as various censuses, surveys, and administrative records. Additionally, the book provides detailed explanations on advanced technical methods in national accounts, including:

- The calculation of **volume indices** and **real growth rates** (Chapters 16–18),
- The compilation of **quarterly national accounts** (Chapter 19),
- The estimation of **capital stock** (Chapter 20),
- The transformation of **supply and use tables into input-output tables** (Chapter 21),
- The **analysis of economic impact** using input-output tables (Chapter 22).

Chapter 2. Understanding basic concepts of national accounts

This chapter aims to introduce several fundamental terms and concepts that are essential for understanding the basic framework of the account system before delving into the detailed aspects of national accounts. As some of the content of this chapter may overlap with other chapters in this book, readers already familiar with these concepts may choose to skip this chapter.

Understanding and compiling national accounts requires familiarity with many basic concepts. Among these, this chapter focuses on introducing the following: the concept of production as defined in the SNA, the product balance identity, types of taxes and subsidies, price types applied in national accounts, the product balance identity incorporating these price types, the concept of residency, the distinction between establishments (industries) and institutional units (institutional sectors), as well as the types of output and their valuation methods.

2.1 The production boundary

In the SNA, the fundamental starting point for measuring production activities is to measure the output, which is the result of those activities. For this purpose, it is essential to define the scope of production. **Production**, in an economic sense, is generally defined as the activity of producers who use capital, labor, and intermediate goods and services as inputs to produce output. However, the concept of production as defined by the SNA is applied in a somewhat more restricted sense compared to this definition.

The **production boundary** includes both market production (goods and services produced by market producers for sale or barter) and non-market production (goods and services produced by government or non-profit institutions). This category encompasses not only the production of goods and services provided to other economic entities other than their producers but also the production of goods and services used in the process of producing such outputs. However, the issue arises with the household's production. According to the SNA, households are also classified as producers engaged in small-scale production. While **goods** produced by households for their own use (i.e., final consumption and gross fixed capital formation) are included in the production boundary, **services** produced for their own use are excluded. The criterion for this distinction is whether the output can be provided to other economic entities. Goods produced for their own use can be offered to other economic units, but services produced for own use generally cannot. Nonetheless, there are exceptions: the production of imputed services by owner-occupied dwellings and the production of domestic and personal services by employing paid domestic staff (i.e., housekeeper, private chauffeurs) are still included within the scope of production under the SNA, although they are services for the household's own use. To reiterate the above explanation, the production boundary includes the following activities:

- The production of all goods and services intended to be provided by producers to other economic entities. (This includes the production of goods and services used in the process of producing such outputs.)
- The production of all goods intended for the producer's own use[3]. (This is called "own-account production.")
- Own-account production of housing services by owner-occupiers.
- Production of domestic and personal services by employing paid domestic staff.

2.2 Product Balances

The economic activities of a country over a specific period are fundamentally carried out in the forms of production, investment expenditure, consumption expenditure, and imports and exports, through which income is generated, distributed, and used. In the SNA, these main components of economic activity are interconnected and expressed as an identity. That is, the **total supply** of goods and services in a national economy is equal to the total output supplied domestically by producers plus the imports supplied from abroad. This can be expressed in the form of an identity as follows:

(2.1) **Total supply = total domestic output + imports**

On the demand side, the **total use** of a country's products must equal its total supply, and its components can be classified into several categories in the following way. That is, total use consists of intermediate consumption used by enterprises as material and supplies for their production, gross capital formation (gross investment) that enterprises repeatedly use for production or hold in inventories, final consumption expenditure by final consumers such as households, and exports to foreign countries. This relationship can be expressed as an identity as follows:

(2.2) **Total use = intermediate consumption + gross capital formation + final consumption expenditure + exports**

[3] This category also includes "intellectual property products."

Therefore, as total supply equals total use, the following identity is derived from expressions (2.1) and (2.2).

Total domestic output + imports = intermediate consumption + gross capital formation + final consumption expenditure + exports

This identity is referred to as the **product balance identity**. (See Figure 2.1.)

Figure 2.1 Product balance

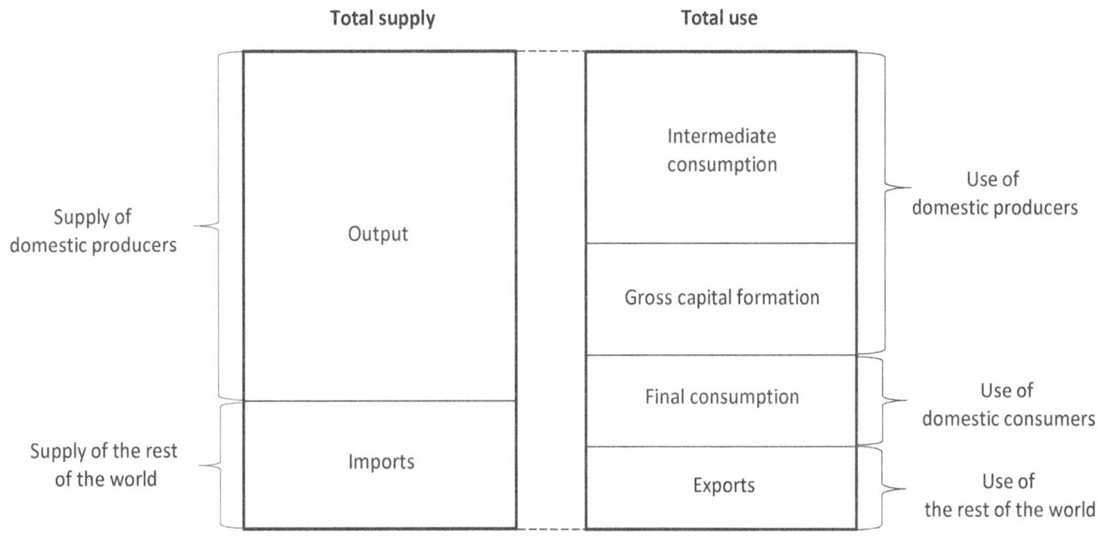

While detailed definitions for each component will be discussed in later chapters, a brief explanation is presented here. First, on the supply side, the **output** represents the aggregate value of goods and services produced by domestic economic entities (i.e., institutional units or institutional sectors) over a specific period of time. This figure reflects production activities during the period and does not necessarily correspond to sales value. For example, in industries such as manufacturing or mining, unsold products that remain in inventories influence total output. Specifically total output is affected by the opening inventories carried over from the previous period and the closing inventories at the end of the current period. This relationship can be expressed as follows.

Opening inventories + output – closing inventories = sales

In this equation, the output is derived as follows:

Output = sales + change in inventories (= closing inventories – opening inventories)

In industries where inventories do not arise (i.e., service industries), total output directly corresponds to the sales value. In addition, the value of non-market output (e.g., that of government or NPISHs) that is not sold on the market and is provided free of charge or at a significantly lower price than the market price is calculated based on the total costs incurred in their production.

Imports refer goods and services supplied to residents from the rest of the world. For goods, it includes items brought into the country by importers or travelers. For services, it encompasses transport and insurance services associated with the imports and exports of goods, as well as a wide range of other service imports. It also includes expenditures by domestic residents for the purchase goods and services abroad. While import statistics for goods are estimated using customs data, imports of services lack a dedicated statistical source and thus require data collection through various alternative methods.

In terms of the **use side** on the product balance identity above, total use is categorized into intermediate consumption and gross capital formation in relation with the production activities of domestic producers, final consumption expenditure by final consumers, and exports demanded by non-residents. **Intermediate consumption** refers to the costs incurred for inputs consumed in the production of output. This includes both direct costs, such as raw material expenses, and indirect costs arising from ancillary activities, such as sales, accounting, transportation, and storage of products. However, depreciation of fixed assets (e.g., buildings and machinery) and depletion of natural resources (e.g., minerals and oil) is excluded from intermediate consumption.

Gross capital formation occurs within domestic producers and consists of gross fixed capital formation, changes in inventories, and net acquisitions of valuables. **Gross fixed capital formation** refers to the net acquisition of fixed assets required for production (acquisitions minus disposals), and also includes the costs of ownership transfers of these fixed assets and non-produced assets such as land. Unlike intermediate consumption, which represents inputs consumed during the production process within the year, gross fixed capital formation involves assets used repeatedly in production activities for more than one year.

In the SNA, non-produced assets such as land or subsoil resources are excluded from the category of fixed assets and, therefore, are not included in gross fixed capital formation. Fixed assets, however, experience a decline in value each year as they are used or deteriorated, which is called **depreciation** (*consumption of fixed capital*). This cost is not treated as intermediate consumption. This amount is relatively significant because it arises from the entire stock of fixed assets held by the enterprise or producing unit. If the value of depreciation is deducted from gross fixed capital formation, it is referred to as **net fixed capital formation**.

Changes in inventories represent the sum of the increase (or decrease) in the stock of finished goods not sold and work-in-progress produced by producers, the increase (or decrease) in the stock of materials or supplies purchased by producers for inputs in production, and the increase (or decrease) in the stock of goods held by the wholesalers and retailers for resale purposes. While gross fixed capital formation refers to the increase or decrease in fixed assets used in production, changes in inventories represent the increase or decrease in products that remain unsold or unconsumed in the process of production or distribution. This includes all products regardless of their intended use, whether for intermediate consumption, gross fixed capital formation, or final consumption.

Acquisitions less disposals of valuables refer to the category that records various assets (excluding financial assets) that are held for investment purposes rather than for direct use in production. This includes all investment assets such as precious metals, jewelry and works of art, which are not intended for sale or as intermediate inputs for production. Acquisitions less disposals of valuables are calculated as the net concept of acquisitions minus disposals.

Final consumption expenditure refers to the consumption of goods and services produced, either purchased by households for their own use or consumed by entities such as governments or NPISHs that are imputed to consume the products they produce by themselves. For households, the value of services produced by owner-occupied dwellings and the value of household services provided by paid domestic staff are also treated as final consumption expenditure. Final consumption expenditure is based on the consumption of domestic residents, which means it includes purchases made by domestic residents abroad, while excluding purchases made and consumed by non-residents within the domestic territory.

Exports, in contrast to imports, refer to the value of goods and services sold to non-residents abroad. Purchases of goods and services within the domestic territory by non-residents, such as foreign tourists, are also treated as exports of goods and services. Exports of goods are typically recorded in customs data while exports of services are more challenging to investigate comprehensively using a single data source. Therefore, estimates for exports of services are made by referencing various data sources, such as remittance data from financial institutions.

The components mentioned above have been briefly explained to aid in understanding the identity of product balances. However, these will be examined in detail in Chapter 4 (Components of the supply table) and Chapter 5 (Components of the use table).

2.3 Types of taxes and subsidies

Taxes and subsidies are components of income or expenditure that arise from the general government's influence on the price formation of goods and services produced by producers and its intervention in the income distribution activities of economic agents (units). In the SNA, they serve as an indicator to measure the macroeconomic role of the government in monetary terms. **Taxes** arise from the government's authority to impose compulsory levies and are generated through its influence on the prices of goods and services produced by producers and on the ex-post distribution of income. **Subsidies**, on the other hand, are provided by government exclusively to support the production activities of producers. Government support for activities other than production activities is treated under current transfers or capital transfers. This section examines the nature of taxes and subsidies as outcomes of the general government's intervention in private economic activities.

2.3.1 Types of taxes

The reason why it is essential to first understand the types of taxes in national accounts is that this serves as a prerequisite for correctly comprehending the types of prices and the concept of income as defined in the SNA. Generally, taxes encountered by economic entities can be categorized into the following four types:

1. **Taxes on the sale of goods and services**: This type of tax is imposed by tax authorities on a certain percentage of the sales value of goods and services produced by enterprises. These are taxes applied to individual goods and services, calculated based on the sales amount, and subsequently paid to the tax authorities by the selling enterprise. Examples include excise taxes, commodity taxes, fuel taxes, and similar taxes levied on individual commodity sold by suppliers, including value-added tax (VAT).

2. **Taxes on production inputs**: These taxes are levied on production activities, specifically on the use of production factors such as machinery, buildings, and labor. Examples include property taxes, vehicle taxes, and payroll taxes.

3. **Taxes on final income**: This category includes corporate tax and personal income tax, which are imposed on the final income of enterprises or employees. These taxes involve the mandatory collection of a certain percentage of income earned by economic entities over a certain period.

4. **Taxes on asset transfers**: This type of tax applies when one economic entity transfers assets to another economic entity as a gift without compensation. In such cases, the recipient is taxed a certain amount.

The first and second types are defined in the SNA as **taxes on production and imports**. Specifically, the first type is referred to as **taxes on products**, as these are levied on the sales value of goods and services. The second type is termed as **other taxes on production**, which are taxes imposed by the government on enterprises for the use of production factors (e.g., machinery, buildings, and employees) during the production process. Unlike taxes on products, other taxes on production are unrelated to the sales value of goods and services but are incurred by production activities within the enterprise. Examples include property taxes on buildings and factories, as well as automobile taxes on business-use vehicles. The third type involves **current taxes on income, wealth, etc.**, which are unilateral taxes imposed by the government on the income of enterprises or households. These taxes are not levied directly on production activities but rather on income distributed after production. Examples include corporate tax and personal income taxes, which are compulsory taxes applied to all forms of income. The fourth type pertains to **capital taxes**, which are imposed by the government on the gratuitous transfer of capital between economic entities. Unlike income taxes, these are levied on capital transfers rather than current income. Examples of capital transfers include inheritance and gifts, which do not occur on a regular basis to the taxpayer.

In summary, taxes in the SNA are compulsory levies imposed by the central or local governments on their people. They are broadly classified into taxes on production and imports, current taxes, and capital taxes.

Types of taxes

<table>
<tr><td rowspan="5">Taxes on production and imports</td><td rowspan="4">Taxes on products</td><td>Value added tax (VAT)</td></tr>
<tr><td>Import taxes</td></tr>
<tr><td>Export taxes</td></tr>
<tr><td>Other taxes on products</td></tr>
<tr><td>Other taxes on production</td><td></td></tr>
<tr><td>Current taxes</td><td colspan="2" rowspan="2"></td></tr>
<tr><td>Capital taxes</td></tr>
</table>

2.3.1.1 Taxes on products

Taxes on products require a more detailed explanation because they affect the valuation of all goods and services subject to measurement in national accounting. Taxes on products are levies imposed per unit of goods or services. The unit can be either the quantity or the value of a good or service. Taxes on products are further categorized into **value added tax** (VAT), **import taxes** imposed on imported goods, **export taxes** imposed on exported goods, and **other taxes on products**, which are imposed when domestically produced goods and services are sold within the domestic market. Import taxes are further subdivided into import duties and other import taxes, excluding value added taxes imposed on imports. **Import duties** (tariff) are taxes levied on specific imported goods, and are classified into two types of duties; one is ad valorem taxes which are applied as a percentage of the value of imported goods, and the other is specific taxes which are applied based on the quantity of imported goods. **Other import taxes** refer to all taxes levied on imported goods and services, excluding import duties and VAT. These include taxes such as excise taxes and sales taxes, which are of the same type as those imposed on domestically produced goods and services. For instance, even the same excise tax is classified as either "other import taxes" or "other taxes on products," depending on whether it is levied on imported goods and services or on domestically produced goods and services[4].

Among taxes on products, **value added tax** (VAT) and **other tax on products** differ in nature, and these differences are reflected in the types of prices used in national accounts. A brief explanation of the distinction between these two tax categories is as follows.

As a first example, let us assume that there is no VAT, and only other taxes on products exist (Figure 2.2). Suppose that a beverage manufacturer uses barley as a raw material to produce beer (150), sells it to a trader, and the trader then sells it to a consumer. The beverage manufacturer adds an excise tax on the beer (10) and delivers it to the trader. The trader purchases it at a price that includes the excise tax (10), and the beverage manufacturer pays the excise tax (10) collected from the trader to the tax office. The accounting entries made by the beverage manufacturer are as follows: at the point of sale, sales revenue of 150 is recognized along with a liability (excise tax) of 10 to be paid to the tax office.

(Debit)	Accounts receivable	160	(Credit)	Sales	150
				Excise tax payable (liability)	10

[4] Taxes on products are displayed only as total amounts in the sequence of economic accounts, as there is no need for a breakdown by institutional sector. Similarly, in the supply and use tables, taxes on products do not require industry-specific details, and only total amounts are derived. However, for the compilation of the "use table at basic prices," which is necessary for preparing the input-output table, taxes on products (less subsidies) need to be calculated by industry and product.

Then, when the excise tax is paid to the tax office, the following entry is made:

(Debit) Excise tax payable (liability) 10 (Credit) Cash 10

The consumer purchases the beer from the trader at a price that includes the excise tax (10). As a result, while the beverage manufacturer, as the producer of the product, acts as the taxpayer, the entire burden of the excise tax (10) is ultimately passed on to the consumer.

Figure 2.2 Payment process of other taxes on products

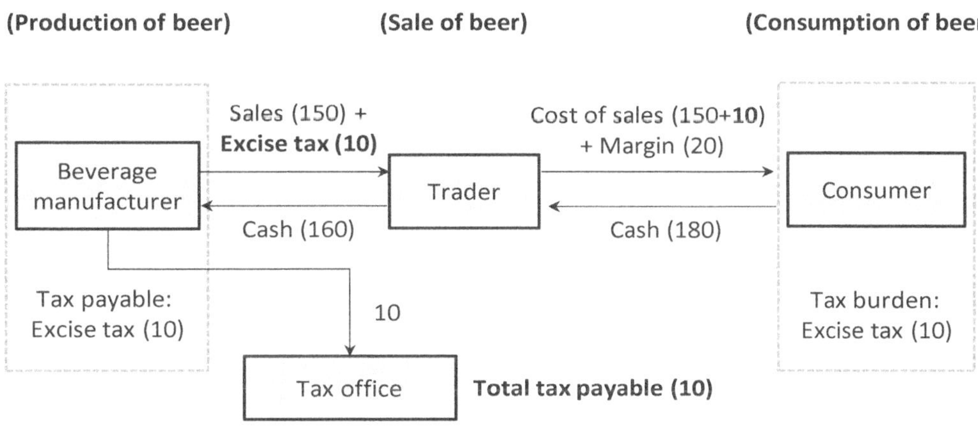

In contrast, value added tax (VAT) is applied at a fixed rate to the sales value at every stage of the transaction. This means that every seller is obligated to pay taxes, but the amount of VAT already paid in previous transaction stages is deducted, ensuring there is no double taxation. For example, suppose a farmer produces wheat and sells it to a miller (agricultural products are generally not subject to VAT). The miller uses the wheat as a raw material to produce flour and sell the it to a baker for a sales amount of $200 (Figure 2.3). Assuming that a VAT rate of 10% on sales value, the miller collects $20 in VAT (10% of $200) from the baker and pays this amount to the tax office. When the baker uses the flour to produce bread and sells it to consumers for $300, including VAT of $30, the baker deducts the $20 already paid to the miller from the $30 collected from the consumer and pays the remaining $10 to the tax office. Consequently, the consumer bears the full VAT of $30 paid to the baker, which corresponds exactly to the sum of the amounts paid to the tax office by the miller and the baker ($20+$10).

Figure 2.3 Example of the treatment process of VAT

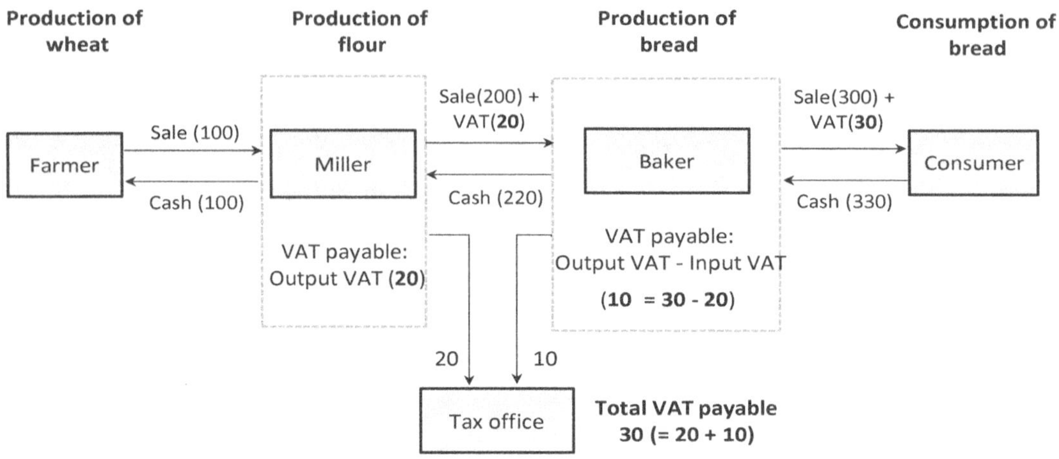

In the tax accounting, the VAT received by a seller from his customers is referred to as **output VAT**, while the VAT paid by the seller when purchasing raw materials or other goods from suppliers is called **input VAT**. The amount of VAT that the seller (producer or trader) must pay to the tax office is the difference between the output VAT collected from customers and the input VAT paid to suppliers for raw materials.

VAT payable to the tax office by a seller = output VAT – input VAT

Let us examine how the baker in the above example records VAT in the book-keeping. First, the expense of $220 incurred by the baker to purchase raw materials such as flour is recorded as following entries.

(Debit)	Inventories (Assets)	200	(Credit)	Cash	220
	Input VAT	20			

Next, the revenue of $330 received by the baker from selling bread to consumers is recorded as follows:

(Debit)	Cash	330	(Credit)	Sales revenue	300
				Output VAT (liability)	30

Thus, the VAT payable by the baker to the tax office is $10 (=30-20). For the final consumer, neither output VAT nor input VAT applies. The consumer bears the entire VAT charged on the purchased products and cannot pass this tax on to any other party. However, there are cases where even non-final consumers cannot deduct the VAT (input VAT) paid to their suppliers. This occurs when the VAT on goods they sell (output VAT) is exempt. Examples of such exemptions include industries such as agriculture, forestry, fisheries, printing and publishing, banking and insurance, public transportation, government services, and non-profit institutions (NPIs). This type of businesses (except for government and NPIs, which are classified as non-market producers.) is referred to in tax accounting as **VAT-exempt entities**. These exempt entities are not required to charge output VAT on the goods and services they sell, but in exchange, they are also not allowed to deduct input VAT paid on goods and services they purchase.

Then, let us examine how the SNA explains the nature of these types of VAT. The SNA categorizes VAT into the following three types based on its characteristics: First, the VAT that a seller charges to customers (purchasers) is called **invoiced VAT**. This is generally calculated by applying a specific tax rate (e.g., 10%) to the price of goods and services sold and corresponds to **output VAT (A)** in tax accounting. This amount is recorded as a liability for the seller, who must remit it to the tax authority. Second, the VAT (B) imposed on raw materials or fixed assets purchased by producers for production activities, or on goods purchased by traders for resale, can be deductible by the producers (or traders) when they pay their invoiced VAT (A) to the tax authority. This is called **deductible VAT**, which corresponds to **input VAT** in tax accounting. Third, as mentioned above, there are cases where economic entities cannot deduct the VAT paid when purchasing goods and services. For instance, final consumers, VAT-exempt entities, government and non-profit institutions are unable to claim deductions for the VAT paid on their purchases. This is referred to as **non-deductible VAT**. Since non-deductible VAT cannot be deductible when remitting VAT to the tax authority, it is not recorded separately in accounting.

Examples of non-deductible VAT include cases where VAT cannot be passed on to other economic entities, such as for final consumers, or expenses incurred by certain producers (e.g., VAT-exempt entities, government and non-profit institutions). Additionally, even for businesses that are not VAT-exempt, specific expense items like "business entertainment expenses" may fall under non-deductible VAT. Therefore, the VAT paid by a purchaser is categorized in national accounting as either deductible VAT or non-deductible VAT.

In the example shown in Figure 2.4, when Enterprise Y deducts the deductible VAT (B) from the gross VAT (A) paid during the purchase of goods, the remainder is the non-deductible VAT (C). By summing up this non-deductible VAT across economic entities, the total VAT imposed on the goods can be calculated. Additionally, the VAT that enterprise Y must remit to the tax authority is determined by subtracting the deductible VAT (B) from the invoiced VAT (D) collected from its customers (Z).

Figure 2.4 Description of Value added taxes in the SNA

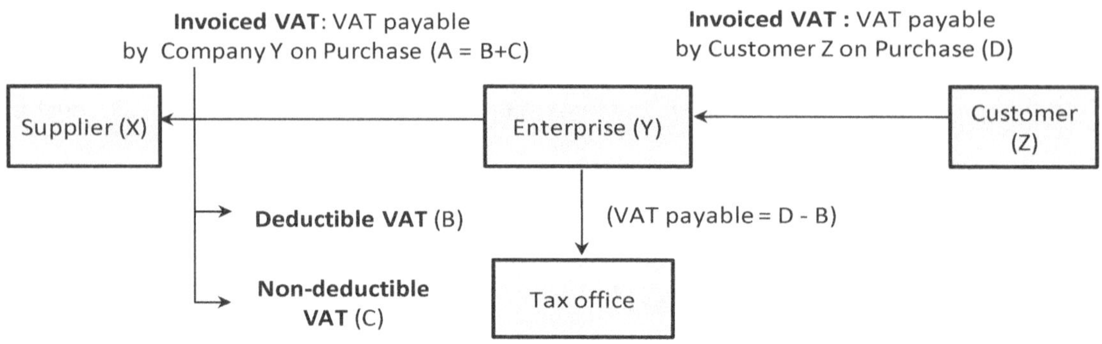

If the purchaser of the products is a final consumer, government, non-profit institutions, or a VAT-exempt enterprise, the deductible VAT is zero. In contrast, if the purchaser is a regular enterprise, the deductible VAT typically equals the VAT paid during the purchase of goods. This distinction is essential for understanding the characteristics of the VAT system, the different types of prices in the national accounts (i.e., basic price, producer price, purchaser's price), and the compilation of supply and use tables.

2.3.1.2 Gross or net recording of value added tax

In the SNA, there are two methods for incorporating VAT into prices. The first method involves including the invoiced VAT in the total transaction value between the transaction parties (sellers and purchasers). Under this method, the selling price and the purchase price are treated as identical, ensuring that the transaction value remains consistent between the purchaser and seller. This approach is commonly referred to as the **gross system** in recording VAT. However, in the practical business accounting, the invoiced VAT is viewed as deductible VAT from the purchaser's perspective and is therefore separated from the transaction value. Instead of being included in the overall transaction value, it is recorded separately. As a result, the gross system does not align with the way VAT is actually recorded in accounting practices. Because of this discrepancy, the gross system is not adopted by most countries.

The SNA adopts another method of recording VAT, known as the **net system**. Under this method, VAT on output, imports and purchases is recorded in the following ways.

- **Output and imports**: Recorded as values excluding invoiced VAT.
- **Purchases**: Recorded as values that include non-deductible VAT. Examples of this include VAT on expenditures incurred by final consumers, VAT-exempt enterprises, government units,

non-profit institutions, and specific corporate expenses such as entertainment costs. If the invoiced VAT included in the value of purchased goods and services is deductible VAT, the price after deducting this amount is recorded as the purchase price. (Therefore, in such case, the seller's sales value and the purchaser's value are recorded as equal.)

Under the net system, except for certain transactions (where VAT is deductible), there is a mismatch between the sales value and the purchaser's value recorded by the transacting parties, as mentioned above. Therefore, at the aggregate level, it is necessary to add non-deductible VAT to the output values to derive the purchaser's value. Since output in the SNA is valued at market prices, and the market price is calculated at the purchaser's price, non-deductible VAT must be added to the output values. (For more details, refer to Section 2.4, "Types of prices applied in the SNA.")

2.3.1.3 Special types of taxes

The types of tax in the national accounts can be categorized into two types: The first type is "taxes on production and imports" (i.e., taxes on products, other taxes on production), which are a component of value-added. The second type includes "current taxes" and "capital taxes" which are transferred to the government without compensation. However, in practice, the classification of these taxes may vary depending on the economic entity being taxed (Table 2.1). For instance, the automobile tax is classified as other taxes on production when it is levied on enterprises, but current taxes when it is levied on households. Similarly, poll taxes are considered current taxes when uniformly levied on individuals, but are other taxes on production when levied on employees of enterprises (as payroll taxes).

Table 2.1 Examples of tax classification changes

Type of tax	Institutional sector	Tax category
Automobile tax	Enterprise	Other tax on production
	Household	Current tax
Poll tax	Enterprise	Other tax on production (as payroll taxes)
	Household	Current tax (as poll taxes)
Property tax	Enterprise	Other tax on production (including the industry of owner's occupied dwelling services)
	Household	Taxes on pure land is classified as "current taxes". The taxes on land attached to housing is classified as "other taxes on production."

There are also taxes that are added to existing taxes and collected for specific policy purposes by applying an additional rate to the original tax (these are called **sur-taxes**). Examples of such taxes include the education tax and the special tax for developing rural area, which are classified in the same category as the original tax. For instance, surtaxes added to taxes on production are classified as taxes on production, and surtaxes added to current taxes are classified as current taxes.

2.3.2 Types of subsidies

Subsidies refer to the monetary amounts provided by the government to enterprises for the production of goods and services or their production activities, granted without compensation and primarily for the industrial policy-supporting purposes. Subsidies, like taxes on production and imports, can be divided into two categories. The first is **subsidies on products**, which are directly provided for specific products and imports (or exports). The second is **other subsidies on production**, which are granted to support production activities rather than specific products (e.g., subsidy on employment). Subsidies on products are monetary amounts provided per unit of goods or services, where the unit can be based on the quantity or value of the product.

Types of subsidies

<table>
<tr><td rowspan="3">Subsidies on products</td><td>Import subsidies</td></tr>
<tr><td>Export subsidies</td></tr>
<tr><td>Other subsidies on products</td></tr>
<tr><td>Other subsidies on production</td><td></td></tr>
</table>

There are also items that must be distinguished from subsidies, as they are provided without compensation and unrelated to production activities. Examples include unconditional transfers from government or non-profit institutions to private individuals, grants from central governments to local governments, and donations from international organizations. Since these items are not related to direct production activities, they are recorded as **current transfers** or **capital transfers**, as discussed later.

2.4 Types of prices applied in the SNA

This section seeks to provide a detailed explanation of the key price types essential for understanding the valuation of goods and services in the framework of the fundamental concepts employed in the SNA. There are three types of prices applied for valuation of products to be measured in the SNA: **basic price**, **producer's price** and **purchaser's price**. These types of prices are derived from the valuation method currently used in business accounting. Therefore, understanding the price types applied in the SNA requires a comparison with the valuation methods used in business accounting (see Box 2.1).

Unlike business accounting, which records prices from the perspective of enterprises, the SNA classifies price types based on the characteristics of economic agents (units). Therefore, prices observed in the national accounts differ depending on the economic agent involved. The following section offers an in-depth discussion of the price types applied in the national accounts.

2.4.1 Basic price

In the SNA, the **basic price** is defined as the price at which a seller sells a product, excluding any taxes on products imposed by government on the sales value (e.g., VAT, import taxes and other taxes on products) and adding any subsidies on products provided by the government for that product. In other words, the basic price is the amount the seller effectively retains after deducting **taxes less subsidies on products** (i.e., taxes on products less subsidies on products) from the price charged to the purchaser. This price generally corresponds to the sales value recorded in business accounting, reflecting the standard accounting practices.

If specific taxes are included in the sales price (e.g., excise tax or VAT charged to the purchaser), those taxes are excluded from the seller's revenue. For instance, when an excise tax is included in the sales price, it is recorded as an unpaid liability that the seller collects from the purchaser at the time of sale and remits to the tax authority afterwards. Similarly, in the case of VAT, the seller calculates the net VAT liability by subtracting the deductible VAT (referred to as **input VAT** in tax accounting) paid on purchases from the VAT collected from purchasers (referred to as **output VAT**). The resulting net VAT is recorded as a liability payable to the tax authority. In the SNA, the **basic price** is the standard used for valuing the **output** of goods and services.

Figure 2.5 Types of prices in the SNA

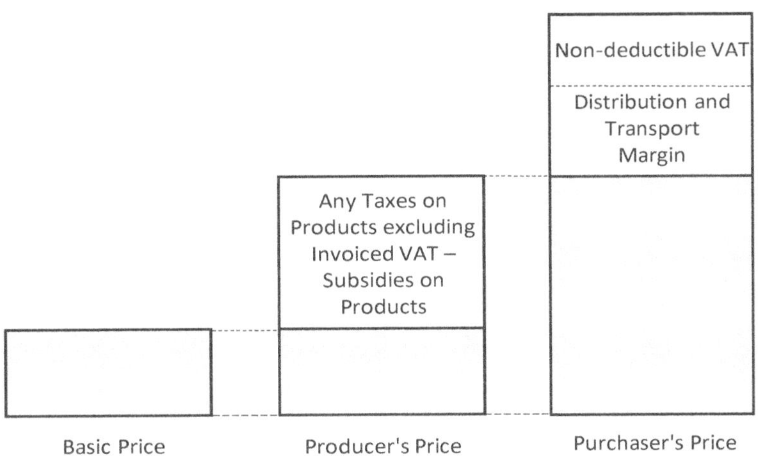

2.4.2 Producer's price

The **producer's price** refers to the price derived by adding any taxes on products (excluding invoiced VAT) to the basic prices and subtracting any subsidies on products. Producer' price is commonly observed in cases where the seller cannot separately identify taxes on products at the time of sale, and instead record the total amount including the taxes on products as sales value. In such cases, since the taxes on products are already included in the sales value, the seller subsequently determines the exact amount of taxes on products at a later point, deducts it from the sales value, and records it as a liability to be remitted to the tax authority. The producer's price is also normally observed in business accounting practices. For this reason, the previous version of the SNA allowed for the application of both the basic price and the producer's price. However, from the perspective of ensuring consistency between business accounting and the SNA practices, the basic price is considered more appropriate. Accordingly, the basic price is now used as the valuation standard for output in the framework of national accounts including the supply and use tables and the sequence of economic accounts.

2.4.3 Purchaser's price

The **purchaser's price** refers to the price of a product measured from the purchaser's perspective, encompassing any costs incurred by the purchaser during the purchasing process. The purchaser's price aligns with the general recording practices in business accounting, which also stipulates that all costs incurred during the purchasing process be included in the cost of purchases. In the SNA, the purchaser's price is calculated by adding **non-deductible VAT** to the **producer's price** and including any distribution margins and transport margins, if any. For VAT, when the purchaser is a producer (or wholesaler/retailer), the VAT paid at the time of purchase is deductible. However, for final consumers, the VAT-exempt enterprises, or government, the VAT paid during the purchase is non-deductible and is therefore included in the purchaser's price. Additionally, transport charges are normally included in the seller's sales price. However, if a separate bill for transport charges is invoiced due to specific contractual arrangements, these charges are also added to the purchaser's price. (This is called the **transport margin** mentioned above.) Such recording practices reflect the conventions of business accounting. On the other hand, if there is no involvement of wholesalers or retailers in the purchasing process and the transaction occurs directly between the producer and the purchaser, no distribution margins (wholesale or retail margins) are incurred.

- **Purchaser's price = basic price + non-deductible taxes less subsidies on products (= any taxes on products excluding VAT + non-deductible VAT – any subsidies on products) + distribution margins + separately invoiced transport charges**

The three items added to the basic price, as described above, must be distinguishable in order to compile the use table at basic prices, which will be explained later. However, these items are not separately identified in the sequence of economic accounts by institutional sectors.

In the SNA, all expenditure items, such as intermediate consumption, gross fixed capital formation, and final consumption expenditure are valued at **purchasers' prices**. In particular, gross fixed capital formation includes any costs incurred for the purchase of fixed assets in addition to purchaser's price.

Box 2.1: Comparison of price valuation in business accounting and national accounts

This section introduces the valuation methods used in business accounting and compares them with those employed in the national accounts. The prices commonly observed in everyday transactions include the prices of agricultural and fishery products sold by farmers or fishers, as well as the prices of goods and services produced by enterprises and sold to customers. For many agricultural and fishery products, taxes on products are often zero or negligible. In such cases, the sales revenue received by producers corresponds closely to the price at which the product leaves the farm or fishing operation (commonly referred to as the **ex-farm gate price**). In the absence of taxes or subsidies on products, this price corresponds to the basic price in the SNA.

However, in the case of goods and services sold by enterprises, the sales price includes excise taxes and value added taxes (VAT), which are charged to the purchaser. The following example illustrates the accounting entries recorded in business accounting when a company sells goods or services. Suppose that a company records a sales amount of $11,000, where the supply value is $10,000 and the VAT (10% of the supply value) is $1,000, and the excise tax of $1,150 is embedded within the supply value. The accounting entries for this transaction are as follows:

(Debit)	Accounts receivable 11,000	(Credit)	Sales revenue	8,850
			Excise tax (Liability)	1,150
			VAT (Output tax)	1,000

In this case, the amount recorded as sales revenue excludes taxes on products and is recognized as revenue in the income statement, while excise taxes and VAT are recorded as liabilities payable to the tax authorities. Assuming that the excise tax is a tax on products and that no subsidies on products apply, the sales revenue of $8,850 corresponds to the **basic price** in the SNA. In addition, the price including the excise tax (i.e., the supply value of $10,000) corresponds to the **producer's price** in the SNA. The producer's price is the basic price plus excise taxes (e.g., liquor tax, fuel tax, tobacco tax, and other excise taxes, collectively referred to as **other taxes on products**.), excluding the VAT levied on the sales value (invoiced VAT). If subsidies are paid from government for the goods and services sold, the net product tax (= taxes on products – subsidies on products) must be added to the basic price to derive the producer's price.

When a company purchases goods and services, the **purchase price** recorded in business accounting includes all costs incurred at the time of purchase, excluding any deductible VAT. For example, if the company pays $8,800 for goods intended as raw materials (comprising a purchase price of $8,000 for goods and deductible VAT of $800), the accounting entries are as follows:

(Debit)	Inventory asset	8,000	(Credit)	Accounts payable	8,800
	VAT (Input tax)	800			

Additionally, any separately incurred transport costs during the purchase are included in the purchase price. In the SNA, this is called the **purchaser's price**. If the company purchases a non-business vehicle (with a purchase price of $550 which includes VAT of $50), the VAT is non-deductible. The journal entry would be recorded as follows:

(Debit) Vehicle (Fixed asset) 550 (Credit) Cash 550 8,800

When the company above files its VAT return, the following accounting entries are recorded:

(Debit)	VAT (Output tax)	1,000	(Credit)	VAT (Input tax)	800
				Cash (Tax payment)	200

2.5 Product balance reflecting the types of prices

When the price concepts of basic prices and purchasers' prices are applied to the product balance identity introduced above, it becomes possible to explain the national accounts from a more professional, compiler-oriented practical perspective. Reflecting this practical perspective, the identity of product balance can be reformulated as shown in Figure 2.6 below.

From the perspective of **total supply**, output is valued at basic prices. This follows the convention in business accounting, where sales value is recorded at basic prices. If one wishes to derive the basic price from the purchaser's price, it is necessary to subtract the non-deductible taxes less subsidies on products (defined as all taxes on products excluding invoiced VAT + non-deductible VAT – subsidies on products) from the purchaser's price. Additionally, wholesale and retail margins and any transport costs separately borne by the purchaser must also be excluded. Therefore, when calculating the total supply in the **product balance identity**, it is essential to add back the excluded taxes less subsidies on products, distribution margins, and separately invoiced transport costs (transport margins) to the output at basic prices. However, since distribution margins and transport margins are already included in the total output as the output of trade services and transport services, only taxes less subsidies on products need to be added.

Figure 2.6 Product balance reflecting the types of prices

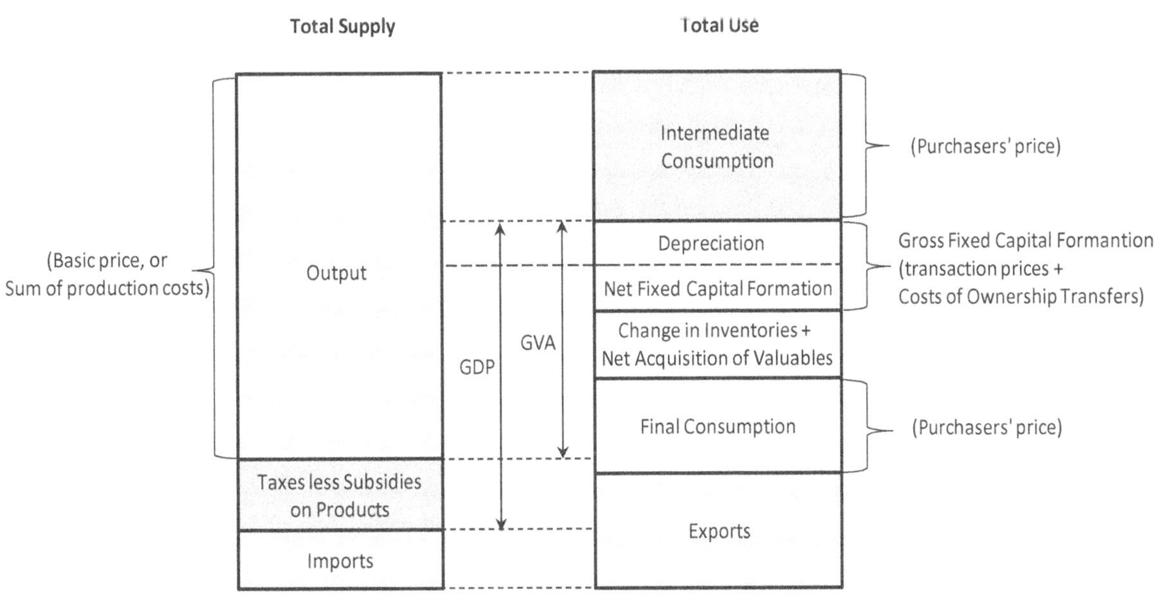

Moreover, as will be explained later, **non-market output** produced by government or NPISH is not subject to market transaction prices (It is valued using the sum of production costs method), and therefore, there is no need to adjust it to purchasers' prices.

Imports are categorized into imports of goods and imports of services. **Imports of goods** are typically recorded in the supply and use tables at **basic prices** when they are brought into the domestic territory. The basic price of imported good refers to the price before import taxes are imposed. However, unlike the basic price of domestically produced goods, the coverage of the basic price for imported goods may vary depending on the data sources. The import price data for imported goods is primarily based on customs records, which are generally recorded at **CIF prices** (Cost, insurance premiums, and freight included). The CIF price serves as the basis for customs to levy import duties and is commonly used for valuing imported goods. However, the basic price of imported goods can vary depending on who bears the freight charges of imports (the foreign exporter or the domestic importer). For instance, if the freight charges for transporting goods across borders are borne by the **exporter**, and the goods are carried by the exporting country or a third country, the CIF price is approximated to the basic price of the imported goods. Conversely, if the freight charges are borne by the **importer**, and the goods are transported by a domestic shipping company, the basic price for imported goods is best represented by the **FOB price** (Free on board price, recorded at the Customs Service of the exporting country) which is excluding the import freight charges. In such cases, the freight charges are reflected in the output of domestic transport enterprises, and it is reasonable to use FOB prices for imported goods to prevent double-counting.

Imports of services are valued based on "market transaction prices". However, imports of services cover imports of freight charges and insurance premiums that may arise during the import of goods, which can result in double counting with the import value of goods recorded at CIF prices. To avoid this double-counting, as will be described in later chapter, a separate row and column referred to as "CIF/FOB adjustment" is created in the supply and use tables to adjust the value. The primary goal of the SNA is to intended to cover all transactions, so it does not matter if relevant transactions are not omitted after setting certain criteria. In the SNA, regardless of the data source's standard, both exports and imports of goods are priced on FOB basis, and the remaining items such as freight charges and insurance premiums are adjusted to imports or exports of services. (Refer to 4.2 "Imports" for more details.)

From the perspective of **total use**, the SNA value both **intermediate consumption** and **final consumption** at **purchaser's prices**, while gross fixed capital formation (GFCF) is valued at actual transaction prices plus costs of ownership transfer. These valuation methods also follow business accounting practices. Specifically, in business accounting, when a company purchases raw materials for intermediate consumption, it calculates the purchase cost by including all associated costs, such as additional transport charge, transaction costs, and taxes on products excluding deductible VAT. Similarly, for fixed assets classified as gross fixed capital formation, the acquisition cost is calculated by adding all expenses associated with ownership transfers (e.g., legal service charges, any separately paid transport charge, taxes, and installation costs). The valuation of changes in inventories may differ depending on the types of inventories. Goods produced by producers that have not yet been sold are valued at basic prices, while inventories of raw materials purchased for production inputs and goods purchased for resales are recorded at the purchaser's price. Exports are categorized into exports of goods and exports of services. For exports of goods, customs data is used, which is recorded at FOB prices. Exports of services, like imports of services, are valued at market transaction prices.

2.5.1 The goods and services account, gross value-added, and GDP

By applying the price types outlined in the above section, the product balance identity can be restructured as follows:

Product balance (when price types are applied):

- Output (basic price) + imports (basic price) + taxes on products (less subsidies on products) = intermediate consumption (purchaser's price) + final consumption expenditure (purchaser's price) + gross fixed capital formation (transaction price + costs of ownership transfer[1)]) + changes in inventories + acquisitions less disposals of valuables (purchaser's price) + exports (goods: FOB price, services: market transaction price)

Footnote: 1) Costs of ownership transfer may already be included in intermediate consumption, leading to potential double counting. To prevent this, a separate adjustment process is necessary. (See 6.6.1.2 for the details.)

In the above expression, by moving imports from the left-hand side to the right-hand side and transferring intermediate consumption on the right-hand side to the left-hand side, the following expression is derived. This expression is known as the **goods and services account**, a fundamental identity in the SNA.

(2.3) Output (basic price) – intermediate consumption (purchaser's price) + taxes on products (-subsidies on products) = final consumption expenditure (purchaser's price) + gross fixed capital formation (transaction price + costs of ownership transfer) + changes in inventories

+ acquisitions less disposals of valuables (purchaser's price) + exports – imports (basic price)

In this expression, the difference between output at basic prices and intermediate consumption at purchasers' prices is referred to as **gross value added (GVA)**, which represents the value of total output produced domestically, after subtracting the intermediate consumption counted twice.

Figure 2-7 Output and gross value-added

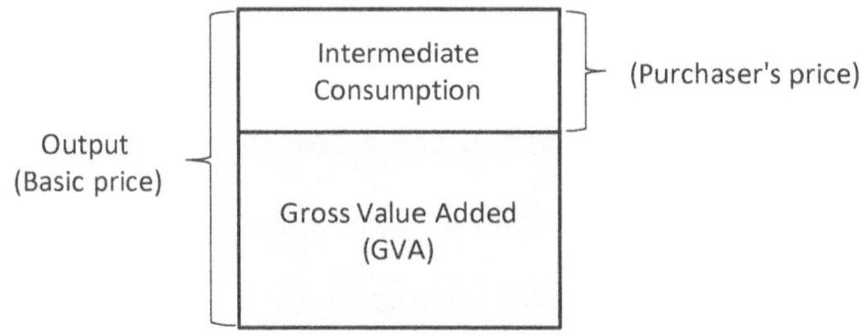

Adding the taxes less subsidies on products, which are excluded from the basic price, to the gross value added results in **Gross Domestic Product** (GDP). In other words, the left-hand side of the goods and services account in Expression (2.3) represents the total value added produced domestically, which reflects GDP at market prices. This is called the **production approach** for estimating GDP. On the other hand, the right-hand side of Expression (2.3) represents the amount of GDP valued at purchaser's price from the expenditure side. That is, GDP is equal to the sum of the final uses of goods and services (all "uses" excluding intermediate consumption), measured at purchasers' prices, less the imports of goods and services at basic prices. This is referred to as the **expenditure approach** for estimating GDP. Among the difference between the basic price and purchaser's price, distribution margins and transport margins are already included in the output of the relevant industries to which they belong (trade industry and transport industry), so there is no need to add them separately. The value obtained by subtracting depreciation and depletion from GDP is referred to as **Net Domestic Product** (NDP)[5].

Now, let's examine how GDP is calculated when data on basic prices for output is unavailable, and only data on producers' prices is provided. Since the difference between the basic price and

[5] In the 2025 SNA, the derivation of NDP from GDP has been revised to include the *deduction of depletion* in addition to depreciation. This change addresses a limitation of the previous framework, under which the reduction in the value of natural resources was not reflected in net income, despite the fact that natural resources are economic assets that are depleted in the production process. Depletion represents the decline in future economic benefits resulting from the extraction of natural resources and, like depreciation, is regarded as a cost that must be covered in order to maintain the asset base.

producer's price is taxes less subsidies on products (= product taxes except the invoiced VAT – product subsidies), GDP is derived as follows. First of all, non-deductible VAT has been excluded from the producer's price, so this item should be added. And since the output (at the producer's price) is the amount occurred in domestic economy, import taxes (less import subsidies) have been excluded, so this item must also be added.

- **GDP = output at producers' prices - intermediate consumption at purchasers' prices + non-deductible VAT + import taxes (less import subsidies).**

To summarize the above discussion, the relationship between gross value added and GDP is expressed as follows:

(2.4) **GDP = GVA at basic price + all taxes on products (less subsidies on products),**

GDP = GVA at producer's price + non-deductible VAT + import taxes (less import subsidies)

Figure 2.8 GVA and GDP

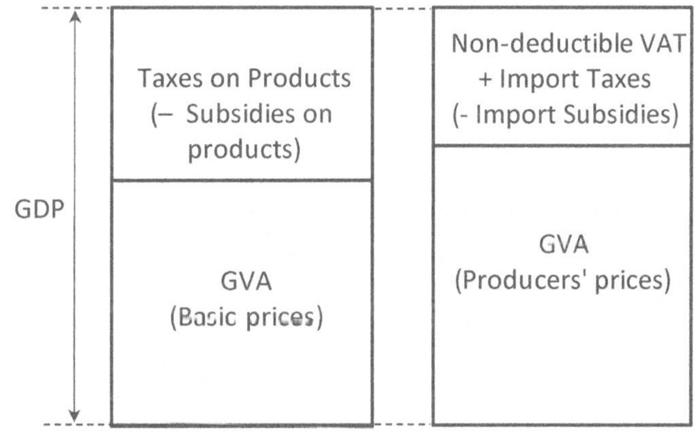

2.5.2 Components of gross value-added

Gross value added at basic prices consists of **remuneration of employees, gross operating surplus, and other taxes on production (less subsidies on production)**. In other words, the output at basic prices minus intermediate consumption at purchasers' prices constitutes remuneration of employees equivalent to labor costs, gross operating surplus measured by surplus in the production process (including gross mixed income, which is a mixture of remuneration of employees and operating surplus), and other taxes on production (less subsidies on production). Gross operating surplus (and gross mixed income) includes *depreciation* and *depletion* that are not included in intermediate consumption[6]. Gross operating surplus minus depreciation and depletion is called **net operating surplus** (and net mixed income). Other taxes on production (less subsidies on production) are expenses born by enterprises, but are not included in intermediate consumption; they are treated as part of value added that accrues to government. Therefore, combining this result with the previous equation (2.4), gives the following:

- GDP = remuneration of employees + gross operating surplus and gross mixed income + other taxes on production (less subsidies on production) + all taxes on products (less all subsidies on products) = remuneration of employees + gross operating surplus and gross mixed income + all taxes on production and imports (less all subsidies on production and imports)

The above method of estimating GDP is called the **income approach**.

Figure 2.9 Components of Gross value-added at basic prices

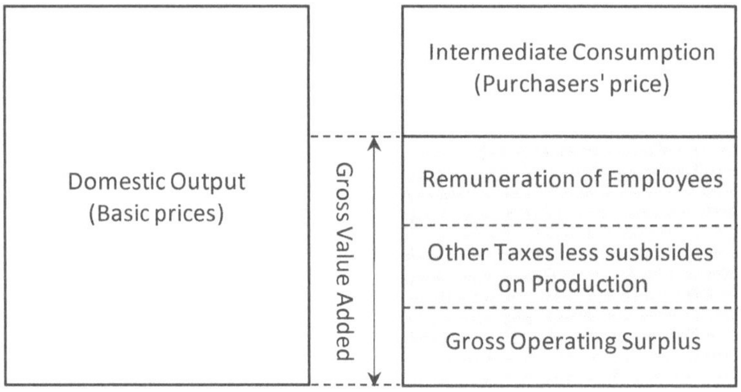

2.6 Residence and GDP

In the SNA, the concept of **residence**, which distinguishes whether an economic unit is a resident or non-resident, is a key criterion in determining the coverage of GDP. National accounts do not classify economic units as residents or non-residents based on nationality or legal status. The criterion for determining whether an economic unit is a resident is whether the **center of its predominant economic interest** is sustained within a particular economic territory. In other words, if an economic unit engages in economic activities or transactions in a specific country on a significant scale, for an extended period (more than one year) or indefinitely, it is considered a

[6] The 2025 SNA introduces the concept of **resource rent**, the portion of gross operating surplus attributable to the use of natural resources, and outlines the method for its measurement. For further details, see 5.5.3.

resident of that country. This concept of residence aligned with the definition in the IMF's BPM6 (Balance of payments and international investment position manual, 6th edition). Transactions between residents and non-residents are separately treated in the **rest of the world account**, which deals with the external sector in the sequence of economic accounts.

GDP, the aggregate indicator of production, is measured based on residence, not on the geographical territory. That is, GDP is the sum of gross value added created by all resident economic units engaged in production within a country, plus taxes less subsidies on products which are not included in the output valued at basic prices. Therefore, the scope of GDP includes the production activities of residents conducted abroad (e.g., when residents provide services overseas), while production activities conducted by non-residents within the domestic economy (e.g., foreign embassies, foreign military bases) are excluded.

Similarly, GDP from the expenditure side is also measured on the basis of residence. For household final consumption expenditures, it is measured based on the expenditures incurred by resident households, rather than by territory. Accordingly, final consumption expenditure of households includes expenditures made by resident households abroad and subtracts expenditures made by non-residents within the country. This calculation method involves first determining the total expenditure of all households (including both residents and non-residents) within the country, then adding the expenditures of resident households abroad (which is treated as "imports"), and subtracting the expenditures of non-residents within the country (which is treated as "exports").

In addition, all non-financial assets within a national economy are assumed to be owned or purchased by resident units only. For example, the owners or purchasers of all buildings, structures, domestic land, and natural resources are considered residents. If the legal owner of such assets is a non-resident, a **notional resident unit** is created, and this notional resident unit are assumed to have purchased the asset, while the actual legal owner, a non-resident, is treated as acquiring an equivalent equity of financial assets from the notional resident unit. In this case, the notional resident unit is classified as **corporations (quasi-corporations)** in the institutional sector classification.

2.7 Establishments and industries, institutional units and institutional sectors

In the process of compiling national accounts, the units in which various basic statistical data are collected play a crucial role in determining the level of aggregation for the statistics. Most of the basic source data collected by statistical agencies are prepared at the factory level within an enterprise or at the enterprise level, and the types of data collected at these units are not consistent. Legally reported data to external entities consists of financial statements at the enterprise level. However, if there are multiple establishments within an enterprise (factories, branches, etc.), accounting data for managerial purposes are prepared for each establishment site, including production value by types of output, detailed costs incurred, inventories, number of employees, and fixed assets. This section aims to examine the **establishment** as the basic production unit and **institutional unit** at the enterprise level as collection units of basic data, as well as the higher-level groupings of these units, such as **industries** and **institutional sectors**. Prior to compiling national accounts, it is essential to understand the characteristics of the data collected from the establishments and institutional units. Depending on the unit of data collection, it will be determined whether to gather production-oriented data or overall economic activity data, and the purpose of the compilation will vary depending on the nature of the collected data.

2.7.1 Establishments and industries

In the SNA, the basic unit for collecting production data is the **establishment**. While the enterprise is a decision-making unit that performs all production activities, the most detailed basic unit for production is the establishment. An establishment as a basic unit of statistical collection has a location in a particular area and produces one or more products. Establishments are classified based on the nature of the products they produce, including market producers, non-market producers, and producers for own final uses (this classification will be further explained in section 2.8 along with "types of output"). An establishment may exist in multiple numbers within a single enterprise or institution. Examples of establishments include individual farms, mines, factories, shops, warehouses, and offices. In addition, an establishment may produce **secondary products** other than its **primary products**. For example, a stee manufacturing plant may produce other steel-related processed goods based on its primary product. In this case, the primary product of the establishment is considered to be steel, while the secondary products are other steel-related goods. The determination of whether a product is the primary product is based on the product that contributes the largest share of output value at the establishment. Typically, when statistical agencies collect data from establishments, they classify both primary products and secondary products by type.

At the enterprise level, in addition to the primary or secondary production activities, a variety of supporting tasks are also carried out, such as accounting, employee recruitment and management, raw material procurement, product sales, advertising, and transportation services. These activities are generally performed by supporting departments of the headquarter, rather than the individual establishments, and are referred to as **ancillary activities**.

Statistical agencies regard the ancillary activities conducted at the enterprise headquarters as contributing to the overall production process of other establishments, and as such, they allocate the costs incurred by the headquarters to the establishments that directly engage in production activities. The allocation process to each establishment begins by first recognizing the output of the headquarters' ancillary activities and then distributing this amount to the respective establishments. At this time, the output of the ancillary activities of the headquarters is calculated by the **sum of costs method**, which includes costs of capital services (= depreciation + net operating surplus from capital investment). Specifically, the output of headquarters is treated as intermediate consumption of other establishments, and the allocation criteria used include the output, value added, and number of employees of each establishment. However, if data on the ancillary activities of the headquarter is not available, there is no need to artificially recognize the establishment.

In the SNA, industries are defined based on the concept of establishments. An **industry** refers to a group of establishments engaged in the same or similar types of production activities. The SNA follows the ISIC (*International Standard Industrial Classification of All Economic Activities*, UN) as the classification standard for industries. Therefore, the detailed classification criteria of ISIC, including Section, Division, Group, and Class, are equally applied to the national accounts. However, in applying to each country, the ISIC may be adjusted or modified under the country' circumstance. The industrial classification includes not only market producers but also non-market producers, such as government or non-profit institutions, and own-account producers who produce for their own consumption.

In particular, some caution is needed when classifying government activities in industries according to ISIC. For government activities, public administration, diplomacy, defense, public order and safety of a nation are allocated to the subcategories of Public Administration and Defense (Division 84), while other government activities are classified into their respective industry activities. For example, public school services are classified under Education services (Division 85), public hospital services under Health activities (Division 86), and public broadcasting services under Programming and Broadcasting activities (Division 60).

2.7.2 Institutional units and institutional sectors

In the SNA, **institutional units** are introduced as the entities that engage in all economic activities. Unlike establishments, which are confined to production units, an institutional unit is a separate economic entity that can independently make all economic decisions. Examples of institutional units include enterprises as production entities and households as consumption entities, as well as government or non-profit institutions that engage in non-market activities. The SNA defines an institutional unit as "an economic entity that can own assets and incur liabilities, in its own right, and engage in economic activities, and enter into transactions with other entities. Among institutional units, households are primarily considered consumers, but are also recognized as entities capable of performing small-scale production activities (which are "household unincorporated enterprises"). Institutional units other than households include corporations, non-profit institutions and government, all of which are recognized as legal entities.

Additionally, when an institutional unit participates in domestic economic activities, it is important to identify whether the unit is a resident or non-resident which is, therefore, excluded from the scope of domestic economy. The criterion for determining whether an institutional unit is a domestic unit (resident) or a foreign unit (non-resident) is based on whether the **center of predominant economic interest** is located in domestic country or abroad. This criterion aligns with the definition presented in the Balance of Payment Manual (BPM6).

In the SNA, **institutional sectors** refer to groupings of institutional units that are identical or similar in nature. In other words, institutional sectors represent the upper-level categories of institutional units, and the SNA subdivides them into five institutional sectors as follows:

- Non-financial corporations
- Financial corporations
- General government
- Non-profit institutions serving households (NPISHs)
- Households

These institutional sectors serve as the minimum basic classifications for distinguishing economic entities based on their characteristics when compiling the SNA sequence of economic accounts. They are used to identify economic activities and transactions between these economic entities. The establishment (or industry) mentioned in the preceding section is a basic statistical unit for collecting data on production activities. However, the institutional unit (or institutional sector) functions as a foundational statistical unit (or sector) for measuring not only its production activities but also other economic activities such as expenditure, capital accumulation, and financial transactions. As a result, in the sequence of economic accounts compiled based on the institutional sector classifications, data from establishments (or industries) are primarily used for the compilation of the production account and the generation of earned income account, while basic statistics at the institutional sector level must be collected to compile all other accounts, including these two accounts.

2.8 Types, valuation and use of output

2.8.1 Definition of output

In the SNA, **output** refers to the total value of goods and services produced by an individual unit, typically an establishment, during a given accounting period. Output is the result of production activity and provides the starting point of the production account within the sequence of economic accounts. Output is compiled on the basis of the accounting unit, that is, the *establishment*, rather than by production process. Accordingly, if a single establishment undertakes multiple production processes, the output of all such process is aggregated. However, output is defined in a way that excludes the following two categories:

1. Goods and services used for activities for which the establishment does not bear the economic risk. Even if goods or services are produced by the establishment, they are not recorded as its output when the economic risk associated with production activity is not borne by that establishment.

2. Goods and services consumed within the same establishment as intra-establishment intermediate consumption. These are not recorded as output. Exceptions are made for (i) goods entering inventories, i.e., goods produced but not used during the period and carried forward as inventories, (ii) goods and services used for own-account gross fixed capital formation, and (iii) the own final consumption of household unincorporated enterprises (for example, the portion of rice produced and consumed directly by a farming household).

The SNA classifies output into three broad categories according to the valuation method and the economic significance of the price at which the output is supplied: **market output**, **non-market output**, and **output for own final use**. In the following section, the definitions of these types of output and the valuation methods applied to each of them are examined.

2.8.2 Types and valuation of output

The SNA defines and establishes accounting procedures for market output, non-market output, and output for own final use as follows:

Market output

If output whose price in the market is an "economically significant price", is defined as **market outputs,** referring to goods and services produced mainly by enterprises (corporations, quasi-corporations, unincorporated enterprises owned by households) for the purpose of selling in the market. The economically significant price, which is the criterion for valuing the market output, is defined by the SNA as "prices that have a significant effect on the amounts that producers are willing to supply and on the amounts purchasers wish to buy." In other words, producers are willing to supply products to the market at this price, but at any price lower than this, they are not willing to supply, while consumers have the freedom to purchase or not purchase and make the choice on the basis of the prices charged. The valuation of market output is primarily based on basic prices at which it is traded in the market, excluding any taxes less subsidies on products imposed on the purchaser at the time of sale. If the data on basic prices is unavailable, producers' prices may be used instead.

Non-market output

Output provided free of charge or at an **economically insignificant price** is referred to as **non-market output**. This primarily refers to goods and services produced by government or non-profit institutions[7], which are not traded in the market but are provided to unspecified general public or specific groups. Examples of non-market output include government services such as public safety, defense, and public administration services, as well as private services by religious institutions. These services are provided to beneficiaries free of charge, or some amounts are charged in return for the services, but the amounts charged are generally far below the actual costs. The distinction between economically significant and insignificant prices is conceptually difficult to define; therefore, in practice, it is determined by how much of the production costs is covered by sales value. This is called the "cost recovery ratio" where **50% rule** is applied. That is, if "sales value/production cost" > 50%, it is assumed as economically significant price, and if "sales value/production cost" < 50%,

---

[7] However, some non-profit institutions sell their products at economically significant prices, and in the SNA, these non-profit institutions are classified as corporations sector.

it is assumed as economically insignificant price. The 50% rule is recommended by the 2008 SNA and the European System of Accounts (ESA).

As such, while the valuation of non-market output is based on whether its price is economically significant or economically insignificant; however, such output does not, in practice, have observable market prices. Consequently, the SNA employes the **sum of costs** approach as an alternative method for valuing non-market output. The 2025 SNA explicitly specifies the components of the sum-of-costs method.

- **Non-market output = intermediate consumption + remuneration of employees + depreciation and depletion + other taxes less subsidies on production + net return to capital + rent payable on non-produced non-financial assets**

In estimating the net return to capital, the 2025 SNA recommends the use of a capital rate of return based on the opportunity-cost concept. Recommended approaches include (i) a rate of return derived from a normal operating surplus (a mark-up-based rate) and (ii) a borrowing-rate-based rate of return. Under the latter, the rate used is the rate at which the producer would borrow, reflecting differences in institutional or industry-specific risk. Rent payable on non-produced non-financial assets refers to payments made for the use of land or natural resources and is classified in the national accounts as a form of property income. The sum-of-costs method is applied to output for which market prices cannot be observed, namely the non-market output of government units, NPISHs, and central banks. It is also applied to own-account gross fixed capital formation and to output for own final use for which no comparable market output exists and therefore cannot be observed at market prices, as discussed later.

Output for own final use

This refers to cases where the producer has produced output but does not sell it in the market, instead, consume it for its own use. For example, a farmer may consume a portion of the crops they have harvested, or a construction company may build and use an office building for its self. This is referred to as **output for own final use**, and the valuation method for this output is to use the average basic price of an identical or similar product if it is traded in the market. If such data is unavailable, the **sum of production costs** method is used, including the return on investment capital[8].

---

[8] When a **non-market producer** such as general government produces intellectual property products for its

Table 2.2 Valuation methods by types of output

Type of output	Description	Valuation method
Market output	Products traded at economically significant prices	Valued at basic prices
Non-market output	Products produced by government or NPISH, and provided free of charge or at economically insignificant prices	"Sum of production costs"
Output for own final use	Products produced by the producer for their own final use	Valued at the "average basic price" of similar products. If such data is unavailable, valued using "sum of production costs" method.

2.8.3 Use of output

As stated above, output is classified into market output, non-market output and output for own final use, accordingly, the methods for valuing these outputs differ. Additionally, the entities that consume (or purchase) the produced outputs vary by type of output, and the method for valuing the consumption amount also differs.

In the case of market output, the economic entity that purchases or uses the output is considered the trading counterpart. However, with non-market output, it is difficult to specify purchasing entities because they acquire it free of charge or at economically insignificant prices. In such case, the SNA introduces a special imputation method to deal with it. This section provides a brief explanation of the entities (institutional units) that use the three types of output mentioned above, as well as how to value the amount of their use.

Use of market output

First, the institutional units that use market output can be divided into the production units that have purchased the output, including enterprises (such as corporations, quasi-corporations, household unincorporated enterprises), government and NPISHs, as well as households and the rest of the world sector as consumption units. The market output consumed by households as sole consumption units is recorded as final consumption expenditure, while the expenditure of that output by other institutional sectors (including households unincorporated enterprises as producers) are treated as intermediate consumption or gross fixed capital formation, and exports. In addition,

own final use (for example, own-account R&D or software), the depreciation and return to capital arising from the existing stock of intellectual property products should not be included in the sum-of-costs method (2025 SNA, 4A.10).

the amount accounted as intermediate consumption by government and NPISHs is again reclassified as final consumption expenditure of themselves.[9]

The expenditure of market output is valued at purchasers' prices, and in the case of gross fixed capital formation, it is recorded at "actual transaction price plus costs of ownership transfers."

Figure 2.10 Use of market output

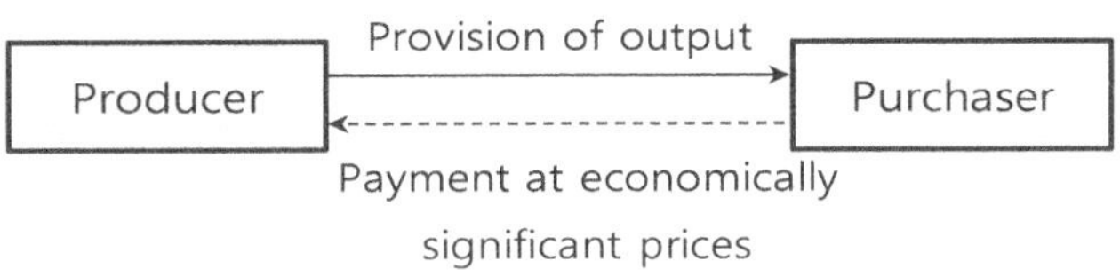

Use of non-market output

The institutional units that use non-market output differ from those using market output. The output produced by government and NPISHs is mostly provided to households or businesses, but the beneficiaries of this output cannot be clearly identified because it is provided free or at economically insignificant prices. Therefore, in the SNA, the institutional units who produce non-market output (that is, non-market producers) are assumed to use the output for themselves. In other words, the output produced by government is attributed to final use of government, and output produced by NPISHs is attributed to final use of NPISHs themselves.

The valuation of the final use of non-market output follows the sum of costs method applied equally for production. However, if beneficiaries (or purchasers) pay a portion of the amount to the non-market producers in exchange for purchase, or if the non-market producers sell any market output, the amount received is deducted, and the remaining amount is treated as final consumption of the non-market producers themselves. On the other hand, the amounts paid by the purchaser to the non-market producer for both market and non-market outputs are recorded as the consumption of the purchaser (enterprises, households etc.). For more details, refer to Chapter 12, the government account, and the NPISHs account.

[9] There are cases where the government purchases market output from private producers simply to provide them to households (this is treated as final consumption of government). An example of this is when the government covers part of the household's hospital treatment costs through a social security system. In such cases, the expenditure is not accounted as intermediate consumption by the government but is only recorded as its final consumption expenditure.

Figure 2.11 Use of non-market output

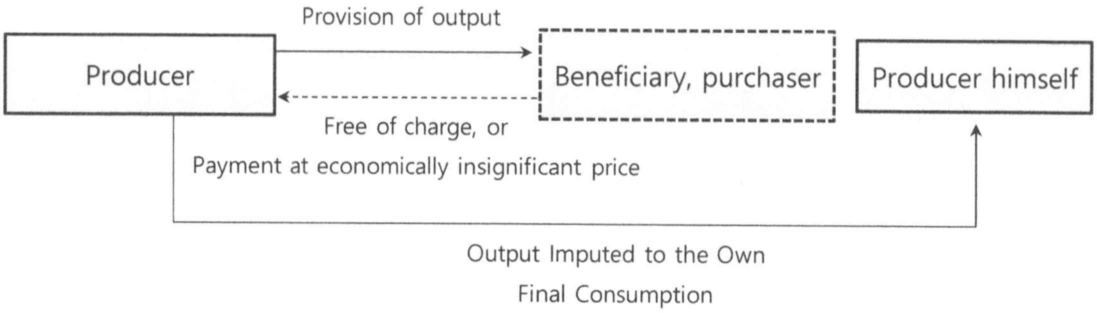

In this way, the amount of consumption attributed to the final consumption by the non-market producer itself is further divided into two parts, one where the beneficiary (purchaser) can be identified and another where it is difficult to identify the beneficiary. An example of the identifiable part is the free healthcare services provided by health clinics and the free or low-cost educational services offered by public education institutions (i.e., public schools) to households. These services allow the identification of the beneficiaries, and in the SNA, they are called **individual consumption**. On the other hand, an example of the unidentifiable part is services such as defense, public safety, and public administration services, where the beneficiaries cannot be specifically identified. These are referred to as **collective consumption**. In the SNA, individual consumption is treated as implicit transfers to households, while only the remaining collective consumption is treated as actual final consumption by non-market producers. (Individual consumption and collective consumption are discussed in detail in Sections 5.2.2 and 5.2.3.)

Output for own final use

Lastly, the users of **output for own final use** are producers themselves, and this output is treated as the final consumption or gross fixed capital formation of the producers. If we look into it by institutional sector, corporations do not incur final consumption; instead, they may generate gross fixed capital formation (e.g., the construction of buildings for their own use). Household unincorporated enterprises may generate both final consumption and gross fixed capital formation for their own final use. For instance, this includes final consumption of agricultural products by farmers themselves, production of fruit trees and dairy cattle for their own use, owner-occupied dwelling services, and household services provided by paid domestic staff. Additionally, government and NPISHs may also generate gross fixed capital formation for their own use (e.g., production of research and development for own use).

Figure 2.12 Use of output for own final use

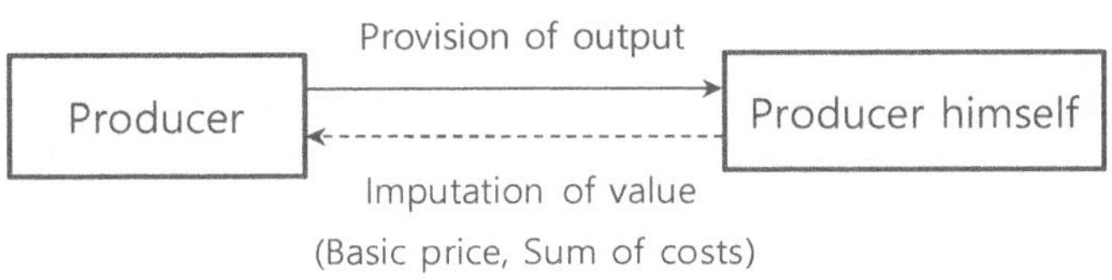

This type of production activity for one's own use is referred to as the **own-account production** in the SNA. In the example above, when a farmer consumes the rice he has produced himself, it is treated as final consumption expenditure by the household sector as a final consumer. However, if the farmer uses part of the rice he has produced as input for the next farming season, it is treated as intermediate consumption by the producer. When a producer uses his own output as intermediate consumption, both the output and intermediate consumption are recorded, so there is no change in terms of net output, and no impact on value added. The amount used for the output for own final use is valued the same as the way for valuing output for own final use described above.

Output for own final use differs in nature from non-market output. The output for own final use is produced and used for the final consumption or gross fixed capital formation of producers by themselves, whereas non-market output is assumed to be consumed by producers themselves, although the benefits of its consumption return to other economic entities.

Chapter 3. Supply and use tables: their functions and structure

Supply and use tables are matrix tables that display all items of total supply and total use by products on the basis of the product balance identity. These tables measure the flow of goods and services in a national economy in terms of production and expenditure, and measure the distribution of income, so that production, expenditure, and generation of earned income can be connected and viewed at a glance. The source data used in the supply and use tables are collected and processed by statistical agencies, and through this compilation process, these basic statistics can be systematically connected, thereby improving the consistency between statistical data in terms of quality. Supply and use tables are displayed by industry in the columns and by product in the rows, and they serve as the basis for compiling the sequence of economic accounts, which is classified by institutional sectors. This chapter aims to explore the functions performed by the supply and use tables and how the tables are structured. Additionally, it will examine how the supply and use tables are constructed from a practical compilation perspective when applying price types (basic prices, purchasers' prices) and discuss how the components of these tables are valued and reflected in the tables.

3.1 Functions of supply and use tables

Supply and use tables (SUTs) are fundamental tables that belong to the core framework in the SNA and serve as basic data for the compilation of the sequence of economic accounts. The sequence of economic accounts records all the activities of a national economy in a series of accounts ranging from the production account to the balance sheet, and supply and use tables provide basic data necessary for the compilation of production account, generation of earned income account, use of income account and capital account among them. In particular, to compile production account and generation of earned income account which are the starting point of the sequence of economic accounts, data from supply and use tables are indispensable. Therefore, it is advisable to compile the supply and use tables in advance before compiling the sequence of economic accounts.

By using the supply and use tables, it is possible to examine flows of supply and use of goods and services within a national economy by industry for a specific period, as well as identify the generation of earned income by industry. Consequently, through the supply and use tables, gross domestic product, which is the primary purpose of compiling national accounts, can be derived in terms of production, expenditure, and income, and the real growth rates can be calculated by combining time-series value data with price data. In other words, these tables can provide estimates of gross domestic product (GDP) in a comprehensive and systematic way.

In addition, the derived effects that arise from compiling supply and use tables are as follows. First, in terms of the quality management of statistics, they serve as a powerful tool for verifying the consistency of economic statistical data by comparing source data. In other words, by reconciling the differences between supply-side and expenditure-side data, and thereby resolving inconsistencies, they help address the weaknesses of basic statistics. Furthermore, when compiling the supply and use tables, it becomes possible to complete insufficient statistics from both the production and expenditure sides. For example, when data on the supply side are known but data on the use side are not available, unmeasured data can be estimated using the product balance identity. Therefore, using the framework of supply and use tables increases the interconnection between various source data.

Second, the supply and use tables are used as source data for deriving weights for key economic indicators. For instance, the values in the supply and use tables are used in selecting the weights for the components when compiling the price indices or GDP for the base year. The reason for using the weights of the supply and use tables is that they provide balanced and refined data between production and expenditure sides, leading to more accurate statistics.

Third, supply and use tables are used as a preliminary data for compiling input-output tables. As will be explained later, input-output tables show the structure of product inputs, income generation, and expenditures under the premise that each industry produces only one product, and consists of the same dimensions in rows and columns (that is, product-by-product or industry-by-industry). By transforming the supply and use tables using matrix formulas, input-output tables can be derived.

The source data required to compile supply and use tables is typically sourced from industry-specific data. To obtain this data, it is necessary to gather information from establishments, which are the basic units of each industry. If data for each institutional sector, such as corporate financial statements, are available, the task of converting this data into industry-specific data must be carried out at the same time to ensure accurate integration into supply and use tables.

3.2 Structure of supply and use tables

In this section, the basic structure of the supply and use tables will be described in order to provide a general understanding of them. This section will introduce the simplest form of the tables that do not take into account the type of prices used in the supply and use tables, while the following section will discuss the practical supply and use tables that incorporate the types of prices.

3.2.1 Structure of the supply table

Supply and use tables consist of the supply table and the use table. The **supply table** presents the total value of goods and services supplied to a national economy during a specific period, categorized by product. In terms of its structure, the columns represent the total supply items from the product balance identity, which include **domestic output** and **imports**, while the rows display the individual products themselves. (See Table 3.1.) The domestic output in the columns is subdivided by industry (categorized by ISIC), and the rows display the various products produced by each industry, classified into their primary products and any secondary products (categorized by "Central Product Classification"). For instance, in Table 3.1, if the manufacturing industry produces manufactured goods ($30) as its primary products, and rental services and trade services ($5) as secondary products, the corresponding cells under the manufacturing industry column will show the output value for both manufactured goods ($30) and services ($5) in their respective rows.

Since the output data in the supply table is collected from establishments, which are the basic unit of industry, the supply table aggregates the products from these establishment and displays them by industry. The bottom row of the supply table shows the total output for each industry, while the right-most column shows the total supply value of each product, calculated as the sum of domestic output and imports.

Table 3.1 Structure of the supply table

Supplies / Products	**Output (by industry)** (A)				**Imports**	**Total supply**
	Agriculture	Manufacturing	Construction	Service	(B)	(A+B)
Agricultural product						
Manufactured product		30				
Building & Structures						
Services		5				
Total output (E)		35				

Imports are divided into two categories: imports of goods and imports of services. Imports of goods are listed by product in rows, and the source data is collected through the Customs Service. The Customs Service's clearance data on imports are recorded under the classification code of HS (Harmonized Commodity Description and Coding System). In order to align this data with the product classification of domestic output (CPC, Central Product Classification), a matching process between the HS and CPC codes must be conducted. To this end, the United Nations publishes the correspondence tables linking between these classification codes on its website.

On the other hand, the customs statistics require the imports and exports of goods to be recorded on the basis of the time of customs clearance, whereas the national accounts are prepared to record the goods based on the time of **change of ownership**. If the timing of the customs clearance and the change of ownership do not coincide, timing adjustments must be made. Specifically, accounting for the delivery of large vessels or aircrafts should be adjusted based on actual changes in ownership, rather than just following data in the customs statistics (BPM6, 3.63~3.64). The timing of change of ownership may be the moment when the goods are entered in the book of the counterpart, or the moment when the ownership is transferred by physical delivery. Moreover, if production is proceeded over a long period of time and payments are made stage by stage, the portion of production completed during the period is treated as having been sold at the end of each period. Therefore, when using customs statistics, technical adjustments should be made to take these issues into account.

3.2.2 Structure of the use table

The **use table** represents the total amount of goods and services used in the national economy, categorized by product. Looking at the structure of the table (Table 3.2), the columns display the items of total use from the product balance identity (such as intermediate consumption, final consumption expenditure, gross capital formation, and exports), while the rows enumerate the used products and value-added items in a matrix form. Intermediate consumption is broken down by industry in the columns, corresponding to the industries in the supply table, and the rows display the details of each product under the items of total use.

Table 3.2 Structure of the use table

Products / Uses	**Intermediate consumption (by industry)** (C)					**Final use** (D)			**Total use** (C+D)
	Agriculture	Manufacturing	Construction	Services	Subtotal	Final consumption	Capital formation	Exports	
Agricultural goods Manufactured goods Buildings, structure Services									
Intermediate consumption total (F)									
Remuneration of employees Net taxes on production Operating surplus									
Value added (G)									
Total output (H = F+G)									

In addition, the value-added for each industry is displayed just below the quadrant of intermediate consumption, and the total output for each industry, which is the sum of intermediate consumption and valued added, is shown in the bottom row. The right-most column of this table shows the amounts of total use by product.

When explaining the use table, it is difficult to describe the use table in isolation. This is because the use table is compiled in connection with the supply table. First, the total output by industry in the supply table (row E in Table 3.1) must correspond to the total output by industry in the use table (row H in Table 3.2). Looking at the process of compiling these tables, typically, once the output values for each industry are derived from the supply table, these values are transferred to the use table as the same output values for each industry, ensuring that outputs of the two tables are consistent. Second, the total supply by product in the supply table (column A+B) must correspond completely to the total use by product in the use table (column C+D). This alignment is required by the product balance identity, which ensures values of total supply and total use are consistent.

The use table can be partitioned into three quadrants as shown in the figure below (Figure 3.1). The *quadrant I* represents intermediate consumption, the *quadrant II* represents final use, and the *quadrant III* represents gross value-added, which is derived by subtracting intermediate consumption from output. The gross value-added quadrant is broken down into its components, which include remuneration of employees, other taxes less subsidies on production, and gross operating surplus. The bottom row of the table shows the output by industry, which is directly transferred from the output values by industry in the supply table. Therefore, the industry-wise totals in the bottom row of the use table must match the industry-wise totals in the bottom row of the supply table. The quadrant I illustrates the industry-wise data to be used for the production account in the sequence of economic accounts, the quadrant II shows the data used for the use of income account and the capital account, and the quadrant III shows the data used for the generation of earned income account, which will be covered later.

Figure 3.1 Quadrants of the use table

Intermediate consumption (I)	Final use (II)
Value-added (III)	

The procedure where the data in the use table is prepared is as follows. Initially, the total output by industry (bottom row) in the supply table are transferred to the bottom row of the quadrant III in the use table. Next, once the values of total intermediate consumption (row) for each industry are recorded, the value-added (row), which is the difference between output and intermediate consumption, is displayed. Subsequently, the gross operating surplus (row) is derived as a balance by subtracting remuneration of employees and other taxes less subsidies on production from the gross value-added (row).

The final use sector (quadrant II), which represents the final expenditure, is further divided by institutional sectors. For instance, final consumption expenditure is divided into expenditures of households, government, and NPISHs in their capacity as final consumers, while gross capital formation is categorized into expenditures by types of producers such as corporations, government and NPISHs. Each column vertically displays the amount of expenditure by product. The last column, representing exports, is split into goods and services. Exports of goods are compiled based on the data of export values for each product from customs statistics, and like imports of goods, the data classified by HS codes is converted into the product classification (CPC) for display in the use table.

3.3 The structure of supply and use tables incorporating price types

Up until now, it has assumed a simplified framework for explaining the supply and use tables, without considering the price elements. However, in practice, these tables are compiled with the inclusion of price elements. Specifically, when preparing the supply and use tables, the prices actually applied to each item in the product balance identity differ, meaning that the product balance identity must be adjusted to reflect the relevant price types. Accordingly, for the items in the product balance identity: the output is valued at basic prices, intermediate consumption and final consumption expenditure are valued at purchasers' prices, and gross fixed capital formation is valued at transaction prices, with the addition of "costs of ownership transfer." A brief overview of the supply and use tables incorporating the types of prices is provided below. (For further details, refer to Chapter 4, Supply Table, and Chapter 5, Use Table.)

Figure 3.2 A supply table reflecting the type of prices

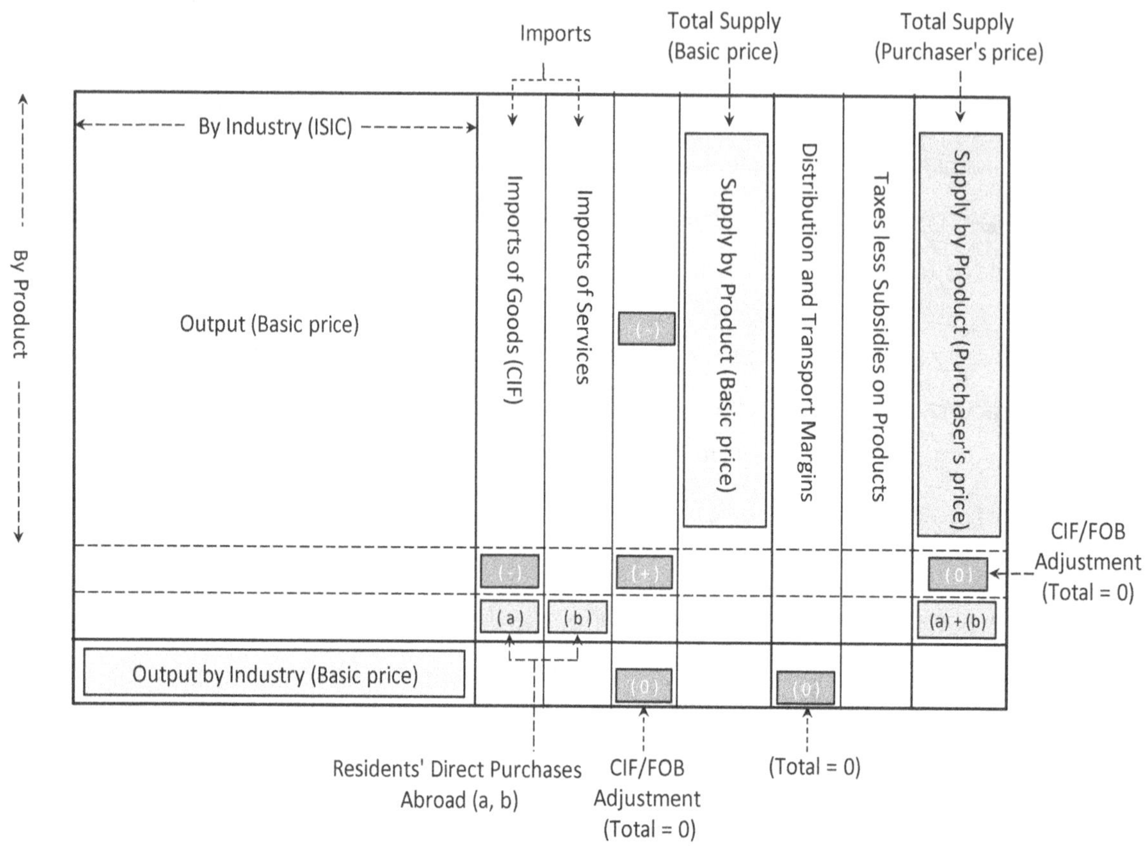

Let's first examine the supply table that incorporates the **types of prices**. As illustrated in Figure 3.2, the values of output and imports are initially prepared at basic prices in the horizontal (columns) direction. Then, to adjust for purchasers' prices, additional columns are added for items such as trade and transport margins, and taxes less subsides on products. These adjustments result in the column of the total supply displayed at purchasers' prices. In the column of trade and transport margins, values of trade and transport margins for each product are shown. However, for trade and transport services, the value of total margins allocated to other products are subtracted (indicated by negative sign), so the sum of this column equals zero. This subtraction is done to avoid double counting, as the margins of trade and transport services have already been added to other products.

The **imports of goods** column is recorded using CIF prices in the customs statistics, and therefore the amounts include the transport and insurance service charges. Since these transport and insurance service charges overlap with the portions recorded as transport services and insurance services within **the imports of services**, they must be deducted from the imports of goods. This adjustment is handled in the special column and row of **CIF/FOB adjustment**. In addition, when domestic residents purchase goods or services from abroad, those amounts are not captured in the customs statistics and must therefore be separately surveyed and added to the imports of goods and services. This procedure is recorded in the row of "direct purchases abroad by residents". The summary of the composition of the supply table is presented in Table 3.3.

Table 3.3 Composition of the supply table

	Output (basic prices)	Imports		CIF/FOB adjustment	Total supply (basic prices)	Price adjustments			Total supply (purchaser's prices)
		Goods	Services			Distribution margins	Transport margins	Taxes less subsidies on products	
Market goods	..	..			a	b	d	g_1	$a+b+d+g_1$
Trade services	..		..		b+c	**-b**			**c**
Transport services	..		..	(-)	d+e		**-d**		**e**
Other products	..		..	(-)	f			g_2	$f+g_2$
CIF/FOB adjust.		(-)		(+)					**0**
Direct purchases abroad by residents		h_1	h_2		h				h
Total	i	j_1	j_2	**0**	$a+b+c+d+e+f+h = i+j_1+j_2$	**0**	**0**	g	a+b+c+d+e+f+g+h

Footnote) a: total supply of market goods, b: distribution margins, c: total trade services - distribution margins, d: transport margins, e: total transport services - transport margins, f: supply of other products, g: taxes less subsidies on products (g1+g2 = g), h: direct purchases abroad by residents (h1: goods, h2: services, h1+h2= h), i: domestic output (basic prices), j: imports (j1: goods, j2: services)

The use table that reflects the different price types is structured as follows (Figure 3.3). Since all items in the use table are displayed at purchasers' prices, no separate adjustments for the price are necessary. The column of total use on the right-most of this table, which represents total amounts by product, must match the total amounts by product at purchasers' prices of the right-most column of the supply table. However, the output values in the bottom row of the quadrant III are recorded at basic prices and are carried over directly from the supply table. As a result, the gross value-added calculated as output minus intermediate consumption represents "gross value-added at basic prices." Therefore, in order to derive GDP, one must sum the gross value added by industry (recorded at basic prices) across the horizontal dimension and then add the taxes less subsidies on products.

Figure 3.3 Use table reflecting the type of prices

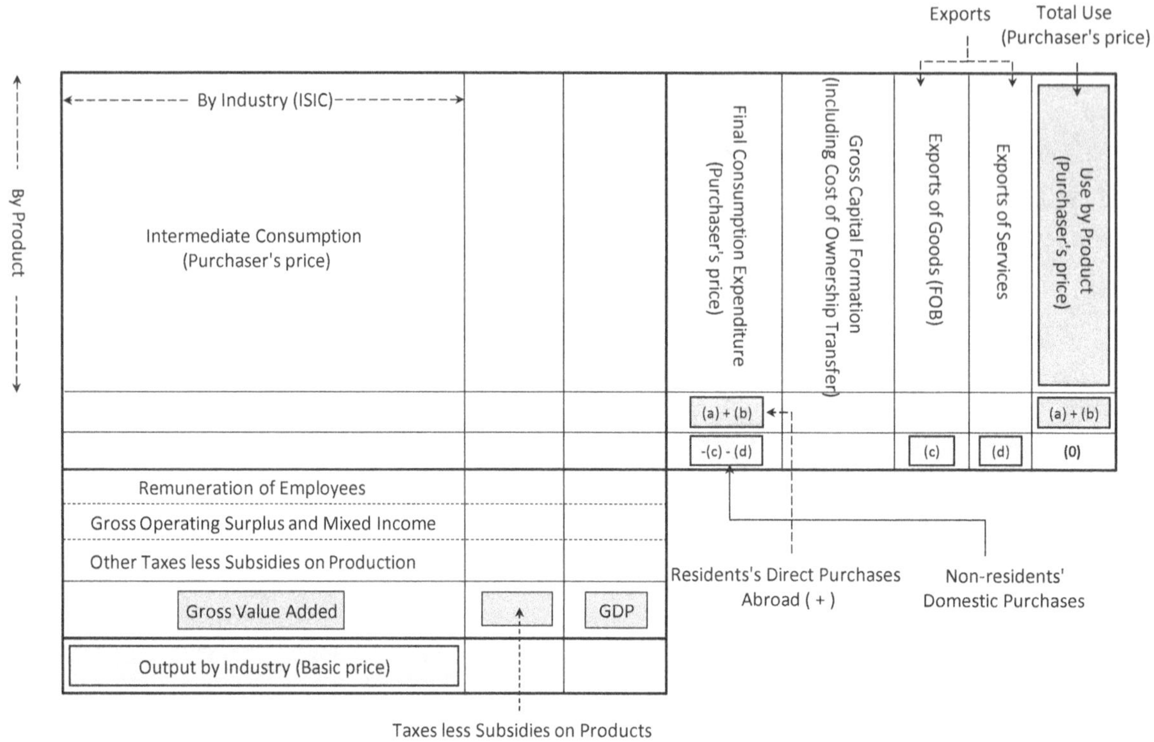

GDP = Gross Value Added + Taxes less Subsidies on Products

A brief summary of the use table is shown in Table 3.4. Here, total supply (at market prices) = a+b+c+d+e+f+g+h = A+B+C+h = total use (at market prices). In addition, A+E = *i* = total output (at basic prices), and E+g = B+C+h – (j1+j2) = GDP.

Table 3.4 Composition of the use table

	Intermediate consumption (purchaser's prices)	Taxes less subsidies on products	Subtotal	Domestic final uses	Exports		Total use (purchasers' prices)
					Goods	Services	
Goods & services	A		A	B	C_1	C_2	A+B+C
Direct purchases abroad by residents				h			h
Domestic purchases by non-residents				**-D**	D_1	D_2	**0**
Subtotal	A		A	B+h – D	C_1+D_1	C_2+D_2	A+B+C+h
Value added	E	**g**	E+g				
Total	A+E	g					

Footnote) A: intermediate consumption of products, B: domestic final uses (final consumption, gross capital formation), C: exports of goods and services (C1: goods, C2: services), D: domestic purchases by non-residents (D1: goods, D2: services), E: value added

3.4 Valuation basis for each component in supply and use tables

In this section, we aim to provide detailed explanations of the valuation principles applied to each component of the supply and use tables. The valuation basis employed in the SNA generally follows the established practices of business accounting, but a significant distinction lies in the fact that, in the SNA, valuation is not conducted on the basis of **historic cost**; rather, **current prices** prevailing at the time of valuation are used. This means that, the SNA reflects the current market value of items at the point of measurement.

3.4.1 Valuation of components in the supply table

Fundamentally, each item in the supply table is recorded at basic prices, and subsequently converted to purchasers' prices through price adjustments (taxes less subsidies on products, distribution margin, and transport margin). First, regarding the valuation of *output*, market output is measured using basic prices, and if no basic price data is available, producers' prices are used. For the valuation of non-market output, the sum of costs method is employed; these costs include intermediate consumption, remuneration of employees, depreciation and depletion, and other taxes less subsidies on production, as well as the net return to capital which corresponds to net operating surplus or net mixed income. For the valuation of the output for own final use, basic prices in the market are used; if this is not feasible, the sum of production costs approach is applied. In this case, the production costs must include depreciation and depletion, other taxes less subsidies on production, and net return to capital employed in production.

Regarding *imports*, the basic price is applied for goods. The basic price of imported goods may vary depending on the party responsible for bearing the freight transport costs. If the foreign exporter bears transport costs for imports, the basic price will be the CIF price (which includes the transport and insurance charges); if the domestic importer bears transport costs, the basic price will be the FOB (free on board) price. In cases where it is unclear who bears the transport and insurance costs, the CIF price must be used as the standard one, but the double counting should be avoided through appropriate CIF/FOB adjustments. Finally, imports of services are measured at the actual prices agreed upon between the supplier and the purchaser (BPM6 3.67, MSITS 3.32).

3.4.2 Valuation of components in the use table

The components in the use table are basically valued on the basis of purchasers' prices. Therefore, unlike the supply table, no price adjustments are applied. As described in the previous chapter, the purchaser's price is calculated as "basic price + taxes less subsidies on products (excluding VAT) + non-deductible VAT + transport charges separately invoiced by the supplier + distribution margins."

Among the items in the use table, *intermediate consumption* (which comprises goods and services consumed as inputs in the production process) is valued at the purchaser's price prevailing at the time the inputs are incorporated into production, rather than at the price when the producer acquired it. However, in practice, the value of intermediate consumption is not measured directly at the time of input; instead, it is derived indirectly by subtracting the changes in inventories from the total purchase amount for raw materials and other parts during the accounting period. At this time, both the purchase amount and changes in inventories are valued at purchasers' prices. Changes in inventories are obtained by subtracting the inventory withdrawals from the inventory entries, with the withdrawals from inventories being valued at the purchaser's price prevailing at the time of withdrawal for the production input (see 5.1 for further details). This approach differs from business accounting, where the withdrawal amount is typically valued at historic costs.

Final consumption expenditure for households is valued at purchasers' prices, which includes all taxes on products (including VAT) as well as any transport charges paid separately by the households. In contrast, non-market producers such as government and NPISHs are deemed to consume their own output as final consumption. Given that the items constituting final consumption expenditures for non-market producers are heterogeneous, it is difficult to establish a uniform valuation method. Nevertheless, any goods and services acquired from the market that form part of these expenditures are invariably valued at purchasers' prices (see 5.2 for further details).

Gross fixed capital formation is valued at the purchaser's price which is the actual transaction price, plus costs of ownership transfers (see Chapters 5 and 6 for details). Regarding *changes in inventories*, inventories of finished goods or work-in-progress are valued at their respective basic prices at the time of entries to and withdrawals from inventories. In particular, the finished goods at the time of entry into inventory is valued based on the basic price that is expected to be sold at the time of entry. Inventories of materials and parts are valued at purchasers' prices at the time of entries into and withdrawals from inventories respectively. As mentioned above, the withdrawal value for materials and parts destined for use as production inputs is determined based on the purchasers' prices anticipated at that time of withdrawals. Inventories of goods for resale are valued at the purchaser's price, both upon entries and withdrawals. In particular, when goods held for resale are withdrawn for the purpose of sale, they are valued at the expected purchaser's price of the same goods at the time of entry into inventory. (See 5.3.2 for details.) The value of *acquisitions less disposals of valuables*, in the same manner as gross fixed capital formation, includes the cost of ownership transfers in addition to the purchaser's price which is the actual transaction price. Lastly, the valuation of *exports* is based on FOB prices for goods, while in the case of services, it is based on actual transaction prices, similar to the treatment for imports of services.

Table 3.5 Valuation criteria for each item in the supply table and use tables

Item		Valuation of item
Output	Market output	Basic price, producer's price
	Non-market output	Sum of production costs
	Output for own final use	Basic price, sum of production costs
Imports	Goods	Basic price
	Services	Market price
Intermediate consumption		Purchaser's price
Final consumption	Households	Purchaser's price
	Own account of households	Basic price
	Government	Sum of production costs etc.
	NPISH	Sum of production costs etc.
Gross fixed capital formation		Actual transaction price, including cost of ownership transfer
Changes in inventories	Inventories of finished goods	Basic price at the time of entry and withdrawal
	Inventories of work-in-progress	For production periods of one year or less: Basic price of finished goods multiplied by the share of production cost
	Inventories of materials	Purchaser's price at the time of entry and withdrawal
	Inventories of goods for resale	Purchaser's price
Acquisitions less disposals of valuables		Actual transaction price, including cost of ownership transfer
Exports	Goods	FOB price
	Services	Market price

Chapter 4. Components of the supply table

The supply table is a matrix table in which the columns represent the supply components of the product balance identity, while the rows display the product details of each supply component. This table shows the details of goods and services supplied by a national economy over a given period of time. The columns of the supply table are composed of output, imports, distribution margins (i.e., wholesale and retail margins), transport margins, and taxes less subsidies on products. Both output and imports are recorded at basic prices, whereas the remaining three components constitute a **valuation matrix** that converts the total supply (= output + imports) at basic prices into purchasers' prices. (See Table 3.7.) The rows of the supply table are arranged according to product mixes of the above column-wise components. This chapter will provide a more detailed examination of each component of the supply table.

4.1 Output

According to the SNA's definition, **output** is the result of production activities, which is measured at the establishment level and represents the total value of goods and services produced by an establishment. However, the following items are excluded from this total.

- The value of goods and services used in activities where an establishment does not assume the risk associated with the use of its products in the production process (for example, when processed items are sent back to the originating establishment, that establishment is deemed to have provided only processing services for those items).
- The value of goods and services consumed within the same establishment (with the exception of goods and services intended for own final use).

If an institutional unit contains more than one establishment, the output of that institutional unit is derived as the sum of the outputs of its establishments, including any output delivered between those establishments. However, intra-enterprise deliveries are recorded as output of the first establishment and as intermediate consumption of the second establishment only when the receiving establishment assumes responsibility for making decisions about the levels of supply and prices at which their output is delivered to the market. If this is not the case, the output of the first establishment is shown as entering inventories while the second establishment delivers a processing service and charges a fee for the service.

In order to value the amount of an output, a transaction price for that output should exist. In the case of ordinary products, such a price can be observed in the market; however, for products that are not traded in the market (such as those produced by government or non-profit institutions), measuring their value becomes problematic. Consequently, the SNA distinguishes the types of output into three types as follows and applies different valuation methods to each type.

- Market output
- Non-market output
- Output for own final uses

4.1.1 Market output

Market output refers to the output produced through production activities for the purpose of selling it at economically significant prices. Market output is represented as the sum of the following items.

- The value of goods and services sold at economically significant prices,
- The value of goods and services exchanged through barter transactions,
- The value of goods and services used for payments in kind (including compensation in kind),
- The value of goods and services supplied as intermediate inputs to other establishments within the same enterprise,
- The value of changes in inventories of finished goods and work-in-progress,
- Distribution margins of goods, transport margins, margins on the acquisition and disposal of financial assets.

If the above items are summarized, they can be expressed as follows:

(4.1) **Market output = market sales + barter transaction + payments in kind + intermediate inputs to other establishments within the same enterprise + changes in inventories of finished goods and work-in-progress + margin services**

In general, market output is traded in the market, and it is valued at *basic prices* in the SNA. This is because the sales records, which serve as the source data for business accounting, are prepared at basic prices. Sales value, barter transaction, payment in-kind, and transfers to other establishments within the same enterprise are all valued at basic prices at which they are sold. The last item, changes in inventories, is primarily applied to industries such as mining and manufacturing, where inventories are generated, and its forms include not only tangible assets but also intangible intellectual property products.

Changes in inventories included in the market output cover those of both finished goods and work-in-progress, and are calculated as follows:

(4.2) **Changes in inventories of finished goods and work-in-progress = entries into inventories of finished goods and work-in-progress – withdrawals from inventories of finished goods and work-in-progress – recurrent losses of inventories**

Changes in inventories of goods are also valued at basic prices. These prices are applied at the time when each activity occurs, regardless of whether the output is sold immediately, entered into inventories or used for other purposes. Therefore, if a good is produced and not sold immediately, and instead enters into inventory, it is recorded at the basic price prevailing at the time of entry. Even when this good is withdrawn from inventories for sale, it is accounted for at the basic price prevailing at the time of withdrawal (sale). This method of valuing inventories by applying the prices at each time of entries and withdrawals is called the **perpetual inventory method** (or **PIM**). The reason for using this method is to eliminate holding gains from inflation by preventing the application of **historic costs** used in business accounting.

Box 4.1: Supplementary explanation of the inventory valuation under the perpetual inventory method

Note that changes in inventories also occur for *materials and supplies* purchased by producers for manufacturing or other purposes. In other words, when a producer purchases materials or supplies, entries into inventories occur; subsequently, when these items are put into the production process, withdrawals from inventories take place. Changes in inventories for materials and supplies are calculated in the same way as those for finished goods: "entries into inventories – withdrawals from inventories – recurrent inventory losses" with the perpetual inventory method being equally applied to these valuation. However, in this case, unlike finished goods and work-in-progress, the prices applied here are the purchasers' prices prevailing at the time of entries into and withdrawals from inventories. Similarly, for goods purchased by wholesalers and retailers for resale purposes, their changes in inventories are also valued using the perpetual inventory method, and in this case, the purchaser's price is used for valuation.

In the SNA, as all inventories are valued using the perpetual inventory method, the difference in price between the entry and withdrawal of the same goods is recorded as a holding gain or loss in the "revaluation account", not in the "production account" (see 11.2.1). Let's illustrate this process with an example. Consider the following manufacturing process at an establishment (Figure 4.1). Suppose that when raw materials are purchased from a supplier, the purchaser's price at the time of entry into inventory is recorded as $20. If, when these raw materials are withdrawn from inventory for inputs into the production process, the purchaser's price is valued at $50, the price difference (50 – 20 = 30) appears as an increase in input costs in the production account, resulting in a decrease in value-added. However, it is recorded as an increase in holding gains in the revaluation account. Similarly, suppose that after the manufacturing process, finished goods that are not immediately sold are recorded as inventory at the basic price of $60, and that when these goods are withdrawn from inventory for sale, they are valued $100. Then, the price difference (100 – 60 = 40) appears as a decrease in output (a decrease in inventory) in the production account, yet is recorded as an increase in holding gain in the revaluation account.

Figure 4.1 Valuation of inventories in the manufacturing process

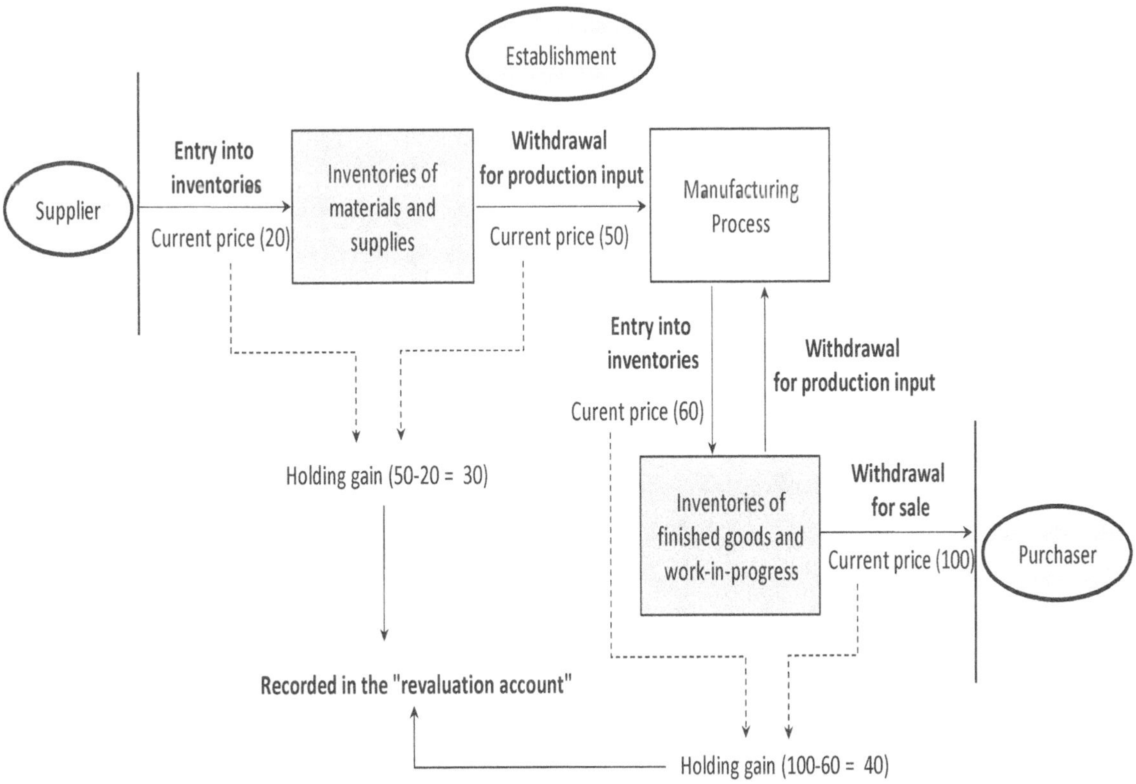

Generally, measuring changes in inventories using entry and withdrawal data on every occasion proves to be cumbersome, making this method far from straightforward. In practice, therefore, changes in inventories are calculated using the stock data on both the opening and closing inventories. This approach also allows output to be derived as follows. In other words, output can be viewed in two ways: **gross output**, which is the output before deducting recurrent inventory losses, and **usable output**, which is the output after such losses have been deducted. The relationship between these two is expressed below:

- Gross output + opening inventory stock = sales + closing inventory stock + recurrent inventory losses
- Gross output = sales + (closing inventory stock – opening inventory stock) + recurrent inventory losses

Based on the above equations, usable output can be determined as follows:

(4.3) **Usable output (= gross output – recurrent inventory losses) = sales + (closing inventory stock – opening inventory stock)**

When applying this formula, the concept of output as defined in the SNA is better represented by usable output which excludes recurrent inventory losses rather than by gross output (see EAA manual rev.1.1, pp. 35-38, Eurostat.) That is, according to equation (4.2), changes in inventories must reflect recurrent inventory losses. However, in equation (4.3), the term "closing inventory stock – opening inventory stock" already has recurrent inventory losses deducted, making it more closely aligned with the definition of changes in inventories.

Figure 4.2 Definition of the gross output and usable output

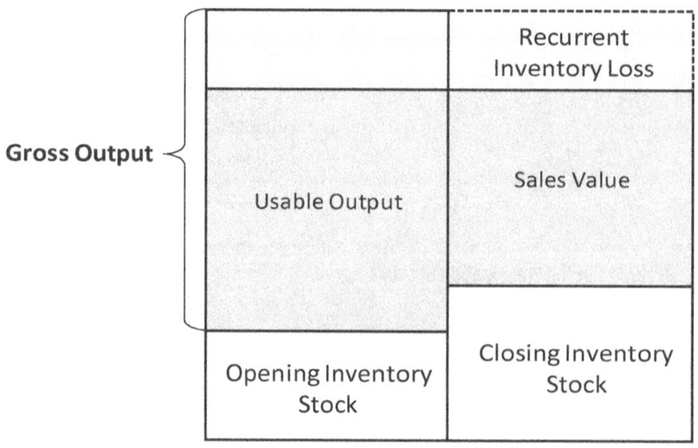

In service industries where inventories do not occur, sales are equivalent output. However, in wholesale and retail services (although part of the service sector), output is affected by changes in inventories of goods, and this is explained separately in Section 14.2.

Treatment of holding gains and losses

The methods mentioned above are based on the historic cost approach used in business accounting, and as such, do not distinguish holding gains or losses; they can be used as a makeshift solution only when detailed accounting data on inventories are not available. Measuring changes in inventories by relying on the opening and closing stock levels has the inherent drawback of not being able to eliminate holding gains and losses of inventories arising from inflation, which is why this approach is not recommended for national accounts.

In practice, business accounting employs inventory valuation methods such as first-in-first-out (FIFO), last-in-first-out (LIFO), and the weighted average method, all of which incorporate holding gains and losses into the inventory values, thereby differing from the perpetual inventory method. Consequently, these valuation methods must be adjusted to conform to the conceptual framework of the national accounts.

The following example (Table 4.1) illustrates how changes in inventories and holding gains or losses are measured according to various inventory valuation methods in business accounting. Assume that the opening stock is priced at 10, the price at the entry into inventory is 12, the price at the withdrawal from inventory is 14, and the closing stock is priced at 11. Also, assume that the quantity of opening stock is 1, the quantity entered into entry is 3, and the quantity withdrawn from inventory is 2. Then, the changes in inventories calculated by the *FIFO*, *LIFO*, *weighted average method*, and *perpetual inventory method* are as follows.

Table 4.1 Numerical example of valuation methods for inventories

	Opening stock			Entries			Weighted average			Withdrawals			Closing stock		
	quantity	price	value	quantity	price	value	quantity	price	value	quantity	price	value	quantity	price	value
FIFO	1	10	10	3	12	36				2	11	22	2	12	24
LIFO	1	10	10	3	12	36				2	12	24	2	11	22
Weighted average	1	10	10	3	12	36	4	11.5	46	2	11.5	23	2	11.5	23
PIM	1	10	10	3	12	36				2	14	28	2	11	22

First, since FIFO, LIFO, and the weighted average method all employ historic costs for valuation, the change in inventories calculated as "entries – withdrawals" formula in this table is identical in amount to that calculated as "closing stock – opening stock" formula. Therefore, as previously noted, "entries – withdrawals" can be replaced with "closing stock – opening stock" to calculate the value of changes in inventories. However, the value of changes in inventories calculated in this manner includes holding gains or losses, and thus does not accurately reflect the true value of changes in inventories. In contrast, changes in inventories under the perpetual inventory method applies the price at the time of entries and withdrawals, thereby eliminating the holding gains and losses.

Since the national accounts recommend the valuation of changes in inventories by the perpetual inventory method, if the value of changes in inventories derived from other methods are used, an **inventory valuation adjustment** must be made to deduct holding gains and losses (Table 4.2). For example, if the changes in inventories measured by the FIFO method is 14 and the changes in inventories calculated by the perpetual inventory method is 8, an adjustment must be made by subtracting 6 to arrive at the value of changes in inventories that conforms to the national accounts concept. In this case, the holding gain of 4 (= closing inventory stock – opening inventory stock – change in inventories) is recorded in the revaluation account (see Section 11.2 for further details).

Table 4.2 Inventory valuation adjustment

	Opening stock (a)	Closing stock (b)	Change in stocks (c=b-a)	Change in inventories (d=entries – withdrawals)	Holding gains (c–d)	**Inventory valuation adjustment**[1)]
FIFO	10	24	14	14	-	**6**
LIFO	10	22	12	12	-	**4**
Weighted average	10	23	13	13	-	**5**
PIM	10	22	12	8	4	

Footnote: 1) Inventory valuation adjustment = d – changes in inventories by PIM.

Next, we introduce another simple method to isolate holding gains and losses when calculating changes in inventories by using the amounts of opening and closing stock of inventories. This method uses the data from opening and closing stocks of inventories, but applies the mid-period average price (the simple average price of the opening and closing periods) to that data, and calculates the change in inventories by multiplying this average price by the change in quantity during the period. In other words, the change in inventories is expressed as follows:

Change in inventories $= (p^0 + p^1)/2 \times (q^1 - q^0)$

where, p^0 and p^1 represent the prices of opening and closing periods, respectively, and q^0 and q^1 represent the quantities of opening and closing periods, respectively. In addition, the following results are obtained by applying the formula of "holding gains and losses = closing inventory stock – opening inventory stock – changes in inventories".

(4.4) **Holding gains and losses of inventories = $(q^0 + q^1)/2 \times (p^1 - p^0)$**

In other words, the holding gains and losses of inventories are equal to the average quantity multiplied by the difference between the prices at the end and beginning periods. For the deriving process of equation (4.4), refer to Sections 5.3.2 and 11.2.1.1.

4.1.2 Non-market output

Non-market output is defined as the output produced by non-market producers such as government units and non-profit institutions serving households (NPISHs), that is provided free or at economically insignificant prices. Governments can finance their production costs through taxes revenues or other income sources, and NPISHs can similarly finance their costs through subscription fees of their members etc., which enable them to offer their output either free of charge or at economically insignificant prices. Since non-market output does not have a market price, the amount of its output is valued by the sum of costs incurred in production. Specifically, items of production cost for non-market output include intermediate consumption, remuneration of employees, depreciation and depletion, and other taxes less subsidies on production, as well as net return to invested capital in the production.

The key issue, then, is how to establish the criteria for determining whether a price is economically significant or insignificant when valuing non-market output. In practice, both the SNA and the EU National Accounts (ESA) recommend applying the **50% criterion** when judging economically significant prices. That is, if the ratio of **sales to production costs** exceeds 50% over a number of years, the output is considered to have been sold at economically significant prices; conversely, if the ratio is below 50%, it is regarded as having been sold at economically insignificant prices. This ratio of sales to production costs is also referred to as the cost-recovery ratio. Consequently, although non-market output is, in principle, produced by non-market producers, the practical judgement on whether it is a market output or a non-market output relies on this criterion.

In this regard, let us examine how the scope of sales and production costs is specifically defined (Table 4.3). Under the SNA and ESA manuals, **sales** are defined as the amount obtained by excluding all taxes less subsidies on products, which is equivalent to the "basic price" of market output. Meanwhile, **production costs**, on the other hand, comprise the sum of intermediate consumption, remuneration of employees, depreciation and depletion, and other taxes on production, rent payable for the use of non-produced non-financial assets (e.g., rent on land, payments for the use of subsoil assets), and the net return to capital used in production. This total corresponds to the value of non-market output when the sum of costs method is applied. However, subsidies on production are not deducted from costs. This is to remove the effect of government support when determining the activity is market or non-market in nature.

Table 4.3 Scope of sales and production costs

	Definition of the 2025 SNA (30.32-33)	Definition of the ESA 2010 (3.33)
Sales	Sales are measured as the amount excluding all taxes on products. They also exclude all payments received from government unless they would be granted to any producer undertaking the same activity. Own-account production is not included in this category of sales.	Sales is measured as the amount excluding all taxes on products, with subsidies on products included. However, government subsidies to compensate for the company's overall deficit are excluded. Holding gains, investment grants and capital transfers are also excluded.
Production costs	Production costs consist of the sum of intermediate consumption, remuneration of employees, depreciation and depletion, other taxes on production, rent payable for the use of non-produced non-financial assets, and net return to capital used in production. Subsidies on production are not deducted from production costs.	Production costs are composed of the sum of intermediate consumption, remuneration of employees, depreciation and depletion, other taxes on production (other subsidies on production are not deducted), plus costs of capital (net interest payments). However, all costs incurred for own-account capital formation are excluded.

Since market output is traded in the market, it constitutes part of intermediate consumption, final consumption expenditure, and gross capital formation in terms of use side. In contrast, the consumption of non-market output is imputed as final uses of non-market producers themselves. That is, non-market output produced by government and NPISHs is attributed respectively to final expenditures of government and NPISHs (this will be discussed in detail in Sections 5.2.2 and 5.2.3).

Mixed production of the market and non-market output

The distinction between market output and non-market output is generally determined by the characteristics of the producers who produce the output. However, in the case of public enterprises run by the government, the nature of their economic activities may make it difficult to clearly distinguish between market output and non-market output. Public enterprises, in pursuit of policy objectives, often provide products at prices consistently lower than market levels and may have their deficits financed by the government. If a public enterprise produces both market and non-market output simultaneously, determining how to measure its total output becomes a significant issue. Such cases are often observed in socialist countries, where state-owned enterprises produce not only market output but also non-market output (at prices below the total production costs on a continuous long-term basis), thereby potentially incurring persistent losses. If the government provides gratuitous financial support to make up for these losses, the SNA treats this support as **subsidies on products**.

Consider the treatment in the national accounts when a public enterprise's output is classified as market output, yet over the long term its sales revenue fails to cover its total production costs, and the government compensates the shortfall through gratuitous financial assistance (see Table 4.4). For example, assume that total cost incurred is \$250 (comprising 200 in intermediate consumption, 30 in remuneration of employees, 0 in other taxes on production, and 20 in depreciation) and that market sales revenue is \$160. In this case, the difference between the total cost (\$250) and sales revenue (\$160) amounts to \$90, which represents the compensation by government. This compensation is treated as the value of non-market output and is covered by the government's subsidy on products. However, since subsidies on products do not have a corresponding entry in the accounts for each institutional sector, they are deducted from gross value added of total economy, resulting in an effect on GDP of – 40 (i.e., gross value added of the public enterprise – subsidy on products, 50 – 90).

Table 4.4 Accounting treatment for public enterprises receiving government subsidies

(Production account)

Public enterprise			
IC	200	Market output	160
GVA	50	Non-market output	90
Total	250	Total	250

Total economy			
IC	200	Market output	160
GVA	**50**	Non-market output	90
Subsidy on products	**-90**	GVA	**-90**
Total	160	Total	160

(Generation of earned income account)

Public enterprise			
Remuneration of employees	30	GVA	50
Depreciation	20		
Total	50	Total	50

Total economy			
Remuneration of employees	30	GVA	**-40**
Depreciation	20		
Subsidy on products	**-90**		
Total	-40	Total	-40

4.1.3 Output for own final use

Output for own final use refers to output produced by producers for their own final use, either for final consumption expenditure or for gross fixed capital formation. This category of output includes various types. A typical example is when a farmer, categorized as a household unincorporated enterprise, consumes the agricultural products he produces as his own final consumption. Also, when an establishment uses its own output for intermediate consumption even though it is not intended for final use, it is included in this category. For example, if a farmer uses the agricultural products produced as intermediate consumption for his own production (e.g., as seeds for crops), such usage is not considered final use and is instead recorded as inventories; however, since such output does not fall under either market output or non-market output, it is included in this category. (If this occurs within the same accounting period, output used for intermediate consumption is recorded both as output and as intermediate consumption, so that the value-added remains unaffected.)

Furthermore, all items produced by household unincorporated enterprises for their own consumption are included in the category of "own account" production. **Own-account production** refers to activities in which an economic unit processes the output it produces solely for its own holding or use, without engaging other economic units. For example, if a producer in the agriculture or livestock industry uses the cultivated biological resources he produces for the purpose of repeated production of his own industry's output, this is recorded as gross fixed capital formation for own final use. In addition, the services by owner-occupied housing are treated as if produced by household unincorporated enterprises in the form of housing rental services and are imputed as final consumption by households. Domestic services provided by household's paid domestic staff (e.g., housemaid, private car driver) are also treated as final consumption expenditure by households unincorporated enterprises. Buildings or other structures constructed by a construction company for its own use constitutes gross fixed capital formation for own final use. Meanwhile, corporate research and development expenses incurred on an own-account basis are included in own-account gross fixed capital formation. However, since these costs can be incurred in every industry, it would be better in practice to establish a separate nominal industry (namely, "own account R&D service industry") to account for them. In addition, services produced by households for their own final consumption are excluded from output because they are not included in the production boundary. This matter remains a subject for further research and review in the SNA.

Based on the foregoing description, output for own final use can be expressed as the sum of the following items:

- The value of goods produced and self-consumed by the households' unincorporated enterprises;
- Imputed services for owner-occupied dwellings;
- The value of services provided to households by the paid domestic staff;
- The value of fixed assets produced by an establishment for own final use (own-account gross fixed capital formation);
- The value of changes in inventories for the above purpose of use;
- The value of output for own intermediate consumption within the same establishment.

Own-account output is valued at the average basic price of the same product traded in the market; if this price information is not available, the total production costs incurred is used instead. The sum of these production costs is expressed as follows:

- **Intermediate consumption + Remuneration of employees + Depreciation and depletion + Other taxes less subsidies on production + Net return to the capital employed in production**[1)]

Footnote: 1): In practice, either the actual interest payments on fixed capital and natural resources (net of FISIM fees) are recorded, or the net operating surplus rate of the industry producing the same product is adopted.

When a producer consumes the output he produces for himself, the accounting treatment varies according to the institutional sectors to which the economic unit belongs. In the case of corporations, since no final consumption expenditure incurs, no final consumption expenditure is recorded for their own-account production as well. In contrast, for household's unincorporated enterprise which is classified as households sector, if the household members consume the own-account output, it is treated as final consumption expenditure. For reference, the table below (Table 4.5) summarizes how products from the own account are handled in the SNA.

Table 4.5 Types of own-account output and their treatment in national accounts

Type of own-account output	Industry (ISIC)[1)]	Institutional sector	Treatment in expenditure side
• Agricultural products produced by farmers for own final consumption	Agriculture (A)	Household	Final consumption
• Agricultural products produced by farmers used as their won seeds or livestock feed	Agriculture (A)	Household	Intermediate consumption

Type of own-account output	Industry (ISIC)[1]	Institutional sector	Treatment in expenditure side
• Goods produced by household's unincorporated enterprises that are consumed by members of the same households	(Relevant industry)	Household	Final consumption
• Cultivated biological resources produced by farmers or stockbreeders for yielding repeat products	Agriculture (A)	Household, corporation	Gross fixed capital formation
• Owner-occupied dwelling service	Real estate services (L)	Household	Final consumption
• Services provided by paid domestic staff	Household's domestic service (T)	Household	Final consumption
• Construction of buildings or structures for own use	Construction (F)	Household, corporation	Gross fixed capital formation
• Own-account R&D	R&D service (M)		Gross fixed capital formation
• Production of domestic services for household's own consumption			Excluded from the production boundary

Footnote: 1) ( ) indicates ISIC classification (Section).

4.1.4 Estimation methods of output by industries

The method of estimating output varies slightly across different industries. Moreover, as each industry engages not only in its primary production activities but also in various secondary production activities, it may simultaneously produce output that is specific to that industry as well as output that is classified under other industries. For example, a manufacturing enterprise may provide not only manufactured products, but also wholesale and retail services, processing services, and rental service for buildings, and all of these individual outputs must be added together to derive total output. Table 4.6 introduces the estimation methods of the output for each industry on the basis of the questionnaire items of the Economic Census conducted by the Ministry of Data and Statistics in Korea every five years. However, since the survey items of the Economic Census often do not achieve the level of detail required by the national accounts, alternative data sources such as corporate financial statement databases from the National Tax Service or from credit rating agencies are sometimes utilized. For more information on this matter, refer to Chapter 15 (Calculation of output and value-added using corporate financial statements). Furthermore, for industries that require special methods of estimating output will be described separately in Chapter 14 in more details.

Table 4.6 Method for estimating output by industry from the questionnaire of Economic Census (for establishments with 5 or more employees)

<table>
<tr><th>Section</th><th>Industry</th><th colspan="2">Classification</th><th>Output (sum of items)</th><th>Market/ Non-market</th><th>Institutional sector</th></tr>
<tr><td>A</td><td>Agriculture, forestry, and fishing</td><td colspan="2">Corporations only (See Chapter 14 for small-scale farmers.)</td><td>Revenue from primary and secondary activities</td><td>Market</td><td>Non-financial corporation</td></tr>
<tr><td rowspan="5">B, C</td><td rowspan="5">Mining and manufacturing</td><td rowspan="2">Manufacturing of goods</td><td>Sales</td><td>Sales value</td><td rowspan="5">Market</td><td rowspan="5">Non-financial corporation</td></tr>
<tr><td>Changes in inventories</td><td>(Closing inventory of finished goods and work-in-progress - opening inventory of finished goods and work-in-progress)</td></tr>
<tr><td colspan="2">Resale trade (wholesale and retail)</td><td>Sales value of purchased goods for resale - cost of goods sold for resale</td></tr>
<tr><td colspan="2">Services</td><td>Income from processing services for goods + income from repair services + rental income + other income</td></tr>
<tr><td colspan="2"></td><td>Sales value of by-products and scrap</td></tr>
<tr><td>D</td><td>Electric power</td><td colspan="2"></td><td>Revenue from sales of electricity + other income</td><td>Market</td><td>Non-financial corporation</td></tr>
<tr><td>D</td><td>Gas</td><td colspan="2"></td><td>Revenue from sales of gas + revenue from gas meter repair + rental income + sales of by-products</td><td>Market</td><td>Non-financial corporation</td></tr>
<tr><td>D</td><td>Water supply</td><td colspan="2"></td><td>Revenue from water supply + revenue from consignment construction + other income</td><td>Market</td><td>Non-financial corporation</td></tr>
<tr><td>D</td><td>Steam/hot water supply</td><td colspan="2"></td><td>Revenue from sales of steam and hot water + rental income + sales of electricity + other income</td><td>Market</td><td>Non-financial corporation</td></tr>
<tr><td>E</td><td>Sewerage, waste management and disposal activities</td><td colspan="2"></td><td>Revenue from primary and secondary activities</td><td>Market</td><td>Non-financial corporation</td></tr>
<tr><td rowspan="2">F</td><td rowspan="2">Construction</td><td colspan="2">Construction[1)]</td><td>Total sales on construction - sales on overseas construction - outsourced construction cost (subcontract)</td><td rowspan="2">Market</td><td rowspan="2">Non-financial corporation</td></tr>
<tr><td colspan="2">Other than construction</td><td>Sales other than construction</td></tr>
<tr><td rowspan="3">G</td><td rowspan="3">Wholesale and retail trade</td><td colspan="2">Commodities</td><td>Sales of goods for resale - (opening inventory of goods + purchase of goods for resale - closing inventory of goods)</td><td rowspan="3">Market</td><td rowspan="3">Non-financial corporation</td></tr>
<tr><td colspan="2">Commissions</td><td>Income from sales agencies</td></tr>
<tr><td colspan="2">Other than trades</td><td>Revenue from non-wholesale/retail activity</td></tr>
<tr><td rowspan="2">H</td><td rowspan="2">Transportation and storage</td><td colspan="2">Transportation</td><td>Revenue from transportation</td><td rowspan="2">Market</td><td rowspan="2">Non-financial corporation</td></tr>
<tr><td colspan="2">Other than transportation</td><td>Revenue other than transportation</td></tr>
<tr><td>I</td><td>Accommodation and food services</td><td colspan="2"></td><td>Revenue from room charge + revenue from sales of food + other income</td><td>Market</td><td>Non-financial corporation</td></tr>
</table>

<table>
<tr><th>Section</th><th>Industry</th><th>Classification</th><th>Output (sum of items)</th><th>Market/ Non-market</th><th>Institutional sector</th></tr>
<tr><td>J</td><td>Publishing, broadcasting, telecommunication, information services</td><td></td><td>Revenue from primary and secondary activities</td><td>Market</td><td>Non-financial corporation</td></tr>
<tr><td>K</td><td>Financial and insurance services</td><td>Refer to Chapter 14</td><td></td><td>Market</td><td>Financial corporation</td></tr>
<tr><td>L</td><td>Real estate activities</td><td>Refer to Chapter 14 on "Dwelling services industry"</td><td>Revenue from primary and secondary activities</td><td>Market</td><td>Non-financial corporation</td></tr>
<tr><td>M</td><td>Professional, scientific, technical activities</td><td></td><td>Revenue from primary and secondary activities</td><td>Market</td><td>Non-financial corporation</td></tr>
<tr><td>N</td><td>Administrative and support services</td><td></td><td>Revenue from primary and secondary activities</td><td>Market</td><td>Non-financial corporation</td></tr>
<tr><td>O</td><td>Public administration and defense</td><td></td><td>Wages and salaries + Retirement benefits + welfare expenses+ depreciation + taxes and dues + rent and rental payment + other operating expenses + net return to capital</td><td>Non-market</td><td>General government</td></tr>
<tr><td rowspan="2">P, Q</td><td rowspan="2">Education, health, and social work</td><td>For market industry</td><td>Revenue + subsidies</td><td>Market</td><td>Non-financial corporation</td></tr>
<tr><td>For non-market industry</td><td>Material input + wages and salaries + retirement benefits + welfare expenses + rent and rental payment + taxes and dues + depreciation + other operating expenses + net return to capital</td><td>Non-market</td><td>NPISH</td></tr>
<tr><td>R</td><td>Arts, entertainment and recreation</td><td></td><td>Revenue from primary and secondary activities</td><td>Market</td><td>Non-financial corporation</td></tr>
<tr><td rowspan="3">S</td><td rowspan="3">Membership organizations, repairs, and other personal services</td><td>Trade unions (942), other membership organizations (949)</td><td>Material input + Wages and salaries + Retirement benefits + Welfare expenses + rent and rental payment + Taxes and dues + depreciation + other operating expenses + net return to capital</td><td>Non-market</td><td>NPISH</td></tr>
<tr><td>Business, employers and professional membership organizations (941)</td><td>Revenue from primary activity (business revenue + subsidies)</td><td>Market</td><td>Non-financial corporation</td></tr>
<tr><td>Repairs and other personal service (95~96)</td><td>Revenue from primary activity</td><td>Market</td><td>Non-financial corporation</td></tr>
</table>

Footnote: ( ) indicates division or group numbers of ISIC.

4.2 Imports

Imports consist of both imports of goods and imports of services. The primary data source for estimating **imports of goods** is the administrative data provided by the Customs Service's export and import statistics. This data includes detailed product-level data classified according to HS codes

(Harmonized Commodity Description and Coding System). In these statistics, the basis for valuing imported goods is the CIF (cost, insurance and freight) price, which is the price of a commodity plus all costs incurred in delivering it to the border of the importing country. This includes the price of the commodity, transport costs to the customs frontier of the importing country and insurance premiums. The customs authorities adopt the CIF price as the valuation basis for imported goods because, following long-established practice, they have used CIF prices as the basis for imposing customs duties.

In contrast, the SNA value both exported and imported goods on an FOB (free on board) basis, which is consistent with the balance of payments. This means that all exported and imported goods are valued based on the price at the customs frontier of the exporting country. The reason for adopting the FOB price in the SNA is to ensure a clear conceptual distinction between goods and services by separately recording freight and insurance charges, which are considered services, rather than including them in the value of goods. Meanwhile, the International Merchandise Trade Statistics (IMTS, UN 2010) manual recommends maintaining the conventional CIF price as the valuation method for imported goods, while also providing additional detailed information on FOB prices and on freight and insurance as supplementary data (IMTS 2010, 4.8-4.9).

When compiling the supply and use tables, imported goods are generally recorded at CIF prices and imports of services are recorded on the balance of payments basis, with adjustments made by deducting the freights and insurance services that are double-counted between imports of goods and imports of services. The reason for using the data of CIF-based imports of goods in the supply table is that the detailed source data for each good collected by the customs authority is prepared at CIF prices, which serve as the basic price from the purchaser's perspective. In contrast, when compiling the supply and use tables, exports of goods are recorded on the FOB price basis and exports of services are prepared on the basis of balance of payments; this aligns with the SNA standards and therefore, no further adjustments are necessary.

Table 4.7 Valuation methods for imports and exports of goods

Type of statistics	Valuation basis		Explanation
	Imports of goods	Exports of goods	
IMTS (2010)	CIF	FOB	Basis for imposing import duties.
Balance of payments (BPM6)	FOB	FOB	Valued at the exporting country's customs frontier.
SNA	FOB	FOB	
Supply and use tables	CIF	FOB	CIF/FOB adjustments are made for comparability with national accounts.

In the supply table, imports of goods are displayed at CIF prices by each commodity, so they must be adjusted to FOB prices. However, since the source data (customs statistics) do not collect FOB prices for individual commodities, a "CIF-to-FOB adjustment" (row) is added to the total value of imported goods to make a global adjustment instead. Moreover, because the import values of services include freight and insurance costs in accordance with the compilation standard of the balance of payments, a separate CIF/FOB adjustment (column) must be added to avoid duplication with imports of goods (column). Accordingly, the supply table incorporates both a CIF/FOB adjustment row and column as part of the adjustment procedure. (See Annex to Chapter 13 for an example of the CIF/FOB adjustment.)

Meanwhile, the treatment of freight and insurance costs on imported and exported goods in the SNA depends on who pays those costs as well as who performs the transportation. In other words, the approach in the national accounts varies depending on whether the freight and insurance costs are born by the exporting country or the importing country, and also on whether the party performing the transportation is from the exporting country, the importing country, or a third country. Accordingly, the following cases can be considered for the treatment of freights and insurance costs. The first case is when the freight carrier is an enterprise from the exporting country. In this case, if the export price already includes freight and insurance costs, then when the exporter contracts its domestic carrier to provide the transportation service, that service is recorded as the production of domestic transport services. However, since the balance of payments compiles export prices on an FOB basis, this transportation service is treated as an export of service (BPM6, Box 10.3). Conversely, if the export price does not include freight and insurance costs and the importer instead contracts a carrier from the exporting country, the transaction is then treated as an import of service for the exporting country and simultaneously as an import of service for the importing country.

The second case is when the freight carrier is an enterprise from the importing country. If the export price of the exporter includes freight and insurance costs and the exporter contracts a carrier from the importing country for transportation, then this transaction is treated as an import of service for the exporting country and as an export of service for the importing country. However, as described above, in the balance of payments, if the carrier for imported good is a domestic enterprise, the transportation service is treated as a domestic transaction, rather than an export of service, and is therefore excluded from the balance of payments. In contrast, in the supply and use tables, it is treated respectively as domestic output in the supply table and as an export of service in the use table.

The third case is when the freight carrier is an enterprise from a third country. If the export price of the exporter includes freight and insurance costs and the exporter contracts a carrier from a third country for transportation, then this is regarded as an import of service of the exporting country from that third country. Conversely, if the export price does not include freight and insurance costs and the importer contracts a carrier from a third country, then it is treated as an import of service of the importing country from that third country.

In practice, however, such detailed information is often not fully available during the compilation process, so general standards must be applied. When compiling the balance of payments which shows international transactions, the following approach is adopted. (See the Annex of Chapter 13 for details.) Specifically, for imports of goods, the 'import declaration' submitted by the importer is indicated at the CIF price, which includes freight and insurance costs of both domestic and foreign carriers. In converting this to the FOB price basis, the freight and insurance costs are deducted: costs for domestic carriers are excluded as they correspond to domestic output, while costs for foreign carriers are treated as imports of services. Conversely, for exports of goods, the 'export declaration' submitted by the exporter is recorded at the FOB price; therefore, costs for domestic carriers are treated as exports of services, and costs for foreign carriers are not separately indicated as they are part of transactions between the third countries. It is important that, in the supply and use tables, the presentation of transactions associated with freight and insurance costs of imports and exports be treated in such a way that they are not double-counted, taking various cases into account, and CIF/FOB adjustments should be understood in this context.

Imports of services are compiled based on the data of the balance of services from the balance of payments. The category of imports of services consists of 12 items as follows (see Table 4.8). This classification is the basis for the international accounts drawn up in the BPM6 and can be applied directly to national accounts. However, although this classification is mostly product-based one, some items (such as travel services, construction services, government goods and services) are classified on a **transactor-basis**, wherein goods and services are mixed; therefore, to utilize these in the supply and use tables, it is necessary to reclassify them on a product-basis. In this regard, the Manual on Statistics of International Trade in Services 2010 (MSITS, UN et al., 2010) proposes an alternative sub-classification that allows for further refinement of the BPM6 classification of the trade in services. For more information, see the Extended Balance of Payments Services Classification (EBOPS 2010), an appendix to the MSITS manual. Meanwhile, the basis for valuing imports of services, like that of other international transactions, is based on market prices (i.e., actual transaction prices).

Table 4.8 Classification of service transactions in the balance of payments

1	Manufacturing services on physical inputs owned by others
2	Maintenance and repair services n.i.e.
3	Transport
4	Travel
5	Construction
6	Insurance and pension services
7	Financial services
8	Charges for the use of intellectual property n.i.e.
9	Telecommunications, computer, and information services
10	Other business services
11	Personal, cultural, and recreational services
12	Government goods and services n.i.e.

4.3 Distribution margin and transport margin

In the supply table, the amounts in the domestic output (columns) and imports (columns) are both presented at basic prices. Therefore, to convert these amounts to purchasers' prices and ultimately derive the total supply at market prices, it is necessary to add distribution margins (= wholesale and retail margins), freight charges (i.e., transport margin), and taxes less subsidies on products which are not included in the suppliers' basic prices.

Constructing and filling out columns of distribution margins and transport margins in the supply table is the first step in converting basic prices of output into purchasers' prices. These margins, which are added to individual products, may or may not occur in actual transactions. For example, when the producer and the purchaser are directly linked, no distribution margins incur. Similarly, when the supplier of the product does not separately charge the purchaser for the transport cost and bears it for himself, or the purchaser bears the transportation cost on his own, no transport margin is incurred. In cases where domestic producers or importers purchase goods, distribution margins and transport margins do not appear as separate costs from the purchaser's perspective; instead, they are included in the price of goods (purchaser's price). This accounting treatment is the same as the approach used in business accounting where the selling price of the supplier is adjusted by adding costs incurred due to wholesale and retail transactions and transportation to derive the purchaser's price.

The process of converting to purchasers' prices in the supply table is as follows. In this table, separate columns are established for the distribution margin and transport margin. Then, the total amounts of distribution margin and transport margin are allocated to cells for other goods (applicable only to agricultural products, minerals, and manufactured goods), excluding the cells for the trade services and transport services in these columns. Subsequently, these total amounts are deducted from the cells corresponding to the trade services and transport services. This procedure ensures that the sum of margins of the trade service and transport service cells and those allocated to the cells for other goods becomes zero. The amounts deducted in the trade and transport services cells represent only the distribution margins and transport margins, not the total output of those services. In what follows, we will discuss each of treatment methods of these margins in detail.

4.3.1 Distribution margins

In this section, we will discuss how the wholesale and retail margins are defined in the SNA, how they are compared with the conventional distribution margin practices in businesses, and how distribution margins are allocated when converting basic price data into purchaser's price data in the supply and use tables.

4.3.1.1 Definition of distribution margin

In general, the production of wholesale and retail services can be categorized into two types. The first type occurs when a wholesaler or retailer purchases goods and resells them, thereby earning wholesale or retail distribution margins. The second type is when an enterprise, acting on the request of another economic entity, sells that entity's goods on its behalf (without transferring ownership of the goods) and receives a commission in return. The former is called a **margin service** in which the wholesaler and retailer purchase goods and resell them by adding distribution margins, while the latter is called a **non-margin service**. Non-margin services include margins on used car sales, margins on waste sales, and other brokerage fees and commissions.

In the supply table, the conversion of output at the basic price into the purchaser's price includes only margin services (that is, distribution margin); non-margin services, although included in the output of wholesale and retail industry, are excluded from the conversion to the purchaser's price. This is because distribution margins reflect only the difference between the trader's selling price and the purchase price from the supplier, whereas for used goods (such as used cars or wastes) that have already been sold and used, either no basic price from the producer exists or no ownership transfer to the wholesaler/retailer occurs.

In the case of wholesale and retail enterprises, any transport costs incurred at the time of purchasing goods are reflected as intermediate consumption without being included in the wholesaler/retailer's purchase cost, even if separately changed by the supplier (SNA 7.163 c, 14.44). Consequently, the difference between the selling price and the purchase price of goods in the wholesaler/retailer is entirely reflected as the distribution margin, and no separate transport margin is incurred (Figure 4.3).

Figure 4.3 Definition of distribution margin in the SNA

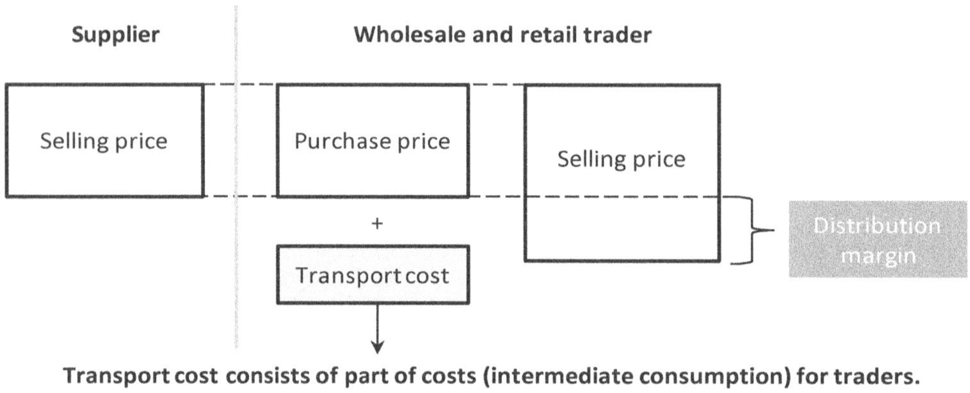

However, under the generally accepted accounting practice of corporations, transport costs incurred in connection with the purchase of goods for resale are included in the purchase cost of those goods. In other words, the conventional method of calculating the distribution margin of wholesaler and retailer enterprises incorporates transport costs incurred at the time of purchase in its cost of goods sold (figure 4.4), which is inconsistent with the aforementioned provisions of the SNA. Therefore, national account compilers must carefully determine, based on appropriate criteria, whether these transport costs should be treated as separate transport margins, as will be further addressed in the following section.

Figure 4.4 Conventional distribution margin in the business practice

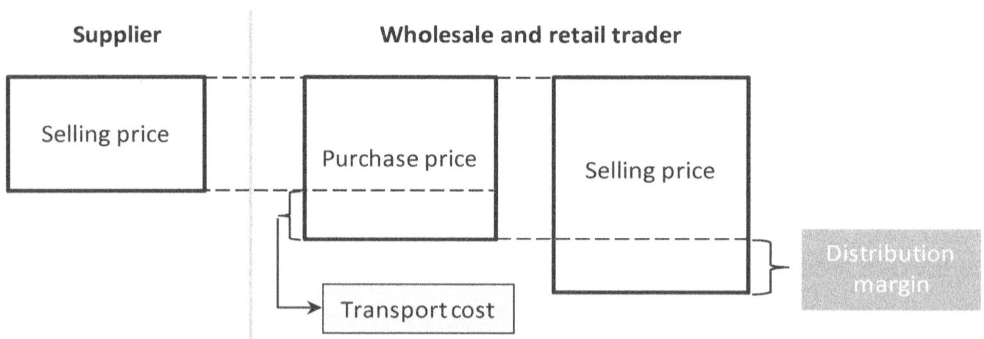

4.3.1.2 Allocation of distribution margins

The procedure for allocating distribution margins in the supply and use tables is in the following way. First, in the use table (at purchaser's prices), all items of intermediate consumption are presented at purchasers' prices, meaning that the wholesale and retail distribution margins have already been reflected; therefore, the distribution margin row appears as "zero." On the other hand, non-margin trade services are recorded as the input cost of the enterprise that requests the service, so the trade service row shows the amount corresponding to the non-margin trade service (for example, the total is 30 in Table 4.9).

Table 4.9 Distribution margin in the use table (at purchasers' prices)

	Agriculture	Manufacturing	Trade industry	Intermediate use	Final consumption	Capital formation	Changes in inventories	Exports .	Total use
Agriculture	…	…	…	…	…	…	…	… .	280
Manufacturing	…	…	…	…	…	…	…	… .	240
Trade service (distribution margin)				0	0	0			0
Trade service (non-margin)	…	…	…	30					30
Total									550

In the supply table, distribution margins that are added to the basic price of individual products to convert them to purchaser's price are displayed in the column of **distribution margin adjustment**. However, in order to estimate these margins, it is necessary to have source data on the margin rate for each individual product, which is not easy to obtain. There are two options for applying the distribution margin rate for each product in the supply table, depending on the source of the margin rate data. The first option is to apply the average margin rate of a specific wholesale and retail industry equally to all traded products in that sector (the industry technology assumption), and the second option is to apply the margin rate of a specific wholesale and retail product equally to the same product regardless of the industry (the product technology assumption). The choice between these methods depends on which one is more appropriate in practice. (Refer to the Eurostat Manual of Supply, Use and Input-Output Tables, 2008, page 177.)

Additionally, in the supply table, the total amount of distribution margin (control total) allocated to individual goods is taken from the overall total in the distribution margin row. The basis for allocating this total amount across the column of distribution margin for each good is determined by the margin rate for the given good in the wholesale and retail sector, calculated as [(sales value – cost of goods sold)/sales value]. For example, in the column of distribution margin of the supply table below (Table 4.10), the total amount of distribution margin ($515) is allocated to the agricultural products ($278) and manufactured products ($237), thereby converting them into purchasers' prices. In the intersecting cell for the trade services row, the total amount of margin is deducted (-$515) so that the sum of the distribution margin (column) equals zero.

Table 4.10 Distribution margin in the supply table

	Agriculture	Manufacturing	Trade	Domestic supply (basic price)	Imports	Distribution margin adjustment	Taxes less subsidies on products	Total supply (purchaser's price)
Agriculture						278	2	280
Manufacturing						237	3	240
Trade service (distribution margin)	5	10	500	515		-515	0	0
Trade service (non-margin)			30	30		0		30
Output	5	10	530	545		0	5	550

4.3.2 Transport margins

In this section, we will discuss how the transport margin is defined in the SNA, describe how it is distinguished from and treated differently than "other transport costs," and then examine how the transport margin is allocated when converting basic price data into purchaser's price data in the supply and use tables.

4.3.2.1 Definition of the transport margin

Transportation services are services in relation to the transportation of goods or passengers, whereas transport margins arise solely in connection with the transportation of goods. The modes of transporting goods include roads, railways, waterways, aviation, and pipelines, and the scope of transport margins also encompass ancillary expenses related to freight transport such as cargo loading and unloading, and insurance.

From the perspective of the purchaser of the freight transportation services, this output is classified into two forms, analogous to the case of wholesale and retail services. The first form is the cost incurred by the purchase of freight transportation services, which is accounted for as the **transport cost** of the enterprise requesting these services (In the business accounting, it is referred to as "transportation-out"). The second form arises when the seller of goods issues a separate freight invoice to the purchaser and charges the freight cost; however, the purchaser then incorporates this freight cost into the purchase price of the goods, without recording it as a separate transportation cost (in the business accounting, it is referred to as "transportation-in"). The former is typical in most transactions, whereas the latter treated in the national accounts as the **transport margin** which is added when converting basic prices into purchasers' prices. In other words, while the provider of the transportation service records its revenue from the transportation services, the user of this service does not account for this expense as an intermediate input cost but includes it in the purchase price of goods, thereby creating a discrepancy between the seller's price and the purchaser's price.

The criterion for distinguishing between transport costs and transport margins in freight transport depends on whether the purchaser of a good incorporates the freight cost into the purchaser's price of the good. Under the practice of business accounting, when a buyer purchases a good, any freight charges separately invoiced from the supplier's selling price is usually added to the purchaser's price. Therefore, if the freight cost incurred at the time of purchase is separately invoiced and included in the purchase price, it is treated as a *transport margin*. In contrast, if the freight cost is not included in the purchase price but is instead recorded as intermediate consumption by either the purchaser or the seller, it is treated as *transport cost*.

Figure 4.5 Transport margin and transport cost

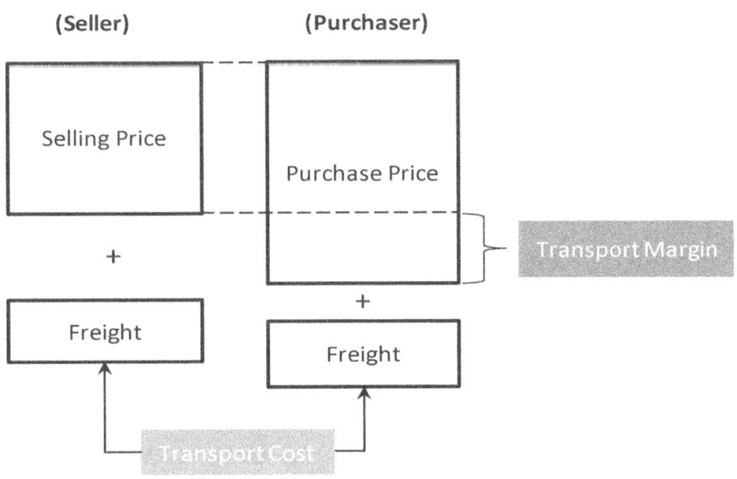

The transport margin is the freight charge separately invoiced to the purchaser in addition to the selling price, which is included in the purchaser's price. However, in practice, it applies only in limited cases, as shown in Table 4.11 below. Specifically, the transport margin arises only when the seller separately invoices the freight charge and treats it as the seller's production of transportation service, or when a third party provides transportation services.

Table 4.11 Accounting for transport margins based on the types of transportation

Type of transportation		Transport margin	Treatment in the national accounts
1. Freight charges are included in the selling price.	Seller's own delivery	Not incur	Ancillary activity of the seller.
2. Freight charges are included in the selling price.	A third party's delivery	Not incur	Seller's intermediate consumption (production of transport services by a third party).
3. Freight charges are separately invoiced in addition to the selling price.	Seller's own delivery	**Incur**	Secondary production activity of the seller.
4. Freight charges are separately invoiced in addition to the selling price.	A third party's delivery	**Incur**	The production of transport services by a third party.
5. The purchaser delivers goods on its own.		Not incur	Ancillary activity of the purchaser.
6. The purchaser contracts a third party for transportation and pays freight charges.		Not incur	Purchase of two products (goods and transport services).

Therefore, among the six cases above, the output related to transportation occurs in cases 2), 3), 4), and 6), and transport costs are incurred only in cases 2) and 6); consequently, transport margins are generated only in cases 3) and 4) after excluding transport costs. However, in case 6), the general accounting practice of business may differ from the SNA accounting treatment because the cost of transportation services may be included the acquisition cost of goods by the purchaser.

Table 4.12 Classification of output, transport cost and transport margin by types of transportation

Type of transportation	Type of output	Treatment of costs in the SNA
1	Not applicable	Cost of the seller
2	Output of transportation industry	Transport cost of the seller
3	Output of transportation service (secondary product of the seller)	Transport margin
4	Output of transportation industry	Transport margin
5	Not applicable	Cost of the purchaser
6	Output of transportation industry	Transport cost of the purchaser

In practical terms, here's a simple method to distinguish and derive the transport margin from the transport cost. The **transport margin** represents the freight cost borne by the purchaser, which is included in the purchaser's acquisition cost of the goods and is not recorded as a separate expense item in the purchaser's financial statements. In contrast, the **transport cost** refers to the freight charge that is not included in the acquisition cost of the goods; these are recorded as the cost of transportation in the financial statements of either the seller or the purchaser. Accordingly, the transport cost is measured using the amount of "transportation cost" item from the input-cost survey, or if the input-cost survey is not conducted, the total transportation costs of enterprise's financial statements are used. By the way, since the addition of transport margins to the purchase price occurs in very limited cases, deriving its total (control total) is not straightforward. However, the control total of transport margin can be indirectly calculated by subtracting the total value of transport cost from the sum of the output of the domestic transportation industry and the output of transport services produced as secondary products in other industries.

4.3.2.2 Allocation of the transport margin

The adjustment of the transport margin to convert to purchasers' prices is arranged in the column of **transport margin adjustment**, where the transport margin is allocated across individual products based on the sum of domestic output and imports. For the detailed allocation, a separate survey is required by each mode of transportation (road, railway, air, waterway, etc.). According to an example as illustrated in the supply table (Table 4.13), in the column of transport margin adjustment, the total amount of transport margin (27) is allocated to agricultural products (7.7) and manufactured products (19.3) to convert them into purchasers' prices, and then the same total amount is deducted (-27) in the intersecting cell for transport services row, so that the column total equals zero.

Table 4.13 Allocation of transport margins in the supply table

	Agriculture	Manufacturing	Transportation	Total (Basic prices)	Imports	Transport Margin Adjustment	…	Total supply (Purchaser's price)
Agriculture						7.7		7.7
Manufacturing						19.3		19.3
Transport service (transport margin)	2	5	20	27		-27		0
Transport service (transport cost)			200	200		0		200
Output	2	5	220	227		0	…	227

Meanwhile, in the use table at purchasers' prices, the value of transport margin in the transport services row is zero, and only transport costs are incurred as intermediate consumption (Table 4.14).

Table 4.14 Transport margin in the use table (at purchasers' prices)

	Agriculture	Manufacturing	Transportation	Intermediate consumption	Final consumption	Fixed capital formation	Exports	…	Total use (purchaser's price)
Agriculture	…	…	…	…	…	…	…	…	7.7
Manufacturing									19.3
Transport service (transport margin)									0
Transport service (transport cost)	…	…	…		…	…	…		200
Total									227

4.4 Taxes on products and subsidies on products

The second step of price adjustment in the supply table to convert the value at basic prices into that at purchaser's prices involves establishing a column of taxes less subsidies on products to add the taxes less subsidies on products imposed on each product. As mentioned earlier, the enterprise's sales data are prepared on the basis of basic prices, which do not include taxes less subsidies on products. Therefore, this adjustment is essential for converting basic prices into purchasers' prices. Moreover, since taxes less subsidies on products are levied directly on the basic price of products, they often take precedence over the distribution margin and transport margin. Therefore, when converting to the purchaser's price, it is necessary to compile data while considering the priority order of adjustments for taxes less subsidies on products, and trade and transport margins. It is also worth noting that other taxes less subsidies on production constitute a component of value-added at basic prices (= output value at basic prices – intermediate consumption at purchaser's prices). Hence, they are excluded from this adjustment process (refer to the use table in Chapter 5).

The column of taxes less subsidies on products, which serves as an adjustment item in the supply table, can be further disaggregated and presented in the form of the following matrix table.

Table 4.15 A matrix table for taxes less subsidies on products

	Non-deductible value added tax (1)	Other taxes on products (excluding VAT and import taxes) (2)	Subsidies on products (3)	Import taxes (excluding VAT) (4)	Total taxes less subsidies on products (5=1+2-3+4)
By product					

The matrix table categorizes taxes on products into non-deductible VAT, other taxes on products (excluding VAT and import taxes), and import taxes (excluding VAT), and then converts them into taxes less subsidies on products by subtracting subsidies on products. In the supply table, the total amount of non-deductible VAT by product (column) is prepared, while in the use table, the detailed breakdown of this VAT is derived by industry and product. (For more detail, refer to "non-deductible VAT" in section 6.7.3.)

4.4.1 Types of taxes on products

The total amount of taxes on products (control total) is obtained from the tax data of the National Tax Service and the Customs Service. To derive this amount, it is necessary to categorize the tax revenue data from the tax statistics and customs statistics by tax type, extract the tax items corresponding to taxes on products, and then allocate them to the relevant products. The types of taxes on products listed in the SNA and their examples can be summarized in the following table (Table 4.16).

Table 4.16 Types and examples of taxes on products

Category		Subcategory	Example
Taxes on products	Value added tax		Value added tax
	Taxes on imports	- Customs duties	Customs duties
		- Taxes on imported goods, except customs duties	Excise taxes on imported goods
		- Profits of import monopolies[1]	
	Taxes on exports	- Export duties	Export duties
		- Profits of export monopolies[1]	
		- Implicit tax imposed on exports as a result of operating a multiple exchange rate system	
	Other taxes on products	- General sales taxes (turnover taxes)	Consumption tax, liquor tax,
		- Taxes on goods (excise duties)	tobacco tax,
		- Taxes on services	transport tax, leisure tax,
		- Taxes on financial and capital transactions	Securities transaction tax, acquisition tax, registration tax
		- Profits of fiscal monopolies[1]	

Footnote: 1) The profits of import monopoly, export monopoly, and fiscal monopoly are the portion of profits transferred to the government from the enterprises to which fiscal monopoly on tobacco, alcohol, etc. is granted by the government.

4.4.2 Types of subsidies on products

Subsidies on products are items that are deducted from the basic price at the time of conversion to the purchaser's price, and they are actually calculated in the form of taxes less subsidies on products (= taxes on products – subsidies on products). Subsidies on products are government subsidies paid per unit of a specified good or service produced, and the producers of these goods and services can be either public or private enterprises. Subsidies to public enterprises occur when the prices of goods and services regularly provided by the enterprise are lower than the average production costs, and the government compensates for the deficit. These subsidies can be calculated as the difference between the actual market price and the government's target price. A example of subsidies for public enterprises includes cases where government continuously compensates for the deficit in the services provided by public enterprises, such as those providing public transportation services, or water supply and sewage services. For private enterprises, the government may also provide incentives to sell their products below market prices and compensate for the deficit (e.g., subsidies for passenger transport services or low-priced coal production).

Subsidies on products differ in nature from the current transfers or capital transfers, which are mentioned later. While the subsidies on products are provided directly to producers, thereby reducing the price burden of a product, current transfers and capital transfers are provided free of charge to economic entities, but are not directly linked to the price of the product. Subsidies on products affect the amount of GDP (= gross value added at the basic price + taxes on products – subsidies on products), but current transfers or capital transfers do not. The data of subsidies on products are obtained from the government's budget and financial statements, and the amounts of subsidies are allocated to each relevant product for the compilation of value-added. The types and examples of subsidies on products can be summarized in the following table (Table 4.17).

Table 4.17 Types of subsidies on products and their examples

<table>
<tr><th colspan="2">Category</th><th>Subcategory</th><th>Example</th></tr>
<tr><td rowspan="4">Subsidies on products</td><td>Subsidies on imports</td><td rowspan="2"></td><td rowspan="2"></td></tr>
<tr><td>Subsidies on exports</td></tr>
<tr><td rowspan="2">Other subsidies on products</td><td>Subsidies on domestic products</td><td>Subsidy on coal price, subsidy on passenger ferry, subsidy on bus transport, subsidy on fuel price, subsidy on fertilizer sales loss.</td></tr>
<tr><td>Subsidies for public corporations and quasi-corporations</td><td>Subsidy on public transportation, subsidy on water and sewage</td></tr>
</table>

4.5 Adjustment of ownership transfer costs

Costs of ownership transfer are costs incurred when acquiring or disposing of fixed assets or non-produced assets (such as land, natural resources, etc.). For example, taxes for acquiring real estate (acquisition tax, registration tax, etc.), various fees for securing legal ownership, and brokerage fees may incur. Additionally, demolition costs may arise at the time of disposing of real estate. In the business accounting, these costs of ownership transfer are required to be included in the acquisition cost of fixed assets. Similarly, in the SNA, as in the recording practice of business accounting, costs of ownership transfer are regarded as part of the fixed capital formation, and they are subject to depreciation over the appropriate useful life. Consequently, to convert the basic prices of products to the purchaser's acquisition prices in the supply table, it is necessary to separate the items of ownership transfer costs (such as various service fees and taxes) and add them to fixed assets or non-produced assets. To this end, the supply table should set up a separate column to adjust these amounts, similar to the adjustment of the distribution margin or transport margin. If this approach is not adopted, as an alternative, the items of ownership transfer costs can be recorded separately from the corresponding gross fixed capital formation in the use table. (Refer to 6.6.1.2 for further discussion.)

4.6 Example of the supply table

Table 4.18 illustrates a simplified version of the supply table of South Korea for the year 2015. In this table, the columns list output (at basic prices), imports, and total supply (at basic prices), consistent with the total supply in the product balance identity. Additionally, the price adjustment columns (taxes less subsidies on products, distribution margin, and transport margin) has been added to convert basic prices to purchasers' prices. The rows display domestic output and imports by product, and the last row records the total values of those products by industry. "Direct purchases abroad by residents" are not shown as a separate row because they have been distributed across the rows of relevant products.

According to this supply table, South Korea's domestic output (at basic prices) in 2015 is KRW 3,717.0 trillion, and imports are KRW 603.4 trillion, resulting in the total supply (at basic prices) of KRW 4,320.5 trillion. In the price adjustment columns, taxes less subsidies on products of KRW 137.1 trillion in, distribution margins of KRW 222.4 trillion, and transport margins of KRW 9.3 trillion are adjusted, resulting in the total supply (at purchasers' prices) of KRW 4,457.6 trillion.

Table 4.18 Example of the supply table (South Korea, 2015)

Unit: KRW trillion

Product \ Industry	A Agriculture, forestry, and fishing	B,C Mining and manufacturing	D,E Electricity, gas, water, and waste	F Construction	G Wholesale and retail industry	H Transportation	I Food and accommodation	J-N Communication, finance, business	O Public admin. and defense	P-T Education, health, and culture	Total output (basic price)	Imports (basic price)	Total supply (basic price)	Taxes less subsidies on products	Distribution margin	Transport margin	Total price adjustment	Total supply (purchasers price)
Agricultural	61.3	0.0	0.0	0.0	0.0	0.0	0.0	0.0	0.0	0.0	61.3	11.6	72.9	0.6	12.2	0.4	13.3	86.2
Mining, manufacturing	0.0	1,661.1	0.0	0.0	0.3	0.2	0.0	0.1	0.0	0.0	1,661.8	494.1	2155.8	69.4	205.1	8.7	283.2	2439.0
Electricity, gas, water	0.0	0.0	107.3	0.0	2.5	0.0	0.0	0.0	0.0	0.0	109.9	0.1	110.0	2.1	0.0	0.0	2.1	112.1
Construction	0.0	0.0	0.0	209.7	0.0	0.0	0.0	0.0	0.0	0.0	209.7	0.1	209.8	13.9	0.0	0.0	13.9	223.7
Trade service	0.0	10.3	0.0	0.0	227.9	0.0	0.0	0.1	0.0	0.0	238.4	3.4	241.8	9.2	-222.4	0.0	-213.2	28.6
Transport service	0.0	0.1	0.0	0.0	0.2	144.2	0.0	0.1	0.0	0.0	144.7	23.4	168.2	-3.4	0.0	-9.3	-12.7	155.5
Food and accommodation.	0.0	0.0	0.0	0.1	0.2	0.0	118.4	0.2	0.0	6.1	125.1	13.6	138.6	6.9	0.0	0.0	6.9	145.5
Communication, finance, business	0.0	3.5	0.6	2.2	2.1	0.6	0.2	705.1	0.0	1.0	715.2	48.5	763.7	31.7	5.1	0.2	36.9	800.6
Public admin. defense	0.0	0.0	0.0	0.0	0.0	0.0	0.0	0.0	123.4	0.0	123.4	0.6	124.0	0.0	0.0	0.0	0.0	124.0
Education, health	0.0	1.0	0.1	0.1	1.0	0.0	0.5	0.6	2.2	322.1	327.6	8.1	335.7	6.7	0.0	0.0	6.7	342.4
Total	61.4	1,676.0	108.0	212.1	234.3	145.1	119.1	706.1	125.6	329.3	3,717.0	603.4	4,320.5	137.1	0.0	0.0	137.1	4,457.6

Chapter 5. Components of the use table

The **use table** shows the detailed use of goods and services by a national economy over a specific period based on the data of output and imports derived from the supply table. This table is structured in a matrix format, with columns representing total use categories from the product balance identity, such as intermediate consumption, final consumption, gross capital formation, and exports, and rows displaying the detailed breakdown of these total use categories by product. In addition, this table includes detailed value-added data by industry.

The use table can be explained in three main quadrants. First, Quadrant I represents intermediate consumption, which shows the value of intermediate inputs used in production by industry and product. Second, Quadrant II represents final use, with columns for items such as final consumption, gross capital formation and exports, and rows showing these breakdowns by product. Third, Quadrant III illustrates the value added by industry, which is derived by subtracting intermediate consumption from output. This value-added can also be obtained by deducting imports in the supply table from the total final use in the use table. In this chapter, we will look into each item that constitutes the use table in detail.

5.1 Intermediate consumption

Intermediate consumption refers to the value of goods and services consumed as inputs in the production process. Gross fixed capital formation is also used in the production process, but it differs from intermediate consumption in that gross fixed capital formation is used repeatedly in production activities for more than one year, whereas intermediate consumption is used either once or for a period of less than one year. Gross fixed capital formation constitutes fixed assets that are used repeatedly in production, and depreciation of fixed assets and depletion of natural resources during the accounting period is not included in intermediate consumption. However, the payment of rentals incurred from the external lease of equipment or buildings is treated as intermediate consumption. On the other hand, the leasing costs of non-produced assets, such as land or subsoil resources, are not treated as intermediate consumption but as the payment of property income as rent.

As illustrated in Table 5.1, the format of the use table is organized with columns distinguishing industries and production types (market production, non-market production, own-account production), and rows displaying the intermediate inputs, categorized by product type (according to the CPC, Central Products Classification).

Table 5.1 Intermediate consumption in the use table (Quadrant I)

		By industry				Final use	Total use
		Market production	Non-market production	Own-account production	Total intermediate use		
Intermediate consumption	Product 1	Quadrant I					
	Product 2						
	Product 3						
	Subtotal				A		
Value added					B		
Total input					A+B		

5.1.1 Types of intermediate consumption

Intermediate consumption can be categorized into three types. The first type refers to materials and supplies directly used in the production process, as well as other manufacturing costs, as seen in the manufacturing industry. The second type involves the costs of ancillary activities that incur commonly across all industries, such as those related to purchasing, sales, accounting, human resources, transportation, storage, and maintenance. The third type of intermediate consumption is the costs that are not explicitly measured, therefore estimated indirectly by national account compilers. Examples include financial intermediation services indirectly measured (FISIM) arising from borrowing or depositing funds with financial corporations, and service charges of non-life insurances. FISIM and non-life insurance service charges are not recorded in the accounting records of individual enterprises; instead, national accounts compilers take the procedure of calculating and allocating them at the level of total economy.

- The value of *Intermediate consumption* = input cost of the materials and supplies + manufacturing costs other than materials and supplies + costs of ancillary activities (purchasing, sales, marketing, accounting, personnel, transportation, storage, and maintenance) + FISIM + non-life insurance service charges

5.1.2 Valuation of intermediate consumption

In the SNA, all goods and services used for intermediate consumption are valued at purchasers' prices. This is because all business accounting data are prepared on the basis of the purchaser's price. Therefore, the purchasers' prices of goods such as materials and supplies include any distribution margins, freight charges separately invoiced by the seller, and non-deductible taxes on products (i.e., other taxes on products, taxes on imports, non-deductible VAT).

The point at which intermediate consumption is valued in the SNA is not when the goods or services are purchased by the producer, but *when these goods or services are input into the production process*. Among the items of intermediate consumption, goods such as materials and supplies should be valued at the "price when they are input into production," rather than at the price when they are purchased. Therefore, the valuation method for intermediate consumption requires measuring the price each time the materials and supplies are withdrawn from inventories and input into production. However, this estimation method differs from current accounting practices of businesses, and due to the nature of the method, it requires extensive data collection. As a result, the method introduced in the following section is more commonly used due to practical limitations in its application.

5.1.3 Estimation of intermediate consumption

The estimates of intermediate consumption of materials and supplies at each establishment can be measured indirectly using the data of changes in inventories as mentioned below. The changes in inventories of materials and supplies are the amount obtained by subtracting the inventory withdrawals for intermediate inputs from the inventory entries, and then further subtracting recurrent inventory losses during the accounting period. **Recurrent inventory losses** reduce the increase in inventories, which in turn increase intermediate consumption.

- Changes in inventories of materials and supplies – entries into inventories – (withdrawals from inventories + recurrent losses of inventories)

In practice, to derive the value of changes in inventories of materials and supplies from stock data, the difference between the closing and opening inventories can be used, as shown in Figure 5.1.

Figure 5.1 Derivation of intermediate consumption for materials (and supplies)

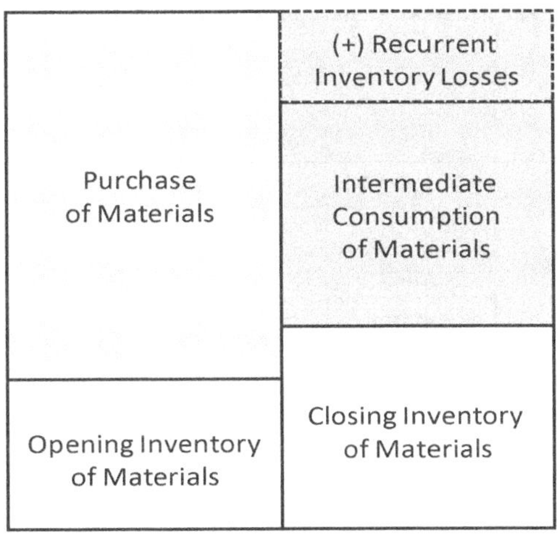

According to Figure 5.1, the following equation can be derived:

(5.1) Purchases of materials and supplies in the current period + opening inventory of materials and supplies = intermediate consumption for materials and supplies + closing inventory of materials and supplies + recurrent inventory losses

Since the total intermediate consumption of materials and supplies includes inventory losses that incur on a recurring basis, equation (5.1) can be rearranged as follows:

(5.2) Total intermediate consumption for materials and supplies = intermediate consumption for materials and supplies + recurrent inventory losses = Purchases of materials and supplies in the current period – changes in inventories (= closing inventory of materials and supplies – opening inventory of materials and supplies)

In other words, in practice, the total intermediate consumption of materials and supplies can be estimated by subtracting changes in inventories from the value of purchases during the period. However, since changes in inventories (= closing stock of inventories – opening stock of inventories) includes holding gains and losses in addition to the volume changes in inventories, these gains and losses must be deducted separately. (For details on this deduction method, see 5.3.2 and 11.2.1.1.)

5.2 Final consumption expenditure

In the use table, **final use** consists of items excluding intermediate consumption from total use. As shown in Table 5.2, this item includes final consumption expenditure, gross capital formation, and exports. In addition, as part of the adjustment process, "direct purchases abroad by residents" are added to final consumption, while "domestic purchases by non-residents" are subtracted from final consumption and add to exports. Below, we will explain each of these items in detail.

Table 5.2 Final use in the use table (Quadrant II)

		By industry	Final consumption	Gross capital formation	Exports	Total use
Intermediate consumption	Product 1		Quadrant II			
	Product 2					
	Product 3					
	Subtotal	A				
Direct purchases abroad by residents						
Domestic purchases by non-residents						
Value added		B				
Total output		A+B				

In the SNA, consumption expenditure is divided into intermediate consumption and final consumption expenditure. The distinction between intermediate consumption and final consumption expenditure is based on whether it is used in the production process. The expenditures of goods and services consumed as intermediate inputs in production activities are recorded as **intermediate consumption**, while those consumed by final consumers are classified as **final consumption expenditure**. The difference between final consumption expenditure and gross fixed capital formation lies in the fact that final consumption expenditure is incurred by final consumers, whereas gross fixed capital formation involves expenditures on goods and services that are used repeatedly in production activities over more than one year.

Final consumption expenditure is further categorized into *household final consumption*, *government final consumption*, and *final consumption by non-profit institutions serving households* (NPISHs) according to the final consumption units. Each of these categories has its own characteristics and estimation methods, which will be discussed below.

5.2.1 Household final consumption expenditure

Household final consumption expenditure refers to as the total expenditure on goods and services for consumption by resident households. This expenditure includes expenditures made by residents both domestically and abroad, while expenditures by non-residents within a domestic economy are subtracted. In this context, the corresponding item of resident's expenditure abroad is recorded as an import, and the corresponding item of non-resident's domestic expenditure is recorded as an export (Figure 5.2).

- Household final consumption expenditure = total domestic expenditure on consumption goods and services by households (both residents and non-residents) for consumption goods and services + expenditures by resident households abroad – expenditures by non-residents within the country

Figure 5.2 Derivation of Household Final Consumption Expenditure

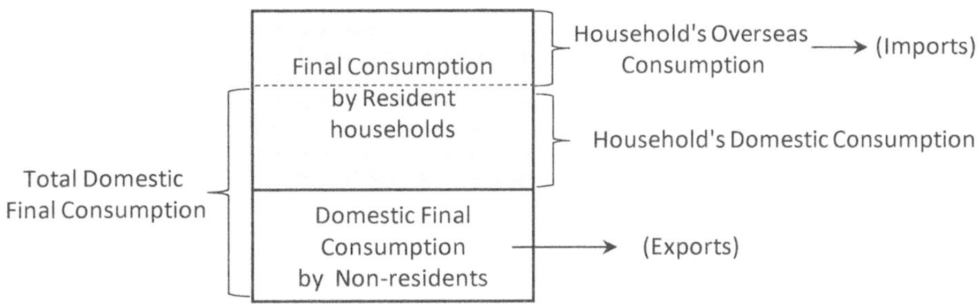

In addition, expenditures by **household unincorporated enterprises** (small enterprises operated by households) on goods and services used in their production activities should be recorded as intermediate consumption. In the SNA, the method of identifying household unincorporated enterprises is determined by whether they maintain complete accounting records, including balance sheets. If they do not prepare complete set of financial statements under double-entry bookkeeping, they are classified as household unincorporated enterprises.

Household final consumption expenditure encompasses not only purchases of goods and services, barter transactions, and acquisitions of in-kind but also all goods produced within the household for own consumption. However, the production of services for own consumption within households is excluded from the production boundary. Furthermore, the scope of household final consumption expenditure excludes purchases of residential buildings and valuables. Residential buildings are regarded as part of gross fixed capital formation, and valuables are included in gross capital formation as acquisitions less disposals of valuables. On the other hand, consumer durables such as home appliances and furniture are included in household final consumption expenditure as consumption goods when they are acquired by households.

There are certain service expenditure items related to households that are difficult to capture through the household expenditure survey and require separate estimation by national accounts compilers. Examples include financial intermediation service fees (FISIM), fees paid for the transactions of foreign exchange and financial instruments, insurance service fees (household portion of life insurance and non-life insurance), and pension-related service fees. In addition, services produced by households for their own consumption are not included in household final consumption expenditures, but the imputed value of owner-occupied dwelling services and the services produced by the paid domestic staff within the household are included in this category.

Household final consumption expenditure is valued at purchasers' prices. This includes not only transport margins separately charged by the seller but also any transport charge paid by the purchaser (e.g., courier).

5.2.1.1 Methods for estimating household final consumption expenditure

Household final consumption expenditure can be estimated using various methods, including the household survey method, product flow method, and retail sales method.

1. **Household survey method**: This direct estimation method involves the national statistical office regularly conducting sample surveys to collect data on household income and expenditure.

The statistical office estimates consumption expenditure per household or per capita using household consumption survey data, then multiplies these figures by the number of households or population to derive total consumption expenditure and its components.

2. **Product flow method**: This is an indirect estimation approach of estimating household consumption expenditure to trace the flow of individual goods and services under the product balance identity, thereby determining the purchase amount of the final consumer. That is, the total amount of final consumption is indirectly derived using the formula "domestic output + imports – (intermediate consumption + gross fixed capital formation + changes in inventories + acquisition less disposal of valuables + exports) = final consumption expenditure." Subsequently, this total is allocated among different sectors, including households, government, and NPISHs. This method is particularly useful for estimating consumption expenditures on items that may be underreported or omitted in direct surveys, such as certain durable goods or services. Moreover, it serves as an alternative method to be used from the production side when the systematic data collection on household consumption expenditures is not conducted.

3. **Retail sales method**: This is a direct estimation approach for household consumption expenditures, where sales figures of specific products are surveyed at the retail store level. Retail stores are selected through sampling techniques, and their sales data are regularly collected and indexed to produce the estimates. This method provides the most up-to-date data obtained from the field, which is highly useful for expenditure analysis of final consumers. If such data is available, it is considered the most preferred method for providing reliable and timely information on household consumption expenditures in national accounts.

5.2.1.2 Actual final consumption of households

As will be mentioned in Chapter 12, among the consumption expenditures incurred by government or NPISHs, expenditures that effectively benefit households, or expenditures paid by government on behalf of households for the purchase of market products by households, can be attributable to household consumption expenditure. In the SNA, they are referred to as **social transfers in kind**. When these social transfers in kind are added to the household final consumption expenditure, the result yields the **actual final consumption of households**, which is an indicator that can measure the true welfare level of household.

- Actual final consumption of households = household final consumption expenditure + government social transfers in kind to households (= government's own products attributable to households + government's payment on behalf of households for part of their purchases of market products) + NPISHs' social transfers in kind to households

5.2.1.3 COICOP Classification of households' expenditure

A more detailed way for categorizing household consumption expenditure is the *Classification of Individual Consumption According to Purpose* (COICOP), which is an internationally recommended classification system by the United Nations[10]. This taxonomy allows us to categorize household consumption expenditures into internationally standardized items. The current version of COICOP, based on the 2018 standards presented by the UN (COICOP 2018), classifies household consumption into the following 15 divisions (Table 5.3).

Table 5.3 Classification of Individual Consumption According to Purpose (division)

Division
01 – Food and non-alcoholic beverages
02 – Alcoholic beverages, tobacco and narcotics
03 – Clothing and footwear
04 – Housing, water, electricity, gas and other fuels
05 – Furnishings, household equipment and routine household maintenance
06 – Health
07 – Transport
08 – Information and communication
09 – Recreation, sport and culture
10 – Education services
11 – Restaurants and accommodation services
12 – Insurance and financial services
13 – Personal care, social protection and miscellaneous goods
14 – Individual consumption expenditure of NPISH
15 – Individual consumption of general government

The sum of divisions 01 through 13 represents the total individual consumption expenditures by households. The last two divisions (14 and 15) represent the consumption expenditures of NPISHs

[10] This special classification was introduced for analytical purposes by establishing a different classification framework separate from the traditional one, reflecting the differing purposes served by each institutional sector. For example, government, households, and NPISHs perform different functions as economic agents, and therefore require new, sector-specific classification systems for their expenditure structures. In line with this rationale, the national accounts apply three different classification systems for expenditure analysis: COFOG for government, COICOP for households, and COPNI for NPISHs.

and general government that are transferred to households as in kind. Adding up all 15 divisions yields the "actual final consumption of households."

Meanwhile, when the COICOP classification is linked with the product classification, it becomes possible to analyze household expenditures by purpose for each product. Table 5.4 is a combination of the product breakdown in rows and the COICOP breakdown in columns. This table shows how much money is spent on each product by the purpose of household expenditure. What should be remembered for preparing this table is that, as described in Figure 5.2, household consumption expenditure of domestic residents must be shown, meaning that expenditures by residents abroad should be added to the product categories, and expenditures by non-residents within the country should be deducted, resulting in an adjustments figure.

Table 5.4 A table linking between COICOP and CPC

COICOP / Products (CPC)	Consumption expenditure of individual consumption by purpose (COICOP)				
	Food and non-alcoholic beverages	Alcoholic beverages, tobacco and narcotics	…	Personal care, social protection and miscellaneous goods	Total (purchaser's price)
	01	02	…	13	01-13
Product 1	xx				xx
Product 2		xx			xx
:			xx		xx
Product N				xx	xx
Total	xx	xx	xx	xx	xx

5.2.2 Final consumption expenditure of general government

Final consumption expenditure of general government is derived in a unique way, unlike that of households. Most of the government's products are non-market output and are not sold to the market, but are subject to final consumption by the government itself, so the government's final consumption expenditure is derived from this treatment method. The value of final consumption expenditure of general government is calculated as total output produced by government minus the value of sales of goods and services to other institutional units, minus the value used to form the government's own capital (e.g., government R&D), plus the value reimbursed on behalf of households for a portion of the market products purchased by households. The government's expenditure on capital formation for its own use is already included in the government's output, but is not final consumption expenditure, so it is subtracted. Here, the value of sales of government products to other institutional units includes both market output (e.g., entrance fees to national or public museums) and non-market output (e.g., tuitions of national and public school). Examples of the government's reimbursement for a portion of household purchases of market products are when the government pays for a portion of the household's medical expenses through health insurance, provides free medical benefits for the low-income class, or reimburses preschool tuition. This portion is not included in the government's output, but is added to the government's final consumption expenditure as it reimburses households for their actual expenditures. (It constitutes part of the government's "social transfers in kind".)

- Final consumption expenditure incurred by government = total government output – government's own-account capital formation – the value of sales of government products (market and non-market) + the value of goods and services purchased from market producers to provide to households for free or at economically insignificant prices.

5.2.2.1 Estimation method of government's final consumption expenditure

The basic data source for the estimation of government final consumption is the budget and financial statements prepared by government units. In particular, in the case of budget documents, detailed breakdowns by product are displayed in the expenditure part, so it is possible to classify the intermediate consumption and final consumption by product. However, expenditures associated with financial services such as FISIM, foreign exchange fees, and non-life insurance service fees must be added through separate calculations.

5.2.2.2 Individual consumption versus collective consumption of general government

On the other hand, the government final consumption can be divided into **individual consumption expenditure** that are attributed to actual benefits to individual households (e.g., education service and healthcare service) and **collective consumption expenditure** for which the target of benefits cannot be clearly attributed (e.g., defense, public order and safety, and public administration service). Individual consumption expenditure is divided into individual consumption on goods and services produced by the government units and the value of compensation paid by government for goods and services purchased by households from market producers. Individual consumption expenditure is added to actual final consumption of households and subtracted from the final consumption of government when calculating the actual final consumption of government. (It will be described in more detail in Chapter 12.)

- Government's actual final consumption = government's final consumption expenditure – individual consumption expenditure of government (= social transfers in kind to households

5.2.2.3 COFOG classification of government expenditure

A more detailed classification of government expenditures is the *Classification of Functions of Government* (COFOG), which is internationally adopted under the recommendation of the United Nations. This classification was initially developed by the OECD, but was published by the United Nations in 2000 as part of an international standard, along with three other purpose-specific expenditure classifications (COICOP, COPNI, and COPP). According to the COFOG classification, government expenditures are divided into ten categories by function[11] as shown in the following table (Table 5.5). Using this classification, it is possible to distinguish between individual consumption and collective consumption in government final consumption expenditure. The category of collective consumption expenditure includes expenditures on General public services (01), Defense (02), Public order and safety (03), Economic affairs (04), Environmental protection (05), Housing and community amenities (06), and sections of health (07.5, 07.6), sections of recreation, culture and religion (08.3~08.6), sections of education (09.7, 09.8), and sections of social protection (10.8, 10.9). On the other hand, the category of Individual consumption expenditure includes expenditures on the remaining sections of Health (07), Recreation, culture and religion (08), Education (09), and Social protection (10).

Table 5.5 Classification of Functions of Government (COFOG)

01	General public services
02	Defense
03	Public order and safety
04	Economic affairs
05	Environmental protection
06	Housing and community amenities
07	Health
08	Recreation, culture and religion
09	Education
10	Social protection

Meanwhile, by linking COFOG with the product classification, it is possible to identify the amounts of government expenditure by function for each product. The expenditures classified under COFOG include all national accounts items, such as final consumption expenditure, gross capital formation, and subsidies, etc. However, for the purpose of this section, we focus only on final

[11] The Government Finance Statistics Manual (GFS 2014, IMF) uses the same classification codes as the UN, but "7" is added as a prefix in front of COFOG codes as a unique GFS classification. For example, 02 (defence) is displayed as 702.

consumption expenditures. Table 5.6 illustrates the government's final consumption expenditure, categorized into collective services and individual services, and shows the amounts by function and product.

Table 5.6 Tables linking between COFOG and CPC (Collective and individual services)

Collective services

COFOG / Products	Collective consumption of general government (COFOG)				
	Public services	Defense	…	Social protection	Total
	1	2	…	10	
Product 1					
Product 2					
:					
Product N					
Total					

Individual services

COFOG / Products	Individual consumption of general government (COFOG)				
	Health	Recreation, culture, religion	Education	Social protection	Total
	07*	08*	09*	10*	
Product 1					
Product 2					
:					
Product N					
Total					

* Refer to UN Handbook on SUTs and IOTs, Table 6.8.

5.2.3 Final consumption expenditure of NPISHs

The method for calculating the final consumption expenditure of non-profit institutions serving households (NPISHs) is similar to that of the government, in that the non-market output produced by NPISHs are considered as being consumed by NPISHs themselves. Therefore, the procedure for deriving final consumption expenditure follows the same method as for the general government. If NPISHs engage in secondary production activities by producing market output for sale or receive payments for the sale of non-market products, these amounts are subtracted when calculating the final consumption expenditure of NPISHs. All of these receipts are recorded as final consumption expenditures of households purchasing the NPISHs' products. If a NPISH (for example, charitable organization) receives donations (e.g., food, clothing, medicine) from other economic entities for the purpose of transferring them to households, these donated goods are recorded as expenditure for households. The accounting treatment in this case assumes that the charitable organization receives cash and then purchases the donated goods from other enterprises that are market producers.

- Final consumption expenditure of NPISHs = NPISHs' output – NPISHs' own-account fixed capital formation – the value of sales of NPISHs (market and non-market) + the value of goods and services purchased from market producers to be provided to households for free or at economically insignificant prices

Unlike general government, the final consumption of NPISHs consists almost entirely of individual consumption expenditures that benefit households, with no collective consumption expenditures considered. Thus, all of the final consumption expenditure of NPISHs is accounted for as social transfers in kind to households, and actual final consumption of NPISHs is considered to be zero.

- Actual final consumption of NPISHs = final consumption expenditure of NPISHs – social transfers in kind from NPISHs to households = 0

5.2.3.1 COPNI classification of NPISHs' expenditure

A more detailed classification on expenditures of NPISHs is provided by a classification set by the UN. This is called the *Classification of the Purposes of Non-profit Institutions Serving Households* (COPNI), which divides expenditures into the following nine categories based on their purposes.

Table 5.7 COPNI Classification

01	Housing
02	Health
03	Recreation and culture
04	Education
05	Social protection
06	Religion
07	Political parties, labour and professional organizations
08	Environmental protection
09	Services n.e.c.

The classification of COPNI includes all expenditures of NPISHs, including final consumption expenditure, gross capital formation, and property income, etc. However, for the purpose of this section, we focus only on final consumption expenditure, and in order to identify the expenditure amounts by purpose and by product, a table can be constructed that links COPNI with the product classification as follows (Table 5.8).

Table 5.8 A Table linking between COPNI and the product classification

COPNI / Products	Final consumption of NPISHs				
	Housing 01	Health 02	… …	Services n.e.c. 09	Total (01-09)
Product 1 Product 2 : Product N					
Total					

Note: Refer to UN Handbook on SUTs and IOTs, Table 6.7.

5.3 Gross capital formation

Gross capital formation represents the amount obtained by subtracting the disposal value from the acquisition value of non-financial assets produced by production activities during the accounting period. Gross capital formation consists of gross fixed capital formation, changes in inventories, and acquisitions less disposals of valuables. Most of the gross capital formation occurs in market producers (like enterprises) and non-market producers, but in the case of acquisitions less disposals of valuables, it may occur within households in their capacity as final consumers. The types of non-financial assets that constitute gross capital formation are shown in Table 5.9, and each type is briefly described below.

Table 5.9 Types of non-financial assets constituting gross capital formation

<table>
<tr><td rowspan="17">Fixed assets</td><td colspan="2">Dwellings</td></tr>
<tr><td rowspan="3">Other buildings and structures</td><td>Buildings other than dwellings</td></tr>
<tr><td>Other structures</td></tr>
<tr><td>Land improvements</td></tr>
<tr><td rowspan="3">Machinery and equipment</td><td>Transport equipment</td></tr>
<tr><td>ICT equipment</td></tr>
<tr><td>Other machinery and equipment</td></tr>
<tr><td>Weapons systems</td><td></td></tr>
<tr><td rowspan="2">Cultivated biological resources</td><td>Animal resources yielding repeat products</td></tr>
<tr><td>Tree, crop and plant resources yielding repeat products</td></tr>
<tr><td colspan="2">Costs of ownership transfer on non-produced assets</td></tr>
<tr><td rowspan="5">Intellectual property products</td><td>Research and development</td></tr>
<tr><td>Mineral exploration and evaluation</td></tr>
<tr><td>Computer software and databases</td></tr>
<tr><td>Entertainment, literary or artistic originals</td></tr>
<tr><td>Other intellectual property products</td></tr>
<tr><td rowspan="6">Inventories</td><td colspan="2">Materials and supplies</td></tr>
<tr><td rowspan="2">Work-in-progress</td><td>Work-in-progress on cultivated biological assets</td></tr>
<tr><td>Other work-in-progress</td></tr>
<tr><td colspan="2">Finished goods</td></tr>
<tr><td colspan="2">Military inventories</td></tr>
<tr><td colspan="2">Goods for resale</td></tr>
<tr><td rowspan="3">Valuables</td><td colspan="2">Precious metals and stones</td></tr>
<tr><td colspan="2">Antiques and other art objects</td></tr>
<tr><td colspan="2">Other valuables</td></tr>
</table>

5.3.1 Gross fixed capital formation

Gross fixed capital formation refers to the amount of fixed assets acquired by a producer during the accounting period in relation to production activities, calculated as the acquisition value minus the disposal value. **Net fixed capital formation** is the amount obtained by subtracting depreciation from gross fixed capital formation. The scope of gross fixed capital formation includes not only newly produced assets but also existing assets. Fixed assets are those used repeatedly in production activities for more than one year, and they must be non-financial assets produced through production activities. Accordingly, non-produced assets such as land and subsoil resources, as well as financial assets, are excluded. The components constituting gross fixed capital formation are listed as follows.

Table 5.10 Components of gross fixed capital formation

	Purchases of new or existing fixed assets
+	Fixed assets produced or retained for producers' own use
+	New or existing fixed assets acquired through barter transaction
+	New or existing fixed assets acquired through capital transfers in kind
+	New or existing fixed assets acquired by the user under financial lease contracts
+	Major improvements to fixed assets
+	Natural growth of natural assets that yield repeat products
-	Existing fixed assets sold
-	Existing fixed assets disposed of through barter transaction
-	Existing fixed assets disposed of through capital transfers in kind

Note: Refer to 3.125, ESA 2010

The category of fixed assets includes the **costs of ownership transfer** associated with the acquisition and disposal of both fixed assets and non produced assets (land, subsoil assets). The costs of ownership transfer include various service fees related to the ownership transfer, any trade and transport costs separately charged to the purchaser, all taxes associated with the ownership transfer, installation and dismantling costs, and terminal costs (i.e., costs associated with the decommissioning power plants, disposal of nuclear wastes, etc.). The depreciation period for the costs of ownership transfer is based on the expected holding period of the owner, but the terminal costs are depreciated over the entire service life of the asset. The costs of ownership transfer, like in the business accounting practice, are included as part of costs when calculating the acquisition cost of a fixed asset. Therefore, the valuation of gross fixed capital formation includes the costs of ownership transfer in addition to the actual market price transacted.

In addition, the disposal of existing fixed assets is recorded as the amount received by the seller minus the cost of ownership transfer incurred at the time of sale. Transactions between domestic residents for existing fixed assets are offset against each other, leaving the seller's un-written off costs of ownership transfer, which are treated as holding losses in the **revaluation**

account described later (section 11.2). In addition, the seller's capital gain or loss from the sale of fixed assets is recorded as a holding gain and loss in the revaluation account. (Further details on fixed capital formation are provided in Chapters 6 and 10.)

Table 5.11 Types of costs of ownership transfer and their depreciation methods

Type	Depreciation method
All service fees related to ownership transfers	Depreciated over the expected holding period of the owner.
Trade and transport costs separately charged to the purchaser	Same as above
All taxes related to the ownership transfer	Same as above
Installation and dismantling costs	Same as above
Terminal costs	Depreciated over the entire service life of the asset

Land and subsoil resources are not included in the category of fixed assets; however, the cost of ownership transfer of these assets is included in the category of fixed assets. Consequently, the incurrence of this cost is included in gross fixed capital formation, with separate provisions in the classification of fixed assets. Specifically, the cost of ownership transfer of fixed assets is included in the acquisition cost, but the cost of ownership transfer of land is classified under "land improvement" (a subcategory of 'other buildings and structures'), while the cost of ownership transfer of non-produced assets, such as subsoil resources, is separately presented under a subcategory of fixed assets. This cost of ownership transfer for non-produced assets (excluding land) is included in the item of gross fixed capital formation; however, as explained later in the balance sheet (section 11.3), no separate account item is shown, and it is combined under the category of *non-produced assets*.

The types of non-financial assets that constitutes gross fixed capital formation include dwellings, other buildings and structures, machinery and equipment, weapons systems, cultivated biological resources, costs of ownership transfer of non-produced assets, and intellectual property products. (See Table 5.9.) A brief overview of the estimation methods for each item is as follows (see Chapter 6 for details).

Both dwellings and, other buildings and structures can be derived from the production-side data in the construction industry based on the **product flow method** (= domestic output + costs of ownership transfer – changes in inventories). For machinery and equipment, the shares of industrial users and general consumers in the total sales of machinery and equipment are investigated to calculate the amount for industrial users, and the amount of imported machinery and equipment is also derived through the "distribution survey on imported products". Intellectual property products, which were referred to as intangible fixed assets in the 1993 SNA, have had their coverage changed since the 2008 SNA. Intellectual property products now include research and development **(R&D)** expenditure, which was previously treated as intermediate consumption by enterprises, but is now recognized as fixed assets and constitutes gross fixed capital formation. Expenditures on **weapons systems** are included in the scope of fixed assets, and are treated as gross fixed capital formation of general government. The scope of weapons systems included in gross fixed capital formation covers those that are continuously provided for the production of defense services, such as warships, military aircraft, tanks, missile carriers and launchers. However, single-use weapons (e.g., ammunition, missiles, bombs, etc.) are treated as **military inventories** and are recorded as intermediate consumption by government after their withdrawals from inventories.

Gross fixed capital formation for own final use (that is, own-account gross fixed capital formation) includes a significant portion of **cultivated biological resources** (i.e., fruit trees, dairy cows, etc.) produced by agricultural and livestock producers for their own use in production. This category also includes buildings constructed for their own use, or own-account R&D for in-house use of enterprises. Own-account gross fixed capital formation is already recorded as the own-account production of output in the supply table, and this output is directly transferred as the gross fixed capital formation in the use table (Table 5.12).

Table 5.12 Presentation of the own-account fixed capital formation in supply and use tables

Supply table

Products	Market output	Own-account output			Non-market output	Imports	Total
		Agriculture	Construction	R&D			
Agriculture		x					
Construction			xx				
R&D				xxx			
…							
Total output		x	xx	xxx			

Use table

Products	Market output	Own-account output			Non-market output	…	Fixed capital formation	Total
		Agriculture	Construction	R&D				
Agriculture							x	
Construction							xx	
R&D							xxx	
…								
Total input								

Capital flow table by industry

The gross fixed capital formation displayed in the use table can be segmented by the industries in which investments are made. It can also be categorized by items of gross fixed capital formation for each industry into groups such as buildings and structures, machinery and equipment, cultivated biological resources, and intellectual property products. To achieve this, the gross fixed capital formation column in the use table can be presented as a matrix table that is cross-classified into columns by industry and rows by type of capital goods (Table 5.13). This matrix table is referred to as the industry-specific gross fixed capital formation table (or **capital flow table**), which can be used not only for national accounts but also for various other purposes. In the SNA, data on gross fixed capital formation by industry in the capital flow table can be used to estimate the capital stocks and capital services by industry through the perpetual inventory method (see Chapter 20). Furthermore, it can serve as source data for estimating depreciation by industry under the perpetual inventory method. The capital flow table itself can also be used to estimate and predict the demand for gross fixed capital formation by industry.

In order to compile the capital flow table, it is necessary to conduct a survey on the fixed capital formation by industry, similar to the survey on intermediate inputs by industry. The estimation method is briefly described as follows: First, for buildings and structures, total output data from the construction industry on the production side can be directly utilized, and based on this data, the acquisition details of buildings and structures by industry are investigated. Machinery, transport equipment, as well as intellectual property products, can be estimated through a survey on the fixed capital formation details, and these control total data can be collected from the economic census or the corporate financial statement databases of the National Tax Service. In addition, when goods classified as capital goods are used for final consumption by households (e.g., durable goods such as household appliances), a supplementary work to survey the distribution ratio between enterprises and households must also be conducted.

Table 5.13 Capital flow table by industry

Industry / Type (Product)	Agriculture	Manufacturing	Construction	Trade, transport, and comm.	Finance, business services	Other services	Total (purchaser's price)
Residential buildings Non-residential buildings Structures Machinery Transport equipment Other equipment Intellectual property products							
Total							

One consideration in preparing the capital flow table by industry is that the assets subject to fixed capital formation may be directly purchased and used by the enterprise, or the assets may be leased from other leasing industries (i.e., operating leases). This means that industries that lease equipment for transportation, construction, communication, and software, etc., may differ from the industries that actually use them. However, in terms of measuring productivity, it may be more appropriate to base the analysis on the industries where the fixed assets are actually put into production activities. Industries that lease fixed assets do not directly apply these assets to production but only provide leasing services, with the revenue from these services as output. Therefore, the capital flow table by industry can be prepared based on either the **user basis** (reflecting the industries that actually use the assets, or the **ownership basis** (reflecting the industries that owns the assets). However, in terms of measurement of the capital productivity, the table based on the user basis is generally preferred.

5.3.2 Changes in inventories

Changes in inventories are defined as the net change during the accounting period, calculated as the value of goods added to inventories minus the value of goods withdrawn and minus recurrent losses. Inventories consist of goods held by producers or wholesalers and retailers for sale or for use as intermediate consumption, covering not only goods intended for single use but also capital goods that can be used repeatedly. The scope of goods includes not only tangible goods but also intangible goods such as intellectual property products. Changes in inventories measure the increase or decrease in goods over a specific period, and therefore correspond to the flow concept as opposed to the stock concept. In this section, we will discuss the types of inventories included in changes in inventories, the valuation and estimation methods for changes in inventories in the national accounts.

5.3.2.1 Types of inventories

The types of inventories include materials and supplies that enterprises put into production, as well as finished goods and work-in-progress that are in the process of production or have been completed as a result of production activities but are still held by the producer. In addition, in relation to the resale of goods, wholesalers and retailers hold goods for resale (also called "distribution inventories," which include imported goods). Work-in-progress is divided into work-in-progress of cultivated biological resources for single use (such as crops, livestock for slaughter, etc.) and other work-in-progress. In the case of government units, there are military inventories.

Figure 5.3 Types of inventories

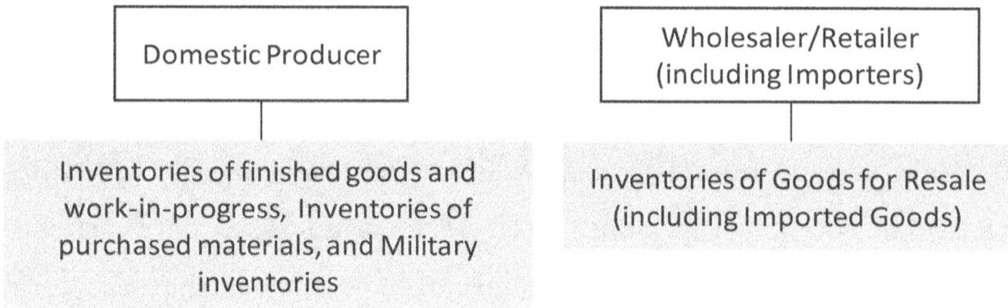

The types of inventories can be further detailed as follows. Materials and supplies are all goods held by enterprises for the purpose of putting them into the production process, with the most common types being fuel, raw materials, parts, and office supplies. **Work-in-progress** refers to output that has not been yet sufficiently processed to be supplied to other institutional units. Work-in-progress is further divided into that on *cultivated biological resources* and *other work-in-progress*. **Cultivated biological resources** refer to the output of animals and plants that are grown through artificial cultivation rather than natural growth, such as agricultural, forestry, fisheries products, and livestock. Cultivated biological resources are classified into **single-use** cultivated assets and **repeated-use** cultivated assets. The former includes crops, timber for logging, and livestock for slaughter, while the latter refers to trees or livestock that are used repeatedly and continuously for more than one year to produce products. Single-use cultivated assets are accounted for as work-in-progress, while the unfinished repeated-use cultivated assets are recorded as fixed assets rather than work-in-progress if they are intended for own use or are provided to other institutional units under specific contracts. *Other work-in-progress* comprises all work-in-progress excluding work-in-progress on cultivated biological resources. Inventories of finished goods refer to output that is no longer intended for further processing and are held by the producer without being sold, and are to be supplied to other institutional units. **Goods for resale** refer to goods acquired by enterprises (wholesalers, retailers, or general enterprises) for the purpose of reselling to their customers. Goods for resale are primarily held by wholesalers and retailers (including importers) as stocks of inventories for resale, and general enterprises may also hold goods for resale as part of operating wholesale and retail businesses as secondary activities. **Military inventories** include single-use items such as ammunition, missiles, and bombs, etc. However, ballistic missiles intended for deterrence in war are excluded from military inventories and are recorded as fixed assets.

Table 5.14 Treatment of inventories by type in national accounts

<table>
<tr><th>Category</th><th colspan="3">Subcategory</th><th>Treatment in national accounts</th></tr>
<tr><td>Materials & supplies</td><td colspan="3"></td><td>Inventories</td></tr>
<tr><td rowspan="4">Work-in-progress</td><td rowspan="3">Work-in-progress on cultivated biological resources</td><td colspan="2">Single-use cultivated assets</td><td>Inventories</td></tr>
<tr><td rowspan="2">Repeated-use cultivated assets</td><td>Own use, Provision to third parties under contract</td><td>Fixed assets</td></tr>
<tr><td>Others</td><td>Inventories</td></tr>
<tr><td colspan="3">Other work-in-progress</td><td>Inventories</td></tr>
<tr><td>Finished goods</td><td colspan="3"></td><td>Inventories</td></tr>
<tr><td>Goods for resale</td><td colspan="3"></td><td>Inventories</td></tr>
<tr><td>Military inventories</td><td colspan="3"></td><td>Inventories</td></tr>
</table>

5.3.2.2 Valuation of changes in inventories

Changes in inventories are measured as the value of entries into inventories less the value of withdrawals from inventories and less the value of recurrent losses of inventories during the accounting period.

- Changes in inventories = entries of inventories – withdrawals of inventories – recurrent losses of inventories

The data in the above equation are collected through financial statements or surveys of enterprises. As the basis for the valuation of changes in inventories, goods produced or in the process of production by enterprises (that is, finished goods and work-in-progress) are valued at basic prices, while goods purchased for inputs into production (that is, materials and supplies) or for resale are valued at purchasers' prices.

The valuation methods for inventories by type are as follows. For goods produced or goods in the process of production, goods transferred to the inventory warehouse are valued at the basic price that can sold at the time of entries of the goods, and goods withdrawn from the inventory warehouse are valued at the basic price that are sold at the time of withdrawals of the goods. This inventory valuation method is called the **perpetual inventory method**, which removes holding gains and losses due to inflation in the calculation of value-added, so that only incomes from normal operating activities are measured. These holding gains or losses are recorded in the revaluation account within "the other changes in assets and liabilities account". However, the perpetual inventory method is based on accounting records and cannot be used unless there is sufficient data on the quantities and prices of the entries and withdrawals of inventories. Therefore, an alternative method for estimating the value of changes in inventories involves *separating and removing the nominal holding gains from the difference between the closing and opening inventories during the period.*

For the valuation of inventories for materials and supplies, goods entering the material warehouse (purchases) are valued at the purchaser's price at the time of entry, and goods withdrawn from the material warehouse (for production purpose) are valued at the purchaser's price at the time of withdrawals. This method also aims to eliminate holding gains and losses due to inflation in materials and supplies.

For work-in-progress, the valuation at the time of entry is derived by multiplying the estimated basic price of the finished goods by the degree of completion (the proportion of incurred costs) during the period, and at the time of withdrawal, it is valued based on the estimated current basic price of the work-in-progress. For work-in-progress of cultivated biological resources, the valuation is done by multiplying the estimated basic price of the finished goods (farm-gate price) by the proportion of physical growth during the period.

The valuation of goods held for resale is based on the following: when goods are entered (purchased from the supplier), they are valued at the actual price or purchaser's price at the time of entry, and when they are withdrawn (sold), they are valued at the expected procurement price that can be purchased from the supplier at that time ("replacement purchaser's price"). However, goods stored for the purpose of increasing their value recognize the quality changes occurring during storage as an increase in the inventory of goods. For example, the activity of storing wine for ageing is considered part of the production process and affect the calculation of wholesale and retail trade as an increase in the output of goods. In this case, the increase in the value of goods held for resale during the period can be recorded as an increase in holding gains (treated in the revaluation account) and as an increase in output due to the production activity of storage services.

Table 5.15 Valuation methods by type of inventories

Category	Valuation method	
	Entry	**Withdrawal**
Finished goods	Basic price at the time of entry (production)	Basic price at the time of withdrawal (sales)
Materials and supplies	Purchaser's price at the time of entry (purchases)	Purchaser's price at the time of withdrawal (input into production)
Work-in-progress	Basic price of finished goods x degree of completion (proportion of incurred costs) during the period	Revalued using the prices and costs of the period in which the production is finished.
Cultivated biological resources	Basic price of finished goods (= farm-gate price) x proportion of physical growth during the period	
Goods for resale	Purchaser's price at the time of entry (purchase)	Replacement purchaser's price at the time of withdrawal (resale)

5.3.2.3 Estimation method of changes in inventories

The method for estimating changes in inventories in the SNA uses the perpetual inventory method, and the actual process of preparing it is briefly described as follows. In practice, it is difficult to obtain data on "the value of inventories entered – the value of inventories withdrawn", so first, the data on closing stock and opening stock of inventories are converted to those at constant prices, and then "the closing stock in constant prices – the opening stock in constant prices = the change in inventories in constant prices" is calculated. Next, deflators are applied to convert this into **changes in inventories in current prices**. Through this process, the formula "the closing stock of inventories in current prices – the opening stock of inventories in current prices – changes in inventories in current prices = holding gains and losses" is derived. If the changes in inventories calculated under the existing historic cost method (e.g., FIFO, LIFO) is to be converted into the change in inventories in current prices, the value of "inventory valuation adjustment" must be subtracted. (See inventory valuation adjustment in section 4.1.1.)

- Inventory valuation adjustment = Changes in inventories at historic costs – changes in inventories in current prices

5.3.3 Acquisitions less disposals of valuables

Valuables are assets held for the purpose of storing value rather than production. Unlike other fixed assets, depreciation on this item does not incur over time. Valuables are durable goods that are not used in production or consumption, and are not included in the final consumption expenditures by households; instead, they are separately accounted for as a subcategory under gross capital formation. The SNA classifies valuables into three categories as follows:

- Precious metals and stones
- Antiques and other art objectives
- Other valuables

The acquisition and disposal of valuables also include non-monetary gold (including gold other than for reserve assets held by monetary authorities and other financial institutions).

5.3.3.1 Valuation and accounting for acquisitions less disposals of valuables

Acquisitions less disposals of valuables are recorded as the value of acquisitions of valuables less disposals of valuables. Acquisitions of valuables are valued at the purchaser's price and any costs incurred in the acquisition process (i.e., appraisal fees, auctioneer's margin) are included in the value of valuables on the balance sheet as with other non-financial assets. These costs arise when valuables are traded, and constitute gross capital formation. Disposals of valuables are recorded at the price receivable by the seller, less any intermediary margins or commissions. The difference between the sale price excluding intermediary fees and the seller's acquisition cost is written off in the revaluation account as explained later. The gains and losses from the sale of valuables by the seller are recorded as holding gains or losses also in the revaluation account. (See 10.1.3.4 for an example of this transaction.)

5.4 Exports

Exports are categorized into exports of goods and exports of services. The source data for compiling exports of goods is derived from the administrative records from the customs office, which are recorded on the basis of FOB prices according to the HS code classification by product. As mentioned earlier, the international manual on trade statistics (*International Merchandise Trade Statistics 2010*, **IMTS 2010**) requires that all exports of goods be recorded on the FOB basis. Since the national accounts also follow the FOB basis, no additional price adjustments are necessary for exports of goods. However, in the case of **merchanting**, since goods move directly from a third country to another third country without passing through the resident country of the merchant, the transaction price (rather than the FOB price) is recorded in the resident country of the merchants. In accordance with this, the SNA records imports of goods in merchanting as *negative exports*, and exports of goods in merchanting as *positive exports*, with the traded value being actual transaction prices.

Exports of services are classified in the same way as imports of services, in accordance with the guidelines of the Manual on Statistics of International Trade in Services 2010 (MSITS 2010). The statistics for exports of services are compiled by collecting various data on foreign exchange transaction, transportation and insurance transactions, and other exports of services. The valuation for exports of services based on market transaction prices, just as it is for imports of services.

In addition, consumption by non-residents within the domestic economy is excluded from the household final consumption expenditure of residents, and is recorded as exports of goods and services. The procedure for this task involves, in the use table, adding a row for "domestic consumption expenditure of non-residents", subtracting the same amount from the cell that intersects with the column of domestic consumption expenditure, and then adding it to the cell that intersects with the column of exports. (Refer to Table 3.4.)

5.5 Gross value added

In the use table, the *value-added quadrant* represents the sector that shows **gross value added** derived as an accounting residual by subtracting intermediate consumption from output. There are three methods for calculating gross value added in the SNA. First, the **production approach**, which subtracts intermediate consumption from output; second, the **expenditure approach**, which subtracts imports from final use (final consumption expenditure + gross capital formation + exports); and third, the **income approach**, which adds all value-added items to calculate gross value added. The components constituting gross value added (based on the basic price for output) include remuneration of employees, other taxes less subsidies on production, and gross operating surplus and gross mixed income. Adding this gross value added (at basic prices) to taxes less subsidies on products yields gross domestic product (GDP). This section will provide a more detailed examination of each of these components.

Table 5.16 Value added quadrant in the use table (Quadrant III)

	By industry				Final use	Total use
	Market production	Non-market production	Own-account production	Total		
Intermediate consumption				A		
Gross value added (Remuneration of employees) (Other taxes less subsidies on production) (Gross operating surplus) (Gross mixed income)	Quadrant III			B		
Output (at basic price)				A+B		

5.5.1 Remuneration of employees

Remuneration of employees refers to all forms of compensation that an employee receives in return for providing labor services during the production process of an enterprise. Remuneration of employees consists of two types. The first type includes wages and salaries (both cash and in-kind) and stock options received from the employer. The second type is social insurance contributions payable by the employer for the employee.

Wages and salaries include not only regular wages and salaries but also all allowances and bonuses, commissions, and service fees. This category also includes in-kind benefits, which are goods and services provided to employees and their families for the discretionary use outside of work (e.g., canteen subsidies, transportation for commuting, and childcare services).

Social insurance contributions relate to pension and non-pension contributions paid by the employer to social insurance schemes on behalf of the employee, either legally or under the employment contract between the employer and the employee. The social insurance system is a mechanism that requires the state or individual enterprises to operate pension and non-pension insurance schemes through legal mandates. Social insurance schemes under this system include both **social security schemes** that manage pension and non-pension insurance (e.g., National pensions, National health insurance, Industrial accident insurance, etc.), and **employment-related pension schemes** that are legally mandated by enterprises or organization units to entrust pension management to financial institutions (e.g., Civil servant pension, Military pension, Teachers' pension).

Employers' social contributions for employees are subdivided into two types: **actual** social contributions and **imputed** social contributions. Employer's actual social contributions are those that the employer directly pays to social insurance schemes on behalf of the employee. In this category, there are pension contributions (e.g., National pension contributions, Retirement pension contributions, Civil servant pension contributions, Military pension contributions, etc.) and non-pension contributions (e.g., health insurance contributions, unemployment insurance contributions, industrial accident insurance contributions, etc.). Imputed social contributions include retirement benefit and other similar payments made by the employer from its own resources, rather than being paid to a separate social insurance scheme. Further details are provided in section 9.3.3.

Table 5.17 Types of remuneration of employees

Type			Description
Wages and salaries	Wages and salaries in cash		
	Wages and salaries in kind		Goods and services to employees for discretionary use outside of work for themselves or their families.
	Stock options		A form of in-kind income. The corresponding entry is recorded in the financial account.
Employers' social contributions	Actual social contributions	Pension contributions	Contributions made by the employer to pension-related schemes such as National pension or other pension-related contributions.
		Non-pension contributions	Contributions made by the employer to social insurance schemes other than pension schemes.
	Imputed social contributions	Pension contributions	It arises when there is a difference between the pension contributions and the actual pension payments under a defined benefit (DB) scheme. It is the portion borne by the employer when the actual pension payments exceed the pension contributions.
		Non-pension contributions	It is paid from the employer's own resources without a separate insurance scheme.

5.5.2 Other taxes on production and other subsidies on production

Other taxes on production are taxes incurred in connection with the production activities of enterprises, excluding taxes directly levied on products (i.e., taxes on products). Taxes included in this category are recurrent taxes levied on an enterprise's non-financial assets (e.g., land, buildings, structures, and automobiles), including taxes on owner occupied dwellings, taxes on remuneration of employees (such as payroll taxes), business license taxes, and stamp taxes. Corporate tax arising in relation to corporate profits and income tax are excluded from other taxes on production, as these taxes are recorded as an item of current transfer payable to the government in the "income transfers other than transfers in kind account." Other taxes less subsidies on production are part of the items that constitute gross value added at basic prices. Data on other taxes on production can be found in individual business financial statements, but a more efficient method is to take the total amount (control total) from the tax data of the National Tax Service and allocate it by industry or product.

As a practical matter, the classification of other taxes on production may vary depending on the entity being taxed. For example, the automobile tax, when levied on an enterprise, is considered part of other taxes on production, but when it is levied on households, it is classified as a current tax. Similarly, taxes on land are classified as other taxes on production when levied on enterprises, but as current taxes when levied on individuals (households). Furthermore, there are **sur-taxes**, which are added at a certain rate to the existing tax amount for specific policy purposes, and these sur taxes are classified in the same category as the original taxes.

Other subsidies on production refer to all subsidies that are paid by the government in connection with production activities of enterprises, excluding subsidies on products. Examples include payroll subsidies for hiring specific groups of people, such as disabled individuals or unemployed seniors, and subsidies on pollution prevention.

There are items with similar in nature to government subsidies but not treated as subsidies, such as government's current transfers or capital transfers to the private sector. Examples include funds provided by government to households in their capacity as consumers (which are treated as current transfer.), investment grants provided by government to other institutional units for their acquisition of fixed assets (which are treated as capital transfer.), and exceptional financial support to public enterprises to cover their accumulated operating losses (which are also capital transfer). Current transfers and capital transfers are recorded in the income transfers other than transfers in kind account and the capital account, respectively.

5.5.3 Operating surplus and mixed income

Gross value added is derived by subtracting intermediate consumption (at purchasers' prices) from output (at basic prices). From this value of gross value added, after excluding remuneration of employees and other taxes less subsidies on production, **gross operating surplus** or **gross mixed income** is derived, which is the result from the production activities of the institutional unit (or production unit).

Gross operating surplus arises in corporations including quasi-corporations, while gross mixed income arises in household unincorporated enterprises. Gross mixed income includes the value of unpaid labor inputs contributed by the owner and household members of the household unincorporated enterprise. The reason why this item is called mixed income is that the income as of an entrepreneur and the remuneration for unpaid labor as of the household members in a household unincorporated enterprise cannot be separated.

- Gross operating surplus (or gross mixed income) = output at the basic price – intermediate consumption at the purchaser's price – (remuneration of employees + other taxes less subsidies on production)

Distinction between corporations and household unincorporated enterprises

The distinction between corporations (including quasi-corporations) and household unincorporated enterprises is determined by whether income and capital transactions between enterprises and their owners are separated. The practical criterion for distinguishing them is *whether complete sets of accounts including balance sheets are kept* by double entry bookkeeping. If a complete set of accounts through double entry bookkeeping is not maintained, it is not possible to distinguish between the enterprise and its owner from an accounting perspective, so the enterprise is classified as a household unincorporated enterprise. As an exception, owner-occupied dwellings, lessors of dwellings, and households with paid domestic staff are excluded from generating mixed income within the framework of household unincorporated enterprises. In these cases, the value added by owner-occupiers of the houses and lessors of rental houses is treated as operating surplus, while the value added by paid domestic staff is treated as remuneration of employees.

Gross operating surplus and gross mixed income are residual concepts, representing the income of an enterprise before deducting its property incomes payable, and before adding its property incomes receivable. Here, **property income** refers to interest, dividends, rent, and other property income equivalent to the remuneration for using financial assets, land, and other natural resources necessary for production. Gross operating surplus and gross mixed income are the income of an enterprise measured from the perspective of the producer, not from the perspective of the economic entity that provides assets such as financial assets and land. Subtracting depreciation and depletion from gross operating surplus and gross mixed income results in **net operating surplus and net mixed income**.

Concept and measurement of resource rent

The 2025 SNA introduces a method for distinguishing, within gross operating surplus, the portion attributable to the use of non-produced non-financial assets, namely natural resources. The economic surplus generated through the use of natural resources in production is referred to as **resource rent** (or **natural resource rent**). In the SNA, resource rent is derived as a residual by deducting several cost components from gross operating surplus, commonly known as the **residual value method**. The derivation proceeds as follows:

- Output at basic prices – intermediate consumption – remuneration of employees – other taxes less subsidies on production = gross operating surplus
- **Gross operating surplus – specific taxes less subsidies on extraction – (depreciation + net return to fixed capital) = resource rent**

Resource rent consists of two components: *depletion* (the decline in the value of natural resources) and the *net return* attributable to the natural resources. As the present value of the future economic benefits derived from natural resources, resource rent may be used directly as an indicator for valuing natural resource assets. Because resource rent is computed as a residual, it should represent income attributable solely to the natural resources and not to any other asset.

In the production account, resource rent is recorded as part of the internal gross operating surplus of the extractor. Only the amounts payable to the legal owner of the natural resource (typically general government) under contractual arrangements are recorded in the allocation of earned income account as payments of property income (rent) by the extractor and receipts of property income by the government.

5.5.4 Depreciation

Depreciation (or consumption of fixed capital) refers to the decrease in the current value of the stock of fixed assets due to physical deterioration, normal obsolescence, or normal accidental damages caused by using the fixed assets for production purposes. Depreciation is an imputed value that is not based on market transactions, and is measured by estimating the future service life of the asset. Therefore, it does not represent an actual expense incurred. Additionally, depreciation is difficult for international comparisons because the method of its measurement may vary from country to country. Therefore, when comparing the data of value added by country, depreciation is included in the item of gross value added without being deducted. However, when calculating **net value added**, it is excluded and no longer constitutes value-added.

Depreciation applies only to fixed assets among non-financial assets. Fixed assets are produced assets acquired by an economic unit that are used in production repeatedly and continuously for more than one year. They include both tangible and intangible fixed assets (Intangible fixed assets has been renamed intellectual property products). Non-produced assets such as land and subsoil resources are excluded from this category. Moreover, valuables are not classified as fixed assets, and are therefore not eligible for depreciation. However, the cost of ownership transfer of land and subsoil resources is included in the category of fixed assets and is subject to depreciation.

The SNA recommends the methodology for calculating depreciation by measuring the decline in the current value of fixed asset based on its value of future use, rather than applying depreciation rates to historic costs of fixed assets. Accordingly, it adopts a method of calculating fixed assets in volume terms by accumulating gross fixed capital formation in volume terms (perpetual inventory method) and deriving the depreciation of these fixed assets in volume terms during the accounting period, and then transforming the depreciation into the current value. (*OECD, Measuring Capital 2009*). Detailed explanations can be found in Chapter 20 (section 20.4).

5.5.5 Depletion of natural resources

Depletion refers to the decline in the value of non-produced non-financial assets, particularly *non-renewable mineral and energy resources* and *non-cultivated biological resources yielding once-only products*, resulting from their economic use. In the 2008 SNA, depletion was recorded in the *other changes in the volume of assets and liabilities account.* In contrast, the 2025 SNA records depletion as a cost of production in the production account and reflects the corresponding reduction in natural resource assets in the capital account.

The method for calculating depletion differs depending on whether the resources are non-renewable resources or non-cultivated biological resources yielding once-only products (e.g., natural forest logging, wild fish stocks). For *non-renewable resources*, depletion is calculated by multiplying the annual quantity extracted by the average implicit price of the resources. This method ensures that depletion reflects the decline in the economic value of the resources.

- **Annual depletion = annual extraction x average implicit price of the resource**

where average implicit price corresponds to "opening-year price + closing-year price)/2."

Non-cultivated biological resources yielding once-only products are created somewhat differently. Because these biological resources can naturally regenerate, depletion may be either positive or negative. When extraction exceeds natural growth, depletion is positive; when extraction is lower than natural growth, depletion is negative.

5.6 Example of the use table

Table 5.18 illustrates the actual results of the use table in South Korea for 2015 (at purchaser's prices) in an abbreviated form. In the columns, it is structured in accordance with the items of product balance identity, including "intermediate use by industry, final use (final consumption expenditure by institutional sector, gross fixed capital formation, changes in inventories, acquisitions less disposals of valuables, exports), and total use." In the rows, the categories include "intermediate inputs by product, gross value added (remuneration of employees, net operating surplus, depreciation, other taxes less subsidies on production), and output by industry." No row is added to adjust the domestic purchase by non-residents and the direct purchases abroad by residents, which are omitted from the transactions of imports and exports; instead, those amounts have been directly adjusted in the rows of corresponding products.

According to this use table, as of the year 2015, South Korea's intermediate use (at purchasers' prices) amounts to KRW 2,196.1 trillion, and final use (at purchasers' prices) amounts to KRW 2,261.5 trillion. The breakdown of final use is as follows: final consumption expenditure is 1,054.9 trillion (= 804.8 + 250.1), gross fixed capital formation is 481.0 trillion, changes in inventories are 6.7 trillion, net acquisition of valuables are 1.9 trillion, and exports are 717.0 trillion. Therefore, total use is KRW 4,457.6 trillion. Additionally, gross value added is KRW 1,520.9 trillion, and total input amounts to KRW 3,717.0 trillion.

Table 5.18 Example of the use table (South Korea, 2015)

Unit: KRW trillion

Product \ Industry	A Agriculture, forestry, and fishing	B,C Mining and manufacturing	D,E Electricity, gas, water, and waste	F Construction	G Wholesale and retail industry	H Transportation	I Food and accommodation	J~N Communication, finance and business	O Public admin. and defense	P~T Education, health, and culture	Total intermediate use	Private final consumption	Gov't final consumption	Fixed capital formation	Change in inventories	Net acquisition of valuables	Exports	Total final use	Total use
Agriculture	3.5	41.9	0.0	0.6	0.2	0.1	10.1	0.3	0.4	2.4	59.4	24.4	0.0	0.5	1.2	0.0	0.7	26.8	86.2
Mining and manufacturing	19.9	985.1	44.0	96.4	21.2	39.4	54.9	55.5	9.1	78.2	1403.7	253.9	0.0	142.2	6.9	1.9	630.4	1035.3	2439.0
Electricity, gas	0.8	38.9	14.0	1.0	3.8	2.2	3.2	12.7	1.7	10.8	89.3	21.2	1.2	0.0	0.0	0.0	0.5	22.8	112.1
Construction	0.1	1.3	0.4	0.2	0.3	0.2	0.2	7.6	0.6	0.5	11.4	0.0	0.0	213.5	-1.4	0.0	0.2	212.2	223.7
Trade service	0.0	10.9	0.1	0.0	6.7	0.0	0.0	6.5	0.0	0.0	24.2	0.0	0.0	0.0	0.0	0.0	4.4	4.4	28.6
Transport service	0.7	38.1	1.1	1.3	15.9	24.1	0.4	7.6	2.1	1.6	92.9	24.6	0.0	0.0	0.0	0.0	38.0	62.6	155.5
Food & accomm	0.5	10.7	0.5	0.8	8.8	1.7	0.9	15.3	2.1	14.2	55.6	82.8	0.0	0.0	0.0	0.0	7.0	89.9	145.5
Finance, real estate	2.0	96.5	5.6	29.5	50.0	14.9	11.3	168.9	12.4	30.6	421.6	221.1	0.0	124.3	0.0	0.0	33.5	379.0	800.6
Public admin. Defense	0.1	0.4	0.1	0.0	0.1	0.5	0.1	0.2	1.2	0.0	2.8	1.4	119.8	0.0	0.0	0.0	0.0	121.2	124.0
Education, health	0.6	9.0	0.5	1.1	3.9	3.4	1.0	9.3	0.5	5.9	35.1	175.4	129.1	0.5	0.0	0.0	2.2	307.2	342.4
Intermediate consumption	28.2	1232.7	66.3	130.9	110.9	86.6	82.2	284.0	30.1	144.3	2196.1	804.8	250.1	481.0	6.7	1.9	717.0	2261.5	4457.6
Remuneration of employees	5.2	180.3	9.2	66.5	67.0	29.8	23.8	169.7	59.6	139.0	750.2								
Operating surplus	22.6	142.9	16.0	9.8	47.6	7.7	9.6	163.8	0.0	21.6	441.5								
Depreciation	4.8	115.8	16.0	4.4	7.7	20.6	2.8	78.1	35.9	23.4	309.7								
Net taxes on production	0.6	4.2	0.6	0.5	1.1	0.4	0.7	10.5	0.0	1.0	19.6								
Gross value added	33.2	443.3	41.8	81.2	123.4	58.5	36.9	422.2	95.5	185.0	1520.9								
Total input	61.4	1676.0	108.0	212.1	234.3	145.1	119.1	706.1	125.6	329.3	3717.0								

Chapter 6. Practical compilation of the supply and use tables

In the previous Chapters 3 through 5, the structure of the supply and use tables have been explained, and in this chapter, we will examine the actual procedure for compiling the supply and use tables. Specifically, we are going to go over the practical steps of what needs to be done before we can compile the supply and use tables, and how the tables are estimated based on these works. In this chapter, we will discuss the procedure for compiling the supply and use tables, the specific estimation for each item in the tables, the method for filling in missing items using the product flow method, and the derivation of the use table using price types. Finally, we will introduce how to calculate GDP using the use table.

6.1 Selection of the classification systems

Prior to compiling supply and use tables, it is essential to select the appropriate industrial and product classification systems for categorizing the collected data. The current SNA recommends using the **ISIC** (*International Standard Industrial Classification*, established by the UN) for industry classification and the **CPC** (Central Product Classification, also established by the UN) for product classification. However, the ISIC and CPC classification systems assign codes based on separate criteria, rather than correlating them by similarity. As a result, when these codes are arranged in the supply table (with columns representing ISIC codes and rows representing CPC codes), the primary products are not placed along the diagonal cells. As shown in Figure 6.1, the distribution of CPC codes (on the y-axis) and ISIC codes (on the x-axis) does not follow a diagonal pattern from the origin, which could cause issues when converting the supply and use tables into the input-output table. Therefore, when compiling the supply and use tables, it is necessary to reorganize the order of industrial and product codes to ensure they correspond correctly to each other. To resolve this issue, the European classification system has developed its own industrial and product classification codes, which are arranged in the same order. Specifically, the European Industrial Classification system (**NACE**) is aligned with the ISIC, matching up to the two-digit level (division), while the European Product Classification system (**CPA**) follows the same order as the European Industrial Classification system.

Figure 6.1 CPC-ISIC Correspondence

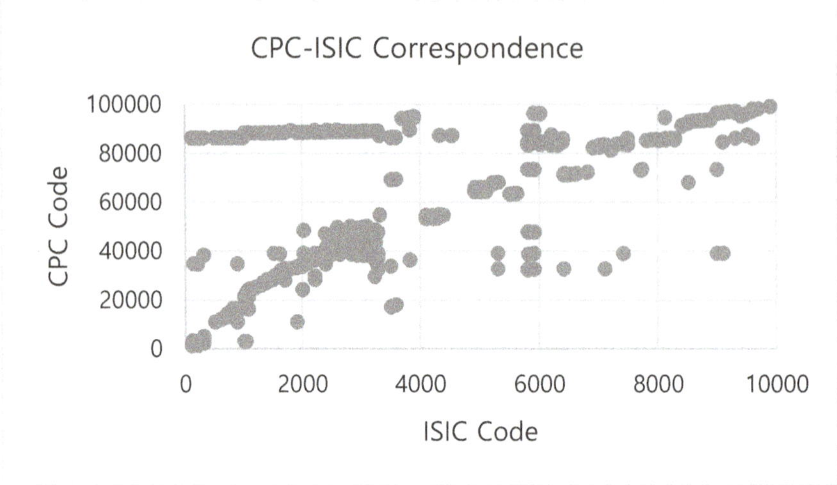

Once the classification systems for industries and products in the supply and use tables are determined, the next step is to decide at what detailed level the data should be collected and compiled. The level of details for data at which industries and products are compiled depends on the availability of the data. This is determined based on the following collectable levels in ISIC or CPC: Section (1 digit), Division (2 digit), Group (3 digit), Class (4 digit), Subclass (5 digit). The level of aggregation is decided by considering both the availability and reliability of the data. However, to ensure that the characteristics of industries and products are well reflected, it is preferrable to compile the data at the most detailed level possible, allowing for flexible adjustments during the aggregation process.

6.2 Collection of source data

To compile the supply and use tables, censuses, surveys or administrative records must first be collected. Initially, in order to compile a supply table, data on the details and amounts of products by industry must be collected. The scope of products produced within an industry includes not only primary products but also secondary products. These data are mostly collected through economic censuses or industrial surveys, and particularly in the manufacturing industry, there is currently no substitute for economic censuses or industrial surveys to obtain specifications of output for each product. The total industrial data (control total value) is most efficiently collected through administrative sources (e.g., corporate financial statements database from the National Tax Service, financial statements database on financial institutions from the financial supervision authority). These data are close to a full enumeration, so they can serve as supplement data to the sample-based surveys. In particular, the financial statements of financial institutions are essential for deriving the FISIM and non-life insurance service charges, which are intermediate consumption items in the use table. The data for estimating taxes on products are collected from administrative records (aggregate data) such as the National Tax Service and the Customs Service, and subsidies on products are obtained from the government's budget and financial statements. Data on wholesale and retail margins and freight transport margins by product must be collected through wholesale and retail surveys and freight rate surveys. For non-market producers such as government and NPISHs, it is difficult to collect product data through industrial surveys, so separate data collection on their financial statements is required. Government data can be investigated through budget documents (fiscal execution plans) and settlement documents (execution reports). For NPISHs, administrative data from the relevant authority or a separate income and expenditure survey is required.

For the compilation of the use table, first, the details and amounts of materials and supplies used for intermediate consumption by industry (corresponding to the *first quadrant* of the use table) must be collected. In addition, through **input cost surveys**, the details of manufacturing costs, sales costs, and general administrative costs by category should be examined. These industry-specific intermediate consumption values are collected through economic censuses or surveys. These data also serve as the source data for applying the product flow method, which will be explained later. This means that by identifying the amount of intermediate use by product, final use can be indirectly derived by subtracting this amount from total use.

The data for the *second quadrant* of the use table, which shows to the **distribution structure** of final use, must also include the value of final consumption expenditure, gross fixed capital formation, changes in inventories, and acquisitions less disposals of valuables by product. To estimate these data, surveys for each component must be conducted. For gross fixed capital formation, buildings and structures data are primarily collected from the production data on construction industry, and the amounts of machinery, equipment, and transportation vehicles, except for exports and household final consumption, are all allocated to gross fixed capital formation. Additionally, data for changes in inventories must be surveyed separately. Distribution inventories held by wholesalers and retailers as well as mining and manufacturing producers must be investigated. Furthermore, for the inventories of agricultural and livestock products, it must be determined whether they are held for sale or used for gross fixed capital formation as cultivated assets. A survey of distribution structure of imports must also be conducted to determine whether they are used for intermediate consumption, final consumption, or gross fixed capital formation by product. Meanwhile, the total values of final use by product are derived using the product flow method, and are adjusted by comparing them with the previously surveyed items.

For the *third quadrant* of the use table, which concerns value-added items, the total amounts are derived using economic census data or administrative sources (such as tax authorities, financial supervisory authority, social security funds, and pension data from financial institutions), and remuneration of employees and other taxes on production need to be allocated by industry. Gross operating surplus and gross mixed income are derived from the value-added amount which is obtained by deducting intermediate consumption of the use table from output of the supply table, and then subtracting remuneration of employees and other taxes less subsidies on production. In order to separate between gross operating surplus and gross mixed income, the distinction between corporations and household unincorporated enterprises is made based on whether business financial statements are available in economic census or tax authorities' data. The corporations data are allocated to operating surplus, while the data on household unincorporated enterprises are allocated to gross mixed income.

Prerequisites for the preparation of the supply and use tables

- Survey on output structure by industry: details and amounts of products by industry
- Survey on input structure by industry: Details and amounts of intermediate inputs by industry
- Compilation of accounts by institutional sectors (government, NPISHs): Income and expenditure data for government and NPISHs
- Survey on distribution structure of domestic final use: Final consumption, gross fixed capital formation, changes in inventories, acquisitions less disposals of valuables
- Details of imports and exports data (breakdown of goods and services)
- Survey on distribution structure of imports: Breakdown of intermediate consumption and final use by imported goods (gross fixed capital formation, final consumption, changes in inventories)
- Composition of value added by industry: Remuneration of employees, taxes less subsidies on production, operating surplus and mixed income, depreciation and depletion
- Data for adjusting types of prices (basic price, producer's price, purchaser's price): Distribution margins, transport margins, taxes less subsidies on products
- Details of types on taxes and subsidies: Taxonomy data of VAT, other taxes less subsidies on products, import taxes, and taxes less subsidies on production

Table 6.1 Basic data for the compilation of supply and use tables

	Data name		Data source
1	Overview by industries	Output by industry and product	Economic census, industrial survey, National Tax Service data
		Breakdown of Intermediate consumption (materials, fuels, indirect costs) by product and industry	ditto
		Remuneration of employees by industry (wages and salaries, employer's social contribution)	Economic census, industrial survey, National Tax Service data. Employers' social contributions from the data of social security funds, and the pension data from financial institutions.
		Operating surplus by industry	Calculated as residual
2	Household unincorporated enterprises data	Output by industry and product	Economic census, industrial survey, National Tax Service data
		Intermediate consumption by industry	Based on the ratio from corporations
		Remuneration of employees by industry (wages and salaries, employer's social contribution)	ditto
		Mixed income by industry	Calculated as residual
3	Government data	Taxes on products by product, subsidies on products by product	National Tax Service data, government's budget and financial statements
		Other taxes on production by industry, other subsidies on production by industry	ditto
		Output, intermediate consumption and value added of government	Government's budget and financial statements, Public NPIs' budget and financial statements
		Expenditure breakdown of government sector (COFOG classification)	Government's budget and financial statements
4	NPISHs account	Output, value added of NPISHs	Economic census, administrative records
5	Exports and imports by commodity	Imports and exports by commodity (HS classification)	Customs statistics data
		Imports and exports by service	Balance of payments
6	FISIM, non-life insurance service charges	Interest income and interest payment by industry	Financial survey of financial institutions
		Deposit and loan balances by industry	ditto
		Non-life insurance fee payments by industry	ditto
7	Final consumption expenditure by institutional sector	Final consumption expenditure by product and by institutional sector (COICOP classification)	Economic census, urban household survey, wholesale and retail business survey

	Data name		Data source
8	Gross capital formation	Gross fixed capital formation by product and institution	Economic census, construction industry survey, mining and manufacturing survey
		Changes in inventories by product (producer's inventory, imported inventory, traders' inventory)	Economic census, mining and manufacturing survey, wholesale/retail survey
		Net acquisition of valuables	Survey on valuables sales
9	Price adjustment (Conversion from the basic price to the purchaser's price)	Distribution margins by industry and product	Survey on wholesale and retail business
		Transport margins by industry and product	Survey on transportation industry
		Taxes on products, and subsidies on products by industry and product	National and local tax data, government's budget and financial statements (data on subsidies)

6.3 Balancing procedure for the supply and use tables

Once the basic data required for the supply and use tables are collected, the next step is to input these data into the format of the supply and use tables and compile the tables. However, since the basic data are collected from various sources such as production-side and expenditure-side data, there are many inconsistencies between them in the aspect of price criteria and data sources. Therefore, it is necessary to reconcile them while adjusting the totals in the rows and columns. This process is known as the **balancing procedure** for the supply and use tables. The balancing procedure primarily involves adjusting the data in such a way that the sum of supply and use of each product row matches, and the sum of inputs and outputs of each industry column is consistent. The balancing procedure adjusts the data entered into the tables in the following three aspects:

- **Balancing the total supply and total use by product**: This ensures that "product balance identity" holds, which allows the total value of GDP to be derived using the expenditure approach.
- **Balancing the total output and total input by industry**: This ensures that the equation "output = intermediate input + gross value added" holds, which allows the total value of GDP to be derived using the production approach.
- **Balancing gross value added by industry**: This ensures that the gross value added and the sum of its constituent item match, which allows the total value of GDP to be derived using the income approach.

Ultimately, the balancing procedure aims to align the aggregate indicators derived from the production, expenditure, and income approaches of GDP. Additionally, this procedure is essential for converting the use table at purchasers' prices into the same table at basic prices, separating the import table and domestic use table from the total use table, and compiling the supply and use tables at both the base year price and the comparative year price. This balancing procedure is initially performed manually by the staff in charge of the supply and use tables (this is called **manual balancing**), followed by automated adjustments using its own software (this is called **automated balancing**, or **mechanical balancing**). This process involves adjusting the figures entered into the columns and rows based on the underlying collected data. During this process, the column totals of industry-specific output in the supply table and the column totals of industry-specific input in the use table are adjusted to be identical with each other (this is called **column adjustment**.), as well as the row totals of product-specific supply in the supply table and the row totals of product-specific use in the use table are adjusted to be identical with each other (this is called **row adjustment**.) (see Figure 6.2).

Figure 6.2 Adjustment of values in the rows and columns of the supply and use tables

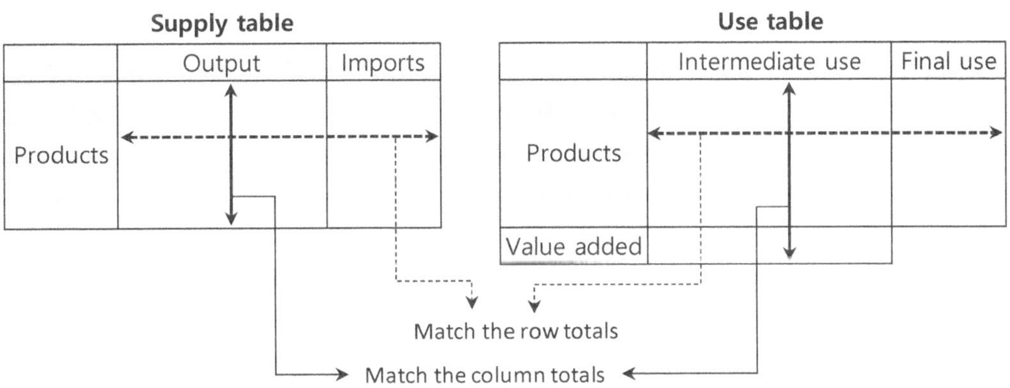

6.3.1 Procedure for the column adjustment

For the column adjustment, the source data used in the supply table include the details of output by product for each industry, imports by product, and price adjustment items (such as margins, and taxes less subsidies on products) by product. Based on these data, the total values corresponding to the bottom row of this table are determined. For column adjustment in the use table, the source data include the details of intermediate input by product for each industry, value added by industry, and final use by product. These data are used to adjust the total input value (the bottom row of the use table), which is the sum of the intermediate input and value added for each industry, to match the total output value in the supply table.

The data required to perform this task are collected from sources such as the economic census, various industry-specific surveys, and household expenditure surveys, which include the values of products, input costs and expenditure details. In this way, the method of compiling in the vertical direction using the details of industry-specific intermediate input and value added, and final use data by product in the use table is called the **input approach** or **column approach**. In this case, most of the details of intermediate inputs are usually derived from sample surveys rather than population data to calculate the input ratios. Therefore, the detailed products of intermediate consumption can be estimated by applying the input ratios of products to the total value of intermediate consumption of each industry.

Table 6.2 Data used in the input approach

Data sources	Supply table	Use table
Economic census, industrial surveys	Details of output by product for each industry	Industry-specific intermediate consumption by product, industry-specific gross value added, product-specific fixed capital formation and changes in inventories
Customs statistics	Import values by commodity	Export values by commodity
Balance of payments	Import values by service	Export values by service
Household expenditure survey		Households' final consumption by product
Government's budget and financial statements	Details of output by government	Final consumption and fixed capital formation by government

Depending on the reliability of the data sources, some basic data may be used as predetermined values without modification, while others may be estimated or sampled data and need to be modified by adjusting the figures in rows and columns. Examples of predetermined values include all the amounts of the items in the supply table. In the supply table, the output value by industry and product, as well as the import value by product, are all collected in fixed amounts. In the use table, the total output by industry, total intermediate consumption by industry, value added by industry, and export value by product are collected as predetermined values. The remaining items in the use table, such as the details of intermediate consumption, final consumption, and gross fixed capital formation may be directly obtained through surveys; however, they may also be derived indirectly in the process of adjusting discrepancies with production-side data.

The amounts for detailed items of intermediate consumption can be estimated using the RAS method once the amount (ratio) for each product in the base year and the total amount in the current year are available. While final consumption expenditures are surveyed annually from the expenditure side, they are likely missing a large portion of the data; thus, to maintain consistency with the production-side data, they can be supplemented using the **product flow method** described below. Gross fixed capital formation is often estimated by the product flow method using production-side data from the output of construction, machinery and equipment, and intellectual property products (e.g., R&D, software).

6.3.2 Procedure for the row adjustment

The source data for the row adjustment include the values of output and imports by product in the supply table, and the values of intermediate use and final use by product in the use table. These data are adjusted using the "product balance identity" to ensure that total supply equals total use. This method is called the **output approach**, or **row approach**. This approach is used to match the total supply of each product in the supply table with the total use of each product in the use table, and to estimate the remaining unmeasured components in the product balance identity. The method used for this is the **product flow method**, which estimates the values of missing products on the use-side based on the product data from the supply-side. In other words, by using the product balance identity, missing items among intermediate consumption or final use for each row in the use table can be estimated based on the total supply of each product row derived from the supply table. The estimation of missing items is done using the residuals or ratios from the product balance identity. For example, in the product balance identity of "output + imports = intermediate consumption + final consumption + gross capital formation + exports", given the values on the left-hand side (= output + imports) and the values for intermediate consumption and gross capital formation and exports on the right hand side, final consumption can be derived as the residual.

6.3.3 Balancing the data for columns and rows

Once the column and row data are populated in the supply and use tables, they need to be internally adjusted to match the sum of the amounts in each entry in the rows and columns (the sum of endogenous values) with the **marginal totals** that represent the row totals and column totals. This is the process of re-adjusting the numerical values of the constituent items in a matrix, so that the sums of their values align with the pre-determined row and column totals. This method is called the "automated balancing technique" as it is performed automatically using statistical software. For this task, the values of endogenous elements are adjusted based on a set of values in the **marginal columns** and **marginal rows**, and the most popular method used for this purpose is the "RAS technique". For example, given the row and column totals of a matrix, and the sum of the elements inside the matrix does not match the row and column totals (Table 6.3), the task is to adjust the values of the internal elements to match the row and column totals as follows (Table 6.4).

Table 6.3 A matrix where the sum of internal elements and the marginal totals are not identical (Before adjustment)

	1	2	3	4	Row total
1	293	21,057	160	61	21,576
2	1,198	17,720	12,180	1,827	32,922
3	1	3,094	19,291	1,793	24,175
4	1,130	6,621	7,228	2,991	17,970
Column total	2,623	48,490	38,860	6,670	96,643

Table 6.4 A matrix where the sum of internal elements and the marginal totals are identical (After adjustment)

	1	2	3	4	Row total
1	293.22	21,061.68	160.09	61.01	21,576.00
2	1,198.36	17,715.79	12,181.36	1,826.49	32,922.00
3	1.00	3,092.64	19,289.23	1,792.13	24,175.00
4	1,130.42	6,619.89	7,229.32	2,990.37	17,970.00
Column total	2,623.00	48,490.00	38,860.00	6,670.00	96,643.00

More advanced forms of the RAS technique have been introduced, such as GRAS (generalized RAS) and TRAS (three-stage RAS). The RAS technique is also used in the input-output table, and an example of its application can be found in section 22.4.

An important aspect in this balancing process is that the compilers perform "manual balancing" adjustments to reflect the real-world situation. This process involves adjusting figures through consultation among experienced work-level officials, and in parallel with this work, the mechanical adjustments explained earlier are repeatedly performed, ultimately leading to the completion of the final supply and use tables.

6.4 Compilation of supply and use tables for the benchmark year

The supply and use tables are first compiled for the benchmark year, followed by the tables for other years (non-benchmark years). In this section, we will closely examine the process of compiling the supply and use tables when a particular year is selected as the benchmark year for these tables.

First, let's reproduce the **product balance identity**, which serves as the basis for compiling the supply and use tables:

(6.1) Output (basic price) + taxes less subsidies on products + trade and transport margins + imports = intermediate consumption (purchaser's price) + final consumption (purchaser's price) + gross fixed capital formation (transaction price + costs of ownership transfer) + changes in inventories + acquisitions less disposals of valuables (purchaser's price) + exports

The items on the left-hand side of the above identity (6.1), including output (basic price), taxes less subsidies on products, trade and transport margins, and imports should be prepared as items necessary for the compilation of the supply table. Among the items, taxes on products are added to each output as part of the process of converting output at the basic price into the market value, which is the purchaser's price. This total amount must be obtained from the tax data provided by the National Tax Service and allocated by product. Additionally, trade and transport margins are also allocated by separately surveying only the part constituting the purchaser's price of goods. Output for own final use is not identified by industrial surveys. Therefore, own final consumption of agricultural products, imputed services of owner-occupied dwellings, and construction of building for own final use must be estimated using separate survey data. These figures are simultaneously allocated to intermediate consumption and final use in the use table. (See Chapter 4 for details of the supply table.)

To prepare each item in the use table corresponding to the right-hand side of the product balance identity (equation 6.1), the details of intermediate consumption surveyed through the economic census or input cost survey are allocated for each product, and the final use is arranged by distributing the details of final consumption, gross capital formation and net exports (= exports – imports). Below, we will explain the key methodologies applied when compiling the supply and use tables for benchmark year from a practical perspective.

6.4.1 Estimation of output

Output can be estimated by dividing it into market output, non-market output, and own-account output, depending on the nature of their establishments. First, market output is derived indirectly based on the sales and inventories of primary and secondary products for each establishment, surveyed through the economic census or annual surveys. In the case of service industries with no inventories, sales are considered as the output value. Non-market output is surveyed by the sum of costs method for each establishment.

The table below (Table 6.5) shows the breakdown of sales (or shipments) by product at each establishment, which can be obtained from the manufacturing survey questionnaire of the Korean Economic Census. By using this survey questionnaire, the output value of the primary and secondary products at the relevant establishments is obtained, and these values are tabulated in the supply table by entering them in the cells of the corresponding product row and industry column.

Table 6.5 Excerpt of the questionnaire for the sales and inventories in the establishment survey (Ministry of Data and Statistics in Korea)

Annual sales and inventories

No.	Industry Code		(1) Sales	(2) Opening inventory (Finished goods)	(3) Closing inventory (Finished goods)
	Product code	Product name	KRW Million	KRW Million	KRW Million
01					
02					
03					
99	Total				

Annual revenue of processing fees by product

No	Industry code	Product code	Processed product name	Amount (KRW Million)
01				
02				
03				
99	Total			

Inventories

	(1) Opening inventory	(2) Closing inventory
	KRW Million	KRW Million
① Finished goods		
② Semi-finished goods		
③ Work-in-progress		
④ Materials and supplies		
Total		
⑤ Goods for resale		

Based on this survey questionnaire, here is an example of how a practical calculation of output per product might be[12].

- **For market output**: Output = sales (or shipments) + closing inventories of finished goods and work-in-progress – opening inventories of finished goods and work-in-progress
- **For non-market output**: Sum of the costs

[12] This calculation method differs from the one recommended by the SNA (the perpetual inventory method for inventory valuation), but it demonstrates an example of a practical approach based on the available data.

Here's an example of how to calculate the value of **market output**. Suppose a manufacturer's sales and inventories at an establishment are given as follows.

Sales

Manufacturing	Sales of products	1,510
	Sales of by-products	20
	Processing revenue	120
	Repair revenue	30
	Total	1,680
Non-manufacturing	Sales of goods for resale	150
	Costs of goods sold	130
	Rentals received	15
	Other revenue	5

Sales and inventories by product

	Product code	Product name	Sales	Opening inventory (Finished goods)	Closing inventory (Finished goods)
1	0001	TV	350	50	40
2	0002	Refrigerator	500	80	100
3	0003	PC	660	120	150
4					
5					
계			1,510	250	290

Processing income by goods

	Product code	Product name	Processing income
1	0001	TV	30
2	0002	Refrigerator	40
3	0003	PC	50
Total			120

Inventories

	Opening inventory	Closing inventory
Finished goods	250	290
Work-in-progress	220	320
Raw materials	340	350
Fuels etc.	100	95
Subtotal	910	1,055
Goods for resale	80	100

The output of this establishment is calculated as follows. First, looking at the manufacturing sector, the output of finished goods and work-in-progress is calculated as follows.

Output (Finished goods)

TV	350 + (40-50) = 340
Refrigerator	500 + (100-80) = 520
PC	660 + (150-120) = 690
Total	1,550

Output (Work-in-progress)

TV	320×(40/290) – 220×(50/250) = 0.1
Refrigerator	320×(100/290) – 220×(80/250) = 40
PC	320×(150/290) – 220×(120/250) = 59.9
Total	100

Note: It is assumed that the work-in-progress inventory changes at the same rate as the finished goods inventory.

The output of the manufacturing sector can be calculated by summing the output of finished goods and work-in-progress. Therefore, the output of this sector is 1,550+100=1,650. Looking at each product, the output of TVs is 340+0.1=340.1, the output of refrigerators is 520+40=560, and the output of PCs is 690+59.9=749.9. For sectors other than manufacturing, the output is calculated as follows: processing services 120, repair services 30, wholesale and retail services 20 (= sales of goods for resale – cost of goods sold for resale), rental service 15, and other income 5. Therefore, the total output is 1,650+120+30+20+15+5=1,840.

Next, let's look at an example of calculating the value of **non-market output**. This is the process of calculating the output of the government sector if the amounts in the survey for the public administration sector of the economic census are as follows (Table 6.6). Each item in the survey is classified into the following category of national accounts: salaries, retirement benefits, and welfare expenses are classified as remuneration of employees; rentals and other operating expenses are classified as intermediate consumption; depreciation expense remains as depreciation; and taxes and public levies are classified as other taxes on production. Summing these items results in the output of the government sector. That is, the government output is calculated as intermediate consumption plus gross value added (= remuneration of employees + net taxes on production + depreciation), which equals (70 + 560) + (300 + 40 + 150) + 8 + 45 = 1,173.

Table 6.6 Survey items of the government sector and their treatment in national accounts

Survey item	Amount	Category in national accounts
Total salaries	300	Remuneration of employees
Retirement benefits	40	Remuneration of employees
Welfare expenses	150	Remuneration of employees
Rentals	70	Intermediate consumption (Excluding rent on land, which is attributed to property income.)
Taxes and public levies	8	Other taxes on production (In practice, it is derived indirectly from the National Tax Service data.)
Depreciation expense	45	Depreciation
R&D expenses	10	Gross fixed capital formation
Bad debt	2	It is recorded in "the other changes in the volume of assets and liabilities account".
Other operating expenses	560	Intermediate consumption

For reference, the output and intermediate consumption data of the government sector are more efficiently obtained and prepared by directly extracting the relevant data from the government's budget and financial statements rather than relying on the economic survey. The estimation method could be a full enumeration for the central government and a sample survey for local governments to estimate the population. In addition, when categorizing the government sector by industry, as outlined in section 2.7.1, each government activity must be assigned to the corresponding industry. Specifically, output associated with the collective consumption of government (such as public administration, defense, foreign affairs, and public order) should be classified under *public administration and defense service* (ISIC 84), while other government activities related to individual consumption, such as public schools, are classified under *educational services* (ISIC 85), and public hospitals are classified under *health services* (ISIC 86).

6.4.2 Estimation of imports and exports

The data for estimating imports and exports are primarily based on customs statistics for imports and exports of goods, as well as the balance of payments, and these are adjusted to fit the framework of the supply and use tables. The SNA recommends that estimates of imports and exports be consistent with the concepts and classifications of the balance of payments. Therefore, figures associated with international transactions in the national accounts are based on the balance of payments, and the detailed information on product-specific import and export transactions recorded in customs statistics must be adjusted in accordance with the national accounts.

6.4.2.1 Estimation of imports and exports of goods

For estimating imports and exports of goods, detailed data by product are only available from customs statistics, so this data is used as the base and adjusted to comply with national accounts standards. For example, instead of adjusting imports from CIF data in customs statistics to FOB price on a per-product basis, the entire value of imports is globally adjusted to FOB basis by setting up a CIF/FOB adjustment row at the bottom of the supply table. To adjust this source data to the SNA standards, customs statistics must be reconciled to the balance of payments basis, as mentioned earlier. This involves various adjustments such as converting basic statistics to the change-in-ownership basis, subtracting the exports of goods for processing, and reflecting goods for merchanting. (See 13.3.2.2 for the reconciliation methods in the balance of payments.)

The product classification in customs statistics generally adopts the *HS or SITC* classification. To align these classifications with the domestic products categories in the supply and use tables, a code matching process between these different classification systems is required. Since domestic output is categorized by CPC, imports must also be classified in accordance with this system to ensure that the classification of products is consistent across rows. This process can be carried out by referring to the code correspondence tables between HS, CPC, ISIC, and BEC classifications provided by international organizations such as the United Nations. Furthermore, while merchanting is categorized as exports of goods in the SNA, it essentially corresponds to trade services. Therefore, to align it with domestic services, it should be allocated to the category of services.

6.4.2.2 Estimation of imports and exports of services

The classification of the import and exports of services is characterized by the fact that most of them are on a **product basis**, but items such as travel, construction, and government goods and services are classified on a **trader basis**, which means that they represent a mixture of goods and services. Therefore, items classified on a trader basis need to be adjusted by disaggregating them by each type of goods or services when classifying products in the supply and use tables.

To align travel, construction, and government goods and services with domestic output, more detailed data for these items must be surveyed and allocated to their corresponding goods and services categories. For example, travel services consist of various components such as transportation, accommodation, food services, and vehicle rentals, so their expenditure details should be surveyed and then appropriately allocated to the relevant goods and services categories. In addition, the two rows in the supply and use tables, "direct purchases abroad by residents" and "domestic purchases by non-residents" represent total amounts of final consumption that are not disaggregated, therefore, unless separate surveys are conducted for these items, they cannot be allocated to individual products.

Table 6.7 Reclassification of the imported and exported products in the supply and use tables

Supply table

Item	**Output**	**Imports**	**Reclassification of imports**
Goods	CPC	Commodities	Convert HS codes to CPC codes.
Services		Services (excluding travel, construction, government products)	Match to corresponding CPC codes.
		Travel, construction, government products	Reallocate to corresponding products.
Direct purchases abroad by residents			If not disaggregated by product, count it as a single item under final consumption expenditure.
Total output			

Use table

Item	Intermediate consumption	Final consumption	Gross capital formation	Exports	**Reclassification of exports**
Goods	CPC			Commodities	Convert HS to CPC.
Trade services				Merchanting	Categorize as trade services.
Other services				Services (excluding travel, construction, gov't goods and services)	Match to corresponding CPC codes.
				Travel, construction, gov't goods and services	Reallocate to corresponding goods and services.
Direct purchases abroad by residents					
Domestic purchases by non-residents					If not disaggregated by product, count it as a single item of exports.
Value added					
Total input					

6.4.3 Estimation of intermediate consumption

The estimation of intermediate consumption can be categorized into market products and non-market products. Generally, the total value of intermediate consumption by industry for market output is surveyed through the economic census or annual establishment survey. However, the details of intermediate consumption, specifically intermediate input items in each industry, are prepared through the **input cost survey** (or **input structure survey**) conducted in the benchmark year, and the intermediate input details of subsequent years are estimated by extending the data of the benchmark year. The input details for non-market producers, such as government, can be obtained annually through the government's budget and financial statement data, which are more easily accessible than those of market producers.

Then, let's look at how the details of intermediate input are estimated through the input cost survey of the benchmark year. The table below (Table 6.8) is part of the questionnaire used for establishment surveys by the U.S. Department of Commerce during the Economic Census. This table shows an example of investigating the intermediate consumption details of materials used at an establishment producing automobile parts. The details of these intermediate inputs gathered in this census are aggregated by industry and product, and then, after applying the "expansion factors," the amount of intermediate input details for the relevant industry is estimated (in the vertical direction).

Table 6.8 Sample questionnaire of the input cost survey by the U.S. Department of Commerce

2017 Economic Census

MC-33637 - Other Motor Vehicle Parts Manufacturing

Item 18: Detailed Cost of Materials, Parts, and Supplies

Description	Value		Census Material Code
1. Automotive stampings (including body parts, hubcaps, fenders, etc.)	$	,000.00	33637000
2. Other engine equipment (including turbochargers, injection fuel pumps, machine engine blocks, etc.)	$	,000.00	33361819
3. Air-conditioning and warm air heating equipment and commercial and industrial refrigeration equipment	$	,000.00	33341500
4. Metal crowns, closures, and other stamped metal products	$	,000.00	33211900
5. Metal forgings	$	,000.00	33211000
6. Miscellaneous fabricated metal products (excluding hardware, containers, screw machine products (bolts, nuts, screws, etc.), bearing components,	$	,000.00	33200091
7. Aluminum and aluminum-base alloy castings	$	,000.00	33152401
8. Copper and copper-base alloy pipe and tube	$	,000.00	33142030
9. Nonferrous metal shapes, forms, sheet, strip, powder, and wire (excluding castings and forgings), excluding aluminum and copper	$	,000.00	33141000
TOTAL	$	,000.00	77100000

The following table (Table 6.9) is a questionnaire for the input structure survey used for preparing the benchmark-year input-output table in South Korea (compiled every 5 year). This survey questionnaire is divided into the **questionnaire for material costs** and the **questionnaire for other expenses**. The questionnaire for material costs primarily investigates the composition and value of materials used in the manufacturing process, and the relevant data can be extracted from the cost statement. This survey questionnaire is designed differently for each industry because each industry has different details of materials. The questionnaire for other expenses investigates both the details of expenses incurred in the production process and expenses incurred in selling and general administration. The former can be extracted from the cost statement, while the latter can be derived from the income statement. This survey questionnaire is designed to be used in common across all establishments, regardless of their industries.

Table 6.9 Sample questionnaires for the input cost survey in South Korea

1. A questionnaire of materials input costs for gasoline manufacturing industry

(Unit: KRW thousand)

Serial No.	Name of material (Primary product: gasoline)	I/O code	Total	Values of raw materials and parts used by product		
			Product name			
1	Crude oil (petroleum, bituminous oil, etc.)	28				
2	Naphtha	103				
3	Ethylene, propylene, butadiene, butylene	113				
4	Benzene, toluene (methylbenzene), xylene	114				
5	Hydrocarbon derivatives, alcohols and related derivatives, styrene monomer (SM), dinitro toluene (DNT)	115				
6	Carboxylic acids and related derivatives (industrial fatty acids, acetic acid, ethyl acetate, acrylic acid, maleic anhydride, phthalic anhydride, terephthalic acid, dimethyl terephthalate, acrylate)	115				
	Total					

2. A questionnaire of other expenses (General purposes)

(Unit: KRW thousand)

No.	**Fuel cost**	I/O code	Income statement	Cost statement
1	Gasoline	134		
2	Kerosene	136		
3	Diesel	137		
4	Fuel oil	138		
5	Liquefied petroleum gas	139		
6	Liquefied natural gas	302		
7	Lubricant	140		
8				
9				
10				
	Total			

No.	**Employee benefits**	I/O code	Income statement	Cost statement
1	Staff meal	405		
2	Subsidy for canteen expense	402		
3	Sports event expenses	402		
4	National Pension, Health Insurance costs	405		
5	Employment insurance, Accident insurance costs	405		
6	Long-term care insurance premium	405		
7	Hospital expenses	405		
8	Public health institution checkup expenses	377		
9	Hospital check-up expenses	379		
10	Clothing expenses	101		
	Total			

(Unit: KRW thousand)

No.	**Transport and travel expenses**	I/O code	Income statement	Cost statement
1	Car fare	329		
2	Airfare	334		
3	Rail fare	327		
4	Water freight	332		
5	Outward travel	333		
6	Courier fee	402		
7	Accommodation expenses	402		
	Total			

No.	**Fees and commissions payable**	I/O code	Income statement	Cost statement
1	Legal and accounting fees	361		
2	Sales commission			
3	Other engineering services	365		
4	Guarantee fee			
5	Bank fee	348		
6	Product brokerage fee	321		
7	Cleaning and disinfection service	369		
	Total			

In most countries, the intermediate cost survey is conducted through sampling rather than a full enumeration, and the results of this sample survey are used to estimate the population values. In practice, according to this industry-specific sampling method, establishments with sales above a certain threshold are all selected, and those below this threshold are selected through a sampling design. Then, the details of intermediate input costs for these selected establishments or enterprises are surveyed. The types of the survey questionnaire include the material cost survey form, the expense survey form as explained above, and other auxiliary survey forms. Based on the sample results of the intermediate input costs surveyed in this way, statistical methods are used to estimate the intermediate input amounts for the industry population or derive the composition ratios of intermediate input items by industry. Since the total values (= control totals) of intermediate consumption by industry are already secured through the economic census or industrial surveys, the values of components of the intermediate inputs are re-adjusted based on these totals by industry. The adjustment procedure is generally as follows:

1. Adjust the industry total for intermediate inputs in the columns (vertical direction).
2. Based on the previous result, adjust the total amount for each product in the rows by comparing it with the difference between the product-specific total supply in the supply table and the product-specific total final use in the use table (horizontal direction).

However, there is no clear rule on which of the rows or columns should be reconciled first in this adjustment method.

Figure 6.3 Adjustment of the values of intermediate consumption

	Intermediate consumption by industry	**Total**
By product	Population estimates based on sampling data	Semi-determined values
Total intermediate consumption	Pre-determined values (CT)	

Derived from economic census or survey data.

Reconciled using both the total supply by product (column) in the supply table and the total final use by product (column) in the use table.

Additional cost items that need to be considered in the estimation of intermediate consumption are FISIM (financial intermediation services indirectly measured) and non-life insurance service charges. These data are not directly derived from the input cost survey, so they must be estimated and allocated by the compilers afterwards.

The intermediate input structure for non-market products is surveyed for the government and NPISHs. Government data are primarily sourced from the budget and financial statements, while NPISHs' data are collected through administrative records or surveys. To obtain the government's intermediate consumption data, (similar to estimating output), the central government is fully enumerated, and local government data are estimated through a sampling survey method.

6.4.4 Estimation of final consumption expenditure

Final consumption expenditure represents the amount of expenditure in relation to final use by residents units of an economy, excluding gross domestic capital formation and exports to the rest of the world sector. Final consumption expenditure can be broken down by institutional sectors (households, government and NPISHs), with households accounting for the largest share.

The core source data for estimating household consumption expenditure are the **household expenditure survey** data conducted regularly or irregularly by statistical agencies on urban households. These data provide estimates of the expenditure per household or per capita for a sample of selected urban households based on the COICOP classification, which can be used to estimate the population amount of household final consumption expenditure. To use these data in the use table, the first step is to match the product groups in the COICOP classification with those in the supply and use tables. In addition, a supplementary survey is needed to account for the final consumption expenditure of products that are missing in the urban household survey.

In many cases, this survey is conducted in the form of a sample survey, and is heavily influenced by the reliability of household responses. Due to the limited range of survey items, there are limitations in directly using this survey data. Therefore, it is necessary to supplement the survey data with estimates based on the "product flow method." However, when using the product flow method for estimation, it is also necessary to survey the proportion of goods or services produced that are used as intermediate consumption. Specifically, goods or services intended to be used as intermediate consumption in the production process of other enterprises cannot be allocated to final consumption expenditure.

Under the product flow method, as shown in figure 6.4, consumption expenditure for consumption goods and services is calculated by adding the domestic output value to imports value, and then allocating these values to each institutional sector in the domestic economy and exports.

Figure 6.4 Flow of consumption expenditure

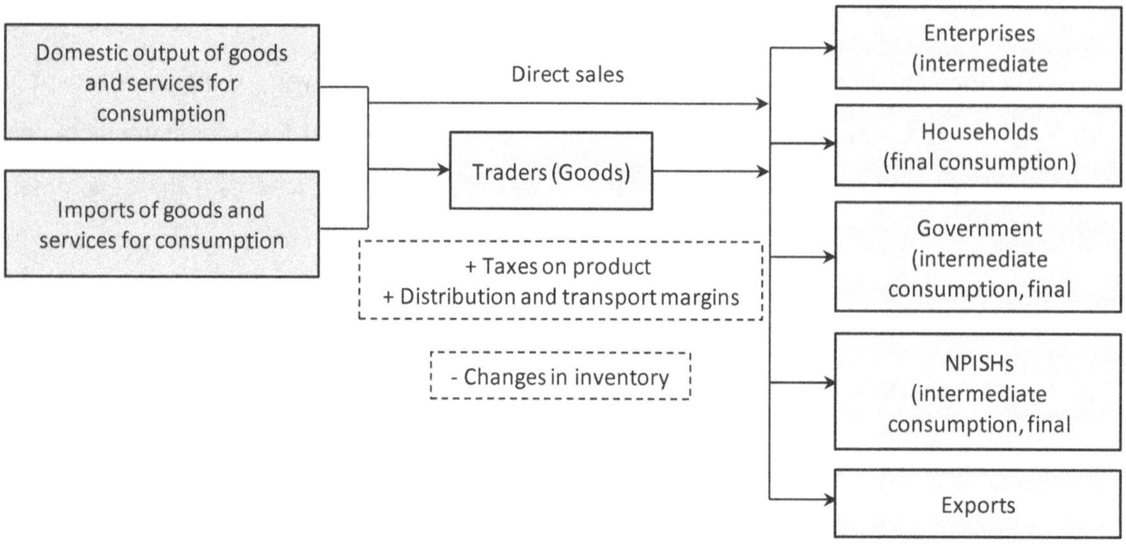

Looking at the type of consumption expenditures by institutional sector, those of enterprises are allocated to intermediate consumption, those of government and NPISHs to both intermediate consumption and final consumption expenditure, and those of households to final consumption expenditure, respectively. The output value is expressed at basic prices, so it must be adjusted to purchasers' prices by adding taxes less subsidies on products, and trade and transport margins. In addition, changes in inventories held by producers and traders should also be accounted for.

The method for estimating final consumption expenditure under the product flow method is as follows:

- **Consumption expenditure for goods**: Output for consumption goods (basic price) + other taxes less subsidies on products + non-deductible VATs + trade and transport margins + imports − exports − changes in inventories held by producers and traders → Allocated to intermediate consumption and final consumption
- **Consumption expenditure for services**: Output for consumption services (basic price) + other taxes less subsidies on products + non-deductible VATs + imports − exports → Allocated to intermediate consumption and final consumption

For items that can be used for both gross fixed capital formation and final consumption among products, their allocation ratios must be obtained through a separate survey. For example, refrigerators are recorded as gross fixed capital formation when used by enterprises, but as final consumption when used by households. Therefore, such items must be selected, and their allocation ratios by institutional sector must be surveyed.

The amounts of consumption expenditure derived in this way are then allocated to each institutional sector (households, corporations, and government), with households accounted for as final consumption expenditure, corporations as intermediate consumption, and government and NPISHs as both intermediate consumption and final consumption. The allocation for households (including NPISHs) and government include non-deductible VAT. In addition, items allocated to households must include the consumption of own-account products, such as the consumption of agricultural products for their own final use and the production of imputed services of owner-occupied dwellings (see Table 4.5 in Chapter 4).

If sufficient data is not available through household expenditure surveys and the product flow method, a third option, "retail sales method," should be considered. This method estimates the expenditure amounts by product for final consumers by surveying the retail sales value or retail sales index of consumption goods actually sold. The retail sales survey is conducted by collecting data from retail stores on sales value or sales index, categorized by the unit or group of consumption goods, and by institutional sector of purchasers. In practice, this survey allows us to estimate the ratios of the intermediate consumption to final consumption of goods, and thus to estimate household's final consumption expenditure.

Government final consumption expenditure is obtained by subtracting the market and non-market sales from the government output and adding market products purchased by government to provide to households for free or at economically insignificant prices. The market and non-market sales deducted from the government final consumption expenditure are recorded as consumption expenditure for other institutional sectors (mainly households). The table below (Table 6.10) shows an example of how the government final consumption expenditure is displayed in the supply and use tables. In this example, suppose that the government output is 100 (public administration 35, education 45, health 20), sales of government services to households are 5, and the purchase of private medical services provided to households is 30. As a result, the government final consumption expenditure is 125 (=100–5+30), and the final consumption expenditure for households is recorded as 5.

Table 6.10 Presentation of government's output and final consumption in supply and use tables

Supply table

	..	Health	Public services	..	Total
..					
Public administration			35		35
Education services			45		45
Health services		30	20		50
..					
Output total		30	100		130

Use table

	..	Health	Public services	..	Household final consumption	Government final consumption	..	Total
..								
Public administration						35		35
Education services					5	45-5		45
Health services						20+30		50
..								
Total					5	125		130

Government final consumption expenditure is further divided into individual consumption expenditure that is attributable to households and collective consumption expenditure that is not attributable to households, which are classified by the COICOP breakdown described earlier. (See section 5.2.1.3.) For NPISHs, similar to government final consumption expenditure, the product-specific output of NPISHs in the supply table is allocated to their final consumption expenditure in the use table. (See section 12.2 for details.)

6.4.5 Estimation of gross fixed capital formation

The category of gross fixed capital formation can be divided into buildings and structures, machinery and equipment, cultivated assets, and intellectual property products. Below, the estimation methods for each of these items are explained.

6.4.5.1 Estimation of buildings and structures

The estimation method for gross fixed capital formation is generally more efficient using the product flow method, which tracks production-side data rather than expenditure-side data. Buildings and structures, as immovable assets, can also be derived using production-side data by contractors. Their estimates of gross fixed capital formation are directly obtained from the domestic output of the construction industry (excluding duplicated output such as domestic subcontracting), but since the construction industry data is prepared at basic prices, it needs to be adjusted to purchasers' prices. In addition, the cost of ownership transfer for buildings and structures must be separately calculated and added, but this cost must not be included in intermediate consumption to avoid double counting.

Figure 6.5 Flow of construction investment

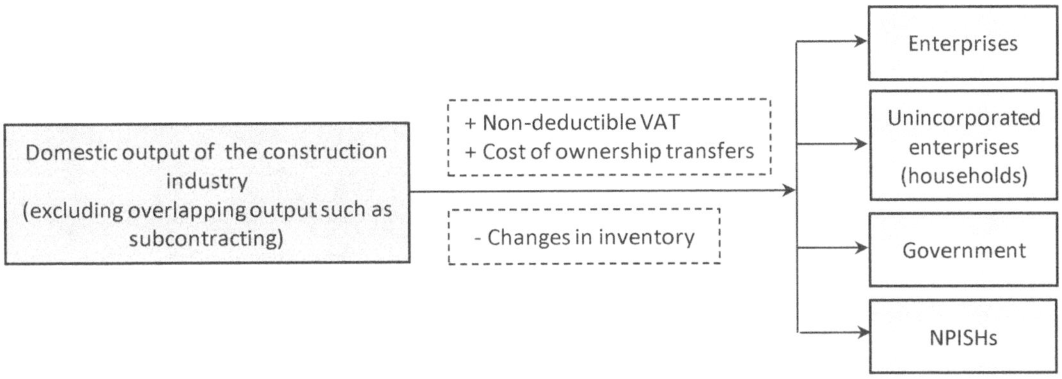

The cost of ownership transfers for buildings and structures is included in the category of gross fixed capital formation. This cost includes various transaction taxes (e.g., acquisition tax, registration tax, etc.), separately invoiced transport costs, brokerage fees, legal fees, and others. In business accounting, the cost of ownership transfers is required to be included in the acquisition cost. However, when applying the product flow method using production-side data, this cost must be separately estimated and included in the acquisition value of buildings and structures, or, if that is not feasible, it should be presented as a separate item under gross fixed capital formation. (Refer to Table 6.17 in 6.6.1.2.) Finally, to calculate gross fixed capital formation, the changes in inventory of buildings must be subtracted, as this represents the increase or decrease in unsold buildings. Buildings and structures under construction are considered to be sold as fixed assets if an installment payment has been made through a sales contract. In this case, the portion of the buildings or structures constructed during the period is considered to have been delivered to the purchaser, and is treated as the purchaser's gross fixed capital formation. However, if installment payments have not been made in stages, or if there is no sales contract, it is treated as the producer's work-in-progress or inventories of finished goods. For buildings or structures under construction intended for own final use, even if they are not completed, the portion completed during the period is treated as an acquisition of fixed assets.

- Gross fixed capital formation for buildings and structures = Output of buildings and structures (basic price) + non-deductible VAT + cost of ownership transfers – changes in buildings inventory

6.4.5.2 Estimation of machinery and equipment

The value for machinery and equipment in gross fixed capital formation is derived mostly by the product flow method, with some items estimated by surveying actual expenditures. The value of expenditure on machinery and equipment under the product flow method is derived by adding up domestic output and imports, subtracting exports, and excluding the amount used for intermediate inputs by domestic enterprises and household consumption. The total amount derived in this way is then allocated to producers by institutional sector.

The procedure for estimating machinery and equipment investment is as follows. First, from the domestic production-side data, separate the product items of machinery and equipment classified as fixed assets and obtain their output (at basic prices). Then, the value of the output is allocated to gross fixed capital formation after deducting the amounts that are exported, used as intermediate inputs by enterprises, consumed as durable consumption goods by households, and changes in inventory. The same procedure is followed for imports of goods.

Figure 6.6 Flow of machinery and equipment investment

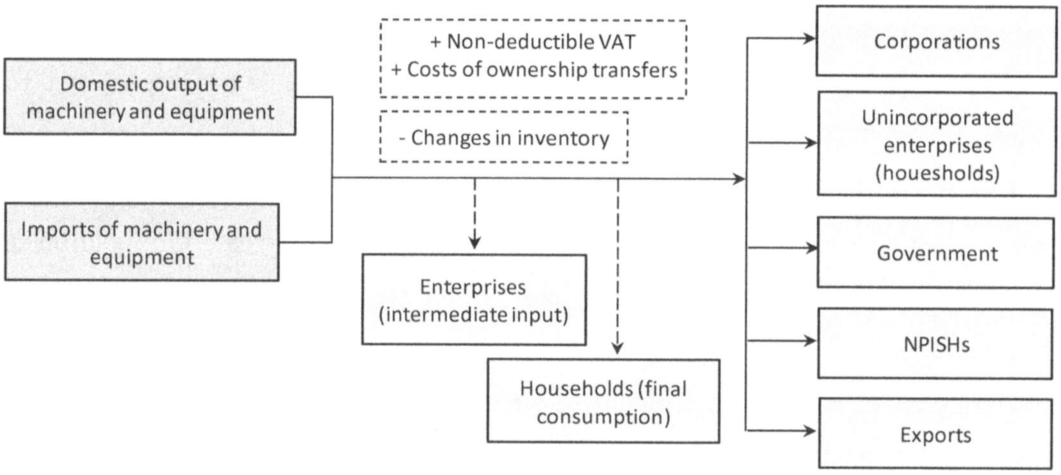

All purchases of machinery and equipment used for production activities are exempt from value added tax (VAT), but government, NPISHs and tax-exempt businesses are subject to non-deductible VAT. These amounts must also include other taxes on products, excluding VAT, as well as costs of ownership transfers. Parts used as intermediate inputs for enterprises are allocated to intermediate consumption, while transportation equipment and home appliances purchased by households are allocated to household final consumption expenditure.

- Gross fixed capital formation of machinery and equipment = Output and imports (basic prices) – (exports + intermediate inputs such as parts, etc. + final consumption as durable consumption goods) + non-deductible VAT + other taxes less subsidies on products + costs of ownership transfers – changes in inventories (producer's inventory and trader's inventory)

6.4.5.3 Estimation of cultivated assets as gross fixed capital formation

Cultivated assets refer to livestock or trees that are raised and produced by livestock farmers or foresters. In the national accounts, these assets are categorized into two types. First, there are cultivated assets produced for sale, similar to other products. Second, there are assets that are cultivated for own final use (gross fixed capital formation), such as breeding livestock, draft animals, dairy cattle, fruit trees and rubber trees. In the former case, cultivated assets intended for sale are recorded as work-in-progress until the immature animals or plants mature and are sold, similar to other products. However, in the latter case, cultivated assets for own final use, are regarded as the acquisition of fixed assets and classified as part of gross fixed capital formation, even if they have not yet matured during the period (i.e., even if they remain in work-in-progress).

The estimation method of cultivated assets for gross fixed capital formation is as follows:

- **Gross fixed capital formation (livestock)**: Net increase in the number of breeding animals, draft animals, and dairy cattle (both mature and immature) x production cost per unit
- **Gross fixed capital formation (fruit trees, etc.)**: Increase in the area of fruit trees cultivated x cost per unit area

6.4.5.4 Estimation of intellectual property products

The term, **intellectual property products** (formerly intangible fixed assets) was first introduced in the 2008 SNA, and this category includes research and development (R&D), computer software and databases, entertainment, literary and artistic originals, and mineral exploration and evaluation.

Gross fixed capital formation for **computer software** covers software that is used repeatedly in production activities for more than one year, and is divided into 'purchased software' and 'own-account software.' **Purchased software** includes the acquisition of licenses to use ready-made copies of the software (packaged software), and the acquisition of custom-made software from software developers. The gross fixed capital formation for purchased software is derived from the value of purchasers' expenditures using the product flow method. In addition, the portion of software used for household consumption is excluded from gross fixed capital formation as it is treated as final consumption expenditure, while regular maintenance costs for software (e.g., professional consulting, computer equipment management services) are considered intermediate consumption and are also excluded from gross fixed capital formation.

- Gross fixed capital formation (purchased software) = sales of the software development and supply industry + imports + distribution margins and taxes less subsidies on products – software installed on computer hardware, duplication due to subcontracting (intermediate consumption) – software for household consumption – maintenance costs (intermediate consumption) – exports

Own-account software includes the production of software originals for internal use, or for the sale of licenses to use or to reproduce. Software originals developed for the purpose of selling copies is also included in the own account software. The estimation method for own-account software uses the **sum of costs method**. To calculate gross operating surplus under this method, the user cost of fixed capital, (i.e., depreciation and net operating surplus) is estimated and added together. In addition, the costs incurred in producing the originals for custom-made software and copies for sale by the software development and supply industry corresponds to the intermediate consumption of the same industry, so these values must be deducted to prevent double-counting in gross fixed capital formation.

- Gross fixed capital formation (own-account software) = intermediate consumption of own-account software production + remuneration of employees + other taxes on production + gross operating surplus – other maintenance costs – (production costs of custom-made software originals and production costs of software copies for sale by the software development and supply industry)

Table 6.11 Estimation method of gross fixed capital formation for computer software

	Type	Estimation method
Purchased software	Packaged software	Product flow method
	Custom-made software	
Own-account software	Production of originals for sale of copies	Sum of costs method
	Production of originals for own use	

R&D expenditure, which was previously treated as intermediate consumption, has been changed to gross fixed capital formation starting from the 2008 SNA. R&D expenditure is estimated using the sum of costs method, the same approach used for own-account software (See section 14.6 for more details).

Entertainment, literary and artistic originals have been explicitly classified as fixed assets, rather than intermediate consumption since the 1993 SNA. Items included in this category are originals of films, TV and radio programs (which are valued by the sum of production costs method), and originals of literature, music, and photographs/images (which are valued by the method of net present value of future income).

Regarding **mineral exploration and evaluation**, the 1993 SNA requires only mineral exploration to be valued as fixed assets, but this scope was expanded in the 2008 SNA to include "evaluation" as a fixed asset. The scope of mineral exploration and evaluation is in accordance with the International Financial Accounting Standards (IFRS 6) set out by the International Accounting Standards Board (IASB). Mineral exploration is valued at market price when purchased from other specific enterprises, and when produced on own-account, it is valued at the sum of costs basis.

6.4.6 Estimation of changes in inventories

In practical terms, there are three examples of methods to estimate changes in inventories, depending on what underlying data is available. The first case is when the inventory data provided in business accounting is available only at book value. For instance, when the amounts for the opening and closing inventories, as well as the price indices for those inventories, are provided, these data can be used to calculate the changes in inventories and holding gains or losses separately in terms of national accounts. The formula for this process is as follows:

Let the book values of the opening and closing inventory stocks in business accounting be denoted as BV^{t-1} and BV^{t}, and let the price indices for the opening and closing inventory stocks be denoted as PI^{t-1} and PI^{t} respectively, then the changes in inventories and holding gains and losses are expressed as follows:

- **Changes in inventories =** $(\boldsymbol{BV^t / PI^t - BV^{t-1} / PI^{t-1}}) \times \overline{\boldsymbol{PI}}$

where $\overline{PI} = 1/2\ (PI^t + PI^{t-1})$

- **Holding gains and losses =** $(\boldsymbol{BV^t - BV^{t-1}})$ **– changes in inventories**

The second case is when the data on prices and quantities of the opening and closing inventory stocks are provided. For example, if price and quantity data for opening and closing inventory stocks are available, such as for agricultural, forestry and fishery products, livestock or minerals, then changes in inventories and holding gains and losses can be separately accounted for as follows. Here, P^{t-1} and P^{t} denote the opening and closing prices, respectively, and Q^{t-1} and Q^{t} denote the opening and closing quantities, respectively.

- "Closing inventory – opening inventory" at book value = $P^tQ^t - P^{t-1}Q^{t-1}$

- Changes in inventories = $1/2(P^{t-1} + P^t)(Q^t - Q^{t-1})$

- Holding gains and losses = ("closing inventory – opening inventory" at book value) – changes in inventories = $(P^tQ^t - P^{t-1}Q^{t-1}) - 1/2\,(P^{t-1} + P^t)(Q^t - Q^{t-1})$ $= 1/2\,(P^t - P^{t-1})\,(Q^{t-1} + Q^t)$

For example, given the following quarterly price and volume data for livestock products, the annual value of changes in inventories by the "book-keeping approach" is 210, and the changes in inventories is 112.5, and the holding gain is 97.5 by the national accounting approach.

Table 6.12 Derivation of changes in inventories and holding gains

	Quantity		Price		Value in $t-1$	Value in t	Change in inventory (Book value)	Change in inventory	Holding gain
Quarter	q^{t-1}	q^t	p^{t-1}	p^t	$p^{t-1}q^{t-1}$	p^tq^t	$p^tq^t - p^{t-1}q^{t-1}$	$1/2(p^{t-1}+p^t)\,(q^t - q^{t-1})$	$1/2(p^t - p^{t-1})\,(q^{t-1}+q^t)$
Q1	100	105	10	11	1,000	1,155	155	52.5	102.5
Q2	105	110	11	12	1,155	1,320	165	57.5	107.5
Q3	110	115	12	10	1,320	1,150	-170	55	-225.0
Q4	115	110	10	11	1,150	1,210	60	-52.5	112.5
Total					4,625	4,835	210	112.5	97.5

The third case to estimate changes in inventories uses the product flow method, which is derived from the product balance identity. That is, changes in inventories can be derived as follows:

- Changes in inventories = (domestic output + imports) – (intermediate consumption + final consumption + gross fixed capital formation + acquisition less disposal of valuables + exports)

This method requires the availability of data on other items, excluding changes in inventories. However, the limitation of this method is that, unlike the previous two methods, it does not allow for the separate calculation of holding gains or losses that can be derived from the changes in inventories in the book-keeping approach.

6.5 Compilation of supply and use tables for non-benchmark years

When compiling the supply and use tables for non-benchmark years, detailed data are often not collected compared to benchmark-year tables. Therefore, it is common to use the product flow method, and extrapolate ratios of the benchmark year. However, to prepare supply and use tables for non-benchmark years, it is essential to have basic data from the supply-side, including total value of output by industry, details of imports and exports, taxes less subsidies on products, and total of trade and transport margins. Additionally, the use-side data must include changes in inventories. When compiling the supply and use tables, the use-side data are usually estimated based on the supply-side data, and the following **product flow table** can be used for this purpose.

Table 6.13 Product flow table

Details of products (CPC)	Output (basic price) (1)	Imports (2)		Margins (3)		Taxes less subsidies on products (4)	Exports (5)		**Total domestic supply** (purchaser's price) (1+2+3+4-5)	Intermediate consumption (6)	Changes in inventories (7)			Gross fixed capital formation (8)	Net acquisition of valuables (9)	Final consumption (10)			**Total domestic use** (purchaser's price) (6+7+8+9+10)
		Goods	Services	Distribution margin	Transport margin		Goods	Services			Producer's inventory	Trader's inventory	Imports inventory			Households	Government	NPISHs	
Raw materials																			
Processed goods																			
Capital goods																			
Services																			

For the compilation of the supply table, the values of output by industry and by product should be available as the basic data. If these data are not available, the total values of output by industry can be used temporarily, assuming that the production structure of products by industry in the benchmark year remains unchanged, and the allocation can be made proportionally across the products. Imports are estimated directly using data on imports of goods from the customs statistics and imports of services from the balance of payments. Estimates of distribution margins, transport margins, and taxes on products are also based on actual data for the current year; however, if these data are not available, the ratios from the benchmark year can be applied.

For the compilation of the use table, once the total value of intermediate consumption by industry is surveyed, the value for each input is derived by applying the product-specific input ratios in the benchmark year, assuming that the input cost structure by industry remains the same as in the benchmark years. Then, the amounts for inputs are summed by row to obtain the value of intermediate use for each product (row total), and are adjusted afterward. The estimates for final use items are directly obtained from the expenditure-side data if available. For exports, the estimates are directly obtained using data on exports of goods from customs statistics and on exports of services from the balance of payments. Other items of final use that cannot be directly estimated are approximated using the product flow method and extrapolating year-on-year growth rates. For example, gross fixed capital formation is estimated using the production-side data (e.g., construction industry output, machinery and equipment, and intellectual property products), or by extending the values of these items from the benchmark year using their year-on-year growth rates. Private final consumption expenditure can be adjusted by comparing the value remaining after excluding other expenditure items from the production-side data with the value of benchmark year extrapolated by the year-on-year growth rate. Government final consumption expenditure is estimated by the sum of costs method using the government's budget and financial statement data.

Table 6.14 Compilation methods of the supply and use tables in non-benchmark years

	Item	Methodology	Data source
Supply table	Output (Basic price)	Industry-specific, product-specific output is calculated based on actual survey data. If this data is unavailable, the ratios of output by product to total output in the benchmark year is applied under the assumption that the product structure by industry in the benchmark year is unchanged.	Surveys on mining and manufacturing industries, surveys on service industries.
	Imports	Actual data are used.	Customs statistics, balance of payments
	Distribution margin, transport margin	Actual data are used. If this data is unavailable, extrapolate the values of the benchmark year by the sales growth rates.	Surveys on Trade and Transport services. Trade and transport margins in the benchmark year.
	Taxes less subsides on products	Same as above	National tax statistics report, government's budget and financial statements.
Use table	Intermediate inputs by industry	If the total value of intermediate inputs by industry is available, the product-specific input ratios in the benchmark year can be applied to allocate the amounts for non-benchmark years under the assumption that the input cost structure by industry in the benchmark year remains unchanged, and then adjusted by adding up the amounts of inputs by row.	Surveys on mining and manufacturing industries, surveys on service industries, corporate financial statements databases in the National Tax Service.
	Final consumption expenditure	Actual survey data are used.	Urban household survey, retail sales survey.
		Adjustments are made by comparing the value of final consumption expenditure derived by the product flow method with the value of final consumption in the benchmark year extrapolated by the year-on-year growth rates.	Final consumption in the use table of benchmark year.
	Gross fixed capital formation	Actual survey data are used. If this data is not available, extrapolate the gross fixed capital formation in construction, machinery and equipment, and intellectual property products with the year-on-year growth rates.	Surveys of construction industry, Surveys on mining, manufacturing and R&D industry.
	Changes in inventories	Changes in inventories held by producers: actual data are used.	Surveys on mining and manufacturing industries.

	Item	Methodology	Data source
		Changes in inventories held by wholesalers and retailers: actual data are used.	Survey on trade industry.
	Net acquisition of valuables	Actual data, or extend the value from the benchmark year using the year-on-year growth rate.	Ratios in the use table of benchmark year.
	Exports	Actual data are used.	Customs statistics, balance of payments

6.6 Compilation of supply and use tables by the product flow method

To define again the product flow method mentioned in the previous section, it is a process of estimating the value of expenditure items based on the production data, using the product balance identity in the supply and use tables. In this section, we will explore the method of estimating expenditure-side items using the product flow method when it is difficult to obtain the expenditure-side data or when the reliability of the data is low.

6.6.1 Estimation of expenditure-side GDP items by the product flow method

To estimate *expenditure-side* items using the product flow method, it is necessary to obtain supply-side data, including output (at basic prices), import values, and taxes less subsidies on products for conversion to purchasers' prices. In addition, once the export data are collected from expenditure-side sources, intermediate consumption, final consumption, and gross capital formation can be estimated based on the supply-side data and this information.

To cite again the product balance identity used in the product flow method:

- Output (basic price) + imports + taxes less subsidies on products = intermediate consumption (purchaser's price) + final consumption (purchaser's price) + gross fixed capital formation (purchaser's price) + changes in inventories + acquisition less disposal of valuables + exports

The left-hand side of this expression uses supply-side data, while the right-hand side uses expenditure-side data. The product flow method estimates expenditure-side data based on supply-side data, which forms the basis for estimating the expenditure-side values. Expenditure-side data can be classified based on the "end-use" of products, and as far as goods are concerned, it can be classified much easier by using the **Broad Economic Categories** classification (BEC revision 5) established by the United Nations. In the BEC, goods are divided into seven categories, with codes distinguishing industrial and household uses. This classification can be linked to the SNA's classification based on **use**, allowing goods to be categorized as "intermediate goods, consumption goods, capital goods, and intermediate and consumption goods." Thus, by classifying the supply-side individual product and imported goods in accordance with their end-use, intermediate goods are generally allocated to intermediate consumption, consumption goods to final consumption, capital goods to gross fixed capital formation, and intermediate and consumption goods that can be used for both intermediate and final consumption are allocated to intermediate and final consumption. However, there many items in domestic products and imported goods that can be allocated to two or more end-use purposes. Therefore, it is necessary to survey supplementally the end-use ratios for these items and allocate their amounts to appropriate expenditure items. For example, passenger cars can be used both as durable consumption goods for households and as capital goods for the transportation or leasing industry, so the proportions of their actual end-use must be surveyed and allocated appropriately.

Table 6.15 Linking between BEC and SNA classification by use

	Category of goods	BEC code	Subcategory	SNA classification by use
1	Food and beverages	111	Mainly for industry	Intermediate goods
		112	Mainly for household consumption	Consumption goods
2	Industrial supplies not elsewhere specified	21	Primary	Intermediate goods
		22	Processed	Intermediate goods
3	Fuels and lubricants	31	Primary	Intermediate goods
		321	Motor spirit	Intermediate goods and consumption goods
		322	Other	Intermediate goods
4	Capital goods (except transport equipment), and parts and accessories thereof	41	Capital goods (except transport equipment)	Capital goods
		42	Parts and accessories	Intermediate goods
5	Transport equipment, and parts and accessories thereof	51	Passenger motor cars	Intermediate goods and consumption goods
		521	Industrial	Capital goods
		522	Non-industrial	Consumption goods
		53	Parts and accessories	Intermediate goods
6	Consumer goods not elsewhere specified	61	Durable	Consumption goods
		62	Semi-durable	Consumption goods
		63	Non-durable	Consumption goods
7	Goods not elsewhere specified	7	Goods not elsewhere specified	

6.6.1.1 Selection of the product classification

In order to prepare a flow table for each individual product by the product flow method, a uniform product classification must be selected to allow the allocation of the supply-side products to the end-use on the expenditure side. The table below (Table 6.16) illustrates the process of estimating expenditure items by product according to the product flow method. To allocate the products in the leftmost column to their end-use, it is advisable to apply the most detailed classification system, which currently requires a distinction between goods and services. For goods, there are classification criteria such as HS, CPC, and SITC, with the HS classification being the most detailed. Therefore, it is preferrable to use the HS classification criteria to allocate end-use items. For services, since only the CPC classification is available at present, the end-use items are allocated based on this taxonomy. In this way, goods classified according to this product classification are then linked to the BEC classification through the code correspondence to determine their end-use.

Table 6.16 Preparation of the product flow table by product codes

Product name	Output (basic price) (1)	Imports (2)	Adjustment of margins and taxes on products (3)	**Total supply** (1+2+3)	Exports (4)	Intermediate consumption (5)	Final consumption (6)	Gross fixed capital formation (7)	Changes in inventories (8)	**Total use** (4+5+6+7+8)
Goods 1 (HS)										
Goods 2 (HS)										
…										
Service 1 (CPC)										
Service 2 (CPC)										
…										

6.6.1.2 Estimation methods by the expenditure item

Estimation of intermediate consumption

Intermediate consumption by product corresponds to intermediate goods in terms of their end-use classification (BEC), and products considered as intermediate goods are allocated under the product flow method. However, certain products are used in both intermediate consumption and final consumption, or in both final consumption and gross fixed capital formation, and these products should be carefully distinguished. For instance, rice is categorized as a consumption good in terms of its end-use, but the raw rice harvested by farmers is processed through milling and packaging, so it is allocated to intermediate consumption in the manufacturing industry as intermediate goods. Additionally, products such as home appliances, cars, and furniture are used by both households and enterprises. Therefore, the proportion of users should be surveyed, with the portion used by households allocated to final consumption as durable consumption goods, while the portion used by enterprises allocated to gross fixed capital formation. Similarly, electricity should be allocated according to proportions of their users, with intermediate consumption (for enterprises, government and NPISHs) and final consumption (for households) clearly separated.

Estimation of gross fixed capital formation

Gross fixed capital formation by product can be derived from the business investment surveys, but it can be more accurately estimated by supplementing it with the product flow method described above. For example, the gross fixed capital formation of buildings and structures is calculated by using the total output of the construction industry excluding changes in inventories, while the gross fixed capital formation of machinery and equipment are allocated based on the BEC classification of relevant capital goods and imports. However, since the production-side data is valued at basic prices, it is necessary to convert it to purchasers' prices by adjusting for trade and transport margins and adding taxes less subsidies on products. Furthermore, gross fixed capital formation must include the cost of ownership transfer, so transaction costs not included in the purchasers' prices adjustment must be allocated to the gross fixed capital formation of enterprises.

Presentation of the costs of ownership transfer

When gross fixed capital formation is shown in the supply and use tables using the product flow method, a discrepancy arises between the values of the product items in the supply table and the gross fixed capital formation in the use table due to the inclusion of the cost of ownership transfer in addition to the price adjustment items. Therefore, to reconcile the cost of ownership transfer for each product to the corresponding fixed capital formation item (e.g., buildings) in the supply and use tables, the following two options can be considered. The first option involves adjusting the cost of ownership transfer while converting the basic price of the product item in the supply table to the purchaser's price by adjusting the margins and taxes less subsidies on products. For example, as shown in the table (Table 6.17, option 1), an adjustment column for the cost of ownership transfer can be added in the supply table, subtracting the amount corresponding to ownership transfer costs for service items (e.g., real estate service 6, legal services 4) and adding this amount to buildings (+10). In this case, in the use table, the value for buildings will be displayed as the amount including the cost of ownership transfer (buildings 110).

If this procedure is too complicated, a second option (option 2) may be adopted, under which the costs of ownership transfers are not adjusted in the supply table, but are instead shown separately in the gross fixed capital formation column of the use table. This method can be more convenient in practice as it allows the costs of ownership transfer to be displayed separately in the use table without going through the adjustment procedure in the supply table.

Table 6.17 Presentation of the cost of ownership transfer in the supply and use tables

(Option 1)

Supply table

	Output	Imports	Adjustment of costs of ownership transfer
Buildings	100		**10**
Real estate services	6		**-6**
Legal services	4		**-4**
Total	110		0

Use table

	…	Final consumption	Fixed capital formation	Changes in inventories	Exports
Buildings			110		
Real estate services			0		
Legal services			0		
Total			110		

(Option 2)

Supply table

	Output	Imports	
Buildings	100		
Real estate services	6		
Legal services	4		
Total	110		

Use table

	…	Final consumption	Fixed capital formation	Changes in inventories	Exports
Buildings			100		
Real estate services			6		
Legal services			4		
Total			110		

Estimation of final consumption expenditure

Final consumption expenditure can be allocated by government, households, and NPISHs. The estimates for government final consumption expenditure by product are directly derived from the same product data prepared in the government accounts. The largest share of government output consists of public administration and defense services, with other sectors including education, health, entertainment and arts, and telecommunication and broadcasting services. Government output can be classified according to the COFOG categories based on the government's budget and financial statements, which allows for relatively accurate estimates of final consumption expenditure to be derived directly. Government final consumption expenditure is calculated as the value of government output, minus government's sales to private sector and government's own-account fixed capital formation, plus the in-kind payments that government purchases from market producers and provides to households. (See 12.1.4 for detailed examples.) The final consumption expenditure for NPISHs is also derived and accounted for in the same manner as for government.

Household final consumption expenditure by product is derived by subtracting the final consumption expenditure of government and NPISHs from the total value allocated to final consumption expenditure by the product flow method. The resulting amount is compared with the amount derived from the household consumption expenditure survey to determine the most reliable data. In the case of household survey data, estimates of the population may vary depending on the sample size, and there is a significant potential for missing data by items due to inaccurate reporting by respondents. Particularly for durable consumer goods, the data in the short-term survey may exhibit substantial variation, so it is not advisable to rely entirely on this data. Therefore, the use of the product flow method based on production-side data is more accurate method for deriving data alongside these surveys. However, it is important to note that underground economic activities, which are not captured in production-side data, should be accounted for by adjusting and combining with household survey data for a more complete estimate.

Figure 6.7 Derivation of household final consumption expenditure

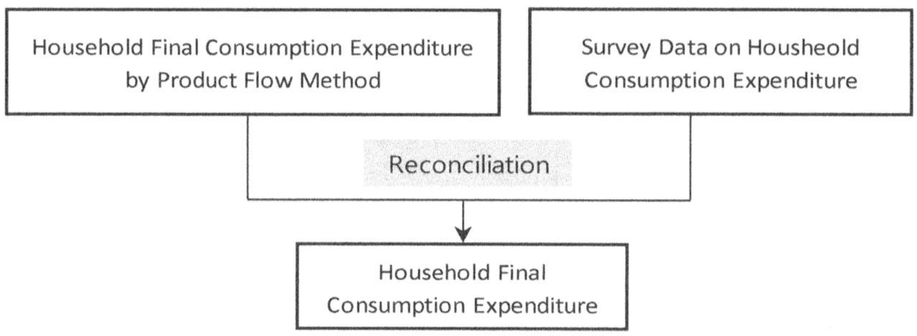

Estimation of exports

Export statistics by product are estimated more accurately compared to other items, as the data are obtained from customs statistics for goods and balance of payments for services. Since the customs office's statistics on exported goods are recorded at FOB prices, they are consistent with the price valuation system of the supply and use tables and do not require separate adjustments. However, the original data of the customs office is collected in accordance with the customs clearance basis, it must be adjusted to match the standards of the *balance of payments*. In the balance of payments, goods are recorded on the basis of **change in economic ownership**, not of customs clearance. For example, if the ownership of a ship is transferred even though they are not physically cleared through customs, the change in ownership occurs in national accounts' perspective and this should be adjusted. In addition, items excluded from exports, such as re-exports and exports of goods for processing, should also be adjusted to align with the balance of payments standards.

Among the categories of exports of services in the balance of payments, "travel" and "government goods and services" are characterized as a mixture of various types of goods and services. Therefore, when applying the product flow method, it is necessary to break these categories down into the specific corresponding goods and services items and redistribute them accordingly. (For details, refer to "Imports and exports of services in the balance of payments" in 13.3.3.)

The customs office's statistics on exported goods are recorded in accordance with the HS classification, thus to align them with the CPC classification used in the product flow method, it is required to convert them to the CPC codes using the HS-CPC correspondence table. Similarly, exports of services must also be matched with CPC codes. As described above, the "travel" and "government goods and services" categories must be reallocated to CPC codes corresponding to the appropriate detailed goods and services. The classification by type of end-use (BEC) can also be used to allocate amounts for the domestic use items (such as intermediate consumption, final consumption, and gross fixed capital formation) by subtracting exports from the supply-side data (= output + imports).

6.7 Compilation of the use table at basic prices

The method for compiling the supply and use tables is based on the principle that the supply table is converted into a purchaser's price table by adding price adjustment items (trade and transport margins, and taxes less subsidies on products) to the supply items at the basic price, while the use table is compiled based on use items at the purchaser's price. However, another way of compiling the use table is to convert the table at purchasers' prices to basic prices and display margins and taxes less subsidies on products separately. This table is referred to as the **use table at basic prices**, and it can be used when converting the supply and use tables into an input-output table, as it is compatible with the supply table at basic prices in terms of price aspects. As explained later (see Chapter 21), in order to convert the supply and use tables to an input-out table using matrix formulas, the supply table (excluding imports column) and the use table (excluding the final use) must be compatible in terms of the price basis. The use table at basic prices is also used when compiling the use table in volume terms, which helps eliminate price fluctuations between periods and enables the analysis of volume growth. To compile the use table in volume terms, it is considered that using basic prices is more suitable than using purchasers' prices for the conversion to input-output tables. (Refer to 17.2.2.) In this section, we will explain briefly how to prepare the use table at basic prices.

The use table at basic prices is derived from the use table at purchasers' prices. The specific procedure involves extracting the values of price adjustment items (distribution margins, transport margins, and taxes less subsidies on products) from the cells of the intermediate consumption quadrant (Quadrant I) and the final use quadrant (Quadrant II) of the use table at purchasers' prices. These extracted values of items are then placed into a new matrix table (**a table of margins and taxes less subsidies on products**). Afterward, the table of margin and taxes less subsidies on products is subtracted from the use table at purchasers' prices to create the use table at basic prices. In the use table at basic prices, a new row (on taxes less subsidies on products) is added below the row of total intermediate consumption and final use at basic prices to record the sum of extracted taxes less subsidies on products. For the trade and transport services row, the extracted values of trade and transport margins are added to the values of existing trade and transportation services rows. (See Figure 6.8.)

Figure 6.8 Conversion of the use table at purchasers' prices to the use table at basic prices

Use table at purchaser's prices

	By product	Intermediate consumption	Final use
Purchaser's Price			
	Trade and transport services **(Excluding distribution and transport margins)**		
	Total (purchaser's price)		

⇨

Distribution and transport margins, and net taxes on products

By product	Adjustment item	Intermediate consumption	Final use
Agriculture	Distribution and transport margins		
	Taxes less subsidies on products		
Mining and manufacturing	Distribution and transport margins		
	Taxes less subsidies on products		
Trade and transport services	Taxes less subsidies on products		
	Distribution and transport margins	(-)	(-)
Other services	Taxes less subsidies on products		
Total distribution and transport margins		0	0
Total taxes less subisides on products			

(Subtraction)

Use table at basic prices

	By product	Intermediate consumption	Final use
Basic Price			
	Trade and transport services **(Including distribution and transport margins)**		
	Total (basic price)		
	Total taxes less subsidies on products		
	Total (purchaser's price)		

Therefore, among the adjustment items, distribution margins of each product are added to the trade service row, transport margins are added to the transport service row, and taxes less subsidies on products are recorded in the newly inserted row on taxes less subsidies on products. It is important to note that, in the use table at purchasers' prices, the values of the trade and transport services rows do not include total value of the trade and transport margins, but only represent the value of costs used for intermediate consumption of these services. However, in the use table at basic prices, the values of trade and transport services rows include both the costs used for intermediate consumption and the trade and transport margins extracted above. Table 6.18 shows the format of this adjusted use table at basic prices. This table separates intermediate consumption and final use into domestic products and imports. If the imports row is removed and a new table (**imports use table**) is created, the remaining part will form the **domestic use table**. Generally, the rows of "residents' direct purchases abroad" and "non-residents' domestic purchases" displayed in the use table can be directly allocated to the corresponding product rows if these amounts are investigated by product, similar to the case of the supply table. Removing these two rows may be more advantageous for the presentation format and will also facilitate the conversion to the input-output table.

Table 6.18 A format of the use table at basic prices

<table>
<tr><th rowspan="2">Industry
Product</th><th colspan="4">Intermediate use</th><th colspan="4">Final use</th><th rowspan="2">Total use at basic prices</th></tr>
<tr><th>Agriculture</th><th>Manufacturing</th><th>Other industries</th><th>Total</th><th>Final consumption expenditure</th><th>Gross capital formation</th><th>Exports</th><th>Total</th></tr>
<tr><td>Agricultural
Manufacturing
Trade service
Transport service
Other products</td><td></td><td></td><td></td><td></td><td></td><td></td><td></td><td></td><td></td></tr>
<tr><td>**Total at basic prices**</td><td></td><td></td><td></td><td></td><td></td><td></td><td></td><td></td><td></td></tr>
<tr><td>**Taxes less subsidies on products**</td><td></td><td></td><td></td><td></td><td></td><td></td><td></td><td></td><td></td></tr>
<tr><td>**Total at purchasers' prices**</td><td></td><td></td><td></td><td></td><td></td><td></td><td></td><td></td><td></td></tr>
<tr><td>**Gross value added**</td><td></td><td></td><td></td><td></td></tr>
<tr><td>Remuneration of employees
Net operating surplus
Depreciation and depletion
Other taxes less subsidies on production</td><td></td><td></td><td></td><td></td></tr>
<tr><td>**Total input at basic prices**</td><td></td><td></td><td></td><td></td></tr>
</table>

6.7.1 Extraction of distribution margins

The method for calculating **distribution margins** follows a two-step approach: first, the total value of distribution margins is derived from the supply table, and then it is allocated to individual products in the use table. The total value (control total) of distribution margins can be obtained from the sum of amounts recorded as the primary and secondary products in the row of trade services in the supply table. If the total value of trade services is not available, it can be estimated obtained from total sales data for resale. This estimation method can be divided into domestic distribution margins and imports margins. Domestic distribution margins can be calculated by estimating the output of the relevant industry's products (such as agricultural products, minerals, and manufactured goods), multiplying the estimated value of output by the distribution ratios of those products traded domestically through wholesalers and retailers, and then, multiplying these amounts by the respective **wholesale and retail margin rates** [= (margin/(cost of sales + margin)] (see Table 6.19). In this case, the domestic distribution amount is the cost of sales excluding the margin, so the calculation is adjusted by including the margin.

Table 6.19 Sales and distribution margins (Supply side)

Industry / Product	Agriculture	Mining and manufacturing	Construction	Services	Imports	**Total sales of trade**	**Sales margin rates**	**Sales margins**
Agricultural products								10
Mining products	Sales of domestic products				....	A	B	60
Manufactured goods								30
Total sales of trade								
Sales margin rates								
Sales margins								100

Similarly, the distribution margins of imports can be estimated by calculating the portion of imports values for each product that is distributed to wholesale and retail transactions and multiplying it by the respective distribution margin rates for each product. As a result, the sum of distribution margins of domestic products and imports is derived.

- Distribution margins of domestic products (i) = $\sum_i(\text{Sales value}_i \times \text{domestic distribution ratio}_i \times \text{margin rate}_i)$
- Distribution margins of imported goods (i) = $\sum_i(\text{Imports value}_i \times \text{domestic distribution ratio}_i \times \text{margin rate}_i)$

The reconciliation is made by comparing these distribution margins to the total distribution margins extracted from the supply table. These distribution margins data are used as distribution margins for each product for adjusting to purchasers' prices in the supply table and as the total value to convert purchasers' prices to basic prices in the use table.

To prepare a **distribution margin table** from the use table, it is necessary to estimate distribution margins from the use table at purchaser's prices. However, it is preferrable to use distribution margin rates derived from the supply side as alternative data. The reason for this is that it is difficult to estimate the amounts of margins from the purchasers' perspective, and the data provided by the supply side is reliable and easy to use. Table 6.20 shows the format of distribution margin table used to derive distribution margins in the use table. The wholesale margin rates are applied to the intermediate consumption sector, and both the wholesale and retail margin rates are applied for the final use sector.

Table 6.20 Distribution margin table (Use side)

Industry / Product	Agriculture	Mining and manufacturing	Construction	Services	Final consumption	Fixed capital formation	Exports	**Total trade purchases**	**Sales margin rates**	**Sales margins**
Agricultural products										10
Mining products		.....								60
Manufactured goods										30
Total trade purchases										
Sales margin rates										
Sales margins										100

The distribution margin table is subdivided into wholesale margin and retail margin tables. The data source for **wholesale margins** is obtained from the wholesale trade service industry on the supply side, and the total value of wholesale margins by product, arising from domestic economy and imports, is allocated to the wholesale margin table. The data source for **retail margins**, similarly to wholesale margins, is obtained from the retail trade service industry on the supply side, and it is primarily allocated to final consumption expenditure on the use side, while it is rarely allocated to intermediate consumption, fixed capital formation, and exports.

6.7.2 Extraction of transport margins

Transport margins refer to the freight charges separately paid by the purchaser when purchasing goods. These costs are recorded as the output of the seller providing the transportation services or a third-party transportation service provider. At the same time, this amount is included in the cost of goods purchased by the buyer. This amount is reflected as a secondary product of the seller of the goods or as the primary product of the transportation service provider. However, in many cases, the seller does not charge the purchaser separately for freight cost but includes them in the selling price, meaning transport margins rarely occur separately. Therefore, it can be seen that the proportion of transport margins is not that large in reality.

The total value of transport margins must, in practice, be equivalent to the value obtained by subtracting the total use amount in the row of freight transportation services in the use table at purchasers' prices from the total supply amount in the corresponding row in the supply table. This value is allocated to each cell in the **transport margin table** during the preparation of the use table at basic prices. Moreover, transport margins do not arise from changes in inventories or exports. The sectors where transport margins arise need to be surveyed separately, but they are limited to agricultural, forestry and fishery products, minerals, and manufactured goods.

The method for constructing the transport margin table is as follows. First, from the supply table, the total transport margins by transport mode (land, water, and air) are derived, and these amounts are then allocated to each product (agricultural, forestry, and fishery products; mineral products; manufactured goods) though the margin adjustment process. The allocation by product in the supply table is based on transport statistics by transport mode, using the data "distance per product x freight rate per unit of product." The product-specific transport margins derived from this supply table are used as control totals for each product in the transport margin table and are subsequently allocated to intermediate consumption by industry and domestic final use.

Table 6.21 Example of preparing a transport margin table

Supply table

	By industry	Imports	Total	Transport margin	…	Supply total
Agriculture				15		15
Mining				8		8
Manufacturing				52		52
…						
Transport margin			75	**-75**		0
(Land)			(40)	(-40)		0
(Water)			(25)	(-25)		0
(Air)			(10)	(-10)		0
Total			75	**0**		**75**

Transport margin table

	Intermediate consumption by industry	Domestic final use	Exports	Total transport margin
Agriculture	…	…		15
Mining	…	…		8
Manufacturing	…	…		52
…				
Transport margin				-75
(Land)				(-40)
(Water)				(-25)
(Air)				(-10)
Total				0

6.7.3 Extraction of taxes less subsidies on products

The process of extracting **taxes less subsidies on products** is as follows: taxes less subsidies on products are extracted from the values at purchasers' prices in each cell of the Quadrant I and II of the use table, these totals are then displayed in a newly added row of "taxes less subsidies on products" at the bottom of these quadrants. The method for extracting taxes on products or subsidies on products included in each cell of product is as follows: For taxes on products, the total amounts (CT) are calculated by tax type, and then they are allocated in proportion to the quantity or value of the corresponding product. The total amount of taxes on products is derived from the revenue data for national and local taxes. Subsidies on products are items that must be deducted when deriving the taxes less subsidies on products, and these amounts are generally granted to specific industries or products, so these items must be identified individually. The total amount (CT) of subsidies on products is derived from the government's budget and financial statements, and is applied to the relevant sectors. Through this process, **tables of taxes on products and subsidies on products** to be deducted for each item of intermediate consumption and final use in the use table are prepared as follows.

Table 6.22 Taxes on product table and subsidies on products table

Taxes on products table (excluding VAT)[1)]

Intermediate consumption	Final consumption	Fixed capital formation	Exports	Total
By industry				
..	...	...		...
..	...	...		...
..	...	...		...

Subsidies on products table

Intermediate consumption	Final consumption	Fixed capital formation	Exports	Total
By industry				
..	...	...		...
..	...	...		...
..	...	...		...

Note: 1): The Table of VAT is displayed below.

When extracting taxes on products, other taxes on products and value-added tax (VAT) are distinguished. Other taxes on products are extracted by tax category for all products in intermediate consumption and final use, while, in the case of value-added tax, only non-deductible VAT is extracted. The total value of non-deductible VAT (CT) is derived from the column of taxes on products in the supply table, and this value must match the sum of the values extracted from the sector in the use table where non-deductible VAT occurs. The sectors where non-deductible VAT arises include almost all final consumption expenditures (excluding VAT-exempt or zero-rated goods and services), valuables, and expenditures (of intermediate consumption and gross fixed capital formation) in the VAT-exempted industries. For reference, the **VAT-exempt goods or services** (or **industries**) refer to those where the VAT (output tax) on the sold products is exempt, but the VAT (input tax) on materials and fixed assets purchased to produce these products is not exempt. Examples of the VAT-exempt industries include agriculture, forestry, fisheries, passenger transport services, medical and health services, education, finance and insurance services, government, and NPISHs. On the other hand, **zero-rated goods** are items for which the value added tax on the products sold is exempt, while the VAT (input tax) imposed on materials and fixed assets for use in production is refunded to the purchasers. Examples of zero-rated goods include equipment provided to farmers and fishermen, and exported goods. Therefore, non-deductible VAT does not arise from intermediate consumption of zero-rated goods.

Non-deductible VAT corresponds to the value-added tax included in the goods and services (excluding VAT-exempted and zero-rated products) purchased by VAT-exempt industries and final consumers. Additionally, the VAT included in certain fixed capital formation (fixed assets purchased by VAT-exempt industries) and valuables also falls under non-deductible VAT. Furthermore, since the government and NPISHs cannot claim the exemption for the VAT imposed on goods and services they purchase, non-deductible VAT applies to these products as well. These are summarized in the table below.

Table 6.23 Sectors subject to non-deductible VAT in the use table

	Intermediate consumption		Final consumption, valuables	Gross fixed capital formation	
	VAT-exempted industries, government, NPISHs	Other industries		VAT-exempted industries, government, NPISHs	Other industries
VAT-exempted or zero-rated products					
Other products	O		O	O	

Note: 'O' indicates the sectors where non-deductible VAT arises.

Non-deductible VAT may also arise in certain cost items even in intermediate consumption of industries other than the VAT-exempted industries. For example, expense items for which the base for input tax cannot be estimated (e.g., entertainment expenses) are subject to non-deductible VAT. However, most non-deductible VAT arises from the goods and services purchased by VAT-exempted industries, non-market producers and final consumers.

To compile the use table at basic prices, the **non-deductible VAT table** should be prepared and the amounts of this table should be subtracted from the use table at purchasers' prices as follows.

Table 6.24 Non-deductible VAT table by purchasers

Supply table

	Output by industry (Basic price)	Price adjustment				Total supply (Purchaser's price)
		Non-deductible VAT	Other taxes less subsidies on products	Distribution margin, transport margin		
		…				…
		…				…
Total output		200				

Non-deductible VAT table by purchasers

	Intermediate consumption		Final consumption	Fixed capital formation	Exports	Total use (Purchaser's price)
	Other industries	VAT-exempted industries				
	..	…	…	…		
	..	…	…	…		
Total intermediate consumption	..	…	…	…		200

6.7.4 Derivation of the use table at basic prices

Once all the tables necessary for converting to the basic price basis have been prepared as described above, the use table at basic prices must be derived based on the use table at purchasers' prices. The procedure is as follows: First, the margins and taxes less subsidies on products from the corresponding cells in the distribution margin table, transport margin table, other taxes less subsidies on products table and non-deductible VAT table are subtracted from the amounts in each cell of the use table at purchasers' prices. Next, the total amounts of trade and transport margins by industry and final use are added to the trade services row and transport services row, respectively. The total amounts of taxes less subsidies on products by industry and final use are then recorded in the newly inserted row of taxes less subsidies on products at the bottom of the table. As a result, the amounts in each element in the use table are converted to basic prices, the trade and transport margins are added to the rows of trade and transport services, and the total amount of taxes less subsidies on products are included. Ultimately, the bottom row of the use table at basic prices matches that of the use table at purchasers' prices (See Figure 6.8).

Figure 6.9 summarizes the procedure for converting the use table at purchasers' prices to the use table at basic prices, as discussed in this section. As shown in the figure, the use table at basic prices is derived by subtracting the price adjustment items (i.e., distribution margins, transport margins, other taxes less subsidies on products, and non-deductible VAT) from the use table at purchasers' prices. Then, the domestic use table at basic prices is finally obtained by subtracting the imports use table from the use table at basic prices (this part is explained in the next section).

6.7.5 Separation of the imports use table and domestic use table

Finally, the use table at basic prices can be separated into domestic and imports sectors. The method of separation is to first prepare the **imports use table** and then subtract the amounts in this table from the total use table to derive the **domestic use table**. The imports use table is a table that details how the imported values are used in intermediate and final use by product. The total values of imports by product in this table match the values of the imports column in the supply table. The details of imports by product in the supply table are based on CIF values at basic prices, they can be used without any further price adjustments. In addition, taxes on imported goods are estimated using data from customs and tax authorities. The taxes less subsidies on imported goods can be displayed in a separate row in the imports use table.

The primary purpose of separating the imports use table and the domestic use table is, first, to distinguish the structure in which imported goods and domestic products are distributed and used, and second, to analyze the induced impact on domestic production for each imported goods and domestic products individually by separating them in the input-output table. (See 22.2.2.2 for more details.)

To compile the imports use table, it is necessary to survey the industry-specific intermediate consumption or final use of imported goods and services through the **imports distribution survey**. Imports of goods can be allocated using the importers' information from customs declaration records, but imports of services are not clear where they are used, so a separate survey must be conducted.

Information on which intermediate consumption in a particular industry or final use the imported goods are distributed to can be obtained through a separate imports distribution survey, or to some extent, through the analysis of importers' information in the customs declaration records (such as business registration number, industrial classification) when using administration data. In addition, it is also possible to distribute imported goods into intermediate consumption, final consumption, and fixed capital formation in accordance with the BEC (Broad Economic Categories) classification, following the distribution method of domestic products. Goods can be categorized into **direct imports**, where they are imported for direct use by producers or consumers, and **indirect imports**, where intermediary traders import the goods and resell them to domestic users. Therefore, when analyzing databases on importers in customs statistics, this distinction should be taken into account.

Table 6.25 Formats of the imports table and domestic use table

Imports Use Table (at basic prices)

	Intermediate consumption					Final consumption expenditure			Gross capital formation				Total imports (Basic price)	
	Agriculture	Manufacturing	Electricity, gas	Construction& Services	Total	Households	General government	Total	Fixed capital formation	Changes in inventories	Acquisition of valuables	Total	Goods	Services
Agriculture														
Mining, electricity														
Manufactured														
Construction, services														
Total imports (basic prices)														
Taxes less subsidies on Imports														
Total imports (purchaser's price)														

Domestic Use Table (at basic prices)

	Intermediate consumption					Final consumption expenditure			Gross capital formation				Total (Basic price)	
	Agriculture	Manufacturing	Electricity, gas	Construction& Services	Total	Households	General government	Total	Fixed capital formation	Changes in inventories	Acquisition of valuables	Total	Goods	Services
Agriculture														
Mining, electricity														
Manufactured														
Construction, services														
Total (at basic prices)														
Taxes less subsidies on Domestic products														
Total (purchaser's price)														

Figure 6.9 Conversion procedure from the use table at purchasers' prices to the use table at basic prices

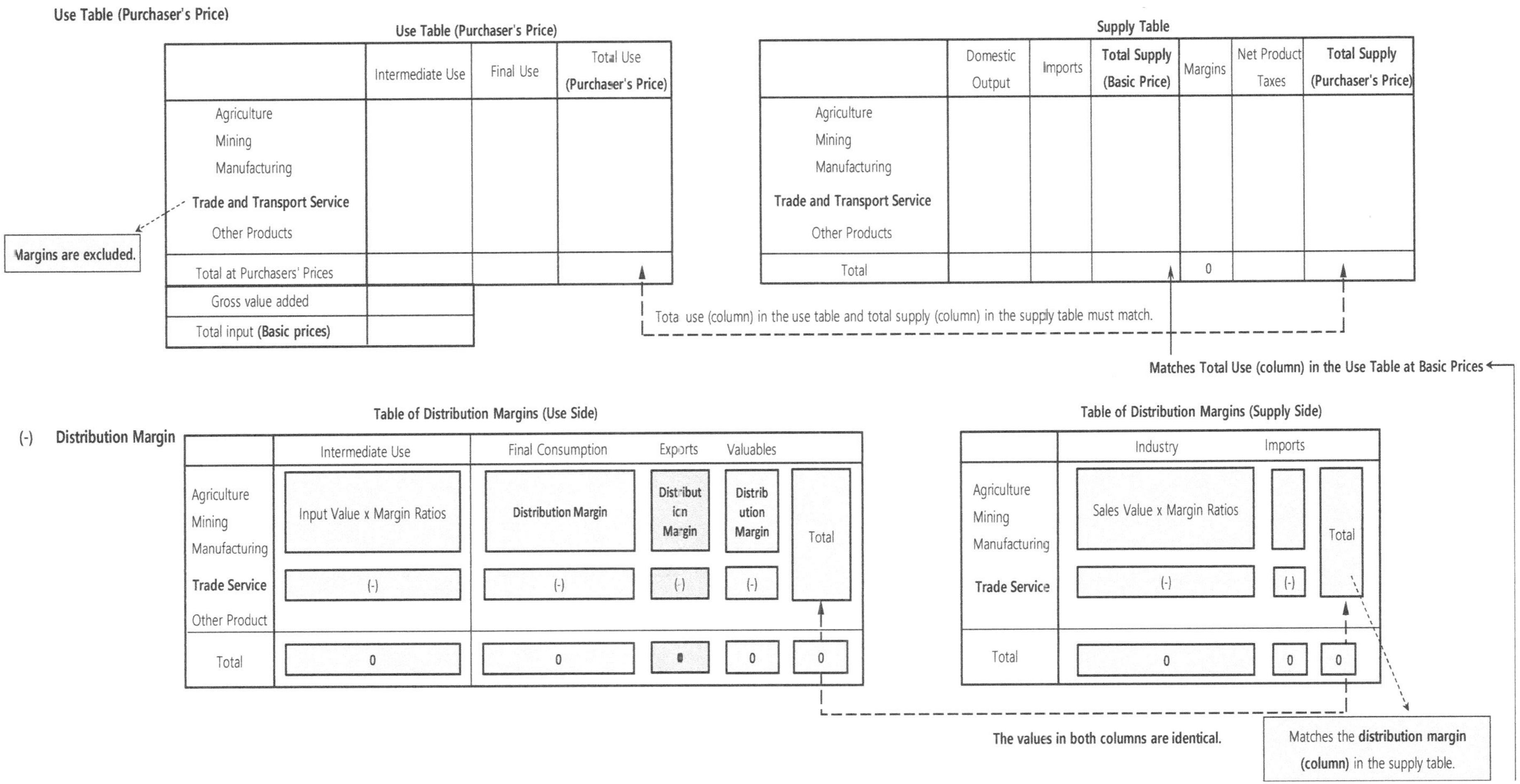

(-) **Transport Margin**

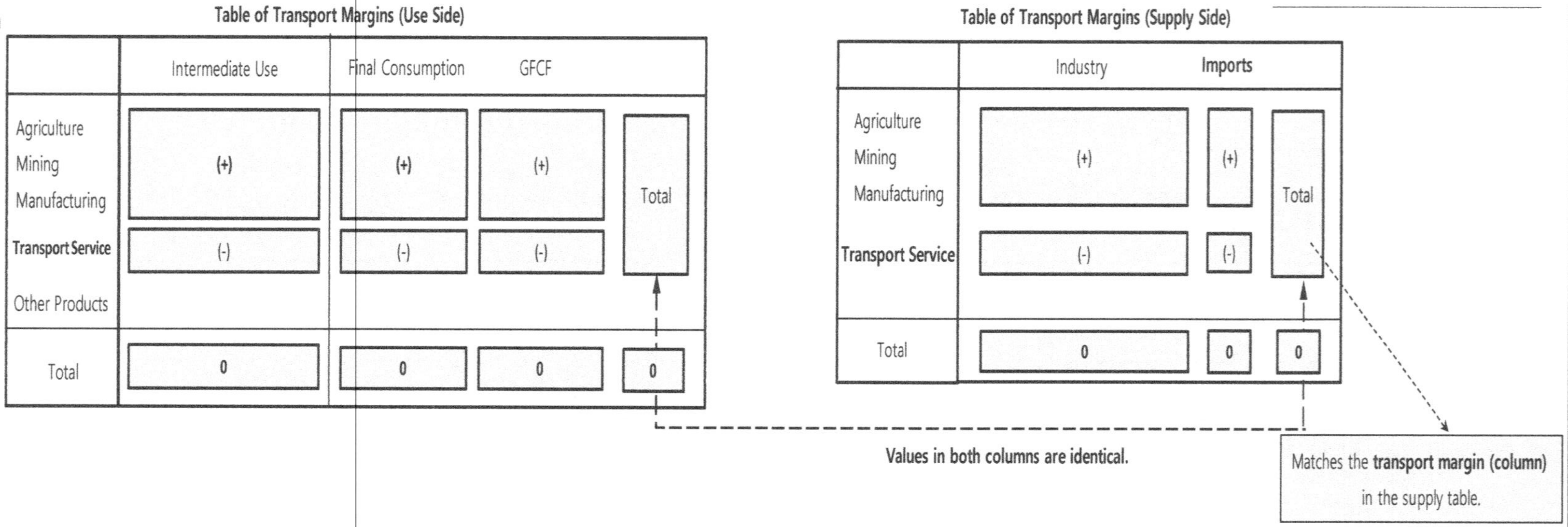

(-) **Taxes Less Subsidies on Products (Including Import Taxes, Excluding Non-deductible VAT)**

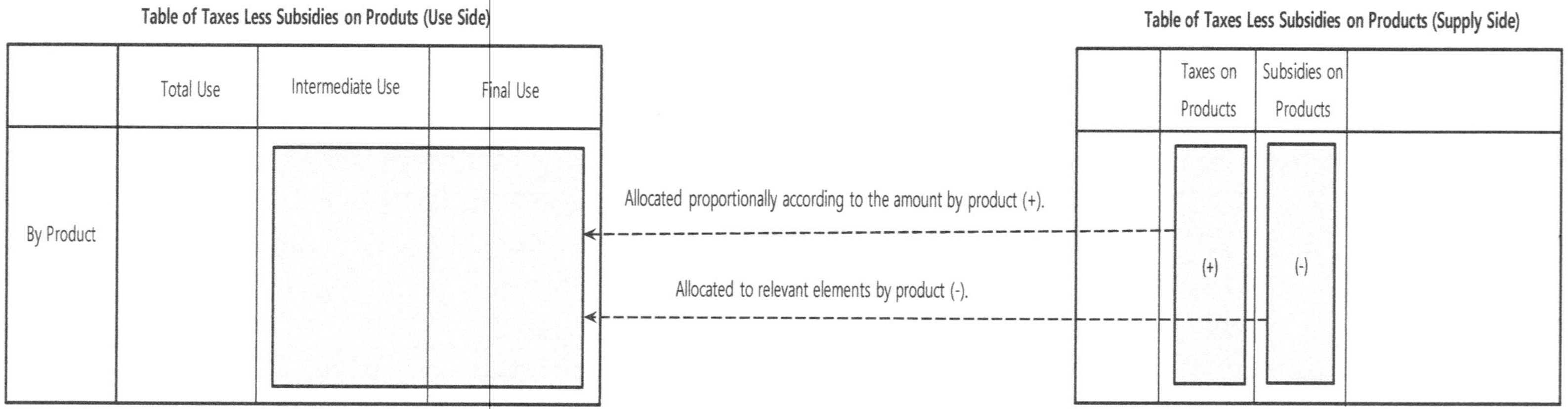

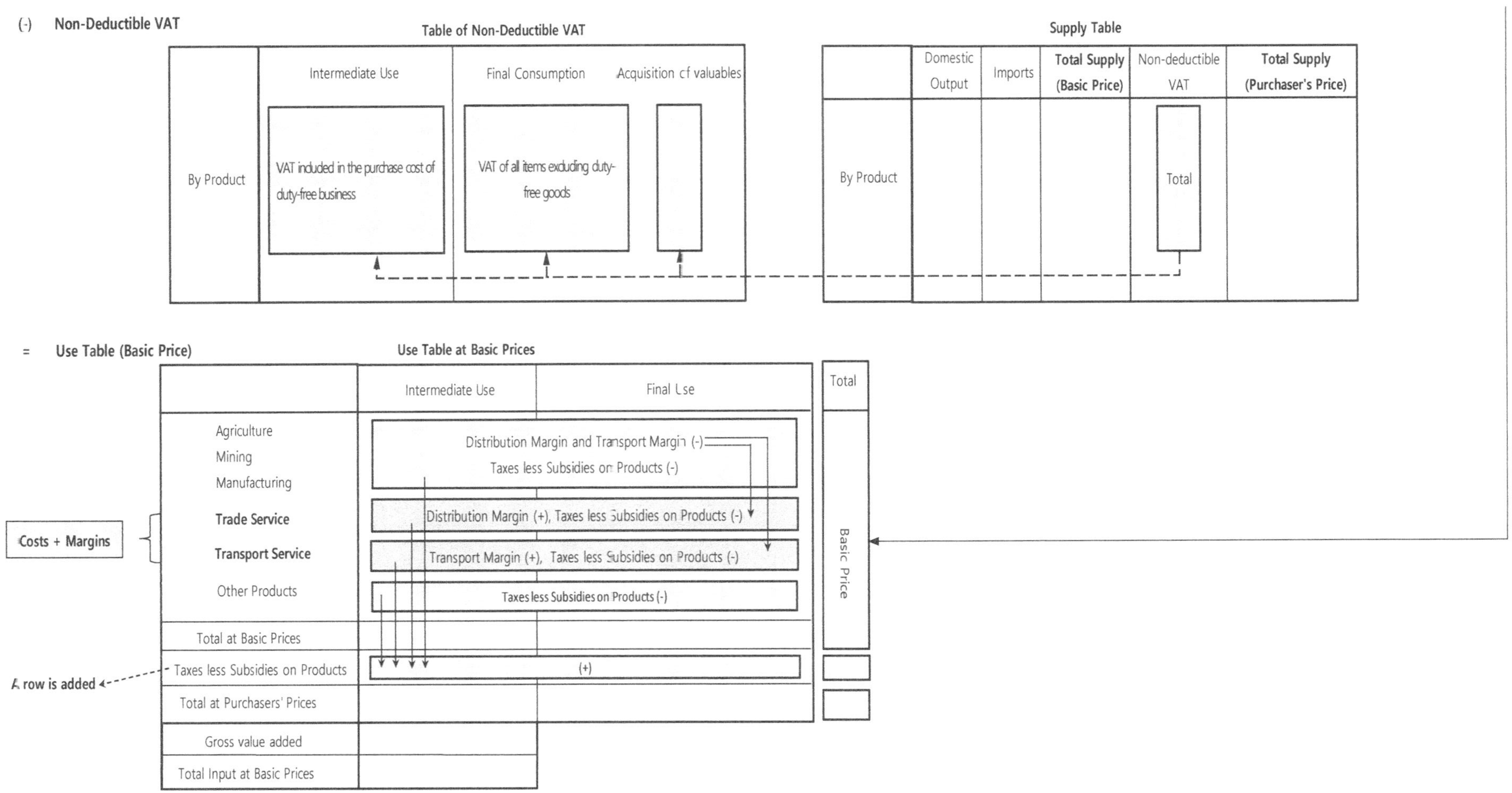
(-) Non-Deductible VAT
Table of Non-Deductible VAT
By Product
Intermediate Use
Final Consumption
Acquisition of valuables
VAT included in the purchase cost of duty-free business
VAT of all items excluding duty-free goods
Supply Table
Domestic Output
Imports
Total Supply (Basic Price)
Non-deductible VAT
Total Supply (Purchaser's Price)
By Product
Total
= Use Table (Basic Price)
Use Table at Basic Prices
Intermediate Use
Final Use
Total
Agriculture
Mining
Manufacturing
Trade Service
Transport Service
Other Products
Costs + Margins
Distribution Margin and Transport Margin (-)
Taxes less Subsidies on Products (-)
Distribution Margin (+), Taxes less Subsidies on Products (-)
Transport Margin (+), Taxes less Subsidies on Products (-)
Taxes less Subsidies on Products (-)
Basic Price
Total at Basic Prices
Taxes less Subsidies on Products
(+)
A row is added
Total at Purchasers' Prices
Gross value added
Total Input at Basic Prices

(-) **Import Use Table (Basic Price)**

Import Use Table at Basic Prices

	Intermediate Use (Basic Price)	Final use (Basic price)			Total Imports (CIF)
		FC	GCF	Exports	
By Products					
Total imports (Basic price)					
Taxes less subsidies on Imports					
Total Imports (Purchaser's price)					

= **Domestic Use Table (Basic Price)**

Domestic Use Table at Basic Prices

	Intermediate Use	Final Use	Total
Agricultral Products Manufactured Products Other Products			Basic Price
Total Domestic products (Basic Price)			
Taxes less subsidies on Domestic products			
Total Domestic products (Purchaser's price)			

6.8 Calculation of GDP using the use table

Using the use table, GDP can be derived according the production approach, expenditure approach, and income approach mentioned earlier. Table 6.26 summarizes the supply table and use table (converted to basic prices) of South Korea discussed in sections 4.6 and 5.6. Table 6.27 illustrates an example of how to derive GDP using the use table of South Korea (year 2015) under the three approaches.

In this table, the production approach yields GDP by subtracting intermediate consumption at purchasers' prices from output at basic prices and adding total taxes less subsidies on products. Under the expenditure approach, GDP is derived by adding final consumption, gross capital formation and exports, and subtracting imports. In the income approach, GDP is derived by summing remuneration of employees, other taxes less subsidies on production, and gross operating surplus and gross mixed income to obtain gross value added, and then adding the total taxes less subsidies on products. The GDP values obtained by these three approaches should be consistent.

Table 6.26 Supply and use tables (summary table, South Korea, 2015)

(Unit: KRW trillion)

Supply table

	By industry	Total domestic output (Basic price)	Imports (Basic price)	Total supply (Basic price)	Taxes less subsidies on products	Distribution margins	Transport margin	Total price adjustment	Total supply (Purchasers)
By product	...	...	...	...	...	...	...	...	...
Total output	...	3,717.0	603.4	4,320.5	137.1	0.0	0.0	137.1	4,457.6

(Unit: KRW trillion)

Use table (at basic prices)

	By industry	Total intermediate consumption	Private consumption	Government consumption	Gross fixed capital formation	Changes in inventories	Acquisitions less disposals of valuables	Exports	Total final use	Total use at basic prices
By product	...	...	...	...	...	...	...	...	...	...
Intermediate input at basic prices		2,149.9	749.6	250.1	445.7	6.4	1.8	717.0	2,170.5	4,320.5
Taxes less subsidies on products		46.2	55.2	0.0	35.3	0.3	0.1	0.0	91.0	137.1
Intermediate input at purchasers' prices	...	2,196.1	804.8	250.1	481.0	6.7	1.9	717.0	2,261.5	4,457.6

Remuneration of employees	…	750.2
Net operating surplus	…	441.5
Depreciation	…	309.7
Net other taxes on production	…	19.6
Gross value added	…	1,520.9
Total input at basic prices	…	3,717.0

Table 6.27 Three approaches to GDP

(Unit: KRW trillion)

Production approach		Income approach		Expenditure approach	
Output (basic price)	3,717.0	Remuneration of employees	750.2	Private consumption	804.8
– Intermediate consumption	-2,196.1	+ Net operating surplus	441.5	+ Government consumption	250.1
= Gross value added	1,520.9	+ Depreciation	309.7	+ Gross fixed capital formation	481.0
+ Taxes less subsidies on products	137.1	+ Net other taxes on production	19.6	+ Changes in inventories	6.7
= GDP	1,658.0	= Gross value added	1,520.9	+ Net acquisition of valuables	1.9
		+ Taxes less subsidies on products	137.1	+ Exports	717.0
		= GDP	1,658.0	= Final use (purchaser's price)	2,261.5
				– Imports (basic price)	-603.4
				= GDP	1,658.0

Chapter 7. Classification of industry and institutional sector

The production-side data required to compile the supply and use tables discussed above are primarily relied on data collected from **production units**, such as output, intermediate consumption (materials and supplies), and remuneration of employees (wages and salaries). In contrast, the expenditure-side data, such as final consumption expenditure and gross fixed capital formation are based on data collected mostly from **institutional units** that represent economic agents, such as households, government, and corporations. In addition to traditional classification of outputs by industry, the national accounts also require that output be categorized into market producers, non-market producers, and own-account producers, depending on whether market prices exist for the output.

The supply and use tables adopt all three of the classification categories mentioned above (see Figure 7.1). For example, domestic products and intermediate consumption are categorized by industry and by market production status (market or non-market production), while final consumption and fixed capital formation are classified by institutional sectors. However, compared to the mixed classification criteria, the basic data required to prepare these tables are collected from different sources, necessitating the work of linking these classification categories. In other words, it is necessary to first classify the production data by industry and market production status, while simultaneously aligning the industry and institutional sector classifications to organize the data. Nevertheless, if the characteristics of the units for data collection are different, it becomes challenging to maintain the consistency of the data.

Figure 7.1 Links between types of economic units

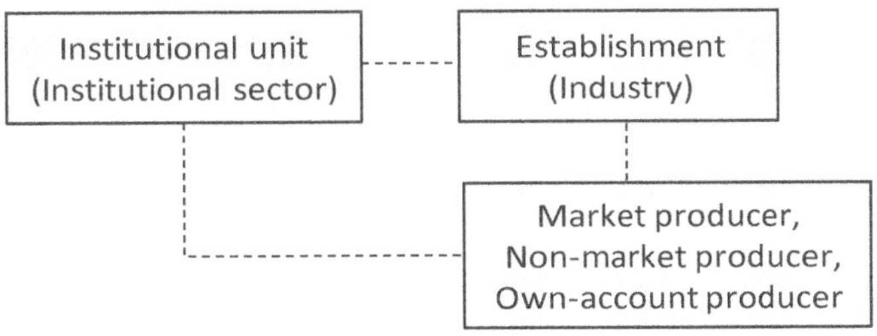

Production-side data are primarily collected at the establishment level, which focuses mainly on production activities (a broader classification is by industry), but data encompassing on all economic activities, including production, consumption, investment, and saving are ultimately collected at the institutional unit level (a broader classification is by institutional sector). Therefore, in order to measure all economic activities, including not only production but also consumption expenditures, financial transactions, and capital accumulation, it is necessary to prepare **accounts by institutional sector**. For this reason, the output, intermediate consumption, and value-added by industry derived from the supply and use tables must also be prepared by institutional sector so that the accounts can encompass not only production activities but also other economic activities. To reclassify the industry-specific production data by institutional sector, it is necessary to create a **cross-classification table by industry and institutional sector**, which serves as a bridge table. This chapter will explore the process of matching industry-specific production data with institutional sectors to prepare the production data by institutional sector. To do this, it is essential to first understand the characteristics of industries and institutional sectors.

7.1 Establishment as a production unit, and industry

The most fundamental data for measuring economic activity in national accounts is the production-side data, which are collected from production units such as corporations, government, non-profit institutions, and household unincorporated enterprises. An enterprise as a production unit operates single or multiple **establishments** and engages in the production of **primary products** as the main purpose of the enterprise, as well as the production of secondary products. In addition, there may be establishments within the enterprise that do not directly produce marketable products, but support production activities, such as those engaged in marketing, accounting, and human resources management, etc. These establishments (usually headquarters) provide auxiliary support for the production activities of other establishments.

An establishment is the most basic unit for collecting production-side data, and is grouped into **industry** according to the similarity of the production activities performed by this establishment. The types of production activities are specified in detail in the *International Standard Industrial Classification* (ISIC), which is an international classification standard set by the United Nations. Each country adopts its own classification system based on the ISIC to suit its specific economic structure and needs.

In the SNA, the industrial classification is only applied to the production account and the generation of earned income account among the sequence of economic accounts, which will be explained later. In other words, output, intermediate consumption, gross value added, and the components of gross value added (such as remuneration of employees, operating surplus and mixed income, and other taxes on production) are measured by industry and recorded in these two accounts only.

7.2 Institutional unit and institutional sector

While the classification of establishments and industries is limited to production activities, economic activities within an economic territory encompass not only production but also expenditure, final transactions, and capital transactions, and a broad range of other activities. Given the limitations of using this classification system to measure all such activities, the SNA has introduced the concepts of 'institutional units' and 'institutional sectors' to capture the entities responsible for performing these economic activities.

An **Institutional unit** refers to an entity that can make autonomous decisions and engage in economic activities, such as a household, corporation, and government. According to the SNA, an institutional unit is defined as "an economic entity that is capable, in its own right, of owning assets, incurring liabilities and engaging in economic activities and in transactions with other entities." The concept of the institutional unit extends beyond economic units engaged solely in production activities, providing a means to measure all economic activities. An institutional unit has the following attributes (BPM6 4.13):

1) It is entitled to own goods and assets in its own right, and therefore, is able to exchange the ownership of goods or assets in transactions with other institutional units.
2) It is able to take economic decisions and engage in economic activities for which it is directly responsible and accountable at law.
3) It is able to incur liabilities on its own behalf, to take on other obligations or future commitments, and enter into contracts.
4) A complete set of accounts, including a balance sheet, exists for the unit, or it must be possible, from both an economic and legal viewpoint, to compile a complete set of accounts if required.

Institutional units are primarily classified into households and non-households for economic activities, with non-households referring to **legal** or **social entities** rather than natural persons. Non-household institutional units include corporations, government, and non-profit institutions (NPIs). Moreover, institutional units are further categorized as residents or non-residents based on their **residence**, which is determined by whether their predominant economic interest is in the country or abroad. Non-residents are classified as the rest of the world sector, not the domestic economic sector.

Figure 7.2 Classification of institutional units

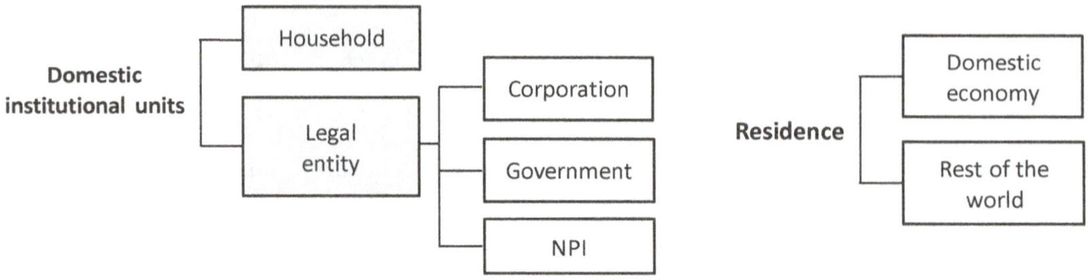

The **institutional sector** is a concept that groups institutional units at a higher level. In the SNA, the domestic economy is broadly classified into five sectors: non-financial corporations, financial corporations, general government, non-profit institutions serving households (NPISHs), and households. In addition, the rest of the world sector is established to handle the transactions with foreign countries. The classification by institutional sector is applied across all accounts in the SNA, including the production account, income accounts, financial account, capital account, other changes in assets account, and balance sheet. The accounts that encompass all these accounts by institutional sector are referred to as the **sequence of economic accounts**. (See Chapter 8 for details.)

7.3 Classification of domestic institutional sectors

In this section, we will briefly examine the characteristics of the domestic institutional sectors, including corporations, government, non-profit institutions (NPIs), unincorporated enterprises and quasi-corporations, households, and the public sector.

7.3.1 Corporation

First, a **corporation** is an enterprise that is legally registered and engages in market production activities, while not participating in final consumption activities. A corporation is a legal entity separate from its owners, and the profits generated from its economic activities can be distributed to the owners. Corporations primarily include legally constituted corporations, and the concept extends beyond its legal definition to include cooperatives, limited liability partnerships, quasi-corporations, and notional resident units within the corporations. In addition, as will be discussed later, *non-profit institutions (NPIs) that engage in market production activities* are also included in the category of corporations for the convenience of classification.

Corporations are divided into for-profit and non-profit entities based on their purpose, and further subdivided into public corporations, private corporations, and foreign-controlled corporations according to the type of ownership structure. Foreign-controlled corporations include subsidiaries owned by foreign companies (with foreign ownership exceeding 50%), branches of foreign companies (with foreign ownership of 100%), and associates effectively controlled by foreign companies (with foreign ownership between 10% and 50%).

Figure 7.3 Classification of corporations by type

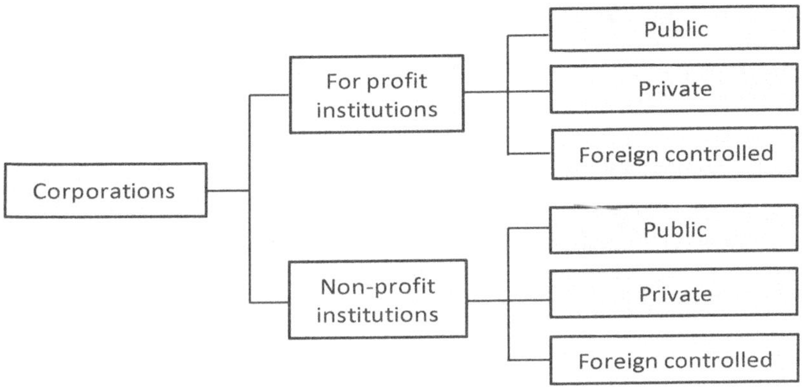

Corporations are classified into **non-financial corporations** which produce goods and non-financial services in the market, and **financial corporations** which produce financial services such as financial intermediation, insurance, and pensions. The definition of non-financial corporations is straightforward, and in practice, it refers to all corporations excluding financial corporations. The scope of financial corporations includes central bank, deposit-taking corporations, other financial intermediaries, investment funds, financial auxiliaries, insurance corporations, and pension funds (financial institutions that manage pensions such as retirement pensions).

The central bank is an institution responsible for overseeing a country's financial system and implementing various market operations in relation to currency and financial intermediation policies. Deposit-taking corporations and other financial intermediaries are entities mainly in charge of financial intermediation through deposits and loans, and also provide other financial services. Investment funds are financial entities that raise funds from unspecified investors in the form of shares, and invest them in short and long-term financial instruments or non-financial assets, and redistribute the profits to the investors. Financial auxiliaries are corporations whose primary function is to provide services that facilitate financial transactions, without acquiring ownership of financial assets being traded. This category includes units engaged in financial transaction intermediation, brokerage, and advisory services (e.g., securities brokers, insurance brokers), entities involved in the issuance, underwriting, and guaranteeing of securities, financial market infrastructure institutions (such as securities depositories), and financial transaction platforms (e.g., foreign exchange brokers, securities exchanges, and exchanges for crypto assets with a corresponding liability). Financial supervisory authorities are also included when they exist as separate institutional units. Insurance corporations are categorized into three categories: life insurance, non-life insurance (e.g., fire insurance, casualty insurance etc.) and reinsurance. **Pension funds** are social insurance organizations in which government or employers directly manage pensions on behalf of their employees, or entrust the management and payment of pensions outside. In the case of government, this includes the civil servant pension funds or military pension funds, while in the case of private pension funds, such as defined contribution (DC) and defined benefit (DB) pension funds, it includes the retirement pensions department of financial institutions.

7.3.2 General government

General government holds legislative, judicial, and executive powers and has the authority to collect taxes. This includes the authority to collect 'taxes on production and imports' as a value-added item, as well as current and capital taxes related to transfer transactions. Types of government include not only central government, local government, and social security funds but also non-profit institutions controlled by government. The criteria in the SNA for determining whether non-profit institutions are controlled by government include the following: the authority to appoint executives, approve budgets and statues, and provide financial support. In practice, it can be determined by whether the institution is controlled by the government (through control over decision-making and over 50% of budget support) and whether it engages in the sale of non-market products (either free or at economically insignificant prices).

7.3.3 Non-profit institution

Non-profit institutions are legal entities constituted in accordance with legal procedures, and they cannot distribute the profits accrued from their production activities to the members of the institution; instead, the profits must be retained within the institution. The types of non-profit institutions are listed in Table 7.1.

Table 7.1 Types of non-profit institutions

	Type	Example
1	Non-profit service providers	Hospitals, higher education institutions, day-care centers, schools, social service providers, environmental groups.
2	Non-governmental organizations (NGO)	Organizations for economic development and poverty reduction in less developed countries.
3	Arts and culture organizations	Museums, performing arts centers, orchestras, libraries.
4	Sports clubs	Amateur sports training, physical fitness.

	Type	Example
5	Advocacy groups	Groups to improve civil rights and social and political interests of constituencies.
6	Foundations	Organizations that donate to other organizations or perform specific activities using assets or income accrued from donated assets.
7	Community-based or grass-roots associations	Associations that are member-based and offer services to members of a particular community or area.
8	Political parties	Organizations formed to realize a specific political ideology and gain political power.
9	Social clubs	Organizations established to provide recreational services to individual members and communities.
10	Unions, business and professional associations	Associations that promote labor, business and professional interests.
11	Religious congregations	Religious institutions (excluding institutions affiliated with official national organizations and maintained by taxes).

* Note: Quoted from the 2025 SNA, paragraph 31.18

Non-profit institutions are primarily engaged in non-market production activities, but they can also participate in market production activities. Examples of non-profit institutions that engage in market production activities and offer their products at "economically significant prices" include medical institutions and private schools. In addition, "non-profit institutions serving enterprises" (e.g., chambers of commerce) are operated by receiving membership dues (subscriptions) or contributions from a group of related businesses; however, these dues are treated as payments for services rendered, rather than current transfers. These institutions engaged in market activities are classified as corporations in the SNA. Non-profit institutions under government control are classified as the government sector, as mentioned above. However, non-profit institutions that are not controlled by the government and provide their output at economically insignificant prices are classified as **non-profit institutions serving households** (**NPISHs**); the national accounts treats these institutions as separate and distinct institutional units (or institutional sector).

Figure 7.4 Institutional sectoring of non-profit institutions

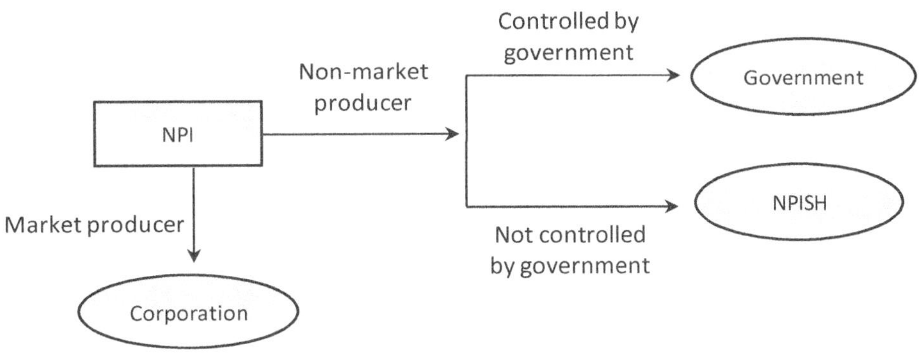

7.3.4 Unincorporated enterprise and quasi-corporation

Unincorporated enterprises refer to enterprises that engage in production activities without being legally incorporated. They include all enterprises that are not registered as corporations, regardless of whether they are registered with the national tax authorities. They can be divided into two categories: **quasi-corporations** which function similarly to corporations, and **household unincorporated enterprises** which are small-scale enterprises operated by households. Quasi-corporations can be further divided into two types: resident-owned enterprises that operate like corporations while maintaining a complete set of accounts, and unincorporated enterprises owned by non-residents that engage in long-term production activities within an economy such as branches.

In the first case, there can be **government-owned unincorporated enterprises** and **privately-owned unincorporated enterprises**. An example of government-owned unincorporated enterprises is the Corporate Special Accounts of the central government and local government, which though not in corporations form, have an independent and complete set of accounts and engage in market activities. This type of enterprise is not a public corporation, but does participate in market activities.

The criteria for classifying privately-owned unincorporated enterprises as quasi-corporations are, in practice, difficult to apply, as the distinction between these enterprises as quasi-corporation and small-scale household unincorporated enterprises as household sector is ambiguous. Nevertheless, privately-owned unincorporated enterprise may be classified as a quasi-corporation if they maintain double-entry bookkeeping and prepares a complete set of accounts. The criterion for classifying an unincorporated enterprise as a quasi-corporation is not determined by the size of the enterprise, but by whether the owner of the enterprise and the accounting entity can be distinguished. In other words, if the enterprise has a complete set of accounts, including balance sheet, it can be treated as a quasi-corporation separate from its owner. A **branch**, by definition, is not a legal entity, but it is exceptionally treated as a quasi-corporation because it is considered a resident performing continuous economic activities in the resident's economy for an extended period. As mentioned earlier, quasi-corporations are classified as corporations in terms of the institutional sectoring.

Figure 7.5 Classification of quasi-corporations

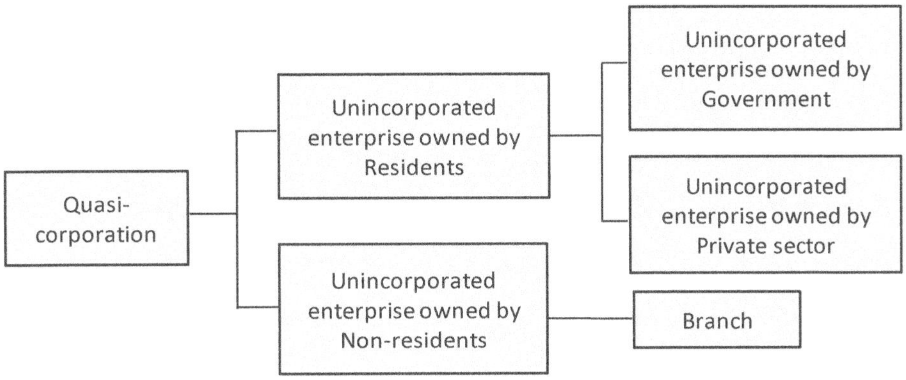

On the other hand, it may happen that the legal owner of real estate (e.g., land including its associated buildings and structures, and natural resources) is a non-resident unit. However, The SNA does not recognize the ownership of domestic real estate by non-resident units. Instead, for statistical purposes, a **notional resident unit** is created, and the legal owner of the real estate, being a non-resident, is deemed to acquire an ownership equity (recorded as a financial asset of the non-resident) from the notional resident unit. Thus, all purchases and sales of land and natural resources normally take place between residents units. The only exception is when the boundaries of the economic territory itself are changed (e.g., when a foreign government or international organization purchases or sells real estate to establish or close its embassy or office), such transactions are excluded from this treatment.

The notional resident unit, like the branch, does not meet the criteria for being an institutional unit, but is exceptionally treated as an institutional unit. The notional resident unit is classified as a corporation (which includes a quasi-corporation) in the institutional sectoring. However, the industry classification is determined by the activities performed by this unit, and for example, if it is engaged in the rental of buildings, it is classified under real estate services.

7.3.5 Household

In the SNA, households are defined as groups of persons who share the same living accommodation, pool some or all of their income and wealth, and collectively consume certain types of goods and services, mainly housing and food. From the perspective of the national accounts, households function as institutional units that are final consumers, producers, and income recipients.

Households are the key actors in final consumption expenditure, accounting for the largest share of such expenditure. Since the expenditure data in the national accounts primarily rely on administrative income data, the details of comprehensive consumption expenditures are not easily accessible, most countries collect data through household consumption expenditure surveys.

In addition, households also function as producers in the institutional sectoring, with household unincorporated enterprises falling under this category. **Household unincorporated enterprises** are unincorporated enterprises engaged in market production by households. They include typically small-scale enterprises that do not prepare financial statements, as well as those producing owner-occupied dwelling services, and producers of paid domestic services. Household unincorporated enterprises are classified as households in the institutional sectoring. Thus, in the SNA, the scope of households includes not only their role as consumers within the institutional sector but also their function as producers.

In the SNA, Households, like other institutional units, are income recipients. When classifying households by their income sources, they are divided into four categories: owners of household unincorporated enterprises with paid employees, owners of household unincorporated enterprises without paid employees (referred to as **own-account workers**), employees, and recipients of property income and transfer income.

The types and examples of the institutional sector classifications so far can be summarized in the following table.

Table 7.2 Institutional sectoring by type

Institutional sector	Description	Type	Example	Institutional sectoring
Corporation	1) A legal entity separate from its owner, providing profits to the owner. 2) Engaged in market production.		Corporation, cooperative, limited liability partnership, quasi-corporation, notional resident unit.	Corporation
Government	Holds public power and the authority to collect taxes.		Central and local government, social security funds, government-controlled NPI.	Government
NPI	No profit sharing	Government-controlled NPI		Government
		NPIs that provide products at economically significant prices.	Medical institution, private school, NPI serving corporations (ex.: chamber of commerce).	Corporation
		Others (not under government control, providing products at economically insignificant prices)		NPISH
Unincorporated enterprise	Quasi-corporations	A resident-owned enterprise that keeps a complete set of accounts and operates like a separate corporation.	Government-owned unincorporated enterprise.	Corporation
			Privately-owned unincorporated enterprise.	
		An unincorporated enterprise that is owned by a non-resident	Branch	

Institutional sector	Description	Type	Example	Institutional sectoring
		and engages in long-term, substantial -scale production within an economy.		
		Notional resident unit		
	Household unincorporated enterprises		Household unincorporated enterprise	Household
			Owner-occupied housing services	
			Paid domestic services	
Household		Subdivision by the source of income	Employer (Owner of household unincorporated enterprise with paid employees.	Household
			Own-account worker	
			Employee	
			Recipients of property income and transfer income.	

7.3.6 Scope and classification of public sector

In the SNA, the **public sector** refers to the sector under the control or supervision of the government, and its scope does not distinguish between market producers and non-market producers. The classification of the public sector is important because there is an increasing demand for data on the public fiscal activities of an economy, which affects not only the government sector in a narrow sense but also the economic activities of public enterprises under the government control. As a result, comprehensive economic indicators covering government-controlled public enterprises as well as government are required for the formulation of public policies.

The classification criteria of the public sector in the SNA are determined by whether the unit is under the control of government. The indicators for determining government controls are listed in the 2025 SNA, paragraphs 5.115–5.119. (These include the ownership of the majority of voting interest, control of the board or other governing body, control of the appointment and removal of key personnel, control of key committees of the entity, holding golden shares and options, regulation and control, control by a dominant customer, and control attached to borrowing from the government.) Units that are controlled by government and act as market producers are classified as *public corporations*, whereas those controlled by government and acting as non-market producers are classified as general government. However, all these units are categorized under the public sector.

7.4 Correspondence between institutional sectors and industries

The supply and use tables are based on the data of industries and products, while the sequence of economic accounts which is the final stage of national accounts, is composed of the data by institutional sectors. In order to reclassify the industry-specific data of the supply and use tables into that of the sequence of economic accounts by institutional sectors, it is necessary to first align the industries with the corresponding institutional sectors. In addition, producers are categorized as market producers, non-market producers and producers of own final use, depending on whether they engage in market sales. Therefore, all of these must be taken into account and matched with the corresponding institutional sectors. The specific details will be introduced in turn, but the basic classifications are as follows:

In the institutional sectoring, the non-financial corporations sector includes all market industries except for those in the financial corporations, regardless of whether the enterprise is a corporation or a quasi-corporation. Non-profit institutions that engage in market production (e.g., education, healthcare, social services, arts) are also classified under the non-financial corporations. The financial corporations sector is relatively straightforward, and includes all corporations and quasi-corporations in the financial and insurance industries. The general government sector includes all non-market activities performed by the government, such as public administration, defense, social protection, public education and healthcare, social services activities in the industrial classification. It also includes non-profit institutions controlled and financed by government. The NPISHs sector corresponds to all non-profit institutions, excluding market NPIs classified as corporations and NPIs controlled by government. Finally, the households sector includes all industries participating in market production except for corporations and quasi-corporations, as well as the owner-occupied dwelling service industry, paid domestic services, and production for own consumption by agricultural households.

For the intermediate stage of using data to match industrial data to institutional sectors, the institutional unit data are most suitable. The government, financial corporations, NPISHs, and households sectors rely heavily on the data from institutional units. The non-financial corporations sector has traditionally used establishment-based censuses and surveys, but recently, with the increasing access to institutional unit-based information through administrative data (e.g., from the national tax authorities, financial supervisory authorities, etc.), collecting data based on administrative records has become more efficient or a complementary method. The table below outlines the criteria for classifying institutional sectors based on the institutional unit data discussed earlier.

Table 7.3 Correspondence between institutional sectors and institutional units

Institutional sector	Institutional unit
Non-financial corporations	Corporations engaged in market production activities (excluding financial and insurance corporations)
	Quasi-corporations engaged in market production activities (excluding financial and insurance corporations)
	NPIs engaged in market production activities (education, medical care, social welfare business, etc.)
Financial corporations	Corporations engaged in the financial and insurance businesses
	Quasi-corporations engaged in the financial and insurance businesses
	NPIs engaged in the financial and insurance businesses
General government	Non-market industries of government that engage in public administration, national defense, social protection, education, medical care, social work, and other social service activities
	NPIs controlled by government
NPISHs	NPIs engaged in non-market production, and not controlled by government (education, medical care, social welfare, etc.)
Households	Household unincorporated enterprises engaged in market production activities
	Own account industries (i.e., owner-occupied dwelling services, own-account production of farmers, paid domestic services)

7.5 Procedure for classifying the data of production unit into that of institutional sector

This section will provide a detailed explanation of the procedure for converting establishment or industry data into institutional sector data. In order to convert the data from establishments (or industries), which are the basic units of production, into the institutional sector data, several economic classifications must be considered, in addition to industrial classification of production units and the marketability of the output. First, the institutional sectoring of a production unit may vary depending on whether it belongs to a private or a public producer, whether it is a corporation or an unincorporated enterprise, and in the case of a non-profit institution, whether it provides services to corporations, households, or government. For example, if the unit is a private producer, it will belong to either households, corporations, or NPISHs sector, while if it is a public producer, it will be classified under government or corporations sector.

For private producers, the first step is to classify them as households or non-households sector, depending on whether they are unincorporated enterprises or corporations (including quasi-corporations). This classification can be judged by checking whether business financial statements are provided in statistical surveys or administrative statistics (e.g., business financial statements data from the National Tax Service). In addition, the owner-occupied dwelling service industry, whose output is intended for its own final use, is classified as household unincorporated enterprises. Private producers other than households are divided into corporations and NPISHs, but the distinction between these two institutional sectors needs to be more carefully examined, as non-profit institutions (NPIs) include both market and non-market producers.

The importance of non-profit institutions is increasing in terms of their share as well as economic analysis, therefore, the United Nations has also published a classification manual for NPIs. NPIs were often classified as "private sector" without being separated from the households sector in the past, but now they tend to be classified as an independent institutional sector.

Table 7.4 Criteria for the stepwise application of institutional sectoring

<table>
<tr><th>Private/ public</th><th>Corporation/ Unincorporated</th><th>Industrial classification</th><th>NPI status</th><th>Market/ Non-market 2)</th><th>Institutional sectoring</th></tr>
<tr><td rowspan="8">Private producer</td><td rowspan="2">Household unincorporated enterprise</td><td rowspan="2">All industries</td><td rowspan="2"></td><td>For own final use</td><td rowspan="2">Household</td></tr>
<tr><td>Market producer</td></tr>
<tr><td rowspan="6">Corporation (including quasi-corporation)</td><td rowspan="5">Q, R, S, T 1)</td><td>NPIs serving corporations</td><td>Market producer</td><td>Corporation</td></tr>
<tr><td>NPI serving household</td><td>Non-market producer</td><td>NPISH</td></tr>
<tr><td rowspan="2">Other NPI</td><td>Market producer</td><td>Corporation</td></tr>
<tr><td>Non-market producer</td><td>NPISH</td></tr>
<tr><td>Corporation other than NPI</td><td>Market producer</td><td>Corporation</td></tr>
<tr><td>Industries other than Q, R, S, T</td><td></td><td>Market producer</td><td>Corporation</td></tr>
<tr><td rowspan="3">Public producer</td><td rowspan="3"></td><td>All industries</td><td></td><td>Market producer</td><td>Corporation</td></tr>
<tr><td></td><td>Government-controlled NPI</td><td>Non-market producer</td><td>Government</td></tr>
<tr><td>Public administration services (P)</td><td></td><td>Non-market producer</td><td>Government</td></tr>
</table>

Footnote: 1) ISIC section categories: Q (Education), R (Human health and social work activities), S (Arts, entertainment, and recreation), T (Other service activities).

2) Market producer: cost recovery ratio (= sales / production cost) ≥ 50%. Non-market producer: cost recovery ratio < 50%.

In the case of NPIs, separate surveys are required to determine whether they should be classified as corporations, government-controlled NPIs in the government sector, or NPISHs. NPIs that provide services to businesses are classified as market producers and fall under corporations sector. A typical example is "Activities of business, employers and professional membership organizations" in the industrial classification (ISIC: S 941). NPIs that are controlled by government and are non-market producers are classified into the government sector. NPIs providing goods and services to households are classified as **non-profit institutions serving households** (**NPISHs**) if they provide the products free or at an economically insignificant price (= sales < cost x 0.5). This includes not only typical NPISHs but also entities in the social services (P, Q, and R sections in the ISIC classification) with a cost recovery ratio below 0.5. Specifically, this includes non-market producers in the following industries: trade unions (S 942) and other membership organizations (S 949) in the 3-digit levels of ISIC, and education (P), human health and social work (Q), arts, entertainments, and recreation (R) in the sections of ISIC. On the other hand, if non-profit institutions engaged in the P, Q, or R industries sell their products at economically significant prices (= sales ≥ cost x 0.5), they should be classified as market producers and as corporations. For example, profit-seeking hospitals and private schools in the form of non-profit institutions are included in this category.

Table 7.5 Institutional sectoring of non-profit institutions

<table>
<tr><th>Type</th><th>Market/ Non-market</th><th>Institutional sectoring</th><th>Examples of industry</th></tr>
<tr><td>NPIs serving businesses</td><td>Market producer</td><td>Corporations</td><td>Business and employers' membership organizations (ISIC: S 941)</td></tr>
<tr><td>Government controlled NPIs</td><td>Non-market producer</td><td>Government</td><td></td></tr>
<tr><td rowspan="4">NPIs providing goods and services to households</td><td>Market producer</td><td>Corporations</td><td>Market producers in P, Q, and R industries</td></tr>
<tr><td rowspan="3">Non-market producer</td><td rowspan="3">NPISHs</td><td>Non-market producers in P, Q, and R industries</td></tr>
<tr><td>Trade unions (ISIC: S 942)</td></tr>
<tr><td>Other membership organizations (ISIC: S 949)</td></tr>
</table>

Public producers are classified as a corporation when they are public corporations controlled (governed) by government. To be classified as a **public corporation**, two conditions must be met: it must be under government control, and be a corporation that engages in market production activities. **Government control** is defined as the government holding a majority of voting rights, controlling the board of directors, or appointing key personnel. As for market producers, as mentioned above, the cost recovery ratio (=sales/production cost) must be 0.5 or higher.

7.6 Cross-classification by industry and institutional sector

In order to convert the production-side data in the supply and use tables (such as industry-specific output, intermediate consumption, and value added) into data by institutional sector for the compilation of the sequence of economic accounts, it is necessary to classify them using the correspondence table between industries and institutional sectors described above. To convert industry-specific production data into the institutional sector data, a **cross-classification table by industries and institutional sectors** (**CCIS**) can be created with industries in the columns and institutional sectors in the rows, acting as a bridge table.

The cross-classification table by industries and institutional sectors takes the format of Table 7.6, and this table is used to construct the production account and the generation of earned income account by institutional sectors in the sequence of economic accounts (which will be described later). In this table, the detailed amounts for output, intermediate consumption, and value-added are displayed by industries and institutional sectors. When output is expressed at basic prices, value-added is also shown at basic prices, and therefore, taxes less subsidies on products are excluded.

That is, the value-added items include remuneration of employees, operating surplus (with 'mixed income' allocated to the households sector), and other taxes less subsidies on production.

Table 7.6 Cross-classification table by industries and institutional sectors

(Unit: KRW billion)

	By institutional sectors	By industries												Total
	Output, intermediate consumption, and value-added	Agriculture	Mining and manufacturing	Electricity, gas, and water	Construction	Trade, restaurant, and accommodation	Transportation, storage, and communication	Finance and insurance	Real estate, and business services	Public admin., defense, and social protection	Education	Human health, and social	Other services	
1	**Nonfinancial corporations**													
	Output													
	IC													
	Value added													
	Remuneration of employees													
	Net operating surplus													
	Depreciation and depletion													
	Other taxes on production													
2	**Financial corporations**													
	Output													
	IC													
	Value added													
	Remuneration of employees													
	Net operating surplus													
	Depreciation and depletion													
	Other taxes on production													
3	**General government**													
	Output													
	IC													
	Value added													
	Remuneration of employees													
	Net operating surplus													
	Depreciation and depletion													
	Other taxes on production													
4	**NPISHs**													
	Output													
	IC													
	Value added													
	Remuneration of employees													
	Net operating surplus													
	Depreciation and depletion													
	Other taxes on production													
5	**Households**													
	Output													
	IC													
	Value added													
	Remuneration of employees													
	Net operating surplus													
	Depreciation and depletion													
	Other taxes on production													

6	Total economy		
	Output		
	IC		
	Value added		
	Remuneration of employees		
	Net operating surplus		
	Depreciation and depletion		
	Other taxes on production		

Note: Basic price basis (excluding taxes less subsidies on products and import tax)

Chapter 8. Basic concepts of the sequence of economic accounts

This chapter aims to explain some of the key concepts necessary to understand the sequence of economic accounts, which will be discussed in detail in Chapters 9 to 13. Specifically, it introduces several basic accounting concepts required to understand the sequence of economic accounts, explains the concept, structure, and characteristics of these accounts. It will also introduce the statistical sources needed to compile the sequence of economic accounts.

8.1 Some basic concepts for the sequence of economic accounts

To compile the sequence of economic accounts which is the integral part of the national accounts, it is essential to have some basic accounting knowledge in advance. This section aims to help better understand the SNA sequence of economic accounts by explaining these essential accounting concepts.

8.1.1 Flows and stocks

National accounts can be viewed as an accounting system designed to measure the economic activities during the period and the economic states at a particular point in time of a country in terms of economic value. The measurement of this economic value is reflected in monetary amounts, which can be classified into two categories: flows and stocks. **Flows** measure changes in economic value over a specific period, while **stocks** measure the economic value (balances) at a particular point in time. Specifically, flows represent the creation, transformation, exchange, transfer or extinction of economic value, leading to changes in the volume, composition, and value of assets and liabilities held by institutional units. This is represented as the value accrued, transacted, or increased (decreased) over a specific period. In contrast, stocks represent the accumulated balance at a specific point in time (either the end or beginning of the period). The accounts that measure flows in the SNA are the current accounts (the production account, the generation of earned income account, the distribution of income account, the use of income account) and the accumulation account (the capital account, the financial account, the other changes in volume of assets account, the revaluation account), while the account that measure stocks is the balance sheet.

Flows can be further divided into two types. First, there are **transactions**, which are economic activities carried out by mutual agreements between institutional units. Second, there are **other flows**, which arise from unilateral actions that do not involve mutual agreement (e.g., wars, natural disasters, price changes due to holdings of assets). Illegal transactions are economic activities prohibited by law, but when carried out by mutual consent among economic agents, they are treated as transactions, while illegal activities without mutual consent are treated as other flows.

Transactions include both those expressed in monetary value and those that are not. Examples of transactions expressed in monetary value include the sales and purchases of goods and services, buying and selling of financial assets and nonfinancial assets, the payment of wages in exchange for labor, and the payment of taxes to government. Examples of non-monetary transactions include barter, payments in kind, transfers in kind. To express non-monetary transactions in monetary terms, the price of similar products or the sum of costs can be used as an approximation.

Other flows refer to events that cause changes in assets or liabilities due to factors other than transactions between economic entities. Other flows are broadly divided into two categories. The first category involves changes in the volume of assets due to the appearance of new assets or the disappearance of existing assets, not due to mutual agreements between economic units. The second category involves holding gains or losses occur due to changes in the value of holding assets or liabilities. The production account, income account, capital account, and financial account are accounts that record transactions, while the other changes in volume of assets account, and revaluation account are accounts that record other flows.

8.1.2 The accrual basis of recording

An important thing to mention in association with distinguishing stocks and flows in accounting data is when an economic unit records transactions resulting from its economic activities. The reason why the timing of recording is important is as follows. First, economic records apply only to events that occur during the accounting period, and thus it must be determined which accounting period the records belong to. Second, while stocks are recorded based on a specific point in time, flows record economic events during a specific period, so it is necessary to clarify the timing of recording in order to measure the changes in net worth or the holding gains due to price changes within the accounting period.

The SNA requires that economic value be recorded when it is created, transformed, exchanged, transferred, or extinguished. This is called the **accrual basis**, which is the same accounting practice applied in business accounting. The production of goods is recorded at the point when the goods are produced, intermediate consumption is recorded when materials and supplies are used, the acquisition of goods is recorded when the economic ownership of the goods is changed, and services are recorded when they are rendered. The point at which the economic ownership of a good changes is when the transaction is recorded in the book of the counterparty, or if this is not feasible, when the physical ownership is transferred. In the SNA, the transfer of ownership is judged based on **economic ownership**, not legal ownership. For example, when a good is purchased under an installment purchase contract or financial lease, the change in ownership is deemed to occur at the time the good is delivered. Moreover, government tax claims are recognized when the sale or use of a product actually occurs, not when the tax return or tax notice is issued. This is because enterprises issue invoices at the time of sales, so the tax liability is recognized at this time. However, taxes that are confirmed ex post, such as income taxes, are flexibly determined.

Foreign transactions involve the acquisition of goods and services, and as with domestic transactions, the acquisition of goods is recorded when the economic ownership changes, and the acquisition of services is recorded when they are provided or delivered. In the case of overseas processing of goods, since the actual ownership of goods is not transferred, it is not treated as an import or export of goods. Instead, only the processing service fees is treated as an import or export of services. Therefore, this transaction is recorded at the point when the services are provided, not when the goods are exchanged. Merchanting is recorded when changes in economic ownership of goods occur (BPM6, 3.46). The acquisition of goods in cross-border transactions is recorded when they are declared with customs. However, in the case of goods with progressive payments under long-term contracts (e.g., ships), they are recorded at the time of being delivered when they are manufactured in stages.

8.1.3 Double entry versus quadruple entry accounting

Since national accounts are compiled based on accounting principles, it is difficult to understand the overall accounting system without understanding basic accounting principles. Before delving into the details of national accounts, I will briefly introduce the business accounting principles and explain them in relation to the national accounting.

When an institutional unit performs economic activities such as production or consumption, and records them in its accounts, the national accounts, as in the case of business accounting, record the amounts on the left-hand and right-hand sides of the T-form account, and the difference between the amounts of left-hand and right-hand sides is displayed on the side with smaller amount to balance the amounts on both sides. Table 8.1 below shows the basic accounting entries for business accounting. In business accounting, economic entities record changes in assets, liabilities and capital as well as accruals of revenues and expenses, and these amounts are displayed on the left-hand side (debit) and right-hand side (credit) of T-form accounts. For example, when an enterprise purchases materials for production, the asset of materials increases, and at the same time, the payment to the material supplier causes a decrease in assets of cash. When an enterprise sells its output to an outside party, it records a revenue as sales (credit side), and in exchange, an increase in accounts receivable (debit side). This simultaneous recording of transactions on the left-hand and right-hand sides of accounts is known as **double-entry accounting**, and the total on the left-hand must match the total on the right-hand side. If the amounts on the left-hand and right-hand sides do not match, the difference is calculated and recorded on the side with smaller amount to balance their totals. In the SNA, this difference is called the **balancing item**.

Table 8.1 T-form account

Debit	Credit
Increase in assets	Decrease in assets
Decrease in liabilities	Increase in liabilities
Decrease in capital	Increase in capital
Incurrence of expenses	Occurrence of revenues
Total (A)	Total (B)

Total A = Total B

In the national accounts, the terms used for the left-hand and right-hand sides of accounts are expressed differently from those in business accounting. Specifically, the current accounts use the term **expenditures** for the left-hand side and **revenues** for the right-hand side. The accumulation accounts use the term **increase in assets** for the left-hand side, and **increase in liabilities and net worth** for the right-hand side. In addition, the balance sheet uses the term **assets** for the left-hand and **liabilities and net worth** for the right-hand side.

In the SNA, every transaction must involve two parties, so both economic entities' activities must be recorded. Similar to how an enterprise records its own transactions by double-entry bookkeeping, national accounts require simultaneous recording of transactions between two economic entities, which is referred to as **quadruple-entry accounting**. For example, when an enterprise sells a product to government, the enterprise records the sale of the product (revenue) and the receipt of cash (increase in assets) while the government, as the counterparty, records the purchase of the product (expense) and the payment of cash (decrease in assets). As a result, four transactions are recorded (see Figure 8.1). However, sometimes there are economic phenomena where no two economic entities are involved. In such case, instead of quadruple-entry accounting, only double entries of a single economic entity are made. For example, **other flows** that are not transactions, such as the occurrence of natural disasters or the discovery of resources, do not have a corresponding economic entity, therefore, only the activities of the economic entity that experiences the event are recorded in the accounts.

Figure 8.1 Example of quadruple-entry accounting

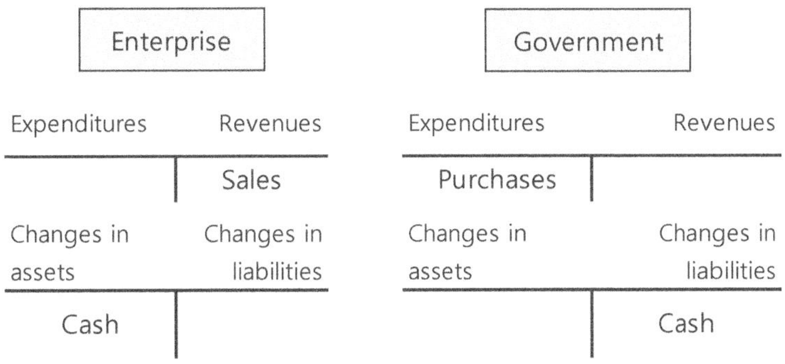

One of the characteristics of quadruple-entry accounting is that it always involves **financial transactions** for both parties in the transaction, except in special cases. There are two forms of quadruple entry: first, one pair involves a non-financial transaction while the corresponding other pair involves a financial transaction; second, both pairs of transactions are financial transactions. The former case occurs in most non-financial transactions, such as the transaction between the enterprise and the government in the previous example. In other words, the sales by the enterprise and purchases by government are non-financial transactions, while the cash transactions occurring for both parties are financial transactions (note that financial transactions are recorded in the financial account). Additionally, in the case of in-kind transactions (e.g., barter or payment in-kind), they also, in principle, involves financial transactions. For example, let's consider a case where company A engages in barter with company B. First, when A provides goods to B, A will record accounts receivable from B, and B will record accounts payable. Later, when company B provides the corresponding goods to company A, A's accounts receivable and B's accounts payable will be extinguished. However, if there is no time lag in the exchange of goods, the financial transactions may be omitted.

In the case when both pairs of transactions are financial transactions, they involve the acquisition of financial assets or the repayment of liabilities. These transactions are recorded exclusively in the financial account. For example, if a bank issues certificates of deposit (CDs) and sells them to individuals, the quadruple-entry transaction would show an increase in CD liability and an increase in cash assets for the bank, while the households that purchase the CDs would show an increase in CD assets and a decrease in cash assets.

Figure 8.2 Example of quadruple entry accounting in financial transactions

Bank		Household	
Changes in assets	Changes in liabilities	Changes in assets	Changes in liabilities
Cash	CD	CD	Cash

8.1.4 Netting, consolidation, and "net" concepts

In the SNA, the amounts arising from transactions during an accounting period are recorded cumulatively and are sometimes offset depending on the underlying data. For example, "changes in inventories" are the concept of entries less withdrawals of inventories, and fixed capital formation represents the net amount of acquisition less disposal of fixed assets. Similarly, in financial transactions, assets of financial instruments are shown net of acquisitions and disposals, and liabilities are shown net of incurrence of a new debt and redemption of an existing debt. This type of offsetting of debits and credits within the same asset type (or liabilities type) is referred to as **netting**. However, in the SNA, netting beyond certain levels within the accounting system is not encouraged. Specifically, in financial transactions, netting of increases in financial assets and counterpart increases in liabilities is avoided, because **gross recording** allows for more detailed analysis of transactions.

In the balance of payments, netting is not used for analytical purposes, and gross reporting is recommended instead. For example, in merchanting, imports of goods are not netted against exports of goods, and imports are shown as negative value. Similarly, acquisitions and disposals of non-produced non-financial assets and receivables and payables of capital transfers are also required to be presented on a gross basis (BPM6 3.113).

In the SNA, the amounts of the same transaction may differ depending on the level of the economic unit (or institutional unit) being aggregated. For example, in the financial account for the government sector, grants from the central government to the local government are recorded as payments by the central government and receipts by the local government, respectively. However, in the financial account that shows transactions between the government sector and the private sector, the grant transaction between the central and local governments is offset, showing the net effect of the transaction. In the case of financial institutions, internal transactions between the head office and branches within the same financial institution are offset in the financial statements for the public disclosure. In this way, when there are multiple sub-units within an economic unit, transactions between these sub-units are netted out for external reporting. This is called **consolidation**. Consolidation is a method used to present statistics by aggregating multiple economic units into a single economic unit. the SNA generally does not encourage consolidation, but it can be prepared for the purpose of providing supplementary data or further analysis.

The third type of "net" indication is when the prefix "net" is added to terms such as net worth or net lending (+)/net borrowings (-). As concepts derived from balancing items, net worth is the amount of assets minus liabilities, and net lending (+)/net borrowings (-) is the right-hand side value minus the left-hand side value of the capital account. Another concept of "net" is used when specific items are deducted, as in the case of gross domestic product (GDP) and gross national income (GNI), where the deduction of depreciation and depletion results in net domestic product (NDP) and net national income (NNI). Net taxes on products are the result of subtracting subsidies on products from taxes on products, and net premiums refer to premiums less the insurance service charge.

8.2 Characteristics of the sequence of economic accounts

The sequence of economic accounts (*integrated economic accounts* in the 2008 SNA) is the most essential set of accounts that form the integrated framework of the national accounts. They provide a comprehensive representation of the economic activities and positions of all institutional units within an economy, presented in the form of accounts. The sequence of economic accounts consists of three main parts: current accounts, accumulation accounts, and balance sheets. The **current accounts** consist of the production account, the generation of earned income account, the allocation of earned income account, the distribution of secondary income account, and the use of income account. The **accumulation accounts** include the capital account, the financial account, and the other changes in assets and liabilities account. Finally, there are **balance sheets**, which represent stock accounts. This chapter aims to introduce the characteristics of the sequence of economic accounts before delving into each of these accounts in detail in the following chapters.

First, the sequence of economic accounts is structured all by institutional sectors as the agents of economic activities. In contrast to the supply and use tables, which are classified mainly by economic activities, the sequence of economic accounts is compiled by institutional sectors, covering from production, generation and distribution of income, capital transaction, financial transactions, to the balance sheet. The institutional sectors are categorized into five groups: non-financial corporations, financial corporations, households, government, and NPISHs. In addition, the **rest of the world account** is added to the institutional sectors, representing transactions between the domestic economy and the external sector. However, the rest of the world account differs from the balance of payments, as the balance of payments is measured from the perspective of the domestic economy, which is the compiling entity, whereas the rest of the world account measures transactions with the domestic economy from the perspective of the rest of the world sector. As a result, the amounts in the rest of the world account are displayed in the opposite way to the debit and credit entries in the balance of payments.

Second, the sequence of economic accounts resembles business accounting in terms of the structure of accounts. Specifically, these accounts divide into current accounts, accumulated accounts, and the balance sheet. The current accounts correspond to the cost statement, income statement in business accounting, while the accumulation accounts correspond to the extraordinary income and expenses in the income statement, as well as the statement of changes in equity and the statement of cash flows. The balance sheet in the sequence of economic accounts mirrors the statement of financial position in business accounting. The left-hand side of business accounting (debit) corresponds to the expenditures, changes in assets, and assets (stocks) in the national accounts, while the right-hand side of business accounting (credit) corresponds to the revenues, changes in liabilities and net worth, and liabilities and net worth (stocks) in the national accounts.

Figure 8.3 Presentation of the left-hand and right-hand sides in the sequence of economic accounts

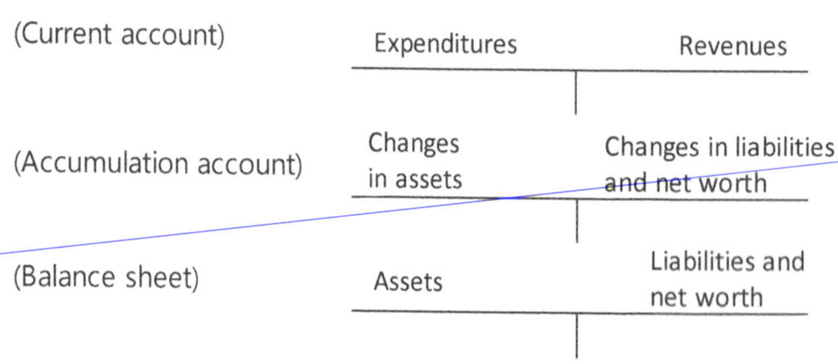

Third, one of the key features of the sequence of economic accounts is the setting of **balancing items**. To match the amounts on the left-hand and right-hand sides of the account, the difference between the amounts on the right-hand and left-hand sides is displayed as a balancing item on the left-hand side (Table 8.2).

These balancing items represent the most important economic indicators to be derived from the national accounts. For example, gross domestic product/net domestic product (GDP/NDP) is derived from the production account of the domestic economy, gross operating surplus and gross mixed income/net operating surplus and net mixed income from the generation of earned income account, gross national income/net national income (GNI/NNI) from the allocation of earned income account, gross national disposable income/net national disposable income (GNDI/NNDI) from the income transfers other than transfers in kind account, and gross saving/net saving from the use of income account.

Table 8.2 Balancing items by account in the sequence of economic accounts

Domestic Economy

Account	Balancing item
Production	Gross or net value added (GDP/NDP)
Generation of earned income	Gross or net operating income
Allocation of earned income	Balance of earned incomes (GNI/NNI)
Income transfers other than transfers in kind	Gross or net disposable income
Use of income	Gross or net saving
Capital	Net lending/net borrowing
Financial	Net lending/net borrowing
Other changes in the volume of assets and liabilities	Changes in net worth due to other changes in the volume of assets and liabilities
Revaluation	Changes in net worth due to holding gains/losses
Balance sheet	Net worth

Rest of the World Sector

Account	Balancing item
Goods and services	Balance of goods & services
Earned income	Balance of earned income
Transfer income	Balance of transfer income
Use of income	Current external balance
Capital	Net lending/net borrowing
Financial	Net lending/net borrowing
Other changes in assets and liabilities	Changes in net worth due to other changes in assets and liabilities
Balance sheet	Net worth

Net lending (+)/net borrowing (-) are derived from the capital account and the financial account. In addition, in the other changes in the volume of assets and liabilities account, the item recorded is the *changes in net worth due to other changes in the volume of assets and liabilities*; in the revaluation account, the item recorded is the *changes in net worth due to nominal holding gains and losses*; and in the balance sheet, *net worth* is derived as the balancing item. For the **rest of the world sector**, the following balancing items are derived: "balance of goods and services" is derived from the goods and services account, "balance of earned incomes" from the earned income account, "balance of transfer income" from the transfer income account, "current external balance" from the use of income account, and "net lending (+)/net borrowing (-)" from the capital account and the financial account. The net lending (+)/net borrowing (-) of the domestic economy is equal in absolute values to that of the rest of the world sector, only the sign reversed. The balancing items derived in each account are carried forward to the next account.

Figure 8.4 Balancing items between accounts in the Sequence of economic accounts

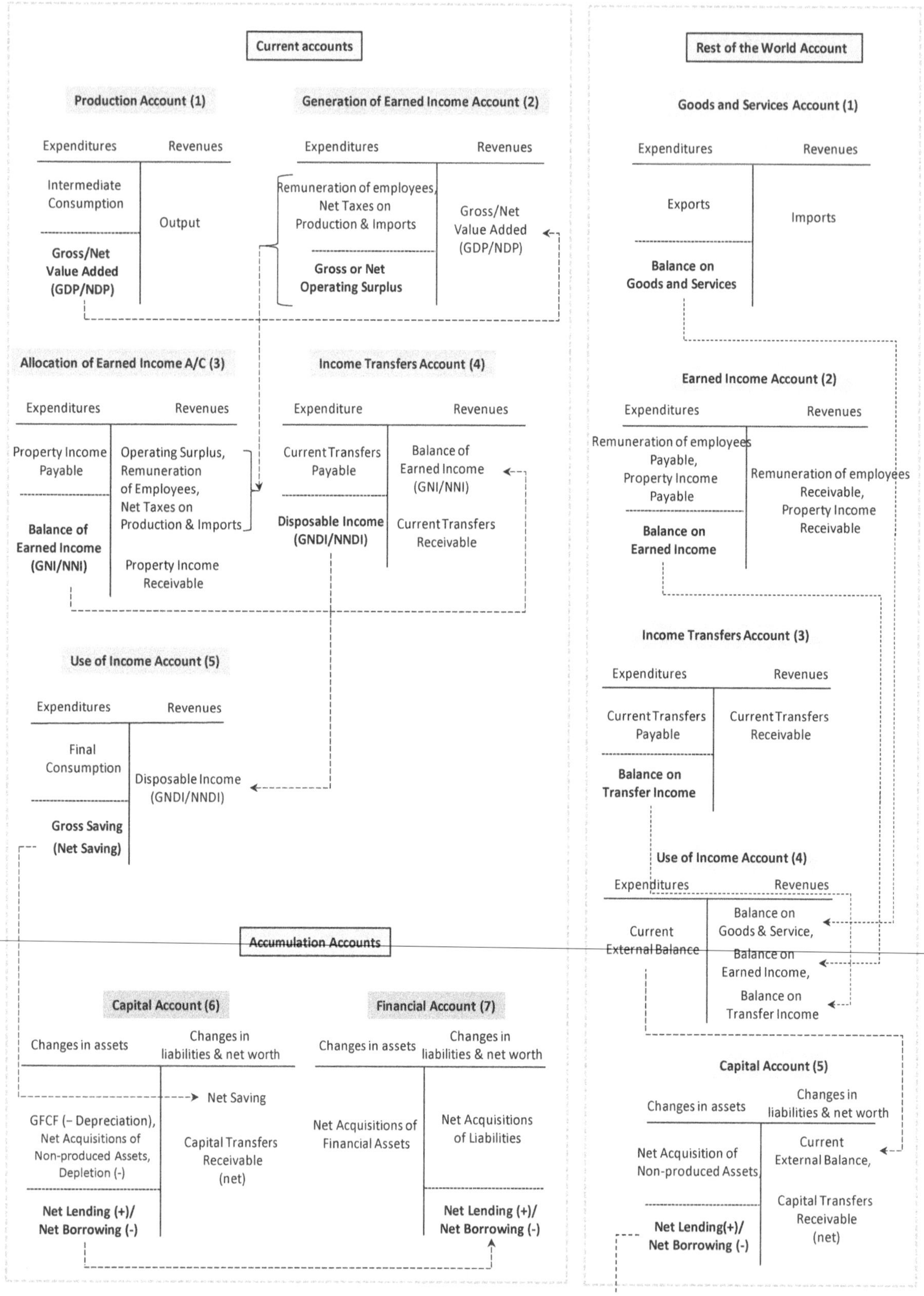

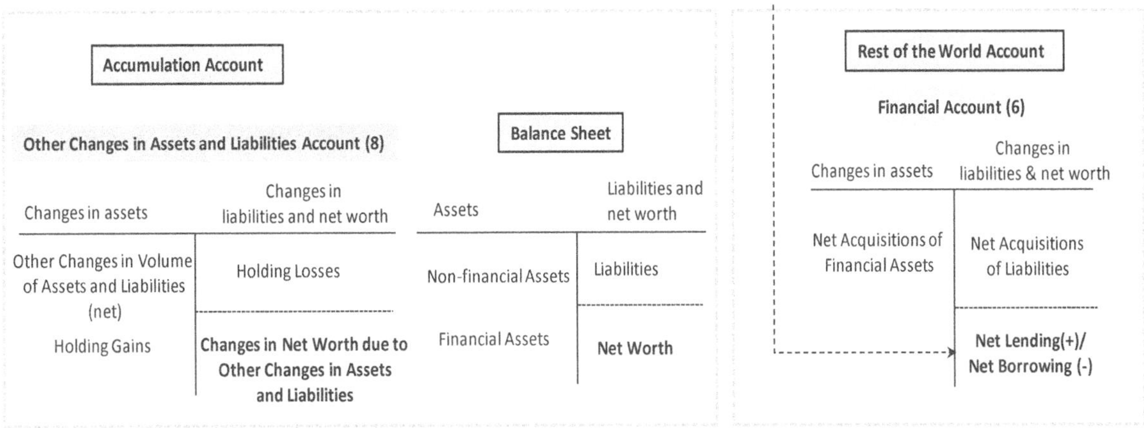

Fourth, the **goods and services account** is added as a column along with other institutional sectors. The goods and services account represents a formula derived from the product balance identity to calculate GDP. Recalling the product balance identity, it is as follows:

- Output + imports = intermediate consumption + final consumption + gross capital formation + exports

If the types of prices are applied to this identity, it becomes:

- Output (basic price) + taxes less subsidies on products + imports = intermediate consumption (purchaser's price) + final consumption expenditure (purchaser's price) + gross capital formation (purchaser's price) + exports

Here, the goods and services account is displayed as follows:

- Output (basic price) – intermediate consumption (purchaser's price) + taxes less subsidies on products = final consumption expenditure (purchaser's price) + gross capital formation (purchaser's price) + exports – imports

This account can be represented as a T-form as follows.

Table 8.3 The goods and services account

Expenditures	Revenues
Intermediate consumption	Output
Final consumption expenditure	Imports of goods and services
Gross capital formation	Taxes on products
Exports of goods and services	Subsidies on products (-)
Total expenditures	Total revenues

This identity is the same as the formula used to derive GDP. In the sequence of economic accounts, the goods and services account is presented with *opposite signs* of the debits and credits of institutional sector accounts. The table below (Table 8.4) illustrates an example set of integrated economic accounts for South Korea in 2015, from the current accounts to the balance sheet. (However, the other changes in assets and liabilities accounts are currently not compiled.)

Table 8.4 Example of the sequence of economic accounts (South Korea, 2015)

Current accounts

Production account

Expenditures (Unit: KRW trillion) Revenues

Nonfinancial corp.	Financial corp.	Government	Households & NPISHs	Total economy	ROW	Goods & services	Total	Transactions and balancing items	Nonfinancial corp.	Financial corp.	Government	Households & NPISHs	Total economy	ROW	Goods & services	Total
						3,729	3,729	Output	2,879	150	221	479	3,729			3,729
1,888	64	64	191	2,208			2,208	Intermediate consumption							2,208	2,208
						137	137	Taxes less subsidies on products					137			137
992	85	157	287	1,658			1,658	**Gross value added/GDP**								
207	8	47	49	310			310	Depreciation								
785	78	110	238	1,348			1,348	***Net value added/NDP***								

Generation of earned income account

Expenditures (Unit: KRW trillion) Revenues

Nonfinancial corp.	Financial corp.	Government	Households & NPISHs	Total economy	ROW	Goods & services	Total	Transactions and balancing items	Nonfinancial corp.	Financial corp.	Government	Households & NPISHs	Total economy	ROW	Goods & services	Total
								Gross value added/GDP	992	85	157	287	1,658			1,658
								Net value added/NDP	785	78	110	238	1,348			1,348
489	37	109	115	750			750	Remuneration of employees								
				164			164	Taxes on production & imports								
				-8			-8	Subsidies (−)								
493	47	48	163	751			751	**Gross operating surplus & mixed income**								
287	40	1	114	441			441	***Net operating surplus & mixed income***								

Allocation of earned income account

Expenditures (Unit: KRW trillion) Revenues

Nonfinancial corp.	Financial corp.	Government	Households & NPISHs	Total economy	ROW	Goods & services	Total	Transactions and balancing items	Nonfinancial corp.	Financial corp.	Government	Households & NPISHs	Total economy	ROW	Goods & services	Total
								Gross operating surplus & mixed income	493	47	48	163	751			751
								Net operating surplus & mixed income	287	40	1	114	441			441
					1		1	Remuneration of employees				750	750	1		751
								Taxes on production & imports			164		164			164

Nonfinancial corp.	Financial corp.	Government	Households & NPISHs	Total economy	ROW	Goods & services	Total	Transactions and balancing items	Nonfinancial corp.	Financial corp.	Government	Households & NPISHs	Total economy	ROW	Goods & services	Total
								Subsidies (-)			-8		-8			-8
136	125	25	33	319	25		344	Property income	36	117	28	143	325	17		342
394	39	207	1,023	1,663	-7		1,663	**Balance of earned incomes, gross / GNI**								
187	32	161	974	1,354	-7		1,354	***Balance of earned incomes, net / NNI***								

Income transfers other than transfers in kind account

(Unit: KRW trillion)

Expenditures / **Revenues**

Nonfinancial corp.	Financial corp.	Government	Households & NPISHs	Total economy	ROW	Goods & services	Total	Transactions and balancing items	Nonfinancial corp.	Financial corp.	Government	Households & NPISHs	Total economy	ROW	Goods & services	Total
								Balance of earned incomes, gross/GNI	394	39	207	1,023	1,663			1,663
								Balance of earned incomes, net/NNI	187	32	161	974	1,354			1,354
94	66	134	317	611	12		622	Current transfers	36	63	287	221	607	16		622
336	37	361	926	1,659	4		1,659	**Gross disposable income**								
129	29	314	877	1,349			1,349	***Net disposable income***								

Use of disposable income account

(Unit: KRW trillion)

Expenditures / **Revenues**

Nonfinancial corp.	Financial corp.	Government	Households & NPISHs	Total economy	ROW	Goods & services	Total	Transactions and balancing items	Nonfinancial corp.	Financial corp.	Government	Households & NPISHs	Total economy	ROW	Goods & services	Total
								Gross disposable income	336	37	361	926	1,659			1,659
								Net disposable income	129	29	314	877	1,349			1,349
		250	805	1,055			1,055	Final consumption							1,055	1,055
0	14	0		14	0		14	Adj. for changes in pension entitlements				14	14	0		14
336	23	111	135	604			604	**Gross saving**								
129	15	64	86	294			294	***Net saving***								

Social transfers in kind account

(Unit: KRW trillion)

Expenditures / **Revenues**

Nonfinancial corp.	Financial corp.	Government	Households & NPISHs	Total economy	ROW	Goods & services	Total	Transactions and balancing items	Nonfinancial corp.	Financial corp.	Government	Households & NPISHs	Total economy	ROW	Goods & services	Total
								Gross disposable income	336	37	361	926	1,659			1,659
								Net disposable income	129	29	314	877	1,349			1,349
		136	28	163			163	Social transfers in kind				163	163			163
336	37	225	1,061	1,659			1,659	**Gross adjusted disposable income**								
129	29	178	1,013	1,349			1,349	***Net adjusted disposable income***								

Use of adjusted disposable income account

(Unit: KRW trillion)

Expenditures / **Revenues**

Nonfinancial corp.	Financial corp.	Government	Households & NPISHs	Total economy	ROW	Goods & services	Total	Transactions and balancing items	Nonfinancial corp.	Financial corp.	Government	Households & NPISHs	Total economy	ROW	Goods & services	Total
								Gross adjusted disposable income	336	37	225	1,061	1,659			1,659
								Net adjusted disposable income	129	29	178	1,013	1,349			1,349
		114	941	1,055			1,055	Actual final consumption							1,055	1,055
0	14	0		14	0		14	Adj. for changes in pension entitlements				14	14	0		14
336	23	111	135	604			604	**Gross saving**								
129	15	64	86	294			294	***Net saving***								

Accumulation accounts

Capital account

(Unit: KRW trillion)

Changes in assets: Nonfinancial corp.	Financial corp.	Government	Households & NPISHs	Total economy	ROW	Goods & services	Total	Transactions and balancing items	Changes in liabilities and net worth: Nonfinancial corp.	Financial corp.	Government	Households & NPISHs	Total economy	ROW	Goods & services	Total
								Net saving	129	15	64	86	294			294
								Current external balance						-114		-114
321	10	72	86	490			490	Gross capital formation							490	490
316	10	72	83	481			481	Gross fixed capital formation							481	481
-207	-8	-47	-49	-310			-310	Depreciation (-)							-310	-310
5	0	1	1	7			7	Changes in inventories							7	7
0	0	0	2	2			2	Net acquisition of valuables							2	2
34	1	8	-43	0	-0		0	Net acquisition of non-produced assets								
								Net capital transfers receivable	5	-0	-11	5	0	-0		-0
								Changes in net worth due to saving and capital transfers	134	15	54	91	294	-114		180
-14	12	20	97	114	-114		-0	**Net lending (+)/net borrowing (-)**								

Financial account

(Unit: KRW trillion)

Changes in assets: Nonfinancial corp.	Financial corp.	Government	Households & NPISHs	Total economy	ROW	Goods & services	Total	Transactions and balancing items	Changes in liabilities and net worth: Nonfinancial corp.	Financial corp.	Government	Households & NPISHs	Total economy	ROW	Goods & services	Total
								Net lending (+)/net borrowing (-)	-15	16	19	95	114	-114		0
94	474	84	224	875	-16		859	**Net acquisition of financial assets**								
								Net acquisition of liabilities	108	459	65	129	761	98		859
0	-0	0	0	-0	0		-0	Monetary gold & SDRs	0	0	0	0	0	-0		-0
57	42	5	110	214	-9		205	Currency & deposits	0	194	12	0	205	0		205
13	130	9	5	157	-7		150	Debt securities	-14	85	50	0	121	29		150
0	215	5	0	220	-0		220	Loans	87	-4	1	128	212	8		220
-10	34	56	17	96	-3		94	Equity & investment fund shares	21	52	2	0	76	18		94
5	3	-0	90	98	0		98	Insurance, pension & guarantee schemes	0	98	0	0	98	0		98
0	0	0	0	0	0		0	Financial derivatives	0	0	0	0	0	0		0
29	51	9	3	91	2		93	Other receivable/payable	14	35	0	1	49	44		93

Balance sheets

(Unit: KRW trillion)

Stocks and changes in assets: Nonfinancial corp.	Financial corp.	Government	Households & NPISHs	Total economy	ROW	Goods & services	Total	Transactions and balancing items	Stocks and changes in liabilities and net worth: Nonfinancial corp.	Financial corp.	Government	Households & NPISHs	Total economy	ROW	Goods & services	Total	
3,705	128	2,790	5,284	11,907			11,907	**Nonfinancial assets**									**Opening balance sheet**
2,752	80	1,158	1,491	5,481			5,481	Produced nonfinancial assets									
954	48	1,632	3,793	6,426			6,426	Non-produced nonfinancial assets									
2,140	6,090	1,303	2,901	12,434	1,090		13,524	**Financial assets/liabilities**	4,209	6,020	820	1,296	12,345	1,174		13,519	
								Net worth	1,637	198	3,272	6,889	11,996	-84		11,912	
153	7	143	280	582			582	**Nonfinancial assets**									**Total**
114	4	32	60	210			210	Produced nonfinancial assets									

39	3	111	220	372		372	Non-produced nonfinancial assets								
193	486	94	281	1,055	11	1,066	**Financial assets/liabilities**	220	477	81	127	904	161	1065	
126	16	156	434	733	-150	582	***Total changes in net worth***	126	16	156	434	733	-150	582	
							Savings & capital transfers	134	15	54	91	294	-114	180	
							Other changes in volume of assets	-50	-1	32	114	95	-36	59	
							Nominal holding gains/losses	42	2	71	228	343	0	343	
3.858	135	2.932	5.564	12.489		12.489	**Nonfinancial assets**								Closing balance
2.866	84	1.190	1.551	5.691		5.691	Produced nonfinancial assets								
992	50	1.742	4.013	6.797		6.797	Non-produced nonfinancial assets								
2.334	6.576	1.397	3.182	13.489	1.101	14.590	**Financial assets/liabilities**	4.429	6.497	901	1.423	13.250	1.335	14.585	
							Net worth	1.763	214	3.428	7.323	12.728	-234	12.494	

8.3 Statistical data sources of the sequence of economic accounts

The sequence of economic accounts must be compiled by institutional sector, so the underlying statistical data for each account should be collected from data sources that can be compiled by institutional sector. A brief introduction to the statistical data sources for compiling the Sequence of economic accounts by institutional sector is as follows. First, for the compilation of the production account and the generation of earned income account in the current accounts, data from the supply and use tables and the "cross-classification table by industry and institutional sector" are utilized. The allocation of earned income account and the income transfers other than transfers in kind account, which record the income distribution by institutional sector, rely on income-related data sources such the National Tax Service database, government accounts, and financial statements of financial institutions. For the compilation of the use of income account, data from household surveys and retail sales surveys are used for the private sector, while the government budgets and financial statements of government are referenced for the government sector. In addition, balance of payments must be used exclusively for the external sector transactions. In the accumulation accounts, both the capital account and the financial account are compiled using the balance sheets of non-financial enterprises and financial institutions. The capital account can utilize the fixed capital formation table by product derived from the use table as an auxiliary data. The financial account is prepared by institutional sector, with the financial corporations sector using the balance sheets of financial institutions (from the financial supervisory authority database), and the non-financial corporations sector and government sector extracting financial assets and liabilities items from the corporate balance sheets (from the National Tax Service) and the government's budget and financial statements, respectively. Financial account data for the households sector can be obtained either by using the households asset surveys or by extracting the households' financial assets and liabilities based on the total financial assets and liabilities of the financial institutions. Finally, the balance sheet is compiled using the financial statement databases mentioned earlier or, using estimates of capital stocks based on the perpetual inventory method. (For methods of estimating capital stocks, see Chapter 20.)

Figure 8.5 Data sources for the compilation of the sequence of economic accounts

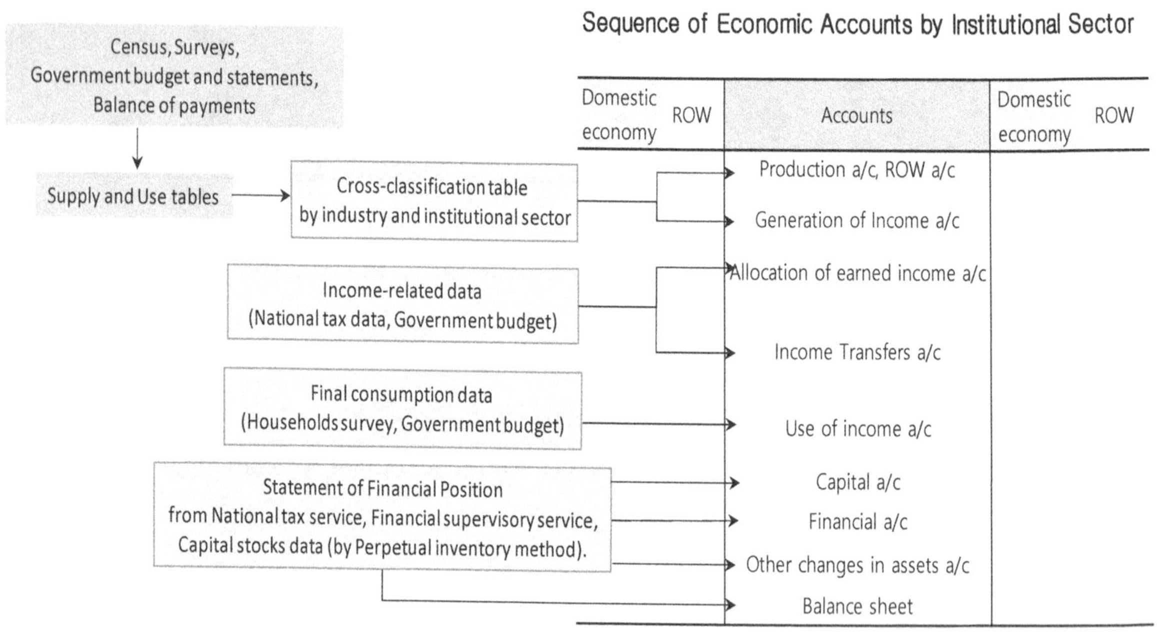

Chapter 9. Current accounts

This chapter provides a detailed discussion of the current accounts among the SNA sequence of economic accounts introduced in the previous chapter. The current accounts record information on production, generation of earned income, and use of income. These accounts encompass the production account, the generation of earned income account, the distribution of income account, and the use of income account for each institutional account (and the rest of the world sector) in the sequence of economic accounts. These accounts generate balancing items, such as value added, operating surplus (and mixed income), balance of earned incomes, disposable income, and savings, which are the most important aggregate indicators of the national accounts. In the following, we will examine each account of these current accounts in detail.

9.1 The production account

The **production account** is an account that shows domestic output and intermediate consumption, which are the starting points of production activities, and serves as the account for deriving the balancing item, **gross value added** (or net value added). Like other accounts, it is classified by institutional sectors. However, when the data sources for the production account are collected at the establishment level, this account can be compiled by industry.

In the table below (Table 9.1), output is displayed on the right-hand side (revenues), while intermediate consumption is shown on the left-hand side (expenditures), and the balancing item, gross value added, appears on the left-hand side. Net value added is gross value added minus depreciation and depletion. The sum of gross value added of domestic institutional sectors (valued at basic prices) plus taxes less subsidies on products (= taxes on products – subsidies on products) gives **gross domestic product** (GDP). GDP minus depreciation and depletion equals **net domestic product** (NDP). The balancing items of the production account, gross value added (or net value added) and GDP (or NDP) are carried forward to the right-hand side (revenues) of the income account, as described in the subsequent section.

Table 9.1 The format of the production account

Expenditures	Revenues
Intermediate consumption	Output
Value added (Depreciation and depletion)	

In the production account, transactions involving goods and services in the **rest of the world sector** can be additionally recorded. This can be done by adding entries for exports and imports of goods and services within the production account, without setting up a separate rest of the world account, thus reflecting external transactions. Exports of goods and services are recorded as expenditures of the rest of the world sector, while imports of goods and services are recorded as revenues of the rest of the world sector, and the difference is shown as the balancing item "balance of goods and services" on the left-hand side.

Transactions of goods and services in the rest of the world sector

Expenditures	Revenues
Exports of goods and services (B)	Imports of goods and services (A)
Balance of goods and services (A–B)	

The table below (Table 9.2) illustrates the production account by institutional sector for South Korea in 2015. The output at basic prices (unit: KRW trillion) for the entire domestic economy is 3,728.7, when taxes less subsidies on products of 137.1 is added, the output at purchasers' prices amounts to 3,865.8. The gross value added (at basic prices) is 991.5 (= 2,879.2–1,887.7) for non-financial corporations, 85.3 for financial corporations, 156.9 for general government, and 287.2 for households and NPISHs. The total gross value-added of institutional sectors (991.5+85.3+156.9 +287.2=1,520.9) plus taxes less subsidies on products (137.1) results in the gross domestic product (GDP) of 1,658.0. The value of net domestic product is 1,348.4 (= 1,658.0–309.7).

Table 9.2 Example of the production account (South Korea, 2015)

Expenditures (Unit: KRW trillion) **Revenues**

Nonfinancial corp.	Financial corp.	General government	Households & NPISHs	Total economy	ROW	Goods & services	Total	Transactions & balancing items	Nonfinancial corp.	Financial corp.	General government	Households & NPISHs	Total economy	ROW	Goods & services	Total
						3,728.7	3,728.7	Output	2,879.2	149.5	221.3	478.7	3,728.7			3,728.7
						3,374.6	3,374.6	Market output	2,879.2	149.5	34.8	311.0	3,374.6			3,374.6
						70.7	70.7	Own final consumption				70.7	70.7			70.7
						283.4	283.4	Nonmarket output			186.5	97.0	283.4			283.4
1,887.7	64.2	64.4	191.5	2,207.8			2,207.8	Intermediate consumption							2,207.8	2,207.8
						137.1	137.1	Taxes less subsidies on products					137.1			137.1
						599.3	599.3	Imports of goods and services						599.3		599.3
					712.8		712.8	Exports of goods and services							712.8	712.8
991.5	85.3	156.9	287.2	1,658.0			1,658.0	**Gross value added /GDP**								
206.5	7.7	46.6	48.9	309.7			309.7	Depreciation								
785.0	77.6	110.3	238.3	1,348.4			1,348.4	***Net value added /NDP***								
					-113.5		-113.5	***Balance of goods and services***								

9.2 Income accounts

The **income accounts** in the SNA comprise a sequence of accounts that records how income is generated in each industry or institutional sector (and in the rest of the world), how it is distributed to the respective institutional sectors, and how it is ultimately used by those sectors. These accounts show the processes through which earned income and transfer income are allocated to the institutional sectors and the rest of the world, and how that income is used. The income accounts are divided into three main categories. The first category consists of the generation of earned income account and the allocation of earned income account, which record the generation and distribution of earned income. The second category comprises the income transfers other than transfers in kind account and the social transfers in kind account, which record the distribution of transfer income. The third category includes the use of disposable income account and the use of adjusted disposable income account, which record the use of income.

The balancing items of these accounts are as follows: operating surplus and mixed income are derived from the generation of earned income account; the balance of earned income is derived from the allocation of earned income account; disposable income is derived from the income transfers other than transfers in kind account; adjusted disposable income is derived from the social transfers in kind account; and saving is derived, in an identical manner, from both the use of disposable income account and the use of adjusted disposable income account. Each of these accounts is described below.

9.2.1 Earned income accounts

Earned income accounts record incomes that arises by institutional sector from participation in the production process or from the ownership of assets used in production, and how those incomes are distributed. They are divided into two accounts: the generation of earned income account and the allocation of earned income account.

9.2.1.1 The generation of earned income account

The generation of earned income account records the components of value added generated by institutional units. In this account, the components of value added such as remuneration of employees, taxes less subsidies on production and imports, and operating surplus and mixed income are recorded. Among these, operating surplus and mixed income constitute the balancing item that is derived as a residual. Because the source data for this account can be collected at the establishment level, the account may be compiled not only by institutional sector but also by industry, in the same manner as the production account.

In the presentation of the generation of earned income account, value added carried over from the production account is displayed on the right-hand side (revenues), while remuneration of employees, and taxes less subsidies on production and imports are recorded on the left-hand side (expenditures); the balancing item, operating surplus and mixed income, also appears on the left-hand side. (When value added on the right-hand side is *net value added*, the corresponding balancing item is *net operating surplus and net mixed income*.) **Operating surplus or mixed income** measure the surplus arising from the production process and represent income before property income receivable (including explicit interest, implicit interest (such as dividends), rent, and other property income on assets used in production) is added, and before property income payable is deducted. The amount of operating surplus or mixed income, as the balancing item of the generation of earned income account, is carried forward to the right-hand side (revenues) of the allocation of earned income account, which is described in the following section.

Table 9.3 The format of the generation of earned income account

Expenditures	Revenues
Remuneration of employees Taxes on production and imports Subsidies (-)	Value added
Operating surplus & Mixed income (Depreciation and depletion)	

The table below (Table 9.4) illustrates the generation of earned income account for South Korea in 2015 (unit: KRW trillion). In this example, for the entire national economy, remuneration of employees is 750.2, taxes on production and imports are 164.3, subsidies are -7.6, and the balancing item, gross operating surplus and gross mixed income, is 751.1 (with net operating surplus and net mixed income at 441.5). By institutional sector, remuneration of employees is 488.9 in the non-financial corporations sector, 36.8 in the financial corporations sector, 109.2 in the general government sector, and 115.3 in households and NPISHs. The remuneration of employees in the households sector is attributed to the household unincorporated enterprises, and there is no remuneration of employees in the owner-occupied dwelling service industry. Other taxes on production are 9.9 in the non-financial corporations sector, 1.3 in the financial corporations sector, and 10.1 in households and NPISHs. Taxes on product are not disaggregated by institutional sector in the sequence of economic accounts, but are instead shown as a total of 143.0. Similarly, subsidies are treated in the same way, with other subsidies on production (-1.7) allocated by institutional sector, and subsidies on products (-5.9) deducted as a total.

Table 9.4 Example of the generation of earned income account (South Korea, 2015)

Expenditures (Unit: KRW trillion) **Revenues**

Nonfinancial corp.	Financial corp.	General government	Households & NPISHs	Total economy	ROW	Goods & services	Total	Transactions & balancing items	Nonfinancial corp.	Financial corp.	General government	Households & NPISHs	Total economy	ROW	Goods & services	Total
								Gross value added/GDP	991.5	85.3	156.9	287.2	1,658.0			1,658.0
								Net value added/NDP	785.0	77.6	110.3	238.3	1,348.4			1,348.4
488.9	36.8	109.2	115.3	750.2			750.2	Remuneration of employees								
				642.2			642.2	Wages and salaries								
				108.0			108.0	Employer's social contributions								
				87.4			87.4	Actual social contributions								
				20.6			20.6	Imputed social contributions								
				164.3			164.3	Taxes on production & imports								
				143.0			143.0	Taxes on products								
9.9	1.3	0.0	10.1	21.3			21.3	Other taxes on production								
				-7.6			-7.6	Subsidies (-)								
				-5.9			-5.9	Subsidies on products								
-0.4	-0.0	-0.0	-1.3	-1.7			-1.7	Other subsidies on production								
493.1	47.2	47.6	163.1	751.1			751.1	**Gross operating surplus & mixed income**								
206.5	7.7	46.6	48.9	309.7			309.7	Depreciation								
286.6	39.5	1.1	114.3	441.5			441.5	*Net operating surplus & mixed income*								

9.2.1.2 The allocation of earned income account

The generation of earned income account records the process of income generation from the *perspective of the producer*, rather than from that of the income recipient. By contrast, the **allocation of earned income account** records the items of income receivable arising from the generation of earned income from the *perspective of the income recipient*. **Earned incomes** (or primary income in the 2008 SNA) are incomes that accrue to institutional units as a consequence of their involvement in processes of production or ownership of assets used for production.

The components of earned income include remuneration of employees accruing to households in return for their labor input; operating surplus and mixed income of enterprises; taxes less subsidies on production and imports levied by government on enterprises; and property income receivable and property income payable (-) of the institutional sector. Property income is classified into investment income arising from financial assets and rents arising from land and natural resources.

In addition, under the 2025 SNA, as *depletion* of natural resources has newly been introduced as a component of gross value added, the allocation of earned income account includes an additional deduction item, **depletion borne by legal owners**, to adjust for this element and to present net property income. This adjustment is introduced to deduct the portion of depletion embedded in the *resource rent* that is allocated to the legal owner of the natural resource (typically government), thereby allowing the recording of payments and receipts of property income on a net basis.

Table 9.5 The format of the allocation of earned income account

Expenditures	Revenues
	Operating surplus & mixed income
	Remuneration of employees
	Taxes on production and imports
	Subsidies (-)
Property income payable	Property income receivable
Depletion borne by legal owners (–)	Depletion borne by legal owners (–)
Balance of earned incomes	

9.2.1.2.1 Components of earned income

The components of earned income differ depending on the institutional sectors (Table 9.6). For households, earned incomes include remuneration of employees, mixed income, property income receivable, property income payable (-), as well as the operating surplus from dwelling services produced by homeowners for their own final consumption. For corporations, earned incomes include operating surplus, property income receivable, and property income payable (-). For general government, earned incomes include taxes on production and imports received from other institutional sectors, subsidies paid to other institutional sectors (-), property income receivable, property income payable (-), and operating surplus of the government sector. For NPISHs, earned incomes include property income receivable, property income payable (-), and operating surplus of NPISHs.

For each institutional sector, the balancing item of the allocation of earned income account is obtained by deducting totals expenditures on the left-hand side from total revenues on the right-hand side, yielding the **balance of earned incomes**. This balance, when summed across domestic institutional sectors, gives the balance of earned incomes of the total economy. If depreciation and depletion are included in the balance of earned incomes, the resulting aggregate is referred to as *gross balance of earned incomes*, and if depreciation and depletion is excluded, it is called *net balance of earned incomes*.

Meanwhile, transactions of earned incomes also take place between the domestic economy and the rest of the world sector. For example, there are payments and receipts of remuneration of employees and property incomes between the domestic and external sectors. These transactions appear as counterpart transactions of earned incomes in the rest of the world account, and in the balance of payments, these amounts are shown in reverse.

Table 9.6 Derivation of the balance of earned incomes by institutional sector

Institutional sector	Balance of earned incomes [1]
Corporations	Operating surplus + property incomes receivable - property incomes payable
General government	Taxes on production and imports receivable - subsidies on production and imports payable + property incomes receivable - property incomes payable + operating surplus
Households	Remuneration of employees + mixed income + property incomes receivable - property incomes payable + operating surplus of the owner-occupied dwelling services industry
NPISHs	Property incomes receivable - property incomes payable + operating surplus
Rest of the world	Property incomes receivable - property incomes payable + remuneration of employees receivable - remuneration of employees payable + taxes less subsidies on production and imports receivable – taxes less subsidies on production and imports payable

Note: 1) The gross balance of earned incomes includes depreciation and depletion, which are components of gross operating surplus, whereas the net balance of earned incomes excludes these amounts.

Gross national income and net national income

When earned incomes are aggregated at the level of the national economy as a whole, their amounts of property incomes (receipts and payments of property incomes) exchanged between institutional sectors are netted out. Then, the following amounts remain: (a) the total gross value-added generated by resident institutional units, and (b) the net earned incomes receivable by the domestic economy from transactions with the rest of the world, including remuneration of employees, taxes less subsidies on production and imports and property incomes. The item in (b) represents the net income (= inflows – outflows) accrued to the domestic economy in transactions with the rest of the world sector, and it is called the **net earned incomes from the rest of the world**. The sum of these two items ((a)+ (b)) is called **gross national income** (GNI). Item (a) is gross domestic product (GDP), which represents the total gross value added created by resident institutional units. In contrast, gross national income represents the aggregate value of the gross balances of earned incomes received by resident institutional units. When depreciation and depletion is subtracted from gross national income, **net national income** (NNI) is obtained.

- **GNI = GDP + net earned incomes from abroad (remuneration of employees + taxes less subsidies on production and imports + property incomes)**

Example of the allocation of earned income account

The table below (Table 9.7) illustrates the allocation of earned income account for South Korea in 2015 (unit: KRW trillion). Here is an example of how to calculate the balance of earned incomes from this table. The breakdown of earned incomes for the entire domestic economy is as follows: gross operating surplus 751.1, remuneration of employees 749.8 (=750.2+1.0–1.4), taxes on production and imports 164.3, subsidies 7.6, property income receivable 324.8, and property income payable 319.2, resulting in the gross balances of earned incomes (GNI) of 1,663.2 (= 751.1+749.8+164.3–7.6+324.8 – 319.2). By institutional sector, non-financial corporations account for 393.6 (= 493.1+36.3–135.9), financial corporations account for 39.5 (=47.2+117.2–125.0), general government accounts for 207.5 (=47.6+164.3–7.6+28.4–25.2), and households and NPISHs account for 1,022.7 (=163.1+749.8+142.9–33.2). The amount contributed to GNI by the rest of the world is 7.3, which is receipts by the rest of the world (1.0+25.2 = 26.2) less payments to the rest of the world (1.4+17.5 = 18.9). Note that the rest of the world in the sequence of economic accounts is interpreted in the opposite direction from the perspective of the domestic economy. In other words, the expenditures side of the rest of the world becomes the revenues side of the domestic economy, and the revenues side of the rest of the world become the expenditures side of the domestic economy. The balance of earned incomes becomes the balancing item in the allocation of earned income account and is carried forward to the next account, the right-hand side (revenues) of the income transfers other than transfers in kind account.

Table 9.7 Example of the allocation of earned income account (South Korea, 2015)

Expenditures (Unit: KRW trillion) **Revenues**

Nonfinancial corp.	Financial corp.	General gov't	Households & NPISHs	Total economy	ROW	Goods & services	Total	Transactions & balancing items	Nonfinancial corp.	Financial corp.	General gov't	Households &	Total economy	ROW	Goods & services	Total
								Gross operating surplus & mixed income	493.1	47.2	47.6	163.1	751.1			751.1
								Net operating surplus & mixed income	286.6	39.5	1.1	114.3	441.5			441.5
					1.0		1.0	Remuneration of employees				749.8	749.8	1.4		751.2
					1.0		1.0	Wages and salaries				641.8	641.8	1.4		643.2
								Employer's social contributions				108.0	108.0			108.0
								Actual social contributions				87.4	87.4			87.4
								Imputed social contributions				20.6	20.6			20.6
								Taxes on production & imports			164.3		164.3			164.3
								Taxes on products			143.0		143.0			143.0
								Other taxes on production			21.3		21.3			21.3

								Subsidies (-)			-7.6		-7.6			-7.6
								Subsidies on products			-5.9		-5.9			-5.9
								Other subsidies on production			-1.7		-1.7			-1.7
135.9	125.0	25.2	33.2	319.2	27.4		346.6	Property income	36.3	117.2	28.4	142.9	324.8	21.7		346.5
43.8	78.5	25.2	31.7	179.3	13.8		193.1	Interest	18.6	108.4	23.2	36.5	186.7	6.5		193.2
88.3	12.6			100.9	9.2		110.1	Income on equity	13.1	8.6	4.5	71.0	97.1	13.0		110.1
35.0	12.6			47.6	9.2		56.8	Dividends	13.1	8.6	4.5	17.6	43.8	13.0		56.8
53.3	0.0			53.3			53.3	Withdrawals from income of quasi-corporations				53.3	53.3			53.3
2.0	0.2			2.2	4.3		6.5	Reinvested earnings on FDI	4.0	0.3	0.0	0.0	4.3	2.2		6.5
0.0	33.5			33.5			33.5	Investment income disbursements	0.5	0.0	0.0	33.0	33.5			33.5
1.7	0.1	0.0	1.4	3.2			3.2	Rent	0.1	0.0	0.7	2.4	3.2			3.2
393.6	39.5	207.5	1,022.7	1,663.2	-5.2		1,663.2	**Gross balance of earned incomes /GNI**								
187.0	31.8	160.9	973.8	1,353.5	-5.2		1,353.5	***Net balance of earned incomes /NNI***								

9.2.1.2.2 Property income

As for the components of the allocation of earned income account, remuneration of employees, operating surplus and mixed income, taxes on production and imports, and subsidies have been explained in Chapters 4 and 6. Therefore, this section will focus more on property incomes (Table 9.8).

The categories of **property income** include **investment income** and **rent**. Investment income is further subdivided into interest, income on equity (i.e., dividends, withdrawals of income from quasi-corporations, reinvested earnings on foreign direct investment) and other investment income (i.e., investment income disbursements). Investment income disbursements will be covered in more detail later, but for now we will focus on interest, income on equity, and rent.

Table 9.8 Types of property incomes

Investment income	• Interest	
	• Income on equity	• Dividends
		• Withdrawal of income from quasi-corporations
		• Reinvested earnings on foreign direct investment
	• Investment income disbursements	• Investment income attributed to insurance policyholders
		• Investment income payable on pension entitlements
		• Investment income attributed to collective investment funds shareholders
Rent		

Interest

The interest recorded in the allocation of earned income account is not the actual interest receivable or payable. In the SNA, it is assumed that financial intermediaries receive interest on loans with the financial intermediation fee added and pay interest on deposits with the financial intermediation fee deducted. In reality, financial intermediaries receive interest on loans adjusted for the financial intermediation fee and pay interest on deposits similarly adjusted. However, the interest initially accrued to the financial intermediaries is the hypothetical interest receivable and payable before the implicit financial intermediation fees are applied. This is referred to as **SNA interest**, while the interest actually received or paid is called **bank interest**. The "SNA interest receivable" is the actual amount of interest received by the financial corporations less the implicit financial intermediation service charges. On the other hand, the "SNA interest payable" refers to the actual amount of interest paid by the financial corporations plus the implicit financial intermediation service charges. Financial intermediation service charges are considered to be added to the interest receivable to, or subtracted from the interest payable by financial corporations, and since these intermediation charges cannot be measured directly, they are referred to as **financial intermediation services indirectly measured** (FISIM). In the SNA, FISIM is considered as the output of financial intermediaries, and this output is treated as the cost for the depositors and borrowers who purchase it. If the purchaser of FISIM is a producer, it is recorded as an intermediate consumption item for the producer, and if the purchaser of FISIM is a final consumer, it is recorded as a final consumption item. As a result, the interest recorded as property income in the allocation of earned income account is the SNA interest, which reflects property income before the application of FISIM. Interest other than SNA interest, such as interest on bonds or interbank interest, is recorded as property income without the deduction of the intermediation fee, as no fees are applied to these items.

Dividends

Dividends are property income provided by corporations to their shareholders in return for the use of funds raised through the issuance of shares. Occasionally, there are stock dividends (where shares are issued as dividends), but this does not fall under the category of dividends because it is not a direct withdrawal of income but merely a reclassification of the own capital within the corporation. Dividends are distributed from operating surplus for the current period (more specifically, from distributable income) and are recorded as a payment of property income. However, in the case of exceptionally large dividends, referred to as "*super dividends*" that are disproportionately large compared to normal dividends, they are treated as a financial transaction because they are of the same nature as a withdrawal of equity in a corporation. **Withdrawal of**

income from a quasi-corporation measures the withdrawal of property income from a quasi-corporation (an unincorporated enterprise that prepares a complete set of financial statements) and cannot exceed its distributable income. If funds are withdrawn through the sale or disposal of assets, they are recorded not as a withdrawal of income, but as a withdrawal of equity from the quasi-corporation and a receivable by its owner, in the financial account.

Box 9.1: Recording of super dividends in the SNA

Super dividends refer to large, irregular dividend payments made by a corporation that exceed the distributable income of the current period. These payments are often financed from accumulated reserves, or from the proceeds of the sale of financial or non-financial assets. In the national accounts, the recording of super dividends differs between domestically controlled corporations and foreign direct investment (FDI) enterprise.

1. **Domestically controlled corporations**: Super dividends are recorded as withdrawals of equity rather than as dividends. In other words, payments that cannot be explained by current-period performance are treated as a return of capital to the shareholders.

- Super dividends = total payments – distributable income = withdrawals of equity

2. **Foreign direct investment (FDI) enterprises**: FDI enterprises comprise two types of units. The first is the branch of a non-resident enterprise operating domestically, which is treated as a quasi-corporation in the national account. The second is a resident corporation in which a non-resident investor holds sufficient equity to exercise control or significant influence, typically interpreted as a shareholding of 10 percent or more.

For FDI enterprises, the concept of super dividends is not applied. That is, all distributions made out of accumulated reserves, whether recorded as dividends or as withdrawals of income from quasi-corporations, are not treated as withdrawals of equity. (The only exception is when an FDI enterprise distributes the proceeds from the sale of assets; such payments are recorded as withdrawals of equity.) The rationale for treating these distributions as dividends (or withdrawals of income from quasi-corporations) rather than as withdrawals of equity lies in the particular characteristics of FDI: investment income must be measured consistently as "dividends + reinvested earnings" to facilitate international comparability and to maintain coherence with the balance of payments framework.

Reinvested earnings on foreign direct investment

Reinvested earnings on foreign direct investment refers to the retained earnings accrued either to direct investment by non-residents in domestic economy or direct investment by residents in foreign countries. The distributable income generated from a foreign direct investment (FDI) enterprise is allocated in two ways. One component consists of actual distribution (that is, dividends or withdrawals of income from quasi-corporations) which are recorded as actual international transactions. The other component arises when the enterprise retains part of its earnings; in the SNA, these retained earnings are imputed as if they were distributed to the direct investors and subsequently reinvested in the same enterprise. These imputed reinvested earnings are classified as a component of investment income. This imputation reflects the need for consistency with the treatment applied in the balance of payments framework[13]. Reinvested earnings of an FDI enterprise are calculated as follows:

- **Reinvested earnings of the FDI enterprise = direct investor's ownership share x retained earnings (= distributable income – dividends payable or withdrawals of income from quasi-corporations)**

For example, if the distributable income of an FDI enterprise is 100, the actual dividends payable is 30, and the foreign direct investor owns 70 percent of the equity, then total retained earnings are 100 – 30 = 70, and the reinvested earnings attributable to the foreign investor are 70 percent x 70 = 49.

Reinvested earnings can be divided into the following two cases depending on whether the investor is a resident or a non-resident. The first case is when **reinvested earnings on inward direct investment** are deemed to be treated as property income payable to a non-resident investor. This occurs when a non-resident investor receives the retained earnings from an enterprise in the domestic economy that was the result of inward direct investment. Subsequently, it is assumed that the non-resident reinvests this amount back into the domestic direct investment enterprise (which is recorded in the financial account as an increase in the "direct investment share" of the rest of the world). The rationale behind this treatment is that a direct investment enterprise is, by definition, under the control or influence of the direct investor and, therefore, it is assumed that the retention

[13] This treatment is also recommended in the 2025 SNA for all domestic corporations other than foreign direct investment enterprises, by compiling supplementary items that record the retained earnings as being distributed and subsequently reinvested.

or reinvestment of invested earnings within the enterprise is considered a decision made by the direct investor (BOP6, 11.41). Accordingly, the accounting treatment is carried out as follows.

Table 9.9 Accounting for reinvested earnings on inward direct investment

	Domestic sector (Direct investment enterprise)		**The rest of the world**	
	Expenditures/Changes in assets	Revenues/Changes in liabilities	Expenditures/Changes in assets	Revenues/Changes in liabilities
Allocation of earned income account	Reinvested earnings payable			Reinvested earnings receivable
Financial account		Increases in liabilities of direct investment shares	Increases in assets of direct investment shares	

The second case, contrary to the first case, is when the **reinvested earnings on outward direct investment** (i.e., a domestic resident's direct investment abroad) are deemed to be treated as property income receivable by the resident investor, thereby recorded as reinvested earnings for the investor. At the same time, the resident investor is treated as reinvesting this amount in the non-resident direct investment enterprise in the financial account. The accounting treatment in this case is opposite to that for the reinvested earnings on inward direct investment.

Reinvested earnings on foreign direct investment are imputed values and should be added or subtracted when calculating the **net earned incomes receivable from abroad** for the purpose of deriving GNI. In other words, reinvested earning on inward direct investment is recorded as "payments to the rest of the world", while reinvested earning on outward direct investment is recorded as "receipts from the rest of the world". The following table (Table 9.10) shows the details of property income by institutional sector for South Korea in 2015. By looking at this table, one can understand how reinvested earnings on foreign direct investment is treated. According to this table (unit: KRW trillion), the reinvested earnings payable from the inward direct investment is recorded as 2.2 on the expenditures side of the domestic economy, with the corresponding record is 2.2 on the revenues side of the rest of the world. Conversely, the reinvested earnings receivable for the outward direct investment is recorded as 4.3 on the revenues side of the domestic economy, with the corresponding record 4.3 on the expenditures side of the rest of the world.

Table 9.10 Details of property incomes by institutional sector (South Korea, 2015)

Expenditures (Unit: KRW trillion) **Revenues**

Nonfinancial corp.	Financial corp.	General government	Households & NPISHs	Total economy	ROW	Goods & services	Total	Transactions & balancing items	Nonfinancial corp.	Financial corp.	General government	Households & NPISHs	Total economy	ROW	Goods & services	Total
135.9	125.0	25.2	33.2	319.2	27.4		346.6	Property income	36.3	117.2	28.4	142.9	324.8	21.7		346.6
43.8	78.5	25.2	31.7	179.3	13.9		193.2	Interest	18.6	108.4	23.2	36.5	186.7	6.5		193.2
88.3	12.6			100.9	9.2		110.1	Income on equity	13.1	8.6	4.5	71.0	97.1	13.0		110.1
35.0	12.6			47.6	9.2		56.8	Dividends	13.1	8.6	4.5	17.6	43.8	13.0		56.8
53.3	0.0			53.3			53.3	Withdrawals from income of quasi-corporations				53.3	53.3			53.3
2.0	0.2			2.2	4.3		6.5	Reinvested earnings on foreign direct investment	4.0	0.3	0.0	0.0	4.3	2.2		6.5
0.0	33.5			33.5			33.5	Investment income disbursements	0.5	0.0	0.0	33.0	33.5			33.5
1.7	0.1	0.0	1.4	3.2			3.2	Rent	0.1	0.0	0.7	2.4	3.2			3.2
-99.6	-7.7	3.2	109.8	5.6	-5.6		0.0	**Balance of property incomes**								

Rent

Rent refers to the property income receivable by the legal or economic owner of a non-produced non-financial assets (i.e., land, subsoil assets, and other natural resources) for allowing another institutional unit to use the asset in production (this is called *resource lease*). Rent is classified into three categories: (i) rent on land, (ii) rent on mineral and energy resources (i.e., payments for extraction rights), and (iii) rent on other non-produced non-financial assets.

In the SNA, rent is classified as property income payable for the use of a non-produced asset. In contrast, payments for the use of fixed assets such as building and machinery are classified as **rentals**, which represent the purchase of produced services. Rentals are recorded as the output of the lessor and as intermediate or final consumption of the lessee.

1. **Rent on land**: Rent arising from the leasing of land is recorded on an accrual basis for the period, regardless of whether payment is actually made. When a portion of agricultural output is provided in kind to the landowner as payment (i.e., share-cropping), the rent is valued at the basic price of the crops delivered. Land does not undergo depletion in the production process. In relation to leasing of land, taxes and other expenses that are legally borne by the landowner are conventionally treated as being paid by the tenant, and the rent on land is recorded on an **after-tax basis**, net of these amounts. This convention avoids the need to construct a notional enterprise for the landowner for accounting purposes. When a contract covers land together with building

and the payments does not distinguish between the two, the entire payment is classified based on the dominant component. If the value of land is judged to exceed the value of building and improvements, the whole amount is treated as rent; otherwise, it is classified as a rental.

2. **Payments for extraction rights to mineral and energy resources**: These are payments made by the owner of the resource (e.g., government) in exchange for granting permission to extract the resource for a specified period. This category includes royalties, sur-taxes, and permits in relation to extraction.

In the SNA, rent on natural resources is distinct from **resource rent**. Resource rent is the excess return attributable to natural resources used in production and is recorded as part of the gross operating surplus of the extractor in the production account. Rent on extraction rights, on the other hand, is property income payable to the legal owner (usually government). It is recorded in the allocation of earned income account as rent payable by corporations and rent receivable by government. Under the 2025 SNA, the rent recorded as property income must reflect the **depletion-adjusted rent**. Thus, the rent receivable by the legal owner is recorded gross, and the portion attributable to the owner's share of depletion is recorded as a negative entry in the same account. This ensures that the owner's income is recorded net of depletion.

The 2025 SNA adopts the **split-asset approach** for the allocation of rent on natural resources and the recording of depletion in the sequence of economic accounts (For further details, see section 10.1.3.6).

3. **Rent on other non-produced non-financial assets**: This category includes payments for the rights to use marketing assets and in the digitalized economy, payments made to individuals who allow enterprises to access or collect their personal behavior data.

Box 9.2: The entrepreneurial income account and the allocation of other earned income account

In the SNA, the allocation of earned income account is partitioned into two sub-accounts: the "entrepreneurial income account" and the "allocation of other earned income account" in order to measure income from market activities of enterprises separately from other income. In the entrepreneurial income account, **entrepreneurial income** is derived as a balancing item, which measures the income of market producers, and is defined as "operating surplus plus property income receivable minus property income payable (excluding dividends payable, withdrawals of income from quasi-corporations, and reinvested earnings payable)". This income is similar to corporate income before tax familiar in business accounting. Entrepreneurial income is not measured at the establishment level but can only be measured at the institutional unit level, such as for enterprises. In addition, the entrepreneurial income account applies only to corporations, and unincorporated enterprises in the households and government sectors are included in the corporations sector only when they are recognized as quasi-corporations with a complete set of accounts. For enterprises other than corporations, this account is not compiled because the assets that contribute to production activities cannot be distinguished from the total assets, and therefore, property incomes related to production activities cannot be identified separately.

9.2.2 Transfer income accounts

Transfer income accounts comprise the *income transfers other than transfers in kind account*, which records, for each institutional sector, current transfers receivable and payable in addition to the balance of earned incomes carried forward from the allocation of earned income account, and the *social transfers in kind account*, which records, for each institutional sector, social transfers in kind receivable and payable. These corresponds to the *secondary distribution of income account* and the *redistribution of income in kind account* in the 2008 SNA, respectively.

9.2.2.1 The income transfers other than transfers in kind account

The income transfers other than transfers in kind account (the *income transfers account* hereafter) is the account that shows the amount of balance of earned income plus current transfers receivable minus current transfers payable. The balancing item, **disposable income** is derived by subtracting total expenditures from total revenues of this account (Table 9.11). A **transfer** in the SNA is a transaction in which one institutional unit provides goods, services or assets to another institutional unit without receiving anything in return as a direct counterpart. **Current transfers** refer to transactions in which goods, services, or assets are provided on a regular basis, without any counterpart payment. These transactions are recorded in the opposite direction depending on whether they are received or paid. Examples of current transfers include current taxes on income and wealth, net social contributions, social benefits, and other current transfers.

Current taxes on income and wealth are taxes levied recurrently by the government on the households' income or corporate income, or on properties such as land and buildings, excluding taxes directly related to production activities. These taxes are transfers that are unilaterally collected by the government through its coercive taxing authority. Capital taxes, which are levied irregularly and occasionally on capital, are excluded from this category and are classified as capital transfers.

Net social contributions and social benefits arise when social insurance schemes receive social contributions from households and enterprises, manage these funds, and pay social benefits to households under the social insurance system. In the SNA, the payments of social contributions by households and their employers and the receipts of social benefits from social insurance schemes are treated as current transfers. **Net social contributions** (social transfers less service charges) refer to the amount of insurance premiums collected by the social insurance schemes from households and enterprises minus the management fees of the insurance schemes under the social insurance system (i.e., social security funds, pension funds etc.). Social contributions received by social insurance schemes are used to pay pensions to insured households, or to provide social transfers in kind, such as subsidizing medical expenses. Under the social insurance system, pensions are paid to households that are members of social insurance schemes, or social assistance benefits can be paid to non-members under certain conditions, all of which are referred to as **social benefits**. (See section 9.3.5 for more details.)

Social insurance schemes can be organized by employers of enterprises or by government (such as the national pension funds and the national health insurance administration, which are social security organizations), or they can be operated by financial institutions. The primary role of these organizations is to hold and manage assets to be used for social insurances, and to distribute the earnings from those assets. (See section 9.3.3 for more details.)

The national disposable income of the economy as a whole is derived by summing all the disposable incomes of institutional sector. Current transfers are offset within domestic institutional sectors, and only **net current transfers receivable from abroad** (= all current transfers receivable by resident institutional units from nonresident units - all current transfers payable by resident institutional units to non-resident units) remains from transactions with the rest of the world. The result is the sum of gross national income (GNI) and net current transfers from abroad, which is called **gross national disposable income** (GNDI). *Net national disposable income* (NNDI) is obtained by deducting depreciation and depletion from gross national disposable income.

- GNDI = GNI + net current transfers with the ROW (= current transfers receivable from abroad – current transfers payable abroad)

Table 9.11 The format of the income transfers other than transfers in kind account

Expenditures	Revenues
	Balance of earned incomes
Current transfers payable	**Current transfers receivable**
(Current taxes on income and wealth, payable)	(Current taxes on income and wealth, receivable)
(Net social contributions, payable)	(Net social contributions, receivable)
(Social benefits other than social transfers in kind, payable)	(Social benefits other than social transfers in kind, receivable)
(Other current transfers payable)	(Other current transfers receivable)
Disposable income	

9.2.2.1.1 Current transfers versus capital transfers

In the SNA, among the items involving unrequited transfers, there are two types of transfers: current transfers and capital transfers. **capital transfers** are recorded in the capital account and are not included in the income concept of the SNA. The distinction between current transfers and capital transfers affects the determination of the value of national income. Both items involve unrequited transfers between economic units, but current transfers are included in disposable income, whereas capital transfers are not. The distinction between capital transfers and current transfers is determined by whether they occur on a regular basis, or their scale is abnormally large. (See 10.1.3.8 for more details on capital transfers.)

Current transfers are recorded in the income transfers other than transfers in kind account, and their types include the following items (Table 9.12): current taxes (personal income tax, corporate income tax, and capital gains tax) and taxes on household properties such as land and buildings (However, taxes on corporate assets are excluded as they are classified as other taxes on production. Also, "capital taxes" such as inheritance tax are excluded from the category of current taxes.), social benefits, and net social contributions. Other items classified as current transfers include net premiums and claims related to non-life insurance, net premiums and net claims related to reinsurance, grants between the central and local governments, and current international aids.

Table 9.12 Types of current transfers

Item	Example
Current taxes	Personal income tax, corporate income tax, taxes on capital gains
Other current taxes	Current taxes on capital (excluding taxes levied on enterprises, which are classified as other taxes on production. "Capital taxes" are also excluded and classified as capital transfers).
Miscellaneous current taxes	Poll tax levied on individuals

Item	Example
Net social contributions	
Social benefits	
Other current transfers	Net non-life insurance premiums
	Non-life insurance claims
	Net reinsurance premiums and claims
	Current transfers within general government
	Current international cooperation
	Miscellaneous current transfers

Other types of current transfers (**miscellaneous current transfers**) are comprised of remittances between households, lotteries, and fees levied by the central bank on financial corporations in relation to providing services (see Table 9.13).

Table 9.13 Types of miscellaneous current transfers

Item	Example
Current transfers to NPISHs	Current transfers to NPISHs such as membership dues, subscriptions and donations. (Membership dues or donations to non-profit market institutions such as the chamber of commerce are treated as "intermediate consumption" by donating institutions.
Current transfers between households	Regular remittances to family members residing in other regions or countries.
Fines and penalties	They are compulsory payments imposed by courts or judicial bodies. (Fines or penalties levied by tax authorities are classified as "taxes.")
Lotteries	
The central bank's fees received from financial corporations	Fees levied by the central bank on financial corporations in relation to providing services.
Charitable contributions	They include charitable contributions paid by government or NPISHs in response to natural disasters.

Example of the income transfers other than transfers in kind account

The following table (Table 9.14) illustrates the income transfers other than transfers in kind account for South Korea in 2015 (unit: KRW trillion). The balancing item in this account, gross disposable income (or net disposable income), is derived by adding net current transfers receivable from abroad (= current transfers receivable – current transfers payable) to the balance of earned incomes.

For the domestic economy as a whole, gross national income (1,663.2) carried over from the allocation of earned income account, plus current transfers receivable (606.5) minus current transfers payable (610.8), yields gross national disposable income (GNDI) of 1,659.0 (=1,663.2+606.5–610.8).

In the rest of the world sector, payments to foreign countries (15.8) exceed receipts from abroad (11.6), resulting in a negative net current transfers receivable from abroad of 4.2 (=15.8–11.6). Gross disposable income by institutional sector is as follows: 335.6 (=393.6+35.7–93.6) for non-financial corporations, 36.8 (=39.5+63.2–65.8) for financial corporations, 360.8 (=207.5+287.1–133.9) for general government, 925.7 (= 1,022.7+220.5–317.5) for households and NPISHs. Gross disposable income (or net disposable income) is carried forward to the right-hand side (revenues) of the use of income account as described in the following section.

Table 9.14 Example of the income transfers other than transfers in kind account (South Korea, 2015)

Expenditures (Unit: KRW trillion) **Revenues**

Nonfinancial corp.	Financial corp.	General government	Households & NPISHs	Total economy	ROW	Goods & services	Total	Transactions & balancing items	Nonfinancial corp.	Financial corp.	General government	Households & NPISHs	Total economy	ROW	Goods & services	Total
								Balance of earned incomes, gross/GNI	393.6	39.5	207.5	1,022.7	1,663.2			1,663.2
								Balance of earned incomes, net/NNI	187.0	31.8	160.9	973.8	1,353.5			1,353.5
93.6	65.8	133.9	317.5	610.8	11.6		622.4	**Current transfers**	35.7	63.2	287.1	220.5	606.5	15.8		622.4
49.0	8.2	0.0	65.0	122.2	0.0		122.2	Current taxes on income & wealth			122.2		122.2	0.0		122.2
40.1	6.8	0.0	57.7	104.7	0.0		104.7	Taxes on income			104.7		104.7	0.0		104.7
8.9	1.3	0.0	7.3	17.5			17.5	Other current taxes			17.5		17.5			17.5
			175.7	175.7			175.7	Net social contributions	12.6	36.4	126.7	0.0	175.7			175.7
			87.4	87.4			87.4	Employers' actual contribution	0.0	31.8	55.6	0.0	87.4			87.4
			20.6	20.6			20.6	Employer' imputed contribution	12.6	1.4	6.5	0.0	20.6			20.6
			67.7	67.7			67.7	Household' actual contribution	0.0	3.2	64.6	0.0	67.7			67.7
			0.0	0.0			0.0	Social insurance charges	0.0	0.0	0.0		0.0			0.0
12.6	22.7	75.4	0.0	110.8	0.0		110.8	Social benefits				110.8	110.8	0.0		110.8
		24.5		24.5	0.0		24.5	Social security benefits				24.5	24.5	0.0		24.5
12.6	22.7	21.3	0.0	56.6			56.6	Other social insurance benefits				56.6	56.6			56.6
		29.6		29.6			29.6	Social assistance benefits				29.6	29.6			29.6
32.0	34.9	58.4	76.7	202.0	11.6		213.6	Other current transfers	23.0	26.7	38.3	109.7	197.8	15.8		213.6
335.6	36.8	360.8	925.7	1,659.0	4.2		1,659.0	**Gross disposable income**								
129.1	29.1	314.2	876.9	1,349.3			1,349.3	***Net disposable income***								

9.2.2.2 The social transfers in kind account

The **social transfers in kind account** is an account that derives **adjusted disposable income** by adding the receipts of "social transfers in kind" for each institutional sector or subtracting the payments of social transfers in kind from the balancing item, disposable income, in the income transfers other than transfers in kind account. The purpose of compiling the social transfers in kind account is to measure the actual final consumption (the amount of final consumption actually acquired by each institutional sector) by adding social transfers in kind to the final consumption expenditure by institutional sectors, as explained in the use of income account in the following section.

Social transfers in kind refers to goods and services provided to households by non-market producers (such as government or NPISHs), for free or at economically insignificant prices, and delivered in kind rather than in cash. Social transfers in kind are the final consumption expenditure made by non-market producers for households, and this expenditure is called **individual consumption expenditure**. This contrasts with the **collective consumption expenditure** by government. Collective consumption expenditures are final consumption expenditures by non-producers excluding individual consumption expenditures, and are consumption expenditures that cannot be attributed to households. (For more details on individual consumption and collective consumption, see 12.1.4.)

Table 9.15 The format of the social transfers in kind account

Expenditures	Revenues
	Disposable income
Social transfers in kind, payable	Social transfers in kind, receivable
Adjusted disposable income	

9.2.2.2.1 Social transfers in kind

There are two types of **social transfers in kind**. The first type involves non-market producers who produce goods and services for their final consumption, but the actual benefit of this consumption accrues to households. For example, health and education services are examples of non-market producers' goods and services that can be attributed to households. Specifically, the government's free medical care and education for households fall into this category, and if these services are provided to households at prices significantly lower than market prices, the difference between the market price and the price paid by the household is treated as social transfers in kind. In the case of NPISHs, all non-market products are provided to households for free or at economically insignificant prices.

The second type of social transfers in kind involves cases where households receive medical treatments at hospitals, and part of the medical expenses are reimbursed by the government, such as health insurance or medical benefit. In this case, the government is treated as purchasing a certain portion of medical services from market producers (such as hospitals) and providing them to households free of charge. Thus, the first type of social transfers in kind involves the transfer of non-market products to households, while the second type involves the transfer of market products to households. The first type is recorded as the output of government, whereas the second type is recorded as government purchases of the market output from private producers. Both types are recorded as final consumption by government or NPISHs, but since the benefits ultimately go to households, they are recorded as social transfers in kind receivable by households and social transfers in kind payable by government or NPISHs in the social transfers in kind account.

The household's disposable income plus the value of social transfers in kind receivable gives the household's **adjusted disposable income**. In addition, the adjusted disposable income of the government and NPISHs is obtained by subtracting the value of social transfers in kind payable from the disposable income of government and NPISHs. The social transfers in kind account does not apply to corporations that do not receive or pay social transfers in kind.

- Government's adjusted disposable income = government's disposable income – government's social transfers in kind payable
- NPISHs' adjusted disposable income = NPISHs' disposable income – NPISHs' social transfers in kind payable
- Households' adjusted disposable income = households' disposable income + social transfers in kind receivable

Example of the social transfers in kind account

The table below (Table 9.16) illustrates an example of the social transfers in kind account for South Korea in 2015 (unit: KRW trillion). In this example, due to social transfers in kind to households, total adjusted disposable income changes only for households, general government and NPISHs: 225.1 (= 360.8-135.7) for general government, 1,061.5 (= 925.7+163.5-27.7) for households and NPISHs, and no changes for the total domestic economy and corporations sector.

Table 9.16 Example of the social transfers in kind account (South Korea, 2015)

Expenditures (Unit: KRW trillion) **Revenues**

Nonfinancial corp.	Financial corp.	General government	Households & NPISHs	Total economy	ROW	Goods & services	Total	Transactions & balancing items	Nonfinancial corp.	Financial corp.	General government	Households & NPISHs	Total economy	ROW	Goods & services	Total
								Gross disposable income	335.6	36.8	360.8	925.7	1,659.0			1,659.0
								Net disposable income	129.1	29.1	314.2	876.9	1,349.3			1,349.3
		135.7	27.7	163.5			163.5	Social transfers in kind				163.5	163.5			163.5
335.6	36.8	225.1	1,061.5	1,659.0			1,659.0	**Gross adjusted disposable income**								
129.1	29.1	178.5	1,012.6	1,349.3			1,349.3	***Net adjusted disposable income***								

9.2.3 Use of income accounts

The use of income accounts derive the balancing item, gross saving or net saving, by deducting final consumption expenditure (and actual final consumption) from disposable income (and adjusted disposable income) carried forward for each institutional sector from the transfer income accounts, and by adding or subtracting the adjustments for the change in pension entitlements. This category comprises the *use of disposable income account* and the *use of adjusted disposable income account*.

9.2.3.1 The use of disposable income account

The **use of disposable income account** is an account that shows how the disposable income carried over from the income transfers other than transfers in kind account is allocated between final consumption expenditure and saving by households, government, and NPISHs. Unlike the adjusted disposable income (disposable income adjusted for social transfers in kind), the disposable income used in this account is based on the income and consumption expenditure that actually occurred within the institutional sectors. (This part will be covered in more detail in the use of adjusted disposable income account.)

In the use of disposable income account, disposable income, which is the balancing item carried over from the income transfers other than transfers in kind account, is further adjusted to derive the final disposable income by adding or subtracting the **adjustment for the change in pension entitlements** for each institutional sector. After this adjustment, final consumption expenditure is subtracted from this total disposable income to derive the balancing item, **saving**. If the amount carried forward from the income transfers other than transfers in kind account is gross disposable income, the balancing item will be **gross saving**; if it is net disposable income, the balancing item will be **net saving**. The adjustment for the change in pension entitlements represents the adjustment made for employees' accrued pension rights arising from employment-related social insurance schemes. From the household perspective, this adjustment is added to disposable income, while from the perspective of the financial corporations managing the pension schemes, the same amount is subtracted in order to derive their disposable income.

The adjustment for the change in pension entitlements is introduced to account for the dual nature of "pension entitlements." The dual nature refers to the fact that some pensions have characteristics of both social insurance and life insurance. Therefore, this item is treated as a current transfer under social insurance (payable in households, receivable in financial corporations) in the income transfers other than transfers in kind account, and it is processed as the change in pension entitlements in the use of income account (receivable in households, payable in financial corporations) and the changes in financial assets and liabilities in the financial account (pension entitlement claims in households, and pension entitlement liabilities in financial institutions). (For more details, see 9.3.3.) The balancing item, saving, is carried forward to the right-hand side of the capital account (under changes in liabilities and net worth), as described in the next section.

Table 9.17 The format of the use of disposable income account

Expenditures	Revenues
	Disposable income
Final consumption expenditure	
Adjustment for the change in pension entitlements, payable	Adjustment for the change in pension entitlements, receivable
Saving	

The savings ratio in the national accounts is calculated as follows:

- **Savings ratio = 1 – final consumption expenditure/(disposable income + net adjustment for the change in pension entitlements)**

For the national economy as a whole, the net adjustment for the change in pension entitlements becomes zero because the amounts of pension entitlements held by households and the liabilities of financial corporations who owe the pension entitlements offset each other. Therefore, the savings ratio is calculated as "1 – final consumption expenditure/disposable income." The calculation of the savings ratio varies by institutional sector. In the case of corporations, final consumption expenditure does not incur, and it only applies to the other institutional sectors, such as households, government, and NPISHs. Thus, for non-financial corporations, disposable income equals the amount of saving, and the savings ratio is 'one.' In the case of financial corporations, the amount of total disposable income is the disposable income minus the adjustment for the change in pension entitlements payable, and this amount also represents the saving.

Meanwhile, in the use of income account, **current external balance** is added as the balancing item for the rest of the world sector. This item represents the balancing item for the current accounts as a whole of the rest of the world, which is derived from the amount of "balance of goods and services + balance of earned income + balance of transfer income (secondary income)".

The following table (Table 9.18) shows the use of disposable income account for South Korea in 2015 (unit: KRW trillion). In this table, final consumption expenditure is 250.1 for general government, 804.8 for households and NPISHs, and 1,054.9 for the total domestic economy. The ratio of final consumption expenditure to gross disposable income for the total economy is 0.636 (= 1,054.9/1,659.0). The current external balance for the rest of the world is -114.5 (= -113.5 - 5.2+4.2), which is the sum of the balance of goods and services, the balance of earned income, and the balance of transfer income.

The results of calculating the **gross savings ratio** using this table is as follows. The gross saving ratio for non-financial corporations is 335.6/335.6=1.0; for financial corporations, it is 23.1/(36.8-13.7)=1.0; for general government, it is 110.7/360.8=0.307; and for households and NPISHs, it is 72.1/(925.7+13.7)= 0.143. The gross saving ratio of the total domestic economy is 604.1/(1,659.0 + 13.7 – 13.7)=0.364. Similarly, the **net saving ratio** is equal to 1.0 for both non-financial corporations and financial corporations, 0.204 for general government, 0.096 for households and NPISHs, and 0.218 for the total domestic economy.

Table 9.18 Example of the disposable use of income account (South Korea, year 2015)

Expenditures (Unit: KRW trillion) Revenues

Nonfinancial corp.	Financial corp.	General government	Households & NPISHs	Total economy	ROW	Goods & services	Total	Transactions & balancing items	Nonfinancial corp.	Financial corp.	General government	Households & NPISHs	Total economy	ROW	Goods & services	Total
								Gross disposable income	335.6	36.8	360.8	925.7	1,659.0			1,659.0
								Net disposable income	129.1	29.1	314.2	876.9	1,349.3			1,349.3
		250.1	804.8	1,054.9			1,054.9	Final consumption							1,054.9	1,054.9
0.0	13.7	0.0		13.7	0.0		13.7	Adjustment for change in pension entitlements				13.7	13.7	0.0		13.7
335.6	23.1	110.7	134.6	604.1			604.1	**Gross saving**								
129.1	15.4	64.1	85.8	294.4			294.4	***Net saving***								
					-114.5		-114.5	***Current external balance***								

9.2.3.2 The use of adjusted disposable income account

The **use of adjusted disposable income account** shows how the adjusted disposable income, which is the balancing item in the social transfers in kind account, is allocated into **actual final consumption** and **saving**. This account is used to measure how social transfers in kind affect actual final consumption by institutional sectors, with social transfers in kind being added to disposable income. This account is not sequential or hierarchical to the use of disposable income account but is compiled for the purpose of policy analysis.

The final consumption expenditure of the government and NPISHs minus their social transfers in kind to households is called **actual final consumption** of the government and NPISHs. The actual final consumption of government corresponds to its **collective consumption expenditure**, which contrasts with individual consumption expenditure. Collective consumption expenditure includes expenditures on defence, public safety, and public administration, which cannot be directly attributed to households. NPISHs do not have collective consumption expenditure, so all final consumption expenditure of NPISHs is considered social transfers in kind attributed to households, resulting in an actual final consumption of 'zero.' The actual final consumption of households is equal to final consumption expenditure of households plus social transfers in kind from the government and NPISHs.

- Government's actual final consumption = government's final consumption expenditure – government's social transfers in kind = government's collective consumption expenditure
- Actual final consumption of NPISHs = final consumption expenditure of NPISHs – social transfers in kind of NPISHs = 0
- Households' actual final consumption = households' final consumption expenditure + social transfers in kind from the government and NPISHs

The use of adjusted disposable income account derives the final adjusted disposable income by adding (as in the case of the use of disposable income account) the adjustment for the change in pensions entitlements to the adjusted disposable income. Then, the actual final consumption is subtracted from this amount to derive the balancing item, **saving**. Adjusted disposable income in this account differs from disposable income by institutional sector, but the total for domestic economy is consistent with the amount of disposable income in the use of disposable income account. In addition, savings for institutional sector are derived by subtracting actual final consumption from total adjusted disposable income, and are unchanged compared to the amount of savings in the use of disposable income account.

Table 9.19 The format of the use of adjusted disposable income account

Expenditures	Revenues
	Adjusted disposable income
Actual final consumption Social transfers in kind, payable	Social transfers in kind, receivable
Saving	

The table below shows the use of adjusted disposable income account for South Korea in 2015 (unit: KRW trillion). In this example, actual final consumption is 114.4 (=250.1-135.7) for general government and 940.5 (=804.8+163.5-27.7) for the households and NPISHs. The balancing item, saving, matches that in the use of disposable income account, both by institutional sector and for the total domestic economy.

Table 9.20 The use of adjusted disposable income account (South Korea, year 2015)

Expenditures (Unit: KRW trillion) **Revenues**

Nonfinancial corp.	Financial corp.	General government	Households & NPISHs	Total economy	ROW	Goods & services	Total	Transactions and balancing items	Nonfinancial corp.	Financial corp.	General government	Households & NPISHs	Total economy	ROW	Goods & services	Total
								Gross adjusted disposable income	335.6	36.8	225.1	1,061.5	1,659.0			1,659.0
								Net adjusted disposable income	129.1	29.1	178.5	1,012.6	1,349.3			1,349.3
		114.4	940.5	1,054.9			1,054.9	Actual final consumption							1,054.9	1,054.9
0.0	13.7	0.0		13.7	0.0		13.7	Adjust. for the change in pension entitlements				13.7	13.7	0.0		13.7
335.6	23.1	19.7	134.6	604.1			604.1	**Gross saving**								
129.1	15.4	64.1	85.8	294.4			294.4	***Net saving***								
					-114.5		-114.5	***Current external balance***								

9.3 Supplementary explanations on income accounts

In the previous section, a general explanation of the income accounts was provided, but there were insufficient details regarding the individual items included in each account and their institutional background. In this section, we aim to provide supplementary explanations for these items.

9.3.1 The concepts of income in the SNA

In the SNA, "the coverage of **income** is limited to income accrued in the income accounts," and capital transfers receivable or payable accrued in the capital account are not included in the income definition. In addition, other flows accrued in the other changes in assets and liabilities account (i.e., holding gains or losses, other changes in the volume of assets and liabilities) are also not included in income. In other words, the income concept in the SNA is confined to "disposable income" derived from the income accounts[14]. Moreover, income in the SNA is measured from the perspective of what economic entities receive. Accordingly, the income accrued to resident producers through production activities is reflected in the gross value added, which constitutes

[14] The *economic theoretic concept of income* is the sum of disposable income in the income accounts, plus net capital transfers receivable in the capital account, plus other changes in the volume of assets and liabilities and real holding gains and losses accruing in the other changes in assets and liabilities account.

gross domestic product (GDP), while the income received by resident economic entities (institutional units) is recorded as **gross national income (GNI)**. In other words, GDP is measured in terms of the income accruing, while GNI and GNDI are measured in terms of the income receipt.

Understand the following concepts of income introduced in the SNA will help clarify the income accounts explained earlier. Below, we will take a closer look at income concepts in the income accounts that were insufficiently explained earlier, including property income, transfer income, income in kind, entrepreneurial income, as well as distributed income, and distributable income.

9.3.1.1 Accounting treatment of property income

Earned income refers to the income accrued to institutional units as a consequence of participating in the production process or providing assets required for production. Among earned incomes, income generated by lending financial assets used for production purposes in other institutional units or by leasing natural resources is referred to as **property income**[15].

Property income is divided into two main categories: **investment income**, which is the return for providing financial assets, and **rent**, which is the return for providing natural resources. Investment income consists of interest, income on equity (i.e., dividends, withdrawals of income from quasi-corporations, reinvested earnings on foreign direct investment), and investment income disbursements.

Figure 9.1 Types of property income

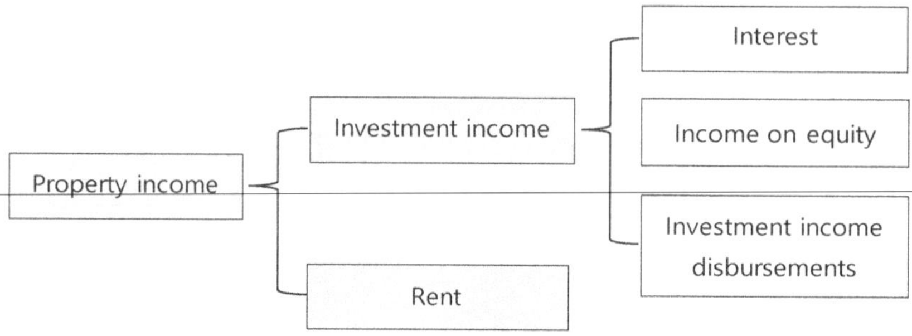

Interest and *income on equity* among investment income have been explained previously. However, to understand investment income disbursements, a comprehensive understanding of the nature of non-life and life insurance scheme, social insurance schemes, and the treatment of imputed

[15] On the other hand, income accrued by providing produced assets (i.e., machinery, buildings etc.) is recorded in the output of the rental industry as **rentals**.

transaction in relation to them is required. Therefore, the investment income disbursements will be discussed in greater detail in the following sections (see 9.3.2 to 9.3.4). In this section, we will present a summary table outlining the accounting treatments of property incomes in the national accounts.

Table 9.21 Accounting treatment for property incomes in the national accounts

<table>
<tr><th colspan="3">Type of property income</th><th>Accounting treatment</th></tr>
<tr><td rowspan="8">Investment income</td><td>Interest</td><td></td><td>This records "SNA interest" before adding or subtracting FISIM. (FISIM is the output of financial corporations and is recorded as intermediate consumption by other producers and final consumption by households who use financial intermediation services).</td></tr>
<tr><td rowspan="3">Income on equity</td><td>Dividends</td><td></td></tr>
<tr><td>Withdrawals of income from quasi-corporations</td><td></td></tr>
<tr><td>Reinvested earnings on foreign direct investment</td><td>The retained earnings of foreign direct investment enterprises in the domestic economy are deemed to be remitted to non-resident investors (saving of foreign direct investment enterprises = 0), and are then attributed to be reinvested in the direct investment enterprises. The counterpart transaction is recorded as an increase in the non-resident investor's direct investment equities (= reinvested earnings) in the financial account.</td></tr>
<tr><td rowspan="4">Investment income disbursements</td><td rowspan="3">Investment income attributed to insurance policyholders</td><td>1) Life insurance and annuities: It consists of all the investment income earned on the reserves of the policyholders. It is recorded as a counterpart transaction in the financial account as an increase in the entitlements of life insurance and annuities of households.</td></tr>
<tr><td>2) Non-life insurance: Investment income disbursement attributable to policyholders is deemed to be repaid as a premium supplement to the insurance corporations in the income transfers other than transfers in kind account.</td></tr>
<tr><td>3) Standardized guarantee schemes: Investment income disbursement is deemed to be repaid as a fee supplement to the guarantor in the income transfers other than transfers in kind account.</td></tr>
<tr><td>Investment income attributed to pension entitlements</td><td>Employment-related schemes (DB and DC, etc.): Investment income disbursement is deemed to be repaid to the employment-related schemes in the income transfers other than transfers in kind account.</td></tr>
</table>

Type of property income			Accounting treatment
			Subsequently, it is added to disposable income as an "adjustment for the change in pension entitlements" in the use of income account, and recorded as changes in the "households' pension entitlements" (assets) as a counterpart entry in the financial account.
		Investment income attributed to investment fund shareholders	The remaining retained earnings of the investment funds are treated as being distributed to shareholders (the saving in the investment funds = 0). Thereafter, it is assumed that the shareholders reinvest in the funds. (It is recorded as an increase in the shareholder's equity in the investment funds in the financial account.)
Rent			Only the net rent after deducting taxes and other expenses borne by the landowner is treated as being paid by the tenant. (The taxes and other expenses are recorded in the tenant's production account or generation of earned income account.)

9.3.1.2 Transfer income in the balance of payments

Transfer income is defined, in the balance of payments, as income obtained by current transfers receivable minus current transfers payable in the transfer income account. Current transfers are unrequited transfers between economic units, which include current taxes (i.e., personal income tax, corporate tax, etc.), social contributions, social benefits, and other current transfers (i.e., non-life insurance premiums, non-life insurance claims, current international aid, etc.). Current transfers are explained in more detail in the next section, as it is directly associated with the life and non-life insurance schemes and social insurance schemes.

The transfer income account in the balance of payments corresponds to the income transfers other than transfers in kind account in the SNA. However, since the former account does not include the balance of earned income as an item, only the balance of transfer income is derived as a balancing item. The term "transfer income" is officially used only in the balance of payments.

9.3.1.3 Social transfers in kind

Income in kind refers to income provided by enterprises to employees in the form of goods and services instead of cash. In the SNA, this concept is similarly applied to **social transfers in kind** to households. There are two types of social transfers in kind. The first type is goods and services provided to households by non-market producers (i.e., government or non-profit institutions) either free or at economically insignificant prices, which is referred to as **social transfers in kind from non-market production**. This includes medical services at public health clinics or free education at public schools. In these cases, the portion of the cost paid by households for the government services is excluded from the government's consumption expenditure. The second type involves the government (social security schemes) reimbursing households for the cost of medical services purchased by the households. This is either paid for by social insurance contributions collected by the government from households and enterprises, or provided directly by government from its own budget to households in the form of market products. This is referred to as **social transfers in kind from purchased market production**. Both types are recorded in the "social transfers in kind account" as social transfers paid by the government and NPISHs, and received by households.

9.3.1.4 Entrepreneurial income

Entrepreneurial income is a concept introduced to measure the income generated by enterprises as market producers within their earned incomes. It is derived as a balancing item in the **entrepreneurial income account**, a sub-account of the "allocation of earned income account." Entrepreneurial income is calculated only for institutional units (or institutional sector) in the income accounts and cannot be applied to establishments (or industries). It is the return for market activities, and thus the income of non-market producers such as government or NPISHs is not included in this category. Furthermore, for unincorporated enterprises owned by households or government (excluding quasi-corporations), the property income allocated to their market production activities cannot be separately recognized from the total property income generated by the institutional unit, making it difficult to derive entrepreneurial income specifically for these unincorporated enterprises. Therefore, entrepreneurial income applies only to corporations sector (including quasi-corporations). The definition of entrepreneurial income is expressed as follows:

- Entrepreneurial income = operating surplus + property incomes receivable − property incomes payable, excluding *income on equity*

Property incomes payable, excluding *income on equity*, includes interest payable, investment income disbursements payable, and rent payable.

9.3.1.5 Income on equity, distributable income of corporations, and retained earnings

Income on equity refers to property income received by the owners of financial assets in return for providing capital to corporations (excluding loans). This includes dividends, withdrawals of income from quasi-corporations, and reinvested earnings. On the other hand, **distributable income of corporations** refers to the total income of corporations before distributing its *income on equity* (dividends, withdrawals of income from quasi-corporations). The definition of distributable income of corporations is as follows:

- Distributable income of corporations = entrepreneurial income + current transfers receivable – current transfers payable (such as corporate taxes) – (adjustment for the change in pension entitlements payable in relation to the corporations' pension schemes)

(Note: the adjustment for the change in pension entitlements applies only to the corporations that incur this liability.)

Retained earnings refer to the portion of distributable income that remains after deducting actual dividend payments (or withdrawals of income from quasi-corporations). In the case of foreign direct investment (FDI) enterprises, retained earnings are allocated to foreign direct investors in proportion to their equity share and are recorded as reinvested earnings, followed by an imputed reinvestment in the enterprise. In this treatment, reinvested earnings are recorded in the allocation of earned income account as investment income receivable by the investor and payable by the FDI enterprise, and then, in the financial account, as an increase in the equity asset of the investor and a corresponding increase in the equity liability of the FDI enterprise.

For example, if an FDI enterprise has distributable income of 100, pays actual dividends of 30, and the non-resident investor holds 70% of the equity, the total retained earnings amount to 70 (= 100 – 30). The portion of dividends attributable to the non-resident investor is 21 (= 30 x 70%), and the reinvested earnings attributable to the investor amount to 49 (= 70% x 70). Accordingly, in the allocation of earned income account, the foreign direct investor's dividend and reinvested earnings, the associated in equity positions, are recorded as follows.

Direct investor

Allocation of earned income account

		Dividends receivable	21
		Reinvested earnings receivable	49

Financial account

Equity of direct investment	49		

Foreign direct investment enterprise

Allocation of earned income account

Dividends payable	21		
Reinvested earnings payable	49		

Financial account

		Equity of direct investment	49

9.3.2 Life insurance and non-life insurance

Insurance is a system in which the entity operating the insurance receives premiums from a large number of unspecified policyholders and operates the funds, and pays insurance claims or benefits to the policyholders when specific contract conditions occur. There are two types of insurance: life insurance and non-life insurance operated by insurance corporations, and social insurance operated publicly by government or law. The accounting for insurance is very complex, but from the perspective of the SNA, it is essential to understand the production and income flows of insurance services and to reflect them in each account. This section will address life insurance and non-life insurance, while the next section will explain social insurance schemes.

Life insurance is a contract under which a policyholder pays premiums to an insurance company over a specified period and, upon the occurrence of a contractual event (such as death or maturity) receives insurance benefits from the insurance company. As a contract that provides for the payment of a lump sum or periodic benefits at maturity, the **net premiums** (= premiums – insurance service charges) that the insurance company regularly receives from the policyholder and the benefits paid to the policyholder at maturity correspond to financial assets and liabilities arising between the insurance contracting parties. This transaction is a financial transaction, so it is recoded as changes in the financial assets and liabilities of households and insurance companies in the "financial account" (explained later). Furthermore, investment income arising from the insurance technical reserves managed by insurance companies is attributed to the earned income receivable by policyholders (households) in the allocation of earned income account, which is, in turn added to the household's disposable income.

In the SNA, the output of life insurance companies corresponds to insurance service charges, which are calculated as "**insurance premiums earned + premium supplements – insurance benefits due – changes in life insurance technical reserves**." Premium supplements are the investment income accrued from the technical reserve for policyholders, which are retained within the insurance company. Life insurance technical reserves are reserves that are attributed to policyholders among the funds held by the insurance companies. They increase due to the receipt of new premiums received every year and the income allocated to the policyholder out of total investment income of premiums, and decrease due to the payment of insurance benefits. In addition, the change in life insurance technical reserves is the increase or decrease in liabilities that life insurance companies must pay to households (insurance policyholders) during the period. This is recorded as changes in the "life insurance entitlements" that households can claim from life insurance companies in the financial account. (For details on life insurance, see 14.3.3.)

Annuities are a similar type of life insurance. With annuities, the policyholder pays a lump sum to the insurance company, and in return, the insurance company provides the policyholder a fixed amount in the form of an annuity for a certain period of time.

Non-life insurance refers to a contract in which the policyholder pays premiums for a certain period of time and receives insurance claims from the insurance company if a specific event covered by the contract occurs during that period. If no such event occurs during the period, the insurance claims expire. The payment of premiums and receipt of claims by insurance policyholders correspond to the transactions of current transfers, so they are recorded in the income transfers other than transfers in kind account. In this account, only "net premiums" (premiums less service charges) are recorded, excluding insurance service charges. Insurance service charges are the output of non-life insurance companies and are recorded in the production account. The output of non-life insurance is calculated as "**premiums earned + premium supplements – adjusted claims incurred**." Premium supplements are a type of imputed premiums that arise when an insurance company retains the investment income within the company instead of paying it to the policyholders. Adjusted claims are "the actual insurance claims incurred plus the change in equalization provisions." The change in equalization provisions is a fund that insurance companies typically set aside to prepare for a large-scale payment of claims in the future. Adjusted claims are calculated by taking into account the historical actual claim rates.

The "investment income" attributable to the premium supplements in non-life insurance is investment income arising from non-life insurance technical reserves. Non-life insurance technical reserves refer to the sum of prepayment of insurance premiums (premiums paid but not yet lapsed at the end of the accounting period) and claims that have occurred but remain unsettled or unpaid at the end of the accounting period. This investment income is imputed as earned income receivable by policyholders in the allocation of earned income account as is the case with life insurance. However, unlike life insurance, it is treated as being paid back to the non-life insurance company as premium supplements in the income transfers other than transfers in kind account. This treatment is due to the fact that the investment income is not attributable to the policyholders but remains as income for the non-life insurance company. As a result of this treatment, there is no impact on the disposable income of the policyholders from the investment income. Reinsurance is also treated in the same way as non-life insurance. (See 14.3.3 for further details on non-life insurance.)

Table 9.22 Accounting for the life insurance and non-life insurance in the SNA

Item	Life insurance and annuities	Non-life insurance and reinsurance
Premiums and benefits (or claims)	Insurance premiums payable and insurance benefits receivable are recorded as financial transactions in the financial account. (The insurance premiums account for "net insurance premiums" excluding insurance service charges.)	Insurance premiums payable and insurance claims receivable are recorded as current transfers in the income transfers other than transfers in kind account. (The insurance premiums account for net insurance premiums excluding insurance service charges.)
Investment income	The Investment income accrued as a result of the management of insurance technical reserves is attributed to the receipt of the earned income for the insurance policyholders (households), and is added to the disposable income for them.	The investment income accrued as a result of the management of insurance technical reserves is imputed as earned income received by the policyholders, but is treated as being repaid to the insurance company in the form of "premium supplements" in the income transfers other than transfers in kind account. As a result, it does not affect disposable income for beneficiaries.
Insurance service charges	Insurance service charges (output) are calculated as premiums earned + premium supplements - benefits due - changes in insurance technical reserves.	Insurance service charges (output) are calculated as premiums earned + premium supplements - adjusted insurance claims.

9.3.3 Social insurance schemes

Social insurance is a type of insurance operated by social insurance schemes, which, unlike private insurances operated on the basis of individual contracts, are administered by law or through the exercise of public authority. An insurance scheme is classified as a social insurance scheme if it satisfies one or more of the following conditions:

- The insurance coverage is a legal obligation or a mandatory requirement of an employment contract.
- The insurance is operated collectively and its membership is limited to a specific employee group.
- The employer pays contributions on behalf of their employees.

Social insurance schemes can be broadly divided into two types: **Social security schemes**, which are financed, managed, and supervised by the government, and **employment-related schemes**, which provide pensions through the employer-employee relationship. The former includes social insurance schemes that cover all or most of the population, such as social security pension funds, national health insurance, industrial accident insurance, and unemployment insurance run by public authorities. The latter, on the other hand, is social insurance schemes linked to employment, where the government is not responsible for the payment of social benefits. However, insurance schemes organized by government for its own employees are included in this category.

There are three types of social insurance schemes that are linked to employment: First, the employer owns and operates the social insurance scheme, second, a third-party insurance management organization receives fees from the employer, and operates the social insurance on behalf of the employer, and third, a third-party insurance management organization manages the social insurance scheme on behalf of multiple employers, and any income exceeding a certain amount of accrued property income is retained by the insurance organization. Specific examples of employment-related social insurance schemes include defined contribution (DC) pension scheme, defined benefit (DB) pension scheme, civil servant pension, military pension, and private school pension etc.

Table 9.23 Types of social insurance scheme (I)

Type	Description
Social security scheme	It is a social insurance scheme that is financed, managed, and supervised by government. It covers all or most of the community.
Employment-related scheme	Pensions are provided through the employer-employee relationship. Responsibility for the payment of benefits is not transferred to general government. However, schemes organized by the government for its own employees are included in this category.

Social insurance is categorized into pension and non-pension types, depending on the form of payment. Pension type social insurance includes the National Pension administered by social security funds, and retirement pensions (DC, DB) and civil servant pensions which are handled by employment-related pension schemes. Non-pension type social insurance includes National Health insurance, unemployment insurance, and industrial accident insurance operated by social security schemes, and other social insurance-related benefits provided by employment-related schemes.

Table 9.24 Types of social insurance scheme (II)

Type		Example
Pension	Social security scheme	National Pension scheme
	Employment-related scheme	Retirement pension (DC, DB), civil servant pension, military pension, private school pension
Non-pension	Social security scheme	National health insurance, unemployment insurance, industrial accident insurance
	Employment-related scheme	Other social insurance benefits

Social insurance is considered a form of income redistribution among households. Therefore, it shares characteristics similar to current taxes or non-life insurance, and its accounting treatment follows a similar approach. In the national accounts, what corresponds to the premiums of social insurance are called **social contributions,** while what corresponds to claims or benefits of social insurance are called **social benefits**. Both social contributions and social benefits are treated as current transfer transactions, and social contributions are only recorded as "net contributions" excluding insurance service fees charged by insurance management organizations. However, social security schemes, as non-market service producers, do not charge insurance service fees.

Employment-related pension schemes versus social security schemes

In the SNA, **pension schemes** require special attention as their accounting treatment differs from other pensions or insurance. Pension schemes in the SNA are considered part of social insurance schemes. Unlike pensions or social assistance provided by social security schemes (government), pension schemes are restricted to defined contributions (DC) and defined benefits (DB) schemes operated by "employment-related schemes" (2025 SNA, paragraph 8.154). While pension schemes are part of the social insurance schemes, it functions similarly to life insurance or annuities (financial transactions). Although the contributions to and benefits from pension schemes are treated as current transfer transactions, in reality, the payment of pension contributions and the receipt of pension benefits by households correspond to the acquisition and disposal of financial assets (the "changes in pension entitlements" in the financial account). That is, the SNA classifies them as social insurance but then restores them to disposable income for households. This process initially records the pension contributions to and pension benefits from pension schemes as social contributions and social benefits in the income transfers other than transfers in kind account. Then, it is processed as "adjustment for the change in pension entitlements" in the use of income account (as it actually affects the level of disposable income for households).

Meanwhile, pensions by **social security schemes** are treated as follows. First, the employers' pension contributions are recorded as part of remuneration of employees in the generation of earned income account as the employer's contributions payable, and in the allocation of earned income account as the employers' contributions receivable. The employees then pay the employers' pension contributions receivable together with their own pension contributions to the social security fund as pensions contributions. This amount is recorded as payable by households and receivable by government in the income transfers other than transfers in kind account. Pension benefits payable by the government and receivable by households are also recorded in the income transfers other than transfers in kind account. However, unlike employment-related pension schemes, no adjustment is made to the change in pension entitlements in the use of income account. This is because in the SNA, government-run social security funds are treated as receiving pension contributions in a period and paying them out as pension benefits in the same period, and no future liability for pension entitlements is accrued. (This is known as the "pay-as-you-go basis.")

The **investment income from employment-related pension schemes** is also recorded as the earned income receivable by household pensioners in the allocation of earned income account, but it is attributed to be reimbursed to insurance corporations in the form of households' social contribution supplements in the income transfers other than transfers in kind account. However, since pension entitlements for this social insurance arise for households, an increase corresponding to this amount is added to the households' disposable income in the use of income account. Currently, DC and DB pension schemes, which are considered a type of social insurance but function similarly to life insurance, are recorded as current transfers in the income transfers other than transfers in kind account, and then processed as an increase in disposable income for pensioners through the adjustment of the change in pension entitlements in the use of income account. In the financial account, a transaction is recorded that reflects the increase in the pensioner's assets in response to the adjustment for the change in pension entitlements. On the other hand, social security pension schemes do not record investment income. Table 9.25 shows an example of how the investment income from the employment-related pension schemes, excluding social security pension schemes, is accounted for in each account.

Table 9.25 Accounting for the investment income of employment-related pension schemes (excluding social security schemes)

	Insurance beneficiaries (households)		Financial corporations	
	Expenditures/Changes in assets	Revenues/Changes in liabilities	Expenditures/Changes in assets	Revenues/Changes in liabilities
Allocation of earned income account		Investment income receivable 5	Investment income payable 5	
Income transfers other than transfers in kind account	Pension contribution supplements payable 5			Pension contribution supplements receivable 5
Use of income account		Adjustment for the change in pension entitlements 5	Adjustment for the change in pension entitlements 5	
Financial account	Increase in financial assets (pension entitlements) 5			Increase in liabilities (pension entitlements) 5

The amount of the adjustment for the change in pension entitlements is calculated as follows:

- Adjustment for the change in pension entitlements = pension contributions + investment income of pension schemes – (service fees of pension schemes + pension benefits)

Table 9.26 summarizes how social insurance schemes described above are accounted for in the SNA.

Table 9.26 Accounting for social insurance schemes in the SNA

Items	Accounting treatment of social insurance schemes
Contributions and benefits	Social contributions and social benefits are recorded as current transfers in the income transfers other than transfers in kind account. (Employment-related social contributions are calculated as "net contributions" excluding insurance service charges.)
Investment income	1) Employment-related pension scheme: Investment income is recorded as earned income receivable by insurance beneficiaries (households), but it is treated as being repaid to the insurance corporations in the form of household's social contribution supplements in the income transfers other than transfers in kind account. However, since a pension entitlement arises for this portion, the increase (or decrease) is added to the household's disposable income in the use of income account.
	2) Social security scheme: Investment income is treated as not accruing.
Insurance service charge	Insurance service charges (output) vary depending on the type of insurance schemes: Employment-related pension schemes incur insurance service charges like life insurance, while no insurance service charges arise in social security schemes (which are treated as government's production and final consumption).
Changes in pension entitlements	Changes in pension entitlements by employment-related pension schemes are recorded in the financial account.

9.3.4 Imputation and rearrangement of transactions

Imputation is the process of treating a transaction as if it had occurred, even if it did not actually occur or was not actually undertaken. In the context of national accounts, imputation is a technique that is used to explain economic phenomena in a more logical and systematic way by basing them on causal relationships rather than superficial observations. This is done more clearly by setting up hypothetical transactions and amounts.

The typical form of imputation is hypothetical transactions, which establishes that a transaction and an amount are assumed to have occurred even though there is no actual identifiable transaction. For example, estimating rentals from owner-occupied dwelling services as if they had occurred (See section 14.4), estimating and recording depreciation due to of declines in the value of fixed assets (See section 20.4) are representative examples of imputed transactions.

National accounts use the term "rearrangement of transactions" specifically for the following cases of imputation: **rerouting transactions** and **partitioning transactions** (Table 9.27). Rerouting a transaction refers to imputing a transaction through a different process than the one that actually occurred, or imputing a transaction that did not actually take place but is assumed to have occurred in an economic sense. Examples of rerouting transactions include assuming social contributions paid by employers for their employees as remuneration of employees and then treating they are paid to social insurance schemes, handling reinvested earnings on inward or outward foreign direct investment, accounting for investment income disbursements, and acquiring domestic real estate by non-residents. Partitioning a transaction refers to the process of dividing a single transaction into two or more transactions. Examples of partitioning transactions include setting up FISIM (financial intermediation services indirectly measured), calculating the output of wholesale and retail industries by accounting only for trading margins rather than gross value of transactions, and treating the rental payments of financial leases as separating principal and interest for the acquisition of fixed assets. Below, we will explain in more detail the rerouting transactions and partitioning transactions respectively.

Table 9.27 Types of imputations

Type	Description	Example
1) Simple imputation of transactions	Setting up a transaction when there is no identifiable transaction between the parties.	Estimation of imputed rentals for owner-occupied housing
		Recording depreciation
		Transferring the production of central bank's monetary policy services to the government
2) Rerouting of transactions	Imputing a direct transaction between A and C as having been traded first from A to B, and second from B to C.	Employer's social contributions
		Reinvested earnings on foreign direct investment
		Investment income disbursements
		Acquisition of domestic real estate by non-residents
3) Partitioning of transactions	Splitting a single transaction between two parties into two or more transactions.	FISIM
		Calculating margins for wholesale and retail industries as output
		Recording rental payments on financial leases separately as principal and interest

9.3.4.1 Rerouting transactions

This section will provide a more detailed explanation of items related to rerouting transactions. Examples of rerouting transactions occurring in the income accounts include the treatment of employer's social contributions, reinvested earnings on foreign direct investment in the domestic economy, the treatment of investment income disbursement from pension entitlements for pensioners, standardized guarantee schemes, and collective investment fund shareholders.

Employers' social contributions

The employers' social contributions (both actual and imputed) are payments made by employers directly to social insurance schemes on behalf of their employees. However, in the SNA, it is treated as a rerouted transaction, where it is assumed that employers pay the contributions to the employees, who then pay them back to the social insurance schemes. The accounting procedure for the employers' social contributions starts with recording payments of remuneration of employees by employers in the generation of earned income account, and as receipts of remuneration of employees by households in the allocation of earned income account. Then, they are recorded as social contributions payable by households and the social contributions receivable by government (or financial corporations) in the income transfers other than transfers in kind account.

Table 9.28 Accounting for employer's social contributions

	Employer		Household		Government or financial corporation	
	Expenditures	Revenues	Expenditures	Revenues	Expenditures	Revenues
Generation of earned income account	Payments of remuneration of employees					
Allocation of earned Income account				Receipts of remuneration of employees		
Income transfers other than transfers in kind account			Employer's social contribution payable			Employer's social contribution receivable

Reinvested earnings on foreign direct investment

Reinvested earnings on foreign direct investment are derived from the retained earnings of foreign direct investment enterprises owned by non-resident investors in the domestic economy. In the SNA, these retained earnings are imputed to be distributed to the non-resident investors in proportion to their ownership of corporate shares, then remitted abroad, and reinvested in the direct investment enterprises in the domestic economy. The remittance of retained earnings to investors is a form of *income on equity* and is accounted for separately as an item of the same type as payments of dividends or withdrawals of income from quasi-corporations. The accounting treatment of reinvested earnings on foreign direct investment is recorded as property income payable by the direct investment enterprise on the expenditures side and as property income receivable by the direct investors on the revenues side, both in the allocation of earned income account. As a corresponding entry, the amount of reinvested earnings is recorded under the heading "additions to equity" in the financial account. (An increase in liabilities of the direct investment enterprise and an increase in assets of direct investors.) **Reinvested earnings of outward foreign direct investment by resident direct investors** are accounted for in the opposite way to the reinvested earnings of inward foreign direct investment by non-resident direct investors.

Retained earnings of corporations or quasi-corporations are also known as **undistributed income**, which is "the distributable income of corporations or quasi-corporations less dividends payable (for corporations) or withdrawals of income (for quasi-corporations)." Distributable income is derived as follows:

- Distributable income = entrepreneurial income + current transfers receivable – current transfers payable – (adjustment for the change in pension entitlements of the enterprise)

Entrepreneurial income refers to income that occurs only in the corporations sector, calculated by adding all property incomes receivable to operating surplus and subtracting interest payable, investment income disbursements payable and rents payable from the property incomes payable. In the case of corporations sector, since final consumption expenditure does not incur, the disposable income of corporations in the "use of income account" is equal to the value of saving, and this disposable income becomes retained earnings. However, in the case of foreign direct investment enterprises, retained earnings are imputed to be remitted abroad, so the retained earnings become zero, and thus their disposable income and savings are also zero. As reinvested earnings are derived ex post, the recording of earned income must also be adjusted ex post in the allocation of earned income account, and consequently, the reinvested earnings calculated in the use of income account must be retroactively reduced.

The retained earnings of direct investment enterprises are distributed in proportion to the direct investors' equity shares. However, the Balance of Payment Manual (BPM6) stipulates that reinvested earnings are only recorded for direct investment enterprises in which the investors' shares are 10 percent or more, and those under 10 percent are excluded (BPM6 11.40). The calculation method for the retained earnings of direct investment enterprises is as follows (BPM6 11.43).

- Retained earnings of direct investment enterprise = net operating surplus + property income receivable [1)] – property income payable [2)] + current transfers receivable – current transfers payable = distributable income − *income on equity* excluding reinvested earnings (= dividends payable + withdrawals of income from quasi-corporations)

where, property incomes receivable [1)] = dividends receivable + interest receivable + rent receivable + share of reinvested earnings of direct investment enterprises, property incomes payable [2)] = dividends payable + interest payable + rent payable. It is assumed that direct investment enterprises have no investment income disbursements.

If there are no reinvested earnings, the retained earnings themselves become the enterprises' disposable income and, at the same time become savings. However, in the case of foreign direct investment enterprises, reinvested earnings are generated, which are imputed to be distributed to equity holders. This transaction is recorded in the distribution of earned income account as property incomes payable by the direct investment enterprise (in proportion to the investor's equity share), and the same amount is recorded again in the financial account as "reinvestment of earnings" (increase in equity).

Table 9.29 Accounting for reinvested earnings

	Direct investment enterprise		**Direct investor**	
	Expenditures/Changes in assets	Revenues/Changes in liabilities	Expenditures/Changes in assets	Revenues/Changes in liabilities
Allocation of earned income account	Reinvested earnings payable			Reinvested earnings receivable
Financial account		Increase in liability (Reinvestment of earnings)	Increase in equity (Reinvestment of earnings)	

Investment income disbursements

Investment income disbursements are a notional accounting item that reallocates the investment income accrued by the financial institutions (such as insurance companies or investment funds) from the funds received from policyholders or fund investors back to the policyholders or fund investors as part of their property income for the current period. In other words, the portion of the funds paid in by policyholders or fund investors that is available for investment is managed by financial institutions, and the resulting investment income is accounted for as being distributed to the policyholders or fund investors. This treatment is implemented in the SNA to clarify the actual disposable income of each institutional sector in terms of the distribution and use of property income.

Types of investment income disbursements include the investment income attributable to insurance policyholders (covering both life insurance and non-life insurance), investment income attributable to guaranteed entities of standardized guarantee schemes, investment income attributable to pension entitlements of pensioners, and investment income attributable to equity holders of investment funds. Investment income disbursements are treated as earned income payable or receivable for the relevant institutional sectors in the allocation of earned income account.

However, in the case of insurance, there is a difference in the treatment of investment income disbursements between life insurance and non-life insurance. life insurance has the nature of a financial asset where the insured amount is repaid at maturity as insurance benefits, whereas non-life insurance has the nature of a current transfer in which insurance claims are paid only upon the occurrence of an insured event. While both of them are accounted for as investment income disbursements in the allocation of earned income account, they are treated differently in subsequent accounts. Specifically, the investment income disbursement from life insurance (including annuities) is recorded in the financial account as an increase in the financial assets of policyholders, while the investment income disbursement from non-life insurance is not linked to an increase in policyholders' income but is treated as being retained within the insurance company. Consequently, in the latter case, the income attributed to the policyholders as investment income disbursements in the allocation of earned income account is returned to the insurance company's income as a current transfer called "premium supplements" in the income transfers other than transfers in kind account. Examples of such investment income disbursements being returned to financial institutions include non-life insurance and standardized guarantee schemes. Conversely, investment income disbursements for policy holders of life insurance and shareholders of investment funds are not returned as income of financial institutions, but are recorded as an increase in the disposable income and an increase in financial assets of the policyholders and investors.

Defined contributions and **defined benefits** of pension schemes are accounted for in the SNA as having both the characteristics of life insurance and social insurance. Specifically, investment income disbursements of these pension schemes are recorded as current transfers in the income transfers other than transfers in kind account, and are then converted back to disposable income (as adjustment for the change in pension entitlements) in the use of income account. At the same time, this amount is shown as an increase in the pension entitlements of pensioners in the financial account.

Table 9.30 Examples of imputation accounting for property incomes

Imputation item			Account name	Direct investor/Insurance policy holder/Investment funds shareholder		Direct investment enterprise/Insurance corporation/Investment fund		Relevant item in the financial account
				Expenditures/Changes in assets	Revenues/Changes in liabilities	Expenditures/Changes in assets	Revenues/Changes in liabilities	
Reinvested earnings on foreign direct investment			Allocation of earned income account		Investment income receivable	Investment income payable		
			Financial account	Increase in the asset of investment equity			Increase in the liability of investment equity	Equity and investment shares
Investment income disbursements	Investment income attributed to policyholders	Life insurance and annuities	Allocation of earned income account		Investment income receivable	Investment income payable		
			Financial account	Increase in the asset of life insurance entitlement			Increase in the liability of life insurance entitlement	Life insurance, annuities
		Non-life insurance	Allocation of earned income account		Investment income receivable	Investment income payable		
			Income transfers account	Premium supplement payable			Premium supplements receivable	
	Standardized guarantee schemes		Allocation of earned income account		Investment income receivable	Investment income payable		
			Income transfers account	Fee supplement payable			Fee supplements receivable	
	Investment income on pension entitlements (Investment income		Allocation of earned income account		Investment income receivable (A)	Investment income payable (A″)		

Imputation item		Account name	Direct investor/Insurance policy holder/Investment funds shareholder		Direct investment enterprise/Insurance corporation/Investment fund		Relevant item in the financial account
			Expenditures/Changes in assets	Revenues/Changes in liabilities	Expenditures/Changes in assets	Revenues/Changes in liabilities	
	accrued from retirement pension schemes)	Income transfers account	Household's pension contribution supplements payable (A)			Household's pension contribution supplements receivable (A")	
		Use of income account		Adjustment for the change in pension entitlements (A)	Adjustment for the change in pension entitlements (A")		
		Financial account	Increase in the asset of pension entitlements (A)			Increase in the liability of pension entitlements (A")	Pension entitlements
	Investment income attributed to investment fund shareholders	Allocation of earned income account		Investment income receivable (Excluding dividends, only retained earnings)	Investment income payable (Excluding dividends, only retained earnings)		
		Financial account	Increase in the asset of investment fund shares			Increase in the liability of investment fund shares	Equity and investment shares

The investment income disbursement associated with social insurance schemes can be explained by dividing it into two categories: **social security schemes** and **employment-related social insurance schemes**, which have different accounting treatments. Employment-related social insurance schemes, such as DC and DB, generates the investment income disbursement in the allocation of earned income account, whereas social security schemes do not generate any investment income disbursement. Therefore, in employment-related social insurance schemes, an increase in the earned income (of investment income disbursement) is returned to the current transfer item called "pension contribution supplements payable" by households in the income transfers other than transfers in kind account. In contrast, no such item is recorded in the case of social security schemes.

On the other hand, employment-related pension (DC and DB) is a social insurance in nature, but it creates a liability to pay the pension contribution supplements to the pensioners. Therefore, the investment income disbursement accrued by the employment-related insurance scheme is recorded as an increase in financial assets of the pensioners (treated in the financial account) because, like life insurance, it is actually payable to the pensioners. In addition, this amount is also treated as an increase in "the adjustment for the change in pension entitlements" of the pensioners in the use of income account. Unlike social security schemes, "the adjustment for the change in pension entitlements" is an item set up to reflect the increase of pension entitlement of the employment-related scheme as an increase in the disposable income of the pensioners.

Table 9.31 Accounting for investment income disbursements of insurance policyholders or pensioners

	Non-life insurance and reinsurance	**Social security scheme**	**Life insurance and annuities**	**Pension scheme (DC, DB)**
Allocation of earned income account	Investment income receivable	-	Investment income receivable	Investment income receivable
Income transfers other than transfers in kind account	Premium supplements payable	-	-	Premium supplements payable
Use of income account	-	-	-	Adjustment for the change in pension entitlements
Financial account	-	-	Increase in insurance entitlement	Increase in pension entitlement

Acquisition of real estate by non-residents

If a non-resident owns domestic real estate (i.e., land, buildings, structures, and natural resources), the SNA establishes a **notional resident unit** for statistical purposes. In this case, the non-resident is considered to own the equity of the notional resident unit, and the notional resident unit is deemed to own the real estate. The notional resident unit conducts its business activities (e.g., receives rentals and incurs expenses) similar to a domestic branch owned by a non-resident, with the non-resident owning the equity of the notional resident unit. The accounting treatment in the national accounts is that the acquisition of real estate by a non-resident is recorded as an increase in equity asset and a decrease in financial asset of the non-resident and as an increase in gross fixed capital formation or non-produced non-financial asset (land etc.) and an increase in equity liability of the notional resident.

Table 9.32 Accounting for acquisitions of real estate by non-residents

Account name	Notional resident		Non-resident (The rest of the world)	
	Changes in assets	Changes in liabilities	Changes in assets	Changes in liabilities
Capital account	Increase in fixed capital formation/non-produced nonfinancial assets			
Financial account		Increase in equity (liabilities)	Increase in equity (assets)	Decrease in financial assets

9.3.4.2 Partitioning transactions

Partitioning of a transaction refers to the process of recording a transaction as two or more separate transactions, even though it is considered one transaction from the perspective of both parties involved. Examples include separating the interest receivable and interest payable between financial intermediaries and their users into the pure interest and the brokerage fees (which is called FISIM), or separately identifying only wholesale and retail margins as the output of the wholesale and retail trade industries rather than their total value of transactions. (See 14.3.2 and 14.2 respectively for more details.) These examples will be discussed in their respective topics.

A financial lease is a transaction in which the lessee pays rentals for a certain period of time in exchange for using a specific product and receives ownership of the product at maturity. While the legal ownership of the product is transferred to the lessee at the end of the lease term, in the SNA, economic ownership is deemed to be transferred at the point of sale of the lease, and the lessee is considered to incur a liability to the lessor during the lease term. Therefore, the rental payment by the lessee is not treated as an incurrence of expenses, but is accounted for as the repayment of principal and interest on a loan to the lessor.

9.3.5 Social contributions and social benefits

Social contributions and social benefits are one of the typical items of current transfers, which are recorded in the income transfers other than transfers in kind account. These items generally appear in countries with established social security systems, and the accounting treatment in the SNA suggests a standardized method under the assumption that the social insurance system is in place in a country. However, since social insurance systems vary by country, their accounting treatment may also differ.

9.3.5.1 Social contributions

Social contributions are contributions paid to social insurance schemes by employees enrolled in social insurance, and the funds come from remuneration of employees. Social contributions are divided into two parts: employers' contributions and households' contributions. The employers' contributions are actually paid by the employer to the social insurance schemes without being paid directly to the employee, but in the national accounts, they are attributed to the employees' income as remuneration of employees and then, to the payment to the social insurance schemes by the employee. Therefore, the employer's social contribution is recorded as remuneration of employees payable by the employer in the generation of earned income account and as revenues of income for households in the allocation of earned income account. Thereafter, in the income transfers other than transfers in kind account, these contributions, along with the social contributions payable by households, are added up and treated as a current transfer payable to social insurance schemes.

The employers' social contributions can be divided into two categories: those payable to **social security schemes** and those payable to **employment-related social insurance schemes**. The former is further divided into pension contributions (such as national pension contributions), non-pension contributions (such as national health insurance, national unemployment insurance and industrial accident insurance). The latter is further divided into pension contributions (such as contributions of the DC and DB) and non-pension contributions paid in cash.

The insurance service charge, which is the cost of services provided by social insurance schemes for operating social insurance, constitutes the output of these schemes. Therefore, net social contributions (= social contributions – insurance service charges) are recorded as a current transfers item in the income transfers other than transfers in kind account. However, the service charge of the social security schemes operated by government is accounted for as government final consumption expenditure and are thus not deducted from social contributions. Consequently, only service charges of social insurance schemes (i.e., employment-related social insurance schemes), excluding social security schemes, are deducted from social contributions, and these charges are treated as households' final consumption expenditures. The accounting treatment of charges for social insurance schemes other than social security schemes is shown in Table 9.33 below.

Table 9.33 Accounting for charges of social insurance schemes (except social security schemes)

	Household		**Financial corporations**	
	Expenditures	Revenues	Expenditures	Revenues
Production account				Charges receivable 20
Income transfers other than transfers in kind account	Charges payable (-20)			Charges receivable (-20)
Use of income account	Final consumption expenditure 20			

Social insurance contributions consist of the following three components. The first is social contributions payable by employers, the second is contributions payable by employees, and the third is the insurance service charge, which is one for services provided by social insurance schemes. (See Table 9.34.) In the income transfers other than transfers in kind account, the **net social contributions** which are the sum of the employer's social contribution and the employee's social contribution, less the insurance service charge of the social insurance scheme are recorded as the portion paid by households.

Employers' social contributions can be classified into two types: **actual social contributions**, which are paid to social security schemes or employment-related social insurance schemes, and **imputed social contributions**, which are not paid as social contributions but are used for that purpose. The employers' actual social contributions can be divided into pension and non-pension types, depending on whether the amount is paid to households as social benefits (in cash). The pension type contributions include those paid through social security pension schemes, as well as those paid to employment-related schemes such as DC, DB and civil servant pensions. Non-pension type contributions include those paid to social security schemes (i.e., national health insurance, national unemployment insurance, industrial accident compensation insurance etc.), as well as other social contributions paid in cash.

Table 9.34 Types of social contributions

<table>
<tr><th colspan="4">Type</th><th>Example</th></tr>
<tr><td rowspan="7">Employers' social contributions (A)</td><td rowspan="4">Employers' actual social contributions</td><td rowspan="2">Pension contributions</td><td>Social security scheme</td><td>National pension contributions</td></tr>
<tr><td>Employment-related scheme</td><td>Contributions for DC, DB, Civil servant pension, Private school pension, and Military pension</td></tr>
<tr><td rowspan="2">Non-pension contributions</td><td>Social security scheme</td><td>Contributions for national health insurance, unemployment insurance, industrial accident compensation insurance</td></tr>
<tr><td>Employment-related scheme</td><td>Premiums for private social insurance (health)</td></tr>
<tr><td rowspan="3">Employers' imputed social contributions</td><td rowspan="2">Pension contributions</td><td rowspan="2">Employment-related scheme</td><td>For DC scheme, the operating costs of the insurance scheme run directly by the employer are applicable.</td></tr>
<tr><td>For DB scheme, the employer's residual contributions (= planned benefit - actual benefit paid) are applicable.</td></tr>
<tr><td>Non-pension contributions</td><td>Employment-related scheme</td><td>One-off retirement payment</td></tr>
<tr><td rowspan="4">Households' social contributions (B)</td><td rowspan="2">Households' actual social contributions</td><td>Pension contributions</td><td>Social security scheme</td><td>National pension contributions</td></tr>
<tr><td>Non-pension contributions</td><td>Social security scheme</td><td>Contributions for national health insurance, unemployment insurance, and industrial accident compensation insurance</td></tr>
<tr><td rowspan="2">Households' social contribution supplements</td><td>Pension contributions</td><td>Employment-related scheme</td><td>Investment income from employment-related social insurance schemes (DC and DB only)</td></tr>
<tr><td>Non-pension contributions</td><td>Employment-related scheme</td><td></td></tr>
<tr><td>Social insurance scheme service charges (C)</td><td></td><td></td><td>Employment-related scheme</td><td></td></tr>
<tr><td>Net social contributions (A+B-C)</td><td></td><td></td><td></td><td></td></tr>
</table>

Imputed social contributions paid by employers do not arise in social security schemes, but only in employment-related social insurance schemes. These imputed social contributions paid by employers are also divided into a pension type and a non-pension type, depending on the form of social benefits that are paid in return. For the pension type, in the case of defined contribution scheme, where the employer directly operates the insurance scheme, operating costs borne by the employer are accounted for as imputed pension contributions. This amount is treated as financial service cost for households and is recorded as household's final consumption expenditure in the use of income account. In the case of defined benefit pension scheme, if the employer pays any shortfall in the fixed amount of pension benefit on behalf of the employees is recorded as an imputed pension contribution (Table 9.35). In the non-pension type, for example, there is a retirement allowance that is paid in a lump-sum. In this case, it is accounted for simultaneously as a non-pension contribution and a non-pension benefit in the income transfers other than transfers in kind account.

Table 9.35 Types of the employer's imputed pension contribution

Type		Description	Accounting treatment
Defined contribution scheme (DC)	Operating costs of the pension scheme[1)]	Imputed contribution by the employer for employees.	It is treated as household's final consumption expenditure (financial service costs).
Defined benefit scheme (DB)	Employer's contribution for insufficient benefit	Recording shortfalls in the planned benefit payments[2)].	Treated as employer's imputed social contribution payable in the generation of earned income account, allocation of earned income account, and income transfers other than transfers in kind account.

Footnote: 1) It incurs only if the employer directly operates its own pension scheme.
2) Employer's imputed contribution = increase in benefits for the current period + operating costs of the pension scheme - employer's actual contribution - employee's other contribution (actual contribution + investment income).

9.3.5.2 Social benefits

Social benefits are current transfers in the form of "cash" that households receive from social insurance schemes or government. They can be either payments made to households after retirement in return for social contributions paid to social insurance schemes, or payments made unilaterally by the government as part of social security. The scope of social benefits includes not only pensions but also non-pension benefits such as cash payments for medical treatment for illness, injury or old age, allowances for family support, wage compensation for retirement and unemployment, and benefits for housing and education.

Social benefits, just like social contributions, are classified into those provided by social security schemes and those provided by employment-related schemes, and they are also divided into pension and non-pension types (Table 9.36). Social security schemes provide pension type benefits, such as national pensions, as well as non-pension type benefits such as unemployment benefits by the employment insurance scheme, and industrial accident compensation benefits. Employment-related social insurance schemes provide pension benefits such as retirement pensions (DC, DB), civil servant pensions, military pensions, and private school pensions, as well as non-pension benefits such as lump-sum retirement benefits or private health insurance benefits.

Retirement pension benefits are paid under two schemes: the **defined contribution scheme** and **defined benefit scheme**. The defined contribution (DC) scheme allocates social benefits based on the contributions actually accumulated in the social insurance schemes, while the defined benefit (DB) scheme allocates social benefits based on the payment criteria that the social insurance scheme has confirmed at the time of the contract. Under the DB scheme, if there is a shortfall in the amount of benefit to be paid compared to the planned amount of benefit, the employer must cover the difference (referred to as "imputed contributions"). On the contrary, if the benefit is left over, the employer is exempted from paying contributions.

All benefits from employment-related social insurance schemes other than social security are recorded in the national accounts as if they are received in cash, even when they are provided in kind. For example, in the case of benefits in kind provided to employees, such as health services, the amount paid by the social insurance scheme directly to the hospital is recorded as a cash benefit received by the employee, and the expenditure on the health service is recorded as final consumption expenditure of the employee. The rationale for this treatment is that employment-related social insurance schemes are regarded as insurance institution (financial corporations) in the national accounts, and financial corporations cannot incur final consumption expenditure. However, medical services provided at the workplace to deal with accidents or illnesses arising in the course of work are recorded as intermediate consumption of the employer. The "benefits in kind" in relation to health insurance provided by social security schemes to households is not considered social benefits, but is treated as a "social transfer in kind" from government to households, which is recorded in *the social transfers in-kind account*.

On the other hand, **social assistance benefits in cash** paid unilaterally to households by the government, where households do not burden any social contribution, are also included within the scope of social benefits. These refer to a form of social benefits payment where the households are not required to pay social contributions, but the government, other than social insurance schemes, provide social benefits to households through "means-testing" which is a method by government to determine whether households are eligible for certain financial assistance or benefits based on their income, assets, or financial situation. Examples include basic security benefits for the old-aged, and veterans' benefits. However, compensation paid by the government to households (cash and in-kind) for damages caused by natural disasters etc., which is not related to social insurance schemes, is recorded under the "miscellaneous current transfers" category.

Table 9.36 Types of social benefits

<table>
<tr><th colspan="2">Type</th><th>Example</th></tr>
<tr><td rowspan="2">Social security benefits (A)</td><td>Pension benefits</td><td>National pension scheme</td></tr>
<tr><td>Non-pension benefits</td><td>Unemployment insurance benefit, and industrial accident compensation insurance benefit (excluding Health insurance)</td></tr>
<tr><td rowspan="3">Other social insurance benefits (B)</td><td rowspan="2">Pension benefits</td><td>Retirement pension (DC, DB)</td></tr>
<tr><td>Civil servant pension, private school pension, military pension</td></tr>
<tr><td>Non-pension benefits</td><td>Severance benefits, private health insurance benefits</td></tr>
<tr><td colspan="2">Social assistance benefits in cash (C)</td><td>Basic security benefits for the old aged, veterans' benefits</td></tr>
<tr><td colspan="2">Total social benefits (A+B+C)</td><td></td></tr>
</table>

9.3.5.3 Distinction between social benefits and social transfers in kind

Social benefits are current transfers paid by social insurance schemes or government to households, allowing the households to use these benefits to purchase or exchange any other goods or services at their discretion. In contrast, social security systems are sometimes operated in which the government provides individual services to households either free or at economically insignificant prices, such as public healthcare or public education, or in which households pay part of the cost of private healthcare or education services and the government covers the remainder on behalf of households. These are called "social transfers in kind" by government and are treated as transfers of income in-kind, not as social benefits, and are therefore, recorded in the social transfers in kind account, rather than the income transfers other than transfers in kind account. (For more details, refer to section 9.3.6.4 on "Accounting treatment of social transfers in kind by social security schemes.")

9.3.6 Accounting treatment by insurance types (Comprehensive summary)

This section provides a comprehensive summary of how the life insurance, non-life insurance and social insurance schemes, as described above, are accounted for in the national accounts.

9.3.6.1 Accounting treatment of non-life insurance

The insurance service charge for non-life insurance constitutes an output of the insurance company in the production account, and is recorded as intermediate consumption by the insured enterprise (in the production account) and final consumption by the insured household (in the use of income account), respectively. This insurance service charge is deducted when calculating the *non-life insurance premium less service charges* (= non-life insurance premium + premium supplements – insurance service charge) in the income transfers other than transfers in kind account.

Table 9.37 Accounting for non-life insurance service charges

	Other sectors except insurance companies		**Insurance companies**	
	Expenditures	Revenues	Expenditures	Revenues
Production account	Charges payable (excluding households) 15			Charges receivable 20
Income transfers other than transfers in kind account	Charges payable -20			Charges receivable -20
Use of income account	Charges payable (households) 5			

Changes in non-life insurance technical reserves are recorded in the financial account as an increase in the policyholder's asset and an increase in the insurance company's liability. The investment income accrued from the technical reserves is recorded in the allocation of earned income account as the property income receivable by policyholders and the property income payable by the insurance company. However, since this income is not actually returned to the policyholder, it is treated as being paid to the insurance company in the form of premium supplements in the income transfers other than transfers in kind account. Consequently, in the income transfers other than transfers in kind account, net premiums payable by the policyholder and net premiums receivable by the insurance company are recorded.

Table 9.38 Accounting for non-life insurance

	Net insurance premium [1]	Insurance investment income	Insurance claim	Insurance service charge [2]	Changes in insurance technical reserve [3]
Production A/C				Output [2] (insurance corp.) / intermediate consumption (policyholders excluding households)	
Allocation of earned income A/C		Investment income receivable (policyholder) / investment income payable (insurance corp.)			
Income transfers A/C	Net premium payable (policyholder) / net premium receivable (insurance corp.)		Claim payable (insurance corp.) / claim receivable (policyholder)		
Use of income A/C				Final consumption (household)	
Financial A/C					Increase in assets (policyholder) / increase in liabilities (insurance corp.)

Footnote: 1) Net premium = actual premiums (earned premium) + premium supplements – insurance service charges

2) Output = premiums earned + premium supplements – adjusted insurance claims

3) Changes in insurance technical reserves = prepayment of net insurance premiums + reserves for insurance claims outstanding

9.3.6.2 Accounting treatment of life insurance

Insurance service charges for life insurance are recorded as an output of the insurance company in the production account and as final consumption expenditure of household in the use of income account. Net premiums are recorded in the financial account as an increase in the household's financial asset and an increase in the insurance company's liability. Investment incomes accrued from insurance companies are recorded in the allocation of earned income account as investment income disbursements receivable by the household and investment income disbursements payable by the insurance company, which is included in net insurance premiums as premium supplements. The payment of insurance benefits is recorded in the financial account as a decrease in the entitlements to life insurance by households and a decrease in the corresponding liability of the insurance company. In conclusion, the amount of life insurance entitlements in the financial account is recorded as "net premiums – benefits," where net premiums are derived as "actual premiums + premium supplements – insurance service charges."

Table 9.39 Accounting for life insurance

	Net premiums[1)]	Investment income	Insurance service charges[2)]	Insurance benefits
Production account			Output (insurance corp.)	
Allocation of earned income account		Investment income disbursement receivable (household) / investment income disbursement payable (insurance corp.)		
Income transfers account				
Use of income account			Final consumption (household)	
Financial account	Increase in the asset of life insurance entitlement (household) / increase in liability (insurance corp.)			Decrease in the asset of life insurance entitlement (household) / decrease in liability (insurance corp.)

Footnote: 1) Net premium = actual premium + premium supplement – insurance service charge
2) Output = premium earned + premium supplement – benefit – change in life insurance technical reserve

9.3.6.3 Accounting treatment of social contributions and social benefits in social security schemes

The insurance service charges of the social security schemes operated by government are not separately charged to households, but constitutes the government's output, and are recorded as final consumption expenditure of this sector. Social contributions of social security schemes are similar to the premiums of life or non-life insurance, and they appear as the employer's social contribution in the generation of earned income account, and as a counterpart entry, are recorded as household's remuneration of employees in the allocation of earned income account. These, in turn, are combined with the households' social contributions and recorded as "social contributions payable by households" sector in the income transfers account, with a counterpart entry as social contributions receivable by government. Social benefit, other than social transfers in kind, are recorded as payable by government and receivable by households in the income transfers account.

Social insurance schemes other than social security schemes, such as civil servant pensions, military pensions, and private school pensions, fall under employment-related schemes. However, since they share characteristics similar to social security schemes, their accounting treatment is aligned with that of social security schemes.

Table 9.40 Accounting for social contributions and social benefits of social security schemes

	Social contribution	Investment income	Social benefit
Generation of earned income A/C	Employer's social contribution payable (corporation, government, NPISH)		
Allocation of earned income A/C	Employer's social contribution receivable (household)	Not applicable	
Income transfers A/C	Social contribution[1] payable (household) / social contribution receivable (government)		Social benefit receivable (household)/ social benefit payable (government)
Use of income A/C			

Footnote: 1) Social security contribution = employer's social contribution + households' social contribution

9.3.6.4 Accounting treatment of social transfers in kind by social security schemes

Some social insurance items treated by social security schemes are paid as social security contributions but are not directly received by households as social benefits in the income transfers account. Instead, they are treated as social transfers in kind in the social transfers in kind account. An example of this is the National Health insurance, where the government (social security scheme) purchases products from market producers and provides them to households as a form of benefits in kind. For example, when an individual patient receives treatments at a private hospital, a portion of the hospital costs is paid in kind by the social health insurance schemes on behalf of the patient.

Figure 9.2 Receipts and payments of social security schemes

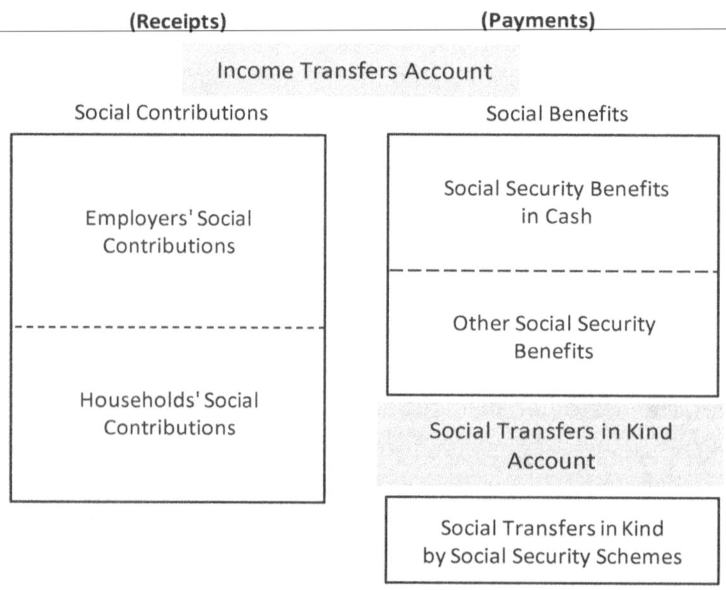

The following is an explanation of the treatment of social health insurance scheme in the national accounts. Assume that the employer pays 60% of the health insurance premiums and the employee pays the remaining 40%, and that the government reimburses 70% of medical expenses incurred when the employee receives medical services. In the generation of earned income account, the employer's 60% contribution is recorded as remuneration of employees, which is carried forward onto the revenues side of the household sector in the allocation of earned income account. In the income transfers account, the employer's 60% contribution and the employee's 40% contribution are combined and recorded as **non-pension social contributions** payable. The benefits of this health insurance are recorded in both the use of income account and the social transfers in kind account. Specifically, payments in kind to households by the national health insurance scheme (70% government-funded) are treated as final consumption expenditure of the government sector in the use of income account, and as the social transfer in kind payable by government and receivable by households in the social transfers in kind account.

Thus, while the social contributions payable to non-pension social security schemes such as social health insurance is treated in the income transfers account, the benefits (70%) are processed in the social transfers in kind account. The remaining 30% of the expenditure is recorded as household final consumption expenditure in the use of income account.

Table 9.41 Example of accounting for the social security health insurance

		Employer		Employee		Government		Private hospital	
		Expenditures	Revenues	Expenditures	Revenues	Expenditures	Revenues	Expenditures	Revenues
Health insurance premiums	Generation of earned income A/C	Employers' social contribution 60							
	Allocation of earned income A/C				Employers' social contribution 60				
	Income transfers A/C			Non-pension contribution payable 100			Non-pension contribution receivable 100		
Health insurance benefits	Production A/C								Health service 100
	Use of income A/C			Final consumption 30		Final consumption 70			
	Social transfers in kind A/C				Social transfers in kind receivable 70	Social transfers in kind payable 70			
	Use of adjusted disposable income A/C			Actual final consumption 70		Actual final consumption -70			

In summary, the government-run social security schemes provide social benefits in both pension and non-pension forms in return for social contributions receivable. Pension-type benefits include the National Pension, while non-pension type benefits include the unemployment insurance and industrial accident compensation insurance. In addition, there are health insurance schemes in which the government compensates households in the form of social transfers in kind in return for the social contributions receivable.

9.3.6.5 Accounting treatment of employment-related pension

In the SNA, the treatment of employment-related pension entitlements (DC or DB), which are a form of pension scheme other than the social security funds, differs from that of social security pensions. Since the employment-related pension entitlements have both the characteristics of both life insurance and social insurance, the accounting methods for these two types of insurances are applied together. In the general accounting treatment, insurance service charges are recorded as output of financial corporations in the production account, and as final consumption expenditure of households in the use of income account. In addition, pension contributions are recorded as employers; social contributions payable in the generation of earned income account and the remuneration of employees receivable by households (employers' social contributions) in the allocation of earned income account. Investment incomes attributable to policyholders arising from the operations of the pension insurance are recorded as receivable by households and payable by financial corporations in the allocation of earned income account.

However, due to the nature of employment-related pensions as social insurance, it is recorded as households' net social contributions payable (= employers' pension contributions + pension supplements – insurance service charges) and net social contributions receivable by financial corporations in the income transfers account. In addition, when payments of insurance benefits are made, it is recorded as social benefits payable by financial corporations and social benefits receivable by households in the same account. Furthermore, due to the nature of employment-related pension schemes as life insurance, the adjustment for the change in pension entitlements receivable (= net social contributions – social benefits) by households and the adjustment for the change in pension entitlements payable by financial corporations are recorded in the use of income account, respectively. At the same time, the same amount of this transaction is recorded in the financial account as an increase in financial asset (pension entitlements) by households and an increase in liability by financial corporations. (See Tables 9.42 and 9.43.)

Table 9.42 Accounting for employment-related pensions by items

	Pension contributions	Investment income	Insurance service charge	Pension benefits	Change in pension entitlements
Production A/C			Output[1] (financial corp.)		
Generation of earned income A/C	Employers' social contributions payable (producers)				
Allocation of earned income A/C	Employers' social contributions receivable (household)	Investment incomes attributable to pension entitlements receivable (household)/ investment incomes payable (financial corp.)			
Income transfers A/C	Net social contributions [2] payable (household) / net social contributions receivable (financial corp.)			Social benefits receivable (household) / social benefits payable (financial corp.)	
Use of income A/C			Final consumption (household)		Adj. for change in pension entitlements[3] receivable (household) / adj. for change in pension entitlements payable (financial corp.)
Financial A/C					Pension entitlement asset (household) /pension entitlement liability (financial corp.)

Footnote: 1) Output: Depending on the type of contract, it can be either a fee-based or a life insurance-based contract.

2) Net social contributions = employers' pension contributions + pension supplements – insurance service charges.

3) Adjustment for the change in pension entitlements = net social contributions – social benefits payable by pension schemes.

Table 9.43 Accounting for employment-related pensions by institutional sectors

Sector / Account	Household		Financial corporation		Employer sector	
	Expenditures / changes in assets	Revenues / changes in liabilities	Expenditures / changes in assets	Revenues / changes in liabilities	Expenditures/changes in assets	Revenues / changes in liabilities
Production A/C				Output of pension service charges (A)		
Generation of earned income A/C					Employers' social contributions (B)	
Allocation of earned income A/C		Employers' social contribution(B)+investment incomes (C)	Investment incomes payable (C)			
Income transfers A/C	Employers' net social contributions payable (D)	Pension benefits receivable (E)	Pension benefits payable (E)	Employers' net social contributions receivable (D)		
Use of income A/C	Final consumption expenditure (A)					

Use of income A/C		Adj. for the change in pension entitlements (F)	Adj. for the change in pension entitlements (F)			
Financial A/C	Pension entitlements (F)			Pension entitlements (F)		

Footnote) A: pension service charges, B: pension contributions, C: investment incomes, D: net pension contributions (=B+C−A), E: pension benefits, F: adjustment for the change in pension entitlements (F=D−E).

Chapter 10. Accumulation accounts (I)

Accumulation accounts are a set of accounts that measure the increase or decrease in assets, liabilities, and net worth that occur between the opening and closing balance sheets. These accounts classify the causes of changes in balance sheets items during the accounting period into two categories: changes "due to transactions" in non-financial and financial assets and liabilities, and changes "due to other flows." Changes resulting from transactions in non-financial and financial assets and liabilities arise between institutional units or within the same unit for analytical purposes. Transactions occur when the economic parties engage in economic activities under mutual agreements between economic entities or internal decisions for analytical purposes within an economic entity. Other economic changes that do not meet this requirement of transaction are recorded as other flows.

The accumulation accounts consist of the following three components (Figure 10.1):

1. the **capital account**, which records transactions in non-financial assets.
2. the **financial account**, which records transactions in financial assets and liabilities
3. the **other changes in assets and liabilities accounts**, which record changes in other flows other than transactions.

The other changes in assets and liabilities accounts are further divided into the **other changes in the volume of assets and liabilities account**, which records changes in the volume of assets due to the appearance of new assets or the disappearance of existing assets, and the **revaluation account**, which records changes in the value of assets and liabilities due to changes in prices or exchange rates. Unlike current accounts, the T-account format for accumulation accounts is structured such that the left-hand side represents "changes in assets," and the right-hand side represents "changes in liabilities and net worth." The following section provides detailed explanations of each of these accounts.

Figure 10.1 The relationship between the accumulation accounts and balance sheets

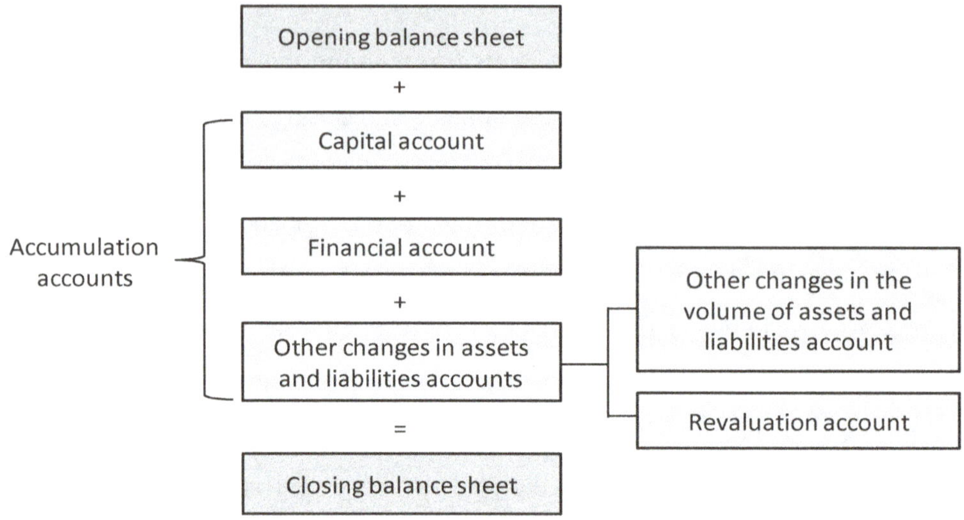

10.1 The capital account

This section describes the nature and structure of the capital account, as well as the detailed components related to its compilation. The first sub-section presents the classification of non-financial assets recorded in the capital account. The second subsection discusses the compilation method of the capital account. The third subsection explains the accounting standards applied to the items recorded in the capital account.

10.1.1 Classification of non-financial assets

The capital account records the transactions involving the acquisition and disposal of non-financial assets and the resulting changes in net worth during a given accounting period. Non-financial assets refer to all assets other than financial assets, and this category is further divided into **produced assets** and **non-produced assets** (Table 10.1). Produced assets are non-financial assets that are produced as output through the production process, and non-produced assets are non-financial assets that occur naturally without undergoing the production process.

In the 2025 SNA, natural resources are identified as a separate category within non-financial assets, and the classification is reorganized into three categories: **produced assets (excluding natural resources)**, **non-produced assets (excluding natural resources)**, and **natural resources**. Accordingly, non-financial assets in the system of national accounts are classified as shown in Table 10.1.

The scope of **produced assets** (excluding natural resources) comprises three types: fixed assets, inventories, and valuables. **Fixed assets** are further categorized into dwellings, other buildings and structures (including land improvements), machinery and equipment, weapons systems, costs of ownership transfer on non-produced assets, and intellectual property products (such as R&D; mineral exploration and evaluation; computer software; data and databases; entertainment, literary and artistic originals). Inventories are classified into raw materials and supplies used in the production process, work-in-progress which is not unfinished in the production process, finished goods held for sale, military inventories held by government for defense purposes, and goods for resale held by wholesalers and retailers.

The scope of non-produced assets (excluding natural resources) comprises three types: contracts, leases and licences; crypto assets without a corresponding liability; and goodwill and marketing assets. Natural resources are classified into: fixed assets of biological resources; costs of ownership transfer on non-produced natural resources; work-in-progress on cultivated biological resources; and non-produced natural resources, including land, mineral and energy resources, non-cultivated biological resources yielding once-only products, water resources, and other natural resources (e.g. radio spectra). Specific examples for contracts, leases, licences, crypto assets without a corresponding liability, and goodwill and marketing assets are discussed in 10.1.3.6. The appearance and disappearance of non-produced assets are recorded in the "other changes in the volume of assets and liabilities account", which will be explained in section 11.1.

Table 10.1 Classification of non-financial assets

<table>
<tr><th>Type</th><th>Subitem (1)</th><th>Subitem (2)</th><th>Subitem (3)</th></tr>
<tr><td rowspan="16">Produced assets (excluding natural resources)</td><td rowspan="16">Fixed assets</td><td>Dwellings</td><td></td></tr>
<tr><td rowspan="3">Other buildings and structures</td><td>Non-residential buildings</td></tr>
<tr><td>Other structures</td></tr>
<tr><td>Land improvements</td></tr>
<tr><td rowspan="3">Machinery and equipment</td><td>Transport equipment</td></tr>
<tr><td>ICT equipment</td></tr>
<tr><td>Other machinery and equipment</td></tr>
<tr><td>Weapons systems</td><td></td></tr>
<tr><td>Costs of ownership transfer on non-produced assets (excluding natural resources)</td><td></td></tr>
<tr><td rowspan="5">Intellectual property products</td><td>Research and development</td></tr>
<tr><td>Mineral exploration and evaluation</td></tr>
<tr><td>Computer software</td></tr>
<tr><td>Data and databases</td></tr>
<tr><td>Entertainment, literary and artistic originals</td></tr>
</table>

Type	Subitem (1)	Subitem (2)	Subitem (3)
			Other intellectual property products
	Inventories	Materials and supplies	
		Work-in-progress (excluding produced natural resources)	
		Finished goods	
		Military inventories	
		Goods for resale	
	Valuables	Precious metals	
		Antiques and art objects	
		Other valuables	
Non-produced assets (excluding natural resources)	**Contracts, leases and licences**	Marketable operating leases	
		Permits to undertake specific activities	
		Entitlements to future goods and services on an exclusive basis	
		Non-fungible tokens (NFTs)	
	Crypto assets without a corresponding liability		
	Goodwill and marketing assets		
Natural resources	**Fixed assets**	Biological resources yielding repeat products	Animal resources yielding repeat products
			Tree, crop and plant resources yielding repeat products
		Cultivated biological resources yielding once-only products	
	Costs of ownership transfer on non-produced natural resources		
	Inventories	Work-in-progress on cultivated biological resources	Work-in-progress on cultivated biological resources yielding repeat products
			Work-in-progress on cultivated biological resources yielding once-only products
	Non-produced natural resources	Land	
		Mineral and energy resources	Non-renewable mineral and energy resources
			Renewable energy resources
		Non-cultivated biological resources yielding once-only products	
		Water resources	
		Other natural resources	Radio spectra
			Permits to use natural resources
			Other

10.1.2 Compilation of the capital account

For the compilation of the capital account, transactions during the accounting period in non-financial assets, namely produced assets (excluding natural resources), non-produced assets (excluding natural resources), and natural resources are recorded (Table 10.2). The capital account is a flow account, meaning it records the increase or decreases in non-financial assets during the period. On the right-hand side of this account, **net saving**, the balancing item carried forward from the previous account (the use of income account) is recorded, along with **net capital transfers** (= capital transfers receivable – capital transfers payable). On the left-hand side, items such as net fixed capital formation (= gross fixed capital formation – depreciation), changes in inventories, acquisitions less disposals of valuables, acquisitions less disposals of non-produced non-financial assets, and depletion (–) during the period are recorded. The balancing item of the capital account is shown on the left-hand side as **net lending/net borrowing**, which is netted out across institutional sector within the domestic economy as a whole, leaving only net lending/net borrowing with the rest of the world. The sum of the right-hand side, "changes in net worth due to saving and capital transfers", is added to the opening balance sheet to derive the closing balance sheet which is described in the next chapter.

Table 10.2 The format of the capital account

Changes in assets	Changes in liabilities and net worth
	Net saving
Acquisitions less disposals of produced assets (excluding natural resources)	
Gross fixed capital formation	
Depreciation (-)	
Changes in inventories	
Acquisitions less disposals of valuables	
Acquisitions less disposals of non-produced assets (excluding natural resources)	
Acquisition of natural resources	**Capital transfers receivable**
Depletion (-)	**Capital transfers payable (-)**
Net lending (+) / net borrowing (-)[2]	Changes in net worth due to saving and capital transfers[1]

Note: 1) The total on the right-hand side, 2) Balancing item (= the total on the right-hand side – the total on the left-hand side).

For each institutional sector of the domestic economy, the capital account is compiled in the same format as described above. However, in the case of the rest of the world sector, instead of carrying forward the saving from the use of income account, the **current external balance** is brought forward. The current external balance is the balancing item in the current account for the rest of the world sector and is calculated as "balance of goods and services + balance of earned income + balance of transfer income." In the capital account for the rest of the world sector, the **capital external balance** is derived from the non-residents' "net capital transfers receivable – acquisitions less disposals of non-produced assets (excluding natural resources)." The sum of the current external balance and capital external balance represents the net lending or borrowing of the rest of the world sector. The amount of this net lending/borrowing is equal to the aggregate of the domestic economy, but with the opposite sign.

Table 10.3 The capital account of the rest of the world sector

Changes in assets	Changes in liabilities and net worth
	Current external balance
Acquisitions less disposals of non-produced assets (excluding natural resources)	Net capital transfers receivable
	Changes in net worth due to saving and capital transfers [1]
Net lending(+) /net borrowing(-) [2]	

Note: 1) The total on the right-hand side, 2) Balancing item (= the total on the right-hand side – the total on the left-hand side).

Table 10.4 illustrates the capital account of South Korea for 2015 (unit: KRW trillion). In this example, gross capital formation (=gross fixed capital formation + changes in inventories + net acquisition of valuables) amounts 321.5 for non-financial corporations, 10.1 for financial corporations, 72.4 for general government, 85.6 for households and NPISHs, respectively. Acquisitions less disposals of non-produced non-financial assets are 33.8 for non-financial corporations, 0.8 for financial corporations, 8.1 for general government, and –42.6 for households and NPISHs. To finance capital formation and acquisitions less disposals of non-produced non-financial assets, non-financial corporations have net borrowing of 14.3, while financial corporations have net lending of 12.0, general government has net lending of 19.6, and households and NPISHs have net lending of 97.1, respectively. In the domestic economy as a whole, transactions among domestic institutional sectors are offset against each other, resulting in net lending of 114.4 to the rest of the world sector, and conversely, net borrowing of 114.4, the same amount by the rest of the world sector.

Table 10.4 Example of the capital account (South Korea, 2015)

Changes in assets (Unit: KRW trillion) **Changes in liabilities and net worth**

Nonfinancial corp.	Financial corp.	General government	Households & NPISHs	Total economy	ROW	Goods & services	Total	Transactions & balancing items	Nonfinancial corp.	Financial corp.	General government	Households & NPISHs	Total economy	ROW	Goods & services	Total
								Net saving	129.1	15.4	64.1	85.8	294.4			294.4
								Current external balance						-114.5		-114.5
321.5	10.1	72.4	85.6	489.6			489.6	Gross capital formation							489.6	489.6
114.9	2.4	25.9	36.7	179.9			179.9	Net capital formation							179.9	179.9
316.0	10.1	71.8	83.1	481.0			481.0	Gross fixed capital formation							481.0	481.0
-206.5	-7.7	-46.6	-48.9	-309.7			-309.7	Depreciation (-)							-309.7	-309.7
5.5	0.0	0.6	0.6	6.7			6.7	Changes in inventories							6.7	6.7
0.0	0.0	0.0	2.0	2.0			2.0	Net acquisition of valuables							2.0	2.0
33.8	0.8	8.1	-42.6	0.1	-0.1		0.0	Net acquisition of non-produced assets								
								Net capital transfers receivable	5.4	-0.2	-10.6	5.4	0.0	-0.0		-0.0
								Changes in net worth due to saving and capital transfers	134.5	15.2	53.5	91.2	294.4	-114.5		179.9
-14.3	12.0	19.6	97.1	114.4	-114.4		-0.0	**Net lending (+)/net borrowing (-)**								

10.1.3 Components of the capital account

Since the previous section 5.3 already explained gross capital formation, one of the main components of the capital account, this section will focus on important considerations in the accounting treatment of the various items comprising the capital account, including gross capital formation. However, natural resources are not presented as a separate category but are described as being included within produced and non-produced assets.

10.1.3.1 Gross fixed capital formation

Gross fixed capital formation (GFCF) refers to a technical term that represents the acquisitions or disposals of fixed assets within the national accounts framework. Fixed assets in the SNA include only produced assets; non-produced assets such as land and subsoil assets are not included in the category of fixed assets. Gross fixed capital formation encompasses not only acquisitions of new assets but also purchases and disposals of existing assets. Some important accounting standards in association with gross fixed capital formation are explained as follows:

- Consumer durables used by households are excluded from fixed assets. This is because the services provided by consumer durables are classified as domestic services, which are not included in the production boundary of the SNA. Consequently, purchases of consumer durables by households are treated as final consumption. However, owner-occupied dwellings are included in fixed assets of households' unincorporated enterprises that produce housing services. *Houseboats, mobile homes, and campers* used as the principal residences of households also fall under this category of dwellings. The production of housing services by owner-occupied dwellings is attributed to "household unincorporated enterprises" in the institutional sectoring, and is classified under the industry of "real estate rental activities."

- Small-scale tools may be classified as fixed assets depending on their relative importance in a country's industrial context, although in practice the criterion of their classification is often based on their amounts.
- When a resident unit sells real estate (buildings or structures for fixed assets; land or subsoil resources for non-produced assets) to a non-resident unit, the transaction is treated as the establishment of a **notional resident unit** that purchases the real estate, while the non-resident unit is deemed to acquire the equity (financial asset) representing a claim on that notional unit. However, as an exception, land purchased by a foreign government for the purpose of the *embassy* or *military base* is treated as a direct sale of non-financial asset to a non-resident unit. In addition, the sale of movable fixed assets such as existing airplanes or ships to non-residents is treated as negative fixed capital formation and positive exports.
- Major improvements to existing fixed assets are included in gross fixed capital formation. Likewise, **land improvements** are treated as the creation of new fixed assets.
- Construction activities and cultivated biological resources are treated differently depending on the circumstances. For example, incomplete construction projects or immature plants and animals, which are intended for sale are recorded as work-in-progress inventories by the producer, and when completed and delivered to the institutional unit that will use them as fixed assets, they are recorded as fixed assets of the purchaser. However, construction activities or cultivated biological resources for one's own use (that is, own-account production) are treated as fixed capital formation even if partially completed. In addition, when fixed assets are acquired through **stage payments** according to the progress, only the amounts actually paid are recorded as the acquisition of fixed assets.

- Newly produced fixed assets that are not sold are recorded as inventories of finished goods held by the producer.
- The amount of gross fixed capital formation for cultivated assets, specifically livestock, is calculated as "net acquisitions of livestock (= acquisitions – disposals) plus costs of ownership transfer arising from transactions between livestock producers." Acquisitions include the own account natural growth (including immature animals) and external acquisitions (including imports). Disposals include on-farm slaughter, sales for slaughter, and exports. The increase in immature animals must be captured first as the output of livestock industry.
- Own-account final use of R&D is valued on the basis of its total production costs.
- The acquisition of licenses to produce copies (as distinct from the originals) of the computer software is recognized as a fixed asset. The fees paid by the licensee of such copies to the licensor are recorded as intermediate consumption for the licensee enterprise and as final consumption expenditure for the household.

10.1.3.2 Costs of ownership transfers

The costs of ownership transfer arising from the acquisition and disposal of fixed assets are treated as part of gross fixed capital formation. The following types of ownership transfer costs falls into this category.

- All fees incurred in connection with the acquisition and disposal of fixed assets (i.e., legal, architectural, real estate, appraisal, and auction fees);
- All the costs of trade and transport incurred by the purchaser;
- Taxes related to the acquisition and disposal of fixed assets;
- Delivery, installation and dismantling costs not included in the price of acquired and disposed assets;
- Terminal costs arising from dismantling and disposing of assets at the end of their useful lives.

The accounting treatment rules for the costs of ownership transfer are as follows:

- The depreciation for costs of ownership transfer is applied only over the "expected holding period" of the asset by the owner.

- Anything other than the costs of ownership transfers is depreciated over the service life of the asset
- The costs of ownership transfer on valuables are added to the value of the valuables, but no depreciation for valuables incurs.
- The costs of ownership transfer on non-produced assets (excluding land) are recorded as a separate item of gross fixed capital formation.
- The costs of ownership transfer on land are included in "land improvements" and are depreciated over the holding period.

The costs of ownership transfer on financial assets are recorded as intermediate consumption if incurred by enterprises or government, and as final consumption expenditure if incurred by households. In addition, the costs of ownership transfer incurred by non-residents when acquiring financial assets are treated as exports of services.

Table 10.5 Treatments of costs of ownership transfers in the national accounts

Asset type	Treatment of ownership transfer costs	National accounts item
Fixed assets	Added to the value of fixed assets	Gross fixed capital formation
Valuables	Added to the value of valuables	Valuables (depreciation is not incurred.)
Land	Treated as land improvements	Gross fixed capital formation
Non-produced assets (excluding land)	Treated as "costs of ownership transfer in non-produced assets" which is a separate item of gross fixed capital formation	Gross fixed capital formation
Financial assets (purchased by resident units)	Treated as intermediate consumption or final consumption	Intermediate consumption (enterprises, government and NPISHs), final consumption (households)
Financial assets (purchased by non-resident units)	Treated as exports of services	Exports of services

10.1.3.3 Changes in inventories

The scope of inventories includes those acquired or disposed of through direct transactions between institutional units, as well as those arising internally during the production process within enterprises. The categories classified as inventories include: finished goods and work-in-progress inventories held by producers, inventories of materials or supplies held by producers, inventories of goods for resale held by wholesale and retail traders, inventories of cultivated biological resources held by agricultural and livestock producers, and military inventories held by government.

Here are several accounting treatment methods in association with the valuation of inventories below:

- Inventories of the output (finished goods) produced by producers are valued at basic prices prevailing at the time of entry into the warehouse of the finished goods. Work-in-progress is valued by multiplying the basic price of finished goods by the degree of completion of the work-in-progress (the proportion of costs incurred relative to the total costs of finished goods). When finished goods are withdrawn for sale from the warehouse, they are valued at the basic price prevailing at the time of withdrawal.
- Goods for intermediate consumption (such as materials and supplies) held in their capacity as producers are valued at the purchaser's price prevailing at the time of entry into the materials warehouse. In addition, when the materials are withdrawn from the warehouse for production input, they are valued at the purchaser's price prevailing at the time of withdrawal.
- Goods for resale are valued at the purchaser's price at the time of entry into inventories. (The accounting practice typically includes transport charges paid at the time of acquisition.) When the goods for resale are withdrawn from inventories for sale, etc., they are valued at the prices at which the wholesale and retail traders could reprocure the goods at the time of withdrawal, as distinct from the original prices when they were acquired.
- Standing timbers and livestock intended for slaughter are treated as work-in-progress during their growth period. Standing timbers are typically cultivated over a long period of time, so they are valued by deducting the necessary costs incurred (from planting to logging) from the future sales revenue and discounting the remaining amount to their present value.

10.1.3.4 Acquisitions less disposals of valuables

The acquisition value of valuables includes the costs of ownership transfer such as appraisal fees and auctioneer's margins. The disposal value of valuables is recorded as the value of the sales minus brokerage fees. Since valuables are not classified as fixed assets, their costs of ownership transfer are not subject to depreciation.

Example of transaction for the acquisition less disposal of valuables

Let us examine how the acquisition and disposal of valuables are handled in the national accounts. For example, suppose that A purchases a valuable from a producer at $800 and pays a brokerage fee of $200. In this case, A's acquisition value of the valuable is recorded as $1,000 (=800+200).

Purchaser A

	Changes in assets	Changes in liabilities
Capital account	Valuables 800 Valuables (fee) 200	
Financial account		Currency 1,000

Now, assume that during the same period, A resells the valuable to B for $1,000 and pays a brokerage fee of $100, while B pays a brokerage fee of $300 in connection with the purchase of the valuable. Then, the disposal value of the valuable by A, the seller, is recorded as $1,200 (=1,300–100), and B's acquisition value of the valuable is recorded as $1,600 (=1,300+300).

	Seller A		Purchaser B	
	Changes in assets	Changes in liabilities	Changes in assets	Changes in liabilities
Capital account	Valuables (fee) 100	Valuables 1,300	Valuables 1,300 Valuables (fee) 300	
Financial account	Currency 1,200			Currency 1,600

Thus, the acquisition less disposal of valuables during this period would be $-200 (=1,000–1,200) for A and $1,600 for B, resulting in the total net acquisition of valuables during the period is $1,400 (= -200+1,600). Meanwhile, since A holds no assets at the end of the accounting period, a net acquisition of valuables of $200 is recorded under the revaluation account (as described later), resulting in a holding gain of $200.

Seller A

	Changes in assets	Changes in liabilities
Revaluation account	Valuables 200	Holding gain 200

Summarizing the above transactions, the valuables held by A and B are recorded as follows in the national accounts.

	A	B
Opening balance sheet	0	0
Changes during the period	-200	1600
Holding gain	200	
Closing balance sheet	0	1,600

10.1.3.5 Depreciation

The measurement of depreciation (consumption of fixed capital) is essential for estimating net value added and net fixed capital formation in the national accounts. Specifically, net value-added is derived by subtracting depreciation and depletion from gross value added, and net fixed capital formation is derived by subtracting depreciation from gross fixed capital formation respectively. In the SNA, net value added is preferred over gross value added as a concept of value added because deducting depreciation, which is the decline in the value of fixed assets, provides a more appropriate measure of value added.

The necessity of measuring depreciation also arises in other contexts. In the national balance sheet, fixed assets are shown net of depreciation. Furthermore, as will be explained later, depreciation must also be estimated to calculate "capital income" (capital services), which represents the payment for the use of non-financial assets.

Definition and measurement of depreciation

Depreciation is defined as the decline in the current value of fixed assets owned by producers during an accounting period due to *physical deterioration, normal obsolescence, or normal accidental damage*. Depreciation in the SNA is estimated based on the current value of fixed assets, whereas depreciation in business accounting is determined by historic costs of the assets. Depreciation is an imputed value, not based on actual market transactions, and it is estimated based on the expected future service lives of assets, which may lead to variations in the estimation methods across countries. Accordingly, the value of gross fixed capital formation is calculated first, and then net fixed capital formation is derived by subtracting depreciation, and GDP in gross terms is commonly used for international comparisons. However, net domestic product (NDP) is more appropriate from an economic perspective, which highlights the need for a more refined measurement of depreciation.

The scope of depreciation is restricted to fixed assets among non-financial assets. That is, it applies to tangible fixed assets and intellectual property products (formerly intangible fixed assets) and also includes the costs of ownership transfer of non-produced assets such as land and subsoil resources. However, valuables and non-produced assets are excluded from the scope of depreciation because they do not meet the definition of fixed assets. Depreciation covers not only physical deterioration due to the use of fixed assets, but also normal obsolescence and accidental damage. However, irregular losses caused by events such as wars or catastrophic natural disasters are excluded and are instead recorded in the *other changes in the volume of assets and liabilities account*.

10.1.3.6 Non-produced assets

In the 2008 SNA, non-produced assets were classified into two categories: natural resources and other non-produced assets (contracts, leases and licences; crypto assets without a corresponding liability; and goodwill and marketing assets). In the 2025 SNA, however, natural resources are identified as a separate category. Nevertheless, the following section reviews the main components of non-produced assets for each category, *including natural resources*.

Natural resources

Natural resources refer to *non-produced tangible assets* such as land, mineral and energy resources, non-cultivated biological resources (e.g., natural forests, natural fish stocks), and water resources, and the income generated from leasing these assets is classified as "rent."

There are three options of leasing arrangements for natural resources. The first option is a lease that lasts until the asset is fully depleted. The second option is a lease that allows the lessee to use the resource for a specified period of time without intervention from the legal owner. The third option is a lease that is automatically extended each year. The first option corresponds to a sale of the asset, while the second and third options are classified as a **resource lease**, where rent is charged between the lessor and lessee. A resource lease is a contract under which the legal owner of non-produced non-financial asset, particularly a non-produced natural resource, permits another institutional unit to use that asset in production. In the SNA, resource leases apply to the following types of assets:

- Land
- Mineral and energy resources
- Other non-produced natural resources (non-cultivated biological resources, water resources)

For resource leases on **land**, it is assumed that the asset is returned to the owner at the end of the contract. Changes in the value of land reflect only changes in its regenerative potential (use and productivity), and no depletion occurs in the production process. Accordingly, only rent is recorded for land, with no depletion. In contrast, **mineral and energy resources** are not returned to the owner at the end of a resource lease, and production results in a physical reduction of the underlying asset. Therefore, both rent and depletion must be recorded for these types of resource leases.

Land

Land refers to land in its natural state and its surface, including terrain and locational characteristics that may have economic value. Land must be subject to established ownership rights and be capable of being transacted. While land itself is not subject to depletion, resources embedded in or combined with land may be subject to depletion (e.g., land combined with mineral rights).

In the SNA, land is not further disaggregated into more detailed categories. However, the "System of Environmental-Economic Accounting" (SEEA, 2012), the manual adopted by international organizations such as the UN, subdivides land in accordance with the land use as follows.

Classification of the land use (by SEEA)
• Agriculture
• Forestry
• Land used for aquaculture
• Use of built-up and other related areas
• Land used for maintenance and restoration of environmental functions
• Other uses of land n.e.c.
• Land not in use

In the SNA, land is not subject to depreciation because it is a non-produced asset, and the cost of ownership transfer associated with this asset is not included in the acquisition cost of land itself. Instead, this cost of ownership transfer on land is classified as a fixed asset and recorded under the category of land improvement. Unlike fixed assets, the purchase price of land does not include the cost of ownership transfer, so the prices recorded for both the seller and the purchaser of land is the same. Land may be used independently, or in conjunction with buildings or other structures. Therefore, when valuing land, the associated buildings are appraised at their appropriate value, and this amount is then subtracted from the combined market price of the land and buildings. However, if there is no valuation data to separate the land value from the associated building, the entire value is classified, by convention, under the asset category with the larger proportional value.

Mineral and energy resources

Mineral and energy resources consist of confirmed reserves of coal, oil, gas, other fuels, metallic ores, and non-metallic ores located below or on the earth's surface, including under the seabed. In the 2025 SNA, mineral and energy resources are classified into *non-renewable mineral and energy resources* (coal and lignite, oil and natural gas, mineral resources, and other non-renewable resources) and *renewable energy resources* (wind, solar, water, geothermal, and others). Among these, non-renewable mineral and energy resources are subject to depletion. The 2025 SNA recommends that the rent and depletion arising from these non-renewable mineral and energy resources be allocated between the extractor and the legal owner of the resources in proportion to the agreed sharing of resource rents. The natural resources stock is likewise to be recorded as having been moved to the extractor in that same proportion. This treatment is referred to as the **split-asset approach** (see Box 10.1).

Box 10.1 The split-asset approach of natural resources

Natural resources (e.g., oil and minerals) are typically the assets of a legal owner (most often government). However, extraction is carried out by an extractor, and the economic surplus derived from the use of the resource (that is, resource rent) is shared between the legal owner and the extractor. The **split-asset approach** allocates the natural resource assets and its depletion between the legal owner and the extractor in proportion to their shares of the resource rent. For example, suppose the government grants extraction rights to a private corporation, with the agreement that future economic benefits (resource rent) are split 75% to government and 25% to the extractor. The accounting data are provided as follows: opening value of the natural resource 800, extractor's output 110, intermediate consumption 10, remuneration of employees 35, depreciation 30, depletion 20, and total resource rent generated 24. Under the split-asset approach, government's share of resource rent 18 (75%) and extractor's share of resource rent 6 (25%); government's share of depletion 15 (75%) and extractor's share of depletion 5 (25%). Under the split-asset approach, 25% of the natural resource (value 200) is deemed to be moved from the government to the extractor through entries in the *other changes in the volume of assets and liabilities account*, not the *capital account*.

A representation of the complete set of entries in the sequence of economic accounts is provided below:

Table 10.6 Treatment of split-asset approach in the sequence of economic accounts

Extractor				Legal owner (government)	
Production and generation of earned income account				Production and generation of earned income account	
Intermediate consumption	10	Output	110		
Remuneration of employees	35				

Gross operating surplus	65						
(Depreciation)	30						
(Depletion)	20						
(Net operating surplus)	15						
Total	110	Total	110				
Allocation of earned income account				**Allocation of earned income account**			
		Net operating surplus	15				
Rent	18					Rent	18
Depletion of legal owner	-15					Depletion of legal owner	-15
Net saving	12			Net saving	3		
Capital account				**Capital account**			
		Net saving	12			Net saving	3
Depreciation	-30						
Depletion	-5			Depletion	-15		
Net lending	47	Changes in net worth	12	Net lending	18	Changes in net worth	3
Financial account				**Financial account**			
Cash	47	Net lending	47	Cash	18	Net lending	18
Other changes in volume of assets and liabilities account				**Other changes in volume of assets and liabilities account**			
		Other changes	200			Other changes	-200
		Changes in net worth	200			Changes in net worth	-200
Balance sheet				**Balance sheet**			
Cash	47	Net worth	212 (=200+12)	Cash	18	Net worth	603 (=800-200+3)
Fixed assets	-30						
Natural resources	195 (=200-5)			Natural resources	585 (= 800-200-15)		
Total	212	Total	212	Total	603	Total	603

Non-cultivated biological resources

Non-cultivated biological resources refer to naturally occurring fish stock (e.g., wild fisheries), naturally occurring forests (non-cultivated forests), and other unmanaged biological populations. Although the natural growth of these resources increases the value of assets that are treated as economic assets, such growth is not recorded as production. Instead, this natural increase is recorded in *the other changes in the volume of assets and liabilities account.*

Changes in these resources are measured as 'extraction minus natural growth.' When extraction exceed natural growth, the resulting decrease is treated as **depletion**, which is recorded as a cost item in the production account. Conversely, when extractions are less than natural growth, the resulting negative depletion is recorded as an increase in asset value in the other changes in the volume of assets and liabilities account. By contrast, cultivated biological resources (e.g., the growth of trees in managed plantations intended for timber production, or the growth of fish in aquaculture facilities) are under the control and responsibility of owners, and their growth is therefore recorded as production in the form of *work-in-progress*.

Water resources

Water resources refer to surface water and groundwater that are extracted or used for economic purposes, and whose scarcity justifies the establishment of ownership and use rights, market-based valuation, and some degree of economic control. Thus, not all naturally occurring water is included within the asset boundary of the national accounts; only water resources with economic value and enforceable rights are recognized as economic assets.

In some cases, it may be difficult to measure separately the value of water resources from the value of the associated land. For example, the surface of a river or lake and the adjacent land may need to be treated as a single, inseparable asset. When the value of the water resource cannot be clearly distinguished from that of the land, the entire asset is classified to the asset category representing the component with the greater economic value. If water resources are extracted at a rate that exceeds their natural regeneration, depletion may occur, and such depletion is recorded as a cost of production.

Other non-produced assets

Contracts, leases and licences

Contracts, leases and licences constitute a category of non-produced assets, referring to expenditures associated with the acquisition of rights arising from various types of contracts that cannot be recorded as produced assets. Specific examples include:

- Contracts for future production: contracts with football players by football clubs, exclusive rights to release albums by famous musicians, and exclusive publication rights for new books by renowned authors.
- Marketable operating lease: In an operating lease, a lessee can sublease to another economic entity at a price higher than the original contractual rental.
- Licences to use radio spectra: for example, licences held by telecommunication companies to use frequency spectra.

- Licences to use natural resources: In the case where the holder of a fishing quota sells the right to use it to another economic entity.

Contracts, leases and licences are assets arising from non-transactional factors and are first recorded in the "other changes in the volume of assets and liabilities account." Subsequently, they are recorded in the capital account as non-produced asset of the economic entity that acquires this asset. (See section 11.1 for accounting treatment.) In addition, these values decline over the contract period as they expire at the end of the contract period.

Crypto assets without a corresponding liability

Crypto assets without a corresponding liability (e.g., Bitcoin and algorithm-based stablecoins) do not entitle the holder to any legal or contractual claim on an issuer, and because no counterpart liability exists, they are classified as non-produced non-financial assets, rather than financial assets. When such assets are used to purchase goods or services, the transaction is treated as **barter** in the national accounts. For example, if a household purchases accommodation services using Bitcoin, the household is considered to have disposed of a crypto asset, while the enterprise is considered to have provided accommodation services. The transaction value is recorded as the observed market price at the time of exchange.

The value of crypto assets is measured using observable market prices, including direct transaction prices, the market value of the goods and services acquired with the asset, or exchange prices quoted at specific points in time. Changes in the value of crypto assets are recorded as holding gains and losses and captured in the *revaluation account* within the sequence of economic accounts.

Purchased goodwill and marketing assets

Goodwill refers to the value paid by a purchaser of a company that exceeds the fair value of the company's net assets (= assets – liabilities). It can be regarded as the present value of the company's expected excess earnings. Goodwill may sometimes include the value of marketing assets. **Marketing assets** refer to the expenditures incurred to acquire trademarks, logos, and domain names of a company. Goodwill and marketing assets are not transactions that arise from an agreement with another party (i.e., they result from other flows). Therefore, they are first recorded as non-produced assets in the other changes in the volume of assets and liabilities account. Subsequently, the economic unit that acquires these assets records the corresponding amount in the capital account. In addition, these assets are amortized over the expected period of excess earnings, which is handled in the other changes in the volume of assets and liabilities account, not as operating expenses. (Refer to section 11.1 for details.)

10.1.3.7 Depletion

Depletion refers to the decline in the stock of non-produced natural resources during an accounting period, which occurs when economic units extract natural resources at a level exceeding their natural regeneration or growth. In the national accounts, depletion can be defined in both physical and monetary terms. The physical concept refers to the reduction in the physical stock of a natural resource at a rate faster than its natural regeneration, while the monetary concept measures the decline in future income that the resource could generate as a result of depletion, valued using the price of the natural resource in its original place.

Scope of assets to which depletion applies

Depletion applies to those non-produced natural resources that do not provide repeated production service. The application rules differ by resource type as follows:

1. **Non-renewable resources** (minerals, oil, gas, etc.): Depletion is limited to the decline in value attributable to extraction. New discoveries, reappraisals, or the withdrawal of a resource from economic activity due to technological or demand changes are not recorded as depletion but as other changes in the volume of assets and liabilities.

2. **Bare land**: Land itself is not subject to depletion. However, when land is combined with another asset (e.g., land plus mineral rights), the combined asset may be subject to depreciation or depletion depending on its nature.

3. **Renewable resources**: For *non-cultivated biological resources* (e.g., natural fish stocks, timber from non-cultivated forests), if extraction exceeds natural regeneration, depletion is recorded; increases in natural regeneration are recorded as negative depletion. In the case of *cultivated biological resources* (e.g., aquaculture assets or commercial timber grown on plantation forests), their growth does not constitute natural regeneration; therefore, the concepts of depletion and regeneration do not apply. *Biological resources that yield repeat products* (e.g., dairy cattle, fruit trees) are classified as fixed assets; their decline is recorded as depreciation rather than depletion.

Depletion is recorded on the left-hand side of the capital account as a negative change in assets, in a manner similar to the recording of depreciation, although the types of assets involved are different. Net saving already reflects deductions for both depreciation and depletion.

Box 10.2: An example of the accounting treatment of depletion in the SNA

Consider the accounting treatment of depletion in the sequence of economic accounts, given the following data on a natural resource.

Item	Data
(1) Extraction of the natural resource	120
(2) Natural regeneration	40
Physical depletion	120 − 40 = **80**
(3) Price	$1
Monetary depletion	80 × 1 = $**80**

Assume that the output and cost data of the enterprise are as follows:

- Output: 800, intermediate consumption: 300, remuneration of employees: 200, depreciation: 100, Other taxes less subsidies on production: 10

1. Recording in the production and the generation of earned income account

Under the 2025 SNA, depletion is included as a cost in the production account and is incorporated into gross value added.

Production and generation of earned income accounts

Expenditures | Revenues

Item	Amount	Item	Amount
Intermediate consumption	300	Output	800
Gross value added	**500**		
Remuneration of employees Other taxes less subsidies on production Gross operating surplus (Depreciation) **(Depletion)**	200 10 290 100 **80**		
Total	800		800

2. Recording in the allocation of earned income account

Assume that the natural resource is entirely owned by government and that the enterprise uses the resource under a lease arrangement. In this case:

- Government receives resource rent.
- This resource rent includes depletion amounting to 80. Therefore, in the allocation of earned income account, depletion of 80 is deducted from the amount receivable by government in order to derive net property income.

Allocation of earned income account

Item	Enterprise (Expenditures)	Government (Revenues)
Resource rent (gross)	120	120
Depletion of natural resources borne by the legal owner (-)	–	**– 80**
Net resource rent	(Enterprise: payment of 120)	**40**

3. **Recording in the capital account**

Depletion is recorded in the capital account as a reduction in non-produced assets (natural resources).

Capital account

Expenditures / Revenues

Item	Amount	Item	Amount
Depletion (decrease in assets)	**– 80**	Net saving	

10.1.3.8 Capital transfers

Capital transfers are unrequited transfers where the party making transfers provides assets (excluding cash and inventories) or financial assets (excluding accounts receivable), and the party receiving transfers acquires those assets. Capital transfers are typically large in scale, and occur infrequently and irregularly. (In contrast, current transfers are relatively small in scale, and occur frequently and regularly.) Because of these characteristics, capital transfers are recorded in the capital account, not in the current account. Typical examples of capital transfers include capital taxes (i.e., inheritance tax, gift tax), investment grants provided by governments or international organizations to other institutional units, debt forgiveness agreed upon between a creditor and a debtor (excluding debt write-offs by unilateral decision of creditors, which are recorded in the other changes in the volume of assets and liabilities account.), inheritances or gifts, and exceptional insurance claims (see Table 10.7).

Table 10.7 Types of capital transfers

Item	Example
Capital taxes	Capital transfer taxes (i.e., inheritance tax and gift tax)
Investment grants	Free investment grants provided by government or international organizations
Debt forgiveness	Debt forgiveness by agreement between a creditor and a debtor
Other capital transfers	Inheritance, gift, exceptionally large insurance claims, and long-term accumulated losses that government compensates for public enterprises.

Annex to 10.1: Representation of the sequence of economic accounts in a matrix form

The SNA sequence of economic accounts described so far can be represented in a single consolidated matrix that shows at a glance the revenues and expenditures of a set of economic accounts and the balancing items of each account. This matrix format is used in the **Social Accounting Matrix** (SAM) approach, which allows for the abbreviated presentation of accounts ranging from the production account to the capital account. The social accounting matrix integrates data from the supply and use tables and institutional sector accounts and presents them in a single matrix, with each entry in the matrix representing both the receipt and payment of a transaction. In this matrix table, the rows represent receipts for each account, and the columns represent payments for each account. For example, an entry in the matrix denoted as a_{ij} represents the receipt in row i and the payment in column j. The key advantage of this matrix format is that, unlike the traditional presentation of the sequence of economic accounts, where balancing items and major accounting components are displayed separately by account, the matrix consolidates all indicators into a single table, allowing for a comprehensive overview of the national accounts.

The table below shows a condensed matrix form based on South Korea's Sequence of economic accounts for 2015 (from the goods and services account to the capital account). In this table, as in a typical Social Accounting Matrix representation, the figures shown in the rows indicate the incoming amounts for each account, while the figures in the columns represent the outgoing amounts for each account. The row and column totals themselves have no economic meaning, but must be consistent for each account. The generation of earned income account, which serves as an intermediate account linking the production account and the allocation of earned income account, is not shown separately in this table.

Table 10.8 Representation of Integrated Economic Account in a matrix form (Korea, 2015)

(Unit: KRW trillion)

Account \ Account	Goods and services	Production	Allocation of earned income	Income transfers	Use of income	Capital	Rest of the world	Total
Goods and services		Intermediate consumption (2,207.8)			Final consumption (1,054.9)	Gross capital formation (489.6)	Exports of goods and services (712.8)	4,465.1
Production	Output plus taxes less subsides on products (3,865.8)							3,865.8
Allocation of earned income		NDP (1,348.4)	Property income (297.5)				Remuneration of employees plus property income from rest of the world (28.4)	1,674.2
Income transfers			NNI (1,353.5)	Current transfers (595.0)			Current transfers from rest of the world (11.6)	1,960.1
Use of income				NDI (1,349.3)	Adjustment for change in pension entitlement (13.7)		Adjustment of change in pension entitlement from rest of the world (0)	1,363.0
Capital		Depreciation (309.7)			Net saving (294.4)	Net capital transfers receivable less net acquisition of non-produced assets (0)	Net capital transfers less net acquisition of non produced asset from rest of the world (0.1)	604.0
Rest of the world	Imports of goods and services (599.3)		Remuneration of employees and property income to rest of the world (23.2)	Current transfers to rest of the world (15.8)	Adjustment of change in pension entitlement to rest of the world (0)	Net lending of domestic economy/net borrowing (114.4)		752.6
Total	4,465.1	3,865.8	1,674.2	1,960.1	1,363.0	604.0	752.7	

10.2 The financial account

This section describes the nature and structure of the financial account, as well as the specific provisions on how to compile the account. To this end, section 1 explains the classification of financial assets, section 2 describes how financial accounts are prepared, and section 3 presents the accounting rules for recording each item of the financial account. In the final section, a detailed discussion will be provided on the relationship between the financial account and related items in other current accounts.

10.2.1 Classification of financial assets

The financial account is an account that records transactions in financial assets and liabilities that occur during a certain accounting period. Financial assets recorded in the financial accounts follow the classification shown in Table 10.9, which is directly linked to the balance sheet. Explanations of the main items of financial assets are covered in section 10.2.3. The source data for deriving financial assets and liabilities are the statement of financial position (balance sheet) of each institutional sector, but among them, the statement of financial position and accompanying statements of financial corporations play the most important role. Most of these data can be collected from the corporate financial statement databases of the financial supervisory authorities and tax authorities.

Table 10.9 Classification of financial assets

Type	Subitem	Example
Monetary gold, SDRs	Monetary gold	
	SDRs	
Currency and deposits	Currency	
	Crypto-assets with a corresponding liability designed to act as a general medium of exchange	
	Transferrable deposits	Interbank positions
		Other transferrable deposits
	Other deposits	
Debt securities	Short-term	
	Long-term	
Loans	Short-term	
	Long-term	
Equity, Investment fund shares	Equity	Listed shares
		Unlisted shares
		Other equity
	Investment fund shares	Money market fund shares

Type	Subitem	Example
		Non-MMF investment fund shares
Insurance, pension, and standardized guarantee schemes	Non-life insurance technical reserves	
	Life insurance and annuities entitlements	
	Pension entitlements	
	Claim of pension fund on pension managers	
	Entitlements to non-pension benefits	
Financial derivatives and employee stock options	Financial derivatives	Options
		Forwards
	Employee stock options	
Other accounts receivable/payable	Trade credits and advances	
	Other accounts receivable/payable	

10.2.2 Compilation of the financial account

The financial account records the acquisitions and disposals of financial assets, as well as the incurrence and repayment of liabilities, resulting from transactions during the accounting period. The acquisitions and disposals of non financial assets through transactions are recorded in the capital account, while other flows other than transactions are recorded in the other changes in assets and liabilities accounts. Similarly, each item in the financial accounts records an increase or decrease (flow) in financial assets and liabilities arising from transactions during the period, while changes not resulting from transactional events are recorded in the other changes in assets and liabilities account. The financial account must be clearly distinguished from the balance sheet, which record a balance (stock) at the end of the period.

The left-hand side of the financial account records acquisitions of financial assets and repayments of liabilities, while the right-hand side of the same account records disposals of financial assets and incurrence of liabilities. The balancing item, where the total of the left-hand side exceeds that of the right-hand side, is recorded as **net lending** (+); conversely, if the total of the right-hand side exceeds that of the left-hand side, it is recorded as **net borrowing** (-). The amount of this net lending (+) or net borrowing (-) thus derived must be equal to the net lending (+) / net borrowing (-) in the capital account, which records transactions of non-financial assets. Note that these values are shown on opposite sides in the financial account and the capital account.

Net lending (+) / net borrowing (-) arises for each domestic institutional sector within the domestic economy, and when the domestic economy as a whole and the rest of the world sector are aggregated, the total net lending/net borrowing across all sectors should sum to zero. That is, the value of the domestic economy represents the acquisition of financial assets (or liabilities) vis-à-vis the rest of the world sector, while the value of the rest of the world sector represents the incurrence of liabilities (or financial assets) vis-à-vis the domestic economy.

Each item in the financial account has a corresponding liability for every financial asset, and the net acquisition of financial assets on the left-hand side correspond to the net incurrence of liabilities on the right-hand side across both the domestic economy and the rest of the world. However, as explained later, **gold bullion**, which is an exceptional item, does not have a corresponding liability. Therefore, the total increase in assets on the left-hand side will exceed the total increase in liabilities on the right-hand side by the amount of gold bullion. Moreover, the amount of gold bullion is excluded from the category of capital formation in the capital account.

Table 10.10 The format of the financial account

Changes in assets	Changes in liabilities and net worth
	Net lending (+) / net borrowing (-)
Net acquisition of financial assets	Net incurrence of liabilities
Monetary gold and SDRs	Monetary gold and SDRs
Currency and deposits	Currency and deposits
Debt securities	Debt securities
Loans	Loans
Equity and investment fund shares	Equity and investment fund shares
Insurance, pension and standardized guarantee schemes	Insurance, pension and standardized guarantee schemes
Financial derivatives and employee stock options	Financial derivatives and employee stock options
Other accounts receivable/payable	Other accounts receivable/payable

The table below (Table 10.11) presents an abridged financial account of South Korea in 2015. During 2015, the net acquisition of financial assets is KRW 875.4 trillion for the domestic economy as a whole, with KRW 93.5 trillion for non-financial corporations, KRW 474.3 trillion for financial corporations, KRW 83.8 trillion for the government, and KRW 223.7 trillion for households and NPISHs. The rest of the world sector has a net acquisition of KRW -16.2 trillion. During the same period, the net incurrence of liabilities is KRW 760.9 trillion for the domestic economy as a whole, with KRW 108.3 trillion for non-financial corporations, KRW 458.7 trillion for financial corporations, KRW 65.2 trillion for the government, and KRW 128.7 trillion for households and NPISHs. The rest of the world sector has a net incurrence of KRW 98.3 trillion.

The balancing item obtained by subtracting the net incurrence of liabilities from the net acquisition of financial assets for each institutional sector is recorded as either net lending (+) or net borrowing (-). Accordingly, non-financial corporations record KRW -14.7 trillion (=93.5-108.3), financial corporations KRW 15.6 trillion (=474.3-458.7), the government KRW 18.6 trillion (=83.8-65.2), and households and NPISHs KRW 95.0 trillion (=223.7-128.7), resulting in a total of KRW 114.5 trillion for the domestic economy. In principle, this value of net lending or net borrowing must be consistent with the value of the net lending or net borrowing by institutional sectors in the capital account. However, as will be discussed later, discrepancies between these two balancing items occur more commonly due to different data sources for each account.

Table 10.11 Example of the financial account (South Korea, 2015)

Changes in assets (Unit: KRW trillion) **Changes in liabilities and net worth**

Nonfinancial corp.	Financial corp.	General government	Households & NPISHs	Total economy	ROW	Goods & services	Total	Transactions & balancing items	Nonfinancial corp.	Financial corp.	General government	Households & NPISHs	Total economy	ROW	Goods & services	Total
								Net lending (+) / net borrowing (-)	-14.7	15.6	18.6	95.0	114.5	-114.5		0.0
93.5	474.3	83.8	223.7	875.4	-16.2		859.2	Net acquisition of financial assets								
								Net acquisition of liabilities	108.3	458.7	65.2	128.7	760.9	98.3		859.2
0.0	-0.1	0.0	0.0	-0.1	0.0		-0.1	Monetary gold and SDRs	0.0	0.0	0.0	0.0	0.0	-0.1		-0.1
57.3	41.7	5.1	109.9	214.0	-8.6		205.3	Currency and deposits	0.0	193.7	11.6	0.0	205.3	0.0		205.3
13.2	129.8	9.2	4.7	156.9	-7.0		149.9	Debt securities	-13.9	84.9	50.3	0.0	121.2	28.7		149.9
0.0	214.8	5.0	0.0	219.8	-0.0		219.7	Loans	87.3	-4.3	0.7	128.2	211.9	7.9		219.7
-10.1	34.5	55.6	16.5	96.4	-2.6		93.8	Equity and investment fund shares	21.3	51.9	2.3	0.0	75.6	18.2		93.8
4.7	3.1	-0.0	89.8	97.5	0.0		97.5	Insurance, pension and standardized guarantee schemes	0.0	97.5	0.0	0.0	97.5	0.0		97.5
0.0	0.0	0.0	0.0	0.0	0.0		0.0	Financial derivatives and employee stock options	0.0	0.0	0.0	0.0	0.0	0.0		0.0
28.5	50.5	9.0	2.8	90.8	2.2		93.0	Other accounts receivable/ payable	13.6	35.0	0.3	0.5	49.4	43.5		93.0

The net lending or net borrowing shown in the capital account is the sum of saving and net capital transfers less expenditures for the net acquisition of non-financial assets, which is recorded on the left-hand side as a balancing item. In contrast, net lending or net borrowing in the financial account is calculated by subtracting the net incurrence of liabilities from the net acquisition of financial assets, which is recorded on the right-hand side as a balancing item. These relationships can be expressed by the following formulas:

- Net lending (or net borrowing) in the capital account = (saving + net capital transfer) – (net capital formation + acquisitions less disposals of non-produced assets)
- Net lending (or net borrowing) in the financial account = net acquisition of financial assets – net incurrence of liabilities

However, as shown in Table 10.12, the net lending for each institutional sector in the previous capital account (Table 10.4) differs from that in the financial account. This occurs because the amounts of net lending in the capital account and the financial account are derived independently, based on different source data. Therefore, the challenge for statisticians is how to reduce these discrepancies.

In addition, in the financial account, the net lending or net borrowing amounts between the domestic economy and the rest of the world sector are identical in value but have opposite signs. When adding together the amounts for the domestic economy and the rest of the world sector (-114.5), the sum always equals zero. The net lending/net borrowing figure in the rest of the world sector corresponds to "net lending/net borrowing" figure in the balance of payments. However, the signs are reversed because the balance of payments is measured from the perspective of the resident domestic economy, whereas the financial account is measured from the perspective of the rest of the world sector. Therefore, the negative value of the rest of the world sector in the financial account appears as the positive value in the balance of payments. As a reference, in Table 13.4, net lending of South Korea in 2015 on the balance of payments is US$ 103.0 billion, which is equivalent to KRW 114.5 trillion when converted into Korean currency.

Table 10.12 Comparison of net lending/net borrowing between the financial account and the capital account (South Korea, 2015)

(Unit: KRW trillion)

	Non-financial corporations	Financial corporations	Government	Households and NPISHs	Total economy	ROW
Financial account (1)	-14.7	15.6	18.6	95.0	114.5	-114.5
Capital account (2)	-14.3	12.0	19.6	97.1	114.4	-114.4
Statistical discrepancy (1-2)	-0.4	3.6	-1.0	-2.1	0.1	-0.1

10.2.3 Components of the financial account

The followings are the main financial instruments that constitute the financial account. These items are also applied directly to the balance sheet.

Monetary gold

Monetary gold refers to gold held by monetary authorities as part of their reserve assets, and it is distinct from non-monetary gold, which is treated as an ordinary commodity. Monetary gold includes both **gold bullion** held in physical form and **unallocated gold accounts**[16] which are gold accounts held in the form of deposits with foreign monetary authorities or international financial organizations. Since gold bullion is physical asset, unlike other financial assets, it does not have a counterpart liability, making it the only financial asset without a corresponding liability. When gold bullion is held by the monetary authority as a reserve asset, it is classified as monetary gold. However, if it is held in a form of other than a reserve asset, it is treated as an ordinary good (**non-monetary gold**) and recorded as a "valuable" item in the capital account.

The classification of gold bullion as a financial asset when held as a reserve is based on international convention, and because there is no corresponding liability, the financial account will show an imbalance between assets and liabilities to the extent of the increase in gold bullion (i.e., an increase in domestic assets without a corresponding increase in foreign liabilities). This discrepancy is consistent with the exclusion of monetary gold from gross capital formation in the capital account, ensuring consistency in the overall accounting framework.

When an unallocated gold account is held by the monetary authority as part of reserves, it is recorded as a deposit liability for the counterpart non resident financial institution, and thus the amounts of financial assets and liabilities are matched. If such an account is not held as a reserve asset, then it is recorded as a deposit asset for the account holder, and a deposit liability for the provider of the gold account (BPM6, 5.77). Meanwhile, **allocated gold accounts** are classified as monetary gold if they are held by monetary authorities as reserve assets (i.e., included in gold bullion). However, if not held for reserve purposes, they are treated as valuables, i.e., ownership of a good in the same manner as non-monetary gold.

[16] Gold accounts held by financial institutions are categorized into **allocated gold accounts** and **unallocated gold accounts**. Allocated gold accounts are those in which the ownership of physical gold fully belongs to the account holder, who can purchase, store, and sell the gold. In contrast, unallocated gold accounts refer to deposits denominated in gold where the account holder cannot directly hold or dispose of the gold in physical form. When the monetary authority holds the allocated gold account as a reserve asset, it is included in the category of monetary gold (BPM6, 5.74-5.77).

Table 10.13 Accounting for monetary gold

Type	Reserve asset status	Accounting treatment	
		Asset	Liability
Gold bullion (Including allocated gold accounts)	Reserve asset	Monetary gold	
	Not reserve asset	Valuables	
Unallocated gold accounts	Reserve asset	Monetary gold	Deposit liability
	Not reserve asset	Deposit asset	Deposit liability

SDRs

Special Drawing Rights (SDRs) are international reserve assets created by the IMF to supplement existing official reserve assets. They are allocated by the IMF to its member countries in proportion to their quota shares at the IMF. SDRs can be held only by central banks of the IMF member countries and certain designated international financial organizations, and they represent an unconditional right of an IMF member to obtain foreign exchange or other reserve assets from other member countries. In accounting, SDRs are treated in two parts: **holdings** and the corresponding item, **allocations**. SDR holdings refer to the amount of SDRs that a member country holds as part of its reserves, and is recorded as a financial asset (specifically, a reserve asset of the central bank). SDR allocations represent a liability to non-residents by the member country the SDRs from the IMF. Importantly, SDR holdings and allocations are not netted; they are recorded on a gross basis. As a result, the initial allocation of SDRs and the associated increase in SDR holdings do not change the international net worth (net IIP) of SDR holders. However, as countries make use of their SDRs, differences between SDR holdings and allocations can arise due to the following factors (Table 10.14).

Table 10.14 Transaction types of SDR

Account item	Transaction type	
SDR holdings (Asset of the central bank)		New SDR allocations – SDR cancellations
	+	Purchases of SDR – Sales of SDR
	+	Interest receivable on SDR holdings
	–	Payment of charges in SDRs to the IMF
SDR allocations (Liability of the central bank)		New SDR allocations – SDR cancellations
	+	Interest payable on SDR allocations

* Note: See *MFSM 2016*, Table 5.3.

Deposits

Deposits are non-negotiable financial contracts that allow the depositor to place funds with deposit-taking institutions and to withdraw the principal (including any interest accrued) at a later time. In the financial account, deposits on the right-hand side are liabilities of financial institutions, while deposits on the left-hand side are financial assets of depositors. The amount of Interest accrued on deposits is added to the existing deposit amount. When recorded in the allocation of earned income account, **SNA interest** is displayed by adding the FISIM charge to the deposit interest payable by the bank, and this amount is shown as a new deposit in the financial account. The FISIM charge is recorded as the expenditure of depositors (either intermediate consumption of producers or final consumption expenditure of households), and the counterpart entry is recorded in the financial account as a decrease in deposits.

Crypto assets with a corresponding liability designed to act as a medium of exchange

This category includes crypto assets that are not issued or authorized by the central bank or government, but for which a claim on the issuer exists and that are designed to function as a general means of payment. A representative example is stablecoins with a claim on the issuer. Stablecoins are designed to maintain price stability by being backed by specific assets (such as fiat currency or gold), and holders are recorded as holding "deposit-like financial assets." By contrast, payment tokens that are used solely within a specific platform or network are not considered general means of payment and are therefore classified as "debt securities" within financial assets.

Transferable deposits

Transferable deposits are deposits that can be exchanged for cash at face value without additional penalty or restriction upon request for withdrawal such as demand deposit, or that can be paid directly by means of a payment instrument such as cheque or draft. This category includes deposits for inter-bank fund settlement (inter-bank positions), as well as other transferable deposits where either one or both parties to the transaction are not banks. However, in the case of an overdraft agreement that allows withdrawals in excess of the deposit balance, the amount withdrawn in excess of the deposit is treated as a loan.

Loans

Loans are non-negotiable financial instruments that are created when a creditor lends funds to a debtor, who is contractually obliged to repay the principal and interest to the creditor under a loan agreement. Types of loans include overdrafts, installment loans, hire-purchase credit, repurchase agreements, gold swaps and loans via financial leases.

In the financial account, loans are recorded as financial assets of lenders on the left-hand side, and as liabilities of the counterpart borrowers on the right-hand side. The interest accrued on loans consists of SNA interest and FISIM charges; the former is recorded in the allocation of earned income account, while the latter is recorded separately as the output of financial institutions.

The amount of loans recorded on the balance sheets of both creditor and debtor represents the outstanding principal amount and includes any uncollected amounts as accrued interest on loans. **Non-performing loans**, which are loans where principal or interest payments are overdue by 90 days or more, or whose recovery is doubtful even for less than 90 days, are included in loans and not charged off. However, the nominal and fair value of such loans should be reported in footnotes. If the recovery of a loan is doubtful and the loan is written off, it is recorded in the other changes in the volume of assets and liabilities account.

Debt securities

Debt securities are negotiable securities that establish debt relationships, under which the issuer of debt securities is not obligated to repay the principal amount of the securities to the holder until maturity. In return, the issuer pays interest to the holder, either at maturity or at intervals before maturity. Examples include bills, bonds, negotiable certificates of deposit (CDs), commercial papers, and other debt securities. Negotiable loans are reclassified as debt securities, rather than loans.

The issuer of a debt security has a contractual obligation to pay a fixed amount of principal and interest to the holder of the security. However, the principal and interest of the security may be paid in different ways. For example, the principal and interest may be paid in a lump sum at the maturity date of the security, or the security may be initially issued at a discounted price reflecting interest to the maturity and redeemed at face value at maturity, or the security may be issued with periodic interest payments prior to maturity and principal payments at maturity. Since debt securities are negotiable before maturity and are traded freely in the financial market, it is appropriate that both the issuer and the holder value them at market prices.

Stablecoins with a claim on the issuer

Stablecoins with a claim on the issuer are crypto assets designed to maintain a stable value by being linked to specific assets such as fiat currency, gold, or a basket of assets. Stablecoins can be broadly divided into two types:

1. **Stablecoins with a claim on the issuer**: In this case, the holder has a legal or contractual claim on the issuer. For example, the holder may redeem one coin from the issuer for one unit of fiat currency (e.g., USD), or receive a redemption guarantee backed by collateral assets. These stablecoins are designed to function either as a general means of payment or as a

payment instrument within a specific platform. A corresponding liability arises for the issuer, and the holder records an increase in financial assets. In national accounts, stablecoins used as a general medium of exchange are classified under the subcategory *currency and deposits*. Stablecoins used solely within a specific platform are treated as the issuance of *debt securities* between creditor and debtor. Accordingly, only stablecoins with a claim on the issuer are included in the financial account, while stablecoins without such a claim described below are excluded. Stablecoins are valued at market prices (such as exchange prices) or, where applicable, by reference to the value of their underlying assets.

2. **Algorithm-based stablecoins without a claim on the issuer**: These stablecoins maintain price stability by adjusting supply algorithmically, and the holder does not have a corresponding claim on the issuer. In national accounts, they are not recorded in the financial account; instead, as with Bitcoin, they are classified as *non-produced non-financial assets*. When used for transactions, they are treated as barter, and changes in their value are recorded in the revaluation account.

Equity and investment fund shares

Equity refers to securities issued for the purpose of acquiring ownership in a corporation or quasi-corporation, and serves as the equity capital of the corporation. The issuer of equity has no obligation to repay the principal, while the equity holder is entitled to claim residual income, such as dividends, in return for holding the equity. Types of equity are classified into listed shares, unlisted shares, and other equity. Listed shares are valued at market prices, while unlisted shares and other equity are valued using specific valuation methods.

Investment funds are collective investment undertakings that pool money from a number of investors to form funds, which are then invested in a variety of instruments (such as debt securities, shares, real estate, or commodity-linked instruments). The returns generated from these investments are redistributed to the investors. Investment funds are described later in relation to the investment income disbursement.

10.2.3.1 Items related to other current accounts

This section explains items within the financial account that are directly associated with other current accounts (income accounts), focusing in particular on the non-life insurance technical reserves, life insurance and pension entitlements, provisions for calls under standardized guarantees, as well as the reinvestment of earnings.

First, **non-life insurance technical reserves** represent the liability that non-life insurance corporations owe to policyholders. These are equal to prepayments of net non-life premiums to the insurance corporation plus unpaid insurance claims during the accounting period. **Life insurance and annuities entitlements** refer to the financial claims held by policyholders against the life-insurance corporations (corresponding to technical reserves for life insurance or annuities). These are recorded in the financial account as net premiums receivable less benefits payable. **Pension entitlements** are financial claims that pensioners in retirement pension schemes (e.g., DC or DB) hold against the pension schemes. From the perspective of the pension scheme, these represent liabilities to be paid in the future. In the financial account, the net pension contributions receivable less pension benefits payable is recorded, and this amount corresponds to the "adjustments for the change in pension entitlements" item in the use of income account. **Provisions for calls under standardized guarantees** are liabilities that guarantors hold toward the beneficiaries of such guarantees. These are conceptually similar to non-life insurance technical reserves. They are recorded in the financial account as prepayments of net fees plus the amount of outstanding calls not yet settled under standardized guarantee contracts.

In the financial account, the accounting treatments for non-life insurance technical reserves, life insurance (and annuities) entitlements, pension entitlements, and provisions for calls under standardized guarantees reflect an increase in the financial assets of the policyholders, pension beneficiaries, or guarantee beneficiaries, and a corresponding increase in the liabilities of financial institutions that offer these products.

Table 10.15 Technical reserves of insurance, pension and standardized guarantee in the financial account

Item	Formula	Description
Non-life insurance technical reserves	Prepayment of net premiums + unpaid insurance claims	Increase in the liability of insurance corporation to the non-life insurance policyholder.
Life insurance (and annuities) entitlements	Net premium receivable – benefits payable	Increase in the liability of insurance corporation to the policy holder of life insurance or annuities.
Pension entitlements	Net contributions receivable – benefits payable	Increase in the liability of pension schemes to the pension beneficiary (DC and DB).
Provisions for calls under standardized guarantees	Prepayment of net fees + outstanding calls not settled	Increase in the liability of the guarantor to the holder of standardized guarantees.

Reinvestment of earnings is an imputed transaction that arises in the context of the foreign direct investment (both inward FDI and outward FDI) as well as in collective investment funds. This transaction is, as mentioned in the previous chapter (see section 9.3.4), initially recorded in the allocation of earned income account as property income allocated to investors in the form of reinvested earnings. It is then recorded in the financial account as an imputed transaction whereby the investor is deemed to reinvest the same amount of earnings in the foreign direct investment enterprises, or the fund investor is deemed to reinvest earnings in the collective investment funds. In the case of direct investment, the retained earnings of foreign-owned domestic enterprises (or a resident-owned foreign enterprises) are attributed to the direct investors as property income in the allocation of earned income account. The counterpart transaction is then recorded in the financial account as an increase in the direct investor's asset under the item of "equity in direct investors." Conversely, the direct investment enterprise records a corresponding increase in liability. Investment shares may either increase (+) or decrease (-), where an increase represents a new injection of shares, and a decrease represents a withdrawal of shares.

The accounting treatment of the reinvestment of earnings can be illustrated with the following example (see Table 10.16). Suppose reinvested earnings of 10 occur from a resident investor's outward direct investment, and reinvested earnings of 20 arise from a non-resident investor's inward direct investment. Then, each account in the sequence of economic accounts is indicated as follows.

- **For the resident investor's outward FDI**, the allocation of earned income account records reinvested earnings receivable 10 on the revenues side of the resident direct investor (domestic economy), and reinvested earnings payable 10 on the expenditures side of the rest of the world sector. At the same time, the financial account records an increase in assets for the resident direct investor (domestic economy) and a counterpart increase in liabilities for the rest of the world sector.
- **For the non-resident investor's inward FDI**, the reverse entries are shown. That is, the allocation of earned income account records property income receivable of 20 by the non-resident investor (the rest of the world sector) and property income payable of 20 by domestic direct investment enterprises (domestic economy). Simultaneously, the financial account records an increase in assets of 20 in the rest of the world sector and an increase in liabilities of 20 for the domestic economy.

Table 10.16 Accounting treatment for reinvestment of earnings

Allocation of earned income account

Expenditures			Revenues	
Domestic sector	ROW sector	Account item	Domestic sector	ROW sector
20	10	Reinvested earnings	10	20

Financial account

Changes in assets			Changes in liabilities	
Domestic sector	ROW sector	Account item	Domestic sector	ROW sector
10	20	Reinvestment of earnings (Direct investment shares)	20	10

Reinvestment of earnings in collective investment funds is treated in the same way as in the case of foreign direct investment. In the allocation of earned income account, the retained earnings of the funds are imputed as being distributed to the investment fund shareholders as property income, and then the same amount is deemed to be reinvested in the investment funds. This is recorded in the financial account as an increase in the investment fund shareholders. At the same time, the financial institution managing the investment funds records an equivalent increase in its liabilities.

As such, each financial instrument in the financial account is directly related to or affected by the production or income items in the current accounts. This relationship is well illustrated in Table 10.17 below. Looking at the flow items associated with each financial instrument, the production account includes financial trading margins, FISIM, and fees receivable, while the allocation of earned income account includes interest, dividends, withdrawals from income of quasi-corporations, and investment income disbursements (including reinvested earnings on foreign direct investment, investment income attributable to shareholders of collective investment funds, investment income attributable to non-life insurance and standardized guarantees, and investment income attributable to policyholders of life-insurance and annuities and pension schemes).

Table 10.17 Relationship between financial instruments and other current account items

Financial instrument	Production account			Allocation of earned income account						
	Buy/sell margin	FISIM	Fees	Interest	Dividends	Withdrawals from income of quasi-corporations	Reinvested earnings of foreign direct investment	Investment income attributed to investment fund share holders	Investment income attributed to non-life insurance and standardized guarantees	Investment income attributed to life insurance & pension holders
Monetary gold and SDRs										
Gold bullion										
Unallocated gold account				X						
SDR		X		X						
Currency and deposits										
Currency										
Domestic										
Foreign	X									
Transferable deposits										
In domestic currency		X		X						
In foreign currency		X		X						
Inter-bank deposits				X						
Other deposits										
In domestic currency		X		X						
In foreign currency		X		X						
Debt securities	X			X						
Loans										
In domestic currency		X		X						
In foreign currency		X		X						
Equity and investment funds										
Equity										
Listed shares	X				X					
Unlisted shares	X				X					
Other equity						X	X			
Investment fund shares	X		X					X		
Insurance, pension entitlements, standardized guarantee			X							
Non-life insurance technical reserve									X	
Life insurance entitlement										X
Pension entitlement										X
Provisions for calls under standardized guarantees									X	
Financial derivatives and stock options										
Financial derivatives	X									
Employee stock options										

* Note: Excerpt from Figure 17.2 in the 2008 SNA.

Chapter 11. Accumulation accounts (II) and balance sheets

This chapter discusses the account that falls under accumulation accounts, excluding the capital account and the financial account covered in the previous chapter, specifically, **the other changes in assets and liabilities account**, and the stock account known as the **balance sheet**. The other changes in assets and liabilities account records "other flows", which are changes not caused by "transactions" (the latter being recorded in the capital account and the financial account). Together with the capital account and financial account, this account captures the changes in asset, liabilities and net worth between the opening and closing balance sheets.

The other changes in assets and liabilities account is further subdivided into two sub-accounts. One is the **revaluation account,** which records holding gains and losses arising from changes in market prices of assets and liabilities during the accounting period. The other is the **other changes in the volume of assets and liabilities account**, which records changes due to factors other than holding gains and losses (such as changes in quantity and quality changes).

11.1 The other changes in the volume of assets and liabilities account

This section explains the nature and structure of the other changes in the volume of assets and liabilities account, as well as the accounting rules applied to major items recorded in this account.

11.1.1 Main items and structure of the account

The other changes in the volume of assets and liabilities account records all non-transaction items except for holding gains and losses. The main items included here are as follows:

(a) Appearance and disappearance of assets due to non-transaction factors:

- Newly recognized public monuments or valuables (e.g., auctioned items) as economic assets
- Discovery (or upward revaluation) and extinction (e.g., through downward revaluation) of subsoil resources
- Natural growth of non-cultivated biological resources such as virgin forests and fish stocks
- Change of economic use of land (changes in quality) such as agricultural land converted into building or residential land
- Initiation and cancellation of contracts, leases and licences

- Emergence and extinction (via amortization) of goodwill and marketing assets

(b) Debt write-off (including bad debt) not based on mutual agreement between the parties.

(c) Catastrophic losses (natural disaster, war, riot, radioactive leakage) or uncompensated seizures of assets

(d) Incurrence of costs that exceed the normal depreciation due to unexpected physical deterioration and obsolescence of fixed assets.

(e) Exceptional losses in inventories.

(f) Reclassification of institutional sector, assets and liabilities:

- Reclassification of household unincorporated enterprises as quasi-corporations
- Mergers and divisions due to corporate restructuring
- Nationalization or privatization of enterprises
- Change from valuables to monetary gold due to the acquisition of gold by the central bank, or vice versa
- Reclassification of work-in-progress inventories into finished goods

The depletion of natural resources, in physical terms, refers to the decline in the value of non-produced natural resources during an accounting period caused by extraction that exceeds the level of natural regeneration. In the 2008 SNA, the depletion of natural resources was recorded in the other changes in the volume of assets and liabilities account, whereas in the 2025 SNA it is treated as a cost of production, analogous to depreciation, and is recorded in both the production account and the capital account.

Crypto assets without a corresponding liability are classified as non-produced non-financial assets. When newly released as an exchange for the provision of crypto-asset validation services, they are not recorded in the "other changes in the volume of assets and liabilities" account but, instead, are recorded in the capital account as a change of assets from existing holders to validators. Changes in the prices of crypto assets without a corresponding liability are recorded in the revaluation account.

The balancing item in the other changes in the volume of assets and liabilities account is "changes in net worth due to other changes in the volume of assets and liabilities", which is derived as the difference between the total changes in assets (on left-hand side) and the total changes in liabilities (right-hand side). This balancing item is recorded on the right-hand side of this account.

The derived value is then added to the net worth in the opening balance sheet to arrive at the net worth in the closing balance sheet (in section 11.3).

Table 11.1 The format of the other changes in the volume of assets and liabilities account

Changes in assets	Changes in liabilities and net worth
Economic appearance of assets	Economic appearance of assets
Economic disappearance of non-produced assets	Economic disappearance of non-produced assets
Catastrophic losses	Catastrophic losses
Uncompensated seizure	Uncompensated seizure
Other changes in volume n.e.c.	Other changes in volume n.e.c.
Changes in classification	Changes in classification
	Changes in net worth due to other changes in the volume of assets and liabilities

11.1.2 Examples of accounting treatment for main items in the account

The following provides specific accounting treatments to illustrate how the appearance and disappearance of assets due to non-transaction factors are recorded in the national accounts. While the treatment is generally similar across items, the examples below focus on valuables, which are produced assets, and on contracts, leases, and licences as well as goodwill and marketing assets, which are non-produced assets.

Recognition of valuables as newly identified economic assets

Let us examine the accounting treatment procedures applied when valuables (such as precious metals or works of art), previously held by households as durable consumer goods, are newly recognized as economic assets through transactions such as auctions. First, to recognize the valuables as new economic assets, they are recorded in the other changes in the volume of assets and liabilities account as an increase in both assets and net worth. Next, the transaction involving the sale of the valuables to another institutional unit is recorded. If the valuables are sold to another institutional unit in the domestic economy, the sale is recorded in the capital account, and if they are exported abroad, they are recorded as exports of goods to the rest of the world sector.

Table 11.2 Accounting treatment when newly recognized valuables are exported abroad

	Seller		Purchaser (Rest of the world)	
	Changes in assets	Changes in liabilities and net worth	Expenditures/Changes in assets	Revenues/Changes in liabilities and net worth
Other changes in the volume of assets and liabilities account	Valuables xx	Net worth xx		
Rest of the world account			Exports of good	Currency and deposits xx
Capital account		Valuables xx		
Financial account	Currency and deposits xx			

Accounting for the appearance and disappearance of contracts, leases and licences

The accounting procedure for the appearance and disappearance of contracts, leases and licences is as follows. First, when a transaction involving the sale of contracts, leases and licences occurs, the seller records the appearance of the relevant non-produced asset and the corresponding increase in net worth in the other changes in the volume of assets and liabilities account. Subsequently, the seller and the purchaser record the sale and purchase of the contracts, leases and licences, respectively, in the capital account, while the payment and receipt of currency and deposits arising from the transaction are recorded in the financial account. As these assets hold economic value only during the term of the agreement, they must be amortized over the duration of the contract.

Table 11.3 Accounting treatment of transactions in contracts, leases and licences

	Seller		Purchaser	
	Changes in assets	Changes in liabilities and net worth	Changes in assets	Changes in liabilities and net worth
Other changes in the volume of assets and liabilities account	Contracts, leases and licences xx	Net worth xx		
Capital account		Contracts, leases and licences xx	Contracts, leases and licences xx	
Financial account	Currency and deposits xx			Currency and deposits xx

Accounting for the emergence and extinguishment of goodwill and marketing assets

The emergence and extinguishment of goodwill and marketing assets are processed through the following accounting procedures. For example, consider the case of purchasing a company with assets of $6 million and liabilities of $4 million by issuing shares worth $3 million. The net asset value of this company is $2 million (=6 million – 4 million) and the value of goodwill is calculated as $1 million (=3 million – 2 million). First, when this transaction occurs, the seller of the company records the emergence of a new non-produced asset, goodwill, and the corresponding increase in net worth in the other changes in the volume of assets and liabilities account. Subsequently, the seller and the purchaser record the sale and purchase of goodwill in the capital account, respectively. The acquisition and payment of shares in return are recorded in the financial account.

Table 11.4 Accounting for the transaction of goodwill

	Seller		Purchaser	
	Changes in assets	Changes in liabilities and net worth	Changes in assets	Changes in liabilities and net worth
Other changes in the volume of assets and liabilities account	Goodwill 1 million	Net worth 1 million		
Capital account		Goodwill 1 million	Goodwill 1 million	
Financial account	Shares 1 million			Shares 1 million

As the value of goodwill and marketing assets held by the purchaser decrease over time, amortization is carried out over a specified period. In the above example, if the amortization period of goodwill is set to 5 years, $0.2 million will be amortized every year, which will be recorded as a decrease in goodwill of the purchaser ($0.2 million) and a corresponding decrease in net worth ($0.2 million) in the changes in the volume of assets account.

Table 11.5 Accounting for amortization of goodwill by the purchaser

	Purchaser	
	Changes in assets	Changes in liabilities and net worth
Other changes in the volume of assets and liabilities account	Goodwill -0.2 million	Net worth -0.2 million

11.2 The revaluation account

The **revaluation account** is an account that records holding gains and losses arising from price changes of non-financial assets, financial assets and liabilities held by institutional units during the accounting period. These gains and losses reflect pure price changes, excluding those resulting from changes in the volume, quality and classification (which are recorded in the changes in the volume of assets account)., Like entries in the other changes in the volume of assets and liabilities account, holding gains and losses are caused by non-transaction factors without a counterparty.

In the revaluation account, holding gains and losses on assets are recorded on the left-hand side (debit), while those on liabilities are recorded on the right-hand side (credit). The balancing item in the revaluation account is recorded on the right-hand side by subtracting the sum of the right-hand side from the sum of the left-hand side, referred to as the **changes in net worth due to nominal holding gains or losses**. The value of this balancing item is added to the opening balance sheet (as described in the next section 11.3) and used to derive the closing balance sheet.

Nominal holding gains and losses are divided into **neutral holding gains and losses** and **real holding gains and losses**. Neutral holding gains or losses refer to the increase (or decrease) in the value of assets that allow the real value (volume) of goods and services to be kept the same. In order to maintain the same real value, the value of assets must increase by the overall inflation rate, which is measured in practice by multiplying it by the consumer price index. Neutral holding gains and losses are used to measure changes in the real value of assets and liabilities held due to this general inflation. Therefore, by subtracting the neutral holding gains and losses corresponding to overall price increases (or decreases) from the nominal holding gains and losses, the real holding gains and losses, which represent the changes in relative value of individual assets, can be derived. In addition, nominal holding gains and losses arising during an accounting period can be further divided into "realized gains and losses" through transactions during the period and "unrealized gains and losses" arising from holding until the end of the period. Realized gains and losses occur from transactions involving the disposal of assets, whereas unrealized gains and losses arise from transactions involving the acquisition of assets as well as from their continued holding. Although both of these are included in the calculation of nominal holding gains and losses, realized gains and losses are already incorporated into the transaction values recorded during the accounting period. Consequently, only unrealized gains and losses are reflected in the closing balance sheet at the end of the period.

Table 11.6 The format of the revaluation account

Changes in assets	Changes in liabilities and net worth
(Nominal holding gains and losses)	
Non-financial assets	Non-financial assets
Produced assets (excluding natural resources)	Produced assets (excluding natural resources)
Non-produced assets (excluding natural resources)	Non-produced assets (excluding natural resources)
Natural resources	Natural resources
Financial assets / liabilities	Financial assets / liabilities
	Changes in net worth due to nominal holding gains/losses
(Neutral holding gains and losses)	
Non-financial assets	Non-financial assets
Produced assets (excluding natural resources)	Produced assets (excluding natural resources)
Non-produced assets (excluding natural resources)	Non-produced assets (excluding natural resources)
Natural resources	Natural resources
Financial assets / liabilities	Financial assets / liabilities
	Changes in net worth due to neutral holding gains/losses
(Real holding gains and losses)	
Non-financial assets	Non-financial assets
Produced assets (excluding natural resources)	Produced assets (excluding natural resources)
Non-produced assets (excluding natural resources)	Non-produced assets (excluding natural resources)
Natural resources	Natural resources
Financial assets / liabilities	Financial assets / liabilities
	Changes in net worth due to real holding gains/losses

11.2.1 Measurement of nominal holding gains and losses

This section examines the measurement method of nominal holding gains and losses, and the following section explains that of neutral and real holding gains and losses, which are items in the revaluation account. To measure nominal holding gains and losses, it starts with the following basic identity:

(11.1) Value of opening stocks + value of acquisitions less disposals during the period + other changes in the volume of assets and liabilities + nominal holding gains and losses = value of closing stocks

In the above identity, the "acquisition" value includes the cost of ownership transfer, and the "disposal" value is the amount after deducting the cost of ownership transfer and reflects the realized holding gains and losses. Therefore, nominal holding gains and losses include both realized and unrealized holding gains and losses. By rearranging this formula, nominal holding gains and losses can be derived as follows:

(11.2) Nominal holding gains and losses = value of closing stocks – value of opening stocks – value of acquisitions less disposals during the period + other changes in the volume of assets and liabilities

Nominal holding gains and losses can be divided into those arising from non-financial assets and those arising from financial assets, depending on the type of asset. Nominal holding gains and losses on non-financial assets represent the gains and losses accrued to owners due to price changes in non-financial assets. These amounts include both the realized and unrealized gains and losses during the accounting period. However, in practice, it is not easy to calculate the realized part separately. The following is a brief introduction to how to measure the nominal gains and losses on these non-financial assets and financial assets.

11.2.1.1 Measurement of nominal holding gains and losses on non-financial assets

Measurement of nominal holding gains and losses on fixed assets

Fixed assets recorded in the balance sheet are valued net of the accumulated amount of depreciation. Therefore, when measuring fixed assets, the concept of net fixed capital formation (=gross fixed capital formation – depreciation) is applied. The formula for measuring normal holding gains and losses in the identity (11.1) above can be expressed as follows:

- Net capital stock at the beginning of the period + net fixed capital formation + other changes in the volume of assets and liabilities + nominal holding gains/losses = net capital stock at the end of the period

Based on this identity, the nominal holding gains and losses on fixed assets are calculated as follows.

- Nominal holding gains and losses on fixed assets = net capital stock at the end of the period – net capital stock at the beginning of the period – (gross fixed capital formation – depreciation)

In this formula, "other changes in the volume of assets and liabilities" are assumed to be ignored, as they are exceptional events such as natural disasters.

Measurement of nominal holding gains and losses on inventories

Nominal holding gains and losses on inventories are measured in the following way.

(11.3) Nominal holding gains and losses on inventories = value of closing inventories – value of opening inventories – changes in inventories during the period

Changes in inventories here are derived not based on historic costs but through the perpetual inventory method. In other words, changes in inventories are calculated as "additions to inventories less withdrawals from inventories less recurrent inventory losses" at purchasers' prices prevailing at the time of entry or withdrawal. However, in practice, it is very difficult to accurately calculate the "changes in inventories during the period" based on the above formula, and the only available data are typically the inventory values at the end and beginning of periods. Therefore, in practical applications, changes in inventories can be approximated using the average price during the period and quantities of inventory at the end and beginning of the periods, as follows:

- Changes in inventories = average price of inventories during the period x (quantity of inventories at the end of period – quantity of inventories at the beginning of period)

This can be expressed as a formula where the opening quantity is denoted as Q^{t-1}, the closing quantity as Q^t, the opening price as P^{t-1} and the closing price as P^t:

(11.4) Changes in inventories = $1/2\ (P^{t-1} + P^t)\ (Q^t - Q^{t-1})$

Substituting equation (11.4) into the above equation (11.3), it is expressed as follows:

(11.5) Nominal holding gains/losses on inventories = $P^tQ^t - P^{t-1}Q^{t-1} - 1/2\ (P^{t-1} + P^t)\ (Q^t - Q^{t-1}) = 1/2\ (Q^{t-1} + Q^t)\ (P^t - P^{t-1})$

Equation (11.5) can be summarized as follows:

- **Nominal holding gains/losses on inventories = average quantities of inventories during the period x (prices at the end of the period – prices at the beginning of the period)**

Adding the expressions in (11.4) and (11.5) gives the following:

(11.6) **Changes in inventories + nominal holding gains/losses on inventories = $P^tQ^t - P^{t-1}Q^{t-1}$**

Here, changes in inventories represent the increase or decrease due to changes in quantity during the period, while nominal holding gains and losses indicates the increase or decrease due to changes in price during the period. The sum of the two corresponds to the change in the current value of inventories, i.e., the "value of closing inventories (at the current price) less the value of opening inventories (at the current price).

Measurement of nominal holding gains and losses on land

It is often difficult in practice to clearly distinguish holding gains and losses on land that arise from other changes in the volume of assets and liabilities (such as changes in land use) from those that result from pure price changes. Furthermore, since land is frequently transacted together with building as a combined asset, it is not easy to isolate and measure the nominal holding gains and losses for land alone. Therefore, they are measured in the following way, similar to that used for inventories.

- Nominal holding gains and losses on land = average quantities of land during the period x (land prices at the end of the period – land prices at the beginning of the period)

Land prices can be estimated using either the appraised value of individual land from administrative sources or the actual transaction prices. In cases where land and buildings are combined and the land price is not separately indicated, the value of land is derived by estimating the value of building and subtracting it from the combined value.

11.2.1.2 Measurement of nominal holding gains and losses on financial assets

Nominal holding gains and losses on financial assets are recorded when the value of financial assets changes due to factors other than transactions in association with the assets (e.g., interest accruals) and other changes in the volume of the assets. Similarly, nominal holding gains and losses on liabilities are measured by changes in the value of liabilities due to factors other than the transaction of the liabilities and other changes in the volume of the liabilities.

Financial assets with fixed face values, such as cash, deposits, and loans, do not generate nominal holding gains or losses. However, financial instruments that are sensitive to fluctuations in the financial market, such as shares and investment funds, do generate nominal holding gains or losses due to changes in their market prices. Similarly, short-term and long-term debt securities may also generate nominal holding gains and losses along with changes in interest rates over their holding period. The table below (Table 11.7) illustrates whether nominal holding gains and losses occur for each financial instrument. Even financial instruments such as currency, deposits, and loans, which typically do not generate nominal holding gains and losses, may produce the holding gains and losses if denominated in foreign currencies, due to exchange rate fluctuations.

Table 11.7 Occurrence of nominal holding gains and losses on financial instruments

Financial instrument			Nominal holding gains
Monetary gold and SDRs	Gold bullion		o
	Unallocated gold account		o
	SDRs		o
Currency and deposits	Currency	Domestic	
		Foreign	o
	Transferable deposits	Domestic	
		Foreign	o
	Interbank positions		
	Other deposits	Domestic	
		Foreign	o
Debt securities			(o)
Loans		Domestic	
		Foreign	o
Equity and investment fund shares	Listed shares		o
	Unlisted shares		o
	Other equity		o
	Investment fund shares		o
Financial derivatives and employee stock options	Financial derivatives		o
	Employee stock options		o

* Note: Refer to Figure 17.2 in the 2008 SNA.

Example of accounting for holding gains/losses on the acquisitions and disposals of equity

The following illustrates an example of how to measure holding gains and losses arising from the acquisition and disposal of shares when their market prices are fluctuating. Suppose that individual A purchases shares at $30 during the period and then sells all of the purchased shares at $40 within the same period. As a result, the holding gain of $10 (= 40-30) arises from the acquisition and disposal of the shares during the period. Since the transaction value of the share exceeds the acquisition cost by $10, an adjustment must be recorded in the revaluation account to offset this difference in the closing balance sheet. In this way, realized holding gains are adjusted through the revaluation account so that they do not affect the closing stock values.

Table 11.8 Accounting for the acquisition and disposal of equity

	Changes in assets		Changes in liabilities and net worth	
Financial account	Shares	30	Currency	30
	Currency	40	Shares	40
Revaluation account	Shares	10	Net worth	10

Stocks and flows of equity by A

Opening balance sheet	0
Acquisition less disposal of shares	−10
Holding gain	10
Closing balance sheet	0

11.2.2 Measurement of neutral holding gains/losses and real holding gains/losses

Neutral holding gains and losses on assets that continued to be held throughout the accounting period can generally be estimated by multiplying the value of assets in the beginning of the period by the general inflation rate during the period. However, for assets acquired or disposed of during the accounting period, information on the timing of acquisitions or disposals must be available, making it more difficult to measure neutral holding gains and losses.

Neutral holding gains and losses on non-financial assets are derived by subtracting the capital stock at the beginning of the period (at current prices) from the capital stock at the end of the period adjusted for neutral holding gains and losses, and then further subtracting the value of transactions and other changes in the volume of assets and liabilities during the period also adjusted for neutral holding gains and losses. Here, the inflation rate used to estimate neutral holding gains and losses is typically represented by the consumer price indices (CPIs).

To facilitate understanding of neutral holding gains and losses on non-financial assets, it is useful to represent the concepts using formulas that include price and quantity indicators, as introduced in Chapter 16. A simple illustrative formula based on balance sheet data is presented here, drawn from the 1993 SNA. (See 1993 SNA, paragraphs 12.95-12.97.) Assuming that prices and quantities of assets change at a constant linear rate between the beginning and end of the accounting period, the holding gains and losses can be expressed with the following simple formulas. Let the price and quantity at the beginning of the period be noted as P^{t-1} and Q^{t-1}, and at the end of the period as P^t and Q^t, respectively. Then the values of "transactions and other changes in the volume of assets and liabilities" and nominal holding gains and losses during the period can be expressed as follows:

(11.7) *The value of transactions and other changes in the volume of assets and liabilities* = $\bar{P}\,(Q^t - Q^{t-1})$,

The value of nominal holding gains and losses = $\bar{Q}\,(P^t - P^{t-1})$

Where: $\boldsymbol{\bar{P} = 1/2\ (P^{t-1} + P^t)}$, $\boldsymbol{\bar{Q} = 1/2\ (Q^{t-1} + Q^t)}$.

Assuming that the general price index at time t is r^t, and $r^{t-1} = 1$, neutral holding gains and losses can be obtained as follows:

(11.8) Neutral holding gains and losses = $(r^t - 1)\, P^{t-1}\,\bar{Q}$

Real holding gains and losses are derived by subtracting neutral holding gains and losses from nominal holding gains and losses:

- Real holding gains and losses = nominal holding gains and losses – neutral holding gains and losses

Therefore, the formula for real holding gains and losses can be expressed by subtracting equation (11.8) from (11.7) as follows:

- Real holding gains and losses = $(P^t/P^{t-1} - r^t)\ P^{t-1}\ \overline{Q}$

It is assumed that neutral holding gains and losses on financial assets also increase in line with the general inflation rate (CPIs). Even financial assets that do not accrue nominal holding gains and losses, such as currency, deposits and loans denominated in domestic currency, generate neutral holding gains and losses corresponding to the value of general price increase. As a result, the real holding gains and losses are equal in magnitude but opposite in sign to the neutral holding gains and losses.

11.3 The balance sheet

The **balance sheet** is the final account in the SNA sequence of economic accounts. It records the stock values of assets and liabilities by institutional sector at a specific point in time. This account reflects the cumulative results of production, income distribution and use, and accumulation activities during the accounting period. The balance sheet is compiled by adding the entries from the accumulation accounts (capital account, financial account, other changes in the volume of assets and liabilities account, and revaluation account) to the opening balance sheet, thereby deriving the closing balance sheet.

The balance sheet is compiled on the basis of residence, and is structured to distinguish between the total economy and the rest of the world sector. As with other accounts, the total economy is presented from the perspective of resident units, whereas the rest of the world is recorded from the perspective of non-residents. Thus, assets in the rest of the world sector represent the assets of non-residents and, correspondingly, liabilities of resident units. For reference, a balance sheet that presents the external assets and liabilities of resident units from the resident perspective is referred to as the **international investment position** (IIP), which is covered in the balance of payments statistics (see section 13.3.6).

In the balance sheet, assets (both non-financial assets and financial assets) are recorded on the left-hand side, and liabilities are recorded on the right-hand side. The difference between assets and liabilities is called **net worth**, which is shown on the right-hand side as the balancing item of the balance sheet.

11.3.1 Compilation of balance sheets

The process of compiling the balance sheet can be briefly described as follows. The balance sheet consists of financial assets and non-financial assets on the left-hand side, and liabilities and net worth on the right-hand side. Since the totals of the left-hand and right-hand sides of the balance sheet must be equal by identity, this relationship can be expressed as:

Financial assets + non-financial assets = liabilities + net worth

The changes in assets, liabilities, and net worth during the accounting period are expressed as:

(11.9) Δ *financial assets* + Δ *non-financial assets* = Δ *liabilities* + Δ *net worth*

Here, the symbol Δ denotes increases or decreases due to transactions and other flows. In addition, the change in net worth (Δ net worth) corresponds to the sum of:

- saving and net capital transfers recorded in the capital account, and
- balancing items from the other changes in assets and liabilities account, which reflects changes in net worth due to other changes in the volume of assets and liabilities and holding gains and losses.

The stocks of closing balance sheet can be derived by adding the changes shown in equation (11.9) to the stocks of opening balance sheet.

Table 11.9 illustrates an overview of the structure of the balance sheet. The left-hand side shows the stocks and changes in assets (non-financial and financial), and the right-hand side shows the stocks and changes in liabilities and net worth. The balance sheet is compiled by institutional sector, with the rest of the world sector recorded from the non-resident perspective, recording claims on and liabilities to the domestic economy.

The balance sheet consists of three main parts: the opening balance sheet at the beginning of the accounting period, the closing balance sheet at the end of the accounting period, and the "total changes in assets, liabilities and net worth" during the period, which is placed in the middle. This "total changes in assets, liabilities and net worth" is the sum of the capital account, the financial account, and the other changes in assets and liabilities account. It reflects the total flows, both transactions and other flows during the accounting period. In particular, **changes in net worth** are comprised of the sum of the following three items:

- "Changes in net worth due to saving and net capital transfers" in the capital account,
- "Changes in net worth due to other changes in the volume of assets and liabilities" in the other changes in the volume of assets and liabilities account, and
- "Changes in net worth due to nominal holding gains and losses" in the revaluation account.

In the 2025 SNA, non-financial assets in the balance sheets are classified into three categories by identifying natural resources as a separate category, rather than the two-category classification of produced and non-produced assets used in the 2008 SNA.

Table 11.9 The format of the opening balance sheet, changes in assets and liabilities, and closing balance sheet

Stocks and changes in assets	Stocks and changes in liabilities and net worth
Opening balance sheet	**Opening balance sheet**
Non-financial assets	Non-financial assets
Produced assets (excluding natural resources)	Produced assets (excluding natural resources)
Non-produced assets (excluding natural resources)	Non-produced assets (excluding natural resources)
Natural resources	Natural resources
Financial assets/liabilities	Financial assets/liabilities
	Net worth
Total transactions and other flows	**Total transactions and other flows**
Non-financial assets	Non-financial assets
Produced assets (excluding natural resources)	Produced assets (excluding natural resources)
Non-produced assets (excluding natural resources)	Non-produced assets (excluding natural resources)
Natural resources	Natural resources
Financial assets/liabilities	Financial assets/liabilities
	Changes in net worth, total
	(Saving and net capital transfers)
	(Other changes in volume of assets)
	(Nominal holding gains)
Closing balance sheet	**Closing balance sheet**
Non-financial assets	Non-financial assets
Produced assets (excluding natural resources)	Produced assets (excluding natural resources)
Non-produced assets (excluding natural resources)	Non-produced assets (excluding natural resources)
Natural resources	Natural resources
Financial assets/liabilities	Financial assets/liabilities
	Net worth

Table 11.10 illustrates the balance sheet of South Korea for the year 2015. The balance sheet consists of three parts: First, the stock of the opening balance sheet as of the end of 2014 is shown. Second, the changes in assets, liabilities, and net worth by item are presented, based on the combined values of the capital account, financial account, and the other changes in assets and liabilities account. Third, the closing balance sheet as of the end of 2015 is shown.

According to South Korea's balance sheet as of the end of 2015, the domestic total economy has KRW 12,488.8 trillion in non-financial assets, KRW 13,489.1 trillion in financial assets, and KRW 13,249.5 trillion in liabilities, while the rest of the world sector has KRW 1,101.1 trillion in financial assets and KRW 1,335.1 trillion in liabilities, indicating that the rest of the world holds net worth of KRW -234.0 trillion in respect to South Korea.

Table 11.10 Example of the balance sheet (South Korea, 2015)

Stocks and changes in assets (Unit: KRW trillion) Stocks and changes in liabilities and net worth

Nonfinancial corp.	Financial corp.	General government	Households & NPISHs	Total economy	Rest of the world	Total	Stocks, changes in assets, liabilities and net worth	Nonfinancial corp.	Financial corp.	General government	Households & NPISHs	Total economy	Rest of the world	Total	
3,705.3	127.8	2,789.6	5,284.0	11,906.8		11,906.8	**Non-financial assets**								Opening balance sheet
2,751.7	80.2	1,157.8	1,491.2	5,480.9		5,480.9	**Produced nonfinancial assets**								
2,454.8	80.2	1,154.7	1,462.8	5,152.5		5,152.5	Fixed assets								
297.0	-	3.1	28.4	328.4		328.4	Inventories								
-	-	-	-	-		-	Valuables								
953.6	47.7	1,631.8	3,792.8	6,425.9		6,425.9	**Non-produced non-financial assets**								
953.6	47.7	1,631.8	3,792.8	6,425.9		6,425.9	Natural resources								
2,140.4	6,090.2	1,302.8	2,900.9	12,434.3	1,090.2	13,524.4	**Financial assets/liabilities**	4,208.9	6,020.0	820.4	1,296.1	12,345.4	1,173.8	13,519.2	
-	8.9	-		8.9	3.8	12.7	Monetary gold & SDRs		3.8			3.8	3.6	7.4	
457.9	655.7	192.3	1,254.8	2,560.6	26.5	2,587.1	Currency and deposits		2,545.7	41.4		2,587.1		2,587.1	
48.5	1,477.7	284.9	180.1	1,991.2	243.9	2,235.1	Debt securities	552.4	982.1	631.9		2,166.4	68.6	2,235.1	
-	2,327.8	-	-	2,327.8	6.1	2,333.9	Loans	930.6	133.0	15.8	1,199.6	2,279.0	55.0	2,333.9	
622.7	603.2	471.6	560.8	2,258.4	405.8	2,664.2	Equity & investment funds	1,746.1	734.2	27.3		2,507.6	156.5	2,664.2	
12.1	12.2	-	896.0	920.3		920.3	Insurance,pension, guarantee schemes		920.3			920.3		920.3	
4.6	100.1	2.9	0.4	107.9	39.4	147.3	Financial derivatives & stock options	6.1	107.1	0.5		113.7	33.6	147.3	
994.6	904.7	351.1	8.9	2,259.2	364.7	2,623.9	Other receivables/payables	973.6	593.9	103.4	96.5	1,767.4	856.5	2,623.9	
							Net worth	1,636.8	197.9	3,272.1	6,888.8	11,995.7	-83.6	11,912.0	
153.0	6.7	142.7	279.6	582.0		582.0	**Non-financial assets**								Total changes in assets, liabilities and net
114.3	4.2	32.2	59.9	210.5		210.5	**Produced non-financial assets**								
112.0	4.2	31.5	59.2	206.9		206.9	Fixed assets								
2.2	0.0	0.7	0.7	3.5		3.5	Inventories								
0.0	0.0	0.0	0.0	0.0		0.0	Valuables								
38.8	2.5	110.5	219.7	371.5		371.5	**Non-produced non-financial assets**								
38.8	2.5	110.5	219.7	371.5		371.5	Natural resources								
193.2	486.2	94.1	281.4	1,054.9	11.0	1,065.8	**Financial assets/liabilities**	220.0	476.6	80.6	127.0	904.1	161.3	1,065.5	
0.0	0.5	0.0	0.0	0.5	0.1	0.6	Monetary gold & SDRs		0.1			0.1	0.2	0.3	
57.8	42.1	9.1	107.9	216.9	-6.8	210.2	Currency and deposits		198.5	11.6		210.2		210.2	
17.0	141.8	11.4	1.3	171.6	-1.7	169.9	Debt securities	-4.1	83.6	64.1		143.7	26.3	169.9	

0.0	219.1	0.0	0.0	219.1	0.3	219.4	Loans	66.6	5.2	-0.5	124.5	195.9	23.6	219.4	
53.1	30.3	58.1	74.5	216.0	-2.5	213.5	Equity & investment funds	139.6	46.3	3.1		188.9	24.5	213.5	
4.7	3.1	0.0	92.3	100.1	0.0	100.1	Insurance, pension. and guarantee schemes		100.1			100.1		100.1	
1.1	8.7	-1.2	0.0	8.7	4.9	13.6	Financial derivatives & stock options	0.3	12.1	0.3		12.7	0.9	13.6	
59.5	40.5	16.7	5.2	121.9	16.6	138.5	Other receivables / payables	17.6	30.6	1.9	2.5	52.6	85.9	138.5	
126.2	16.4	156.2	434.0	732.8	-150.4	582.4	*Total changes in net worth*	126.2	16.4	156.2	434.0	732.8	-150.4	582.4	
							Saving & capital transfers	134.5	15.2	53.6	91.2	294.4	-114.5	179.9	
							Other changes in volume of assets	-50.3	-1.3	32.0	114.4	94.9	-35.9	59.0	
							Nominal holding gains	42.0	2.5	70.6	228.4	343.5		343.5	
							Neutral holding gains	42.2	1.5	31.8	60.1	135.5		135.5	
							Real holding gains	-0.3	1.0	44.9	112.9	158.6		158.6	
3,858.3	134.6	2,932.3	5,563.6	12,488.8		12,488.8	**Non-financial assets**								Closing balance sheet
2,866.0	84.4	1,190.0	1,551.1	5,691.4		5,691.4	**Produced non-financial assets**								
2,566.8	84.4	1,186.2	1,522.0	5,359.4		5,359.4	Fixed assets								
299.2	0.0	3.8	29.0	332.0		332.0	Inventories								
							Valuables								
992.4	50.2	1,742.4	4,012.5	6,797.4		6,797.4	**Non-produced non-financial assets**								
992.4	50.2	1,742.4	4,012.5	6,797.4		6,797.4	Natural resources								
2,333.6	6,576.4	1,396.9	3,182.3	13,489.1	1,101.1	14,590.3	**Financial assets/liabilities**	4,428.9	6,496.6	900.9	1,423.1	13,249.5	1,335.1	14,584.6	
	9.4			9.4	3.9	13.3	Monetary gold & SDRs		3.9			3.9	3.8	7.7	
515.7	697.7	201.4	1,362.7	2,777.6	19.7	2,797.3	Currency and deposits		2,744.2	53.1		2,797.3		2,797.3	
65.5	1,619.5	296.3	181.4	2,162.8	242.2	2,405.0	Debt securities	548.3	1,065.7	696.1		2,310.1	94.9	2,405.0	
	2,546.9			2,546.9	6.5	2,553.3	Loans	997.2	138.2	15.3	1,324.1	2,474.8	78.5	2,553.3	
675.8	633.5	529.7	635.4	2,474.4	403.3	2,877.6	Equity & investment funds	1,885.7	780.5	30.4		2,696.5	181.1	2,877.6	
16.8	15.3		988.3	1,020.4		1,020.4	Insurance, pension, and guarantee schemes		1,020.4			1,020.4		1,020.4	
5.7	108.8	1.7	0.4	116.6	44.3	160.9	Financial derivatives & stock options	6.4	119.2	0.8	0.1	126.4	34.5	160.9	
1,054.0	945.2	367.7	14.1	2,381.1	381.3	2,762.4	Other receivables/payables	991.3	624.5	105.4	98.9	1,820.0	942.3	2,762.4	
							Net worth	1,763.0	214.3	3,428.3	7,322.8	12,728.4	-234.0	12,494.4	

11.3.2 Valuation of balance sheet items

All items in the balance sheet must be valued at "current prices" as of the reporting date; thus, there are no items on the balance sheet that are presented at constant prices. Since the balance sheet reflects the cumulative results of the accumulation accounts, consistency with the accumulation accounts must maintained. In particular, the values of the items recorded in the other changes in assets and liabilities accounts and in the closing balance sheet are not determined in advance, but are derived ex-post through an adjustment process based on the opening balance sheet and transaction values that occur during the accounting period. In the following, we will explain the specific valuation methods for each item in the balance sheet.

11.3.2.1 General valuation methods for balance sheets

The asset and liability items included in the balance sheet are valued at the amount that each item could be acquired or traded in the market as of the end of the accounting period, not at the historic cost or book value. In other words, the values of assets and liabilities should reflect **market prices** at the time the balance sheet is compiled. In particular, for non-financial assets (excluding land), it is necessary to accurately assess their market values according to the period of their use. Accordingly, the recorded value reflects the decline in the asset value (i.e., depreciation), resulting in a net asset value, and includes costs of ownership transfer in the asset value. In contrast, for financial assets, costs of ownership transfer are not included in the asset value; instead, these costs are recorded as intermediate consumption, final consumption or imports of services, as appropriate.

The SNA suggests the following three methods for valuing the items of the balance sheet at prices that can be acquired as of the reporting date:

1. **Market price valuation method**: For financial assets (such as shares, bonds, investment funds shares), liabilities, newly produced fixed assets, and inventories, observable market prices are available and can be used for their valuation. In addition, in the case of fixed assets, if there is a second-hand market (e.g., used-car market), the estimated value can be directly derived from the transaction prices on the market.

2. **Valuation based on the accumulation and revaluation of past transactions**: For existing fixed assets for which no observable market prices exist, their values can be estimated by the accumulated amounts of past transactions less the price decline due to physical deterioration or obsolescence (i.e., depreciation) through methods such as the perpetual inventory method. The fixed assets have long service lives and it is difficult to assess their market value over the period of their use, so their current prices can be valued using several measurement methods introduced in Chapter 20 (Measurement of capital stocks).

3. **Present value of future income method**: For non-produced assets such as subsoil resources or virgin forests, explicit market prices are often unavailable. In such cases, the asset value may be estimated as the present value of expected future income from extraction or harvesting, discounted at an appropriate rate.

Based on these valuation approaches, the next section briefly reviews the specific valuation methods for main categories in the balance sheet (see Table 11.11).

11.3.2.2 Valuation of produced non-financial assets

Fixed assets, which are representative of produced non-financial assets, are recorded in the balance sheet at their **written-down value** after deducting depreciation. The valuation method of fixed assets will be discussed in more detail in Chapter 20, but the basic valuation principles are introduced here. The general principle applied to the valuation of existing fixed assets is to convert the asset values to the prices at which the new products were acquired at the current valuation date, and then deduct the accumulated amount of depreciation to date. This is called the "written-down replacement cost" approach. Depreciation includes the depreciation of ownership transfer costs and land improvements.

However, in practice, the estimation of the fixed capital stock generally follows a two-step approach: First, capital stock at constant prices is estimated using historical data on fixed capital formation at constant prices and the age-price function; second, the resulting estimates are converted into those at current prices. In addition, depreciation is indirectly derived, based on the data in constant prices of the opening capital stocks, gross fixed capital formation, and closing capital stocks, and then converted into those at current prices. (See Chapter 20 for the detailed methodology.)

Inventories are valued at current prices on the balance sheet date, not on the date of entries into stock. Specifically, materials and supplies are valued at the purchasers' prices, and finished goods and work-in-progress are valued at basic prices as of the balance sheet date.

Valuables are valued at the actual transaction prices (net of dealers' margins or commissions) that could be sold if there are regular markets for the goods, or at the insured value of the goods against fire or theft if there are no regular markets.

11.3.2.3 Valuation of non-produced non-financial assets

Among **non-produced assets**, land, minerals, and energy resources account for the largest shares. **Land** is valued at its market price, but if such price information is unavailable, the official quoted prices provided by authorized institutions may be used. When land and buildings are combined and their values are not separately identified, the value of land can be obtained as a residual by estimating the value of the building and deducting it from the total value. However, if it is difficult to estimate the value of the building attached to the land, the combined asset is attributed to the component with the greater value. Costs of ownership transfer related to land are treated as part of land improvements and are recorded under "other buildings and structures."

Subsoil resources, natural forests and similar assets are valued at observable market prices when such prices exist. When market values are not available, valuation is based on the present value of expected future stream of *resource rent*, calculated by discounting the projected annual resource rent using an appropriate discount rate. Resource rent represents the surplus generated from the use of non-produced natural resources and, in practical terms, is calculated using the residual value method, whereby labour costs, intermediate consumption, the user cost of produced capital and depreciation are deducted from output. Meanwhile, costs of ownership transfer on non-produced assets (excluding land) are treated as gross fixed capital formation in the national accounts, but they are not shown as a separate item in the balance sheet; instead, they are incorporated into the value of the relevant non-produced assets (2025 SNA, paragraph 14.39).

Contracts, leases and licences are amounts paid in connection with the acquisition of specific rights. The payments made by the holder of the contractual right to the provider of the right (e.g., lessor, owner of natural resources, or issuer of a licence) are written down over the contract period. In the balance sheet, net of the written-down value is recorded.

Goodwill and marketing assets arise from expenditures incurred in connection with the acquisition of a company or the purchase of a company's marketing assets (e.g., trademarks, and logos). The accounting treatment of these assets begins with their recognition as the creation of an asset in the other changes in the volume of assets and liabilities account, followed by their recording in the capital account as the sale of an asset to the purchaser. These assets are also written down annually in accordance with accounting standards in the other changes in the volume of assets and liabilities account, and the value remaining after written-down is recorded in the balance sheet.

11.3.2.4 Valuation of financial assets and liabilities

Financial assets and liabilities are valued at the current prices observed in financial markets, provided such markets exist and regular trading occur. If no such financial market exists, they are valued based on the amount that the debtor would have to pay to the creditor to extinguish the claim. Since financial claims are by nature reciprocal, implying a corresponding liability for each asset, they must be recorded at identical values in the balance sheet of both the creditor and the debtor. For the valuation methods applicable to major categories of financial assets and liabilities, refer to Table 11.11.

11.3.2.5 Valuation of net worth

Net worth is the balancing item in the balance sheet, calculated as the total of financial assets and non-financial assets minus the total value of liabilities. In the sequence of economic accounts, the net worth recorded in the balance sheet at the end of the period is derived by adding the net worth of the opening balance sheet to the changes in net worth during the accounting period (namely, changes in net worth recorded in the capital account, the other changes in the volume of assets and liabilities account, and the revaluation account).

The concept of net worth in the SNA differs from somewhat from the concept of **equity** in business accounting. In the national accounts, the liability item "shares and other equity" is treated as a liability of the issuing enterprise. Accordingly, net worth is calculated by subtracting the total liabilities including equity and other shares from the total assets. In contrast, in business accounting, the enterprise's own issued shares and other equity are treated as part of equity, and the equity is calculated as the total assets less liabilities excluding shares and other equity. Thus, the relationship between the two concepts can be expressed as:

- **Equity in business accounting = net worth in the national accounts + shares and other equity**

By institutional sector, the interpretation of net worth differs. For general government, households and NPISHs, net worth is calculated clearly for each institutional unit and can be directly attributed to their owners. However, in the corporations sector, the treatment of net worth differs between quasi-corporations and corporations. **Quasi-corporations** are by convention treated as having a net worth of zero in the national accounts. This reflects the view that the value of the enterprise's net worth is deemed to be fully attributed to the owner's equity, which is itself assessed as the difference between its assets and liabilities excluding its equity. Foreign direct investment enterprises are also treated as quasi-corporations, and their net worth is therefore likewise recorded as zero. In contrast, for **corporations**, all shares and other equity issued by the enterprise are classified as liabilities, and net worth is derived in accordance with the formula above; as a result, the balancing item may make either a positive or negative value.

Table 11.11 Valuation methods of balance sheet items (summary)

Item		Valuation method
Produced assets	Fixed assets	Current values for acquiring a new asset of the same type at the time of valuation, less the cumulative amount of depreciation to date. (See Chapter 20 for the practical method.)

Item			Valuation method
	Inventories		Current values on the balance sheet date. (Purchasers' prices for materials and supplies, and basic prices for finished goods and work-in-progress.)
	Valuables		1) If there is a regular trading market: The transaction price available. 2) If there is no regular trading market: The insured value by the insurance company in the case of fire or theft.
Non-produced assets	Natural resources		Land: 1) Direct method: size of land area x market price (or officially published price) 2) Residual method: combined value of land and structure minus estimated value of structure
			Subsoil resources and natural forests: the present value of expected future resource rents.
	Contracts, leases and licences		Written-down value of contracts, leases and licences
	Goodwill and marketing assets		Written-down value of goodwill and marketing assets
Financial assets and liabilities	Monetary gold and SDRs		Market transaction price or quoted price
	Currency and deposits		Face or nominal value. Items denominated in foreign currency are converted at the mid-point of selling and buying rates of market exchange rates on the balance sheet date.
	Debt securities		Current market prices, generally including accrued interest.
	Loans		Outstanding principal, including accrued but unpaid interest on loans as of the balance sheet date.
	Equity and investment fund shares		Listed shares: market prices at which they are traded. Unlisted shares: estimated prices.
	Insurance, pension & standardized guarantee	Non-life insurance technical reserves	Prepaid insurance premiums plus outstanding insurance claims.
		Life insurance entitlements	Present value of expected future benefits.
		Pension entitlements	DC: The market value of the financial assets held by pension funds on behalf of the future beneficiaries.
			DB: Actuarial estimation of the liabilities of the pension provider.
		Provisions for calls under standardized guarantees	Expected claims minus expected recoveries.
	Financial derivatives		Market value at the valuation date.
	Other receivables/payables		Amount payable by the debtor to the creditor, including principal and interest.
Net worth	Quasi-corporations		Net worth is conventionally assumed to be zero.
	Corporations		Shares and other equity issued by the corporation are classified as liabilities. Net worth is calculated as total assets minus total liabilities including shares and other equity.

Chapter 12. The government account and the NPISHs account

In the sequence of economic accounts by institutional sector, both the government sector and the NPISHs sector are classified as non-market institutional sectors, and they have a unique accounting framework for production and expenditure that is distinct from other institutional sectors. Therefore, these sectors need to be explained using a separate set of accounts, along with the rest of the world sector, which is discussed in Chapter 13. This chapter aims to examine in greater detail the characteristics of these institutional sector accounts and how they are recorded in the SNA.

12.1 The government account

In the SNA, the general government is an institutional sector of the national economy that exercises public authority such as legislative, administrative, and judicial functions, and conducts expenditure activities based on revenues collected through the taxation or other compulsory transfers. The government's expenditure activities enable it to play the role of a producer of government goods and services, and the government belongs to non-market producers because its products are not sold on the market but are attributed to the final consumption of the government itself.

The scope of general government in the SNA includes central government, local governments, social security funds, and non-profit institutions controlled by government. It also includes publicly operated enterprises that do not maintain a complete set of accounts. **Social security funds** are social insurance schemes operated by the government that cover all or most people of a country. Examples include the national pension scheme, national health insurance, national unemployment insurance, and industrial accident compensation insurance. However, social insurance schemes that serve only specific occupational groups such as civil servants, teachers, or military personnel are classified separately as "employment-related social insurance schemes," distinct from social security funds.

On the other hand, quasi-corporations that are under the government's control but operate independently are excluded from the government sector and classified as public corporations. For an entity to be classified as a quasi-corporation, it must not to be a corporation, but operate in a manner similar to a corporation, sell its output as a market producer at economically significant prices, and maintain a complete set of accounts that allows it to be recognized as an independent economic unit.

Non-profit institutions controlled by government are classified as non-market non-profit institutions, and the specific criteria for their classification are set out in the 2025 SNA, paragraph 5.131. According to this provision, whether an institution qualifies as an NPI controlled by government is determined based on a combination of factors, such as the extent of government financial support, the government's authority to appoint the institution's key officers, and its right to approve major regulations and operations of the institution.

This section outlines the specific procedures for compiling the government account as one of the institutional sector accounts within the sequence of economic accounts. Since the economic activities of the government are generally recorded in the budget and financial statements through simple cash-based transactions of revenue and expense, a distinct conversion process is required to align these records with the accounting standards of national accounts. The following will detail the procedures to transform available government data sources to conform to the conceptual and classification frameworks of government accounts.

12.1.1 Data sources for the government account

The government's accounting records are primarily finalized through the budget and financial statements. The budget is a record of the government's projected revenues and expenditures for the following fiscal year. It details the planned revenue and expenditure of each government agency in detail by item, which serves as the basis for reconciling the government data to the national accounts. On the other hand, the government's financial statements document the actual results of budget execution, providing the confirmed amounts but with less detailed breakdowns compared to the budget. Consequently, the final amounts of the national accounts are determined by using the total executed amounts in the financial statements, but the detailed allocations by item are derived by referring to the more comprehensive budget documents.

12.1.2 Revenue and expenditure of the government

Unlike ordinary enterprises, the government does not generate income by selling products in the market, and thus employs a different method of accounting. Government accounts broadly consist of revenue and expenditure. **Government revenue** encompasses items that increase the government's net worth and consist of receipts in the current accounts and capital transfers receivable in the capital account. Specifically, it includes tax revenue (taxes on production and imports, current tax on income and wealth), social security contributions, other current revenue (property incomes receivable, fines, etc.), sales revenue of government goods and services, and capital transfers receivable (such as inheritance tax and gift tax).

Government expenditure (or **outlay**) consists of expenses and "acquisitions less disposals of non-financial assets." **Expenses** represent transactions that decrease the government's net worth and consist of all expenses incurred in the current accounts and the capital transfers payable in the capital account. In contrast, the acquisitions less disposals of non-financial assets do not decrease net worth because they are transactions of asset exchange. Acquisitions less disposals of non-financial assets include gross capital formation[17] and the acquisitions less disposals of non-produced non-financial assets. Within gross capital formation, the own account capital formation produced by the government for its own use is already recorded as production costs in the current account. Therefore, these costs must be excluded when calculating the government's final consumption expenditure.

Meanwhile, government revenue minus government expense is called the **net operating balance**. When government expenditures are subtracted from government revenue, the result is **net lending** (or **net borrowing**). The above contents are summarized as follows:

- Government revenue = tax revenue (taxes on production and imports, current taxes) + social security contributions receivable + other current revenue (property incomes receivable, value of sales of government products, other current transfers receivable) + capital transfers receivable
- Government expense = production expenses (intermediate consumption, remuneration of employees, gross operating surplus, other taxes less subsidies on production) + subsidies payable + property incomes payable + social security benefits payable + social transfers in-kind purchased from market producers + other current transfers payable + capital transfers payable
- **Government revenue – government expense = net operating balance**
- **Government expenditure = government expense + acquisitions less disposals of non-financial assets**
- **Government revenue – government expenditure = net lending (or net borrowing)**

---

[17] Since depreciation (a cost item) has not actually been subtracted, net capital formation is calculated by excluding this amount.

The table below summarizes the fiscal revenues and expenditures (year 2015) of the South Korean government.

Table 12.1 Revenue and expenditure of general government (South Korea, 2015)

(Unit: KRW trillion)

Government expenditure	Amount	Government revenue	Amount
Intermediate consumption[1)]	60.8	Taxes on production and imports	164.3
Remuneration of employees[1)]	106.1	Property incomes receivable	28.4
Other taxes on production payable[1)]	0.0	Current taxes on income and wealth	122.2
Subsidies payable	7.6	Social contributions receivable	126.7
Property incomes payable	25.2	(Actual social contributions)	120.2
Social benefits payable	75.4	(Imputed social contributions)	6.5
Social transfers in kind purchased from market producers and supplied to households	70.8	Other current transfers receivable	38.3
Other current transfers payable	58.4	Sales of government goods and services	34.1
Net adjust. for the change in pension entitlements	0.0	Capital transfers receivable	9.7
Capital transfers payable	20.3		
Gross capital formation	71.2		
(Gross fixed capital formation) [2)]	70.6		
(Changes in inventories and net acquisition of valuables)	0.6		
Net acquisition of non-produced non-financial assets	8.1		
Net lending (+) / net borrowing (-)	19.6		
Total expenditure	523.6	Total revenue	523.6

Note: 1) The value for own-account capital formation has been deducted. Therefore, it differs from that of government sector in the institutional sector accounts in Chapter 9.

2) The value of depreciation for own-account has been deducted.

Based on the data in the above table, the government revenue, expense and expenditure for South Korea in 2015 are calculated as follows. As additional information data, depreciation (45.3) is given. As a result, government revenue amounts to KRW 523.6 trillion, and government expense is KRW 470.0 trillion, resulting in net operating balance of KRW 53.6 trillion (= 523.6 - 470.0). Meanwhile, government expenditure amounts to KRW 504 trillion, resulting in net lending of KRW 19.6 trillion.

Table 12.2 Revenue, expense, and expenditure of general government (South Korea, 2015)

(Unit: KRW trillion)

Government revenue	523.6	Government expense	470.0
Tax revenue[1)]	286.5	Production expenses[3)]	212.2
Social security contributions receivable	126.7	Property income payable	25.2
Other current revenue[2)]	100.7	Other current expenses[4)]	66.0
Capital transfers receivable	9.7	Social security benefits payable	75.4
		Social transfers in-kind	70.8
		Capital transfers payable	20.3
		Net operating balance	53.6

Note: 1) Taxes on production and imports + current taxes,

2) Property incomes receivable + sales of government products + other current transfers receivab

3) Intermediate consumption + remuneration of employees + gross operating surplus + other taxes less subsidies on production,

4) Subsidies payable + other current transfers payable

(Unit: KRW trillion)

Government revenue	523.6	Government expenditure	504.0
		Government expense	470.0
		Gross fixed capital formation	70.6
		Depreciation (-)	(45.3)
		Changes in inventories and net acquisition of valuables	0.6
		Net acquisition of non-produced non-financial assets	8.1
		Net lending	19.6

Looking more closely at the items of **government revenue**, there are taxes on production and imports which are value added item, and current taxes on income and wealth which are current transfer item. In addition to taxes, government revenue also several other components.

Table 12.3 Revenue items of general government (excluding taxes)

Revenue items
Property incomes receivable
(Interest)
(Income on equity)
-Dividends
-Withdrawals of income from quasi-corporations
(Investment income disbursements)
(Rent)
Social security contributions receivable
(Employers' actual social security contributions)
(Households' actual social security contributions)
Other social contributions receivable
(Employers' social contributions)
(Employees' social contributions)
Other current transfers receivable
(Non-life insurance claims)

Revenue items
(Current transfers within government)
(Current international cooperation)
(Other miscellaneous current transfers)
Sales of goods and services
Capital transfers receivable

The government's expenditure items can be cross-classified according to the "classification of functions or purposes of government" (COFOG) as shown in Table 12.4. The items covered by the classification of government functions are divided into current expenditure and capital expenditure. **Current expenditure** is recorded in the current accounts and consists of intermediate consumption, remuneration of employees, taxes less subsidies on production and imports, property income, social security benefits, social transfers in-kind provided to households via market producers, and other current transfers. **Capital expenditure** is recorded in the capital account, which includes gross fixed capital formation, changes in inventories, acquisitions less disposals of valuables, and acquisitions less disposals of non-produced non-financial assets. This functional classification of government expenditures provides a basis for distinguishing between collective and individual consumptions of government (which is described in section 12.1.4).

Table 12.4 Expenditure breakdown by the government functions (South Korea, 2015)

(Unit: KRW trillion)

Account items \ By functions	Economic affairs	Public order and safety	Education	Defence	Health	Social protection	Recreation, culture,religion	General public services	Housing, community amenities	Environmental protection	Total
Intermediate consumption	8.1	2.9	14.3	10.9	1.3	5.6	2.6	8.9	2.6	3.8	60.8
Remuneration of employees	5.3	12.8	38.8	13.0	1.1	4.0	1.7	27.2	1.2	0.9	106.1
Taxes on production and imports payable	0.0	0.0	0.0	0.0	0.0	0.0	0.0	0.0	0.0	0.0	0.0
Subsidies payable	7.6	0.0	0.0	0.0	0.0	0.0	0.0	0.0	0.0	0.0	7.6
Property income payable	1.9	0.0	0.5	0.0	0.0	1.6	0.0	21.1	0.0	0.0	25.2
Social security benefits payable	0.0	0.0	2.9	0.0	0.0	72.6	0.0	0.0	0.0	0.0	75.4
Social transfers in kind: market products	0.0	0.0	6.5	0.0	56.6	7.7	0.0	0.0	0.0	0.0	70.8
Other current transfers	12.9	0.5	7.1	1.3	6.5	14.0	3.2	9.7	0.8	2.4	58.4
Gross fixed capital formation	26.5	2.7	4.4	14.2	0.4	2.0	3.6	2.6	9.4	4.9	70.6
Changes in inventories, net acquisition of valuables	0.6	0.0	0.0	0.0	0.0	0.0	0.0	0.0	0.0	0.0	0.6
Net acquisition of non-produced non-financial assets	3.0	0.4	1.8	0.2	0.1	0.3	0.4	0.4	1.2	0.4	8.1
Capital transfers	9.5	0.1	1.7	0.3	0.4	3.4	1.5	0.7	0.7	1.9	20.3
Total expenditure	75.4	19.3	78.0	39.8	66.3	111.1	12.9	70.7	16.1	14.4	504.0

12.1.3 Government's output, balance of earned income, disposable income

In the SNA, the goods and services produced by the government are not sold on the market but are considered to be consumed by the government itself, so market prices for government output cannot be observed. Consequently, the **sum of costs method** is used as an alternative approach to valuing government output.

- Government's output (at basic prices) = intermediate consumption + gross value added (= remuneration of employees + taxes less subsidies on production + net operating surplus + depreciation)

Similarly, the formulas for deriving the government's balance of earned incomes and gross disposable income are as follows:

- Balance of earned incomes (gross) for government = gross operating surplus + taxes on production and imports receivable – subsidies on production and imports payable + property incomes receivable – property incomes payable
- Gross disposable income for government = balance of earned incomes (gross) + current transfers receivable – current transfers payable

The table below presents the accounts of South Korea's government, from the production account to the income transfers account, based on the data from Table 12.1. It also shows the corresponding balancing items: value added, balance of earned incomes, and disposable income.

Table 12.5 Current accounts of general government (the production account to the income transfers account): South Korea, 2015

Production account

Expenditures	(Unit: KRW trillion)		Revenues
Intermediate consumption	60.8	Output	213.3
Gross value added	152.5		

Expenditures	**Generation of earned income account**		Revenues
Remuneration of employees	106.1	Gross value added	152.5
Other taxes on production (net)	0.0		
Gross operating surplus	46.3		
(Depreciation)	45.3		
(Net operating surplus)	1.1		

Expenditures	**Allocation of earned income account**		Revenues
		Gross operating surplus	46.3
		Taxes on production and imports receivable	164.3
		Subsidies payable (-)	-7.6
Property income payable	25.2	Property income receivable	28.4
Balance of earned incomes (gross)	206.2		
Balance of earned incomes (net)	160.9		

Expenditures	Income transfers account		Revenues
		Balance of earned incomes (gross)	206.2
Current transfers payable	133.9	Current transfers receivable	287.1
Gross disposable income	359.5		
Net disposable income	314.2		

In this example above (Table 12.5), the results of calculating the balancing items (total aggregates) for the general government of South Korea are as follows. For this calculation, the data on the depreciation for government (KRW 45.3 trillion) is additionally provided.

- Government's gross value added: 106.1+0.0+1.1+45.3 = 152.5,
- Government's output: 60.8+(106.1+0.0+1.1+45.3) = 213.3,
- Government's balance of earned incomes (gross): (1.1+45.3) +164.3–7.6+28.4–25.2 = 206.2,
- Government's gross disposable income: 206.2+287.1–133.9 = 359.5

12.1.4 Government's final consumption expenditure and actual final consumption

Government final consumption expenditure is derived through the follow procedure. First, from the value of government output, the revenue received from sales of market and non-market services (e.g., tuition tees for public education, user charges for public services) is subtracted. Next, the value of compensation in-kind by government for the households who purchase the private medical or educational services are added. Finally, the value of output used for government expenditures of the own account fixed capital formation (including intermediate consumption, remuneration of employees, other taxes on production, and gross operating surplus) is subtracted. The reason for excluding the revenue received from sales of government services from the government final consumption expenditure is that the corresponding expenditure is recorded under the respective institutional units that purchase the services. In addition, when the government pays on behalf of households for market services purchased by households, it is recorded as government expenditure as social transfers in kind to households. On the other hand, the expenditure of the own-account fixed capital formation (for example, R&D) is already included in output, and separately recorded under the government fixed capital formation, so it must be deducted from final consumption expenditure to avoid double counting.

- Government final consumption expenditure = government output − government sales revenue + social transfers in kind to households via market producers − output for the government own-account gross fixed capital formation

Based on the previous data (Table 12.1), the calculated result for government final consumption expenditure is as follows. Note that in this dataset, intermediate consumption (KRW 3.6 trillion), gross value added (KRW 4.4 trillion), and output (KRW 8.0 trillion) for the government's own-account gross fixed capital formation have already been deducted.

- Government final consumption expenditure: 213.3 − 34.1 + 70.8 = 250.1

The allocation of government's output and final consumption expenditure in this example is shown in the supply and use table as follows (Table 12.6). In this table, the government's sales revenue (34.1) is recorded as the final consumption expenditure of households, and therefore subtracted from the government's output. The government's payments in-kind for healthcare (70.8) on behalf of households are added to derive the government final consumption expenditure. Note that government own-account capital formation has already been excluded in this dataset, so no further adjustment is necessary.

Table 12.6 Presentation of the government's output and final consumption expenditure using the supply and use tables

Supply table

	..	Health service	Public service	Total
..				
Public service			213.3	213.3
Health service		70.8		70.8
Total output		70.8	213.3	284.1

Use table

	..	Health service	Public service	Household final consumption	Gov't final consumption	Total
..	.	..	..			
Public service	.	..	..	34.1	179.2 (=213.3−34.1)	213.3
Health service	.	..	..		70.8	70.8
Intermediate consumption			60.8	34.1	250.1	284.1
Gross value added			152.5			
Remuneration of employees			106.1			
Net taxes on production			0.0			
Net operating surplus			1.1			
Depreciation			45.3			
Total input		70.8	213.3			

Final consumption as the expenditure basis versus acquisition basis

Within government final consumption expenditure, there is a portion that effectively contributes to the households final consumption expenditure. This occurs, for example, when public education services or public healthcare services are provided to households for free or at prices significantly lower than market prices. In such cases, the government is providing non-market output in kind to households. In the SNA, this is called **social transfers in kind of government output**. These social transfers in kind can be viewed as households receiving education and health services in kind from government at no cost (or at the market value minus the expense paid by households).

Another form of the government's social transfers in kind to households involves cases when the government pays a portion of the medical expenses incurred by households when they use medical services provided by market producers. This occurs as part of social security schemes, where the government makes payments on behalf of households in return for payments of health insurance premiums as social contributions by households. In the SNA, this is recorded as the **government purchasing market products and then transferring them in kind to households**[18].

Both forms of social transfers in kind can be seen as government payments on behalf of households' direct consumption expenditure, and are called "individual consumption expenditure" by government as they provide actual benefits to households.

- Individual consumption expenditure by government (non-market products + market products) = social transfers in kind to households by government

From the perspective of **expenditure basis**, the government individual consumption expenditure represents government spending, however from the perspective of **acquisition basis** of services, it is considered households' consumption. Accordingly, the amount of actual final consumption expenditure by government is the total final consumption expenditure of government minus the individual consumption expenditure for households. This residual amount is called the **government collective consumption expenditure**. Government collective consumption expenditure refers to government services whose benefits cannot be attributed to individual households but are shared by all members of the community, such as government services for public safety, defense, legislation and public administration.

- Government's collective consumption expenditure = government's final consumption expenditure – government's individual consumption expenditure

Conversely, the actual final consumption of households is equal to their original final consumption expenditure plus the individual consumption provided to them by government.

---

[18] This category also includes the "medical assistance system," in which low-income households receive free medical services and the government pays for the costs.

Figure 12.1 Government's output, final consumption expenditure, and actual final consumption

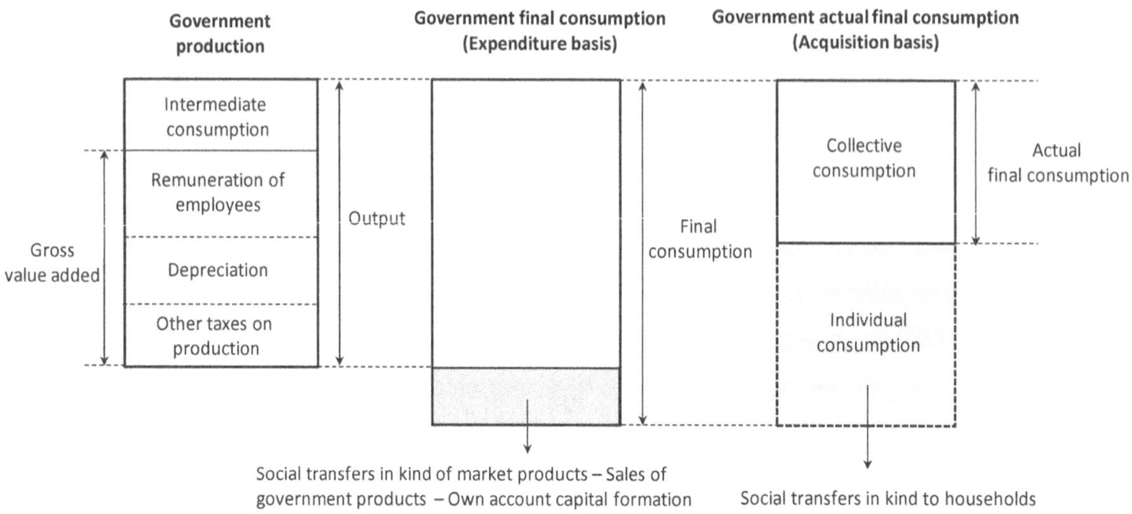

The table below (Table 12.7) illustrates the final part of the current accounts for the South Korean government: the use of income account, the social transfers in kind account, and the use of adjusted income account. Net disposable income and final consumption expenditure were calculated in the previous example; thus, net saving is derived as a balancing item in the use of income account (**Net saving = net disposable income – final consumption expenditure**). It is worth noting that the adjustment for the change in pension entitlements in the use of income account only concerns transactions between households and financial corporations and does not appear in the government sector.

- Government net saving: 314.2 – 250.1 = 64.1

Moreover, as the government provides social transfers in kind to households, its actual net disposable income, which is called **net adjusted disposable income** will decrease. The government's net adjusted disposable income is derived by subtracting social transfers in kind (= social transfers in kind via market products + social transfers in kind via government products) from the net disposable income.

- Government net adjusted disposable income: 314.2 – 135.7 (= 70.8 + 64.9) = 178.5

However, in the use of adjusted income account, the government's actual final consumption is calculated as final consumption expenditure minus social transfers in kind, as a result, the government's net saving remains the same as the value in the use of income account, amounting to 64.1 (**Net saving = net adjusted disposable income – actual final consumption**).

- Government's actual final consumption: 250.1 – 135.7 = 114.4
- Government's net saving: 178.5 – 114.4 = 64.1

Table 12.7 Accounting treatment for the final consumption and actual final consumption of general government (South Korea, 2015)

Use of income account

(Unit: KRW trillion)

Expenditures		Revenues	
Final consumption expenditure	250.1	Net disposable income	314.2
Net saving	64.1		

Social transfers in-kind account

Expenditures		Revenues	
		Net disposable income	314.2
Social transfers in-kind payable	135.7		
(Purchased market products)	70.8		
(Non-market products)	64.9		
Net adjusted disposable income	178.5		

Use of adjusted disposable income

Expenditures		Revenues	
Actual final consumption	114.4	Net adjusted disposable income	178.5
Net saving	64.1		

12.1.5 Government's capital account and financial account

The capital account of general government records transactions related to nonfinancial assets of government. On the right-hand side of this account (changes in liabilities and net worth), net saving carried forward from the current accounts is recorded, and net capital transfer is added. On the left-hand side (changes in assets), net capital formation (including gross fixed capital formation less depreciation, changes in inventories, and net acquisition of valuables) and acquisitions less disposals of non-produced non-financial assets are displayed. The balancing item, net lending of the government, amounts to KRW 19.6 trillion on the left-hand side, which indicates that the government provided lending to other institutional sectors (see Table 12.8).

Table 12.8 Capital account and financial account of general government (South Korea, 2015)

Capital account

(Unit: KRW trillion)

Changes in assets		Changes in liabilities and net worth	
Gross fixed capital formation[1]	70.6	Net saving	64.1
Depreciation (-) [1]	-45.3	Capital transfers receivable	9.7
Changes in inventories & net acquisition of valuables	0.6	Capital transfers payable (-)	-20.3
Net acquisition of non-produced non-financial assets	8.1		
Net lending (+) / net borrowing (-)	19.6		
Total	53.6	Total	53.6

Footnote 1) Excludes depreciation (KRW 1.3 trillion) in the own-account fixed capital formation. Therefore, it differs from the amount of government sector in the institutional sector accounts (Chater 9).

Financial account

Changes in assets	(Unit: KRW trillion)	Changes in liabilities
0.0	Monetary gold and SDRs	0.0
5.1	Currency and deposits	11.6
9.2	Debt securities	50.3
5.0	Loans	0.7
55.6	Equity and investment fund shares	2.3
-0.0	Insurance, pension & standardized guarantee schemes	0.0
0.0	Financial derivatives and employee stock options	0.0
9.0	Other accounts receivable/ payable	0.3
83.8	Net acquisition of assets or liabilities	65.2
	Net lending of financial account (1)	18.6
	Net lending of capital account (2)	19.6
	Statistical discrepancy (1-2)	-0.9

The financial account of the government sector records transactions in financial assets and liabilities that correspond to the transactions recorded in the government's current accounts and the capital account. Accordingly, the entries in the financial account are the counterparts to current and capital transactions, with the sides reversed: the left-hand side records "changes in financial assets," while the right-hand side records "changes in liabilities." The balancing item, which is the difference between the increase in financial assets (left-hand side) and the increase in liabilities (right-hand side) of this account, must be equal to the value of net lending (+) or net borrowing (-) recorded in the capital account.

As shown in the financial account in Table 12.8, the South Korean government's financial assets increased by KRW 83.8 trillion, while the government's liabilities increased by KRW 65.2 trillion, resulting in a net lending of KRW 18.6 trillion (=83.8 – 65.2). However, this figure is less than the net lending of KRW 19.6 trillion recorded in the capital account by KRW 0.9 trillion. This discrepancy arises due to differences in data sources, which is treated as a statistical discrepancy.

12.2 The NPISHs' account

Non-profit institutions serving households (NPISHs) are independent institutional units that produce non-market output and are not controlled by government. If non-profit institutions engaged in non-market production are under the government control, they are classified within the general government sector, while non-profit institutions that engage in market production activities are classified under the corporations sector.

The source data for NPISHs typically come from financial statements that are regularly submitted to the relevant government agencies that oversee them, depending on the nature of the NPISHs. If such data are not readily available, the necessary information may be collected through sample surveys.

12.2.1 Revenue and expenditure of NPISHs

As non-market producers, NPISHs rely primarily on current transfers receivable such as donations from households or government. In addition, they may receive property incomes, sales revenue from goods and services, and capital transfers. Expenditures of NPISHs, like those of general government, consists of expenses and acquisitions less disposals of non-financial assets. Expenses are incurred in the current accounts, while acquisitions less disposals of non-financial assets include gross capital formation and acquisitions less disposals of non-produced non-financial assets.

Table 12.9 Revenue and expenditure of NPISHs

Expenditure	Revenue
Intermediate consumption	Property income receivable
Remuneration of employees	Other current transfers receivable
Other taxes on production payable	Sales of goods and services
Property income payable	Capital transfers receivable
Social transfers in kind: market products	
Other current transfers payable	
Gross capital formation	
Net acquisitions of non-produced assets	
Net lending (+) / net borrowing (-)	

12.2.2 NPISHs' output, final consumption expenditure and actual final consumption

As non-market service producers, non-profit institutions serving households (NPISHs) are treated in the same way as general government in terms of output valuation, their output is calculated using the sum of costs method:

- Output of NPISHs (at basic prices) = intermediate consumption + gross value added (= remuneration of employees + other taxes on production – other subsidies on production + net operating surplus + depreciation)

The output of NPISHs, like government's output, is not sold in the market but is considered to be consumed by the institutions themselves. Therefore, the method for calculating the NPISHs' final consumption expenditure is similar to that used for government's final consumption expenditure.

- NPISHs' final consumption expenditure = output – sales receipts + goods and services purchased from market producers for the purpose of providing them free of charge to households

A representative example of goods and services purchased from market producers to provide to households free of charge is when NPISHs receive donations from other economic units. For instance, if a charitable organization receives donated goods (e.g., food, clothing, or medicine) from other economic units with the intent of distributing them to households, the SNA treats the donation as if the NPISH had received cash. It is then assumed that the NPISH uses this imputed cash to purchase donated goods from market producers and consume them as part of its final consumption expenditure.

This accounting process can be represented across different accounts as follows. First, when the NPISH receives donated goods from another institutional sector, the transaction is recorded as a current transfer receivable in the income transfers account, with a corresponding entry in the financial account as an increase in financial assets. Subsequently, when the NPISH is deemed to use this cash to purchase the donated goods from market producers, it is recorded as final consumption expenditure by the NPISH. This amount is also recorded in the social transfers in kind account as a social transfer in kind from the NPISH to households.

Table 12.10 Accounting for donations to NPISHs by other institutional sectors

	NPISHs		Other institutional sector		Corporations		Households	
	Expenditures/ changes in assets	Revenues/ changes in liabilities	Expenditures/changes in assets	Revenues/ changes in liabilities	Expenditures/changes in assets	Revenues/ changes in liabilities	Expenditures/ changes in assets	Revenues/ changes in liabilities
Income transfers account		Current transfer receivable	Current transfer payable					
Financial account	Increase in financial assets			Decrease in financial assets				
Production account						Output		
Use of income account	Final consumption expenditure				Increase in financial assets			
Financial account		Decrease in financial assets						
Social transfers in kind account	Social transfer in kind payable						Social transfer in kind receivable	

Meanwhile, since most of the final consumption expenditure of NPISHs returns to households' benefits, this consumption is attributed to households' actual final consumption in the form of social transfers in kind. As a result, the actual final consumption of NPISHs become zero.

- NPISHs' actual final consumption = NPISHs' final consumption expenditure – social transfers in kind to households ≒ 0

12.2.3 The case of NPISHs that produce both non-market and market output

Let us consider how to calculate output when an NPISH produces market output as well as non-market output. For example, suppose that an NPISH (e.g., a religious organization) provides food services as a secondary production activity in addition to its primary non-market activity. The following data are given:

Item	Amount
Intermediate consumption	30
Remuneration of employees	50
Depreciation	10
Taxes less subsidies on production	5
Market sales (food services)	20

In this case, the total output of the NPISH = 30+(50+10+5) = 95, of which the output of non-market products = total output – market sales = 95 – 20 = 75. This can be represented in the supply and use tables as follows. In the supply table, the market output of food services (20) and the non-market output of membership organization services (75) are recorded, while in the use table, intermediate consumption (30) and value added (65) make the total input of 95, and final consumption expenditure is shown as 75 consumed by the NPISH (for the non-market output consumed by the institution) and 20 consumed by households (for the market output purchased).

Table 12.11 Accounting for market and non-market products of NPISHs

Supply table

	NPISH	Total
...		
Food services	20	20
Membership organizations	75	75
Total output	95	95

Use table

	.. NPISH ..	NPISH's final consumption	Household final consumption	Total
...				
Food services			20	20
Membership organizations		75		75
Intermediate consumption	30			
Gross value added	65			
Total input	95			

Chapter 13. International accounts and the rest of the world account

In the SNA, economic activities and positions are primarily measured by institutional sector within the domestic economy through the sequence of economic accounts. However, transactions, other flows, and stocks occurring between domestic residents and non-residents are separately measured in a sub-account known as the rest of the world (ROW) account. Unlike domestic economic accounts, the rest of the world account measure all economic activities involving residents from the perspective of non-residents. Here, the **rest of the world** (ROW) includes all non-resident institutional units conducting transactions or other economic relations with resident units, as well as international organizations (BPM6, 4.102, 4.105). In addition, the rest of the world sector is considered the counterparty for all entries within the "international accounts."

However, since all basic statistical data required for compiling the ROW account are derived from the **international accounts** introduced below, it is first necessary to understand the structure of these international accounts to comprehend the ROW account properly. The international accounts follow the framework provided by the Balance of Payments and International Investment Position Manual published by the IMF (BPM6, 2.2). Accordingly, sections 13.1 to 13.3 discuss the compilation methods of the international accounts, and section 13.4 will subsequently explain the methodology for compiling the ROW account based on these international accounts.

13.1 Framework of international accounts

In the SNA, the rest of the world (ROW) account is recorded from the perspective of non-residents, in contrast to the international accounts of BPM6, which are recorded from the perspective of domestic residents. The international accounts, compiled in accordance with the BPM6 manual, are therefore presented with left-hand and right-hand sides reversed compared to the ROW account in the SNA. For instance, imports are recorded on the left-hand side in the international accounts, but appears as revenues (right-hand side) for the rest of the world account. Conversely, exports are recorded on the right-hand side in the international accounts but are presented as expenditures (left-hand side) in the rest of the world account. However, the financial account in the international accounts, as the counterpart to the real transactions described above, has its entries on the left-hand and right-hand sides reversed. (This method of recording the financial account is also applied in the ROW account.) Additionally, there are differences in the terminology used between the two accounts. For example, what is termed "stock" in the ROW account of the SNA is referred to as "position" in the international accounts. Similarly, the balance sheet in the ROW account is called the "international investment position (IIP)" in the international accounts.

In the BPM6 framework, the international accounts systematically represent economic relationship between residents and non-residents of an economy, and consists of the balance of payments (BOP), the international investment position (IIP), and the "other changes in financial assets and liabilities account."

Table 13.1 Comparison of the international accounts and the ROW account

	International accounts of BPM6		Rest of the world account of the SNA
1)	**Balance of payments**: A table that records transactions between residents and non-residents of an economy during a specific period. (The financial account is classified by "functional category", with the left-hand and right-hand sides recorded in reverse.) (Table 13.2)	→	Corresponds to the transaction accounts (current account, capital account, financial account).
2)	**Other changes in financial assets and liabilities account**: A table that records the changes in the value due to economic events other than transactions between residents and non-residents during a specific period. (Table 13.21)	→	Corresponds to "the other changes in assets and liabilities account."
3)	**International investment position (IIP)**: A table that records the positions of residents' financial assets and liabilities with non-residents at a specific point in time (Classified by "functional category."; the balancing item is "net IIP.") (Table 13.21)	→	Corresponds to the balance sheet.

13.2 Accounting principles of international accounts

In the international accounts, the valuation principle applied is **market price**. Market price is defined as the amount of money that a willing buyer pays to acquire something from a willing seller in a transaction conducted solely on the basis of commercial considerations between independent parities. This price reflects the amount actually paid by the buyer in the transaction, taking into account any rebates, refunds, or adjustments from the seller (BPM6, 3.67-3.69).

In the imports and exports of general merchandise, transactions are generally valued on an **FOB** (free on board) basis, which refer s to the price of goods at the customs frontier of the exporting economy). However, the source data used for compiling these accounts, namely customs statistics, report exports on an FOB basis, while imports are compiled on a CIF (cost, insurance, and freight) basis. The reason that imports are also valued on an FOB basis in the international accounts is to separate the freight and insurance costs included in the imports so that these can be properly recorded as international trade in services (for further details, see Annex to 13.3.4). Therefore, it is necessary to adjust the CIF-based import data from customs statistics to the FOB basis required by the international accounts.

When adjusting CIF values to FOB values, the ideal approach is to do so for each individual commodity. However, if detailed data are not available, adjustments should be made at least on the commodity group basis. In addition, when the original data are denominated in different currencies by commodity, it is necessary to convert these into a unified domestic currency or foreign currency. For this conversion, the mid-point exchange rate (the midpoint between the buying and selling rates) at the time of the transaction is applied; while the average rate on the date of transaction is most preferable, if not available, the most recent short-term average rate should be used (BPM6, 3.104-3.105). The exchange rate for positions (stock data) is the mid-point rate prevailing on the balance sheet date.

Financial assets and liabilities are valued at market prices, but commissions and taxes incurred at the time of the transaction are not included in the purchaser's price and are recorded separately. This treatment differs from that of non-financial assets, where all commissions and taxes (i.e., cost of ownership transfer) are included in the purchaser's price.

The time of recording transactions is based on the moment when economic ownership is transferred, consistent with national accounts. In most cases, the transfer of legal ownership coincides with the transfer of economic ownership. However, when only economic ownership is transferred without a change in legal ownership, as in the case of financial leases, the transaction is recorded at the time of transfer of economic ownership. Changes in ownership of high-value capital goods (e.g., ships, aircraft, heavy machinery) should be recorded at the time agreed upon by the parties involved (BPM6, 3.44).

One of the differences between the sixth edition of the *Balance of Payments and International Investment Position Manual* (BPM6, 2009) and the previous edition (BPM5) is the changes in the accounting treatments for merchanting and goods sent abroad for processing. **Merchanting** refers to transactions in which a resident merchant purchases goods from a non-resident and subsequently resells them to another non-resident without the goods ever entering the territory of the merchant's resident economy. Since the goods do not physically cross the resident economy's border, these transactions are not officially recorded as imports and exports by the resident customs authorities. Merchanting commonly occurs within international manufacturing and sales processes. Under BPM5, only the merchant's margin was recorded as a service transaction. However, in BPM6, it is required to record that goods actually flow into and out of the resident economy of the merchant. Specifically, the merchant's acquisition of goods is recorded as negative exports, and the subsequent resale as positive exports. If the acquired goods are not resold during the same accounting period, the unsold goods are recorded as an increase in inventories held by the merchant (even if physically located abroad). When these goods are subsequently sold in the next accounting period, they are recorded as exports accompanied by a decrease in inventories.

Data on merchanting transactions are generally not captured by administrative sources such as customs records, thus it requires separate surveys of enterprises engaging in merchanting, resulting in challenges in data collection.

While merchanting transactions do not involve goods physically entering the resident's territory, **re-exports** are defined as goods produced abroad that were previously imported into the resident economy and then re-exported to another country without any significant transformation. This is different from merchanting in that the goods are brought into the resident economy's territory, and ownership is transferred to the resident, and then re-exported to another country.

Goods sent abroad for processing are goods that are sent to another country for processing and are subsequently re-imported into the resident economy or exported to a third country. Under BPM5, goods for processing abroad were treated as exports and imports of goods, but in BPM6, only processing service fees are reflected in the exports or imports of services.

13.3 Compilation of international accounts

In this section, we will examine the compilation methods of the balance of payments (BOP) and the international investment position (IIP), which are the core tables of the international accounts. With regard to the balance of payments, we will first explain its structure and compilation methods, then review the details by focusing specifically on imports and exports of goods and services. Additionally, we will discuss the accounting treatment of transportation, and insurance services, and financial intermediation services indirectly measured (FISIM), all of which are relevant to the estimation of output in the national accounts.

13.3.1 Compilation of balance of payments

We first examine the types of external transactions recorded in the balance of payments, and then explore its structure along with practical compilation examples.

13.3.1.1 Types of external transactions in the balance of payments

The balance of payments classifies transactions between the domestic economy and the rest of the world sector into several categories (see Figure 13.1 and Table 13.2). First, it records the exports and imports of goods and services, where the difference between these two items (exports minus imports) is shown as the **balance on goods and services**. Next, the earned income account records inflows and outflows of earned incomes (such as remuneration of employees, property income, etc.) between residents and non-residents. The difference between primary receivable by domestic residents from abroad and earned income payable to non-residents yields the **balance on earned income**.

In the SNA, gross national income (GNI) is obtained by adding the balance on earned income to gross domestic product (GDP). Thus, GNI equals GDP plus earned income receivable from the rest of the world minus earned income payable to the rest of the world. As an income concept, GNI represents the total gross earned income earned by domestic residents.

In the balance of payments, the transactions on current transfers record current transfers between residents and non-residents (such as personal remittances and current grant aid between countries). The difference between current transfers receivable from non-residents and current transfers payable to non-residents yields the **balance on transfer income**. Adding the balance on transfer income to GNI results in gross national disposable income (GNDI). Lastly, summing the balance on goods and services, the balance on earned income, and the balance on transfer income provides the **current external balance**.

Figure 13.1 Types of external transactions in the balance of payments

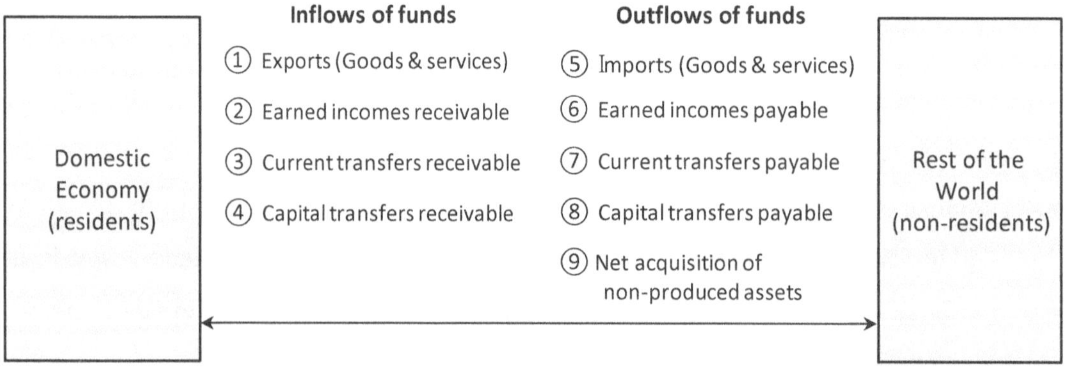

Next, there are two types of capital transactions (which are recorded in the capital account). The first involves capital transfers between residents and non-residents (e.g., investment grants from governments or international organizations, or debt forgiveness between countries), which are recorded as capital transfers receivable and capital transfers payable. The second type includes transactions involving the acquisition less disposal of non-produced non-financial assets between countries (e.g., the acquisition or disposal of embassy premises). In the balance of payments, the **balance on the capital account** is calculated by subtracting capital transfers payable to non-residents from capital transfers receivable from non-residents, and then further subtracting the net acquisition of non-produced, non-financial assets from the rest of the world (acquisitions minus disposals). Adding the balance on capital account to the current external balance yields the economy's **net lending (+) / net borrowing (-)** with the rest of the world. This net lending / net borrowing reflects the balance generated from the current transactions and capital transactions between the domestic economy and the rest of the world, and also represents the change in claims on the external financial assets. This amount should theoretically be equal to the net acquisition of financial assets less the net incurrence of liabilities by residents, as recorded in the financial account of the balance of payments.

13.3.1.2 Example of compiling the balance of payments

Table 13.2 illustrates the structure of the balance of payments (BOP). The left-hand and right-hand sides of the balance of payments are reversed from those of the rest of the world account in the SNA. This is because the balance of payments is compiled from the perspective of the domestic resident economy, whereas the rest of the world account in the SNA is recorded from the perspective of non-residents. In the BOP, the left-hand side (debit) records domestic economy's payments for imports of goods and services, as well as for earned incomes and transfers. The right-hand side (credit) records the domestic economy's receipts from exports of goods and services, and from earned incomes and transfers. The balance of each account is shown as the difference between the right-hand side (credit, revenues of funds for residents), and the left-hand side (debit, expenditures of funds by residents).

The financial account records the corresponding entries to these transactions, with the amounts of financial assets and liabilities recorded on the opposite sides. Specifically, net acquisition of financial assets is recorded on the left-hand side (debit), and net incurrence of liabilities is recorded on the right-hand side (credit). In practice, increases in financial assets and decreases in liabilities are entered as debits, while increases in liabilities and decreases in financial assets are entered as credits. The balancing item in the financial account, net lending(+)/net borrowing(-), is calculated by net acquisition of financial assets minus net incurrence of liabilities. This figure should match the balancing item in the capital account, which also represents net lending (+)/ net borrowing (-). However, in the capital account, the balancing item is calculated by subtracting the left-hand side (debit) from the right-hand side (credit), the opposite of the financial account.

Table 13.2 A format of the balance of payments

	Debits (1)	Credits (2)	Balance (2-1)
Current account ***Goods and services account*** Goods Services *Balance on goods and services* (1)	**Imports**	**Exports**	
Earned income account Remuneration of employees Interest, dividends, and reinvested income *Balance of earned income* (2) *Balance on goods and services and balance on earned income* (3=1+2)	**Payments**	**Receipts**	
Transfer income account Current taxes on income and wealth Other current transfers *Balance on transfer income* (4) *Current external balance* (5=3+4)	**Payments**	**Receipts**	
Capital account Net acquisitions of non-produced assets Capital transfers *Balance on capital account* (6) ***Net lending (+) / net borrowing (-)*** **(7=5+6)**	**Acquisition of assets, and transfers payable**	**Disposal of assets, and transfers receivable**	
	Net acquisition of financial assets (3)	**Net incurrence of liabilities (4)**	**Balance (3-4)**
Financial account (by functional category) Direct investment Portfolio investment Financial derivatives and Employee stock options Other investment Reserves *Total changes in assets/liabilities* *Net lending* ***(+) / net borrowing (-)*** **(8)**			
Statistical discrepancy (9=8-7)			

The difference (balance) between the credit and debit totals for each account in the balance of payments corresponds to the balancing items in the SNA. These differences are summarized by account in Table 13.3. In the balance of payments, the net lending or borrowing in the financial account and the net lending or borrowing in the capital account are derived independently from different data sources. Consequently, there is a significant possibility that the two figures will not match exactly. This discrepancy arises because the underlying data sources for the financial account and capital account are different. The resulting difference between the net lending or borrowing of the financial account and that of the capital account is recorded as **statistical discrepancy**.

Table 13.3 Balances by account in the balance of payments

Account	Balance by account	Calculation
Goods and services account	Balance on goods	Exports of goods – imports of goods
	Balance on services	Exports of services - imports of services
	Balance on goods and services	Balance on goods + balance on services
Earned income account	Balance on earned income	Earned income receivable - earned income payable
	Balance on goods and services, and balance on earned income	Balance on goods and services + balance on earned income
Transfer income account	Balance on transfer income	Current transfers receivable – current transfers payable
	Current external balance	Balance on goods and services + balance on earned income + balance on transfer income
Capital account	Balance on the capital account	(Capital transfers receivable – capital transfers payable) – net acquisitions of non-produced non-financial assets
	Net lending(+)/net borrowing (-)	Current external balance + balance on capital account
Financial account	Net lending(+)/net borrowing (-)	Net acquisition of financial assets – net incurrence of liabilities

Table 13.4 below illustrates a summary of the balance of payments in South Korea for 2015. In this table, the debit side (left) shows imports of goods and service, earned incomes payable, current transfers payable, capital transfers payable, and acquisitions of non-produced non-financial assets. The credit side (right) shows exports of goods and services, earned incomes receivable, current transfers receivable, capital transfers receivable, and disposals of non-produced non-financial assets.

In the goods and services account, exports amount to USD 640.6 billion, while imports are USD 534.9 billion, resulting in the balance of goods and services of USD 105.6 billion. In the earned income account, the earned income receivable from abroad is USD 25.1 billion, and the earned income payable to abroad is USD 20.6 billion with the balance of earned incomes of USD 4.5 billion. In the transfer income account, current transfers receivable from abroad are USD 8.8 billion, while current transfers payable to abroad are USD 13.8 billion, resulting in the balance of transfer income of -USD 5.0 billion. Consequently, the current external balance, which is the sum of the balance on goods and services, the balance on earned incomes, and the balance on transfer income stands at USD 105.1 billion.

In the capital account, the acquisition of non-produced non-financial assets is USD 136.6 billion, the disposal of non-produced non-financial assets is USD 50.7 billion, capital transfers receivable are USD 37.7 billion, and capital transfers payable are USD 12.0 billion, resulting in the balance on the capital account of -USD 60.2 billion. Accordingly, the net lending to the rest of the world is USD 105.1 billion, equal to the sum of the current external balance and the balance of the capital account.

The financial account records the counterpart entries of the current and capital accounts, with debits and credits recorded in reverse. In the direct investment category, financial assets increase by USD 23.7 billion and liabilities increase by USD 4.1 billion, resulting in the net acquisition of financial assets of USD 19.6 billion. In portfolio investment, net acquisition of assets is USD 49.5 billion; in financial derivatives and employee stock options, it is USD 1.8 billion; in other investment, USD 20.0 billion; and in reserve assets, USD 12.1 billion. Altogether, the financial account records net lending of USD 103.0 billion (= 19.6+49.5+1.8+20.0+12.1). Thus, the difference between the net lending recorded in the financial account and that in the capital account is –USD 2.1 billion (= 103.0 – 105.1), which corresponds to statistical discrepancy.

Table 13.4 Example of balance of payments (South Korea, 2015)

(Unit: billion US dollar)

	Debits (1)	Credits (2)	Balance (2-1)
Current account			
Goods and services account	**Imports**	**Exports**	
Goods	422.8	543.1	120.3
Services	112.1	97.5	-14.6
Goods and services (1)	534.9	640.6	105.6
Earned income account	**Payments**	**Receipts**	
Remuneration of employees	1.3	0.9	
Interest	5.7	12.3	
Income on equity	11.6	8.1	
Reinvested earnings	2	3.9	
Earned incomes (2)	20.6	25.1	4.5
Goods, services and earned income (3=1+2)	555.6	665.7	110.1
Transfer income account	**Payments**	**Receipts**	
Current taxes on income and wealth			
Current international cooperation	1.7	0.3	
Miscellaneous current transfers	12.1	8.6	
Transfer income (4)	13.8	8.8	-5
Current account balance (5=3+4)	569.4	674.5	105.1
Capital account	**Acquisition of assets, and transfers payable**	**Disposal of assets, and transfers receivable**	
Net acquisitions of non-produced assets	0.1	0.1	-0.1
Capital transfers	0	0	0
Capital account balance (6)	0.1	0.1	-0.1
Net lending(+)/net borrowing(-) **(7=5+6)**			105.1
	Net acquisition of assets (3)	**Net incurrence of liabilities (4)**	**Balance (3-4)**
Financial account (by functional category)			
Direct investment	23.7	4.1	19.6
Portfolio investment	41.9	-7.7	49.5
Financial derivatives and ESOs	1.8		1.8
Other investment	10.4	-9.6	20.0
Reserve assets	12.1		12.1

	Debits (1)	Credits (2)	Balance (2-1)
Total changes in assets and liabilities	89.8	-13.1	103.0
***Net lending(+)/net borrowing(-)* (8)**			103.0
Statistical discrepancy (9=8-7)			-2.1

13.3.2 Imports and exports of goods in the balance of payments

In this section, we will take a closer look at the current accounts in the balance of payments. In the current accounts, the *earned income account* and the *transfer income account* are similar to the corresponding accounts of the integrated economic account in the SNA, so these accounts will be excluded from discussion here. Instead, we will focus on the explanation of the goods and services account in more detail. In the balance of payments, the goods and services account is further divided into the imports and exports of goods and the imports and exports of services.

13.3.2.1 Classification of the imports and exports of goods

In BPM6, the imports and exports of goods in the balance of payments are classified into three categories: **general merchandise**, **merchanting**, and **non-monetary gold**.

General merchandise includes goods for which there is a change of economic ownership between residents and non-residents, excluding merchanting, non-monetary gold, and certain service-related items (such as travel, construction, and government goods and services). General merchandise is shown as a single item, but it can be disaggregated depending on the circumstances of each country.

The main data sources for general merchandise are customs data, other administrative data (e.g., value-added tax returns), and various surveys. The international standard for recording such data is defined in the *International Merchandise Trade Statistics* (IMTS) manual by the United Nations. (There are two manuals: IMTS: Concepts and Definitions and IMTS: Compilers Manual.)

According to IMTS, export values are to be recorded on an FOB (free on board) basis, while import values are recorded on a CIF (cost, insurance, and freight) basis. Therefore, import statistics need to be adjusted from CIF to FOB to comply with the balance of payments requirements. In addition, some items of goods recorded under the IMTS basis are excluded from the balance of payments, while certain items not captured in customs data must be included additionally in the balance of payments. Consequently, to derive the value of general merchandise on the balance of payments basis, the value on the IMTS basis should be reconciled as follows.

Coverage of general merchandise under the balance of payments basis

According to the BOP basis, the following Items are excluded from the category of general merchandise.

- Goods under merchanting, non-monetary gold, and some service transactions (such as travel, construction, and government goods and services)
- Goods that are not subject to international transactions, including: goods temporarily passing through a territory; migrants' personal effects; goods sent to embassies and military bases; goods temporarily imported or exported without a change in ownership (for repairs, operating leases, goods for exhibition purposes); goods moved abroad for processing, packaging, or assembling by enterprises with no ownership of the goods; and equipment and materials moved abroad for overseas construction projects.

Conversely, the following items may be missing from customs data but should be included in general merchandise in the balance of payments (see BPM6, 10.17):

- Banknotes and coins not in current circulation. (Banknotes and coins in circulation are excluded from goods as they are financial instruments.)
- Electricity, gas, and water.
- Packaged software that is not customized. (Other software is recorded under services.)
- Goods supplied by residents to non-resident transport operators at domestic ports or airports (such as fuel, provisions).
- Fish caught on the high seas by resident vessels and sold directly abroad, and oil or minerals extracted on the high seas by resident enterprises and sold directly abroad
- Goods acquired by lessees under financial lease contracts. (It is deemed to have acquired economic ownership.)
- Goods sent abroad without a change in ownership but subsequently sold (corresponding to the consignment sales).

Time of recording for general merchandise

Transactions of general merchandise are recorded at the time when the change in ownership of the goods occurs. In typical cases, the time of the change in ownership of ordinary goods is assumed to coincide closely with the time of customs clearance. However, for goods that take a long time to produce, such as high-value capital goods (such as ships, heavy machinery), ownership may be transferred in stages according to contract terms. The timing of the ownership change for such high-value capital goods can vary depending on the contract between the parties, which may be based on the gradual transfer of ownership through stage payments or on the complete delivery of the finished goods. Customs data are typically recorded when the finished goods cross the customs frontier, whereas the payments may incur on the basis of stage payments, resulting in inconsistent timing of ownership changes.

Merchanting

Merchanting is essentially regarded as cross-border wholesale and retail trading. It is a form of trade in which a resident enterprise purchases goods from a third country (country A) and sells them to another third country (country C) without the goods passing through the resident's territory. In this process, there is no further processing of the goods, and the transfer of ownership occurs when the resident enterprise sells them from country A to country C. If additional processing of goods by a third country occurs in the course of merchanting, the imports of processing service shall be recorded separately in the resident country of the merchant.

However, since the 2008 SNA, merchanting has been treated as a trade in goods, and is recorded as net exports of goods (which include the merchant's margin) to the rest of the world sector. This treatment was adopted as part of an effort to eliminate discrepancies in the value of goods traded between countries. On the other hand, from the perspective of the domestic industry, the margin earned by the merchant is recorded as output of wholesale and retail services, and goods acquired but not yet sold during the accounting period are recorded as changes in inventories. (For more details, see "Annex to 13.3.2: Merchanting, goods sent abroad for processing, and factoryless goods production.")

The table below shows an example of how transactions in merchanting would be accounted for in the supply and use tables. If a merchant purchases $300 of goods in Country A and resells them all to Country C for $330, and these transactions are completed within one accounting period, the supply and use tables of the country to which the merchant belongs can be displayed as follows.

Non-monetary gold

Non-monetary gold encompasses all gold other than monetary gold. Monetary gold refers to gold held as reserve assets by monetary authorities, such as central banks, and constitutes a financial asset. In contrast, non-monetary gold includes gold bullion (including gold held in allocated gold accounts) and semi-manufactured gold. Purchases and sales of non-monetary gold are valued at the transaction price rather than FOB prices, and this price should include intermediaries' margins and commissions.

13.3.2.2 Deriving the total value of goods in the BOP using customs data

The import and export values of goods recorded in the balance of payments are derived from customs statistics as the primary data source, through a series of adjustment procedures. However, as noted earlier, these customs statistics are compiled according to principles that differ from those used in compiling the balance of payments. Consequently, the following adjustments are made to ensure that the coverage of the data aligns with the requirements of the balance of payments. First, based on the customs statistics, items of general merchandise that are missing from this data must be added, while items that are included in customs statistics but do not fall within the category of general merchandise must be excluded. Next, high-value capital goods are adjusted based on the change-in-ownership basis. In addition, import values in customs statistics, which are reported on a CIF basis, must be converted to an FOB basis. Through these adjustments, the total value of general merchandise is derived. Finally, the net exports of goods under merchanting and non-monetary gold are added to the amount of general merchandise to obtain the total amount of imports and exports of goods.

Table 13.5 Procedures for adjusting customs data to the value of goods on a balance of payments basis[1]

	Adjustment (example)	Exports	Imports
	The amount of merchandise trade statistics provided in the source data		
+	Goods supplied to foreign vessels or aircraft at ports or airports (fuel, stores)		
+	Direct sales of fish and minerals collected by resident vessels on the high seas		
+	Illegally imported and exported goods whose ownership changes		
+	Goods acquired from other economies for processing abroad	Not applicable	
+	Goods sold abroad after processing in other economies		Not applicable
+/-	Goods with ownership changes in customs warehouses or other zones		
-	Migrants' personal effects		
-	Goods imported for construction projects by non-resident enterprises		
-	Goods temporarily exported or imported for repair or storage without change of ownership		
-	Goods sent abroad or returned after processing without change of ownership		
-	Returned goods		
+/-	High-value capital goods (e.g., ships), when delivery differs from change of ownership		
-	CIF/FOB adjustment	Not applicable	
+	Net exports of goods under merchanting		Not applicable
+	Non-monetary gold		
=	Total value of goods on a balance of payments basis		

Footnote: 1) Source: BPM6, Table 10.2

The table below illustrates imports and exports of goods in South Korea's balance of payments for 2015. In that year, the total exports of goods amounted to USD 543.1 billion, and the total imports of goods amounted to USD 422.8 billion, resulting in the total balance of goods of USD 120.3 billion (= 543.1 – 422.8). Of this total, the balance of general merchandise was USD 112.6 billion, net exports of goods under merchanting were USD 8.0 billion, and the balance of non-monetary gold was -USD 0.3 billion.

Table 13.6 Example of balance of payments for goods (South Korea, 2015)

(Unit: billion US dollar)

Item	Debits (1)	Credits (2)	Balance (2-1)
Balance of goods			120.3
Exports of goods (FOB)		543.1	
Imports of goods (FOB)	422.8		
Balance of general merchandise			112.6
General merchandise, exports (FOB)		534.2	
General merchandise, imports (FOB)	421.6		
Net exports of goods under merchanting		8.0	8.0
Balance of non-monetary gold			-0.3
Non-monetary gold, exports (FOB)		0.9	
Non-monetary gold, imports (FOB)	1.2		

Annex to 13.3.2: Merchanting, Goods sent abroad for processing, and Factoryless goods producers

In the 2008 SNA, the treatment of *merchanting* and *goods sent abroad for processing* among the international transactions have been changed in different ways from 1993 SNA. This annex examines the accounting treatment of these two types of international transactions, as well as the treatment of *factoryless goods production*, which has attracted attention as a new form of international production introduced in the 2025 SNA.

1. Merchanting

Merchanting is a trade service activity in which a merchant purchases goods from a third country and sells them directly to another third country without physically passing through the merchant's country. In the 1993 SNA, merchanting was recorded as the export of services by the merchant's country, but in the 2008 SNA, it is treated as a trade in goods as the merchant effectively owns the goods. According to the 2008 SNA, trade in goods is recorded on the basis of the change of ownership rather than the physical movement of goods. Thus, even if goods are exported directly from country A to country B without passing through the merchant's country C, the goods are recorded as imported by country C (the owner) and then exported again by country C.

Figure 13.2 Structure of merchanting*

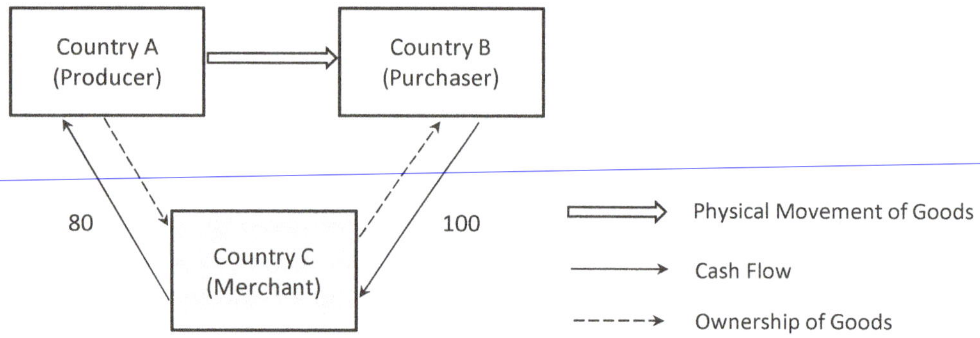

* Footnote: Cited from Chart 6.2, The Impact of Globalization on National Accounts (UNECE, 2011).

In the 2008 SNA, the treatment of merchanting involves recording the purchase of goods by the merchant as a negative entry (-) in export of goods, and recording the sale of these goods to a third country as a positive entry (+) in export of goods. The difference between these two transactions is recorded on a net basis under the item "net exports of goods under merchanting." In this context, the valuation is based on the actual transaction price, and the FOB price standard does not apply. If goods are only purchased without being sold, they are recorded as an increase in inventories in the country where the owner resides (regardless of the physical location of the goods (even if they are abroad). In this case, it is recorded, in the use table, as a negative export and an increase of inventory of the goods. For example, as illustrated in Figure 13.2, if a merchant in country C purchases goods at $80 from country A and sells them to country B at $100, the treatment in the balance of payments of each country is as follows.

Table 13.7 Treatment of merchanting in the balance of payments by country

Country	Transaction	Amount
Country A	Export of goods	80
Country B	Import of goods	100
Country C	**Net exports of goods under merchanting**	20
	(Export)	(-80)
	(Export)	(100)

The main purpose of changing the treatment of merchanting in this way is to eliminate statistical discrepancies between the values of imports and exports of goods across borders. For example, under previous method, if a merchant in Hong Kong purchases a good from China for 80 dollars and sells it to the United States for 100 dollars, China's exports would be recorded as 80 dollars, while the U.S. imports would be recorded as 100 dollars, resulting in a 20-dollar discrepancy in international trade statistics. However, under the new treatment method, an additional export of goods as merchanting (20 dollars) is recorded for Hong Kong, thereby eliminating this discrepancy in international trade statistics.

Despite this change, merchanting is still treated as the output of trade services (merchanting service) within the domestic economy. At this time, in the balance of payments, the net exports of goods under merchanting are also recorded as a single item and not disaggregated by goods.

Next, let us examine how merchanting is specifically presented in the supply and use tables. Suppose the following basic data is provided by the merchant:

Basic data of merchanting (unit: amount)

Opening inventory: 10	Closing inventory: 15
Merchanting purchases: 50	Merchanting sales: 70

From these data, the cost of goods sold from merchanting can be calculated by the following formula:

- Cost of goods sold (C) = opening inventories (A) + Merchanting purchases (B) – Closing inventories (D)

If the merchanting sales (E) are given, the merchanting margin can be calculated as:

- Merchanting margin = Sales (E) – Cost of goods sold (= A + B – D)

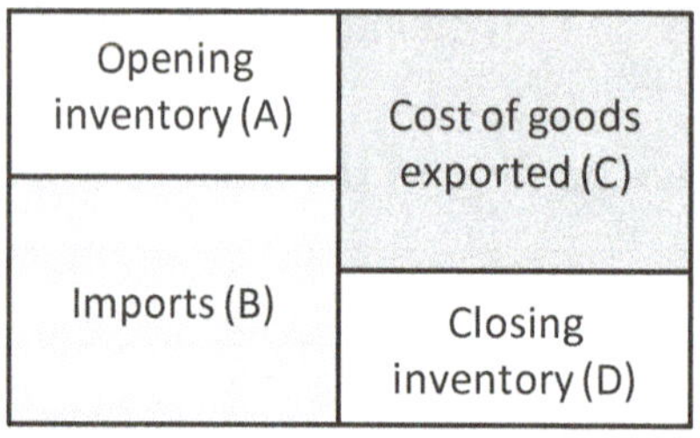

Applying this relationship to the data above, the cost of goods sold for merchanting is 10 + 50 – 15 = 45, and the merchanting margin is 70 – 45 = 25. This situation can be expressed in the supply and use tables as follows. In the supply table, the merchanting margin, calculated as "sales – cost of goods sold" (= E - C), is recorded as output from merchanting. In the use table, the change in inventories, calculated as "closing inventories – opening inventories" (= D – A), and the amount of net exports, calculated as "sales – purchases" (= E – B), are shown in the exports column. The sum of these two items in the use table is (D – A) + (E – B) = E – C, which matches the merchanting margin recorded in the supply table.

Table 13.8 Treatment of merchanting in the supply and use tables

Supply table

	Domestic output	Imports	Total supply
Distribution margin (Merchanting)	E-C		E-C

Use table

	Changes in inventories	Net exports	Total use
Distribution margin (Merchanting)	D-A	E-B	E-C (= E-(A+B-D))

Meanwhile, because data on merchanting transactions does not appear in customs statistics, it can only be obtained through separate surveys of individual enterprises engaged in merchanting. The data items that need to be collected are merchanting exports, merchanting imports, and changes in inventories during the period, as mentioned in the previous example.

2. Goods sent abroad for processing

Goods sent abroad for processing are a type of trade where raw materials or parts are provided to an enterprise in another country for the purpose of processing, and after processing, the finished goods are exported back to the home country or to a third country. For example, if an enterprise in country A (the principal) sends raw materials worth $100 to an enterprise in country B (the processor) for processing, the enterprise in country B may return the processed goods worth $140 to country A or sell them in the domestic market of country B or to a third country. In this case, raw materials or parts needed for processing can be directly provided by country A requesting the processing or may be procured from a third country.

Under the 1993 SNA, these transactions were recorded based on the physical movement of goods. Thus, when country A provided materials to country B, it was treated as exports of goods ($100), and when the processed goods ($140) were returned, it was treated as imports of goods. However, in the 2008 SNA, a change has been made to treat all transactions based on the change of economic ownership rather than physical movement of goods. Accordingly, in both countries, the cross-border movement of goods for processing is no longer recorded as exports and imports of goods. Instead, only the service transactions in relation with processing are recorded. In the example above, country A records only $40 payment for processing services as an import of service, while country B records the same amount ($40) as an export of service (Table 13.10).

With the change to this treatment of goods sent abroad for processing, the practical recording in national accounts can now be aligned with the business accounting practices based on the change of ownership. Moreover, from the perspective of international trade statistics, it prevents situations where simple processing trade transactions that do not involve a change in ownership are still recorded as exports and imports of goods, thus avoiding the problem of overstating trade figures.

Table 13.9 Treatment of goods sent abroad for processing under the 1993 SNA

Country A (Principal)

Supply table		Use table	
Import of processed goods	140	Export of goods for processing	100

Country B (Processor)

Supply table		Use table			
Import of goods for processing	100	IC of goods for processing	100	Export of processed goods	140
Output of processed goods	140				

Table 13.10 Treatment of goods sent abroad for processing under the 2008 SNA

Country A (Principal)

Supply table		Use table	
Import of processing services	40	IC of processing services	40
		IC of goods for processing	100
		Value added	10
		Output of goods	150

Country B (Processor)

Supply table		Use table	
Output of processing services	40	Export of processing services	40

This change in accounting treatment does not affect GDP, but it does alter the composition of intermediate inputs and outputs in both the principle and the processor countries, ultimately affecting the productivity analysis. Specifically, in the principal country, both processing services and goods for processing are counted as intermediate inputs when processing is outsourced. In contrast, in the processor country, goods for processing are excluded from intermediate inputs, and if the goods being processed are in work-in-progress, they are not recorded as changes in inventories. As a result, the composition of inputs and outputs differs between the two countries, which can lead to different outcomes in the productivity indicator analysis.

Types of goods sent abroad for processing and their accounting treatments

Goods sent abroad for processing, including the case above, can be categorized into four types (Figure 13.3). The first type is when the principal country (country A) outsources the processing of raw materials to the processor country (country B) and, after processing, the finished goods are re-imported to the principal country (country A). In this case, as described above, country A records an import of processing service ($40), while country B records an export of processing services for the same amount ($40).

The second type is when the principal country (country A) outsources the processing of raw materials to the processor country (country B), but after processing, the finished goods (processed goods) are not imported back to country A. Instead, they are sold directly in the processor country (country B) or to a third country (country C). In this case, country A still records the processing service fee paid to country B as an import of service ($40), and because the ownership of the finished goods (processed goods, $140) remains with country A, the processed goods are recorded as output of country A and treated as an export of good ($140) of country A.

Figure 13.3 Types of goods sent abroad for processing

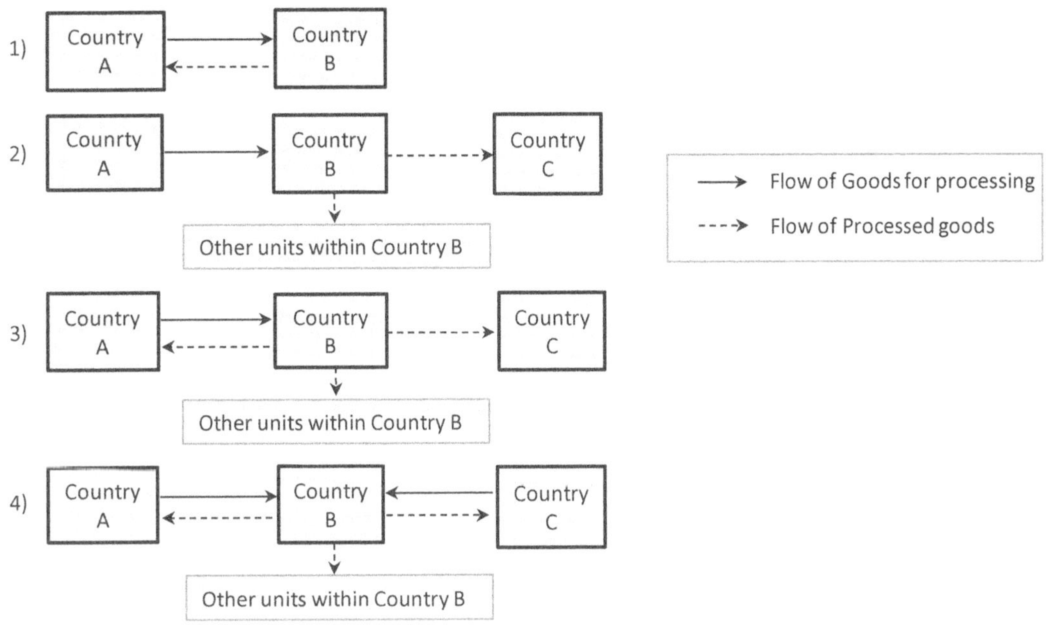

The third type is when the principal country (country A) outsources the processing to the processor country (country B) and re-imports only part of the total output ($90 out of $140), with the remainder ($50) sold in the processor country or to a third country. The accounting treatment for this case is as follows. On the supply side, the principal country (country A) records all of the processed goods as domestic output (90+50=140), while the processing fee paid to country B is recorded as an import of processing service ($40). On the use side, domestic use ($90) and an export of good ($50) are recorded. In the processor country (country B), there is an export of processing service ($40), and if part of the processed goods is used domestically ($50), country B records an import of good ($50).

The fourth type is when the processor country (country B) procures some of the raw materials needed for processing from the principal country (country A), and the rest from the processor country or from a third country. In this case, since the ownership of the processed goods remains with the principal country, all raw materials procured from abroad are treated as imports of the principal country (country A). For example, suppose the following data is given (Table 13.11): the processing fee paid by the principal country to the processor country is $250, and the processor country procures raw materials worth $150 from the principal country and $500 from a third country. The total value of the processed goods is $1,000, and it is also assumed that 10% of the goods are reimported and sold domestically in the principal country, while 90% of them are sold locally in the processor country (on the assumption that all sales of processed goods are for the final use).

Table 13.11 Data on goods sent abroad for processing by the principal country

Output	Destination of processed goods		Processing fee	Origin of raw materials	
	Country A	Country B		Country A	Country C
$1,000	10%	90%	$250	$150	$500

Based on this data, the supply and use tables for the principal country can be compiled as follows (Table 13.12). In the supply table, output of processed goods is recorded as $1,000, an import of raw materials as $500, and an import of processing services as $250. In the use table, intermediate consumption of raw material is recorded as $650 (= 150+500), final use as $100 (=1,000×10%), and export of goods as $900 (= 1,000×90%).

Table 13.12 Accounting treatment of the principal country

Supply table

	Materials	Finished goods	Imports	Total supply
Materials	150		500	650
Processing service			250	250
Finished goods		1,000		1,000
Output	150	1,000	750	1,900

Use table

	Intermediate consumption	Final use	Exports	Total use
Materials	650			650
Processing service	250			250
Finished goods		100	900	1,000
Total	900	100	900	1,900
Value added	100			
Output	1,000			

Meanwhile, the treatment of compiling the supply and use table in the country of processor (country B) is as follows (Table 4.26). In the supply table, the output of processing service is recorded at $250, and the import of processed good at $900. In the use table, the export of processing services is recorded at $250 and the final use of the processed goods at $900.

Table 13.13 Accounting treatment of the processor country

Supply table

	Materials	Finished goods	Imports	Total supply
Materials				-
Processing service		250		250
Finished goods			900	900
Output	-	250	900	1,150

Use table

	Intermediate consumption	Final use	Exports	Total use
Materials				-
Processing service			250	250
Finished goods		900		900
Total	-	900	250	1,150
Value added				
Output	-			

The data required to compile the goods sent abroad for processing can be collected through two channels as follows (Table 13.14). The first source is customs statistics on imports and exports, which provide details on goods sent for processing and finished processed goods. The second source is sample surveys of enterprises, which investigate the following items: For the enterprises commissioning processing (principal country), surveys include the processing service fees paid to the processor, the shares of processed goods sold domestically in the principal country versus abroad, and the shares of raw materials sourced domestically (principal country) versus abroad. For the enterprises undertaking processing (processor country), surveys include revenue from the processing service fees, and the shares of re-export to the principal country versus sales domestically (processor country) or in third countries.

Table 13.14 Details of basic data for estimating goods sent abroad for processing

<table>
<tr><td rowspan="2">Customs statistics</td><td>Export</td><td>·Value of raw materials exported for processing abroad
·Value of goods exported after processing by domestic enterprises</td></tr>
<tr><td>Import</td><td>·Value of goods imported after processing abroad
·Value of raw materials imported by domestic enterprises for processing</td></tr>
<tr><td rowspan="2">Business surveys</td><td>Principal</td><td>·Processing service fees paid
·Value of processed goods: Shares of re-import into the principal country versus overseas sales
·Value of raw materials used for processing: Shares sourced domestically (the principal country) versus abroad</td></tr>
<tr><td>Processor</td><td>·Revenue from processing service fees
·Value of finished processed goods: Shares of re-export to the principal country versus domestic sales (the processor country) or to third countries</td></tr>
</table>

3. Factoryless Goods Production

Factoryless goods production (FGP) refers to an arrangement where an enterprise directly owns manufacturing plants or production facilities abroad and carries out all production activities there, subsequently importing the finished goods into its home country or selling them in third countries. A factoryless goods producer holds intellectual property capital, such as manufacturing technology and designs of goods, provides these technologies to the overseas manufacturing plants it has invested in, while the procurement of raw materials required for production is independently handled by the local manufacturing facility abroad. Thus, goods produced abroad under this arrangement are recorded as imports by the factoryless goods producer and treated as intermediate consumption of this producer. Consequently, factoryless goods producers are classified within the manufacturing industry. The accounting treatment for domestic sales of these imported goods is as follows:

- **If consumed domestically in the FGP country**: The value of imported goods ($100), which reflects raw materials and manufacturing costs abroad, are recorded as intermediate inputs domestically, while the value of output ($150), which includes domestic intellectual property and design costs, is recorded as intermediate or final consumption domestically.
- **If sold directly in the overseas producing country or third countries**: The transaction is recorded as exports of goods by the FGP country. The value of imports from the overseas country of production ($100) is reflected in domestic intermediate inputs, and the corresponding output ($150) is recorded as exports of goods.

An illustrative example of the national accounting treatment of factoryless goods production (FGP) is as follows. Suppose that a principal in country A contracts a manufacturer in country B to produce goods. Country B imports intermediate inputs ($3) from another foreign country, produces finished goods ($7), and supplies them to country A. Country A then incorporates inputs related to intellectual property products and other input costs to produce a new finished good (28), which is exported to a third country. In the supply and use tables, the transactions are recorded as follows. Under the FGP arrangement with the principal in country A, country B imports intermediate inputs ($3), produces finished goods ($7), and exports these goods to country A. The principal in country A records the imported finished goods from country B as intermediate consumption in its production process, while the completed product ($28) is recorded as exports. The resulting value added (28 – 7 =21) is recorded as value added generated without a physical manufacturing process, reflecting the contribution of intellectual property products and related inputs.

Table 13.15 Presentation of factoryless goods production in the supply and use tables

Country A (Principal)

Supply table

	Manufacturing	Imports	Total
Materials		7	7
Finished goods	28		28
Total	28	7	35

Use table

	Manufacturing	Exports	Total
Materials	7		7
Finished goods		28	28
Value added	21		
Total	28		

B 국 (Contractor)

Supply table

	Manufacturing	Imports	Total
Materials		3	3
Finished goods	7		7
Total	7	3	10

Use table

	Manufacturing	Exports	Total
Materials	3		3
Finished goods		7	7
Value added	4		
Total	7		

To qualify as a factoryless goods producer, the enterprise must be the substantive investor in intellectual property capital (such as manufacturing technology) abroad, and the value added generated from this Intellectual property products must exceed 50% of total value-added (Recommendations of Advisory Experts Group on National Accounts, IMF 2014).

Factoryless goods production Is also associated with merchanting or goods sent abroad for processing described above. To distinction between factoryless goods production and merchanting lies in whether the enterprise meets the aforementioned criteria (i.e., the enterprise being the substantive investor in intellectual property capital and the investment returns from this capital exceeding 50% of total value added). If these criteria are met, the activity is classified as factoryless goods production; if not, it is treated as merchanting.

The distinction between factoryless goods production and goods sent abroad for processing is that factoryless goods producers do not engage at all in providing raw materials used in foreign manufacturing processes, while contract manufacturers independently procure the raw materials required for production. Meanwhile Imports of goods by factoryless goods producers are classified as general merchandise imports of the principal in the balance of payments (Table 13.16).

Table 13.16 Distinction between merchanting, goods sent abroad for processing, and factoryless goods production

		Merchanting	Goods sent abroad for processing	Factoryless goods production (IPP investors, Value added of IPP>50%)
Principal	Balance of payments	Export and import of goods (commodities for merchanting)[1)]	Import of services (processing services)	Import of goods (general commodities)
	Domestic industry classification	Wholesale trade	Manufacturing[2)]	Manufacturing[3)]
Contract manufacturer	Balance of payments	Export of goods	Export of services	Export of goods
	Domestic industry classification	Manufacturing	Manufacturing (processing services)	Manufacturing

Footnote: 1) In the supply and use tables, imports of goods are recorded as negative exports and increase in inventories, while exports of goods are recorded as increase in exports and decrease in inventories.

2) In the goods sent abroad for processing trade, processing fees and raw material inputs for processing are treated as intermediate consumption by the principal.

3) Sales by the overseas contract manufacturer are treated as imports of goods and intermediate consumption by the factoryless goods producer.

13.3.3 Imports and exports of services in the balance of payments

The classification of imports and exports of services in the balance of payments follows the examples set out in BPM6. According to BPM6, service items include manufacturing services on physical inputs owned by others; maintenance and repair services; transport services; travel services; construction services; insurance and pension services; financial services; charges for the use of intellectual property; telecommunications, computer, and information services; other business services; personal, cultural, and recreational services; and government goods and services (see Table 13.17). This classification is primarily "product-based", but it also includes "transactor-based" classification such as travel services, construction services, and government goods and services. Since the transactor-based classification is displayed as a mixture of goods and services, additional disaggregation is needed to apply the product-based classification in the supply and use tables.

To meet this need for further disaggregation, the "Manual on Statistics of International Trade in Services 2010" (MSITS 2010, United Nations et al.) presents an alternative classification system that differs from the above classification of balance of payments. This classification, known as the Extended Balance of Payments Services Classification 2010 (EBOPS 2010), is included as an annex to MSITS 2010.

13.3.3.1 Classification of imports and exports of services

Below is a brief overview of service items classified in the balance of payments.

Manufacturing services on physical inputs owned by others refers to transactions in which raw materials are provided to a processor without a change of ownership, processed into finished goods, and then returned to the principal (the owner of the raw materials) in exchange for a processing service fee. Since there is no change of ownership in the import (or export) of raw materials for processing, only the processing fee is recorded as an export of services (or import of services). In the balance of payments, the transactions of this service are recorded in the following way. The debit entries record the fees paid by the domestic principal to the foreign processor for processing the domestic raw materials. Conversely, the credit entries record the fees received for providing the processing services on imported raw materials.

Maintenance and repair services arise when a non-resident provides maintenance and repair services for goods owned by a resident (recorded as debits) or when a resident provides these services for goods owned by a non-resident (recorded as credits). Repairs of ships, aircraft, and other transportation vehicles are included in this category.

Transport services are divided into passenger services and freight services. For passenger services, debits are recorded for payments to non-resident carriers for the international movement of residents, while credits are recorded for payments from non-residents to resident carriers for the international movement of non-residents. Freight services record international freight charges arising from the imports or exports of goods. These freight services can also occur in the imports and exports of materials for processing without a change of ownership, or in personal household moving goods. In both the balance of payments and national accounts, the value of imports and exports of goods is recorded on an FOB basis. Therefore, for imported goods recorded on a CIF basis, the freight costs included in these CIF values are separately extracted and recorded as a service item. Thus, the export values recorded on an FOB basis do not require any adjustment, but the import values recorded on a CIF basis must have the freight costs extracted and allocated to this item. Similarly, in the supply and use tables, CIF/FOB adjustments are made in the import column for goods recorded on a CIF basis to prevent double counting of freight charges. (See 13.3.4 for details.)

Travel services are divided into "business travel services" and "personal travel services" that are performed for purposes other than business. The debit entries of travel services record the amount of goods and services acquired by residents while traveling abroad, and the credit entries of travel services record the amount of goods and services acquired by non-residents while traveling domestically. Travel services also include expenditures for studying abroad or for medical treatment, but exclude goods purchased for resale purpose (which are treated as imports and exports of goods). Travel services as recorded in the balance of payments do not have direct match in the CPC product classification. Unlike other services, travel services encompass all goods and services associated with travel, making them complex services. The category of travel services includes goods, transport services, accommodation, food and beverage services, telecommunications, car rental, and insurances acquired by travelers.

When applying travel services from the balance of payments to national accounts, particularly the supply and use tables, it is necessary to further break them down by type of good or service. (for details, see "14.11 Travel services"). In this process, travel services may be provided with a separate supplementary breakdown by product group as follows: (1) goods, (2) transport services, (3) accommodation services, (4) food-serving services, and (5) other service.

Construction covers the creation, renovation, repair or extension of buildings and structures, as well as land improvements. This category also includes goods and services purchased by construction enterprises in the local country where the construction is taking place. Construction, like travel services, fall under a "transactor-based" classification, so when applied to the supply and use tables, they must be further broken down by products.

In the case of overseas construction, a resident domestic enterprise's participation in foreign construction project is recorded as credits, and the goods and services purchased by the domestic enterprise in the non-resident country where the construction project is performed are recorded as debits. On the contrary, in the case of domestic construction of the compiling country, when a foreign construction enterprise undertakes construction activities in the domestic economy, it is recorded on the debit side. The goods and services acquired by the foreign construction enterprise from domestic enterprises are recorded on the credit side. All of these entries are recorded on a gross basis.

Insurance and pension services include life insurance, pensions, non-life insurance (including freight insurance), reinsurance, standardized guarantees, and auxiliary services to insurance. For detailed calculation methods of service charges for life and non-life insurance, see 14.3.3. **Financial services** include deposit-taking and lending from financial intermediaries and other auxiliary services (such as issuance of letters of credit, credit card services, and other services). The types of service charges for financial services are broadly classified into explicit charges, margins on buying and selling financial instruments, and FISIM. Among these, FISIM is an implicit charge for financial intermediation services provided by financial intermediaries and is recorded separately from interest receivable and interest payable. (For more details, see Section 14.3.2.)

Charges for the use of intellectual property cover charges for the use of proprietary rights (such as patents, trademarks and copyrights), as well as charges for licenses to reproduce or distribute intellectual property embodied in produced originals and related rights. **Telecommunications, computer, and information services** include the following three categories: (1) telecommunication services such as broadcasting, telephone, and e-mail; (2) computer hardware- and software-related services, data-processing services; and (3) information services such as news agency services and database services. **Other business services** include R&D services; professional and management consulting services; technical, trade-related, and other business services; waste treatment and depollution; agricultural and mining services; and operating leasing. **Personal, cultural and recreational services** consist of (1) audiovisual and related services and (2) other personal, cultural, and recreational services.

Finally, **government goods and services** cover (1) goods and services provided by and to enclaves (such as embassies, military bases, international organizations, etc.), and (2) goods and services acquired locally by diplomats, military personnel and their dependents living abroad, and (3) all other services provided by or to governments. Since diplomats, military personnel, and their dependents residing abroad are classified as non-residents of the host country, the goods and services they acquire locally are recorded as imports of government goods and services. Similarly, diplomats, military personnel, and their dependents residing in enclaves in the domestic economy are non-residents, and the goods and services they acquire in the economy are included in exports of government goods and services as international transactions. Visa fees charged by the consulate in the host economy are also included under government goods and services. The supply and acquisition of goods and services by international organizations are classified as government goods and services as well. However, expenditures by employees of international organizations or local nationals employed at embassies and military bases are not included in the government goods and services. (These are classified as resident-to-resident transactions.)

The debit side of this service item records goods and services acquired by embassies, military bases, etc. locating abroad, and the credit side records goods and services acquired by foreign embassies, military bases, and international organizations locating in the domestic economy. When recording government goods and services in the supply and use tables, adjustments must be made to break down the aggregate amounts into the goods and services actually consumed. Since government goods and services are recorded as a mixed total of various consumption goods and services, they must be appropriately allocated to specific categories such as consumption goods, education services, and health services.

13.3.3.2 Example of compiling the imports and exports of services

The table below (Table 13.17) illustrates the balance of payments on the services sector in South Korea for the year 2015. Debit entries represent payments for services made abroad (imports of services), while credit entries represent receipts of services from abroad (exports of services). In 2015, total payments for services to the rest of the world amount to USD 112.1 billion, and total receipts for services from the rest of the world are USD 97.5 billion, resulting in a balance on services of –USD 14.6 billion.

Table 13.17 Example of balance of payments for services (South Korea, 2015)

(Unit: billion US dollar)

Item	Debits (1)	Credits (2)	Balance (2-1)
Services total	112.1	97.5	-14.6
Processing services	8.7	2.6	-6.1
Maintenance and repair services	0.4	0.3	0
Transport	29.5	34.1	4.7
Passenger services	2.7	3.9	1.2
Freight services	12.8	26.5	13.7
Other transport services	14	3.7	-10.3
Travel	25.3	14.8	-10.5
Construction	2.6	12.2	9.6
Insurance and pension services	0.8	0.7	-0.1
Direct insurance services	0.2	0.4	0.1
Reinsurance services	0.6	0.3	-0.2
Auxiliary services to insurance	0	0	0
Financial services	1.7	1.6	-0.1
Explicit charges, and other financial services	0.9	1.3	0.4
FISIM	0.8	0.3	-0.5
Charges for the use of intellectual property	10.1	6.6	-3.5
Telecommunications, computer & information services	2.8	3.5	0.7
Other business services	28.3	19	-9.3
Personal, cultural, and recreational services	0.7	0.9	0.2
Government goods and services	1.3	1.1	-0.3

13.3.4 Derivation of the freight and insurance services in the BOP

The transport and insurance services included in the value of imported goods, as recorded in customs statistics, must be reclassified into imports and exports of services in the balance of payments. In this section, this reclassification procedure is examined in more detail.

In cross-border trade transactions, the accounting treatment of freight services depends on the contractual terms between exporter and importer. The party responsible for freight costs can be stipulated in various ways (i.e., ex-works, FOB, CIF, etc.), and this determines whether the exporter or importer bears the cost. Consequently, whether a resident or non-resident ultimately pays the freight charge directly affects the amount of service transactions in the balance of payments. Because customs statistics report import values simply on a CIF basis, one cannot readily determine from those data alone whether the freight should be attributed to a resident a non-resident in the compilation of balance of payments.

A practical example of converting imported goods valued at CIF price (from customs data) into FOB price (as required by the balance of payments) is as follows. In order to reconcile CIF prices to FOB prices for individual commodities of imports, freight and insurance premiums must first be separated out. The BPM6 recommends estimating them on a commodity-by-commodity basis, but if this is not feasible, they must be disaggregated to the extent that they are available (BPM6 10.34). Let the total freight and insurance on imported cargo be "A", as calculated from customs data. This total A can be split into two components: the portion by resident carriers ("B") and the portion by non-resident carriers ("C"). However, if customs data do not directly report either the total A or the breakdown between resident carriers and non-resident carriers, a separate survey should be conducted targeting resident carriers for which data can be obtained (see Figure 13.4). From such a survey, one should collect:

- B = Freight and insurance earned on imported goods by resident carriers
- The share of resident carriers = the proportion of total imports carried by resident carriers

Using these two pieces of information, the total freight and insurance for all imported goods (A) and the freight and insurance by non-resident carriers (C) can be indirectly estimated as follows:

- Total freight and insurance for imported goods (A) = freight and insurance for goods imported by resident carriers (B) / the share by resident carriers
- Freight and insurance for goods imported by non-resident carriers (C) = total freight and insurance for imported goods (A) x (1– the share by resident carriers)

At this point, the amount C (= A – B), which is obtained by subtracting the freight and insurance for resident carriers (B) from the total freight and insurance for imported goods (A), is treated as imports of services (transport and insurance services in the BOP). The amount B, the portion of resident carriers, is treated as follows:

- The freight portion of B is recorded as output of the domestic transport industry.
- The insurance portion of B is split into (i) insurance service charges and (ii) net insurance premiums; the charges go to the production account (as output), and the net premiums go to the income transfers account.

Figure 13.4 Procedure for converting CIF prices to FOB prices

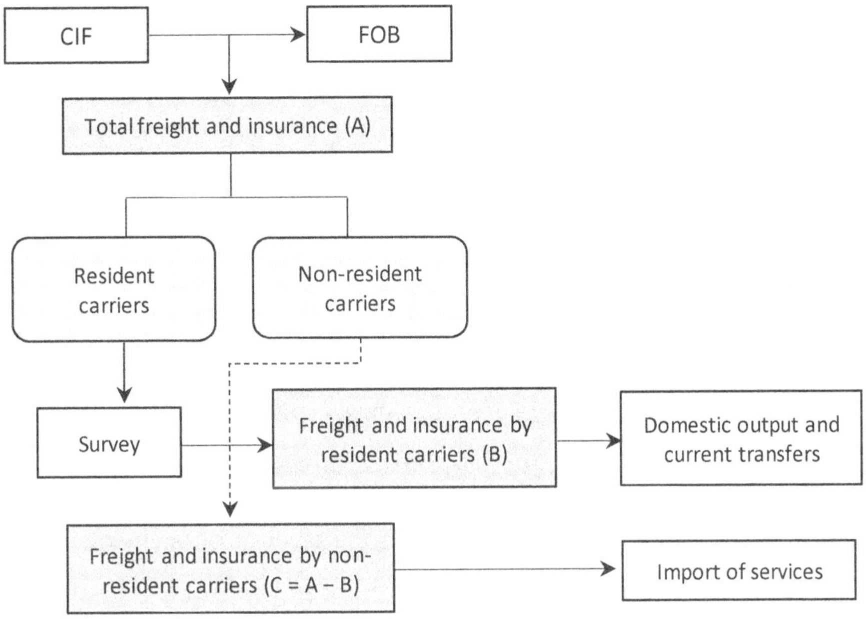

Annex to 13.3.4: Treatments of imports/exports of the freight and insurance in the BOP and the supply and use tables

The balance of payments and the supply and use tables differ in how they treat freight and insurance charges included in imported goods. In summary, in the balance of payments, freight and insurance charges paid to non-resident carriers are recorded as imports of services, while freight and insurance charges paid to resident carriers are recorded as domestic service transactions (i.e., output of the domestic transport or insurance industry). On the other hand, in the supply and use tables, freight and insurance charges paid to non-resident carriers are treated exactly as in the balance of payments, that is, imports of services. However, the freight and insurance charges paid to resident carriers are recorded as imputed exports of services to offset the CIF value of imports.

The statistics on imports of goods used in both the balance of payments and the supply and use tables are based on customs data, which are compiled using the CIF value recorded by the importer on the "import declaration." However, since the balance of payments records both imports and exports of goods on an FOB basis, it is necessary to separate the freight and insurance from the CIF price of imported goods and make the appropriate adjustments. In this process, freight and insurance charges paid to non-resident carriers are deducted from the CIF price and reclassified as imports of services, while freight and insurance charges paid to resident carriers are similarly deducted from the CIF price but treated as "output of the domestic transport and insurance industries."

Figure 13.5 Treatment of freight charges for imported goods in the balance of payments

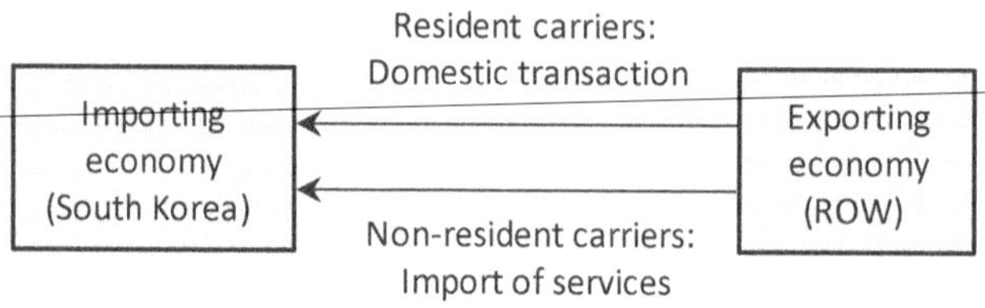

For example, if the CIF value of imported goods is $110, of which $7 is the freight and insurance charges paid to non-resident carrier, and $3 is the freight and insurance charges to resident carrier, the balance of payments will record only $100 (FOB) for imports of goods and $7 for imports of services.

Figure 13.6 Example of treating the freight and insurance for imported goods in the BOP

By contrast, in the supply and use tables, the freight and insurance charge ($7) on goods transported by non-resident carriers is also recorded as an import of services, the same as the balance of payments, but the freight and insurance charge paid to resident carriers is recorded together with an import of goods on a CIF basis, while the equivalent amount of $3 is imputed as an *export of services*. Thus, if the freight by resident carriers is recorded as an export of services in compiling the use table, this amount must be deducted from the use table when converting to the SNA standards through the CIF/FOB adjustment. However, despite this formal compilation guideline, it is also practicable to deduct the entire CIF/FOB adjustment in aggregate in the supply table without recording it as an export of services in the use table. In any case, it is most important to avoid duplication of the value of imports and maintain consistency between the source data and the supply and use tables.

Figure 13.7 Treatment of freight charges for Imported goods in the supply and use tables

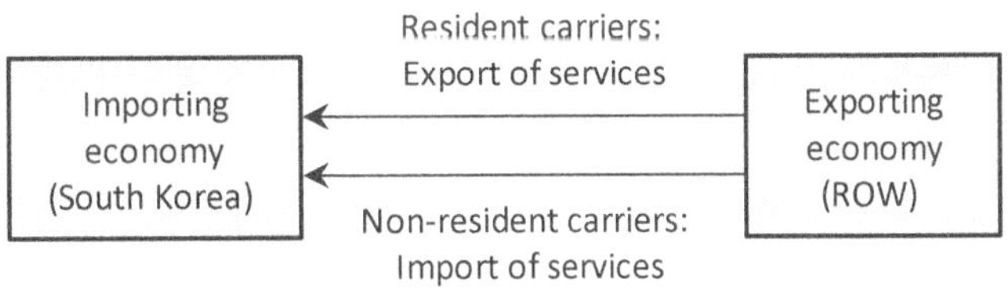

In the case of exports of goods, no separate adjustment is required as the value of exports is displayed at FOB prices in the "export declaration" submitted by exporters to customs office. However, the freight charges paid to resident carriers are treated as "exports of services", while the freight charges paid to non-resident carriers are not reflected in the balance of payments because they are transactions between non-residents.

Figure 13.8 Treatment of freight charges for exported goods in both the BOP and the supply and use tables

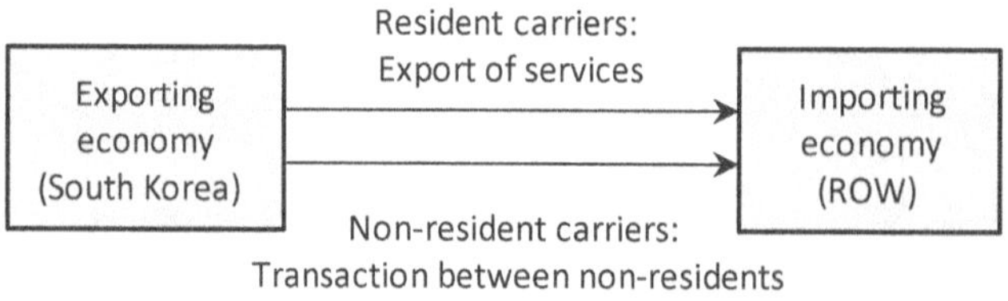

Box 13.1: Example of handling freight charges on imported goods in the SUP

This section examines in detail how freight charges on imported goods are presented in the supply and use tables. Referring back to the previous example, imported goods amount to 110 on a CIF basis, of which the freight of resident carrier is 3 and the freight of non-resident carrier is 7. Let us see how the supply and use tables are compiled and how the CIF/FOB adjustment is made in this case. The supply and use tables undergo the following preliminary adjustment (Table 13.18). First, the balance of payments table is prepared as shown below, and then the supply and use tables are derived based on this. In the balance of payments, an import of goods at FOB value (100) and an import of transport services (7) are recorded. In the supply table, an import of goods is recorded at 110 on a CIF basis (i.e., +10), while an import of transport services is shown as (-7). In the use table, an imputed export of transport services (+3) for the resident carriers is recorded.

Table 13.18 Recording freight services on imported goods in the BOP and the supply and use tables

Balance of payments

Import of goods	100
Import of transport services	7
...	
Total	107

Supply and use tables

	Supply table		Use table
	Import of goods	Import of transport services	Export of services
Goods	(+**10**)		
Services		(-**7**)	(+**3**)
Total	**(+10)**	**(-7)**	**(+3)**

The next step is illustrated in Table 13.19, which shows an example of the supply and use tables after adjustment, with a CIF/FOB row added to align with national accounts standards. In the supply table, the import of goods is adjusted by -10 to become 100 on an FOB basis, and the import of transport services is adjusted by +7 to match the balance of payments. In addition, the export of transport services (3) that had been recorded in the use table is deducted by 3, thereby achieving consistency with the balance of payments.

Table 13.19 CIF/FOB adjustment for freight charges on imported goods in the SUP

	Supply table				Use table		
	Domestic output	Imports: Goods (CIF)	Imports: Import of services	Total supply	Intermediate use and final use	Export of services	Total use
Goods		110		110	110		110
Services	3			3		3	3
CIF/FOB adjustment		**-10**	**7**	**-3**		**-3**	**-3**
Total	3	100 (FOB)	7	110	110	0	110

Box 13.2: Example of handling freight charges on exported goods in the SUP

This box examines in detail how freight charges on exported goods are treated in the supply and use tables. In the case of exports, goods are recorded at FOB prices. Suppose that during the transportation process, freight charges of 4 are paid to resident carriers and charges of 6 are paid to non-resident carriers. In this situation, the supply table records the freight of resident carriers (4) as output of the transport industry, and at the same time, the use table records an export of services (4). In contrast, the freight charge paid to non-resident carriers (6) is treated as a transaction between non-residents and therefore not reflected in the supply and use tables.

Table 13.20 Recording freight charges on exported goods in the supply and use table

	Supply table			Use table	
	Domestic output	Imports	Total supply	Export of services	Total use
Transport service	4		4	4	4
Total	4		4	4	4

13.3.5 Treatment of interest and FISIM in the balance of payments

In the balance of payments, the method of recording the interest receivable and interest payable is identical to that presented in the SNA; for a detailed explanation, see Chapter 14 (Section 14.3.2). In other words, in the balance of payments, actual interest receivable and interest payable are not recorded directly but are instead split into FISIM (financial intermediation services indirectly measured) and "pure interest" (which is called "SNA interest"). The procedure is as follows:

1. The actual interest receivable is divided into the FISIM on interest receivable and the pure interest receivable (SNA interest receivable), and the actual interest payable are divided into the FISIM on interest payable and the pure interest payable (SNA interest payable).
2. The FISIM on interest receivable and FISIM on interest payable are recorded as imports and exports of financial services, respectively.
3. The remaining SNA interest receivable and SNA interest payable are recorded in the earned income account. (See Figure 13.9 and Table 13.21.)

Figure 13.9 Distinction between the SNA interest and FISIM

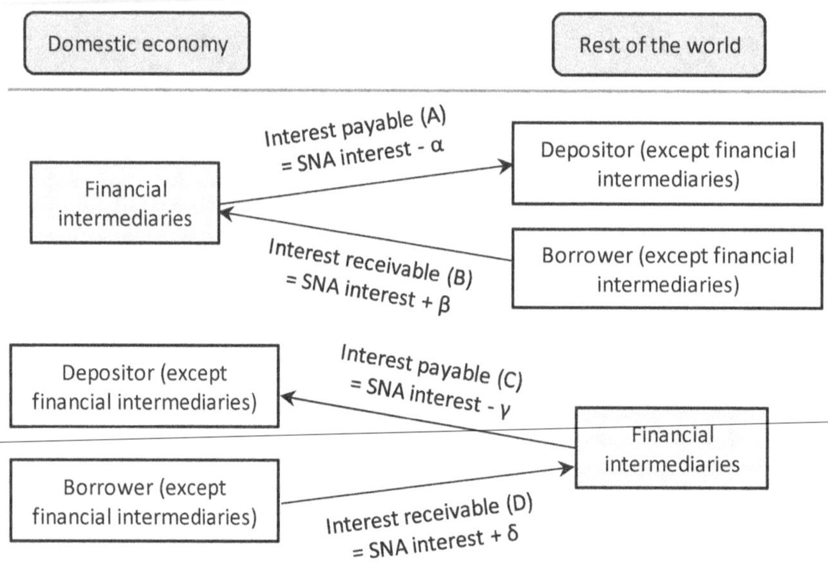

Footnote) α, β, γ, and δ are FISIM components.

Table 13.21 Accounting for the SNA interest and FISIM in the balance of payments

Goods and services account		Debit (imports)	Credit (exports)
	FISIM	$\gamma + \delta$	$\alpha + \beta$

Earned income account		Debit (interest payable)	Credit (interest receivable)
	Interest	$(A + \alpha) + (D - \delta)$	$(B - \beta) + (C + \gamma)$

13.3.6 Compilation of the international investment position

The international investment position (IIP) is a statistical statement that shows at a given point in time the value of external financial assets of residents of an economy (the sum of claims on non-residents and "gold bullion" held as reserve assets), and the value of liabilities of residents of an economy to non-residents. Gold bullion as monetary gold does not give rise to external claims, but is included in financial assets as reserve assets. In the IIP, the difference between the assets and liabilities is called the "net position," which represents either a net claim on or a net liability to the rest of the world. The IIP serves as a primary source for compiling balance sheets of the rest of the world in the SNA. The closing value of the IIP at the end of the period is derived by adding the changes during the period (flow accounts) to the opening value of the IIP at the beginning of the period. The table that shows all of these accounts together is called the **integrated international investment position statement**. The flow accounts for the period are broadly divided into the following two components:

1. Financial account: Derived from the balance of payments, it reflects changes in financial assets and liabilities arising actual transactions.
2. Other changes in financial assets and liabilities account: This account records changes in financial assets and liabilities other than transactions. It is subdivided into (a) *other changes in volume* (such as amortization of assets, economic appearance or disappearance of assets, and reclassification), and (b) *revaluations* (such as changes in exchange rates or other price changes).

Table 13.22 A format of integrated international investment position statement

	Opening IIP	Transaction (Financial account)	Other changes in volume	Revaluations		Closing IIP
				Exchange rate changes	Other price changes	
Assets (functional category) Direct investment Portfolio investment Financial derivatives and ESOs Other investment Reserve assets						
Total assets						
Liabilities (functional category) Direct investment Portfolio investment Financial derivatives and ESOs Other investment						
Total liabilities						
Net IIP						

The international investment position is measured from the perspective of residents, just like the balance of payments. The debit entries record assets of residents to non-residents, and the credit entries record liabilities of residents to non-residents. In this statement, assets and liabilities are presented in a classification by **functional categories** rather than the traditional balance sheet classification. These functional categories are direct investment, portfolio investment, financial derivatives and employee stock options (ESO), other investment, and reserve assets. The reason for using this functional classification is that economic relationships with nonresidents most commonly take the form of financial assets and liabilities. In addition to functional categories, BPM6 allows for the classification by financial instruments, by institutional sector of residents, by maturity of debt instruments (short-term, long-term), by currency (domestic currency, foreign currency), and by interest-rate type of debt instruments (variable rate, fixed-rate) (BPM6 7.12).

The table below (Table 13.23) illustrates South Korea's integrated international investment position statement as of 2015. At the end of 2015, South Korea had external financial assets of USD 1,144.0 billion, and external liabilities of USD 939.5 billion, yielding a net international investment position (net IIP) of USD 204.5 billion.

Table 13.23 Example of the integrated international investment position (South Korea, 2015)

(Unit: billion US dollar)

	Opening IIP	Transactions (Financial account)	Other changes in volume	Revaluation	Closing IIP
Assets (by functional category)					
Direct investment	260.5	23.7	0.0	1.7	285.9
Portfolio investment	204.8	41.9	0.0	-11.3	235.5
Financial derivatives	30.6	-48.0	0.0	46.9	29.5
Other investment	213.2	10.4	0.0	1.6	225.2
Reserve assets	363.6	12.1	0.0	-7.7	368.0
Total assets (A)	1,072.7	40.0	-	31.3	1,144.0
Liabilities (by functional category)					
Direct investment	179.4	4.1	0.0	-4.0	179.5
Portfolio investment	591.0	-7.7	0.0	-32.6	550.7
Financial derivatives	35.8	-49.8	0.0	51.8	37.8
Other investment	185.5	-9.6	0.0	-4.5	171.4
Total liabilities (B)	991.8	-63.0	-	10.7	939.5
Net IIP (A–B)	80.9	103.0	-	20.6	204.5

13.4 Compilation of the rest of the world accounts

Up to the previous sections, we examined how to compile the international accounts based on the BPM6. In this section, using those international account data, we will explain how to compile the rest of the world (ROW) accounts based on the SNA. The rest of the world accounts are the accounts within the sequence of economic accounts that records transactions and other flows between domestic sectors and nonresidents from the perspective of the rest of the world sector. Like other institutional sector accounts, the rest of the world accounts are compiled comprehensively, covering the current accounts, accumulation accounts, and balance sheets. In this section, we will examine how each account for the rest of the world sector is structured and compiled.

13.4.1 Compilation of the current account, capital account and financial account in the ROW accounts

Table 13.24 is the rest of the world account in the SNA format converted from the balance of payments data (Table 13.4). It is shown in US dollar, and the amounts converted to Korean currency are also listed. The rest of the world accounts are recorded from the perspective of non-residents, so the debit and credit entries of the balance of payments are displayed in reverse in the rest of the world accounts. For example, debits in the balance of payments, which record imports, income payable, and transfers payable by the domestic economy, correspond to credits (**revenues**) of the rest of the world account, as these are receipts from the viewpoint of nonresidents. Similarly, credits of the balance of payments, which record exports, income receivable, and transfers receivable by the domestic economy, correspond to debits (**expenditures**) of the rest of the world account, as these are expenditures by nonresidents.

In the rest of the world account, the balancing item of the financial account is calculated as the net acquisition of financial assets by nonresidents minus the net incurrence of liabilities, representing the ROW's net lending (+) or net borrowing (–). This amount should, in principle, be equal to the balancing items of the capital account. In the financial account, it is recorded on the right-hand side, whereas in the capital account, it is shown on the left-hand side.

Table 13.24 Conversion to the rest of the world accounts (South Korea, 2015)

Expenditures | Revenues

Rest of the world: Foreign currency (USD billion)	Rest of the world: Domestic currency (KRW trillion)	Transactions and balancing items	Rest of the world: Domestic currency (KRW trillion)	Rest of the world: Foreign currency (USD billion)
		Goods and services account		
		Imports of goods and services	599.3	534.9
		Imports of goods	478.5	422.8
		Imports of services	120.8	112.1
640.6	712.8	Exports of goods and services		
543.1	620.3	Exports of goods		
97.5	92.5	Exports of services		
-105.6	-113.5	Balance on goods and services (1)		
		Earned income account		
0.9	1.0	Remuneration of employees	1.4	1.3
		Taxes on production and imports		
		Subsidies		
24.2	27.4	Property income	21.7	19.4
12.3		Interest		5.7
8.1		Income on equity		11.6
3.9		Reinvested earnings		2.0
-4.5	-5.2	Balance on earned incomes (2)		
-110.1	-118.7	Balance on goods and services, and earned income (3=1+2)		
		Transfer income account		
8.8	11.6	Current transfers	15.8	13.8
		Current taxes on income and wealth		
		Net non-life insurance premiums		
		Non-life insurance claims		
0.3		Current international cooperation		1.7
8.6		Miscellaneous current transfers		12.1
5.0	4.2	Balance on transfer income (4)		
		Adjustment for the change in pension entitlements		
-105.1	-114.5	**Current account balance (5=3+4)**		
		Capital account		
0.1		Net acquisitions of non-produced non-financial assets	0.1	0.1
		Capital transfers receivable		0.0
0.0	0.0	Capital transfers payable		
0.1	0.1	Capital account balance (6)		
-105.1	-114.4	**Net lending (+)/net borrowing (-) (7=5+6)**		
		Financial account		
-13.1	-15.8	Net acquisition of financial assets		
		Net incurrence of liabilities	100.8	89.8
		Net lending (+)/net borrowing (-) (8)	-116.6	-103.0
		Statistical discrepancy (9= 8-7)	-2.2	2.1

13.4.2 Conversion from the integrated IIP to the rest of the world accounts

In the international accounts framework, the integrated international investment position (IIP) combines the financial account in the BOP, the other changes in financial assets and liabilities account, and the IIP itself. All components are compiled using the functional categories. To convert these international account data into the SNA-based rest of the world accounts, it is necessary to prepare a cross-classification table (see Table 13.25) that links the functional categories used in the international accounts with the classification of financial instruments used in the SNA. Using this table, each component of the identity "opening IIP + financial transactions + other changes in financial assets and liabilities (other changes in volume and revaluations) = closing IIP" can be translated from the functional classification to the national accounts classification. This enables the derivation of the flows and positions of financial assets and liabilities for the rest of the world sector according to the SNA framework.

Table 13.25 Table converting the integrated IIP to the SNA rest of the world accounts

SNA classification of financial assets and liabilities	Functional categories					
	Direct investment	Portfolio investment	Financial derivatives	Other investment	Reserve assets	Total
Assets						
Monetary gold and SDRs						
Currency and deposits						
Debt securities						
Loans						
Equity & investment fund						
Insurance, pension						
Financial derivatives & ESOs						
Other accounts receivable/payable						
Total assets						
Liabilities						
Monetary gold and SDRs						
Currency and deposits						
Debt securities						
Loans						
Equity & investment fund						
Insurance, pension						
Financial derivatives & ESOs						
Other accounts receivable/payable						
Total liabilities						

Chapter 14. Derivation of output for special industries (Supplement to Chapter 4)

The estimation methods of output introduced in section 1 of Chapter 4 are the standard approaches generally applicable to most industries. However, in this chapter, we will examine the methods of calculating output for certain industries that require specialized procedures beyond those conventional approaches. The reason these industries were not discussed together with other in Chapter 4 is twofold: first, because their methods of output estimation are unique; and second, because deriving their output values requires a prior understanding of the several complex concepts in the System of National Accounts. Therefore, the explanations provided in this chapter regarding the estimation of output for special industries are developed under the assumption that the reader has a sufficient understanding of the material covered up to Chapter 13.

14.1 Agriculture, forestry and livestock industry

Agriculture, forestry and livestock production are not corporate-based industries but rather production activities highly dependent on natural conditions, so it is difficult to collect output data directly at the establishment level. Therefore, it is essential to estimate output indirectly, mainly using production statistics from administrative agencies combined with item-specific unit prices. Since agricultural, forestry, and livestock products are well standardized by item and quality, output is generally calculated by multiplying the nation-wide production volume of each item by its corresponding selling price. This section provides a more detailed explanation of how to estimate the output of agricultural crops, livestock products, and forest products.

14.1.1 Estimation of agricultural output

The output of agricultural products is calculated as follows. The production volume is obtained by multiplying the *cultivated area* by the *yield per unit area*, and prices are valued at basic prices. The basic price refers to the amount actually received by the producer per unit of output from the purchaser, excluding any taxes on product and including any subsidies on product receivable per unit of output. In most countries, primary agricultural products that are traded without further processing are not subject to taxes on products. Generally, the **farm-gate price**, the price at which a purchaser buys products directly from the farm, is equivalent to the basic price.

- Output of agricultural product = harvested area × yield per unit area × farm-gate price

Agricultural products can experience inventory losses during the storage process after harvest. Therefore, the amount of the gross output minus recurrent inventory losses is used as the output value (**usable output**). The usable output can be divided into three categories according to its purpose of use: "output for market sales" (sales revenue and changes in inventories), "output for own final use" for which farmers use it for their own final consumption or gross fixed capital formation, and "output for own intermediate consumption" such as seeds for sowing and raw materials for processing.

Figure 14.1 Agricultural output and its uses

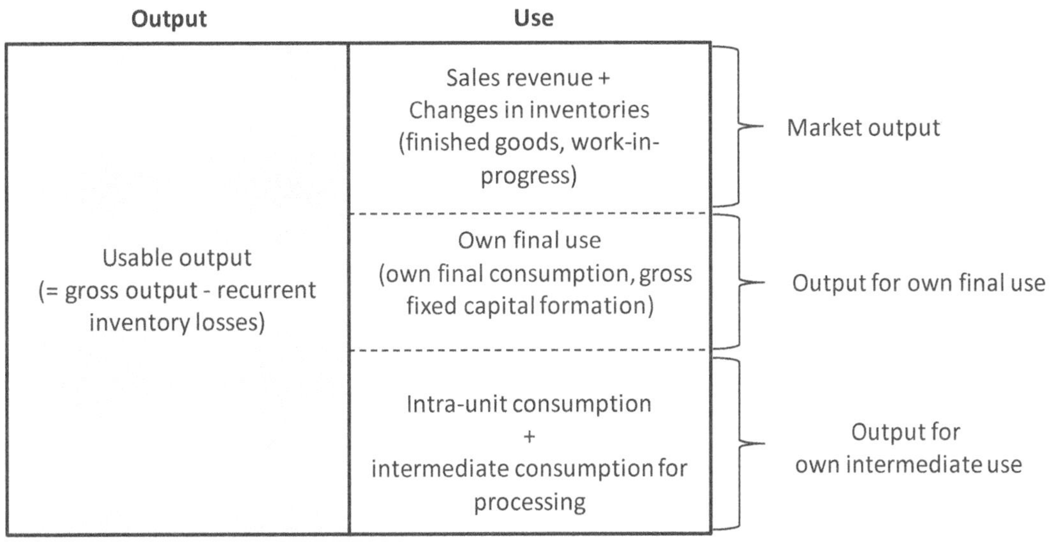

* Source: Eurostat, Manual on the Economic Accounts for Agriculture and Forestry (2000), para. 2.28.1

Presentation in the supply and use tables

The following example illustrates how the output, changes in inventory, sales, and intermediate consumption of a crop (rice) are recorded in the supply and use tables. Suppose that the output of rice for the current period is 100, total sales are 75 (domestic sales 60, exports 15), the farmer's own final consumption is 20, rice used for the farmer's own intermediate consumption (seed for sowing) is 6, closing inventory is 9, and opening inventory is 10.

Table 14.1 Basic data on a crop (rice)

Item	Amount	Item		Amount
Opening inventory	10	Sales	Domestic	60
Output	100		Exports	15
		Own final consumption		20
		Own intermediate consumption		6
		Closing inventory		9
Total	110	Total		110

In the supply table, the value output (100) is recorded in the cell where the "rice" row and the "agriculture" column intersect. In the use table, rice is recorded as: intermediate consumption 6, household final consumption[19] as 80 (= 60+20), changes in inventories -1 (= 9-10), and exports 15 (see Table 14.2).

Table 14.2 Presentation of crops (rice) in the supply and use tables

Supply table

	Agriculture	...	Imports	Total supply
...				
Rice	100			100
...				
Output	100			100

Use table

	Agriculture	...	Final consumption	Changes in inventories	Exports	Total use
...	..					
Rice	6		80	-1	15	100
...	..					
Total						100

For crops such as coffee trees and rubber trees, which are cultivated for the purpose of repeated harvesting, their growth represents the creation of cultivated biological assets and is therefore treated as gross fixed capital formation rather than current output. In the SUT, this is represented as follows (Table 14.3): In the supply table, the value of output (10) is recorded in the cell where the "cultivated crops" row and the "agriculture (own account)" column intersect; in the use table, the same value is recorded in the cell where the "cultivated crops" row and the "gross fixed capital formation" column intersect.

Table 14.3 Presentation of agricultural product for the own fixed capital formation in the supply and use tables

Supply table

	Agriculture (Own account)	Total supply
Cultivated crops	10	10
Output	10	

Use table

	Agriculture (Own account)	Fixed capital formation	Total use
	..		
Cultivated crops	..	10	10
	..		
Total	..		

[19] In practice, rice is treated as intermediate consumption of the manufacturing industry (food and beverage) for milling purposes.

14.1.2 Estimation of livestock output

The output of livestock products is calculated by multiplying the number of heads (number of animals) produced during a given period by their selling prices. However, because it is difficult to directly observe the number of heads actually produced during the period, the output quantity is generally estimated as the sum of the net increase in the number of heads (difference between closing and opening numbers of heads) and the number of heads slaughtered during the period.

- **Output of livestock products = (net increase in number of heads + number of heads slaughtered) × sales price**

For example, as shown in Figure 14.2, if there are 100 heads of animals at the beginning, and 30 heads are produced during the period, with 20 heads of them slaughtered and 10 heads remaining, the ending stock is 110 heads (=100+10). the production quantity during this period is (110–100) + 20 = 30. When 5 heads of the 20 slaughtered animals are used as intermediate consumption for processing, and 15 heads are used for households' final consumption, the accounting treatment on the expenditure side is recorded as 5 for intermediate consumption, and 15 for final consumption. Among the 10 heads of net increase, if 2 heads are used by the livestock farmer himself for breeding or dairy farming (own-account fixed capital formation), and the remaining 8 heads are used for market sales, the accounting treatment on the expenditure side is recorded as changes in inventory of 8, and fixed capital formation of 2.

Figure 14.2 Output and expenditure of livestock products

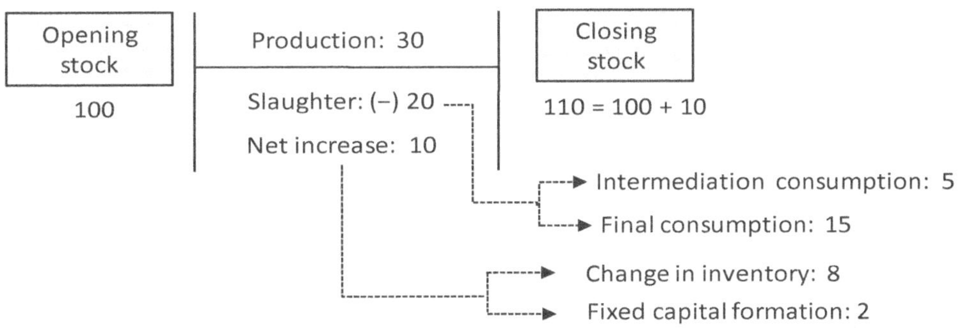

The production and expenditure structure of livestock products can be represented in the use table as follows (assuming no imports of livestock products).

Table 14.4 Presentation of the production and expenditure of livestock in the use table

	..	Livestock industry	Intermediate consumption	Final consumption	Fixed capital formation	Changes in inventories	Exports	Total use
Livestock	. . .		5	15	2	8		30
Value added								
Output		30						

In some cases, the net increase in stock for a particular item of animals may be negative (–), that is, when the number of heads sold or slaughtered during a given period (t) exceeds the number of heads produced. When this happens, the denominator (output in period t) becomes negative, making it impossible to calculate a meaningful growth rate of output between periods t and $(t + 1)$. In such cases, to maintain consistency, the negative denominator should be adjusted by taking its absolute value before calculating growth rates.

Accounting for production spanning multiple accounting periods

When agricultural, forestry, and livestock products are produced over multiple accounting periods, their output is recorded on an accrual basis until completion of the products, while on the expenditure side, the corresponding value is recorded as work-in-progress. Once production reaches the point of completion, such as harvest (for crops), slaughter (for livestock), or felling (for forestry products), the production process is considered finished, and the work-in-progress is reclassified as finished goods. For example, as illustrated in Figure 14.3, suppose the accounting period t ends in December. Products that remain unfinished at the end of the accounting period are recorded as output for the current period, while on the expenditure side they are recognized as inventories of work-in-progress. In the following accounting year $(t + 1)$, once these products are completed, they are reclassified and recorded as inventories of finished goods.

Figure 14.3 Recording of output spanning accounting periods for agricultural, forestry and livestock products

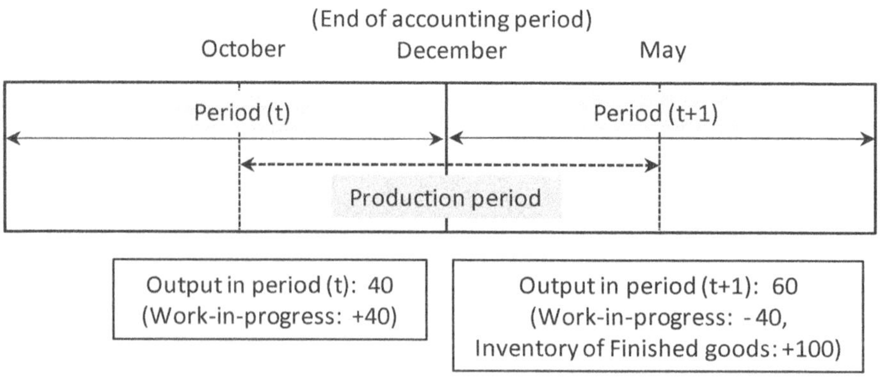

However, the treatment of output between accounting periods may differ slightly depending on the characteristic of the product. For instance, in the case of livestock, the treatment depends on the intended use after birth: livestock retained by the producer for draft, breeding, or dairy farming are recorded as own-account gross fixed capital formation, while livestock raised for slaughter are recorded as increases in work-in-progress inventories. Similarly, in the case of wine production, even if the wine is technically marketable, it remains recorded as work-in-progress inventories until the maturation process is completed.

14.1.3 Estimation of forestry output

The output of forestry products is recorded differently depending on whether the underlying forest resource is a cultivated or non-cultivated biological resource and on whether extraction activities take place. This treatment is grounded in the general principles of the SNA concerning the production boundary and the asset boundary.

Output of forestry products from cultivated biological resources

Cultivated biological resources, such as commercially grown timber in managed plantations under the control, responsibility and management of institutional units, are regarded as produced assets in the SNA. Accordingly, the increase in their value (biological growth) is recorded as an increase in work-in-progress and included in production. Furthermore, timber actually harvested from cultivated forests is treated as a marketable product and valued as:

Output = quantity harvested x basic prices

In addition, trees grown on farms that are intended to produce repeat products are treated as own-account gross fixed capital formation due to the nature of the production process.

Output of forestry products from non-cultivated biological resources

In the case of non-cultivated biological resources, such as natural forests where no institutional units exercise direct control, responsibility, or management, natural biological growth is not recorded as economic production. This natural increase is recorded in the other changes in the volume of assets and liabilities account. However, timber and other forest products harvested from natural forests constitute economic activity and are recorded as production at the time of extraction, valued as:

Output = quantity extracted x basic prices

Non-wood forest products (such as sap, resin, mushrooms, and medical plants) are also recorded as production when extracted. Even in the absence of market transactions, for example, when output is intended for own use, appropriate valuation should be applied using comparable market prices or suitable cost-based methods.

14.2 Wholesale and retail distribution

Wholesale and retail distribution refers to the business activity of purchasing goods from suppliers and reselling them to other purchasers after storing, transporting, and displaying them in order to improve accessibility and choice for customers. Unlike most other industries, this sector generates **margin services** associated with the transfer of ownership, that is, purchasing goods, taking ownership, and then reselling them. The activities of wholesale and retail distribution include both **margin services** and **non-margin services**. Margin services arise from the conventional buying and selling of goods, whereas non-margin services include brokerage fees from the trading of used cars, scrap materials, and other intermediary transactions. This section explains in detail the method used to estimate the output of margin services.

Treatment of wholesale and retail distribution in the national accounts

The accounting treatment of wholesale and retail distribution in the SNA differs from that of other production activities. In this industry, the output is not the total value of goods resold but rather the difference between the selling price and the purchase price of the goods by wholesalers or retailers. This difference is called the **distribution margin**, which represents the payment received for providing wholesale and retail services and simultaneously constitutes the output of the wholesale and retail industry. Therefore, the purchase value of goods acquired by wholesaler and retailers is not recorded as their intermediate consumption. Moreover, any freight charges incurred at the time of purchase are excluded from the purchase value of the good, but are recorded as intermediate consumption (transport costs) of the wholesale and retail enterprise (see section 4.3.1 for this discussion). In the SNA, the distribution margins added when converting from basic prices to purchasers' prices forms part of the output of wholesale and retail distribution. Consequently, when calculating the total output of the economy at basic prices, the output of the wholesale and retail sector is included; but when converting to purchasers' prices, the margin component of that output must be excluded to avoid double counting.

Methods for estimating wholesale and retail output

Two main approaches are used to estimate the output of the wholesale and retail trade industry.

1. Direct survey method using business accounting data

This method relies on financial statements through surveys or censuses. In this case, the output of wholesale and retail distribution is calculated as follows:

(14.1) Output of wholesale and retail distribution = the value of sales (a) + in-kind use of purchased goods (b) − the value of purchased goods (c) + the value of additions to inventories of goods (d) − the value of goods withdrawn from inventories (e) − recurrent losses of goods (f)

For each of the above items, the following valuation criteria are applied.

(a) Sales are valued at actual selling prices, including discounted sales.

(b) In-kind use of purchased goods is valued at the current replacement purchaser's price at the time the goods are provided, with the margin set to zero. If the goods are provided to employees, they are recorded as remuneration of employees (in-kind). If they are provided to other enterprises, they are recorded as intermediate consumption (e.g., advertising and promotional expenses), and if they are provided to households (in the case of household unincorporated enterprises' own final consumption), they are recorded as final consumption.

(c) In measuring the value of goods purchased during the period, any transport costs incurred by wholesalers and retailers are excluded. Freight charges invoiced separately by the supplier are also excluded, all of which are recorded as *intermediate consumption* (transport costs) of the wholesaler and retailer. This treatment prevents double-counting of transport margins, differing from business accounting practice where freight costs are often included in the cost of goods purchased.

(d) Additions to inventories of goods for resale are valued at the purchaser's price at the time of entry into inventories.

(e) Goods withdrawn from inventories for resale are valued at the replacement purchaser's price at the time of withdrawal from inventories. The replacement purchaser's price refers to the cost of purchasing the same goods from suppliers at the time of withdrawal.

(f) Recurrent losses of goods are valued in the same way as goods withdrawn from inventories.

In the above items, "additions to inventories (d) − goods withdrawn from inventories (e) − recurrent losses (f)" corresponds to **changes in inventories**. Therefore, equation (14.1) can be simplified as:

(14.2) **Output of wholesale and retail distribution = the value of sales + in-kind use of purchased goods – the value of purchased goods + changes in inventories**

The basic concept of distribution margins originates from "sales of goods – cost of goods sold." Sales of goods refer to the actual selling prices of goods for resale, while the cost of goods sold is calculated as "the value of purchased goods – changes in inventories". As explained above, changes in inventories are derived from "additions to inventories – goods withdrawn from inventories – recurrent losses". However, in practice, it requires a lot of detailed data to measure this value. Thus, an approximate measure is often obtained using "closing inventories – opening inventories," which implicitly includes recurrent losses (see Figure 14.4).

Figure 14.4 Derivation of cost of goods sold

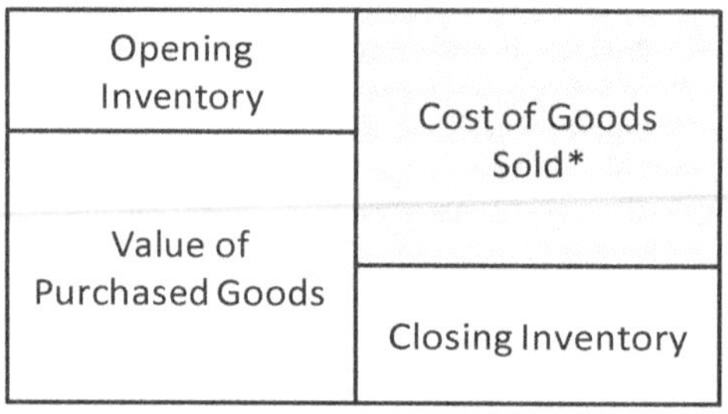

* Cost of goods sold = value of purchased goods + opening inventory – closing inventory

Therefore, the previous equation (14.2) can be further simplified to the following, assuming that there is no "in-kind use of purchased goods" item:

(14.3) Output of wholesale and retail distribution = the value of sales – cost of goods sold = the value of sales – the value of purchased goods + closing inventories – opening inventories

Here, "closing inventories – opening inventories" may include **holding gains and losses**. Therefore, to remove these holding gains or losses, an alternative valuation formula can be applied as is the case with inventories of finished goods or raw materials in the manufacturing industry:

- average price during the accounting period x (the quantity of closing inventories – the quantity of opening inventories)

2. The product flow method

The second method for estimating the output of wholesale and retail distribution is the product flow method. This approach is an indirect method that estimates distribution margins by first determining the **distribution ratio**, the proportion of goods sold by producers that are distributed through wholesalers and retailers, and then multiplying that ratio by the **average margin rate** of the wholesale and retail industry.

Figure 14.5 Sales channels of producer's goods

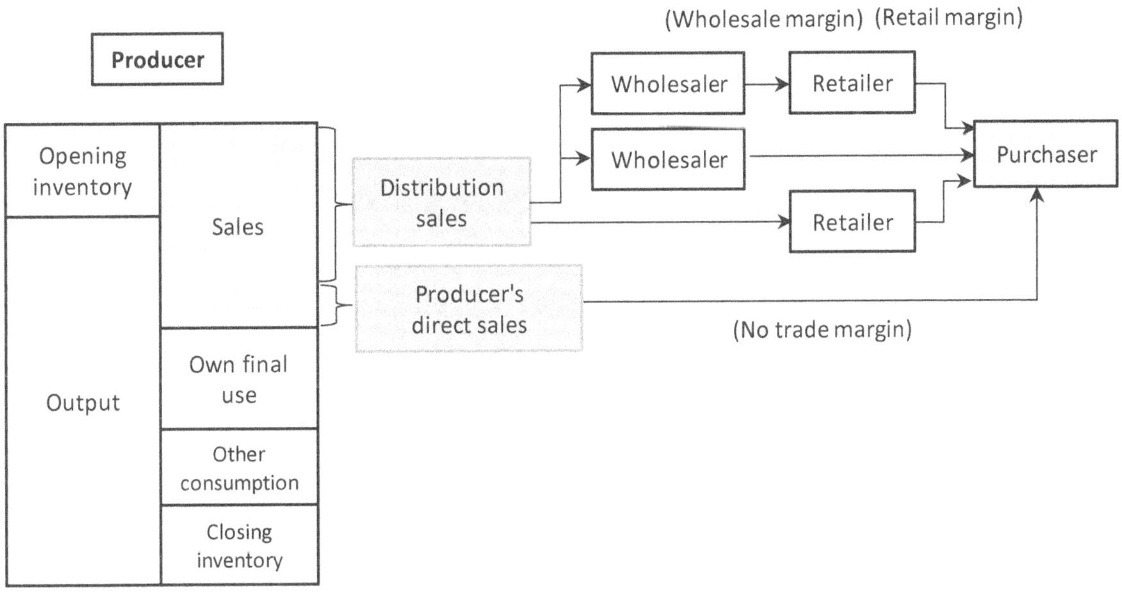

When producers sell their goods in the market, sales can occur either directly to final consumers or through wholesalers or retailers. The sales of the wholesale and retail trade industry correspond to the latter, that is, sales made through distribution channels. Within these distribution channels, transactions can be classified into three types: sales that go through both wholesalers and retailers, sales that go through wholesalers only, and sales that go through retailers only. By calculating the margin rates for each of these channels and multiplying them by the corresponding value of goods sold through distribution, the output of the wholesale and retail distribution can be indirectly estimated.

- Output of wholesale and retail distribution = the value of distribution sales x average margin rates of the wholesale and retail distribution

Treatment of E-commerce platforms

In recent years, e-commerce platforms, which perform the traditional functions of wholesalers and retailers in an online environment, have expanded rapidly. These platforms facilitate transactions by connecting sellers and buyers through digital networks, but unlike traditional wholesalers and retailers, they do not take ownership of the goods being traded. The business models of e-commerce platforms can be broadly be divided into two categories:

1. **Inventory-holding (merchant) model**: The platform purchases goods, take ownership, and resells them to consumers. This model is equivalent to traditional trade, and the distribution margin is calculated in the same way.
2. **Intermediary model**: The platform does not take ownership of goods but intermediates transactions between sellers and buyers, providing services such as payment processing and logistics. In this case, the platform's output consists of transaction fees, advertising revenues, data access fees, and other related charges. These are classified not as distribution margins, but as non-margin services.

Among these, intermediary-type e-commerce platforms are classified separately from traditional wholesale and retail trade in industrial classification systems. According to the *International Standard Industrial Classification* (ISIC Rev.5), they are included under **Web search portals activities and other information service** (6390).

From the perspective of the SNA, merchant-type e-commerce platforms are treated in the same manner as traditional retail trade, and their output is recorded as distribution margins. Intermediary-type e-commerce platforms are classified as **digital intermediation services**, and their output is recorded under "Information and communication service activities." Therefore, in the national accounts, online distribution platforms should be disaggregated as follows: the merchant segment is recorded as the output of the retail trade, and the intermediary segment is recorded as the output of digital intermediation services.

14.3 Financial and insurance services

In the SNA, the institutional sector classification distinguishes financial corporations from non-financial corporations because the production activities of financial corporations are clearly different from those of non-financial corporations. Although financial corporations are service producers, they provide a distinct range of services that are specialized in the financial sector. The financial industry, like wholesale and retail trade, earns most of its income from service margins. However, while wholesale and retail trade generates margins from the distribution of goods, the financial industry derives its margins primarily from financial intermediation and other financial services.

Categories of financial output

The output of financial industry can be classified into four main categories.

1. **Traditional financial intermediation services**: These involves accepting deposits and providing loans, for which the intermediary receives fees. Since such intermediary services are not explicitly reflected in deposit and loan interest rates, the SNA measures them indirectly. This is referred to as **financial intermediation services indirectly measured (FISIM)**.

2. **Pure financial services**: These are explicit-fee-based services such as remittance services or credit card services. For instance, credit card companies charge merchants or stores using their payment systems a fee based on a percentage of the transaction value. This fee constitutes the output of the credit card company, while it is recorded as intermediate consumption for the merchants who use the payment system. However, if this cost is not explicitly identifiable in the data of the merchants using the credit card service, it must be allocated appropriately by the national accountants as intermediate consumption of the relevant industries.

3. **Service margins from the trading of financial instruments**: Financial institutions may earn service margins from buying and selling short-term and long-term securities, shares, or investment fund units. financial instruments. The service margin is calculated as the difference between the selling price and the mid-price, or the difference between the mid-price and the buying price. The mid-price refers to the average of the bid and ask prices at the time of the transaction, and if the securities are purchased and sold at different times, the mid-price will differ accordingly. However, in practice, as is the case with the service margins on the purchase and sale of stocks and investment fund shares, a certain percentage of the buying or selling price is recorded as a service charge. The same principle applies to foreign exchange transactions, where the difference between the buying price and selling price is considered service income. The scope of foreign exchange includes both *cash* and *foreign exchange* used in transactions of imports and exports.

4. **Insurance and pension-related financial services**: These include services for which fees are received exchange for providing insurance and pension-related services. This includes all

types of insurance, including non-life insurance, life insurance and annuities, social insurance schemes, and standardized guarantees.

This section focuses on the measurement methods of output for key components of the financial industry, namely, the central bank, financial corporations generating FISIM, and the insurance industries.

14.3.1 Central bank

The **central bank** is not a governmental unit, but it is a public financial institution responsible for formulating and implementing the key monetary policies directed at deposit-taking corporations in relation to currency issuance and the management of liquidity in financial markets. The central bank provides monetary policy services, carries out financial stability and macro-prudential supervision, manages international reserve assets and oversees the operation of the payments system, and also serves as the banker to government. Although the central bank is generally regarded as a non-market producer, it is classified, in terms of institutional sectoring, as a public financial corporation. Independent institutional units responsible for financial supervision, such as financial supervisory authorities or deposit insurance agencies, are not included within the central bank, but are classified separately as financial auxiliaries.

All services provided by the central bank are treated as non-market output because they are supplied without charge to individual institutional units or, where a fee is charged, at prices that are not economically significant. The output of these services is therefore measured by the **sum-of-costs method**. Moreover, as the authority that sets the policy interest rate, the central bank does not engage in financial intermediation for commercial purposes, and the concept of financial intermediation services indirectly measured (FISIM) is not applied to the central bank's deposits and loans. In some cases, the central bank may sell certain market outputs; even in these circumstances, the output of the central bank continues to be measured on a sum-of-costs basis, and non-market output is derived by deducting the sales revenue of the market output. Moreover, the fees paid by financial corporations to the central bank (e.g., supervisory fees) are treated not as payments for services but as compulsory current transfers. Consequently, these amounts are excluded from the output of the central bank.

In the 2008 SNA, the non-market production of the central bank was regarded as collective consumption of government. In the 2025 SNA, however, the central bank is treated as a public producer in its own right, and its production is deemed to be consumed by the central bank itself rather than by government. Accordingly, the non-market output of the central bank is recorded as the final consumption expenditure (**collective consumption**) of the central bank. Actual final consumption is identical to final consumption expenditure, as the central bank does not supply individual services to households.

For example, the treatment of the central bank's output, derived by the sum-of-costs method, in the national accounts is illustrated as follows. Suppose that the central bank's intermediate consumption is 50, remuneration of employees 120, other taxes on production 5, gross operating surplus 25, market sales 10, and own-account gross fixed capital formation (GFCF) 5. In this case, output amounts to 50 + 120 + 25 + 5 = 200 (with non-market output equals to 200 – 10 = 190). Financial consumption expenditure is then calculated as output (200) minus sales (10) minus own-account GFCF (5), yielding 185. Because the central bank does not provide social transfers in kind, its actual final consumption is identical to its final consumption expenditure, that is, 185.

14.3.2 FISIM

The **financial intermediation service charge indirectly measured** (FISIM) earned by financial intermediaries constitute the most important source of income for financial corporations and form the core of their output. Financial intermediation refers to the process in which financial intermediaries accept deposits from depositors (surplus units) and lend these funds to borrowers (deficit units), thereby providing financial services. This activity involves **liquidity transformation services**, in which funds collected from a large and unspecified number of depositors are made available to borrowers according to their demand for timing and amounts of funds. In this process, financial intermediaries pay depositors interest on their deposits after deducting a certain service charge (α) from a notional base rate, and they charge borrowers interest after adding a service charge (β) to that same base rate. The base rate, referred to as the **reference rate**, represents a pure interest rate for intermediation before taking into account service charges. For example, interbank lending rates are considered typical reference rates because they reflect transactions between financial institutions without intermediation service charges.

Figure 14.6 Interbank borrowing and lending

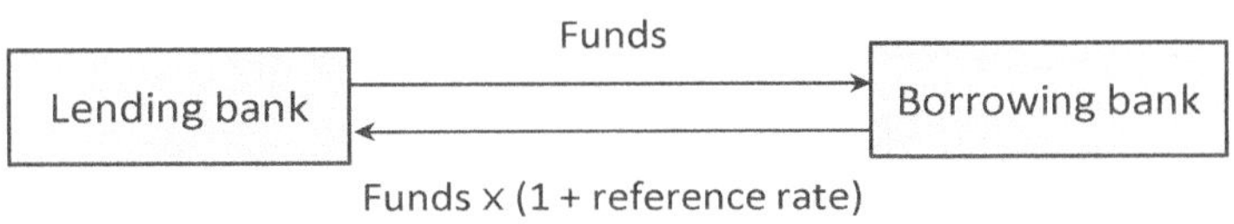

Financial intermediaries, therefore, pay depositors an interest rate on their deposits that is equal to the reference rate minus an intermediation service fee (α). They also charge borrowers an interest rate on their loans that is equal to the reference rate plus an intermediation service fee (β). The total service fees of financial intermediaries, equal to the sum of α and β, represents the value of FISIM.

$$\textbf{FISIM} = \textbf{FISIM on deposits } (\alpha) + \textbf{FISIM on loans } (\beta)$$

The components α and β represent the implicit service charges added to or subtracted from the reference rate. They are not directly observable, therefore, derived indirectly. In this case, the amount of "pure interest" based on the reference rate is called **SNA interest**, and the interest on deposits and interest on loans actually paid or charged to depositors or borrowers after the charges are added or subtracted are called **bank interest**.

Figure 14.7 Flow of interest and FISIM payments

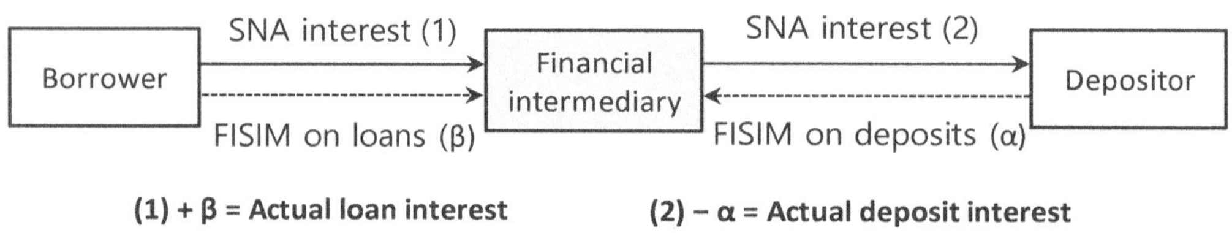

Formula for FISIM calculation

The formula for calculation FISIM can be expressed in more detail as follows:

(14.4) $$\textbf{FISIM} = (R_L - R_f) \times L + (R_f - R_D) \times D$$

where R_L : average loan interest rate, R_D : average deposit interest rate, R_f : reference rate, L: average balance of loans, D: average balance of deposits.

However, if the amounts of loans and deposits are identical (L=D) in this equation, then the SNA interest on loans ($R_f \times L$) and the SNA interest on deposits ($R_f \times D$) are also equal. In that case, FISIM equals the simple difference between the actual interest receivable on loans and the actual interest payable on deposits. In other words, if L = D, then $R_f \times L = R_f \times D$, so the above equation (14.4) can be simplified as follows:

$$\textbf{FISIM} = R_L \times L - R_D \times D$$

However, in practice, the amounts of loans and deposits are usually not equal, and thus the amounts of SNA interest on loans and SNA interest on deposits differ. Therefore, the FISIM in equation (14.4) can be rewritten as:

$$\textbf{FISIM} = (R_L \times L - R_D \times D) - R_f \times (L - D) = \textbf{bank interest margin} - R_f \times (L - D)$$

By rearranging this equation, the following expression (14.5) is obtained. That is, the **bank interest margin** can be divided into two components: FISIM, which represents the output generated from financial intermediation activities, and $R_f \times (L - D)$, which is recorded as property incomes in the allocation of earned income account.

(14.5) **Bank interest margin = FISIM + $R_f \times (L - D)$**

The accounting treatment of this bank interest margin in the SNA us as follows. In the allocation of earned income account, $R_f \times L$ is recorded as interest receivable by financial intermediaries (and payable by borrowers), while $R_f \times D$ is recorded as interest payable by financial intermediaries (and receivable by depositors). The remaining component, FISIM, is recognized as output of financial intermediation services and recorded in the production account.

Deposits and loans that generate FISIM

Next, we examine in more detail which types of financial instruments issued by financial intermediaries give rise to FISIM. First, according to the SNA, the scope of financial instruments that can generate FISIM is limited to **deposits and loans**. In other words, depositors receive interest on their deposits and implicitly pay a service charge to financial corporations, regardless of whether their funds are actually used for lending. Conversely, borrowers pay interest on their borrowings regardless of whether the funds borrowed originate from deposits, borrowings, or the financial corporation's own funds[20], and this interest likewise includes an implicit service charge. Therefore, FISIM arises only from transactions involving deposits and loans.

Second, the range of institutional units that can generate FISIM is restricted to financial corporations engaged in financial intermediation through such deposits and loans. This includes not only resident financial corporations but also non-resident financial corporations. The counterparties to these financial intermediaries (i.e., their clients) do not have to be residents. For example, when a non-resident financial corporation provides intermediation services to resident clients, the resulting FISIM is treated as imports of services. Conversely, when resident financial

[20] In the 1993 SNA, FISIM was applied to all financial instruments that generate property incomes receivable (excluding property income receivable from the investment of the bank's own funds) and all financial instruments that give rise to interest payable. (The definition of FISIM in the 1993 SNA is "total property income receivable (excluding any property income receivable from the investment of the bank's own funds) – total interest payable".) However, after the 2008 SNA, the scope of financial instruments giving rise to FISIM was narrowed and explicitly defined to include only deposits and loans.

corporations provide intermediation services to non-resident clients, the resulting FISIM is recorded as exports of services.

Third, financial corporations are not required to engage simultaneously in both deposit-taking and lending to generate FISIM. *Money lenders* that provide loans exclusively using their own funds (i.e., without taking deposits) are also considered to generate FISIM.

Finally, **interbank transactions** are an exception and are deemed not to give rise to FISIM, because interbank interest rates are typically determined by a pure reference rate that excludes any implicit service charge. However, when a bank accepts deposits from or extends loans to non-bank financial corporations (such as insurance companies or pension funds), these transactions are regarded as involving financial intermediation services and therefore can generate FISIM.

14.3.2.1 Selection of reference rates and calculation of FISIM

There are two main approaches to determining the reference rate used in calculating FISIM: the **single reference rate** method and the **multiple reference rate** method. Under the single reference rate method, one common reference rate is applied uniformly to all deposits and loans for the calculation of FISIM. The interest rate conveniently used as a reference rate is the interbank lending rate. However, if the interbank interest rate is lower than the current deposit interest rate at the time the interbank rate is applied, the calculated FISIM on deposits becomes negative (-), which can make accounting treatment impractical. To overcome this drawback, an alternative approach is to use the "mid-point" between the average deposit interest rate and the average loan interest rate as the reference rate. The procedure for calculating this mid-point reference rate can be illustrated as follows:

1. Calculate the average interest rate on deposits (R_D) and the average interest rate on loans (R_L) for financial corporations:
    - R_D = total interest payable on deposits / average balance of deposits,
    - R_L = total interest receivable on loans / average balance of loans
2. Compute the mid-point reference rate (R_f), as the simple average of the interest rates on deposits and loans:
    - $R_f = (R_D + R_L)/2$
3. Calculate FISIM for each financial instrument by multiplying the difference between the actual interest rate and the reference rate by the corresponding average balance:

- $(R_L^i - R_f) \times L^i$ = FISIM on loan i,
- $(R_f - R_D^j) \times D^j$ =FISIM on deposit j,

where: L^i: average balance of loan i, D^j: average balance of deposit j, R_L^i : interest receivable on loan i divided by L^i, R_D^j : interest payable on deposit j divided by D^j.

4. To derive the FISIM on loans and FISIM on deposits in volume terms, R_L^i, R_D^i, and R_f in the reference year are applied, and L^i and D^j are also deflated to the reference year prices using CPIs (that is, $L^i \times CPI^0/CPI^t$, $D^j \times CPI^0/CPI^t$).

Using the midpoint between the average interest rates on deposits and on loans as the reference rate generally provides stable and balanced results. However, if the interest rate on deposits is higher than the interest rate on loans, the calculated FISIM becomes negative, making this approach inapplicable. Furthermore, for financial corporations that engage exclusively in lending activities without accepting deposits (e.g., moneylenders), a separate reference rate must be established.

Example of applying reference rates

The table below (Table 14.5, column A) illustrates an example of calculating the FISIM on loans and FISIM on deposits using the single reference rate method. Given the following data (an average loan balance of 1,050, an average deposit balance of 800, interest receivable on loans of 17, and interest payable on deposit of 6), the reference rate is calculated as follows, according to the method explained earlier:

$$R_f = (17/1{,}050 + 6/800)/2 = 1.185\%$$

Accordingly,

SNA interest on loans = 1,050 × 1.185% = 12.44, SNA interest on deposits = 800 × 1.185% = 9.48

Therefore,

FISIM on loans = 17 − 12.44 = 4.56, FISIM on deposits = 9.48 − 6 = 3.48, total FISIM = 4.56+3.48 = 8.04.

The difference between the SNA interest on loans and SNA interest on deposits of 2.96 (= 12.44 − 9.48) is recorded in the allocation of earned income account as the net property income receivable for financial corporations sector.

When the risk profiles and maturity structures of deposits and loans held by financial corporations differ, these characteristics should be taken into account in determining the reference rate. Accordingly, instead of applying a single uniform reference rate, one may adopt **multiple reference rates**, one for short-term and another for long-term instruments (as in column B in Table

14.5, "Multiple reference rates"), or compute a **single weighted-average reference rate** based on the relative shares of short-term and long-term deposits and loans (as in column C, "Single weighted average reference rate").

Under the multiple reference rate method (column B), the short-term and long-term reference rates are each derived using the midpoint approach described earlier. From the example in the above table (Table 14.5), the short-term reference rate is (9/600 + 4/500)/2 = 1.15%, and the long-term reference rate is (8/450 + 2/300)/2 = 1.22% respectively. Applying these rates yields a short-term FISIM of 3.85 and a long-term FISIM of 4.17, resulting in total FISIM of 8.02.

If the single weighted average reference rate method (column C) is adopted, the overall reference rate is calculated by weighting the short- and long-term reference rates by the combined values of deposits and loans in each maturity group. That is, the reference rate that is applied equally to both the short-term and long-term funds is:

Weighted average reference rate = $(600 + 500) / [(600 + 500) + (450 + 300)] \times 1.15\%$ + $(450 + 300) / [(600 + 500) + (450 + 300)] \times 1.22\%$ = 1.179%.

Applying this rate produces a total FISIM of 8.05.

In the national accounts, the choice of a reference rate, such as an interbank short-term rate or a maturity-weighted average rate, depends on national circumstances. However, rather than setting separate reference rates for short-term and long-term instruments, the SNA recommends using a single temporal reference rate for each period (2025 SNA, paragraph 7.183).

Table 14.5 Example of calculating FISIM and SNA interest

Item \ Reference rate	Single reference rate (A)	Multiple reference rates (B)			Single weighted average reference rate (C)		
		short-term	long-term	subtotal	short-term	long-term	subtotal
Reference rate	1.185%	1.15%	1.22%		1.15%	1.22%	1.179%
Average balance of loans	1050	600	450	1050	600	450	1050
Average balance of deposits	800	500	300	800	500	300	800
Interest receivable on loans	17	9	8	17	9	8	17
Interest payable on deposits	6	4	2	6	4	2	6
SNA interest on loans (1)	12.44	6.90	5.50	12.40	7.08	5.31	12.38
SNA interest on deposits (2)	9.48	5.75	3.67	9.42	5.90	3.54	9.43
FISIM on loans (3)	4.56	2.10	2.50	4.60	1.92	2.69	4.62
FISIM on deposits (4)	3.48	1.75	1.67	3.42	1.90	1.54	3.43
Total FISIM (5 = 3+4)	8.04	3.85	4.17	8.02	3.82	4.23	8.05
Difference in SNA interest (6 = 1-2)	2.96	1.15	1.83	2.98	1.18	1.77	2.95
Total interest margin (5+6)	11.00	5.00	6.00	11.00	5.00	6.00	11.00

14.3.2.2 Accounting treatment of FISIM

The treatment of FISIM in the SNA has evolved over time. The 1968 SNA treated the total value of FISIM generated by financial institutions as intermediate consumption of a nominal industry and subtracted it from gross value added (GVA) to calculate GDP. Although this approach had the advantage of simplicity, it failed to reflect the actual use of FISIM by individual industries and institutional sectors. In the 1993 SNA, two alternative methods were permitted: (i) to continue using the 1968 SNA approach (allocation to a nominal industry), or (ii) to allocate FISIM directly to the industries and institutional sectors that actually consumed the financial intermediation services, treating it as either intermediate or final consumption. However, the 2008 SNA discontinued the nominal industry approach and required direct allocation of FISIM to the industries and institutional sectors that use the financial intermediation services. That is, FISIM should be explicitly allocated as intermediation consumption for corporations, government, and NPISHs, or as final consumption for households, depending on the nature of the institutional unit that benefits from the service.

Distinction between SNA interest and bank interest

The distinction between **SNA interest** and **bank interest** in the national accounts is essential because "interest", as a type of property income, must be recorded excluding the financial intermediation service component (FISIM). In other words, the components of FISIM on deposits and FISIM on loans represent the output of financial corporations and are simultaneously recorded as expenses of the users of the financial intermediation services. Accordingly, only pure SNA interest (before adding loan FISIM and subtracting deposit FISIM) is recorded as property income. Through this procedure, FISIM and SNA interest are clearly separated and recorded in the appropriate accounts within the SNA.

Allocation procedure for FISIM

However, the accounting treatment of distinguishing between the SNA interest and FISIM for financial intermediaries does not occur at the level of individual institutional units, but only in the process of compiling national accounts, including the derivation of the total values by national accounts compilers. The procedure of allocating FISIM to each institutional sector account in the SNA can be summarized as follows. First, in the production account, both FISIM on deposits and FISIM on loans are recorded as output of financial corporations. The same amounts are recorded as intermediate consumption for corporations, government, and NPISHs (in the production account) or final consumption of households (in the use of income account). If the users of financial intermediation services are government or NPISHs, the amounts are recorded both as intermediate consumption and as final consumption, since the output of these sectors is non-market in nature and is considered to be consumed by the producers themselves.

The following example (Table 14.6) illustrates how the SNA records are organized, assuming that financial corporations earn interest receivable (10) and incur interest payable (5). It is assumed that the interest receivable (10) consists of SNA interest on loans (8) and FISIM on loans (2), and the interest payable (5) consists of SNA interest on deposits (6) minus FISIM on deposits (1). Then, the output of financial corporations is recorded as total FISIM of 3 (FISIM on loans 2 and FISIM on deposits 1) in the production account. This amount is then allocated as intermediate or final consumption to other institutional sectors. In the allocation of earned income account, the SNA interest on loans (8) is recorded as both property income receivable by financial corporations and property income payable by other institutional sectors, while the SNA interest on deposits (6) is recorded as both property income payable by financial corporations and property income receivable by other institutional sectors.

Table 14.6 Example of recording SNA interest and FISIM in the sequence of economic accounts

	Financial corporations		Other institutional sectors	
	Expenditures	Revenues	Expenditures	Revenues
Production account		(Output) FISIM on loans (2) FISIM on deposits (1)	(Intermediate consumption) FISIM on loans (0.5) FISIM on deposits (0.2)	
Allocation of earned income account	SNA interest payable (6)	SNA interest receivable (8)	SNA interest payable (8)	SNA interest receivable (6)
Use of income account			(Household final consumption) FISIM on loans (1.5) FISIM on deposits (0.8)	

14.3.2.3 Accounting treatment of FISIM in external transactions

In the SNA, FISIM can arise not only from domestic transactions but also from cross-border financial transactions. When a resident borrows funds from, or deposits funds with, a financial intermediary in the rest of the world sector, the FISIM service charge implicit in that transaction is regarded as a service imported from abroad, and thus recorded as an import of services. Conversely, when a non-resident borrows funds from, or deposits funds with, a resident financial corporation, the FISIM generated by the resident financial corporation is recorded as an export of services. All of these transactions are treated as service transactions with the foreign sector and are recorded in the rest of the world account.

The method for calculating FISIM in the rest of the world sector is the same as for domestic transactions, except that a reference rate specific to external transactions is used instead of the domestic reference rate. Exports of FISIM ($FISIM^{ex}$) are calculate as follows:

$$\mathbf{FISIM^{ex} = (R_L - R_f^{ex}) \times L + (R_f^{ex} - R_D) \times D}$$

where, L: average balance of loans provided to non-residents by resident financial corporations,

D: average balance of deposits taken from non-residents by resident financial corporations,

R_LxL: total interest receivable by resident financial corporations on loans to non-residents,

R_DxD: total interest payable by resident financial corporations on deposits of non-residents,

R_f^{ex}: reference rate applied to external transactions of resident financial corporations.

Imports of FISIM ($FISIM^{im}$) are calculated as follows:

$$\mathbf{FISIM^{im} = (R_L - R_f^{im}) \times L + (R_f^{im} - R_D) \times D}$$

where, L: average balance of loans provided to residents by non-resident financial corporations,

D: average balance of deposits taken from residents by non-resident financial corporations,

R_L x L: total interest receivable by non-resident financial corporations on loans to residents,

R_D x D: total interest payable by non-resident financial corporations on deposits of residents,

R_f^{im}: reference rate applied to residents' transactions with non-resident financial corporations.

14.3.2.4 Example of recording FISIM in the supply and use tables

This section illustrates how FISIM is recorded in the supply and use tables. Suppose that the output of FISIM generated by resident financial corporations amounts to 100, imports of FISIM are 6, and exports of FISIM are 5. Assume further that total FISIM is allocated as follows: non-financial corporations (51), household final consumption (30), government (17), and NPISHs (3). The recording of these transactions in the supply and use tables is shown in Table 14.7 below. On the supply side, the total supply of FISIM is equal to domestic output (100) + imports (6) = 106. Due to the accrual of FISIM, domestic output increases by the sum of financial corporations (100) and the imputed output of government and NPISHs (17+3), giving a total of 120. On the use side, FISIM is recorded as intermediate consumption of non-financial corporations (51), final consumption of households (30), and as both intermediate consumption and final consumption of government (17) and NPISHs (3), together with exports (5). Thus, the change in gross value added can be confirmed as follows:

- Production approach: Output (120) – intermediate consumption (51+17+3) = 49

- Expenditure approach: Household final consumption (30) + exports (5) + government and NPISHs final consumption (17+3) – imports (6) = 49

Table 14.7 Example of allocating FISIM in the supply and use tables

Supply table

	Financial corp.	Government	NPISHs	Imports	Total supply
FISIM	100			6	106
Gov't service		17			17
NPISHs service			3		3
Total output	100	17	3	6	126

Use table

	Non-financial corp.	Financial corp.	Government	NPISHs	HH final consumption	Gov't final consumption	NPISH final consumption	Exports	Total use
FISIM	51		17	3	30			5	106
Gov't services						17			17
NPISHs services							3		3
Total input	51		17	3					126

14.3.2.5 Example of recording FISIM by institutional sector in the sequence of economic accounts

This section explains how to separate the FISIM on loans and FISIM on deposits, along with their corresponding SNA interest on loans, and SNA interest on deposits, by institutional sector, using the data of the bank interest on loans and deposits. It also describes how these amounts are recorded in the sequence of economic accounts.

Computation and allocation of FISIM by institutional sector

The table below (Table 14.8) shows the results of deriving FISIM on loans and FISIM on deposits for each institutional sector. These are obtained by applying the reference rate to calculate the SNA interest on loans and SNA interest on deposits, and then taking the differences between the bank interest and SNA interest.

- FISIM on loans = bank interest on loans – SNA interest on loans, FISIM on deposits = SNA interest on deposits – bank interest on deposits.)

The sum of FISIM on loans and FISIM on deposits (29+21 = 50) represents the output of financial corporations. This total amount is allocated among the user sectors as follows: non-financial corporations 19 (intermediate consumption), general government 6 (intermediate and final consumption), NPISHs 3 (intermediate and final consumption), households 21 (final consumption), and net exports 1 (exports 4, imports 3). According to Table 14.8, the domestic financial corporations receive interest income of 125 on loans (112 from residents and 13 from non-residents) and pay interest of 77 on deposits. When the reference rate is applied, SNA interest on loans equals 104 and SNA interest on deposits equals 106. From these, the following FISIM values are obtained:

- FISIM on loans 21 (domestic 18 + external 3), FISIM on deposits 29 (domestic 28 + external 1), Total FISM 50 (domestic 46 + external 4)

Table 14.8 Example of the allocation of FISIM and SNA interest by institutional sector (Adapted from the 1993 SNA, Table A.III.1)

	Non-financial corp.	Financial corp.	Government	Households	NPISHs	Total economy	ROW	Total	Transactions items	Non-financial corp.	Financial corp.	Government	Households	NPISH	Total economy	ROW	Total	
Bank interest on loans	66	0	22	17	7	112	13	125	Interest receivable by domestic financial corporations from all borrowers (A)		125				125		125	Bank interest on loans
			17			17		17	Interest receivable by foreign financial corporations from domestic borrowers (B)							17	17	
Bank interest on deposits		77				77		77	Interest payable by domestic financial corporations to all depositors (C)	22	0	12	33	5	72	5	77	Bank interest on deposits
							3	3	Interest payable by foreign financial corporations to domestic depositors (D)	3					3		3	
	66	77	39	17	7	206	16	222	**Total bank interest**	25	125	12	33	5	200	22	222	
SNA interest on loans	56	0	20	12	6	94	10	104	SNA interest receivable by domestic financial corporations from all borrowers (E)		104				104		104	SNA interest on loans
			15			15		15	SNA interest receivable by foreign financial corporations from domestic borrowers (F)							15	15	
SNA interest on deposits		106				106		106	SNA interest payable by domestic financial corporations to all depositors (G)	30	0	14	49	7	100	6	106	SNA interest on deposits
							4	4	SNA interest payable by foreign financial institutions to domestic depositors (H)	4					4		4	
	56	106	35	12	6	215	14	229	**Total SNA interest**	34	104	14	49	7	208	21	229	
FISIM on loans	10	0	2	5	1	18	3	21	Service fees receivable by domestic financial corporations from all borrowers (A-E)		21				21		21	FISIM on loans
			2			2		2	Service fees receivable by foreign financial corporations from domestic borrowers (B-F)							2	2	
FISIM on deposits	8	0	2	16	2	28	1	29	Service fees receivable by domestic financial corporations from all depositors (G-C)		29				29		29	FISIM on deposits
	1					1		1	Service fees receivable by foreign financial corporations from domestic depositors (H-D)							1	1	
	19	0	6	21	3	49	4	53	**Total FISIM**		50				50	3	53	
									Allocation of FISIM									
									Imports							3	3	
									Output		50	6		3	59		59	
	19	0	6	0	3	28		28	Intermediate consumption									
			6	21	3	30		30	Final consumption									
							4	4	Exports									
	19	0	12	21	6	58	4	62	Total allocation of FISIM		50	6		3	59	3	62	

* Note: All FISIM on households sector is assumed to be allocated to final consumption (That is, no household unincorporated enterprise exists in this example).

Impact of FISIM allocation on gross value added

When FISIM is allocated across institutional sectors as shown in the table above, its effect on gross value added (GVA) can be summarized as follows. On the production side, total output increases by 59 (= 50+6+3) due to the output of financial corporations (50) and the additional imputed output of government (6) and NPISHs (3). At the same time, intermediate consumption rises by 28 (non-financial corporations 19, government 6, NPISHs 3), resulting in an overall increase in gross value-added of 31 (= 59 - 28). On the expenditure side, total final consumption increases by 30 (households 21, government 6, and NPISHs 3), exports by 4, and imports by 3, producing the same increase in gross value-added of 31 (= 30 + 4 - 3).

Table 14.9 Effect of FISIM allocation on gross value added

Production side

Output	FISIM output	50
	Government output	6
	NPISHs output	3
	Subtotal	59
Intermediate consumption (-)	Non-financial corporations	19
	Financial corporations	0
	Government	6
	NPISHs	3
	Subtotal	28
Gross value added		31

Expenditure side

Final consumption	Households	21
	Government	6
	NPISHs	3
	Subtotal	30
Exports		4
Imports (-)		3
Gross value added		31

Accounting treatment of FISIM in the sequence of economic accounts

Based on the previous tables, Table 14.10 below presents how FISIM and SNA interest are recorded across each account of the sequence of economic accounts. First, in the production account, the output of financial corporations increases by 50, and with the inclusion of the output of government (6) and NPISHs (3), the total output amounts to 59. Intermediate consumption rises by 28, resulting in an increase of 31 in gross value added. The same amount of operating surplus is recorded in the generation of earned income account. In the rest of the world account, exports of FISIM (4) and imports of FISIM (3) are recorded, producing the balance on services of -1 (= 3-4). In the allocation of earned income account, the SNA interest calculated in Table 14.8 is recorded as follows: on the revenues side of the table, property income receivable (total economy 208, the rest of the world 21); on the expenditures side, property income payable (total economy 215, the rest of the world 14). The operating surplus of 31 (financial corporations 50, non-financial corporations -19) is added to the revenues side of the table. Therefore, in this account, the balance of earned incomes increases by 24 (= 31 + 208 - 215) in the total economy and by 7 (= 21 - 14) in the rest of the world. The balance of earned income is carried forward as disposable income in the use of income account. In the use of income account, after deducting final consumption expenditure of 30 (households 21, government 6, NPISHs 3), the saving of -6 (= 24 - 30) is derived. For the rest of the world, the current external balance is obtained as the sum of the balance on services (-1) and balance on earned income (7), resulting in a surplus of 6.

Table 14.10 Allocation of FISIM and SNA interest by institutional sector in the sequence of economic accounts

Expenditures / Revenues

Accounts	Non-financial	Financial	Government	Households	NPISHs	Total economy	Rest of the world	Total	Transactions and balancing items	Non-financial	Financial	Government	Households	NPISHs	Total economy	Rest of the world	Total	Accounts
Production account/ ROW account								3	Imports							3	3	Production a/c, ROW a/c
							4	4	Exports								4	
								59	Output		50	6		3	59		59	
	19	0	6	0	3	28		28	Intermediate consumption								28	
	-19	50	0	0	0	31		31	Value added	-19	50	0	0	0	31		31	Generation of earned income a/c
Generation of earned income account									Operating surplus									
	-19	50	0	0	0	31		31		-19	50	0	0	0	31		31	Allocation of earned income a/c
Allocation of earned income account	56	106	35	12	6	215	14	229	Interest	**34**	104	14	49	7	208	21	229	
	-41	48	-21	37	1	24		24	Balance of earned incomes	-41	48	-21	37	1	24		24	Income transfers a/c
Income transfers account																		
	-41	48	-21	37	1	24		24	Disposable income	-41	48	-21	37	1	24		24	Use of income a/c
Use of income account	0	0	6	21	3	30		30	Final consumption									
	-41	48	-27	16	-2	-6	6		Saving/Current external balance									

14.3.3 Insurance industry

This section examines how the output of the insurance industry is measured from the perspective of the national accounts. In particular, it focuses on the methods for estimating the output of **private insurance** (life and non-life insurance) and **social insurance** (public insurance schemes of a compulsory nature). While section 9.3.2–9.33 have already provided a general overview of how insurance is treated in the SNA, the present section explains, through concrete examples, how the output of insurance is systematically recorded within the sequence of economic accounts framework.

14.3.3.1 Nature of different types of insurance

From the perspective of national accounting, insurance is classified into three types according to the nature of the transactions involved: (i) life insurance and annuities, which have a characteristic of **financial transactions**; (ii) non-life insurance and social security schemes, which have a characteristic of **transfer transactions**; and (iii) employment-related pension schemes (both defined contribution (DC) and defined benefit (DB) scheme), which combine features of both financial and transfer transactions.

Life insurance and non-life insurance

Life insurance is a form of insurance with the nature of a financial transaction. Under life insurance, an insurance corporation collects premiums from policyholders over a period of time, manages these funds, and pays insurance benefits either as a lump sum or as installments upon maturity. In the SNA, the portion of premiums receivable by life insurance corporations, excluding the service charges, is recorded in the financial accounts as a liability of the insurer and a financial asset of the policyholder during the duration of the contract. Thus, life insurance is treated as a financial service involving the accumulation and management of financial assets.

In contrast, non-life insurance (e.g., automobile or fire insurance) operates similarly in terms of premium payments but provides compensation only when an insured event or loss actually occurs. In the SNA, both the net premiums (i.e., premiums excluding the service charge paid to the insurance corporation) and the claims are recorded in the income transfers account as current transfers. In other words, in non-life insurance, net insurance premiums represent unilateral payments by the policyholder to the insurer, while insurance claims constitute unilateral payments by the insurer to the policyholder.

Nature and accounting treatment of DC and DB schemes in the national accounts

Both **defined contribution** (DC) and **defined benefit** (DB) schemes are forms of social insurance schemes under which employers make regular contributions to financial institutions on behalf of their employees to provide for their retirement. These schemes correspond conceptually to the traditional provision for retirement benefits, but differ from it in important respects. Unlike traditional provisions for retirement benefits, where funds are accumulated internally within the enterprise under a voluntary agreement between the employer and employees, DC and DB schemes are mandated by public regulations and must be deposited with independent third-party financial institutions. This ensures that even if the employer becomes insolvent, employees' right to pension benefits remain protected.

DC and DB schemes are treated as social insurance schemes applicable to employees of resident enterprises. In the SNA, the employers' pension contributions and the pension benefits payable to employees are recorded as current transfers in the income transfers account. However, the net pension contributions of DC and DB (= pension contributions paid – service charges) plus the investment income earned on pension fund assets (treated as contribution supplements), minus pension benefits payable, represent the employees' financial claims on the pension fund, similar to life insurance reserves, and thus increase the disposable income of the households sector. Accordingly, in the use of income account, this amount is recorded as an increase in the household's disposable income and the corresponding payment by financial institutions managing the funds through the item **adjustment for the change in pension entitlements**. The same amount is also recorded as the counterpart transaction in the financial account.

In summary, for DC and DB schemes, the net pension contributions payable and pension benefits receivable by households are treated as current transfers, while the difference between these amounts is reclassified as an adjustment to disposable income and financial claims for the households sector. The processing in the national accounts records the current transfers in the income transfers account, and then the unpaid balance (= net pension contributions – pension benefits) is recorded in both the use of income account and the financial account.

The detailed formula for the "adjustment for the change in pension entitlements" is as follows:

- **Adjustment for the change in pension entitlements** = actual and imputed social contributions payable to pension schemes + the investment income generated by the pension schemes that is attributed to pension beneficiaries (contribution supplements) – pension-related service charges – social benefits payable by pension schemes (pension benefits)

14.3.3.2 Output of non-life insurance and reinsurance

In the case of **non-life insurance and reinsurance**, an insurance contract is concluded between the insurance corporation and the policyholder, under which the policyholder pays premiums over a specified period. If an insured event occurs during that period as defined in the contract, the insurer pays out insurance claims; otherwise, the obligation to pay the claims expires when no event occurs. Non-life insurance contracts generally have short durations (typically one year) and premiums are paid in advance. Consequently, at the end of the accounting period, the insurance corporation treats the portion of premiums that corresponds to the unexpired period of coverage, which has already been paid in advance, as **unearned premiums** and records it as a liability of the insurer. Furthermore, even when insurance claims are incurred, they are not paid immediately, but go through a settlement process over a period of time, so there is a time lag between the incurrence and payment of the insurance claims. The amount that has accrued but not yet been paid is recorded as **claims outstanding** and likewise classified as a liability of the insurance corporation. Aa a result, at the end of the accounting period, the insurance corporation bears total liabilities toward policyholders equal to the sum of unearned premiums and claims outstanding. This combined amount constitutes the **technical reserves** of non-life insurance corporations. In addition, the **investment income** generated from the management of these technical reserves must be attributed to the policyholder's property income. However, since it is not actually distributed to the policyholder but retains within the insurance corporation, it is treated as **premium supplements** payable by the policyholder to the insurance corporation.

Formula for the output of non-life insurance

The output of non-life insurance is measured on a margin basis, calculated as the sum of the actual premiums (premiums earned only) and the part of investment income from the holding of technical reserves that is attributable to policyholders (premium supplements), minus the adjusted claims incurred. This can be expressed by the following formula:

- **Output of non-life insurance = premiums earned + premium supplements – adjusted claims incurred**

Here, **adjusted claims** refer not to the actual insurance claims paid in the current accounting period, but to the expected claims that are likely to occur under normal circumstances. The reason for using adjusted claims instead of actual claims incurred is to minimize fluctuations in the amount of claims arising from unexpected large-scale insurance events, thereby preventing abrupt changes in the measured output of insurance services. In the SNA, two approaches are recommended for estimating adjusted claims. The first approach is to estimate insurance claims by setting up a statistical model based on several years of "historical claims ratios" (= claims payable / premiums earned) to estimate the expected rate of claims and hence the expected amount of claims incurred. This is called the **expectations approach**. The second approach is a retrospective measurement based on actual accounting data, where adjusted claims are calculated as follows:

Adjusted claims = actual claims incurred + changes in equalization provisions

Here, **equalization provisions** refer to reserves set aside by insurance corporations to cover unusually large or unexpected claims. This method is called the **accounting approach**. In circumstances where information about the adjusted claims is not available, the sum of incurred costs (including normal profits) may be used as an estimate of the output of non-life insurance.

Accounting treatment of non-life insurance in the SNA

The output of non-life insurance represents the service charges received by insurance corporations in return for providing insurance services. The economic units that use these services record them as intermediate consumption or final consumption, depending on their institutional sector. Specifically, corporations, government, and NPISHs record the service charges as intermediate consumption, while households record them as final consumption expenditure. Since government and NPISHs are non-market producers, their intermediate consumption is recorded as their own output, which is deemed to be consumed by themselves as final consumption.

In particular, it is important to note that only the service charge for insurance is recorded as intermediate or final consumption, not the total premiums paid by policyholders. The net premiums after deducting service charges from the total premiums (premiums earned + premium supplements) are recorded in the income transfers account as current transfers payable by policyholders to insurance corporations. Similarly, insurance claims payable by insurance corporations are also recorded as current transfers in the same account. However, in exceptional cases, for example in the event of a major catastrophe, the insurance claims payable are treated not as current transfers but as capital transfers, and are therefore recorded in the capital account. On the other hand, in the financial account, the sum of unearned premiums and claims outstanding held by non-life insurance corporations is recorded as a change in technical reserves, representing a liability of the insurance corporations and a corresponding asset of the policyholders.

The accounting treatment of reinsurance follows the same principles as those applied to non-life insurance.

Figure 14.8 Accounting procedure of non-life insurance

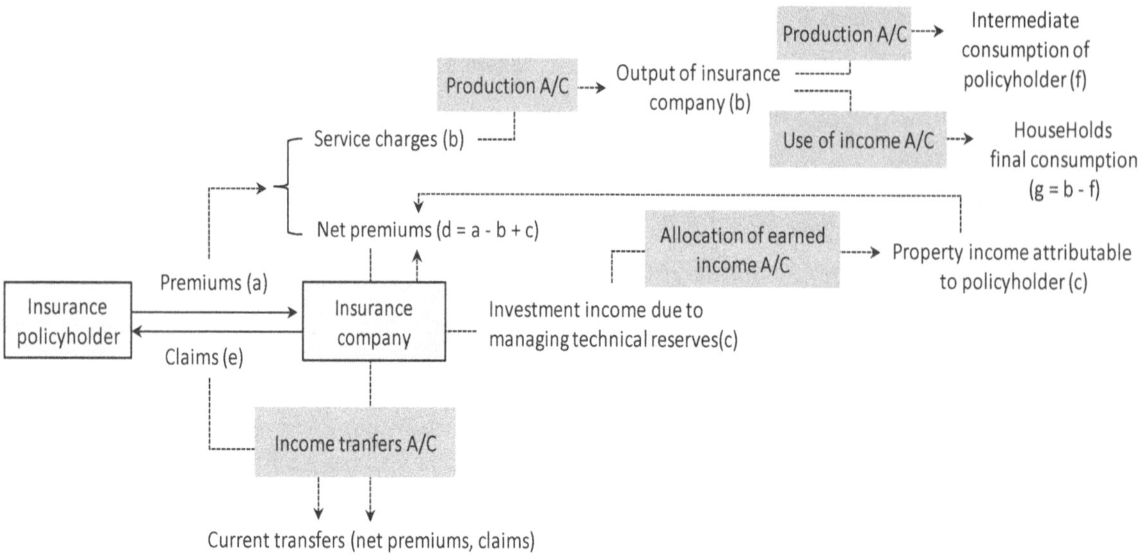

Example of accounting treatment for non-life insurance

Let us illustrate how the output of non-life insurance is calculated and how it is recorded in the sequence of economic accounts, using the following example data. Suppose the following information is given: actual premiums 105 (of which earned premiums 100, and unearned premiums 5), investment income attributable to policyholders 10, and adjusted claims 95 (comprising claims paid 80, claims outstanding 20, and the change in equalization provisions –5). In this case, the output of non-life insurance is 15 (= 100+10–95), the premium supplements by policyholders are 10, and the net insurance premiums equal 95 (= 100+10–15). The accounting entries in the sequence of economic accounts are as follows:

1. Production account: The output of the insurance corporations (15) is recorded.
2. Allocation of earned income account: The investment income (10) receivable by insurance corporations from the operation of technical reserves is recorded, which is attributable to insurance policyholders. This amount is then recorded as the investment income payable by insurance corporations to policyholders.
3. Income transfers account: Policyholders are deemed to pay premiums earned (100) plus premium supplements (10) to the insurance corporations, while the insurance service charge (15) already recorded as output in the production account is deducted. Therefore, net insurance premium of 95 is recorded as a current transfer from policyholders to the insurance corporations
4. Use of income account: The insurance service charge (15) is recorded as expenditure by

the policyholders. If the policyholder is a household, it is recorded as final consumption expenditure in the use account. If the policyholder is a producer, it is recorded as intermediate consumption in the production account.

5. Financial account: The technical reserves of 25 (comprising unearned premium 5, and claims outstanding 20) are recorded as an increase in liabilities of the insurance corporation and a corresponding increase in financial assets of the policyholders.

This accounting treatment procedure applies equally to reinsurance and standardized guarantee schemes.

Figure 14.9 Accounting treatment of non-life insurance in the sequence of economic accounts

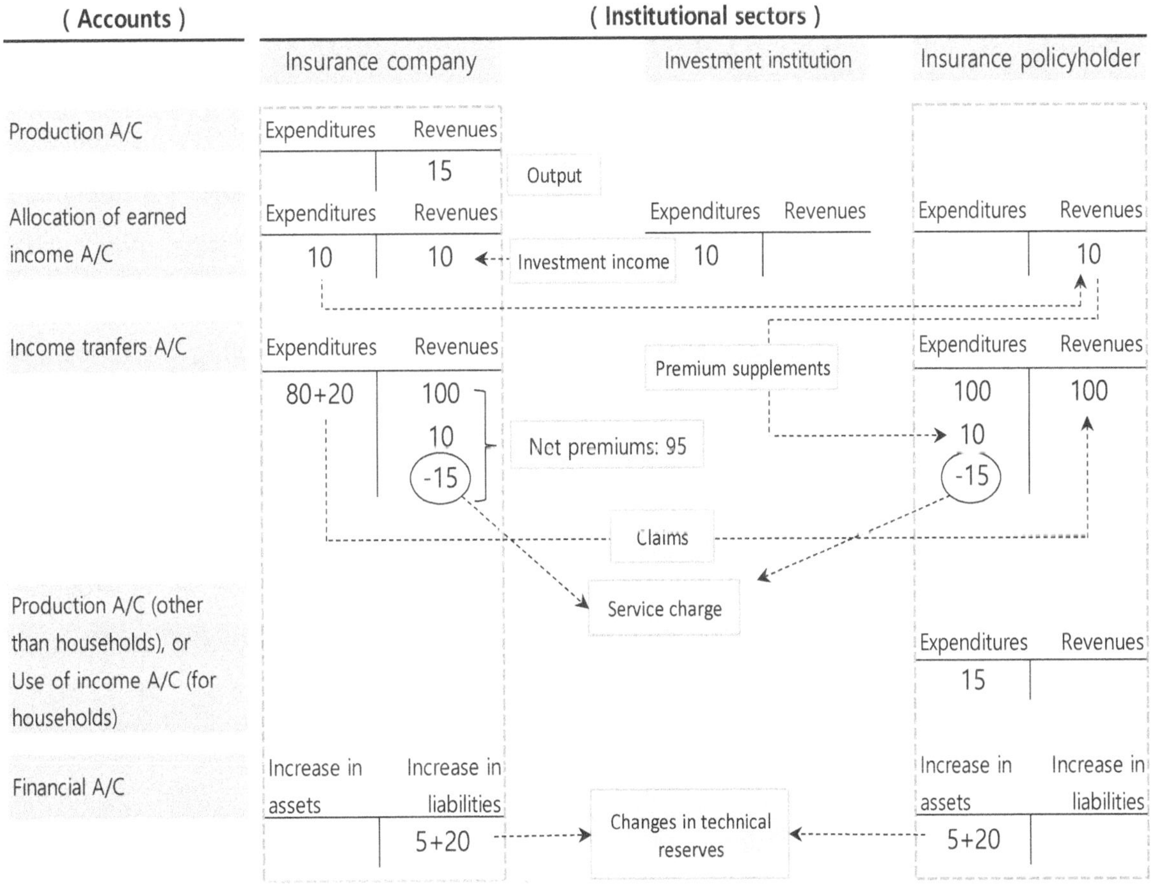

14.3.3.3 Output of life insurance and annuities

Life insurance is a contractual scheme in which a policyholder pays premiums over a specified period of time in exchange for the right to receive a lump sum (or annuity) of benefits at a designated future date. The insurance corporation invests the accumulated premiums, generating investment income, a part of which, after deducting service charges for insurance management, is allocated to policyholders. The part of investment income distributed to policyholders (i.e., insurance bonuses) is retained and managed by the insurance corporation until maturity, forming reserves recorded as liabilities to policyholders.

The **reserves of life insurance** differ somewhat in nature from the technical reserves of non-life insurance. In non-life insurance, contracts are typically short-term, premiums are prepaid in lump sums, and there is usually a time lag between the occurrence and settlement of claims. In contrast, life insurance generally involves regular premium payments over a long period, and the insurance benefits are paid immediately upon maturity. Consequently, unearned premiums and unpaid benefits outstanding are relatively small in life insurance. Instead, because life insurance policies are operated over a long period, insurance corporations accumulate the paid-in premiums to meet future obligations, and a part of the investment income generated from these reserves is allocated to policyholders. Thus, the reserves are accumulated for the purpose of meeting future benefit payments to policyholders and represent households' insurance entitlements.

The reserves of life insurance comprise two components: **Actuarial reserves** and **reserves for with-profit insurance** (i.e., bonus reserves for policyholders). These reserves represent future liabilities of insurance corporations to policyholders, and changes in their value are regarded as changes in households' entitlement of benefits against insurance corporations.

Formula for the output of life insurance

The output of life insurance is measured as a margin concept, similar to that of non-life insurance. However, unlike non-life insurance, life insurance deducts the increase in life insurance reserves, which represents "the amount of liabilities that insurance corporations must accrue for future benefits payable including the part of investment income arising from the management of premiums that is allocated to policyholders" (i.e., changes in life insurance reserves). This amount reflects the increase in the insurance corporations' liabilities to policyholders during the accounting period and must be deducted when calculating the output of life insurance.

Therefore, the output of life insurance is calculated as follows:

- **Output of life insurance = total insurance premiums (= premiums earned + premium supplements) – insurance benefits accrued – changes in life insurance reserves**

The changes in life insurance reserves are conceptually similar to the difference between net premiums and insurance benefits payable by insurance corporations. This amount is recorded in the financial account as an increase in the households' entitlements of life insurance against insurance corporations.

Accounting treatment of life insurance in the SNA

The accounting treatment of life insurance in the SNA follows these steps: In the production account, the output of life insurance is recorded on the revenues side of insurance corporations. The same amount is recorded in the use of income account as final consumption expenditure of households, representing payment for the insurance service. In addition, the part of investment income accrued from the operation of insurance reserves that is allocated to policyholders (as premium supplements) is recorded as property income receivable by households in the allocation of earned income account, and correspondingly, in the financial account, this is recorded as an increase in households' life insurance and annuities entitlements.

Unlike non-life insurance, premiums and benefits in life insurance is not treated as current transfers in the income transfers account; instead, these are treated as financial transactions between households and insurance corporations, and therefore recorded in the financial account. Therefore, the change in life insurance entitlements in the financial account is expressed as follows:

- Change in life insurance entitlements = net premiums (=premiums earned + premium supplements – insurance service charges) – insurance benefits

Figure 14.10 Accounting procedure of life insurance

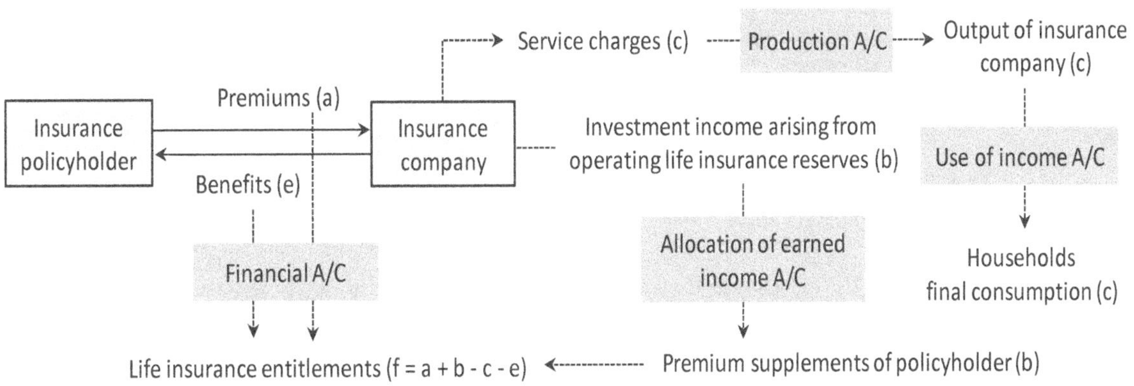

Example of accounting treatment for life insurance

Let us examine how the output of life insurance is calculated and how it is recorded in the sequence of economic accounts, given the following example data. Suppose that the following figures are provided: Actual premiums of 105 (earned premiums 100, unearned premiums 5), investment income of 10, insurance benefits payment of 95, and increase in life insurance reserves of 6. In this case, the output of life insurance is 9 (= 100+10–95–6), and the net premiums are 106 (= 105+10–9). The accounting treatments in each account are as follows:

1. Production account: The output of the insurance corporation (9) is recorded.
2. Allocation of earned income account: the property income (10) earned from operating the life insurance reserves by the insurance corporation is recorded as investment income payable to policyholders.
3. Financial account: On the liability side of the insurance corporation, the net premiums (106), which is actual premiums (105) plus investment income (10 as premium supplements) less insurance service charges (9), are recorded, and the insurance benefits payable (95) are recorded as a decrease in liabilities. Correspondingly, on the asset side of households, an increase in life insurance entitlements 11 (= 106–95) is recorded.
4. Use of income account: The insurance service charge (9) is recorded as final consumption expenditure of households.

Figure 14.11 Accounting treatment of life insurance in the sequence of economic accounts

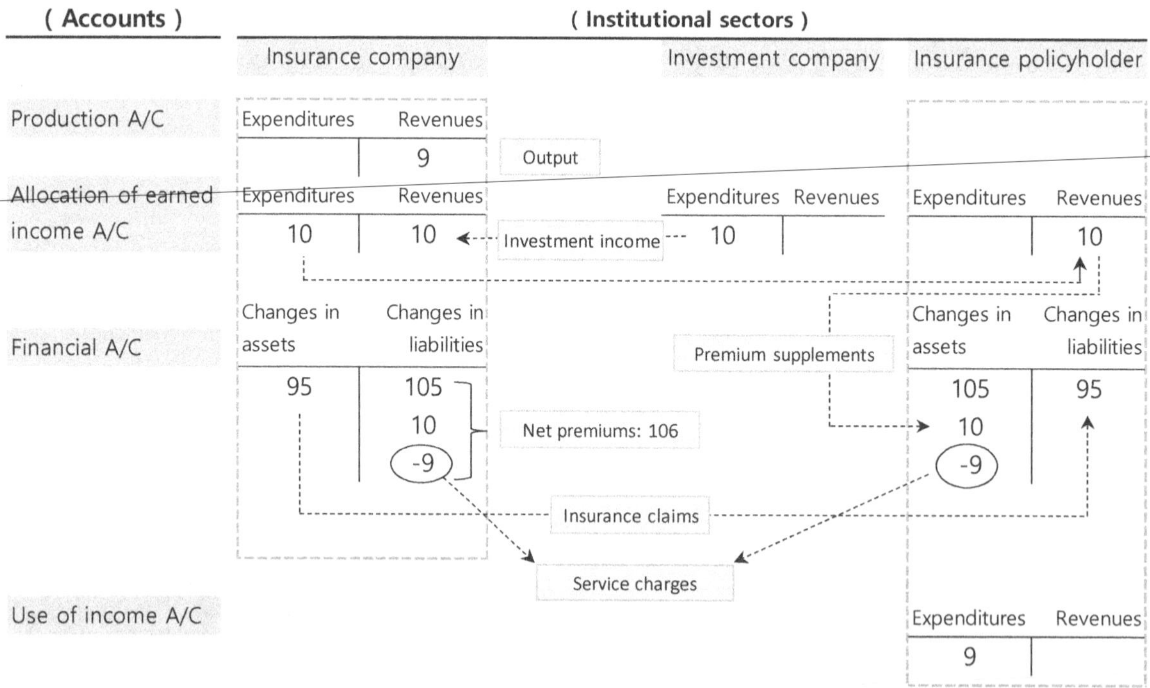

Accounting treatment of annuities in the SNA

Annuities differ from life insurance in that, under an annuity contract, the annuitant (equivalent to the policyholder in the life insurance) pays a lump sum premium to the insurance corporation, and in return, the corporation agrees to make regular periodic payments to the annuitant for fixed number of years or for the remainder of the annuitant's life.

The calculation of annuities can be illustrated as follows. Suppose an annuitant pays $10,000 to an insurance corporation in a lump sum, and the insurer agrees to pay the annuitant $700 annually for 20 years. If the discount rate for future payments is set at 4%, the present value of the 20 annual payments of $700 is calculated as follows:

$$700/1.04 + 700/(1.04)^2 + 700/(1.04)^3 + \cdots + 700/(1.04)^{20} = \$9{,}513.2$$

Thus, the difference between the initial payment (10,000) and the present value of expected payments (9,513.2), or $486.8, represents the present value of the annuity service charge earned by the insurance corporation. If this $486.8 is to be distributed evenly as a service charge over 20 years, the annual service charge amounts to $35.8 (= 700 x 486.8 / 9,513.2). This amount is recorded each year as the output of the insurance corporation.

However, since it is practically difficult in the SNA to obtain detailed data on each individual contract, the output of annuities is generally estimated using the following formula:

- Output of annuities = investment income attributable to annuitants – regular annual annuity payable to annuitants – change in annuity reserves during the period (excluding initial payments for new annuities)

Here, the investment income attributable to annuitants is derived by multiplying the beginning reserve balance of the annuity by the discount rate (without using actual investment income), and the annuity payable to the annuitants is the annuity payment promised each year. In addition, the change in annuity reserves is the change in the values of the total reserves for annuities during the period, which usually has a negative value. Using the aforementioned individual data, the output of annuities for the second period is as follows (Table 14.11). The output for the second period is the investment income of 386.6 (= 9664.2 x 0.04) minus annual annuity payments of 700 minus the change in annuity reserves of (-349.3), which is 386.6–700–(-349.3) = 35.8.

Table 14.11 Example of calculating the output of annuities

Item	Period 1	Period 2
Investment income attributable to annuitants	10,000 x 0.04 = 400	9,664.2 x 0.04 = 386.6
Annual payments due (annual payment of annuity + annual service charge)	700+35.8 = 735.8	700+35.8 = 735.8
Change in annuity reserves	400–735.8 = −335.8	386.6–735.8 = −349.3
Balance of annuity reserves at the end of year	10,000–335.8 = 9,664.2	9,664.2-349.3 = 9,314.9
Output of annuities	400–700–(-335.8) = 35.8	386.6–700–(-349.3) = 35.8

In summary, the output of annuities represents the portion of the investment income earned by the insurance corporation from managing the accumulated funds of annuitants that corresponds to the insurance service provided. This output is recorded in the SNA as part of production of insurance services.

14.3.3.4 Output of the social security pensions and employment-related social insurance pensions

Output of social security pension schemes

Social security pensions are social security schemes that collect social security contributions from households under mandatory regulations and pay pension benefits using their contributions as financial resources. These schemes have the nature of social insurance in which pension contributions and pension benefits are treated as transfer transactions in the SNA. Since social security pension schemes operate on a **pay-as-you-go basis** rather than **funded basis**, no separate financial assets or liabilities are recorded for pension beneficiaries. Therefore, unlike in life insurance, there are no "pension entitlements" entries representing changes in household claims. The output of social security pension schemes is recorded as an expenditure of general government, calculated by the sum of costs method, and classified as final consumption expenditures of general government itself.

Let us illustrate the accounting treatment of a social security pension scheme. Suppose that operating costs of the social security pension scheme are 6, pension contributions are 100 (employer's contribution 50, employee's contribution 50), and pension benefits paid are 90. The accounting entries in the sequence of economic accounts would be as follows:

1. Production account: Output of social security scheme is 6.
2. Generation of earned income account: Remuneration of employees payable by employers

is 100.

3. Allocation of earned income account: Remuneration of employees receivable by households is 100.
4. Income transfers account: Pension contributions payable by households receivable by the social security pension scheme are 100. Pension benefits receivable by households and payable by the social security pension scheme are 90.
5. Use of income account: The output of social security pension scheme (6) is recorded as final consumption expenditure of general government.

Output of employment-related social insurance pension schemes

Employment-related social insurance pension schemes are systems operated by employers as part of their employees' remuneration of employees. Employers either operate the pension funds as pension managers or entrust their operation to independent financial institutions. These pension schemes fall within the category of **social insurance**, but since employees (households) acquire pension entitlements (financial claims), both transfer transactions and financial transactions are recorded in the national accounts.

The accounting procedure in the national accounts is as follows.

1. Payment of pension contributions: Employers pay pension contributions as part of remuneration of employees. This is recorded in the generation of earned income account as remuneration of employees payable by employers and, correspondingly, in the allocation of earned income account as remuneration of employees receivable by households.

2. Transfer to the pension scheme: The pension contributions receivable by households as part of remuneration of employees are transferred to the pensions scheme. At this stage, together with investment income earned from the operation of pension reserves by the scheme (recorded as contribution supplements), these are entered in the income transfers account as pension contributions payable by households and pension contributions receivable by financial corporations. The pension contributions are recorded net of service charges for the operation of the scheme (that is, as net pension contributions).

3. Payment of pension benefits: The pension benefits payable by the pension scheme to beneficiaries (households) are recorded in the same account as pension benefits payable by the pension scheme and pension benefits receivable by households.

4. Service charges and the adjustment for the change in pension entitlements: In the use of

income account, the service charges payable by households to the pension scheme are recorded as final consumption expenditure, while simultaneously the adjustment for the change in pension entitlements is made (as pension entitlements payable by pension schemes and pension entitlements receivable by households). This adjustment for the change in pension entitlements is mirrored in the financial account as an increase in households' pension entitlements (assets) and an increase in the pension scheme's liabilities of the same amount.

There are two types of employment-related social insurance pensions: **defined contribution schemes** and **defined benefit schemes**. The output of pension schemes is calculated as follows. When the employer directly manages the scheme, the output is measured as the sum of the operating costs. If, however, the pension scheme is entirely entrusted to a third-party financial institution (a "multiemployer pension scheme"), the output is derived as:

- **Output of the social insurance pension scheme = pension contributions + contribution supplements – pension benefits – change in pension entitlements**

Here, pension contributions refer to, in the case of DC schemes, the actual contributions payable to the pension schemes, and in the case of DB schemes, the actual contributions plus imputed contributions made by the employer to cover any shortfall in the operating costs of the pension scheme. Contribution supplements represent the investment income arising from the operation of pension reserves (and in the case of DB schemes, additional imputed investment income may also arise). Furthermore, the **net pension contributions** recorded in the income transfers account are calculated as:

- Net pension contributions = pension contributions + contribution supplements – service charges of the pension scheme (= output)

In addition, the adjustment for the change in pension entitlements, which is recorded in the use of income account, is calculated as:

- Adjustment for the change in pension entitlements = net pension contributions – pension benefits

14.3.4 Standardized guarantee schemes

In the national accounts, **standardized guarantees** are guarantees that satisfy the following conditions: similar contracts are issued repeatedly; losses can be estimated statistically; and the guarantor is designed to cover expected losses, administrative costs, and profits through guarantee fees and the investment income earned on those fees. Standardized guarantee schemes constitute a system in which the production of guarantee services, net guarantee fees, and technical provisions are recorded in a systematic manner, in a way analogous to non-life insurance.

The guarantor records "provisions for calls under standardized guarantees," and as the corresponding entry, a notional financial claim of the unit paying the fee is recorded. This recording mechanism is analogous to the treatment of insurance technical reserves as liabilities to policyholders in non-life insurance. Typical forms of standardized guarantees include export credit guarantees that cover the risk of non-payment for exports, loan guarantees, and guarantees on student loans.

The recording of standardized guarantees by account is as follows. In the production account, the guarantor records the output of guarantee services, with the method of valuation being the same as that applied to non-life insurance. On the use side, the service charge component of guarantee fees is recorded as intermediate consumption for enterprises, government, and NPISHs, and as final consumption expenditure for households. In the allocation of earned income account, the investment income generated by the provisions for standardized guarantees is recorded as property income payable by the guarantor and receivable by the unit paying the fee. In the income transfers account, net guarantee fees (defined as guarantee fees plus guarantee fee supplements, that is, attributed investment income, minus service charges) are recorded as receivable by the guarantor and payable by the unit paying the fee. In addition, when a guarantee is called, the amount paid under the guarantee (calls) is recorded in this account as payable by the guarantor and receivable by the guarantee beneficiary (the lender of the debt under guarantee). In the financial account, the net change in provisions for calls under standardized guarantee schemes (equal to net guarantee fees minus calls) is recorded. When a guarantee is called, the lender of the debt under guarantee records a reduction in its asset vis-à-vis the debtor (a loan write-off) in the other changes in the volume of assets and liabilities account.

To illustrate the accounting treatment of standardized guarantees, the following numerical assumptions are used. A guarantor (a public financial institution) provides a guarantee on loans to small and medium-sized enterprise. For a one-year guarantee period, a guarantee fee of 100 is charged, and the value of the guarantee service is assumed to be 30. Investment income earned on the guarantee provisions amounts to 10, and actual calls on guarantees during the period (defaults) amount to 60. Under these assumptions, the recording in the sequence of economic accounts is as follows.

Table 14.12 Example of accounting treatment of standardized guarantee schemes

Account \ Sector	Guarantor (financial institution)		Unit paying the fee		Lender of the debt	
	Expenditures/ changes in assets	Revenues/ changes in liabilities	Expenditures/ changes in assets	Revenues/changes in liabilities	Expenditures/ changes in assets	Revenues/changes in liabilities
Production		Output 30	Intermediate consumption 30			
Allocation of earned income	Property income payable 10					Property income receivable 10
Income transfers	Calls payable 60	Net guarantee fee receivable 80 (=100+10-30)	Net guarantee fee payable 80			Calls receivable 60
Financial		Provisions for calls (liability) 20 (=80-60)	Provisions for calls (asset) 20			
Other changes in the volume of assets and liabilities					Reduction in loans 60	

14.4 Dwelling services industry

Dwelling services refer to the residential services actually received by households from housing. These services are broadly divided into two types. First, **explicit dwelling services**, which arise when a dwelling is rented to another institutional unit, generating actual rental income. Second, **implicit dwelling services**, which occur when the owner of a dwelling occupies the dwelling themselves and thus receives housing services without paying rent.

The output of the dwelling services industry is the monetary value of the services provided by dwellings, which is generally measured based on **rental income**. However, while the rental income generated from leasing dwellings to other institutional units can be directly observed, the dwelling services accrued from owner-occupied housing do not have actual rentals. Therefore, in the SNA, the dwelling services produced and consumed by owner-occupiers are treated as own-account output for own final use, and an imputed rental is recorded to represent the corresponding rental value. In this case, the producers of owner-occupied dwelling services are households that occupy their own dwellings, which is classified as **household unincorporated enterprises** in the institutional sectoring. Since the output of the owner-occupied dwelling services represents a large share of total domestic output, objectivity and consistency in its measurement are crucial for ensuring international comparability.

Owner-occupied dwelling services account for the largest proportion among industries that produce output for own final uses in the national accounts. The source data for this sector can be obtained either from comprehensive economic censuses, population censuses, or through specialized housing and rental surveys. Since owner-occupied dwelling services are measured by imputations, the results can vary significantly depending on the estimation method used.

Table 14.13 Share of housing rental services in major countries (as a percentage of GDP, 2015)

Item	USA	Germany	UK	France
Actual rentals for housing (1)	2.5%	3.6%	4.1%	2.4%
Imputed rentals for housing (2)	7.9%	4.8%	10.2%	7.7%
Total rentals (1+2)	10.4%	8.5%	14.3%	10.2%

Source: OECD, National accounts of OECD countries, detailed tables

14.4.1 Methods for measuring dwelling services

The output of the dwelling service industry is measured on the basis of rental income. For actual rentals, there is no difficulty in measuring the output, since market transactions provide observable prices. However, for owner-occupied dwellings, where non market transactions take place, it is not easy to measure the output because there are no observable market rentals. For actual dwelling services, the rental income reported by landlords registered as housing rental businesses with tax authorities can be used as the basis for estimating output. However, for unregistered rental dwellings and for owner-occupied dwelling services, rental values must be imputed using the rentals of comparable dwellings for which market data are available. This is known as the **equivalent rental approach**. The national statistical office conducts surveys of dwelling rentals through population censuses, stratified by region, types of dwelling, and floor area (number of rooms). These data can be used to estimate the imputed rentals for owner-occupied dwelling.

When information on comparable market rentals is not available, an indirect estimation method, the **user cost approach**, may be applied. Under this approach, the annual user cost of a dwelling is estimated as the present value of the sum of (i) the annual financing cost (interest on the initial investment in the dwelling) and (ii) the annual depreciation of the dwelling.

14.4.2 Accounting treatment of dwelling services in the SNA

The estimation of owner-occupied dwelling services in the SNA can be explained using the supply and use tables (Table 14.14). The output of the owner-occupied dwelling services industry (200) is produced by the household unincorporated enterprises sector, and the entire output of this industry is recorded as final consumption by households (200). Intermediate consumption in this industry includes expenditures on maintenance and repair of dwellings (including provisions for major repairs), fees for housing management, FISIM related to mortgage loans, and insurance service charges. The value added generated by the owner-occupied dwelling services industry consists of gross operating surplus and other taxes on production (such as property taxes), while remuneration of employees does not occur. In addition, depreciation on residential buildings (50) is included in the industry's gross value added.

Table 14.14 Recording of owner-occupied dwelling services in the use table

	...	Construction (residential building)	Owner-occupied dwelling services	Total intermediate consumption	Final consumption (households)	Fixed capital formation (unincorporated enterprises)	....
.....			...				
Residential buildings						(1,000)	
Dwelling services					200		
Total intermediate input			...				
Remuneration of employees							
Depreciation			...				
Other taxes on production			...				
Operating surplus			...				
Gross value added			...				
Total output		(1,000)	200				

The output of actual rental dwelling services (excluding owner-occupied dwellings) includes both the rental income declared by lessors registered with tax authorities and the undeclared rental income of unregistered lessors. The accounting treatment of dwelling services in the sequence of economic accounts is summarized in Table 14.15 below.

Table 14.15 Recording of dwelling services in the sequence of economic accounts

Account	Item in national accounts	Type	Description	Example	
Production account	Output	Rental dwelling services	Rental income from providing dwelling services	Actual rentals	Monthly rentals
				Imputed rentals	Deposits on monthly rentals.
		Owner-occupied dwelling services	Imputed rentals accrued when the owner has assumed to rent the dwelling to others.	Imputed rentals	Owner-occupied or rent-free dwellings
	Intermediate consumption		Input costs incurred by the homeowners or renters.	Maintenance and repair, management fees, mortgage-related FISIM and insurance charge.	
Generation of earned income account	Gross value added	Depreciation	Depreciation of residential buildings (including ownership transfer costs).		
		Remuneration of employees	Occurs only for actual rental dwellings.	Janitor's wages	
		Operating surplus	• Owner occupied dwelling: operating surplus of household unincorporated enterprises. • Rented dwellings: operating surplus of renting corporations or unincorporated enterprises.		
		Other taxes on production		Property taxes	
Use of income account	Final consumption		Output in the production account is treated as final consumption of households.		

As a reference, "own-account transport services" may be considered in the national accounts in the same context as owner-occupied dwelling services. However, unlike dwellings, which are included in gross fixed capital formation and contribute continuously to the production of dwelling services, motor vehicles are mostly treated as "final consumption goods" of households. Therefore, own-account transport services are not separately identified as production activities in the SNA.

14.5 Paid domestic services

Paid domestic services refer to household services provided for remuneration within the household. Examples include maids, nannies, butlers, gardeners, and personal drivers, who are employed by households to perform domestic tasks. By contrast, unpaid domestic services performed by family members without remuneration are not included in the production boundary of the SNA.

The producers of paid domestic services are classified, in terms of institutional sectors, as household unincorporated enterprises. The output of this industry is measured as total amount of wages paid to domestic staff. All intermediate consumption used in the provision of domestic services, such as cleaning supplies, food ingredients, and other consumables, are treated as household final consumption expenditure. This is because it is difficult to distinguish the use of these materials between domestic service workers and household members themselves. Furthermore, since the output of paid domestic services is not sold on the market but produced and consumed within the same household, it is considered the household's own account production. Accordingly, the entire output of paid domestic services is recorded as household final consumption expenditure in the national accounts.

14.6 Research and development (R&D)

This section explains the conceptual nature of research and development and the methods for estimating its output value. It also discusses how basic data on R&D activities are utilized and how these activities are classified and recorded in the supply and use tables.

14.6.1 Nature and valuation of research and development

Research and development (R&D) is a type of intellectual property products. Up to the 1993 SNA, expenditures on R&D conducted by enterprises were treated as intermediate consumption. However, starting from the 2008 SNA, such expenditures have been reclassified as gross fixed capital formation. The SNA defines research and development as follows (2025 SNA, paragraph 11.105):

"Research and development consists of the value of expenditures on creative work undertaken on a systematic basis in order to increase the stock of knowledge, including knowledge of man, culture and society, and use of this stock of knowledge to devise new applications. This does not extend to including human capital as assets."

Human capital refers broadly to expenditures on education in institutions such as schools and training costs for employees incurred by enterprises. Currently, expenditures on education by students at their own cost are recorded as household final consumption, while training costs borne by employers for their employees are treated as intermediate consumption of enterprises.

Measurement and valuation of research and development

Research and development (R&D) can be classified into two types: (i) **own-account R&D output**, produced by enterprises or research institutions for their own use, and (ii) **R&D services output**, produced for sale to other institutional units. Data used to observe R&D output can be obtained in three ways:

1. **From purchasers**, that is, information collected from the demand side,
2. **From own-account producers** by measuring expenditures on internally or externally financed R&D activities,
3. **From producers for sale**, that is, information obtained from the production side.

In the first case, the acquisition of R&D is recorded as gross fixed capital formation of the purchaser. In the second case, it is recorded as gross fixed capital formation of the performers of R&D. In the third case, it is recorded as gross fixed capital formation of the institutional units that purchase the R&D output. The 1993 SNA measured R&D expenditure in cases 1 and 2 as intermediate consumption. However, the 2008 SNA reclassified all such expenditures as gross fixed capital formation. Nevertheless, for case 3, where market producers classified under scientific research and development (ISIC Rev.4 Division 72) undertake R&D for sale, all intermediate inputs used in producing that R&D remain recorded as intermediate consumption. The production of R&D output on own account as in case 2 includes all activities carried out by enterprises for their own use, as well as those conducted by **non-market producers** such educational institutions, public hospitals, and other non-profit research organizations, often financed through government funding.

For valuation purposes of these R&D output, the following principles apply:

- For own-account R&D (case 2), when R&D is produced for internal use within an enterprise, it is valued at the **estimated basic price** that would be paid if the same work were contracted out to another unit. If no comparable R&D outsourcing market exists, the valuation is based on the sum of production costs plus a return to capital equivalent to net operating surplus.
- For own-account R&D by non-market producers, valuation is based solely on production costs, excluding net operating surplus.
- For R&D output produced for sale (case 3), whether conducted by private research institutes specialized in R&D, government units, or non-profit research institutions such as universities, valuation is based on the market transaction price (contract price) at which the R&D is sold.

14.6.2 Recording of research and development expenditure in the SNA

The accounting treatment of R&D expenditure in the SNA differs between market producers (enterprises), and non-market producers (such as government and non-profit institutions). This section explains the accounting procedures separately for these two sectors.

14.6.2.1 R&D expenditure of the corporations sector

R&D expenditure by enterprises can be broadly classified into two types: (i) R&D outputs produced by the specialized unit of R&D (ISIC Division 72) and purchased by other industries, and (ii) R&D expenditure carried out by general enterprises for their own final use. Both types of R&D expenditure are recorded as gross fixed capital formation (GFCF) of the enterprises that incur them. That is, whether a corporation purchases R&D services from a specialized research unit or undertakes R&D on its own account, the associated expenditure is treated as the acquisition of an asset, not as intermediate consumption. However, for specialized producers of R&D, the R&D-related expenditures incurred as inputs in producing R&D outputs are recorded as intermediate consumption.

As an example of the accounting treatment, suppose that the output of specialized producers of R&D (R&D industry) is 100 (with intermediate consumption of 40, and value added of 60), and the output of own-account R&D by general enterprises is 900 (with intermediate consumption of 300, and value added of 600). In this case, the recording in the supply and use tables is shown below. Typically, the own-account R&D conducted by private enterprises may be treated as a secondary product of those enterprises. However, considering the structural characteristics of R&D inputs, it may be more useful for analytical purposes to create a notional industry labeled "own-account R&D" (column) in the supply and use tables. This allows the allocation of R&D-related expenditures (both intermediate consumption and output) arising in all other industries except the R&D industry to this notional R&D-producing activity, providing a clearer picture of R&D activities across industries (see Table 14.16). In the use table, both the R&D output (100) purchased from the R&D industry and the own-account R&D output (900) produced by general enterprises are not recorded as intermediate consumption, but instead as gross fixed capital formation of the enterprises that incur the expenditures.

Table 14.16 Recording of R&D expenditure in the corporations sector

Supply table

	Other industries	R&D industry	Own account R&D
Other products			
R&D product		100	
Own account R&D	(-900)		900
Output	(-900)	100	900

Use table

	Other industries	R&D industry	Own account R&D	GFCF
Other products	...	40	300	
R&D product				100
Own account R&D				900
Value added		60	600	
Input	(-900)	100	900	

* Note: Figures are illustrative. Own-account R&D is shown as a notional industry for analytical clarity.

14.6.2.2 R&D expenditure of non-market producers (government and NPISHs)

The accounting treatment of R&D expenditure for non-market producers is somewhat more complicated than for market producers. This is because the output of non-market producers is estimated using the sum of costs approach, that is, by summing up all input costs. For example, suppose that the government's R&D output on own-account is 90, and that the government purchases of R&D products from the private sector is 60. Additionally, assume that depreciation of 2 arises from the government' gross capital stock of R&D. The SNA records these transactions as follows:

1. The government output on own-account R&D (90) is recorded as gross fixed capital formation of the government, not as government final consumption expenditure.
2. The R&D purchased from private institutions (60, assumed not to be inputs to R&D activities) is also recorded as gross fixed capital formation of government, not as intermediate consumption.

However, the depreciation (2) arising from the government's R&D capital stock represents the depreciation of existing intellectual property products and is therefore excluded from the sum-of-costs method to avoid double counting in the valuation of new IPP output. Accordingly, it is not added to the output of government services.

Table 14.17 Treatment of R&D expenditure by non-market producers

	⋮	Gov't R&D	Private R&D
....			
Gov't service			
Gov't R&D		90	
Private R&D			60
Output		90	60

	Gov't R&D	Private R&D	Gov't GFCF
....			
Gov't service			
Gov't R&D			90
Private R&D			60
Output	90	60	

14.6.3 Derivation of output and gross fixed capital formation for R&D

The most comprehensive data source for R&D expenditure is the statistics compiled in accordance with the OECD Frascati Manual[21]. The OECD's Intellectual Property Product Manual (*Handbook on deriving capital measures of IPPs,* 2010) also recommends deriving national accounts data on R&D based on these Frascati statistics.

Characteristics of Frascati Manual-based R&D statistics

R&D statistics compiled under the Frascati Manual have the following features:

1. Coverage of total R&D expenditure within the reporting unit: The statistics measure all R&D expenditures incurred by R&D performing unit (referred to as "R&D performer") within a specified period. This includes both current expenditures (such as labor costs and operating expenses) and capital expenditures (such as land, buildings, equipment, and software) used for internal R&D activities.

2. Distinction between intra-mural and extra-mural expenditure: Each reporting unit (enterprise, institution, or establishment) reports the total amount spent on R&D, which is divided into two categories:
    - **Intra-mural expenditure**: Expenditure incurred for R&D activities carried out within the unit itself.
    - **Extra-mural expenditure**: Expenditure for outsourcing or funding R&D performed by other units or institutions.

[21] This manual provides the international standard guidelines for the collection of data on research and development, and has undergone a series of revisions since it was first established in Frascati, Italy in 1963.

Intra-mural expenditure is compiled on the basis of enterprises or research institutions that perform R&D (R&D performers). It serves as the primary data source for estimating R&D output produced on own account by these units and is used as the organizing framework for calculating R&D output in the SNA. Extra-mural expenditure includes both expenditures for purchasing R&D from other production units and grants provided to external institutions in support of R&D. To avoid double counting of R&D by the reporting unit, extra-mural expenditure is excluded from the compilation framework.

According to the Frascati Manual, intra-mural R&D expenditure is classified by the following four criteria.

Table 14.18 Classification of intra-mural R&D expenditure (Frascati Manual)

Classification criteria	Main item
By type of cost item	Current costs (labor costs of R&D personnel, other current costs)
	Capital expenditures (land and buildings, instruments and equipment, computer software)
By stage of R&D	Classification by R&D activities (basic research, applied research, experimental development)
By socio-economic objective	Classification of expenditure by socio-economic objective
By institutional sector	Enterprise, government, higher education institutions, and NPISHs

Method for deriving R&D expenditure

Expenditure on research and development (R&D) is derived using the sum of costs approach. The total amount of this expenditure includes net operating surplus (or net return to capital used in production) and depreciation and depletion. To align R&D statistics compiled under the Frascati Manual (abbreviated as **FM**), the following adjustment procedures are required (see IPP handbook, Chapter II, 12-14).

1. Correspondence between institutional sectors in the FM and the SNA

Since the classification of institutional sectors in the Frascati Manual differs from that in the SNA, it is necessary to establish correspondence between them to ensure conceptual consistency of R&D expenditure by institutional sector.

Table 14.19 Linking institutional sectors between the FM and the SNA

FM	SNA
Business enterprise sector	Non-financial corporations
	Financial corporations
Government sector	General government
Private non-profit sector	NPISHs
	Households
	Non-financial corporations
	Financial corporations
Higher education sector	Corporations and quasi-corporations
	General government
	NPISHs
Abroad	Rest of the world

This mapping exercise serves as a preliminary step to consistently integrate R&D expenditure by institutional sector from FM-based statistics into the production structure of the SNA.

2. Converting R&D expenditures by FM into output of the SNA

To align R&D expenditure data compiled from the Frascati Manual (FM) survey with the concepts of the national accounts, adjustments must be made to derive R&D consistent with the SNA framework. In particular, the coverage of R&D expenditure in the FM may include the own-account expenditures of computer software, which should be excluded to avoid double counting, since computer software is treated as a separate intellectual property product. Moreover, R&D products purchased by market producers classified under ISIC Rev.5 Division 72 (Research and Experimental Development Services) are, except in specific cases, treated as intermediate consumption rather than gross fixed capital formation (IPP Handbook 2010, Recommendation 20).

Table 14.20 Derivation of R&D output from FM data

Adjustment	FM item	Additional explanation
	R&D intra-mural expenditure by institutional sector of FM (new R&D development)	Includes both current and capital expenditures.
+	Sales of licenses to use and licenses to reproduce.	Missing from FM data.
–	Payments for licenses to use intellectual property products (e.g., patents) recorded as current costs.	To be treated as capital expenditure.
–	"Intra-mural expenditure" on own-account production of software.	To be transferred to the software industry's own-account production.
+	"Extra-mural expenditures" on R&D services purchased by the R&D service industry (Division 72).	Only applies to R&D purchases recorded as intermediate consumption (excluding those recorded as fixed capital formation).

Adjustment	FM item	Additional explanation
+	Remuneration of employees not included in FM data.	For example: Salaries for graduate students are missing from FM data.
−	Capital expenditure on land, buildings, and machinery	
+	Costs of capital services (= depreciation + net return to capital)	
+	Other taxes less subsidies on production not included in FM data.	
=	**R&D output by institutional sector in the SNA**	

Source: IPP handbook (2010), p. 58 (Table 3)

When corporate accounting data are used as the source for R&D expenditure, additional caution is required. Under business accounting standards, R&D expenditure is recognized as an intangible asset only when future economic benefits are clearly expected; otherwise, it is treated as an expense in the current period. According to these standards, expenditures in the **research phase** are difficult to determine whether they can generate future economic benefits, and thus are recognized as expenses in the current period, while expenditures in the **development phase** are capitalized only if they meet the requirements of intangible assets. All others expenditures except above two cases are treated as current costs (ordinary development expenses).

In contrast, the OECD's IPP handbook (2010, Recommendation 8) recommends that all R&D-related expenditures be included in gross fixed capital formation, regardless of whether the relevant activities ultimately succeed. Consequently, R&D expenditures based on business accounting standards are likely to underestimate gross capital formation in R&D, and therefore, direct use of business accounting data for estimating gross fixed capital formation is not recommended.

3. Deriving total supply, total use, and gross fixed capital formation of R&D using the SUTs

In the final step, the supply and use tables are used to estimate the total supply, total use, and gross fixed capital formation of R&D. In this process, the gross fixed capital formation of R&D is derived using the product flow method instead of obtaining expenditure-side data. The basic formula for this derivation is presented in Table 14.21 below.

Table 14.21 Formula for deriving total supply, total use, and gross fixed capital formation of R&D

Adjustment	Item	Remarks
	R&D output by institutional sector	
+	Imports of R&D	
+	Distribution margins	Close to zero
+	Taxes less subsidies on products	Close to zero
=	Total supply and use of R&D	
–	Intermediate consumption of R&D (only for R&D service producers)	
–	Exports of R&D	
+	Net purchases of R&D gross fixed capital formation between domestic sectors	The total sum equals zero.
–	Changes in inventories of finished and work-in progress R&D	
=	Gross fixed capital formation of R&D by institutional sector	
(+/–)	Adjustments for capital transfers (recorded in the capital account)	

Source: IPP Handbook (2010), p. 58 (Table 4)

14.7 Computer software, data and databases

Computer software is a type of intellectual property product (IPP) that was first introduced in the 1993 SNA, and its scope was later expanded in the 2008 SNA to include databases. In the 2025 SNA, data assets were newly introduced, and the category was further subdivided into *data and databases*, leading to the combined upper category *computer software, data and databases*. The following sections provide separate explanations for computer software and for data and databases.

14.7.1 Computer software

. The term *computer software* encompasses all computer programs, their program descriptions and supporting materials for both systems and applications software. It also includes artificial intelligence systems. Computer software is broadly divided into "original software" and "software copies." The category of the **original software** includes the following items:

- Originals produced for the purpose of reproduction (i.e., those created by specialized software-producing enterprise)
- Own-account software production developed internally by enterprises for use in their own production processes
- Custom-made software purchased from other software development enterprises.

The production or acquisition of such original software is treated as gross fixed capital formation.

Meanwhile, **Software copies** fall into two categories:

- Licenses to use: rights to use specific copies of software, such as packaged software,
- Licenses to reproduce: rights to make additional copies and distribute or sell the software.

The acquisition of such licenses to use and licenses to reproduce is recorded either as gross fixed capital formation or as intermediate consumption, depending on the circumstances. Specifically, it is recognized as gross fixed capital formation only when the license is valid for more than one year and the purchaser bears both risks and rewards of ownership.

14.7.1.1 Output of computer software

The output of computer software consists of the output on own account and the output of the computer software development industry. First, the **output of software development industry** is derived by adding changes in inventories to the industry's sales revenue. The output of this industry includes sales of licenses to use or to reproduce software copies and custom-made software, and the enterprises' financial statements (sales revenue) in the same industry serve as the main data source. Next, the **software output on own-account** includes not only software produced internally by enterprises for their own use, but also software developed internally by the software development enterprises for the purpose of selling licenses to use or to reproduce. Since own-account software is a special case of R&D described in the previous section, it is measured by the sum of costs method in the same way as the R&D, and includes **user costs** (i.e., depreciation and net return to capital used in production).

Figure 14.12 Components of software output

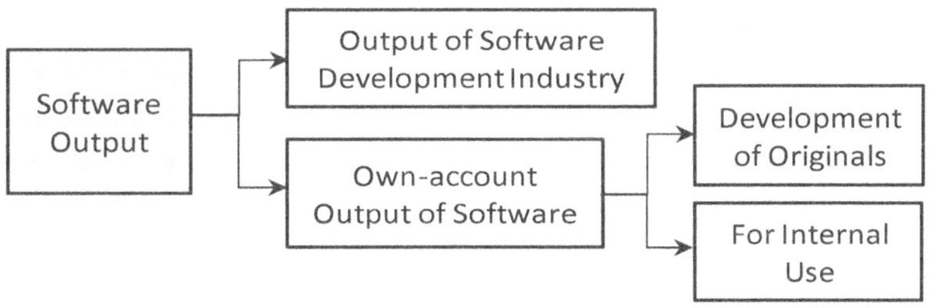

The own-account software output of an enterprise is obtained by summing the wages of software staff, intermediate consumption, and gross operating surplus, and this amount is reflected in gross fixed capital formation. In business accounting, as in the case of R&D, software-related expenditures are treated as intangible assets (capitalized development costs) if they meet the criteria for asset recognition; otherwise, they are recognized as current expenses (current development costs).

According to the OECD IPP Handbook, the production process of own-account software can be divides into eight stages: (1) Feasibility analysis, (2) Functional analysis, (3) Detailed analysis, (4) Programming, (5) Tests, (6) Documentation, (7) Training, (8) Maintenance. When estimating own-account software output, only expenditures corresponding to the core development stages (2)–(6) should be included, while stages (1), (7) and (8) are excluded. In other words, only those stages that create actual assets are included in own-account output and recorded as gross fixed capital formation (IPP Handbook, 2010, Recommendation 31).

If it is difficult to directly estimate own-account software output in industries other than software development industry, it can be estimated indirectly by multiplying the own-account output per employee in the software development industry by the number of software-related employees in the given industry. In addition, the output of own-account software must be adjusted to avoid double counting with own-account R&D output, since R&D statistics often include software development as part of a broader concept of R&D, and thus the software component may already be embedded in R&D data.

14.7.1.2 Measuring gross fixed capital formation of computer software

Gross fixed capital formation (GFCF) of computer software can be divided into two types: (1) **original software** produced internally by production units on **own-account basis**, and (2) **purchased software** obtained from software development enterprises, which includes licenses to use or reproduce software copies and custom-made software developed to order. This section explains the methods used to measure the gross fixed capital formation of these types of software.

Measurement of GFCF for purchased software

Purchases of software supplied by software development enterprises are treated as intermediate consumption if the right to use the software is valid for one year or less, and as gross fixed capital formation if it is valid for more than one year. Although the GFCF of purchased software may be estimated directly through demand-side surveys, it is more commonly derived using the "product flow method" based on supply-side data. Of course, if the supply-side data is available only as aggregated totals, additional information should be obtained to distinguish between contracts lasting one year or less and those exceeding one year. The following table outlines the procedure for deriving the GFCF of purchased software using the product flow method.

Table 14.22 Derivation of GFCF for purchased software (Product flow method)

Adjustment	Item	Description
+	Output of software industry	Software publishing (5821) + Computer programming activities (6219) + Application service provisioning (part of 6310): Only contracts for use exceeding one year included.
+	Imports	Royalties and license fees: Only contracts exceeding one year.
+	Margins and taxes on sales	
-	Intermediate consumption	Software embedded in the hardware (50% of packaged software purchased by hardware industries).
-	Sub-contracting among software enterprises	To avoid double counting.
-	Final consumption	Household consumption on packaged software and games.
-	Exports	Royalties and license fees: Only contracts exceeding one-year.
=	GFCF for purchased software licenses	

Source: OECD, IPP Handbook, pp. 109-110. Industry codes are based on the ISIC Rev.5.

Measurement of GFCF for own-account software

The GFCF of own-account software is obtained by first measuring its output and then directly allocating that amount to gross fixed capital formation. The output of own-account software is measured using the sum of costs method described in the previous section (14.7.1).

14.7.1.3 Presentation of computer software in the supply and use tables

To provide a clearer understanding of the relationship between the production and expenditure of computer software, this section explains it through the framework of the supply and use tables. The estimation method of **own-account software** in the supply and use tables follows an approach similar to that used for own account R&D. First, a notional industry (the own-account software industry) is set up. Then, from all enterprises other than software development industry (i.e., those developing software for their own use), the costs associated with own-account software development are extracted and allocated as the intermediate consumption, value added and output of this notional industry. The resulting output is recorded as the own-account gross fixed capital formation of the same enterprises. On the other hand, the output of the **software development industry** is classified according to the type of purchaser: If the purchaser is a household, it is recorded as final consumption expenditure; if the purchaser is an enterprise, it is recorded either as gross fixed capital formation or intermediate consumption (including software embedded in computer hardware) depending on the purpose and duration of use.

For example, suppose that the software development industry has an output (200) and intermediate consumption (80), while other industries have the output of own-account software (130), intermediate consumption (30), and value added (100). Further, assume that the output of 200 from the software development industry is used for intermediate consumption (50) and gross fixed capital formation (110) of other industries, and for final consumption and exports (40). The results are shown in Table 14.23. In the use table, the output of own-account software (130) derived using the sum of costs method corresponds to the own-account output (130) in the supply table and is recorded as gross fixed capital formation (130) in the use table. Meanwhile, in the supply table, the output of the software development industry (200) is allocated in the use table as intermediate consumption (50) or gross fixed capital formation (110) of other industries, and other final expenditures (40).

Table 14.23 Treatment of computer software in the supply and use tables

Supply table

	Other industries	Software development industry	Own-account software
Other products			
Software products		200	
Own-account software			130
Output		200	130

Use table

	Other industries	Software development industry	Own-account software	Fixed capital formation	Other final expenditure	Total
Other products		80	30			
Software products	50			110	40	200
Own-account software				130		130
Value added		120	100			
Input		200	130			

The accounting treatment of software for non-market producers (such as government and NPISHs) follows the same procedures as for R&D. For details, refer to section 14.6 (Research and development) of this chapter.

14.7.2 Data and databases

Data and databases are a type of intellectual property product and are grouped together with computer software in a single category. This grouping reflects the fact that a computerized database, including the relevant data, cannot be developed independently of a database management system (DBMS), which itself constitutes computer software.

Conceptual treatment and measurement

Database and databases consist of electronic files that contain information content (that is, the data themselves) organized in such a way as to allow resource-efficient access and use of the data. These data and databases can be classified into three types: (i) databases used in production for more than one year (own-use databases), (ii) databases sold as individual items, or (iii) databases sold through licenses granting access to the information contained within them. Data and databases are conceptually distinct, but in practice they are produced using similar inputs and are often difficult to measure separately. Moreover, transactions in databases generally include the value of the data stored in them. For these reasons, data and databases are treated as a single category of intellectual property products. As the production of data and databases is largely undertaken on own account and observable market prices are generally unavailable, their output is in principle estimated using the **sum of costs method**.

The costs included in the output of **data** comprises the costs of planning and designing a data production strategy; the costs of accessing and observing observable phenomena; the costs of recording and storing information; and the costs of cleaning, processing and otherwise preparing the data. The costs included in the output of **databases** comprise the costs of designing, structuring and implementing the database, as well as the costs of transforming and organizing the data into formats suitable for analysis. The cost of the database management system (DBMS) used in the construction of a database is not included in the cost of producing the database and is treated as a computer software asset, unless the DBMS is acquired under an operating lease. By contrast, the costs of organizing and processing data into a format suitable for inclusion in a database are included in the cost of producing the database, while the costs of acquiring or producing the data themselves are excluded from the database. Common cost components in the production of both data and databases include labour input costs, the capital services of non-financial assets, and intermediate consumption.

Data and databases produced for sale are valued at their market prices, which include the value of the information content. If the value of a software component within the database can be identified separately, that value is recorded as the sale of software.

Example of the accounting treatment of data and databases in the SNA

The accounting treatment of data and databases varies depending on the nature of the production activity (own account or market transaction) and the intended use of the asset (own use or sale). In principle, data and databases are classified as intellectual property products, and their production is recognized as gross fixed capital formation (GFCF) at the time of creation. Subsequently, depreciation is recorded over the asset's service life.

1. Own-account data and databases

When an enterprise or public institution develops a database internally for its own production activities, it is treated as **own-account production**. The output of own-account databases is estimated using the sum-of-costs method, which includes the following components:

- Remuneration of employees: salaries and wages of staff engaged in data collection, processing, and management
- Intermediate consumption: goods and services used for data collection, storage, and processing
- Other taxes less subsidies on production
- Depreciation of servers, storage equipment, and other non-financial assets
- Depletion of non-produced assets
- Net return to capital used in production

The output of own-account databases produced in this way is recorded as output in the production account, and at the same time the same amount is recorded as an increase in assets in the capital account as gross fixed capital formation.

2. Market-produced data and databases

When data or databases are sold to external parties, or when licenses granting access to or the right to reproduce data and databases are provided, these activities are classified as market production. In this case, when a user acquires their access license or reproduction rights, the transaction is recorded as intermediate consumption if the period of use is one year or less, and as gross fixed capital formation if the period of use exceeds one year.

3. Example of estimating own-account output

Suppose a data-processing enterprise develops a database internally (own-account) with the following cost structure:

Item	Amount	Description
Remuneration of employees	60	Salaries for staff engaged in data collection, processing, and management
Intermediate consumption	25	Payments for external data collection and cloud services
Depreciation	10	Depreciation of servers and storage equipment
Net return to capital	5	Normal profit margin for a market producer
Other taxes less subsidies on production	0	-
Total	**100**	**Own-account database output = GFCF: 100**

In this case, the following entries are made in the national accounts: in the production account, output of the database industry 100; in the generation of earned income account, net operating surplus 5, depreciation 10, remuneration of employees 60; in the capital account, gross fixed capital formation 100.

14.8 Mineral exploration and evaluation

Mineral exploration and evaluation includes all activities undertaken both by (a) enterprises engaged in the exploration and extraction of mineral resources that carry out exploration work on own account, and (b) specialized exploration enterprises that perform such activities under contract for others. Expenditures on these activities cover all costs related to locating, quantifying, and assessing the quality and economic feasibility of extracting underground resources. These expenditures are not considered ordinary current expenses, but rather investment expenditures made in anticipation of future economic benefits.

Mineral exploration and evaluation is classified, like research and development, as a type of intellectual property product. It was first recognized as an intangible produced asset in the 1993 SNA, and in the 2008 SNA, the scope was expanded by explicitly including "evaluation," leading to the broader term *mineral exploration and evaluation*.

Accounting treatment and valuation method

All costs related to mineral exploration and evaluation are recorded as gross fixed capital formation, regardless of whether the exploration proves to be successful. The expenditures to be included are all costs associated with the acquisition of exploration rights, geological and topographical studies, exploratory drilling, and activities related to evaluating the technical feasibility and commercial viability of extraction.

Since most activities of mineral exploration and evaluation are carried out by enterprises on own-account, market prices are often not directly observable. In such cases, the sum of costs method is used for their valuation:

- Own account output of mineral exploration and evaluation = intermediate consumption + remuneration of employees + depreciation and depletion + net return to capital + other taxes less subsidies on production

It is also reasonable to align the depreciation period of these assets with the economic life of the related mineral resources. Since mineral exploration and evaluation activities are concentrated in specific enterprise, a complete enumeration survey is preferable for data collection.

The treatment of mineral exploration and evaluation in the supply and use tables is shown in Table 14.24. Since most of these activities are performed as own-account production by enterprises within the mining industry, they are recorded as secondary products of the mining industry in the supply table and as gross fixed capital formation for the enterprises' own final use in the use table. For example, suppose the own-account mineral exploration and evaluation of the mining industry amounts to 250, and the contracted exploration work performed by specialized exploration enterprises is 30. In this case, the supply table records 250 as a secondary product of mining industry and 30 as the output of specialized exploration enterprises, while the use table records the combined total (280) as gross fixed capital formation.

Table 14.24 Presentation of mineral exploration and evaluation in the supply and use tables

Supply table

	..	Mining industry	Mineral exploration enterprise	...
Natural gas		300		
Other Mining		100		
Mineral exploration		**250**	**30**	
Total		650	30	

Use table

	..	Mining industry	Mineral exploration enterprise	..	GFCF
Natural gas		..			
Other mining		..			
Mineral exploration		..			**280**
GVA		..			
Total		650	30		

14.9 Military equipment

The treatment of military equipment in the national accounts has evolved over time. Under the 1993 SNA, only expenditures on fixed assets that could also be produced and used for civilian purposes but happened to be employed for military use were recorded as gross fixed capital formation. In the words, only assets similar to those used in the civilian sector were recognized as fixed assets, while strictly military assets such as tanks or combat aircraft were not. However, from the 2008 SNA, this criterion has been broadened to include **all military weapons systems** (such as warships, military aircraft, tanks, and missile launchers) as fixed assets to be recorded as gross fixed capital formation. This reflects the recognition that although such equipment does not directly contribute to production activities in the same way as civilian capital, it provides long-term benefits to the nation by contributing to defense and security services, thereby possessing the essential characteristics of an asset.

On the other hand, **single-use weapons** such as ammunition, missiles, rockets, and bombs are to be treated as military inventories prior to use and as intermediate consumption once they are used. However, weapons such as ballistic missiles with substantial deterrent capability against war are treated as fixed assets due to their long-term service potential.

Table 14.25 Treatment of military equipment in the national accounts

Type	Example	Treatment in the national accounts	
Weapons systems	Warships, submarines, military aircraft, tanks, missile carriers and launchers	Fixed assets	
Single-use weapon	Ammunition, missiles, rockets, bombs	Before use	Military inventories
		After use	Intermediate consumption
	Ballistic missiles	Fixed assets	

Treatment of weapons systems in the use table

For example, let us examine how the purchase of tanks (valued at 10) by the government from the weapons industry is recorded in the use table. Under the 1993 SNA, this expenditure was recorded as intermediate consumption (10) of the government unit, which led to simultaneous increases in both the government's output and its final consumption expenditure. However, from the 2008 SNA, the same expenditure is treated as gross fixed capital formation (10) of the government. While military weapons systems are held as an asset, depreciation on the stock of the weapons systems occurs (2) over time, affecting output by –8 (weapons systems –10, depreciation 2).

Table 14.26 Comparison of the treatment of weapons systems in the use table

1993 SNA

	…	Government	Weapons industry	Gov't final consumption	Gov't GFCF
Government service				10	
Weapons systems		10			
Value added (depreciation)					
Total input		10	10		

2008 SNA

	…	Government	Weapons industry	Gov't final consumption	Gov't GFCF
Government service				2	
Weapons systems		0			10
Value added (depreciation)		2 (2)			
Total input		2	10		

Treatment of single-use weapons in the use table

When the government purchases single-use weapons such as ammunition (valued at 20), the purchase is recorded at that point as an increase in military inventories of the government. Subsequently, when the weapons are used, the entries show a decrease in inventories (– 20), an increase in intermediate consumption (20), and an increase in government final consumption expenditure (20) corresponding to the provision of defense services.

Table 14.27 Treatment of single-use weapons in the use table

At the time of acquisition

	…	Government	Weapons industry	Gov't final consumption	Gov't changes in inventories
Gov't services					
Single-use weapons					20
Value added					
Total input			20		

At the time of use

	…	Government	Weapons industry	Gov't final consumption	Gov't changes in inventories
Gov't services				20	
Single-use weapons		20			-20
Value added					
Total input		20			

14.10 Head offices and ancillary activities

This section explains the concepts and distinctions between **head offices** and **holding companies**, and describe how to measure the output of ancillary activities performed by headquarters and allocate them to each establishment.

Head offices and holding companies

A **head office** is defined as a separate unit within an enterprise or an enterprise group that performs the functions of strategic, organizational, and operational decision-making and management control over other units, including subsidiaries. This category includes not only corporate headquarters but also central administrative offices, regional offices, and subsidiary management offices. The management and support activities undertaken by head offices include services such as legal and accounting support, marketing and IT services, human resources management and training, technical consulting, and real estate management. In terms of industrial classification, head offices are classified under the **professional, scientific and technical activities** (Section N), and in terms of institutional sector classification, they are categorized as *non-financial corporations*. However, when the subsidiaries of a head office are all (or predominantly) financial corporations, the head office is customarily classified under financial and insurance activities (Section L) in the industrial classification, and as financial corporations sector (financial auxiliaries) in the institutional sector classification.

In contrast, a **holding company** is primarily established to own the assets of a group of subsidiaries (holding a controlling level of equity) and its primary purpose is to manage those assets. In other words, unlike a head office, a holding company does not provide managerial or administrative services to its subsidiaries and its main functions are ownership of equity and asset management. Therefore, holding companies are classified under **financial and insurance activities** (Section L) in the industry classification, and in the institutional sector classification, they are treated as financial corporations (captive financial institutions and money lenders), regardless of whether their subsidiaries are financial or non-financial corporations.

Table 14.28 Classification of head office and holding companies

Type	Industrial classification	Institutional sector classification
Head office overseeing and managing other units of the enterprise or enterprise group.	Professional, scientific, and technical activities (N)	Non-financial corporations
Head office where all or most of the other units within the enterprise or subsidiaries are financial corporations.	Financial and insurance activities (L)	Financial corporations (Financial auxiliaries)
Holding company whose principal activity is to own the assets of its subsidiaries, without providing management services.	Financial and insurance activities (L)	Financial corporations (Captive financial institutions and money lenders)

Accounting treatment of establishments performing only ancillary activities

In the SNA, head offices are classified as a separate industry that performs ancillary activities. However, in practice, depending on the organizational structure of the enterprises, it may not always be possible to identify the establishment that performs such functions. The head office is classified under section L or N of the industry classification, and its output and intermediate consumption may be recorded as those of a separate establishment. By contrast, an establishment that performs only ancillary activities (for example, **headquarter unit**) may or may not be identifiable. If the headquarter unit can be identified, its output and intermediate consumption are recorded separately, and its output is allocated as intermediate consumption to other establishments within the enterprise. However, if the headquarters cannot be identified, its output is not recorded separately, and the input costs incurred by the headquarter are allocated directly to the other establishments. The output of headquarter is measured using the sum of costs method, which provides a comprehensive valuation including the cost of capital, as follows:

- Output of headquarter = intermediate consumption + remuneration of employees + other taxes less subsidies on production + depreciation and depletion + net return to capital

An example of allocating the output of a headquarter unit performing ancillary activities to other establishments is illustrated below. As shown in Figure 14.13, suppose an enterprise consists of a headquarter unit and two establishments, and the headquarter unit incurs intermediate consumption of 90 and value added (mainly remuneration of employees) of 60. Accordingly, the headquarter unit's output is recorded as 150 (= 90+60), which must be allocated as intermediate consumption to the other establishments. If the allocation criterion is based on the output value of each establishment (Establishment 1: 1,000; Establishment 2: 500), the output of the headquarter (150) is distributed as follows:

Establishment 1: 150×1,000/(1,000+500) = 100; Establishment 2: 150×500/(1,000+500) = 50

Thus, the output of the headquarter is added as intermediate consumption (100 and 50, respectively) to each establishment, reducing value added of each establishment by the amounts. As a result, the gross value added for the enterprise as a whole is calculated as 360 (= 250+200+60−150).

Figure 14.13 Example of allocating the output of headquarter

<Basic data>

	Establishment 1	Establishment 2	Head quarter
Output	1,000	500	No sales
Intermediate consumption	750	300	90
Value added	250	200	60

<Distribution result>

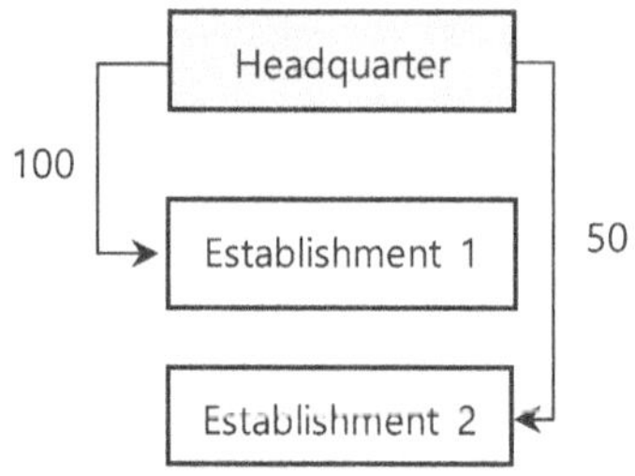

	Establishment 1	Establishment 2	Head quarter	Total
Output	1,000	500	150	1,650
Intermediate consumption	850	350	90	1,290
Value added	150	150	60	360

14.11 Travel agency services

The travel agency industry refers to businesses that arrange and provide various travel-related services on behalf of clients, such as travel agencies or booking intermediaries. These services include the arrangement and brokerage of transport, accommodation, food services, communications, insurance, and travel guide services. In return, travel agencies earn commissions or service fees. (In industry classification, this industry corresponds to "Travel agency and reservation services activities.") The main sources of revenue for travel agencies include commissions from selling package tours, airline ticket commissions, and other service fees. A key feature of the travel agency industry is that the costs of the services intermediated by travel agencies (transport, accommodation, food, etc.) are not recorded as intermediate consumption of the agency. Instead, these services are treated as being purchased and paid for directly by travelers. This treatment is consistent with business accounting practices, in which travel agencies do not recognize the full value of travel-related services as sales revenue, but only record their commission income as operating revenue.

Relationship with travel services in the balance of payments

In the *Balance of Payments and International Investment Position Manual, Sixth Edition (BPM6)*, travel services include all goods and services acquired by residents while travelling abroad (imports of goods and services) and all goods and services acquired by non-residents while staying in the domestic economy (exports of goods and services). **Travel services** in the balance of payments are not represented by a single CPC code but comprise a wide range of items such as goods, transport, accommodation, food services, communication, and insurance. Accordingly, all payments related to travel services intermediated by travel agencies are also included in this category. Therefore, compilers of national accounts must decide whether to disaggregate *travel services* in the balance of payments into multiple product items in the supply and use tables, or to display them as a separate product category. When source data are available by detailed product, it is preferable to allocate travel service expenditures across the relevant product categories.

In the national accounts, travel is classified into **business travel** and **personal travel**. Expenditures incurred by enterprises for business travel purposes are treated entirely as intermediate consumption, whereas expenditures by households for personal travel are recorded as final consumption expenditure.

Recording the imports and exports of travel services in the supply and use tables

When classifying the import and exports of travel services within the supply and use tables, the following guidelines can be applied. In the **supply table**, it is desirable to disaggregate the total imports of travel services, i.e., expenditures by residents travelling abroad for business and personal purposes, by product category (goods and services) and record them under the corresponding *imports* column. If a detailed breakdown by product is unavailable, a separate row titled "Direct purchases abroad by resident" should be created to record the total amount collectively. In the **use table**, expenditures made by non-residents while staying in the domestic economy are recorded as *exports of travel services* in a separate row titled "Domestic purchases by non-residents." If data allow for a breakdown by product, it is preferrable to allocate these amounts across the respective product categories. The export value of travel services is deducted from the final consumption expenditure of total domestic final consumption. Conversely, the "direct purchases abroad by residents" recorded in the supply table are added back in the use table, allocated to household final consumption expenditure (for personal travel) and intermediate consumption (for business travel).

For example, suppose that in the balance of payments, travel services show exports of 6 and imports of 18. That is, non-residents' expenditures in the domestic economy amount to 6, while residents' expenditures abroad amount to 18 (10 by households and 8 by enterprises). The corresponding entries in the supply and use tables are shown below (Table 14.29). First, in the **supply table**, residents' expenditures abroad (18) are recorded in the cell where the *imports* column intersects with the "direct purchases abroad by residents" row. In the **use table**, the amount of direct purchases abroad by residents (18) is allocated between household final consumption (10) and intermediate consumption (8). In addition, *domestic purchases by non-residents* (6) are recorded in the cell where the *exports* column intersects with the *domestic purchases by non-residents* row, and this amount is deducted from household final consumption expenditure to reduce domestic final consumption.

Table 14.29 Adjustment of the imports and exports of travel services in the SUTs

Supply table

	Output	Imports
..		
Direct purchases abroad by residents		18
Total		18

Use table

	Intermediate consumption	Final consumption	Exports	Total
..				
Direct purchases abroad by residents	8	10		18
Domestic purchases by non-residents		-6	6	0
Total	8	4	6	18

14.12 Digital products

The diffusion of digital technologies has brought about structural changes across the entire spectrum of economic activities measured in the national accounts, including modes of production and consumption, transaction structures, and the forms of assets. Nevertheless, despite these transformations, the fundamental principles of the System of National Accounts, namely the production boundary, the asset boundary and the distinction between goods and services, remain unchanged.

In the 2025 SNA, the term "digital" does not denote an independent or entirely new category of products. Rather, it is used as an analytical concept that reclassifies and enhances the identifiability of existing goods, services, and assets from the perspective of digitalization. Accordingly, **digital products** are defined as goods and services that are produced, delivered, or used through digital technologies and infrastructure, or that enable the digitalization of economic activities.

The 2025 SNA recommend identifying digital products by function while maintaining the existing product classification system (CPC). Where appropriate, separate aggregations may be presented through digital supply and use tables or thematic extension accounts. This section summarizes the categories of digital products and their treatment in the national accounts, with particular emphasis on the measurement of output for digital products, such as free online platforms and free software, for which prices are not directly observed or user do not make explicit payments, yet which are nevertheless recorded as market production.

14.12.1 Categories of digital products and national accounts treatment

The 2025 SNA classifies digital products into two functional categories. The first consists of **products enabling digitalization**, which have the character of digital infrastructure. The second comprises **products enabled by digitalization**, which rely on digital technologies for delivery and intermediation. This distinction provides a conceptual and accounting framework for determining how digital products should be recognized and valued as production, consumption, or assets in the national accounts.

Table 14.30 Classification of digital products

	Category	Main content	National account treatment
Products enabling digitalization	ICT goods	Servers, semiconductors, network equipment	Goods
	Software	System software, application software, AI software	Services/Intellectual property assets
	Data and databases	Structured data	Intellectual property assets
	Communication and network services	Internet services, mobile telecommunications	Services
Products enabled by digitalization	Cloud computing	IaaS, PaaS, SaaS	Services
	Digital intermediation services	Platform intermediation fees	Services
	Digital content	Streaming services, online games	Services
	Digital financial services	Electronic payments, fintech services	Services

In the national accounts, digital products are classified into **ICT goods** and **digital services**. ICT goods are tangible goods and may be classified according to the ICT product categories of the Central Product Classification (CPC); they are used either as gross fixed capital formation or as intermediate consumption. Digital services constitute the majority of digital products and may be further grouped as follows:

- ICT services: software development and maintenance, data processing and hosting, systems integration, IT consulting, ICT operation and management
- Digitally delivered services: cloud computing services, digitally delivered content and media services, online communication and collaboration services, artificial intelligence-based serviced delivered remotely, digitally delivered financial and payment services
- Digital intermediation services: non-financial digital intermediation, advertising-based digital intermediation, financial digital intermediation platforms

14.12.2 Output of free platform

The output of free online platforms is measured on the basis of the consideration received from third parties, such as advertisers, rather than from users. In other words, while provision is free from the perspective of users, production is not free from the perspective of the producer. The typical structure of a free platform involves three parties: the digital service producers operating the platform, the users (households or enterprises) who access the platform free of charge, and advertisers who pay for advertising placement. In the 2025 SNA, this structure represents the standard case of **advertising-based digital production**.

The output of free online platforms is measured as follows:

Output = advertising fees + fees for data use + fees for premium services provided to enterprises

On the expenditure side, advertising fees paid by advertisers are recorded as intermediate consumption of the advertisers, while no monetary transaction is recorded as final consumption expenditure in the national accounts. If the free platform is a non-resident unit, advertising services purchased by resident advertisers are recorded as "imports of services," and the attribution of output depends on the residency of the platform.

For example, suppose there is a resident platform (A) and a non-resident platform (B), the latter having no fixed establishment in the domestic economy. The advertiser is a resident enterprise, and users are resident households, all accessing the platforms free of charge. If the advertiser pays advertising fees of 100 to platform A and 150 to platform B, the national accounts treatment is as follows:

Table 14.31 Accounting treatment of free platforms

	Advertiser		**Resident platform (A)**		**Non-resident platform (B)**	
	Expenditures	Revenues	Expenditures	Revenues	Expenditures	Revenues
Production account	Intermediate consumption 250			Output 100		
Rest of the world account						Imports of services 150

14.12.3 Output of free software

The output of free software is determined not by whether the software itself is provided free of charge, but by whether its production is market or non-market in nature, and by how production costs or revenues are financed.

1. Free software financed through advertising or service revenues (e.g., fee applications, free web services, advertising-based and freemium models): The output is treated as market output and measured as follows:

   Output = advertising revenue + subscriptions + premium service fees + revenue from data use

   Although the software itself is provided free of charge, the services produced through the software are provided for payment. Accordingly, output is valued on the basis of actual revenues received. As with free platforms, users' access is not recorded as consumption; instead, advertising and service fees are recorded as intermediate consumption of advertisers and business clients.

2. Software developed internally by enterprise and distributed free of charge (e.g., internally developed software released as open source): No separate output is recorded. Development costs are recorded as own-account gross fixed capital formation. If the distribution serves purely promotional purposes, the costs are recorded as intermediate consumption.

3. Software provided free of charge by government of NPISHs (e.g., public statistical software, free educational programs): Output is measured using the sum-of-costs method and is ultimately recorded as final consumption expenditure of government of NPISHs.

4. Open-source software developed voluntarily and distributed free of charge: When development is carried out in an organized manner by developers affiliated with enterprise or institutions, output is included in the market or non-market production of those units. In contrast, software developed and distributed solely through voluntary individual contributions lies outside the production boundary of the national accounts, and its output is recorded as zero.

Chapter 15. Calculation of output and value-added using business financial statements

In compiling national accounts, production-side data (i.e., output, intermediate consumption, and value-added) have traditionally been derived through economic censuses or industry-specific surveys conducted by national statistical office. However, in recent years, the use of administrative data provided by institutions has been gaining ground, as they offer several advantages in terms of efficiency and accuracy. Key examples of such administrative sources include corporate-level financial statements submitted to the national tax authorities (i.e., income statement, statement of financial position, and statement of cost of goods) as well as financial statements of financial corporations submitted to the financial supervisory authorities. This chapter examines the characteristics of these administrative data sources and discuss methods for estimating output, intermediate consumption, and value-added based on them.

Some key features of administrative data

1. **Enterprise unit vs. establishment unit:** Administrative data are collected at the "enterprise level" and may not coincide with census and survey data which are collected at the "establishment level." If there are multiple establishments within an enterprise, the output from one establishment may be used as an input in other establishments, which may be offset when calculating the enterprise's total output and intermediate consumption. Consequently, when compiling the production account, there may be limitations in substituting industry-specific output and intermediate consumption data with financial statement data, but the amount of gross value-added remains unchanged. Notably, for small businesses, where the enterprise unit and establishment unit mostly coincide, administrative data can be used in place of the census or survey data.

2. **Complete coverage:** Unlike survey data, which are drawn from samples, administrative data cover the entire population and therefore provide definitive figures. National Tax Service data include small-scale enterprises and self-employed individuals that might be missed by conventional sample surveys. However, one limitation is that these data only become available after the conclusion of the tax reporting period. Since corporate tax returns are submitted some months after the fiscal year-end, administrative data may not be immediately accessible, posing challenges for producing timely national accounts estimates.

3. **For-profit enterprises only:** National tax authority data cover only for-profit enterprises that file corporate or personal income taxes. As a result, non-profit institutions are excluded from

these datasets. Thus, such administrative data should be used to supplement production statistics specifically for corporations and households unincorporated enterprises among the institutional sectors of the national economy.

4. **Adjustment of the accounting period:** The closing dates of financial statements may not coincide with the standard accounting period used for national accounts. For instance, if an enterprise's fiscal year ends in June, and only annual financial statements are available, it may be necessary to use two consecutive years of data to reconstruct and align the figures with the national accounts period. Where possible, semiannual or quarterly financial statements are preferable, but they are not always available, especially for small enterprises.

5. **Inventory valuation issues:** Business financial statements are generally prepared based on a historic cost basis. As a result, it is difficult to obtain current price data on the entries and withdrawals of inventories which are necessary for valuing output and intermediate consumption at current market prices. Therefore, separate adjustments must be made to value the inventories according to the perpetual inventory method used in the national accounts.

As outlined above, while administrative data have certain limitations, if these constraints are properly addressed and adjusted for, they can be effectively utilized to improve the efficiency and accuracy to estimate production accounts. The following sections will provide a detailed explanation of how to derive output, intermediate consumption, and value-added using enterprise-level financial statements reported to the national tax authorities. In general, tax authorities distinguish between non-financial corporations and financial corporations, and uses different reporting formats for each. All corporations are required to submit both a statement of financial position and an income statement, and depending on the nature of their business, they are also required to submit additional "cost statements." These include the manufacturing cost statements (for manufacturers), construction cost statements (for construction firms), rental cost statements (for leasing firms), transportation cost statements (for logistics and freight businesses), as well as other sector-specific cost forms. These documents provide a rich data source that, if properly analyzed and adjusted, can serve as a strong foundation for compiling the production account in accordance with the standards of the SNA

15.1 Calculation of output, intermediate consumption, and value added for non-financial corporations

First, let us examine the procedure for calculating output, intermediate consumption, and value-added using the financial statements of non-financial corporations. Table 15.1 below provides examples of the income statement and the manufacturing cost statement submitted by non-financial corporations to the tax authorities.

Table 15.1 Income statement and manufacturing cost statement of non-financial corporations

Income statement (Non-financial corporation)	20XX accounting year		Name of corporation		
			Business registration number		
				(Unit: KRW billion)	
Debit items	code	value	Credit items	code	value
I. Sales	1	120	4.Profit from disposal of securities	41	0
1.Merchandise sales	2	19	5.Securities valuation gains	42	0
2.Product sales	3	95	6.Foreign exchange gain	43	0
3.Construction revenue	4	2	7.Forex conversion profit	44	0
4.Transportation revenue	5	1	8.Equity method gain	45	0
5.Real estate rental revenue	6	2	9.Profit from investment disposal	46	0
6.Dwelling sales revenue	7	0	10.Profit from assets disposal	47	0
7.Other sales	8	1	11.Profit from redemption of bonds	48	0
II. Cost of goods sold	9	71	12.Corporate tax refund	49	0
(1) Cost of goods for resale	10	16	13.Reversal of provisions	50	1
1.Opening stock	11	2	14.Profit from previous error correction	51	0
2.Current purchase cost	12	15	16.Profit from asset donation	86	0
3.Closing stock	13	1	17. Debt waiver profit	73	1
4.Transfers to other accounts	91	0	18.Insurance profit	74	0
(2) Manufacturing, construction, rental, and transportation cost	14	55	19.Other non-operating income	75	1
1.Opening inventory	15	12		52	
2.Cost of finished goods	16	**59**		211	
3.Closing inventory	17	15		212	
4.Transfers to other accounts	18	1		213	
III.Gross profit and loss of sales	19	49		214	
IV.Selling & administrative expense	20	36	VII.Non-operating expense	53	5
1.Salary	21	14	1.Interest expense	54	3
2.Retirement benefit	22	2	2.Other bad debt expense	55	1
3.Insurance premiums	83	1	3.Loss on disposal of securities	56	0
4.Welfare expense	23	1	4.Loss on valuation of securities	57	0
5.Travel expense	84	2	5.Loss of inventory assets	58	0
6.Rental	24	4	6.Foreign exchange loss	59	0
7.Entertainment expense	25	1	7.Loss on forex conversion	60	0
8.Depreciation	26	3	8.Equity method loss	61	0
9.Amortization of intangibles	27	1	9.Long-term securities loss	62	0
10.Taxes and public charges	28	1	10.Loss on disposal of investment	63	0
11.Advertising cost	29	1	11.Loss on disposal of assets	64	0
12.Vehicle maintenance cost	85	1	12.Donations	65	1
13.Research expense	30	0	13.Loss on redemption of bonds	66	0
14.Development expense	31	2	14.Compensation cost	67	0
15.Bad debt expenses	32	1	15.Additional corporate tax	68	0
16.Other selling and administrative expense	33	0	16.Provision for reserve funds	69	0

Manufacturing cost statement (Non-financial corporation)	20XX accounting year	
Account items	code	value
I.Material cost	1	25
1.Material opening inventory	2	7
2.Material purchases	3	24
3.Material closing inventory	4	6
II.Labor cost	5	17
1.Wages and salaries	6	9
2.Daily salary	7	7
3.Retirement benefit	8	1
III.Overhead expenses	9	19
1.Electricity cost	10	3
2.Gas, water, and fuel cost	11	1
3.Transport cost	12	1
4.Depreciation	13	2
5.Repair cost	14	0
6.Consumables	15	1
7.Tax and duties	16	1
8.Rental	17	3
9.Insurance premiums	18	1
10.Welfare expense	19	1
11.Travel expense	20	0
12.Communication cost	21	1
13.Vehicle maintenance cost	35	1
14.Outsourcing cost	22	0
15.Patent royalties	23	1
16Development cost	24	1
17.Research cost	25	0
18.Packaging cost	26	0
19.Entertainment cost	27	0
20.Others	28	1
IV.Total manufacturing cost	29	61
V.Opening work-in-progress	30	4
VI.Total	31	65
VII.Closing work-in-progress	32	5
VIII.Transfer to other accounts	33	1
IX.Cost of finished goods manufactured	34	**59**

17.Outsourcing cost	34	0	17.Loss of previous error correction	87	0
18.Other expense	35	1	18.Disaster loss	78	0
V.Operating income	36	13	19.Other non-operating expense	70	0
VI.Non-operating income	37	6	20.Others	224	
1.Interest income	38	1	VIII.Profit before corporate tax	80	14
2.Dividend income	39	0	IX.Corporate tax	81	2.8
3.Rent	40	2	X.Net profit and loss	82	11.2

* Note: Light grey items are output-related, and dark grey items are cost-related.

For reference, understanding the manufacturing process in manufacturing industry helps us to derive output and intermediate consumption from these two statements. Figure 15.1, shown below, presents a simplified diagram of a typical manufacturing workflow. It illustrates how the cost of finished goods and the cost of goods sold are determined, from the purchase of raw materials through production to the sale of the finished goods.

Figure 15.1 Flowchart of the calculation of the production cost and cost of goods sold in manufacturing

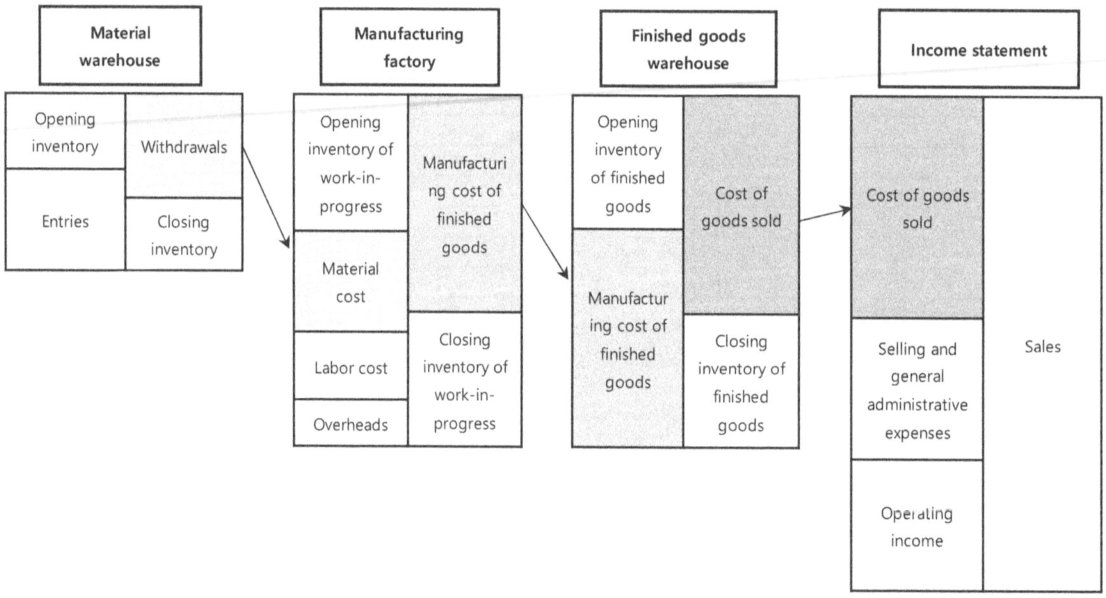

Derivation of the output value

Output for each industry can be calculated by extracting the relevant account items from the financial statements as follows:

- Output of manufacturing = sales of finished goods + closing inventory of finished goods and work-in-progress (including transfers to other accounts) – opening inventory of finished goods and work-in-progress

- Output of wholesale and retail trade = sales of goods for resale – costs of goods sold (= purchases of goods during period + opening inventory of goods – closing inventory of goods – transfers to other accounts)
- Output of other service industries = sales revenue + closing inventory (including transfers to other accounts) – opening inventory

If a single enterprise produces all of the products of the above industries as the primary and secondary products, total output is the sum of each industry's output.

Derivation of intermediate consumption

Here's how to calculate intermediate consumption using the detailed items from the income statement and the cost statement. For example, in the manufacturing enterprise, the sum of intermediate consumption is derived by combining the specific items from the "manufacturing cost statement" and the "income statement". The income statement provides intermediate consumption items related to an enterprise's ancillary activities.

Intermediate consumption for manufacturing industry:

- **Intermediate consumption items from the manufacturing cost statement**: Cost of raw materials consumed during the current period + Manufacturing-related expenses (except for labor costs (wages and salaries, retirement benefits, employee welfare expenses), taxes and duties, depreciation and amortization, current R&D expenditure
- **Intermediate consumption items from the Income statement**: All selling and administrative costs except for labor costs (wages and salaries, retirement benefits, employee welfare expenses), depreciation and amortization, taxes and duties (corresponding to the other taxes on production), current R&D expenditure, and bad debt provisions (recorded in the other changes in assets and liabilities account).

Current R&D expenditure is treated in the national accounts as gross fixed capital formation under research and development. Employee welfare expenses include employers' actual social contributions payable and welfare benefits, so they are classified as remuneration of employees. FISIM is a financial intermediation service charge, so it is separately calculated and added by the national accounts compiler as an intermediate consumption item. Non-life insurance premiums are also excluded from intermediate consumption because in the SNA, only the insurance service fee is included in the intermediate consumption (not the full insurance premiums). Therefore, instead of deducting the full premiums at the enterprise's level, the national accounts compiler allocates the estimated insurance service charges to intermediate consumption at the aggregate level across industries. This approach is similar to the procedure of adding FISIM as an additional item of intermediate consumption. Therefore, the final amount of intermediate consumption is obtained by adding FISIM and non-life insurance service charges to the items of intermediate consumption that can be derived from the financial statements.

- Total intermediate consumption ≈ raw material inputs + manufacturing-related intermediate inputs (other than raw materials) + costs related to ancillary activities + FISIM + non-life insurance service charges

Table 15.2 Formulas for calculating intermediate consumption for manufacturing industry using financial statements

Data source	Calculations
Manufacturing cost statement	**Material inputs** = purchases of materials during the period – changes in inventory of materials (= closing inventory – opening inventory)
	Manufacturing-related intermediate inputs (other than materials) = total manufacturing overheads – employee welfare expenses – taxes and duties – depreciation and amortization – non-life insurance premiums – R&D expenditure
Income statement	**Costs related to ancillary activities** = total selling and administrative expenses – (wages and salaries + retirement benefits + employee welfare expenses) – depreciation and amortization – taxes and duties – non-life insurance premiums – R&D expenditure – bad debt provision

Industries that do not prepare a dedicated manufacturing cost statement, such as service industries, derive their intermediate consumption by using the industry-specific cost statement (e.g., construction cost, transportation cost, rental cost, or other costs statements) together with the income statement. The procedure is as follows:

Intermediate consumption for industries other than manufacturing:

- Intermediate consumption ≈ raw material inputs and other cost items from the relevant industry's cost statement + total selling and administrative expenses in the income statement – (wages and salaries + retirement benefits + employee welfare expenses) – depreciation and amortization – taxes and duties – non-life insurance premiums – R&D expenditure – bad debt expenses + **FISIM[1] + non-life insurance charges***

Note 1) These amounts (FISIM and insurance service charges) must be calculated separately by the national accounts compiler.

Derivation of value added

Once the values of output and intermediate consumption are derived, gross value-added and its components are calculated as follows:

- Gross value added: output – intermediate consumption = remuneration of employees + gross operating surplus + other taxes less subsidies on production
- Remuneration of employees: "wages and salaries + retirement benefits + employee welfare expense" in each cost statement and income statement
- Other taxes and less subsidies on production: Allocated separately using local tax and subsidy data. (In this example, allocated from the financial statement data.)
- Depreciation: "depreciation + amortization of intangible fixed assets" in each cost statement and income statement
- Net operating surplus = gross value added – (remuneration of employees + other taxes less subsidies on production + depreciation)

Using the numerical exampled in the financial statements in Table 15.1, the output and intermediate consumption of non-financial corporations are calculated and presented in Table 15.3.

Table 15.3 Results of calculations for output, intermediate consumption, and value-added using financial statements in Table 15.1

Output	Manufacturing	I/S code (3+17+18–15) + M/S code (32+33–30) = 95+(15+1–12) + (5+1–4) = 101
	Wholesale and retail	I/S code (2–10) = 19–16 = 3
	Construction	I/S code (4+7) = 2+0 = 2
	Other services	I/S code (5+6+8) = 1+2+1 = 4
	Total	110
Intermediate consumption		I/S code (84+24+25+29+85+33+34+35) + M/S code (2+3–4+10+11+12+14+15+17+20+21+35+22+23+26+27+28) = 48
Gross value added	Total	110–48 = 62
	Remuneration of employees	I/S code (21+22+23) + M/S code (5+19) = 35
	Net other taxes on production	I/S code (28) + M/S code (16) = 2
	Depreciation	I/S code (26+27) + M/S code (13) = 6
	Net operating surplus	62–(35+2+6) = 19

* Note) I/S: income statement, M/S: manufacturing cost statement

15.2 Calculation of output, intermediate consumption, and value added for financial corporations

Financial corporations, due to their industry-specific nature, are required by the national tax authorities to submit a specialized format of financial statements. However, in compiling national accounts, it is more common to use the financial statements filed with the financial supervisory authorities. Table 15.4 below shows an abbreviated balance sheet and income statement for a deposit-taking bank.

Table 15.4 Example of financial statements for a deposit-taking bank

Balance sheet Thousand $

Item	Average balance
I. Total assets	216,901.8
1. Currency and deposits	13,110.7
2. Securities	30,714.7
3. Loans	160,412.0
4. Fixed assets	1,864.3
5. Other assets	10,800.1
II. Total liabilities	202,787.6
6. Deposits	146,129.9
7. Borrowing liabilities	39,937.1
7.1 Borrowings	13,453.6
7.2 Debt securities	26,483.5
8. Other liabilities	16,720.5
9. Total equity	14,114.2
III. Total liabilities and equity	216,901.8

Income statement Thousand $

Item	Amount
I. Total expenses	24,304.2
1. Interest payable	5,722.6
2. Commissions payable	1,092.2
3. Trading losses on securities	12,606.1
4. Bad debt	2,274.0
5. Retirement benefits	85.6
6. Wages and salaries	886.7
7. Other fringe benefits	32.0
8. materials and supplies	926.7
9. tax and duties	80.1
10. Depreciation	120.4
11. Other expenses	126.1
12. Corporate tax	271.8
II. Net profit	949.7
III. Total revenues	25,253.9
13. Interest receivable	10,503.7
14. Commissions receivable	843.8
15. Trading gains on securities	13,785.5
16. Other revenues	120.8

Based on these statements, the bank's output, intermediate consumption, and gross value added can be calculated as follows:

- Output = FISIM + fees and commissions receivable + other operating income

Note: Trading gains and losses on securities are not included here but are instead recorded in the revaluation account of the sequence of economic accounts.

FISIM is calculated as follows:

- FISIM = (interest receivable – average balance on loans x reference rate) + (average balance on deposits x reference rate – interest payable)

Where, reference rate = (interest receivable/average balance on loans + interest payable/average balance on deposits)/2, average balance on loans = (opening loan balance + closing loan balance)/2, average balance on deposits = (opening deposit balance + closing deposit balance)/2, and interbank loans and deposits are excluded from these balances.

Intermediate consumption for deposit-taking banks is not directly itemized in the database of financial supervisory authorities (because it appears only as a single item). Therefore, it must be separately estimated using data from the national tax authority's filings on banks.

Table 15.5 Example of deriving the output, intermediate consumption, and gross value added for a deposit-taking bank

	Item	Value	Calculation
FISIM	Average balance on loans	160,412.0	
	Average balance on deposits	146,129.9	
	Interest receivable	10,503.7	
	Interest payable	5,722.6	
	Reference rate	5.23%	(10,503.7/160,412.0 + 5,722.6/146,129.9)/2
	FISIM on loans	2,110.9	10,503.7 – 160,412,0 x 5.23%
	FISIM on deposits	1,923.0	146,129.9 x 5.23% – 5,722.6
Output	Total FISIM	4,033.9	2,110.9+1,923.0
	Commission receivable	843.8	
	Other income	120.8	
Intermediate consumption	Commission payable	-1,092.2	
	Materials and supplies	-926.7	
	Other expenses	-126.1	
Gross value added	Total	2,853.5	
	Remuneration of employees	1,004.2	85.6+886.7+32.0
	Other taxes on production	80.1	
	Depreciation	120.4	
	Net operating surplus	1,648.8	

Chapter 16. Basic concepts for the compilation of volume and real indicators

Thus far, the discussion has focused on the methodology for compiling current-period values at current prices within the framework of the national accounts. In other words, the previous chapters have explained how to compile monetary values for a single accounting period, based on prevailing prices at the time of transaction. Starting from this chapter and continuing through Chapter 18, the focus shifts to methods for measuring of output and value added in volume terms and real income by using multi-period time series data to eliminate the effects of price changes. To this end, this chapter introduces the basic concepts necessary for understanding volume and real indicators, as well as the measurement of prices.

To begin with, section 16.1 explains the concepts of current prices and constant prices, and introduces how values at current prices can be converted into values at constant prices to derive volume or real income indicators. Subsequently, section 16.2 provides a general theoretical overview of index numbers, which are the essential tools for measuring values at both current and constant prices. This section also discusses the characteristics and compilation methods of chain indices, which have become the standard practice in compiling national accounts across many countries. Lastly, section 16.3 deals with the issue of how to treat quality change when measuring prices. It also clarifies the conceptual difference between volume and quantity, and discusses which types of price indices are considered most appropriate for use in the compilation of national accounts, especially in the context of deflating current price values to obtain constant price estimates.

16.1 Current prices and constant prices

In the SNA, all economic activities, except for labor-related measures such hours worked or number of workers, are expressed using monetary values as the common unit of measurement. Monetary unit serves as the only means through which the values of all goods and services can be measured and aggregated in a consistent manner. For example, to aggregate the value of two different products such as 10 kilograms of rice and 10 automobiles, one must convert these into monetary terms, since the physical units "kilograms" and "number of units" (cars) are not directly comparable. In national account, monetary values are represented in the form of "quantity x price per unit." However, when the goal is to measure output in terms of volume or real income based on a certain point in time, it is not sufficient to rely solely on monetary values, which reflect nominal changes. Rather, it is necessary to eliminate the effects of price changes in order to isolate real changes in purchasing power. The approach of fixing prices at a specific point in time and removing the effects of price fluctuations to measure changes in volume or real income is the fundamental method for deriving volume indicators or real indicators in the national accounts.

The following table (Table 16.1) presents an example of measuring the change in volume only, which removes the component of price changes from production values in nominal terms. In the table, column (I) shows the production values based on actual prices that vary from year to year. These are referred to as **values at current prices**. In contrast, column (II) applies a fixed unit price from a particular base year (assumed here to be year xx15, with a unit price of $30) to the quantities of each year. The values in column (II) are thus expressed at the prices of the base year, which in national accounting terminology are called **values at constant prices**.

Table 16.1 Example of calculating values at constant (base year) prices

Year[1]	Quantity (kg)	Price per unit ($)	Value (I) (current price, $)	Value (II) (constant price, $)
xx15	10	**30**	300 (=10×**30**)	300 (=10×**30**)
xx16	20	35	700 (=20×35)	600 (=20×**30**)
xx17	25	40	1,000 (=25×40)	750 (=25×**30**)

Footnote: 1) Base year = xx15

The primary objective of calculating output and value added at constant prices is to derive the growth rate in volume terms (or real growth rate). In general, the economic growth rate, which represents the volume growth of gross domestic product (GDP), is measured in real terms, excluding the effects of price changes. The concept of constant prices is thus an essential tool used in national accounts to remove the influence of price movements and to capture only the changes in volumes.

16.1.1 Distinction between volume terms and real terms

In the SNA, the monetary value of products or materials can be disaggregated into volume and price components. For example, in the case of goods, the total value can be broken down into the volume of output (or consumption) and the price per unit. Similarly, for wages, the total amount paid can be expressed as the product of hours worked (volume) and the wage rate per hour (price). When such a clear distinction between volume and price exists, deflation can be applied to obtain what is referred to as **volume terms**, that is, measures expressed in constant prices reflecting changes in quantities. However, for certain indicators such as income, it is often difficult to distinguish between volume and price components. In such cases, the nominal income is deflated using a general price index to adjust for changes in purchasing power, and the resulting measure is referred to as being expressed in **real terms**. In other words, when deflating nominal values, it is common practice to use "volume terms" for items such as output or consumption, where a clear distinction between volume and price can be made. Conversely, for items such as income, where it is difficult to separate physical quantity from price, the resulting measures are referred to as being in "real terms." Accordingly, gross domestic product (GDP) is typically expressed in volume terms, using constant prices of a base year, while gross national income (GNI) is expressed in real terms, adjusted for changes in purchasing power.

The **growth rates** used in the national accounts refers to the rates of change in values expressed in volume terms or in real terms. That is, the growth rate is defined as the percentage increase in the volume of current period compared to the previous period, valued at the fixed prices of a specific point in time, typically the base year. The growth rate is calculated as follows:

$$\textbf{Growth rate (\%)} = (P^b Q^t / P^b Q^{t-1} - 1) \times 100$$

where P^b refers to prices at a specific point in time (usually the base year), and Q^{t-1} and Q^t denote the volumes in period $t-1$ and period t respectively. (For more detailed explanation of the concept and calculation method of growth rates, see section 18.4.)

16.1.2 Conversion of values at current prices into volume or real measures

In the SNA, when converting indicators expressed in values at current prices into volume or real measures, one of the following three methods is generally used:

Deflation method

The deflation method is the most commonly used approach to convert values at current prices to volume or real measures. In this method, the current value of a product in a given period (expressed as "$p^t \times q^t$") is divided by the price index for the same product (usually expressed as "p^t/p^0"), where p^0 indicates the price in the base period. This method can be used when current values and price indices of the product are available.

- **Values at constant prices in period t by the deflation method: $(p^t \times q^t) / (p^t/p^0)$**

where p^t is the price in period t, q^t is the volume in period t, and p^0 is the price in the base period.

This method has several advantages: First, that it is commonly used when it is difficult to collect the volume indicators of a product. For example, if a product is not precisely distinguished by price and volume components (e.g., in the case of many services), the deflation method provides a more practical means of estimating volume-based value by dividing the current value by a price index, rather than attempting to obtain volume data directly. Second, this method is considered effective in reflecting quality changes in the measurement of volume indicators. As will be discussed later, price indices are usually constructed to remove the effects of quality changes and reflect only pure price changes, so the method of dividing current values by such price indices allows the resulting volume indicators to incorporate the effects of quality improvements. This leads to a more accurate measurement of real changes in volume. Third, in practical applications, deflating current values using a sample-based price index is often more feasible than attempting to survey and aggregate total volumes. While estimating total volumes based on sample surveys has limitations in accuracy, prices tend to move in a similar pattern within product groups, making the sample-based price index a more reliable and efficient deflator. Therefore, the method of deflating the value indicators with a sample-surveyed price indicators is more preferred because it is easier to measure than the method of surveying all volume data. Although this method is widely applicable to all sectors, it is especially useful in the service industries, where direct measurement of volume is inherently more challenging.

Volume extrapolation method

The volume extrapolation method estimates the values at constant prices for the current period (t) by multiplying the value in the base period ($p^0 \times q^0$) by the volume index (q^t/q^0).

- **Values at constant prices in period t by the volume extrapolation method: $p^0 q^0 \times (q^t/q^0)$**

This method is used when volume data are available, and it is particularly suitable for generating preliminary estimates when accurate current value data ($p^t \times q^t$) are not yet available. It is primarily applied in cases where products are standardized and exhibit little variation in quality, such as in the mining sector and some manufactured goods.

Direct method

The direct method estimates the value at constant prices for the current period (t) by directly multiplying the volume in period t (q^t) by the price from the base period (p^0).

- **Values at constant prices in period t by the direct method: $p^0 \times q^t$**

This method is applicable when the variety of products is not diverse and the accurate volume data are available for each time period. It is widely used in sectors that deal with unprocessed raw materials, such as agriculture and mining.

16.2 Concepts of index numbers and their application in the SNA

This section explains how the data of values, volumes, and prices compiled in the national account can be expressed in the form of index numbers. Presenting the national accounts data as index forms facilitates the comparison and analysis of time series data in relative terms, and allows for the convenient calculation of growth rates or rates of change.

16.2.1 Basic understanding of index numbers

Before examining the process of constructing indices and their practical applications within the national accounts, this section first introduces the fundamental concepts and methods of measuring index numbers. An index (plural: indices) refers to a relative measure obtained by setting the value of a particular base period equal to 100 (or 1) which is called a **reference period**, and expressing the values of other periods as a ratio to this reference period value. It is calculated by taking the value of a variable in a reference period and setting it to 100 (or 1), and then converting the values of other periods to ratios relative to the reference period. In other words, the value of the reference period is used as the denominator, and the value for the comparison period is used as the numerator to produce a relative measure. For example, in the table below, if the reference year of index is set to xx15, then the index for each period can be expressed follows: 100 (or 1) for xx15, 125 (or 1.25) for xx16, and 200 (or 2.0) for xx17.

Table 16.2 Example of index calculation

Year[1]	Value	Index
xx15	$**200**	1 (=200/**200**)
xx16	$250	1.25 (=250/**200**)
xx17	$400	2.0 (=400/**200**)

Footnote: 1) Index reference year is xx15.

The primary purpose of using index numbers is to enhance comparability between data from different time periods (or locations) or between different types of items by converting all data into relative values. When time series data are standardized using a common reference period (or reference region), it becomes easier to make objective comparisons across time or across region. In the context of national accounts, expressing values such as volumes and prices in index form enables the analysis of relative changes over time or across different regions.

16.2.1.1 Value index, volume index and price index

In the SNA, the indices commonly used can be categorized into three types: the **value index**, the **volume index**, and the **price index**.

Value index

A **value index** expresses the change in the total value of transactions (where value = volume x price) relative to a specified reference period. It is calculated by dividing the total value in the comparison period by the total value in the reference period. The value index V (0,t) is expressed as follows:

$$\textbf{Value index: } V(0,t) = \Sigma P^tQ^t / \Sigma P^0Q^0$$

where P^0 and Q^0 denote the prices and volumes in the reference period (0), and P^t and Q^t denote the prices and volumes in the comparison period (*t*).

Volume index

A **volume index** measures the relative change in volumes between the comparison period and the reference period. It is calculated by taking the volume of the reference period as the denominator and the volume of the comparison period as the numerator. However, in practice, when multiple heterogeneous items of products are involved, the key issue is how to aggregate the individual volume indices into a single overall volume index. For example, depending on the item, the quantity may be measured in kilograms, liters, units, or other forms. To construct a comprehensive volume index across these items, a common measurement unit is required, and in the national accounts, that unit is **monetary value**. The standard approach is to multiply the quantity of each item in each period by a common price from a specific period (i.e., a constant price), and then sum these values across all items. This results in an aggregate volume measure that reflects the total quantity change. The general formula for a volume index is expressed as follows:

$$\textbf{Volume index: } Q(0,t) = \Sigma PQ^t / \Sigma PQ^0$$

In this formula, the price *P* is fixed at a specific point in time *b*, and the resulting index is called a **Lowe volume index**. At this time, if the price is fixed at the reference year (period 0), it is called a **Laspeyres volume index**, and if the price is fixed at the current year (period t), it is called a **Paasche volume index**. The Laspeyres and Paasche indexes are special cases of the Lowe index. The Lowe volume index $Q_{Lo}(0,t)$ is expressed as:

$$\textbf{Lowe volume index: } Q_{Lo}(0,t) = \Sigma P^bQ^t / \Sigma P^bQ^0$$

where "*b*" denotes a specific time period (or the average of two specific time periods), and if *b* is the reference period of the index (0), it is **Laspeyres** formula, and if *b* is the current period (t), it is

Paasche formula. When there are "n" component items as product *i*, the Lowe volume index can be written as:

$$Q_{Lo}(0,t) = (\sum_{i=1}^{n} P_i^b Q_i^t)/(\sum_{i=1}^{n} P_i^b Q_i^0)$$

Price index

A **price index** compares prices in the comparison period to those in the reference period. It is calculated by dividing the total value at current prices by the total value at reference-period prices, holding volumes constant. However, when multiple items of products are involved, the issue is how to aggregate individual price changes into an overall price index. Similar to the volume index, the price index uses monetary value, assuming fixed volumes across time. The general formula for a price index P (0,t) is expressed as:

$$\textbf{Price index: } P(0,t) = \Sigma P^t Q / \Sigma P^0 Q$$

In this formula, volumes Q are fixed at a specific point in time *b*, resulting in what is called a **Lowe price index**. The Lowe price index $P_{Lo}(0,t)$ is calculated as:

$$\textbf{Lowe price index: } P_{Lo}(0,t) = \Sigma P^t Q^b / \Sigma P^0 Q^b$$

Here, if volumes in the reference period (0) are used for Q^b, it is called a **Laspeyres price index**, and if volumes in the current period (t) are used for Q^b, it is called a **Paasche price index**. If there are "n" component items as product *i*, the Lowe price index can be expressed as:

$$P_{Lo}(0,t) = \sum_i^n P_i^t Q_i^b / \sum_i^n P_i^0 Q_i^b$$

Example of index compilation

The table below presents an example in which two products (product 1 and product 2) are assumed. It illustrates how to calculate individual price indices and volume indices for each product, and then how to derive aggregated indices for the combined set of two products using Laspeyres and Paasche formulas, respectively. To explain the example of the Laspeyres volume index shown in the lower section of the table: the index for the third year is calculated as:

(2.00 x 24+1.10 x 69)/(2.00 x 20+1.10 x 55) = 1.23

Likewise, the Paasche price index for the fourth year is calculated as:

(2.73 x 26+1.27 x 75)/(2.00 x 26+1.10 x 75) = 1.24

Table 16.3 Example of calculating the price indices and volume indices

(Index reference year: 0)

Item	Formula	Year (t)					
		0	1	2	3	4	5
Price of product 1	p_1^t	2.00	2.30	2.42	2.61	2.73	2.89
Volume of product 1	q_1^t	20	22	27	24	26	41
Value of product 1	$p_1^t q_1^t$	40.00	50.60	65.34	62.64	70.98	118.49
Value index 1	$p_1^t q_1^t / p_1^0 q_1^0$	1.00	1.27	1.63	1.57	1.77	2.96
Price index 1	p_1^t / p_1^0	1.00	1.15	1.21	1.31	1.37	1.45
Volume index 1	q_1^t / q_1^0	1.00	1.10	1.35	1.20	1.30	2.05
Price of product 2	p_2^t	1.10	1.20	1.25	1.23	1.27	2.10
Volume of product 2	q_2^t	55	57	62	69	75	75
Value of product 2	$p_2^t q_2^t$	60.50	68.40	77.50	84.87	95.25	157.50
Value index 2	$p_2^t q_2^t / p_2^0 q_2^0$	1.00	1.13	1.28	1.40	1.57	2.60
Price index 2	p_2^t / p_2^0	1.00	1.09	1.14	1.12	1.15	1.91
Volume index 2	q_2^t / q_2^0	1.00	1.04	1.13	1.25	1.36	1.36
Laspeyres price index	$P_L = \Sigma p^t q^0 / \Sigma p^0 q^0$	1.00	1.11	1.17	1.19	1.24	1.72
Paasche price index	$P_P = \Sigma p^t q^t / \Sigma p^0 q^t$	1.00	1.12	1.17	1.19	1.24	1.68
Laspeyres volume index	$Q_L = \Sigma p^0 q^t / \Sigma p^0 q^0$	1.00	1.06	1.22	1.23	1.34	1.64
Paasche volume index	$Q_P = \Sigma p^t q^t / \Sigma p^t q^0$	1.00	1.06	1.22	1.23	1.34	1.59

16.2.1.2 Concept and calculation of modified indices

In practice, it is often difficult to obtain separate data on both prices and volumes of each product when constructing indices. Instead, it is relatively easier to obtain data on the value ($p^t q^t$), which is the product of price and volume for each item. Accordingly, the Laspeyres and Paasche formulas introduced earlier are typically adapted to modified formulas that can be used with value data for each product as follows.

Modified Laspeyres price index

The Laspeyres price index can be transformed as follows by summing the **price relatives** (p_i^t/p_i^0) for each product (i), weighted by the value share of that product in the reference period (year 0). This formula is called the "modified Laspeyres price index":

$$P_L(0,t) = (\Sigma_i p_i^t q_i^0)/(\Sigma_i p_i^0 q_i^0) = \Sigma_i(p_i^t/p_i^0) \times p_i^0 q_i^0 / (\Sigma_i p_i^0 q_i^0) = \Sigma_i(p_i^t/p_i^0) \times s_i^0$$

where $s_i^0 = p_i^0 q_i^0 / \Sigma_i p_i^0 q_i^0$ is the value share of product item i in the reference period.

Modified Laspeyres volume index

Similarly, the Laspeyres volume index can be transformed into a "modified Laspeyres volume index." This is done by summing **volume relatives** (q_i^t/q_i^0) for each product (i), weighted by the value share of that product in the reference period (year 0):

$$Q_L\,(0,t) = (\Sigma_i p_i^0 q_i^t)/(\Sigma_i p_i^0 q_i^0) = \Sigma_i(q_i^t/q_i^0) \times p_i^0 q_i^0/(\Sigma_i p_i^0 q_i^0) = \Sigma_i(q_i^t/q_i^0) \times s_i^0$$

where, $s_i^0 = p_i^0 q_i^0 / \Sigma_i p_i^0 q_i^0$ is the value share of product item i in the reference period.

Modified Paasche price index

The "modified Paasche price index" is calculated by summing the product of the reciprocal of price relatives of each product item (i) and the value share in period t and then, taking the reciprocal of the sum as follows:

$$P_P\,(0,t) = (\Sigma_i p_i^t q_i^t)/(\Sigma_i p_i^0 q_i^t) = \Sigma_i p_i^t q_i^t/(\Sigma_i(p_i^0/p_i^t) \times p_i^t q_i^t) = [(\Sigma_i(p_i^0/p_i^t) \times p_i^t q_i^t)/\Sigma_i p_i^t q_i^t]^{-1}$$
$$= [\Sigma_i(p_i^t/p_i^0)^{-1} \times s_i^t]^{-1}$$

where, $s_i^t = p_i^t q_i^t / \Sigma_i p_i^t q_i^t$ is the value share of product item i in the current period t.

Modified Paasche volume index

The modified Paasche volume index is obtained by summing the product of the reciprocal of volume relative of each item (i) and the value share in period t and then, taking the reciprocal of the sum as follows:

$$Q_P\,(0,t) = (\Sigma_i p_i^t q_i^t)/(\Sigma_i p_i^t q_i^0) = \Sigma_i(p_i^t q_i^t)/[\Sigma_i(q_i^0/q_i^t) \times p_i^t q_i^t] = [(\Sigma_i\,(q_i^0/q_i^t) \times p_i^t q_i^t)/$$
$$\Sigma_i p_i^t q_i^t]^{-1} = [\Sigma_i(q_i^t/q_i^0)^{-1} \times s_i^t]^{-1}$$

where, $s_i^t = p_i^t q_i^t / \Sigma_i p_i^t q_i^t$ is the value share of product item i in the current period t.

When employing the modified formulas, it becomes unnecessary to obtain volume data in order to compute price indices. Provided that information is available on the price relatives for each product item and corresponding value weights for those items (in the reference period for the Laspeyres formula and in period t for the Paasche formula), it is possible to derive upper-level (aggregated) price indices without recourse to volume statistics. Similarly, when compiling volume indices using the modified formula, price data are no longer required. Instead, the necessary inputs are the volume relatives for each product item and the corresponding value weights (in the reference period for the Laspeyres formula and in period t for the Paasche formula). With this information alone, it is feasible to compile upper-level volume indices in a manner consistent with standard index number methodology.

Young index

On the other hand, the index derived by multiplying the price relatives (or volume relatives) by the value weights at a specific point in time (denoted as *b*) is called the **Young index**. The key difference between the Young index and the Lowe index lies in the type of weight used: while the Lowe price index fixes the weight of volume (q), the Young price index fixes the weight of value (pq/Σpq).

$$\textbf{Young price index:}\quad \mathbf{P_Y}\ (0,t) = \sum_i^n \left(\frac{p_i^t}{p_i^0}\right) s_i^b \qquad \text{where } s_i^b = \frac{p_i^b\, q_i^b}{\sum_i^n p_i^b\, q_i^b}$$

Similarly, the Young volume index takes the form:

$$\textbf{Young volume index:}\quad \mathbf{Q_Y}\ (0,t) = \sum_i^n \left(\frac{q_i^t}{q_i^0}\right) s_i^b \quad \text{where } s_i^b = \frac{p_i^b q_i^b}{\sum_i^n p_i^b q_i^b}$$

Here, *b* denotes a specific point in time (referred to as the **weight reference period**), which can be any year. It is possible to use an average of two years as the weight reference.

Meanwhile, the Lowe index mentioned earlier can be transformed in terms of value weights as follows:

$$\textbf{Lowe price index:}\ \sum p^t q^b / \sum p^0 q^b = \frac{\sum(p^t/p^0 \times p^0 q^b)}{\sum p^0 q^b} = \sum\left(p^t/p^0 \times \frac{p^0 q^b}{\sum p^0 q^b}\right) = \sum(p^t/p^0) \times s_i^{0b}$$

where $s_i^{0b} = p_i^0 q_i^b / \sum_i p_i^0 q_i^b$.

Note that the weighting scheme s_i^{0b} can be characterized as having a hybrid nature, as it combines price information from the **index reference year** (period 0) with volume information from the **weight reference year** (period *b*). In practical statistical operations, the weights for price indices are typically derived from expenditure surveys, which require considerable time to compile, verify, and process. Due to these practical constraints, it is common practice to initially employ weights from a period prior to the index reference year, until updated expenditure data aligned with the prices of the index reference year becomes available. Consequently, the weight reference year (*b*) frequently precedes the index reference year (0) by two to three years. Under these circumstances, the available weights initially reflect expenditure shares with prices and volumes both measured in the weight reference year, given by:

$$p^b q^b / \sum p^b q^b$$

To align these weights to the price structure of the index reference year, an adjustment must be performed by multiplying them by the price index covering the interval from the weight reference year b to the index reference year 0, specifically $(\boldsymbol{p^0}/\boldsymbol{p^b})$. The resulting index, known as the adjusted Lowe index, is widely implemented in official statistical practice, notably for compiling consumer price indices (CPIs) and producer price indices, and is preferred over the Young index. (See IMF et al., CPI manual (2020) 1.155, and IMF, PPI manual (2004) 1.23.)

16.2.2 Two-period comparison indices

Indices, by definition, measure relative changes between a reference period and a comparison period. All indices previously discussed adhere to this two-period comparison framework. In contrast, chain indices, discussed separately (see section 16.e.4), incorporate information from each intervening period within a time series between the reference and comparison periods. However, as chain indices fundamentally rely upon two-period indices, this section focuses explicitly on the characteristics of two-period comparison indices.

16.2.2.1 Characteristics of Laspeyres and Paasche indices

The Laspeyres and Paasche indices are representative examples of two-period indices that compare two distinctive points in time $(period\ 0\ and\ period\ t)$ using fixed weights from a specific weight reference period. Due to their computational convenience, these indices have long been employed extensively by statistical agencies, accompanied by substantial theoretical studies. In particular, the Laspeyres-type price index has been broadly applied because it requires only expenditure weights from the reference year. Thus, once the expenditure weights from the reference year are established, subsequent indices can be calculated using only price relatives for an extended period. Typical examples include consumer price indices (CPIs) and producer price indices (PPIs), both commonly compiled using modified Laspeyres formulations. Furthermore, the Laspeyres volume index, which similarly fixes weights at the reference period, has also been extensively used to measure economic growth, notably in deriving GDP volume indices. This section explores the fundamental properties of the Laspeyres and Paasche formulas as standard two-period indices.

In general, a value index V(0,t) can be decomposed algebraically as follows:

$$(16.1)\quad V(0,t) = \Sigma p^t q^t / \Sigma p^0 q^0 = (\Sigma p^t q^t \times \mathbf{\Sigma p^t q^0}) / (\Sigma p^0 q^0 \times \mathbf{\Sigma p^t q^0}) = (\Sigma p^t q^t / \mathbf{\Sigma p^t q^0}) \times (\mathbf{\Sigma p^t q^0} / \Sigma p^0 q^0) = Q_P \times P_L$$

Equation (16.1) demonstrates that the value index can be represented as the product of a Paasche volume index (Q_P) and a Laspeyres price index (P_L). Similarly, the value index can be alternatively expressed as:

(16.2) $V(0,t) = \Sigma p^t q^t / \Sigma p^0 q^0 = (\Sigma p^t q^t \times \mathbf{\Sigma p^0 q^t}) / (\Sigma p^0 q^0 \times \mathbf{\Sigma p^0 q^t}) = (\Sigma p^t q^t / \mathbf{\Sigma p^0 q^t}) \times (\mathbf{\Sigma p^0 q^t} / \Sigma p^0 q^0) = P_P \times Q_L$

Equation (16.2) indicates that the value index may also be represented as the product of a Paasche price index (P_P) and a Laspeyres volume index (Q_L). Combining equations (16.1) and (16.2) yields the fundamental relationship:

(16.3) $\mathbf{V(0,t) = P_L \times Q_P = P_P \times Q_L}$

(Value index = Laspeyres price index x Paasche volume index = Paasche price index x Laspeyres volume index)

This relationship implies that if the value index and the Laspeyres price index are known, the Paasche volume index can be derived; likewise, given the value index and the Paasche price index, the Laspeyres volume index can be determined. Equation (16.3) can be expressed as:

(16.4) $\mathbf{P_P / P_L = Q_P / Q_L}$

The left-hand side of the equation (16.4) can be transformed into the following equation through the manipulation process[22]:

(16.5) $\mathbf{P_P / P_L = 1 + r_{xy}\, \sigma_x \sigma_y / (P_L Q_L) = 1 + cov\,(x, y) / (P_L Q_L)}$

where x denotes price relatives (p^t/p^0), y denotes volume relatives (q^t/q^0), r_{xy} is the correlation coefficient[23] between x and y, σ_x and σ_y represent the standard deviations of x and y, respectively, and $cov\,(x, y)$ is the covariance[24] between x and y.
Modifying equation (16.5) and then combining it with (16.4) leads to the following expression:

(16.6) $\mathbf{P_P - P_L = Q_P - Q_L = r_{xy}\, \sigma_x \sigma_y / Q_L = cov\,(x, y) / Q_L}$

Equation (16.6) reveals essential properties of the relationship between the Laspeyres and Paasche indices. Specifically, if the correlation coefficient (r_{xy}) between price relatives (x) and volume relatives (y) is positive, the standard deviations σ_x and σ_y will also be positive, and therefore, $P_P > P_L$ (or $Q_P > Q_L$) holds on the left-hand sides of the equation. Conversely, if r_{xy} is negative, it follows that $P_P < P_L$ (or $Q_P < Q_L$). Thus, when the covariance between the price relative and the corresponding volume relative of each individual product is positive, implying that the price relative and volume

---

[22] This expression is based on the proof by Bortkiewicz (1923, "Zweck und Struktur einer Preisindexzahl").

[23] $r_{xy} = \frac{cov(x,y)}{\sigma^x \ \sigma^y}$

[24] The covariance is expressed as: $cov(x, y) = \frac{\Sigma_i w_i\,(x_i - P_L)\,(y_i - Q_L)}{\Sigma_i w_i}$, where, $w_i = p_i^0 q_i^0$, $x_i = \frac{p_i^t}{p_i^0}$, $y_i = \frac{q_i^t}{q_i^0}$.

relative move in the same direction, the Paasche price index exceeds the Laspeyres price index (or, analogously, the Paasche volume index exceeds the Laspeyres volume index). Conversely, when the covariance between the price relative and the corresponding volume relative of each individual product is negative (i.e., if the price relative and volume relative move in opposite directions), the Laspeyres price index surpasses the Paasche price index (or similarly, the Laspeyres volume index exceeds the Paasche volume index).

16.2.2.2 Example of constructing modified Laspeyres and Paasche indices

The following illustrates an example of constructing the price and volume indices using Laspeyres and Paasche formulas based on the data of production values and price relatives (see Table 16.4). Suppose that only two products, A and B, are produced. Given the production values of products A and B from year 0 to year 4 (as shown in the light blue area of the table), along with the price relatives calculated with the index reference year "0" (dark blue area), the Laspeyres and Paasche indices can be derived as follows:

First, a value index is computed by setting the index reference year (year 0) equal to 1. Individual indices for A and B are calculated for each year, and these are combined into an aggregate index. The value for each individual product is denoted a p^tq^t (price × quantity in the respective year), and individual value indices are derived using the formula p^tq^t / p^0q^0. The aggregate value index combining products A and B is expressed as $\Sigma p^tq^t / \Sigma p^0q^0$.

The next step involves deriving price indices. Utilizing the given price relatives for products A and B, modified Laspeyres and Paasche formulas are applied to compute the aggregate price indices for both products. Then, based on the value indices and price indices, the Laspeyres and Paasche volume indices can be derived. For individual products, the volume index is calculated as "value index/price index". The overall volume index combining both products can be derived directly using the modified Laspeyres and Paasche formulas, or indirectly using the following relationships:

- **Value index / Laspeyres price index = Paasche volume index**
- **Value index / Paasche price index = Laspeyres volume index**

Indices calculated through this procedure are summarized in the central part of the table (grey area). The calculation results indicates that as the period moves away from the reference year (year 0), both the price and volume indices consistently show higher values for the Laspeyres-type index compared to the Paasche index. This phenomenon arises due to negative covariance between price relatives and volume relatives of products A and B, numerically confirmed by the bottom row of the table.

Table 16.4 Example of compiling the modified Laspeyres and Paasche indices

(Index reference year: 0)

Item	Product	Year 0	1	2	3	4	Formula
Value	A	710.0	755.0	794.0	846.0	911.0	p^tq^t (where p: price, q: volume, t: current year)
	B	340.0	375.0	401.0	433.0	462.0	
	A and B	1050.0	1130.0	1195.0	1279.0	1373.0	Σp^tq^t
Value index	A	1.0	1.0634	1.1183	1.1915	1.2831	p^tq^t / p^0q^0
	B	1.0	1.1029	1.1794	1.2735	1.3588	
	A and B	1.0	1.0762	1.1381	1.2181	1.3076	$\Sigma p^tq^t / \Sigma p^0q^0$
Price relative	A	1.0	1.0300	1.0500	1.0800	1.1200	$p^t/p^0 = (p^tq^t/p^0q^0)/(q^t/q^0)$
	B	1.0	1.0800	1.1300	1.1900	1.2400	
Price index (Laspeyres)	A and B (1)	1.0	1.0462	1.0759	1.1156	1.1589	$P_L(0,t) = \Sigma(p^t/p^0)\, p^0q^0/\Sigma p^0q^0$
Price index (Paasche)	A and B (2)	1.0	1.0461	1.0755	1.1149	1.1577	$P_P(0,t) = [\Sigma(p^t/p^0)^{-1} p^tq^t/\Sigma p^tq^t]^{-1}$
(Difference)	(1-2)	0.0	0.0001	0.0004	0.0007	0.0012	$P_L(0,t) - P_P(0,t)$
Volume relative	A	1.0	1.0324	1.0651	1.1033	1.1456	$q^t/q^0 = (p^tq^t/p^0q^0)/(p^t/p^0)$
	B	1.0	1.0212	1.0437	1.0702	1.0958	
Volume index (Laspeyres)	A and B (3)	1.0	1.0288	1.0582	1.0926	1.1295	$Q_L(0,t) = \Sigma(q^t/q^0)\, p^0q^0/\Sigma p^0q^0$
Volume index (Paasche)	A and B (4)	1.0	1.0287	1.0578	1.0919	1.1284	$Q^P(0,t) = [\Sigma(q^t/q^0)^{-1} p^tq^t/\Sigma p^tq^t]^{-1}$
(Difference)	(3-4)	0.0	0.0001	0.0003	0.0007	0.0011	$Q_L(0,t) - Q_P(0,t)$
Covariance of the price relative and volume relative		0.000	-0.0001	-0.0004	-0.0008	-0.0013	$[\Sigma w(p^t/p^0 - P_L)(q^t/q^0 - Q_L)]/\Sigma w$

Based on the above data, the results of deriving the values in volume terms by the Laspeyres formula are shown in Table 16.5. In the calculation method of Laspeyres volume indices, the price and weight of the index reference year (0) is applied to all subsequent years, and the real growth rate (G) is derived using the annual growth rates of these volume indices.

Table 16.5 Example of calculating Laspeyres volume growth rates

(Weight reference year = year 0)

Item	Product	Year 0	1	2	3	4	Calculation formula
Value at the reference year prices (0)	A	710	733	756.2	783.3	813.4	$p^0q^0 \times (q^t/q^0)$
	B	340	347.2	354.9	363.9	372.6	
	Total	1,050.0	1,080.2	1,111.1	1,147.2	1,186.0	$\Sigma p^0q^0 \times (q^t/q^0)$
Laspeyres volume growth rate (growth rate, G)	A		3.24%	3.16%	3.59%	3.84%	$G=[Q_L(0,t)/Q_L(0,t-1)] - 1$
	B		2.12%	2.20%	2.54%	2.40%	
	Total		2.88%	2.85%	3.25%	3.38%	

16.2.2.3 Superlative indices

According to index number theory, true indices, in the case of a negative correlation between price relatives and volume relatives, are situated between Laspeyres indices (upper bound) and Paasche indices (lower bound). This concept is detailed extensively in the IMF (2004) Producer Price Manual (E. Economic approach) and ILO et al. (2004) Consumer Price Manual (Chapter 17). To measure true indices more accurately, various index formulations have been explored, among which the Fisher index is particularly prominent. The Fisher index is calculated as the geometric mean of the Laspeyres and Paasche indices and is expressed by the following formulas:

Fisher price index: $P_F = (P_L \times P_P)^{1/2}$

Fisher volume index: $Q_F = (Q_L \times Q_P)^{1/2}$

The Fisher index is recommended as an optimal index (which is called "superlative index") due to its capacity to reduce the discrepancy between the Laspeyres index (or Paasche index) and the true index, provided sufficient and detailed data are available. While the Fischer index is fundamentally computed as the geometric mean of the Laspeyres and Paasche indices, practical compilation of the index might involve averaging the weights at a more detailed item-level, for example, by using average weights of the reference year (0) and the comparison year (t).

Building upon this idea of using averaged weights to enhance the accuracy of indices, another notable example of a superlative index is the Törnqvist index. The Törnqvist, like the Fisher index, aims to approximate the true index more closely. However, it introduces an important refinement by applying the average of the value weights from the reference year and the comparison year at the elementary item level and employing geometric averaging to aggregate the price relatives. The formula for the Törnqvist index is as follows:

Törnqvist price index: $P_T(0,t) = \prod (\frac{p^t}{p^0})^{\frac{(w^0+w^t)}{2}}$

In this equation, Π denotes continuous multiplication across items, $\frac{p^t}{p^0}$ is the price relative of each item, and w^0 and w^t are the value weights of each item in the reference period (0) and period t, respectively. The Törnqvist index is characterized by its use of arithmetic averages of the value weights (or expenditure shares) and its reliance on geometric aggregation, rather than arithmetic summation, of price relatives. Similar to the Fischer index, the Törnqvist index is recommended as a superlative measure that minimizes deviations from the true index when appropriate and detailed data are available.

16.2.3 Practical example of index compilation

The construction of indices in practice refers to the step-by-step aggregation process in which indices calculated at the elementary (individual item) level are combined to form indices for higher-level groups. For example, in the construction of a price index, once the price relatives of each component item at the elementary level are determined, these are combined with the corresponding value weights to compute the price indices for aggregate categories.

Let us now examine the process of calculating Laspeyres, Paasche, Fischer, and Törnqvist price induces using an illustrative example. Suppose the prices and production values of agricultural products in 2015 and 2016 are given as follows (Table 16.6).

Table 16.6 Data on the prices and values for agricultural products

Product item	2015	2016	2015 ($)	2016 ($)
	Price (P^0)	Price (P^1)	Value (P^0Q^0)	Value (P^1Q^1)
Total grains			5,789,567	5,989,203
Rice	3,240	3,320	3,623,570	3,752,041
Barley	3,300	3,400	789,270	788,365
Soybeans	11,707	11,950	66,631	67,524
Corn	3,893	4,170	253,768	282,767
Millet	65	66	1,029,406	1,070,126
Wheat	3,127	3,120	25,436	26,921
Red beans	3,147	3,150	1,015	1,069
Others	8,400	8,388	472	392
Total vegetables			639,587	650,721
Cabbage	2,715	2,736	39,362	42,282
Radish	255	268	3,616	3,353
Pepper	2,462	2,479	259,571	269,951
Others	2,001	2,016	337,037	335,135

The data provide the prices for each crop in 2015 (P^0) and 2016 (P^1), along with the corresponding production values in B (P^0Q^0, P^1Q^1). From this information, the price relatives and value weights for each crop can be derived. These are then used to compute price indices for the two broad categories, grains and vegetables, for 2016 relative to 2015 (Table 16.7). As a result, the Laspeyres, Paasche, Fischer and Törnqvist price indices for grains are calculated as 1.025668, 1.025672, 1.025670 and 1.025671 respectively. Similarly, for vegetables, the corresponding price indices in 2016 relative to 2015 are 1.007515, 1.007481, 1.007498, and 1.007499.

Table 16.7 Examples of calculating price indices for individual agricultural items and upper-level aggregates

Product item	Price relative	Weight 2015 (0)	Weight 2016 (1)	Laspeyres price index (P_L)	Paasche price index (P_P)	Fischer price index	Törnqvist price index
	P^1/P^0	$w^0 = P^0Q^0/\Sigma P^0Q^0$	$w^1 = P^1Q^1/\Sigma P^1Q^1$	$\Sigma(P^1/P^0)w^0$	$[\Sigma(P^1/P^0)^{-1}w^1]^{-1}$	$(P_L{*}P_P)^{1/2}$	$\Pi(P^1/P^0)^{(w0+w1)/2}$
(Grains)		1	1	1.025668	1.025672	1.025670	1.025671
Rice	1.0247	0.6259	0.6265	0.6413	0.6114		1.0154
Barley	1.0303	0.1363	0.1316	0.1405	0.1278		1.0040
Soybeans	1.0208	0.0115	0.0113	0.0117	0.0110		1.0002
Corn	1.0712	0.0438	0.0472	0.0470	0.0441		1.0031
Millet	1.0154	0.1778	0.1787	0.1805	0.1760		1.0027
Wheat	0.9978	0.0044	0.0045	0.0044	0.0045		1.0000
Red beans	1.0010	0.0002	0.0002	0.0002	0.0002		1.0000
Others	0.9986	0.0001	0.0001	0.0001	0.0001		1.0000
(Vegetables)		1	1	1.007515	1.007481	1.007498	1.007499
Cabbage	1.0077	0.0615	0.0650	0.0620	0.0645		1.0005
Radish	1.0510	0.0057	0.0052	0.0059	0.0049		1.0003
Pepper	1.0069	0.4058	0.4148	0.4086	0.4120		1.0028
Others	1.0075	0.5270	0.5150	0.5309	0.5112		1.0039

To derive a single price index for the entire agricultural sector (i.e., the aggregation of grains and vegetables), the grain and vegetable indices are treated as if they were individual items. Their price relatives and respective value weights are used to repeat the same procedures of the index calculation. For this calculation, the Törnqvist price indices derived from the above table (Table 16.7) are used as the price relatives between 2015 and 2016.

As a result, the overall price indices for total agricultural products in year 2016 relative to year 2015 are computed as follows: Laspeyres index = 1.023863, Paasche index = 1.023861, Fischer index = 1.023862, and Törnqvist index = 1.023862 (see Table 16.8).

Table 16.8 Overall price indices for total agricultural products

Product group	2015 Value ($)	2016 Value ($)	Price relative	2015 Value weight	2016 Value weight	Laspeyres price index	Paasche price index	Fischer price index	Törnqvist price index
Total	6,429,154	6,639,924		1	1	1.023863	1.023861	1.023862	1.023862
Grains	5,789,567	5,989,203	1.02567	0.9005	0.9020	0.92364	0.87942		1.0231
Vegetables	639,587	650,721	1.00750	0.0995	0.0980	0.10023	0.09727		1.0007

16.2.4 Chain indices

In this section, we examine chain indices, which are currently the most widely used form of indices. Chain indices are also recommended by the SNA as a preferred approach to index construction. Despite their conceptual complexity, chain indices relatively easy to compute with the aid of modern computing tools. International organizations also recommend compiling volume indices based on chain index methods, particularly in the context of constant-price estimation (deflation). For example, the manual on supply and use tables by UN (2018) and the handbook on price and volume measures in national accounts by Eurostat (2016) both advocate for the use of chain indices when compiling volume measures.

16.2.4.1 Characteristics and features of chain indices

All of the indices discussed in the previous sections are two-period comparison indices, meaning they only compare two specific points in time, the reference period and the current (or comparison) period, without considering the intermediate periods. In contrast, a **chain index** is a method of index compilation that incorporates weights from all intermediate periods between the reference and current periods in a continuous sequence. To reflect these weights continuously, price or volume indices are first computed between each pair of adjacent periods (e.g., using the Laspeyres, Paasche, or Fischer formula), and then these indices are multiplied sequentially to obtain a cumulative index. That is, to construct a chain index from period 0 to period t, one must first compute the index between period 0 and 1, then between 1 and 2, then 2 and 3, and so forth, up to t. The final chain index is the product of all these intermediate link indices.

In the following, we explain how to construct chain volume indices using the Laspeyres and Paasche formulas, which are commonly used in national accounts.

Chain Laspeyres-type volume index

Using the Laspeyres approach, the volume index between two periods can be expressed as follows:

- For period 1 relative to period 0: $I_L(0,1) = \frac{\sum p^0 q^1}{\sum p^0 q^0}$
- For period 2 relative to period 1: $I_L(1,2) = \frac{\sum p^1 q^2}{\sum p^1 q^1}$

The chain volume index at the current period (t), denoted as C(0,t), is calculated by multiplying these indices cumulatively from period 0 to period t. The process is as follows:

- Period 1: $C(0,1) = C^0 \times \frac{\Sigma p^0 q^1}{\Sigma p^0 q^0} = \mathbf{C^0 \times \boldsymbol{I_L(0,1)}}$
- Period 2: $C(0,2) = C^0 \times \frac{\Sigma p^0 q^1}{\Sigma p^0 q^0} \times \frac{\Sigma p^1 q^2}{\Sigma p^1 q^1} = C^0 \times I_L(0,1) \times I_L(1,2) = C(0,1) \times I_L(1,2)$
- Period 3: $C(0,3) = C^0 \times \frac{\Sigma p^0 q^1}{\Sigma p^0 q^0} \times \frac{\Sigma p^1 q^2}{\Sigma p^1 q^1} \times \frac{\Sigma p^2 q^3}{\Sigma p^2 q^2} = C^0 \times I_L(0,1) \times I_L(1,2) \times I_L(2,3) =$ $C(0,2) \times I_L(2,3)$
- Period t: $C(0,t) = C^0 \times I(0,1) \times I_L(1,2) \times I_L(2,3) \times \ldots \times I_L(t-1,t) = \mathbf{C(0,t\text{-}1) \times \boldsymbol{I_L}(t\text{-}1,t)}$

The initial chain index at the reference period (0), denoted as C^0, is by definition equal to 1:

$$C^0 = \frac{\Sigma p^0 q^0}{\Sigma p^0 q^0} = 1$$

In this case, the index $\boldsymbol{I_L}$**(t-1,t)**, computed between two adjacent periods, is called a **link**. The weight of the link determines the type of index: Laspeyres-type index if the previous period's weight is used, and Paasche-type index if the current period's weight is used.

Table 16.9 Types of links by weighting method

Previous-period weights (Laspeyres-type)	Volume index	$P^{t-1}Q^t / P^{t-1}Q^{t-1}$
	Price index	$P^tQ^{t-1} / P^{t-1}Q^{t-1}$
Current-period weights (Paasche-type)	Volume index	P^tQ^t / P^tQ^{t-1}
	Price index	$P^tQ^t / P^{t-1}Q^t$

These formulas can be generalized as follows:

- **Laspeyres-type link (volume):** $I_L(t\text{-}1,t) = \frac{\Sigma p^{t-1} q^t}{\Sigma p^{t-1} q^{t-1}}$

- **Chain Laspeyres-type index (volume):** $C_L(0,t) = C^0 \times \frac{\Sigma p_0 q_1}{\Sigma p_0 q_0} \times \frac{\Sigma p_1 q_2}{\Sigma p_1 q_1} \times \frac{\Sigma p_2 q_3}{\Sigma p_2 q_2} \times \ldots \times \frac{\Sigma p_{t-1} q_t}{\Sigma p_{t-1} q_{t-1}} = C^0 \times I_L(0,1) \times I_L(1,2) \times I_L(2,3) \times \ldots \times I_L(t\text{-}1,t) = C_L(0,t\text{-}1) \times I_L(t\text{-}1,t)$

  (where $C^0 = 1$).

Chain volume indices for the periods prior to the reference year can be expressed as follows:

- Period (-1): $C(0,-1) = \mathbf{C^0 / \boldsymbol{I_L}(-1,0)}$
- Period (-2): $C(0,-2) = C^0 / [I_L(-1,0) \times I_L(-2,-1)] = C(0,-1) / I_L(-2,-1)$
- Period (-3): $C(0,-3) = C^0 / [I_L(-1,0) \times I_L(-2,-1) \times I_L(-3,-2)] = C(0,-2) / I_L(-3,-2)$
- Period (-t): $C(0,-t) = C_0 / [I_L(-1,0) \times I_L(-2,-1) \times I_L(-3,-2) \times \ldots \times I_L(-t,-(t-1))] = \mathbf{C(0,-(t-1)) / \boldsymbol{I_L}(-t,-(t-1))}$

The generalized formula of the above equations is expressed as follows:

- $C_L(0,-t) = C^0 \times (\frac{\sum p^{-1}q^0}{\sum p^{-1}q^{-1}} \times \frac{\sum p^{-2}q^{-1}}{\sum p^{-2}q^{-2}} \times \frac{\sum p^{-3}q^{-2}}{\sum p^{-3}q^{-3}} \times \ldots \times \frac{\sum p^{-t}q^{-(t-1)}}{\sum p^{-t}q^{-t}})^{-1}$

  $= C^0 \times [I_L(-1,0) \times I_L(-2,-1) \times I_L(-3,-2) \times \ldots \times I_L(-t,-(t-1)]^{-1} = C(0,-(t-1)) \times I_L(-t,-(t-1))^{-1}$

  (again, $C^0 = 1$).

Chain Paasche-type volume index

Similarly, the Paasche-type link and chain volume indices can be generalized and displayed as follows:

- **Paasche-type link (volume):** $I_P(t-1,t) = \frac{\sum p^t q^t}{\sum p^t q^{t-1}}$
- **Chain Paasche-type index (volume):**

$C_P(0,t) = C^0 \times \frac{\sum p^1q^1}{\sum p^1q^0} \times \frac{\sum p^2q^2}{\sum p^2q^1} \times \frac{\sum p^3q^3}{\sum p^3q^2} \times \ldots \times \frac{\sum p^tq^t}{\sum p^tq^{t-1}} = C^0 \times I_P(0,1) \times I_P(1,2) \times I_P(2,3) \times \ldots \times I_P(t-1,t) = C_P(0,t-1) \times I_P(t-1,t);$

Backward-linked chain Paasche-type volume index can be expressed as:

$C_P(0,-t) = C^0 \times (\frac{\sum p^0q^0}{\sum p^0q^{-1}} \times \frac{\sum p^{-1}q^{-1}}{\sum p^{-1}q^{-2}} \times \frac{\sum p^{-2}q^{-2}}{\sum p^{-2}q^{-3}} \times \ldots \times \frac{\sum p^{-(t-1)}q^{-(t-1)}}{\sum p^{-(t-1)}q^{-t}})^{-1} = C^0 \times [I_P(-1,0) \times I_P(-2,-1) \times I_P(-3,-2) \times \ldots \times I_P(-t,-(t-1)]^{-1} = C(0,-(t-1)) \times I_P(-t,-(t-1))^{-1}$

(where again, $C^0 = 1$)

Advantages and disadvantages of chain indices

Chain indices differ in structural characteristics from traditional two-period comparison indices such as the Laspeyres and Paasche indices. In traditional fixed-weight indices, the weight reference period is fixed to either the reference period or the current period, and the same weights are applied across the entire time series. In contrast, in a chain index, the weight reference period shifts continuously as new links are calculated for each period. As a result, chain indices reflect updated weights at every period.

This feature allows chain indices to overcome the structural limitations of fixed-weight indices. For example, the Laspeyres index, which uses fixed base-year weights, tends to accumulate bias as the time series moves further from the base year. Chain indices mitigate this bias by applying the most current weights at each point in time. Furthermore, chain indices are capable of incorporating the appearance of new products and the disappearance of existing ones in each period along with their weights, making them better suited to represent recent economic situations. There is no need to retroactively estimate weights for new products or continue applying outdated weights for products that are no longer in the market.

However, chain indices also have some disadvantages. A major issue is the lack of so-called **additivity**. In other words, the sum of the subcategory values calculated using chain indices may not match the value of the upper-level aggregate. While the index values for the reference year and the immediately following year maintain additivity, discrepancies may arise for any other years except these two years. Therefore, statistical methods are needed to deal with these inconsistencies when using chain indices. Another potential problem is **chain drift**. This can occur when the price or volume of a product fluctuates irregularly rather than following a monotonic trend. In national accounts, chain drift refers to the phenomenon in which the index does not return precisely to its original value after a period of fluctuation, leading to bias even if prices or volumes revert to their initial levels (1993 SNA, paragraphs 16.46–16.47).

Nevertheless, since long-run trends in economic growth tend to exhibit stable patterns, it is generally considered advantageous to use chain indices overall. In addition, empirical evidence suggests that while the period of the chain indices is monthly or quarterly, the aforementioned chain drift problem may occur due to the seasonality of the links, this issue can be mitigated by adopting benchmarking techniques with annual data. (See section 19.2, "Compilation of quarterly chain indices".)

16.2.4.2 Practical compilation of chain volume indices

This section outlines the practical step for compiling chain volume indices in national accounts. We will explore the process of deriving the annual links and chain indices by applying the chain Laspeyres formula, which is the most commonly used method in compiling chain volume indices. The process of constructing a chain index consists of the following steps:

1) Let's define $PYP^t = P^{t-1}Q^t$, and $CYP^t = P^tQ^t$. PYP^t represents the previous year's prices multiplied by the current year's volumes, while CYP^t represents the current year's prices multiplied by current year's volumes. Then, PYP^t can be rewritten:

$$\mathbf{PYP^t = P^tQ^t \times (P^{t-1}/P^t) = P^tQ^t \times \frac{1}{P^t/P^{t-1}} = CYP^t \times \frac{1}{P^t/P^{t-1}}}$$

This shows that PYP^t is equal to CYP^t divided by the price index for year t relative to year $t-1$.

$$\mathbf{PYP^t = CYP^t \times \frac{1}{P^t/P^{t-1}}}$$

2) Calculate the volume link (I). The result of applying the Laspeyres formula to construct this index is as follows:

- **Annual: $I^t = P^{t-1}Q^t / P^{t-1}Q^{t-1} = PYP^t / CYP^{t-1}$**

According to the above equation, the annual volume link for year t is obtained by dividing PYP^t by CYP^{t-1}.

3) Calculate the chain Laspeyres volume index (C).

- **Reference year: $(C^0) = 1$**
- **For years after the reference year: Annual $C^t = C^{t-1} \times I^t$**
- **For years before the reference year: Annual $C^t = C^{t+1}/I^{t+1}$**

The method of deriving the annual indices from the above expressions can be confirmed as an example of the following expressions. Suppose the annual link series are I^{-3}, I^{-2}, I^{-1}, I^0, I^1, I^2, I^3, and the annual chain index series are C^{-3}, C^{-2}, C^{-1}, C^0, C^1, C^2, C^3, then:

$C^1 = C^0 \times I^1$

$C^2 = C^0 \times I^1 \times I^2 = C^1 \times I^2$

$C^3 = C^0 \times I^1 \times I^2 \times I^3 = C^2 \times I^3$

$C^{-1} = C^0 / I^0$

$C^{-2} = C^0/(I^0 \times I^{-1}) = C^{-1}/ I^{-1}$

$C^{-3} = C^0/(I^0 \times I^{-1} \times I^{-2}) = C^{-2}/ I^{-2}$

4) Calculate the **chain Laspeyres volume measures** (CVM) for year t. The chain volume measure for year t is calculated by multiplying the current value of the reference year (CYP^0) by the chain index for year t.

- **Annual: $CVM^t = CYP^{0\,(ref)} \times C^t$** where ref denotes the reference year (0).

This is conceptually equivalent to constant price values in the fixed-weight indices.

5) Calculate the growth rate (G^t) of year t relative to year $(t-1)$.

- **Annual: $G^t = CVM^t/CVM^{t-1} - 1 = I^t - 1$**

6) Calculate the deflator (Def^t) for year t. The deflator, representing a price index or price level for year t, is calculated as:

   - **Annual:** $\boldsymbol{Def^t = CYP^t/CVM^t \times 100}$

7) Calculate the contribution to GDP growth in year t relative to year $t-1$. The contribution by industry i to the GDP growth (D^t) is:

   - **Annual:** $\boldsymbol{D_i^t = (PYP_i^t - CYP_i^{t-1})/CYP_{GDP}^{t-1}}$

8) Calculate the percentage contribution (or share) by industry i to the GDP growth (Dr^t). This is calculated as *the industry i's contribution to the GDP growth divided by the GDP growth rate.*

   - $\boldsymbol{Dr_i^t = D_i^t/(CVM_{GDP}^t/CVM_{GDP}^{t-1} - 1) = D_i^t/(I_{GDP}^t - 1) = (PYP_i^t - CYP_i^{t-1})/(PYP_{GDP}^t - CYP_{GDP}^{t-1})}$

Example of compiling a chain Laspeyres volume index

This section illustrates a detailed example of how to compile a chain Laspeyres volume index, as shown in Table 16.10. The value data ($CYP^t = p^tq^t$) and price relatives (p^t/p^0) used here are cited from the same figures given in Table 16.4. The first step is to obtain the PYP^t data using the formula $CYP^t/(p^t/p^{t-1})$. The Laspeyres-type volume link is then derived by the formula PYP^t/CYP^{t-1}. Using these results, the chain Laspeyres volume index is calculated. The chain index for year t is calculated by multiplying the chain index for year $t-1$ by the link for year t with the index reference year (year 0) being 1. The chain volume measures (CVM^t) are obtained by multiplying the current value of the index reference year by the chain index for year t. In this way, the Laspeyres-type links, chain indices, and the chain volume measures are calculated respectively. However, it is important to note that the sum of the chain volume measures of individual products (row "C" in the table) does not match the chain volume measures of the corresponding aggregate category (row "D" in the table) except in the reference year and the following year. This discrepancy arises from the non-additivity inherent in chain indices, as mentioned earlier, except for these two years. Therefore, to address this inconsistency, a practical solution is to update the index reference year to a more recent year.

Table 16.10 Example of calculating the chain Laspeyres volume index

Item	Product	Year 0	Year 1	Year 2	Year 3	Year 4	Formula
Value at the price in year t (CYP)	A	710	755	794	846	911	$CYP^t = p^tq^t$
	B	340	375	401	433	462	
	Total	1,050	1,130	1,195	1,279	1,373	$\Sigma_i\ CYP_i^t$
Price index	A	1.00	1.03	1.05	1.08	1.12	p^t/p^0
	B	1.00	1.08	1.13	1.19	1.24	
Value at the price in year $t-1$ (PYP)	A		733.0	778.9	822.5	878.5	$PYP^t = p^{t-1}q^t = p^tq^t \times (p^{t-1}/p^t)$
	B		347.2	383.3	411.2	443.4	$= p^tq^t/(p^t/p^{t-1})$
	Total		1,080.2	1,162.1	1,233.7	1,321.8	$\Sigma_i\ PYP_i^t$
Volume link	A		1.032	1.032	1.036	1.038	$I(t-1,t) = PYP^t/CYP^{t-1}$
	B		1.021	1.022	1.025	1.024	
	Total		1.029	1.028	1.032	1.033	$I(t-1,t) = \Sigma_i\ PYP_i^t/\Sigma_i\ CYP_i^{t-1}$
Chain volume index	A	1.00	1.032	1.065	1.103	1.146	$C(0,t) = C(0,t-1) \times I(t-1,t)$,
	B	1.00	1.021	1.044	1.07	1.096	$C^0 = 1$
	Total	1.00	1.029	1.058	1.092	1.129	
Chain Laspeyres volume measure (CVM)	A (1)	710.00	733.01	756.19	783.33	813.39	
	B (2)	340.00	347.22	354.87	363.87	372.58	$CVM^t = C(0,t) \times CYP^0$
	Total (D)	1050.00	1080.23	1110.95	1146.90	1185.31	
Discrepancy between total and sum of components	C= (1)+(2)	1050.00	1080.23	1111.06	1147.20	1185.97	
	(C-D)	0.00	0.00	0.11	0.30	0.66	
Chain volume growth rate (F)	A		3.20%	3.20%	3.60%	3.80%	$G_C^t = CVM^t/CVM^{t-1}-1$
	B		2.10%	2.20%	2.50%	2.40%	$= I(t-1,t) - 1$
	Total		2.90%	2.80%	3.20%	3.30%	

The following presents another example illustrating the procedure for measuring a chain Laspeyres volume index and growth rates for crop output. In this example, it is assumed that data are available for each year on the values of crop output at current prices, i.e., CYP (P^tQ^t), as well as the price relatives (P^t/P^{t-1}). Table 16.11 shows the values of crops by item at current prices, and Table 16.12 presents the annual price relatives by item.

Table 16.11 Values of crops at current prices (CYP^t)

(Unit: $)

$CYP^t = P^tQ^t$	2015	2016	2017	2018	2019
Cereals	573,736	543,188	536,876	557,972	580,467
Pulses	215,603	205,627	223,743	235,103	246,801
Cooking oil	203,801	196,759	197,335	205,243	215,920
Textile crops	36,598	37,903	32,564	35,498	36,711
Other industrial crops	58,088	64,536	71,542	77,980	82,117
Tobacco	49,768	56,576	60,505	61,480	65,072
Spices	58,645	60,602	63,036	68,598	71,159
Other edible crops	115,078	140,181	149,235	195,481	199,120
Medicinal crops	31	29	26	35	37
Other non-edible crops	42,727	45,583	50,801	53,688	55,727
Total	1,354,075	1,350,984	1,385,663	1,491,078	1,553,131

Table 16.12 Price relatives of crops by item (year-on-year, P^t/P^{t-1})

P^t_i/P^{t-1}_i	2016	2017	2018	2019
Cereals	1.041300	1.009141	1.016070	1.037881
Pulses	1.022018	1.035770	1.011931	1.031229
Cooking oil	1.014959	1.016101	1.007689	1.027882
Textile crops	1.070222	0.983034	0.999352	0.987067
Other industrial crops	1.061046	1.075998	1.021724	0.978049
Tobacco	1.043722	1.011434	1.001548	1.040054
Spices	1.045854	1.028756	1.060477	1.008403
Other edible crops	1.054722	1.052841	1.404661	1.032009
Medicinal crops	1.000000	0.838710	1.346154	1.233333
Other non-edible crops	1.049453	1.079815	1.029097	1.010591
Total	1.038051	1.025074	1.054189	1.027834

Based on the two tables above, the following calculations were performed in sequence for crop output: PYP, link volume indices, chain Laspeyres volume indices, chain Laspeyres volume measures (CVM), and growth rates in chain volume terms. The index reference year is set to 2015. The results of these calculations are summarized in Table 16.13.

Table 16.13 PYP, link volume indices, chain Laspeyres volume indices, chain Laspeyres volume measures, and growth rates of crops by item

(Unit: $)

$PYP^t = P^{t-1}Q^t = P^tQ^t/(P^t/P^{t-1})$	2016	2017	2018	2019
Cereals	521,644	532,013	549,147	559,281
Pulses	201,197	216,016	232,331	239,327
Cooking oil	193,859	194,208	203,677	210,063
Textile crops	35,416	33,126	35,521	37,192
Other industrial crops	60,823	66,489	76,322	83,960
Tobacco	54,206	59,821	61,385	62,566
Spices	57,945	61,274	64,686	70,566
Other edible crops	132,908	141,745	139,166	192,944
Medicinal crops	29	31	26	30
Other non-edible crops	43,435	47,046	52,170	55,143
Total	1,301,462	1,351,769	1,414,431	1,511,072

Volume link (= PYP^t/CYP^{t-1})	2016	2017	2018	2019
Cereals	0.90921	0.97943	1.02286	1.00235
Pulses	0.93318	1.05052	1.03838	1.01797
Cooking oil	0.95122	0.98704	1.03214	1.02348
Textile crops	0.96770	0.87397	1.09081	1.04772
Other industrial crops	1.04708	1.03026	1.06681	1.07669
Tobacco	1.08917	1.05736	1.01454	1.01766
Spices	0.98806	1.01109	1.02618	1.02869
Other edible crops	1.15494	1.01116	0.93253	0.98702
Medicinal crops	0.93548	1.06897	1.00000	0.85714
Other non-edible crops	1.01657	1.03210	1.02695	1.02710
Total	0.96114	1.00058	1.02076	1.01341

Chain Laspeyres volume index (2015 = 1)	2015	2016	2017	2018	2019
Cereals	1.00	0.90921	0.89050	0.91085	0.91299
Pulses	1.00	0.93318	0.98033	1.01796	1.03625
Cooking oil	1.00	0.95122	0.93889	0.96906	0.99182
Textile crops	1.00	0.96770	0.84574	0.92254	0.96657
Other industrial crops	1.00	1.04708	1.07877	1.15085	1.23910
Tobacco	1.00	1.08917	1.15165	1.16839	1.18903
Spices	1.00	0.98806	0.99902	1.02517	1.05458
Other edible crops	1.00	1.15494	1.16782	1.08903	1.07490
Medicinal crops	1.00	0.93548	1.00000	1.00000	0.85714
Other non-edible crops	1.00	1.01657	1.04920	1.07747	1.10667
Total	1.00	0.96114	0.96170	0.98167	0.99483

(Unit: $)

Chain volume measure (CVM^t)	2015	2016	2017	2018	2019
Cereals	573,736	521,644	510,912	522,590	523,816
Pulses	215,603	201,197	211,362	219,475	223,418
Cooking oil	203,801	193,859	191,346	197,495	202,133
Textile crops	36,598	35,416	30,952	33,763	35,374
Other industrial crops	58,088	60,823	62,664	66,850	71,977
Tobacco	49,768	54,206	57,315	58,149	59,176
Spices	58,645	57,945	58,588	60,121	61,846
Other edible crops	115,078	132,908	134,391	125,323	123,697
Medicinal crops	31	29	31	31	27
Other non-edible crops	42,727	43,435	44,829	46,037	47,285
Total	1,354,075	1,301,462	1,302,218	1,329,254	1,347,078

Growth rate in chain volume terms (%)	2016	2017	2018	2019
Cereals	-9.08	-2.06	2.29	0.23
Pulses	-6.68	5.05	3.84	1.80
Cooking oil	-4.88	-1.30	3.21	2.35
Textile crops	-3.23	-12.60	9.08	4.77
Other industrial crops	4.71	3.03	6.68	7.67
Tobacco	8.92	5.74	1.45	1.77
Spices	-1.19	1.11	2.62	2.87
Other edible crops	15.49	1.12	-6.75	-1.30
Medicinal crops	-6.45	6.90	0.00	-14.29
Other non-edible crops	1.66	3.21	2.69	2.71
Total	-3.89	0.06	2.08	1.34

16.3 The measurement of prices and the treatment of quality changes

This section examines the characteristics of prices and volumes used in the measurement of price and volume indices, as well as the methods by which these elements are measured. By gaining a practical understanding of how prices are actually collected and measured in the compilation of price indices, one can more clearly understand the interrelationship between value, price, and volume. Such understanding also facilitates a more comprehensive grasp of the various methods used to construct these indices. In addition, this section aims to explain how the concept of "volume" used in national accounts differs from the commonly understood notion of "quantity," and how the concept of "quality" serves to distinguish between the two. In conclusion, the SNA adopts **volume** rather than **quantity** as the fundamental concept for measuring real growth. "Changes in quality" are considered as part of volume changes, not price changes. Based on this perspective, this section proceeds to discuss the preferred methods for compiling price indices in national accounts and the criteria by which these methods may be selected.

16.3.1 Methods of measuring individual product prices for price indices

To compile price indices, a key technical issue is how to measure the price of individual product items (models) that are collected to compile price indices. In this section, several representative techniques for price measurements are briefly introduced to understand how prices are measured in practice, particularly from the perspective of national accounts[25].

16.3.1.1 Matched-model approach

The **matched-model approach** is a method of measuring price changes by directly comparing the prices of products with identical specifications in two different periods, typically the current and previous periods. This method assumes that the same item (or an item with unchanged characteristics) is available in both periods, allowing for a straightforward comparison. However, in many practical cases, products with the exact same specifications may no longer be available or sold in the market. In such cases, a similar product within the same product category is selected to serve a substitute. When a product substitution occurs, a **splicing technique** is applied to ensure continuity in the price series.

[25] For more information, refer to the PPI manual published by the IMF, the CPI manual published by the ILO et al., and "Handbook on price and volume measures in national accounting (2016) of the EUROSTAT.

To illustrate the splicing procedure, consider the following example: Suppose that at time ($t-1$), product A is available in two different versions, an old model and a new model, which differ in quality. At time t, however the old model is no longer sold, and only the new model remains in the market. In such case, the price index for product A at time t must reflect the shift from the old model to the new model, and is thus calculated based on the change in the new model's price. The procedure can be demonstrated as follows:

The price index of product A at time t is calculated by taking the previously calculated price index at time $t-1$ (which still reflects the old model) and adjusting it using the price change from the old model to the new model. From that point forward, price changes are based on the price movement of the new model only. The resulting calculations would be:

- Price index of product A at time t = 126.5 × (120/100) = 151.8,
- Price index of product A at time $t+1$ = 151.8 × (125/120) = 158.1

Table 16.15 Example of measuring the price index by matched-model approach

Time period (→)	t-2	t-1	t	t+1
Price of product A (old model)	$50	$55		
Price of product A (new model)		$100	$120	$125
Price index of product A	115	126.5	151.8	158.1

The matched-model approach is the most commonly used method in price surveys and is particularly prevalent in the collection of price data for primary sector products, such as agricultural and mining goods. However, in cases where new products are introduced or where quality changes occur rapidly, it becomes difficult to make direct comparisons between items, thereby limiting the applicability of this method.

16.3.1.2 Hedonic approach

While the matched-model approach compares prices through substitution between similar items, a more advanced method involves identifying the quality characteristics embedded in each product and estimating the contribution of these characteristics to the overall price. This enables a decomposition of the price into its underlying components. The **hedonic approach** was developed precisely for this purpose. It is a statistical method for estimating the impact of quality change on the variation in price. Fundamentally, the hedonic method uses "regression analysis" to model the relationship between the price and the product quality.

The procedure begins by identifying the various characteristics inherent in a product and then estimating, through a regression equation, how much each characteristic contributes to the price when it changes by one unit. Using this equation, the price difference between an old item and a new item can be estimated based on differences in the quality characteristics. As a result, the portion of the price change that is attributable to differences in quality is adjusted for (i.e., **quality adjusted**), and only the residual price change, which is unrelated to quality, is treated as a pure price change and reflected in the price index. For example, in the case of computers, the quality characteristics such as CPU processing speed, memory capacity, and information storage size are identified and used as explanatory variables in the price regression model. This regression equation is estimated using a large dataset of actual prices of products, and the coefficients on each variable represent the contribution of that characteristic to the price change. Once the characteristics of the new product are observed, the price change attributable to changes in quality can be adjusted out, and the remaining difference is regarded as the pure price change to be incorporated into the price index. The hedonic price regression model takes the semi-logarithmic form, as shown below (see IMF et al., CPI manual, 2020, paragraph 6.148):

$$\ln price = \beta_0 + z_1\beta_1 + z_2\beta_2 + z_3\beta_3 + \cdots + z_n\beta_n + \varepsilon$$

In this equation, the left-hand side is expressed in logarithmic form, while the right-hand side consists of the coefficients (β_n) of each quality characteristic variable (z_n), a constant term (β_0), and an error term (ε). The hedonic method is a statistical technique that can be used for the construction of a price index, especially in cases where both the quality and the price of a product change simultaneously. However, its application in practice requires the availability of sufficiently detailed and reliable microdata on the quality characteristics of the products in question.

Box 16.1: An example of the compilation of a hedonic price index

Suppose that there is only one type of computer and that its price is determined by two characteristics: processing speed (GHz) and storage capacity (GB).

Period t (old model)

Model	Price	Speed (GHz)	Capacity (GB)
A	1,000	2	256

Period $t+1$ (new model, old model discontinued)

Model	Price	Speed (GHz)	Capacity (GB)
B	1,100	3	512

Assume that a sufficiently large sample is available and that the following hedonic regression equation has been estimated:

$$ln\ (price) = \beta_0 + 0.20\ (GHz) + 0.001\ (GB)$$

This equation implies that an increase of 1 GHz in processing speed raises the price by 20 per cent, while an increase of 100 GB in storage capacity raises the price by 10 per cent.

To convert the price of the old model A into a virtual price with the quality of model B, the quality changes are as follows: processing speed increases by 1.0 GHz (from 2.0 to 3.0), and storage capacity increases by 256 GB (from 256 to 512). The expected rate of price increase due solely to quality change is therefore:

$$\Delta \ln(\text{price}) = 0.20 \times 1.0 + 0.001 \times 256 = 0.20 + 0.256 = 0.456,$$

$$e^{0.456} \approx 1.58$$

Thus, taking quality change alone into account, the price of model B should be about 58% per cent higher. The quality-adjusted price of model A when converted to the quality of model B is therefore:

$$1{,}000 \times 1.58 = 1{,}580$$

However, the actual price of the new model B is 1,100. The pure price change is therefore:

$$1{,}100/1{,}580 \approx 0.70$$

which corresponds to a price decline of about 30 per cent. In other words, although the observed price increased by 10 per cent, one the effect of quality change is removed, the real price fell by about 30 per cent.

Next, consider the price that would prevail in period $t+1$ if the same quality as in period t were applied. If the reference quality is fixed at the period-t level of (2.0 GHz, 256 GB), the price predicted using the hedonic method is as follows:

- Price in period t: 1,000
- Price in period $t+1$ at period-t quality: $1{,}100/1.58 \approx 697$

Accordingly, the **hedonic price index** for period $t+1$ is: 697/1,000 = 0.697.

16.3.1.3 Production cost approach

The production cost approach is used to estimate prices when a product is not traded in the market or when non explicit market price exists. Instead of relying on market transactions, the price is inferred by estimating the cost of production for the item in question. If the product is market output, a more realistic price can be obtained by also estimating the producer's profit margin and adding it the production cost. This method is particularly useful for estimating the prices of non-market output, such as goods and services produced by government units or non-profit institutions, which are not sold in markets and thus lack observable transaction prices.

16.3.1.4 Model pricing versus specification pricing approach

Certain types of products are not produced continuously over time but rather are delivered on a one-off or ad hoc basis, making it difficult to directly compare prices across periods. This discontinuity presents challenges for constructing price indices. Such products typically include capital goods and unique output, such as heavy equipment (e.g., ships, aircraft, and special-purpose machinery), construction projects, R&D outputs, and custom-tailored services. Since these products are usually not standardized and are produced individually at different points in time, they are referred to as **unique products**.

To measure the prices of these types of products, two related approaches are used: **model pricing** and **specification pricing**[26].

Model pricing

Under this method, a standardized reference model with a fixed set of specifications is selected. The prices of key components making up this model are surveyed on a regular basis, and these are used to estimate the total price of the product. For example, in the construction industry, a standard building model, such as a public housing apartment of typical size, is often used. The construction cost per unit is regularly published, and changes in the prices of its major components are used to estimate the overall change in the building's price.

Specification pricing

This method is similar in nature to model pricing but differs in that it involves breaking down an actual product into its primary components, and then estimating the total price by tracking the price movements of those components. It is typically applied to custom-built equipment or complex goods, such as made-to-order machinery or aircraft. In this case, the price survey targets the produced components, not the inputs used in production. Specification pricing resembles the hedonic method in that it also decomposes a product into its constituent parts. However, there are

---

[26] See section 2.5, unique products in Handbook on prices and volume measurements in national accounts (Eurostat, 2016).

important differences between the two approaches. The hedonic method is based on regression analysis and requires a large number of specifications and price observations for a given item. In contrast, specification pricing is applied to individually produced items on a project-by-project basis, which imposes limitations on the availability of a broad set of price data.

16.3.2 Treatment of quality changes

When measuring the price of a product, the first and foremost considerations is whether the good or service in question maintains the same quality over time or whether its quality has changed. If the item being measured does not retain the same quality, it becomes necessary to decide whether the change should be reflected as a price change as a volume change. This section examines how such quality changes are reflected in price indices and volume indices within the SNA, and further discusses the criteria for selecting an appropriate price index.

16.3.2.1 The distinction between volume and quantity

In the index number theory and the SNA, a distinction is made between **volume** and **quantity**. Quantity refers to the aggregation of homogeneous products in terms of measurable units such as number or weight. A typical example would be agricultural or mineral products, where quality is homogeneous and quantities can be directly measured. However, when there are multiple non-homogeneous products, simple aggregation by quantity becomes difficult, and the total quantity of such items is instead expressed as an indirectly derived volume. For instance, in the case of manufactured goods such as automobiles, where products differ in form and price, measurement by quantity is not feasible. In such cases, they should be measured in volume terms. While quantities can be simply aggregated using a common unit of measurement, volumes consist of heterogeneous products and thus cannot be aggregated in a straightforward manner. As a result, volumes cannot be calculated directly; instead, they are derived indirectly when the values and prices of the products are given. Specifically, when a product category includes multiple types of items, the volume is obtained by dividing the total value by the weighted average price. Alternatively, the volume index is obtained by dividing the total value index by the price index.

Another illustrative example of the distinction between volume and quantity involves a product group composed of items A and B, where both items have different quantities and prices. Suppose that in period (0), 80 units of A and 20 units of B are produced, yielding a total quantity of 100 units, and their prices are \$10 and \$20 respectively. Now, suppose that in period (1), the total output remains at 100 units, but the composition changes to 60 units of A and 40 units of B, with prices remaining unchanged.

Data in period (0)

Item	Quantity (unit)	Price ($)	Value ($)
A	80	10	800
B	20	20	400
Total	100		1,200

Data in period (1)

	Quantity (unit)	Price ($)	Value ($)
A	60	10	600
B	40	20	800
Total	100		1,400

Using period (0) as the reference period, the indices for quantity, price, value, and volume for period (1) are calculated as follows. Since the total number of units remains unchanged at 100, the quantity index of period (1) relative to period (0) is 1.0. Likewise, because prices have not changed, the price index is also 1.0, regardless of the weighting method (Laspeyres-type or Paasche type). The value index is 1.167 (= 1,400/1,200), and the volume index, which is not calculated directly, is obtained indirectly by dividing the value index by the price index (1.167/1.0 = 1.167). This example demonstrates that even when the total quantity remains constant, internal changes in the composition of quantities among product items can lead to changes in the total value and the volume index. This phenomenon is called a "compositional change", and such changes are captured in the volume index rather than in the price index.

Table 16.14 Derivation of volume index

Index (period 1 / period 0)

Quantity index	Price index	Value index	**Volume index (=Value index / price index)**
100 units / 100 units = 1	1.0/1.0 = 1	1,400/1,200 = 1.167	**1.167/1 = 1.167**

Concept of unit value index

The value index simply divided by the quantity index is referred to as the **unit value index**. The unit value is calculated by dividing the total sales value of a product by its total quantity. In the example above, the unit value in period 0 is 12 (=1.200/100), and in period 1 it is 14 (=1,400/100). Thus, the unit value index for period 1 relative to period 0 is 1.167 (=14/12). However, in calculating a unit value index, it is assumed that the product in question must be of homogeneous quality. If the product varies in quality or exhibits significant differences in quality, the unit value cannot adequately represent changes in price of the product, and its effectiveness as a price index diminishes.

16.3.2.2 Preferred price indices for the measurement of volumes

To understand how volume indices are calculated in the national accounts, it is important to first understand how quality changes in goods and services are treated when measuring the price index. In the SNA, any change in the quality of a product is reflected in the volume index, not the price index. In other words, the price index is meant to show pure price changes of a product, assuming that the quality of the product remains the same. If the quality improves or worsens, that change is recorded in the volume index.

For example, imagine a new model of mobile phone (Model A) is introduced with better features than an older model (Model B) and is sold at a higher price. In this case, the higher price of Model A does not affect the price index for mobile phones because it results from improved quality. Instead, the total increase in production value due to the sales of Model A is treated as a volume increase. This method assumes that the price difference comes from a difference in quality, and it attributes the impact to volume rather than price.

Based on this approach, the national accounts do not calculate volume indices directly. Instead, they are indirectly derived by dividing the value index by the price index. This ensures that the effects of quality changes are properly included in the volume measure.

Why unit value indices are inappropriate as deflators

The reason why unit value indices are not used in place of price indices in the deflation process is that unit value indices do not adjust for quality changes. A unit value index is derived by simply dividing the total value by the total quantity, and it represents changes in average unit price without distinguishing between the differences in quality between products. As in the previous example, if the quantities of model A and model B (which differ in quality) are simply aggregated to compute a unit value, the resulting increase in the price of model A due to quality improvement would be incorrectly reflected as a general price increase.

Therefore, because unit value indices fail to account for quality differences, they are not suitable as deflators and make it difficult to obtain accurate volume indices. However, in cases where products are relatively homogeneous, such as agricultural or mineral products, unit value indices can be used as an alternative indicator for volume measurement.

Chapter 17. Compilation of volume measures in the SNA

Following the previous chapter, this chapter will explore how to deflate each component in the national accounts. The approaches for deriving volume measures in the SNA include deflating output, intermediate consumption, and value added by industries from the production side, and final consumption, gross capital formation, exports and imports from the expenditure side. Additionally, an approach can be adopted to deflate inputs and expenditures by products. The former approach obtains volume measures from the perspective of the columns (industries) of the supply and use tables, whereas the latter approach obtains volume measures from the perspective of the rows (products) of the same tables.

However, these two approaches are not applied independently, but rather describe the sequencing of deflation for deriving volume measures. In practice, deflation in national accounts is primarily conducted at the individual product level because price indices are typically available at this detailed level, and hence the corresponding values in volume terms are also compiled at the product level. The output of an industry is measured as the sum of the outputs of its primary and secondary products, and intermediate consumption is similarly derived as the total value of the inputs used. Value added is then calculated as the difference between output and intermediate consumption. Thus, the values of an industry's output and intermediate consumption in volume terms or in constant prices are obtained by aggregating the deflated values of the individual products, which enables the application of volume measurement techniques at the product level. Likewise, value added in volume terms is derived as a residual. Among its components, remuneration of employees and other taxes on products are deflated using wage indices and tax rate indices, respectively, while operating surplus is obtained residually. On the expenditure side, deflation is also applied at the product level, based on the uses of each product (final consumption, gross fixed capital formation, and exports). In this process of compiling production and expenditure components, implicit deflators for higher-level aggregates may be computed ex post as the ratio between current price and constant price values.

Ultimately, volume estimates are compiled with the framework of the supply and use tables, which integrates data on production, and expenditure by industry and by product, and income distribution by industry. Since discrepancies may arise from the aggregation of deflated components, reconciliation and balancing adjustments are required, just as in the current price accounts (see section 6.3).

This chapter, based on these principles of deflation, outlines the methods used to derive volume measures. Section 17.1 presents a general overview of deflation methods from the perspectives of production, expenditure, and income distribution. Section 17.2 then describes the actual procedures for compiling the supply and use tables in volume terms.

17.1 Volume measurement in the national accounts

In the SNA, the most commonly used method for measuring volume is the Laspeyres-type approach. This approach involves applying base-period prices to current-period volumes, which is known as fixed-weighted method. Alternatively, in the case of chain indices, the method applies prices from the previous period to current-period, resulting in volume measures based on annual chain-linked weights. If this is expressed in a formula, the current volume measure at the price of reference year (0) is expressed as $\sum p^0 q^t$, and the current volume measure at the previous year's price (PYP) is expressed as $\sum p^{t-1} q^t$ [27].

This section discusses how GDP or gross value added in volume terms is derived based on the Laspeyres approach. Specifically, it explains the methods used to calculate GDP at constant prices from the perspectives of production, expenditure, and income distribution.

17.1.1 Volume measurement of GDP from the production side

Double deflation method

In order to derive volume measures (i.e., constant price estimates) of gross value added (GVA) and GDP from the production side, both output and intermediate consumption must first be converted into volume terms separately. The volume measure of gross value added is then obtained by subtracting intermediate consumption in volume terms from output in volume terms. This approach is referred to as the **double deflation method**, which is considered the most conceptually sound method for compiling GVA and GDP in constant prices. Let us denote the volume measures of output in year t as $\sum_i P_i^0 Q_i^t$, and the volume measures of intermediate consumption as $\sum_i p_i^0 q_i^t$, where i indicates individual products or industries. Then, the volume measure of gross value added in year t is calculated as:

[27] The current volume measure at the reference year prices can be derived as $\sum_i p_i^0 q_i^t = \sum_i [p_i^t q_i^t / (p_i^t / p_i^0)]$. In addition, the current volume measure at the previous year prices (PYP = $\sum_i p_i^{t-1} q_i^t$) can be derived as $\sum_i [p_i^t q_i^t / (p_i^t / p_i^{t-1})]$, or $\sum_i [p_i^0 q_i^t \times (p_i^{t-1} / p_i^0)]$.

$$\textbf{Gross value added in volume terms in year } t = \sum_i P_i^0 Q_i^t - \sum_i p_i^0 q_i^t$$

Alternatively, when current value data and deflators are available, the gross value added in volume terms can be derived by dividing values in current prices by their corresponding price indices (deflators), as follow:

$$\textbf{Gross value added in volume terms in year } t = \sum_i P_i^t Q_i^t / (P_i^t / P_i^0) - \sum_i p_i^t q_i^t / (p_i^t / p_i^0)$$

Once the volume measures of GVA is obtained, GDP in volume terms can be derived by adding the taxes less subsides on products, also expressed in volume terms.

- **GDP^t in volume terms = GVA^t in volume terms + taxes less subsidies on products^t in volume terms**

In this context, the Laspeyres volume index, based on fixed base-year weights, is computed as:

$$\textbf{Volume index in year } t = \frac{\sum P^0 Q^t - \sum p^0 q^t}{\sum P^0 Q^0 - \sum p^0 q^0}$$

If a **chain Laspeyres volume index** is compiled, it is necessary to first calculate the annual link, which represents the volume level in year t relative to year t-1, using the previous year as the weight base. This index for year t is calculated as:

$$\textbf{Link in year } t = \frac{\sum P^{t-1} Q^t - \sum p^{t-1} q^t}{\sum P^{t-1} Q^{t-1} - \sum p^{t-1} q^{t-1}}$$

This link serves as the year-on-year volume ratio, with the value for the previous year set equal to 1. The real growth rate for the period can be obtained by subtracting 1 from this index.

Although the double deflation method provides the accurate conceptual framework for estimating gross value added in volume terms, it can result in significant volatility in volume estimates if the deflation of intermediate consumption is unstable. This is because both output and intermediate consumption are deflated separately, and any imprecision in deflating intermediate consumption directly affects the accuracy of gross value added in volume terms.

Thus, an alternative to address this limitation, a simplified method may be applied whereby the volume growth rate of output is used as a proxy for the growth rate of value added, without separately estimating intermediate consumption in volume terms. Specifically, this can be done either by applying the same deflator used for output also to intermediate consumption (this is commonly referred to as the **single deflation method**), or by directly applying the volume growth rate of output to value added (which is known as the **single extrapolation method**, or the **single**

indicator method). These simplified approaches are often used in situations where detailed source data are lacking or insufficient and they are particularly useful in the compilation of quarterly national accounts, where timely indicators must be used in place of full-scale deflation procedures.

Single deflation method

When calculating a Laspeyres-type volume index using the single deflation method, gross value added (GVA) in volume terms for year t is first estimated using the following formula:

$$\textbf{GVA in volume terms in year } t = \textstyle\sum_i (P_i^t Q_i^t - p_i^t q_i^t)/(P_i^t/P_i^0), \text{ or } \sum_i (P_i^0 Q_i^t - p_i^t q_i^t/P_i^t/P_i^0)$$

where P_i^t/P_i^0 denotes the deflator for output in year t relative to the reference year (0) in industry i. In this equation, if the output deflator (P_i^t/P_i^0) is larger than the (unavailable) deflator for intermediate consumption, the resulting estimate of gross value added in volume terms may be overstated. Conversely, if the output deflator is smaller than the actual intermediate consumption deflator, gross value added in volume terms may be understated.

The Laspeyres-type volume index of gross value added under the single deflation method is expressed as:

$$\textbf{Volume index in year } t = \frac{\sum(P^t Q^t - p^t q^t)/(P^t/P^0)}{\sum(P^0 Q^0 - p^0 q^0)}$$

If a chain Laspeyres volume index of gross value added is to be constructed under this approach, the link for year t is computed as:

$$\textbf{Link in year } t = \frac{\sum(P^t Q^t - p^t q^t)/(P^t/P^{t-1})}{\sum(P^{t-1} Q^{t-1} - p^{t-1} q^{t-1})}$$

Single extrapolation method

The single extrapolation method applies the volume growth rate of output directly to gross value added, without separately deflating intermediate consumption. Under this method, GVA in volume terms for year t is estimated as:

$$\textbf{GVA in volume terms in year } t = \textstyle\sum_i (P_i^0 Q_i^0 - p_i^0 q_i^0) \times P_i^0 Q_i^t/P_i^0 Q_i^0 = \sum_i (1 - p_i^0 q_i^0/P_i^0 Q_i^0) \times P_i^0 Q_i^t$$

where $P_i^0 Q_i^t/P_i^0 Q_i^0$ denotes the volume index of output in industry i for year t relative to the reference year (0), and $(1 - p_i^0 q_i^0/P_i^0 Q_i^0)$ represents the value-added ratio in the reference year for industry i.

17.1.1.1 Deflation of output

This section discusses how to deflate different types of outputs: market output, non-market output, and output for own final use. The deflation methods, i.e., the procedures for deriving volume indicators, are described for each type of output. In particular, for market output, additional attention is given to the deflation of two special types output: FISIM and distribution margins.

Deflation of market output

In the national accounts, volume measures for output are generally not obtained by directly surveying volume data, but rather by deflating current price values using appropriate price indices. This indirect method is preferred for practical and conceptual reasons. As noted in the previous chapter (see 16.3.2.2), directly measured volume indices often fail to adequately account for changes in quality. In contrast, when current price values are deflated using price indices that are adjusted for quality changes, the resulting volume estimates are likely to be more appropriate and reliable for national accounting purposes. Furthermore, collecting data on volumes which are the basis for the construction of the volume index is often challenging in practice. Volumes must be measured in heterogeneous physical units and comprehensively collected across all products. In contrast, price indices are based on a common unit of value (price), and proxy indices can often be used for similar products, reducing the burden of data collection and compilation.

As explained in the previous chapter (see 16.2.2.1), there is a mathematical identity between value, price, and volume indices:

Value index = Laspeyres volume index × Paasche price index

= Paasche volume index × Laspeyres price index

Therefore, it is usually preferable to use the Paasche price index to derive the Laspeyres volume index from the value index. Specifically, the Paasche price index as a deflator is given by $\sum \boldsymbol{P^tQ^t}/\sum \boldsymbol{P^0Q^t}$ to derive the Laspeyres volume index. In the case of deriving a chain Laspeyres volume index, the corresponding link for Paasche-type price index is calculated as $\sum \boldsymbol{P^tQ^t}/\sum \boldsymbol{P^{t-1}Q^t}$.

To construct an output deflator for a given industry, each individual product produced by that industry is matched with its corresponding priced index, and a weighted average deflator is then derived using the respective current values as weights.

In the following paragraphs, we turn to the deflation methods applied to financial intermediation services and distribution margins, which differs from the standard approach used for general market output.

Deflation of Financial intermediation services

The deflation of financial intermediation services, particularly the output known as FISIM, is constructed by applying the margin rates of FISIM on deposit and FISIM on loan in the base year to the current year data. The formula is as follows:

$$\mathbf{FISIM^t\ in\ volume\ terms = (R_L{}^b - R_f{}^b) \times L^t/Def^t + (R_f{}^b - R_D{}^b) \times D^t/Def^t}$$

where, $R_L{}^b$: interest rate on loan in the base year,

$R_D{}^b$: interest rate on deposit in the base year,

$R_f{}^b$: reference interest rate in the base year,

L^t : average stock of loans in year t,

D^t : average stock of deposits in year t,

Def^t : domestic deflator, or consumer price indices (CPIs)

Deflation of distribution margins

The standard method for deflating distribution margins, which represent the primary output of wholesale and retail trade industries, involves applying deflators separately to the individual components of the identity used to calculate output directly: sales of goods for resale – purchases of goods + (closing inventory – opening inventory). Specifically, the sales and purchases of goods for resale, as well as opening and closing inventories, are deflated individually by product. The distribution margins in constant prices are then calculated as follows:

- Distribution margin (in constant prices) = sales of goods for resale (volume terms) – purchases of goods for resale (volume terms) + closing inventory (volume terms) – opening inventory (volume terms)

To apply this method, data must be available on sales, purchases, and changes in inventories by product, along with the corresponding deflators for each item.

Another way for deriving distribution margins in volume terms is to indirectly estimate their output in volume terms by using the data measured at the macroeconomic level, such as total supply of goods, the distribution ratios through wholesale/retail channels, and the wholesale and retail margin rates in the base year. The formula for this method is as follows:

- **Distribution margin^t (in constant prices) = (total supply of goods^t/deflator of goods^t) × distribution ratio^t × markup rate^b**

where the distribution ratio^t denotes the proportion of the domestic supply of goods in period t that is supplied to the wholesale and retail trade industries (= value of wholesale and retail sales^t/ total supply of goods^t), and the markup rate^b denotes the markup rate in the base year b (= (value of sales – cost of goods sold)^b/cost of goods sold^b).

Deflation of non-market output

Non-market output, such as government services that are not sold at market prices, is typically valued using the sum of costs approach. Since there are not market transactions, output cannot be directly separated into price and volume components. The only areas where government output in volume terms can be recognized are "individual services" such as healthcare and education, etc. For collective services, such as defense and public administration, it is practically impossible to measure output in volume terms.

Therefore, in "collective service" areas, a practical alternative is to deflate each component of their inputs individually and then add them up to obtain total output. For example, in the healthcare sector, measurable volume indicators include the number of medical treatments and hospitalized patients. In education, the number of students or teachers may be used. For such services, the **output approach** can be applied, in which the "unit cost" is calculated by dividing the total cost in the reference year by the volume indicator in the same reference year. This unit cost (as a constant price) is then multiplied by the volume indicator in each year to obtain the value in volume terms. In contrast, for "collective services" (such defense, public safety, and public administration), the **input approach** is used. This involves deflating the following components of individual inputs individually: intermediate consumption, remuneration of employees, depreciation, and other taxes on production. The sum of these deflated values represents the government output in volume terms.

Deflation of output for own final use

Output for own final use refers to products produced by an institutional unit for its own consumption or capital formation. If there is a market for similar goods, the output is valued at the corresponding market price, and deflation is carried out using the appropriate price index for those goods. If no such market exists, the sum of costs method is adopted, and deflation is done via the input approach, deflating each input cost items separately and summing them to obtain the output in volume terms. It is important to note that taxes on products must be excluded when applying deflation to own-use output, as such taxes are not part of the underlying value being deflated.

17.1.1.2 Deflation of intermediate consumption

When deflating intermediate consumption for obtaining volume measures, it is appropriate to apply input price indices that reflect prices at purchasers' prices, since intermediate inputs are recorded on that valuation basis. As a general principle, intermediate consumption should be deflated by product, and it is also desirable to distinguish between domestically produced and imported products. If dedicated input price indices for intermediate consumption are not available, deflation should be carried out by applying suitable price indices such as consumer price indices (CPIs), import price indices (MPIs), and producer price indices (PPIs) to each product group, using the corresponding intermediate input values as weights. An **aggregate deflator for total intermediate consumption** by industry can be derived by calculating a weighted average of the price indices for all goods and services used by that industry, including both domestic and imported products. In constructing such a composite index, either a Paasche-type fixed-weight index or a chain Paasche index may be applied, following the same methodology used for calculating the volume index (see section 16.2 for formulas and procedures).

The value weights of intermediate inputs by product can be derived from the use table at purchasers' prices for the relevant year, based on the expenditures recorded for goods and services used as intermediate inputs in each industry. When using output price indices such as PPIs to deflate intermediate consumption, one must take care to adjust for price components not covered in the output index. These typically include transport costs, distribution margins, and taxes on products, all of which may be embedded in purchasers' prices but not in basic prices. If these components are not separately adjusted, the deflated values may understate or overstate the volume of intermediate consumption.

Table 17.1 below presents an example of how to derive an intermediate consumption deflator for a specific industry, using a Paasche-type fixed-weight index based on the expenditure shares and price indices of individual input items.

Table 17.1 Example of deriving an industry-level intermediate consumption deflator (Paasche-type price index)

(Reference year of price index: 2015)

Item of intermediate input (i)	Value in 2019 ($)	Weight (s_i^t)	Price index and price relative (p^t/p^0)				
			2015	2016	2017	2018	2019
Agricultural products	6,129	0.0357	1.000	1.0492	1.0975	1.1489	1.1499
Mining	28,713	0.1671	1.000	0.9649	1.0110	1.0331	1.0229
Manufactured products	44,430	0.2586	1.000	1.0022	1.0147	1.0191	1.0255
Electricity, gas, and water supply	18,259	0.1063	1.000	1.0004	1.0130	1.0175	1.0232
Transport and storage	7,637	0.0444	1.000	1.0117	1.0276	1.0329	1.0448
Rental and lease services	15,406	0.0897	1.000	1.0000	1.0000	1.0000	1.0000
Business services	43,373	0.2524	1.000	1.0072	1.0115	1.0175	1.0284
Financial and insurance services	7,891	0.0459	1.000	1.0039	1.0084	1.0165	1.0290
Total intermediate inputs	171,838	1.0000					
Intermediate consumption deflator: $[\Sigma_i(p_i^t/p_i^0)^{-1} \times s_i^t]^{-1}$			1.000	0.9987	1.0148	1.0237	1.0282

17.1.2 Volume measurement of GDP from the expenditure side

All components of GDP on the expenditure side are valued at purchasers' prices, and therefore, it is appropriate to derive their volume measures by deflating current price values using price indices that reflect purchasers' prices. However, in practice, price indices compiled at purchasers' prices are limited, except for the consumer price indices (CPIs), so a combination of different indices, including producer price indices (PPIs) and other available price indices, must often be used.

Expenditure items should be separated into domestically produced good and services, and imports. Domestic products are deflated by CPIs or PPIs, while imports are deflated by import price indices (MPIs), and the deflated items are then aggregated. Through this process, the volume measure of GDP (real GDP) at time t on the expenditure side can be expressed as:

- **Real GDP^t = real final consumption expenditure^t + real gross capital formation^t + real export^t – real imports^t**

The following sections describe how each of the items that constitute the expenditure side of GDP are deflated.

17.1.2.1 Deflation of final consumption expenditure

Final consumption expenditure is broken down by institutional sector, particularly distinguished between households and non-market producers such as general government and NPISHs.

Deflation of household final consumption expenditure

Household final consumption expenditure at current prices is derived by the formula:

- Total household consumption expenditure = domestic expenditure by all households (residents and non-residents) + direct purchases abroad by residents – domestic purchases by non-residents".

Its value "in real terms" can be derived by the same formula after deflating each of these items. Since household final consumption expenditure is valued at purchasers' prices paid by households, deflation should be conducted accordingly. Specifically, for domestically produced goods and services, consumer price indices (CPIs) are used to remove the effects of price changes, while imported products are adjusted using the import price indices (MPIs). Direct purchases abroad by residents are deflated by a composite index constructed from the CPIs (or PPIs) of major partner countries with the weights of expenditures in the corresponding countries. Owner-occupied dwelling services are estimated using the **rental-equivalent approach**, and the deflation is performed by applying the price indices for actual rentals. This component represents the largest single item with household consumption.

Deflation of final consumption expenditure of government and NPISHs

The final consumption expenditure of non-market producers, including general government and NPISHs, at current prices is defined as:

- Final consumption of non-market producers = output – sales (market and non-market) – own-account fixed capital formation + purchases from market producers for social transfers in kind to households

To obtain the value in constant prices, each component of output, sales, own-account fixed capital formation, and purchases from market producers for the social transfers in kind is deflated separately, and the results are combined in accordance with the above formula. Although output accounts for the largest share among these components, its volume measure does not need to be re-estimated here, since it directly corresponds to the volume measures of products for the individual consumption and collective consumption already derived from the production side mentioned in the previous section.

17.1.2.2 Deflation of gross capital formation

Deflation of gross fixed capital formation

Gross fixed capital formation (GFCF) is deflated separately according to three main categories: buildings and structures, machinery and equipment, and intellectual property product (IPP).

Gross fixed capital formation in buildings and structures at current prices is calculated according to the product flow method as follows:

- GFCF in buildings and structures = output of the construction industry (at basic price) + non-deductible VAT + costs of ownership transfer (e.g., acquisition taxes, registration taxes, real estate agent fees, legal fees, etc.) – changes in construction inventories

To obtain the volume measures of GFCF in buildings and structures, each of the above components is individually deflated, and then combined by addition and subtraction as indicated in the equation.

Gross fixed capital formation in machinery and equipment at current prices is also calculated in accordance with the product flow method as follows:

- GFCF in machinery and equipment = output and imports of the machinery and transport equipment (at basic price) + non-deductible VAT + other taxes on products + costs of ownership transfer (such as trade and transport margins, acquisition taxes, registration taxes, etc.) – changes in inventories of machinery and transport equipment (including both producers' and distributors' inventories)

In practice, some items, such as trade and transport margins, and non-deductible value added tax, may not arise or may be negligible, and thus may be omitted from actual calculations. To derive the volume measures of GFCF in machinery and equipment, each components listed above is deflated separately and then combined according to the identity. The deflation should distinguish between domestically produced items and imports, applying PPIs to domestically produced items and import price indices to imported items.

Intellectual property products are defined in the OECD manual (OECD 2010) to include R&D, computer software and databases, mineral exploration and evaluation, entertainment, literary or artistic originals. The deflation methods for these products generally differ between R&D and other types of IPP. Here, we describe specifically the deflation methods for computer software and R&D, as representative examples.

Computer software can be divided into two main types: the developers and suppliers of software and the own-account software. Gross fixed capital formation via the developers and suppliers of software (at current prices) is derived by the product flow method, expressed as follows:

- GFCF in computer software = output of the software developers and supplier + imports of software + distribution margins – intermediate consumption – purchases by households – changes in inventories of software

To obtain the volume measures, each component in the above formula is deflated separately and then combined. Gross fixed capital formation of own-account software (at current prices) is calculated using the sum of costs approach by summing up the production costs of originals used for reproduction and other own account software. The deflation method of this category is similar to that of "output for own final use", which uses the deflated market price data of similar products if available or deflates individual input costs and then aggregates them. GFCF in **R&D** can similarly be categorized into two categories: purchased R&D (from specialized suppliers) and own-account R&D production. Purchased R&D is measured at current prices according to the product flow method and subsequently deflated. In contrast, the own-account R&D at current prices is measured using the sum of costs method, where the costs of each individual component are separately deflated and then aggregated to obtain the volume measure.

Deflation of fixed assets and depreciation

When the perpetual inventory method (PIM) is applied to estimate fixed assets and depreciation, the values in constant prices are first derived, and the corresponding estimates in current prices are subsequently are derived based on these volume measures. The basic identity used in this calculation is as follows (see section 20.3.3 for detailed methodology):

- Opening net stock of fixed assets (in volume terms) + gross fixed capital formation (in volume terms) – depreciation (in volume terms) = closing net stock of fixed assets (in volume terms)

Deflation of changes in inventories

Changes in inventories (at current prices) are, in principle, measured as the value of "entries into inventories – withdrawals from inventories – recurrent losses from inventories" following the perpetual inventory method. However, due to the frequent unavailability of such detailed data, a alternative identity is often used:

- Opening stock of inventories + changes in inventories + holding gains and losses of inventories = closing stock of inventories".

Since changes in inventories may sometimes take on negative values, their volume measures are obtained by deflating the opening and closing inventory stocks and taking the difference between them. That is:

- Changes in inventories (in volume terms) = closing stock of inventories (in volume terms) – opening stock of inventories (in volume terms)

To deflate both the opening and closing inventory stock, asset price deflators should be applied. These deflators reflect price indices at the respective opening or closing points in time.

17.1.2.3 Deflation of exports and imports

Deflation of exports and imports of goods

In the supply and use tables (SUTs), exports of goods are recorded at FOB prices, while imports of goods are recorded on a CIF basis at the individual product level, although they are adjusted to FOB prices at the aggregate level. Accordingly, for volume estimation, it is appropriate to deflate exports of goods using FOB-based export price indices, and imports of goods using CIF-based import price indices.

In the case of merchanting, which was introduced in the 2008 SNA, its values in current prices are not recorded at FOB prices but at actual transaction prices. Therefore, volume measures for merchanting must be treated differently from standard exports. Specifically, the "negative export" (i.e., import from the country of origin) should be deflated using the producer price indices (PPIs) of the origin country, and the "positive export" (i.e., export to the destination country) should be deflated using PPIs of the destination country. In both cases, exchange rate effects must be adjusted accordingly.

Ideally, export and import price indices should be complied as Paasche-type price indices, since this format is more suitable for deriving Laspeyres volume indices. In the absence of official export and import price indices, unit value indices for exports and imports may be used as substitutes. However, these unit value indices often fail to serve as optimal deflators because they are sensitive to changes in product mix and quality of traded goods.

Deflation of exports and imports of services

The deflation method for exports and imports of services depends on the availability of relevant service price indices. If service export and import price indices are unavailable, PPIs or CPIs for similar domestically produced services can be used as proxies for deflating exports of services. For deflating imports of services, the export price indices of trading partner countries should be applied, and exchange rate effects must also be taken into account.

Processing services related to *goods sent abroad for processing*, which were newly introduced in the 2008 SNA, are treated as part of exports and imports of services, and should be deflated accordingly. Specifically, exports of this processing service may be deflated using price indices for similar domestic processing services. For imports of such services, price indices from the relevant processing industries in the exporting country may be used, and exchange rate effects are also adjusted.

17.1.3 Volume measurement of GDP from the income side

To measure GDP in volume terms from the income side, each component of GDP, namely gross value added (GVA) and taxes less subsidies on products, must be deflated separately and then summed up. Since GVA at current prices is derived as a residual, its volume measure is also calculated residually by subtracting intermediate consumption in volume terms from output in volume terms. Because GVA derived in this way is not explicitly decomposed into separate volume and price components, estimating GDP in volume terms through the income approach requires applying appropriate deflators to each component of GVA, except for the residual item (operating surplus and mixed income), which cannot be deflated independently. Therefore, the estimation of GDP based on the income approach is referred to in real terms rather than volume terms.

Under the income approach, GDP in real terms in year t can be expressed by the following identity:

- GDP in real terms^t = remuneration of employees in real terms^t + net operating surplus and net mixed income in real terms^t + depreciation and depletion in real terms^t + other taxes less subsidies on production in real terms^t + taxes less subsidies on products in real terms^t

The following sections provide a brief overview of the methods used to derive volume measures for the individual components of gross value added.

17.1.3.1 Deflation of remuneration of employees

The most appropriate deflator for converting remuneration of employees into real terms is the hourly wage index that incorporates the weights in detailed industry-level compensation shares. The weights should reflect the proportion of compensation for each industry relative to the total. Moreover, the wage index must be compiled in a "Paasche-type" format to be suitable for deriving Laspeyres-type volume indices.

Wage indices, depending on how they are compiled, can be classified into two types, similar to price indices: (i) **price index-type** and (ii) **unit value index-type**. The former is constructed by stratifying workers according to wage levels and then calculating indices based on representative hourly wage rates within each stratum (this method aligns with the general approach to compiling price indices). The latter is used when both total wage and working hours data are available (for example, for government employees based on administrative data), and is calculated by dividing total wages by total working hours to obtain an average hourly wage (i.e., the unit-value method). If information on hourly wages is not available and deflators cannot be applied directly, an alternative is to use data on the number of employees, by converting this into full-time equivalents of employees, as a volume indicator. This can then be extended to estimate remuneration of employees in real terms.

17.1.3.2 Deflation of taxes less subsidies on production

Deflation of other taxes less subsidies on production

These items refer to taxes and subsidies that are related to production activities of enterprises but are not directly linked to specific products. Since they cannot be broken down into price and volume components, they may be deflated using relevant volume indicators. For example, payroll taxes may be deflated using the number of employees; property taxes based on the size or area of assets; and business license taxes based on the number of licensed firms.

Deflation of taxes less subsidies on products

Taxes on products and subsidies on products can be more systematically deflated, as they are separable into price and quantity components. Taxes on products are generally divided into **specific taxes** (per unit) and **ad valorem taxes** (based on value), with the following deflation methods:

- Specific tax (in real terms) = current quantity × tax rate per unit in the base year
- Ad valorem tax (in real terms): current value of tax / price index × ad valorem tax rate in the base year

Subsidies on products are also deflated in a similar way to taxes on products to derive their volume measures.

17.1.3.3 Deflation of operating surplus and mixed income

Gross operating surplus and mixed income, as well as net operating surplus and mixed income (after subtracting depreciation and depletion), are derived as residuals from gross value added. Unlike remuneration of employees or depreciation, these items cannot be directly separated into price and volume components and therefore cannot be deflated using specific deflators. As such, they must be derived indirectly using the following identity:

- Net operating surplus and mixed income (in real terms) = gross value added (in real terms) – remuneration of employees (in real terms) + depreciation and depletion (in volume terms) + other taxes les subsidies on production (in volume terms).

17.1.4 Deflation using the chain index method

When deflating items of national accounts using the chain index method, values in volume or real terms are obtained by multiplying together the links for each period from the reference period up to the current period. If the chain Laspeyres volume index is adopted for the deflation process, the calculation of PYP^t (i.e., $P^{t-1}Q^t$, the numerator of the link) can be performed using one of the following three approaches, depending on the availability of data:

1) When the current price value in the current period (CYP^t) and the price index are available:

$$\mathbf{PYP^t = P^tQ^t \times \frac{1}{P^t/P^{t-1}} = CYP^t \times \frac{1}{P^t/P^{t-1}}}$$

2) When the current price value in the previous period (CYP^{t-1}) and the volume growth rate in the current period relative to previous period are known:

$$\mathbf{PYP^t = P^{t-1}Q^{t-1} \times \frac{Q^t}{Q^{t-1}} = CYP^{t-1} \times \frac{Q^t}{Q^{t-1}}}$$

3) When the volume measures based on the fixed-weight method of the reference period ($COP^t = P^0Q^t$) and the price index are available:

$$\mathbf{PYP^t = P^0Q^t \times \frac{P^{t-1}}{P^0} = COP^t} \times \text{deflator}^{t-1}$$

where P^0Q^t denotes the value in the current period at constant prices in reference period 0.

17.2 Compilation of the supply and use tables in volume terms

The supply and use tables (SUTs) are the first stage in compiling national accounts statistics that organize the data on production, income, and expenditure in a way that maintain consistency through the product balance framework. It processes source data to align with the national accounts framework. By compiling the SUTs, essential source data are made available for compiling the production account, the generation of earned income account, and most of the capital account within the sequence of economic accounts. Especially when the SUTs is compiled annually, it serves as a basis for calculating annual growth rates in constant prices (i.e., in volume terms).

This section introduces the various types of price indices used in the deflation of the SUTs and describes how these indices are applied to deflate the SUTs by year.

17.2.1 Price indices used to compile the supply and use tables in volume terms

The values of goods and services produced or consumed are typically measured at current prices prevailing in the respective year. However, since prices change continuously over time, it is necessary in the SNA, to eliminate the effects of price changes in order to measure changes in production or expenditure in volume terms. The deflators used to derive such volume measures are price indices, and a commonly used method is to deflate current values by dividing them by the appropriate price indices.

This indirect method is widely adopted because measuring volume indices directly is statistically very complex and burdensome, whereas price indices can be compiled through sample surveys rather than full enumeration and can incorporate appropriate adjustments for quality changes. For this reason, the indirect method of deflation using price indices is considered more efficient and practically applicable in national accounting.

Price indices have long been compiled independently as indicators for measuring changes in prices of goods and services in their own right. Prominent examples are consumer price indices (CPIs), producer price indices (PPIs), and export and import indices (XMPIs). However, within the context of the SNA, these indices serve primarily as deflators for converting current values measures into volume or real terms. This function is particularly important in the compilation of the supply and use tables at constant prices.

To construct the **supply and use tables at constant prices**, it is necessary to compile appropriate price indices by product for each detailed item. For the supply table, price indices are required to deflate output at basic prices, imports, and taxes less subsidies on products on a "product" basis from the supply side. In the use table, price indices are needed to deflate intermediate consumption, final consumption, gross fixed capital formation (all expressed at purchasers' prices), and exports on a "product" basis from the use side.

From a practical standpoint, the most efficient approach is to use existing official price indices as they are or to make suitable adjustments to tailor them for the purpose of national accounts. In the process of deflating national accounts data, not only official price statistics but also price data constructed through other means can be employed, and such data play an important role not only in the supply and use tables but across various domains of the accounts.

The following sections briefly describe the main types of price indices currently in use and show how they are applied to the areas of national accounts, including the supply and use tables.

Consumer price indices

Consumer price indices (CPIs) are generally defined as composite price indices that measure changes in prices of goods and services classified as final consumption products, with weights based on household expenditures for each item. In order for these indices to be used to measure changes in household consumption expenditures within the framework of the SNA, the coverage of prices surveyed must be properly aligned with the concepts of the SNA. Since households' expenditures in national accounts are measured at purchasers' prices, it is appropriate that the CPIs also be compiled at the purchasers' prices. The purchasers' prices include all expenditures paid by consumers to acquire ownership of goods and services, including, among others, nondeductible taxes on products, distribution margins, and transport margins. However, in practice, certain components may be omitted depending on the availability of data collection from the compiling institution. Accordingly, adjustments may be necessary when applying the CPIs for national accounts purposes.

CPIs may be applied not only to deflate household final consumption expenditure, but also to deflate intermediate consumption of enterprises in the use table. However, when using CPIs for such purposes, it is essential to confirm whether the indices include taxes on products (such as VAT and excise taxes) and subsidies on products, depending on the analytical purpose. While intermediate consumption is recorded at purchasers' prices in the use table, in certain analytical applications, it may be converted to basic prices. Since taxes on products can fluctuate with changes in tax rates, they may influence the movement of price indices. Moreover, the treatment of value-added tax (i.e., inclusion or exclusion of VAT) may differ depending on whether the purchaser of the products is a household or an enterprise.

Producer price indices

Producer price indices (PPIs) are composite price indices calculated by applying weights based on the value of shipments for each item of goods and services to their prices sold by domestic producers to other producers, distributers, or consumers. Since PPIs cover all products produced domestically, it may include both products destined for export and products sold in the domestic market. The indices have a broad coverage of products, and prices are collected based on actual transaction prices, including discounts or surcharges where applicable. The price for each surveyed item is typically based on the "basic price" (or producer's price) actually received by the producer. However, in practice, statistical offices may apply various exceptions depending on data availability or practical constraints.

PPIs is mainly used to deflate the value of output in the supply table as they are measured at the basic price (or producer's price) sold by producers. They can also be applied to deflate gross fixed capital formation (GFCF) in the use table, particularly for capital goods such as machinery and equipment that are not well covered by CPIs. Furthermore, since PPIs include prices of goods and services used as intermediate inputs, they are also applicable to the deflation of intermediate consumption by enterprises. However, when applying PPIs based on basic prices to the deflation of GFCF or intermediate consumption, appropriate adjustments should be made to convert the basic prices to purchasers' prices.

Export and import price indices

Export and import price indices (XMPIs) are composite price indices compiled by applying weights based on the transaction values of export and import items to the prices of those transactions. While their intended coverage may include both goods and services, most countries currently compile these indices only for goods. The price data used in compiling XMPIs are collected directly from exporters or importers. Specifically, for imports, prices are usually collected on a CIF basis, while export prices are gathered on an FOB basis.

Unlike XMPIs, unit value indices (UVIs) for exports and imports are calculated indirectly using customs data on transaction values and quantities. However, UVIs do not reflect changes in product quality or shifts in product composition and therefore have limitations in being used as deflators.

XMPIs are used as a measure of the terms of trade with foreign countries in its own right, but in the national accounts, they are primarily applied to deflate current values of exported and imported goods. For international trade in services, XMPIs are not commonly compiled, thus it is often necessary to use price indices for similar domestic services as proxies or conduct separate price surveys.

Unit value indices

Unit value indices can be used as an alternative indicator for price indices in areas where data on the value and quantity of all items of commodities are available. A **unit value** is calculated simply as the ratio of value to quantity, and a **unit value index** is calculated by dividing the unit value in a given period by the unit value in the base period. A typical example is trade statistics, where detailed information on the value and quantity of imported and exported goods is available, allowing for the calculation of unit values and unit value indices by goods.

However, unit value indices are valid only if the goods included are homogeneous and can be measured using the same physical unit. Different measurement units such as weight, number, and volume etc., must not be mixed, and a single consistent unit must be applied throughout. Moreover, as can be seen from the formula, unit value indices are compiled on the basis of quantity, not volume, so they fail to adjust for quality changes in the product mix, attributing such changes entirely to price variation. Consequently, unit value indices are not generally recommended for broad use but may be appropriate for items with relatively uniform quality.

Preferred criteria for price indices in national accounts

The price indices described above have developed independently for their own compilation purposes, but in order to be used for compiling volume estimates of the SNA, the basis of price surveys must be adjusted to suit that purpose. In other words, it is preferable that the price indices used to deflate the inputs of enterprises and outputs for final use be compiled at purchasers' prices, and the price indices used to deflate output be compiled at basic prices or producers' prices. However, in practice, these indices are not always compiled in a way that reflects the valuation principles required in national accounts. For example, CPIs are compiled using purchasers' prices and are therefore directly applicable to deflating household final consumption expenditure. But when used to deflate intermediate consumption by enterprises, it is necessary to check whether the index includes deductible VAT. Similarly, PPIs are generally compiled at basic prices, and when applied to intermediate consumption or gross fixed capital formation in the use table, appropriate adjustments are necessary to bring them to purchasers' prices level.

Although, in theory, separate price indices should be constructed for inputs and outputs based on the valuation principles of the SNA, practical constraints often make this unfeasible. In such cases, it is usually more practical and operationally efficient to adapt existing PPIs and CPIs after adjustments are processed.

The following table lists the types of price indices that can be applied to each item in the supply and use tables for estimate volume measures. Although these indices may not precisely match the valuation principles required by national accounts, they can still be reasonably used to reflect trends in price movements.

Table 17.2 Price indices applied for each item in the supply and use tables

(Supply table)

Domestic Output	Imports	Distribution & Transport Margins	Net Taxes on Products
Deflators at basic prices (PPIs)	Deflators at basic prices (MPIs)	Margin deflators	Deflators for taxes on products

(Use table)

Intermediate Consumption and Value Added	Final Consumption	Capital Formation	Exports
Deflators at purchasers' prices (Adjusted-PPIs, CPIs, MPIs)	Deflators at purchasers' prices (CPIs, MPIs)	Deflators at purchasers' prices (Adjusted-PPIs, CPIs, MPIs)	(XPIs)
Remuneration of employees: Wage indices			
Net operating surplus: Residual			
Depreciation: Deflators for fixed capital formation			

17.2.2 Compilation of the supply and use tables in volume terms

The supply and use tables in volume terms are compiled for the purpose of providing time series of the tables based on volumes by removing the factor of price changes in the SUTs at current prices. When compiling the volume-based SUTs, a key initial decision is whether to use the version of the use table valued at basic prices or the one valued at purchasers' prices. While the supply table is compiled exclusively at basic prices, and thus does not allow for a choice, the use table may be compiled in two versions, one at purchasers' prices and the other at basic prices, requiring a choice between the two depending on the purpose. The preference for using either version of tables may depend on the nature of the price indices used to convert the current values into volume terms.

Producer price indices (PPIs) and consumer price indices (CPIs) are most commonly used price indices for deflation. PPIs are compiled at basic prices excluding trade and transport margins and taxes less subsidies on products, and CPIs are compiled at purchaser's prices, reflecting the prices actually paid by consumers, including trade and transport margins and taxes on products.

Therefore, the use table should be selected so that these price indices can be used appropriately, taking into account their characteristics[28]. If the compiler wants to derive a symmetric input-output table based on the supply and use tables, then it is preferable to choose the **use table at basic prices**. This is because consistency in valuation is required when deriving an input-output table through the supply and use tables, using a supply table at basic prices alongside a use table also at basic prices ensures that the resulting input-output table is likewise expressed in basic prices, thereby maintaining internal coherence.

When the supply and use tables are compiled annually, they serve as the basis for deriving all indicators related to GDP in the national accounts. Chapter 6 has already illustrated an example of calculating GDP in current prices from the production, income distribution, and expenditure sides by using the supply and use tables (see section 6.8). This current section will focus on how to compile the supply and use tables in volume terms, using the supply and use tables in current prices and the relevant price indices, and how to derive growth rates in real terms from the production, income distribution, and expenditure approaches.

When applying the chain volume index approach recommended by the SNA, the supply and use tables in volume terms can be compiled through the following procedure. As a concrete example, let's look at the process of deriving the supply and use tables at the current year (2016) expressed in the previous year's price (2015), and the corresponding annual volume growth rate by the link volume indices in the current year relative to the previous year. This example is based on the supply and use tables at the current prices for two consecutive years (2015, 2016) (see Table 17.3). There compilation process requires the following three sets of source data:

- Supply and use tables in 2015 (at the current prices, $\mathbf{CYP^{15}} = \mathbf{P^{15}Q^{15}}$)
- Supply and use tables in 2016 (at the current prices, $\mathbf{CYP^{16}} = \mathbf{P^{16}Q^{16}}$)

---

[28] The 2008 SNA states that the supply and use tables at basic prices are more appropriate for the compilation on a volume basis (2008 SNA paragraphs 14.138-14.139).

- Price index matrix for 2016 relative to 2015 in the supply and use tables ($\mathbf{P^{16}/P^{15}}$)

Step 1: Divide the supply and use tables in 2016 at current prices (CYP^{16}) by the price index matrix in 2016 relative to 2015 to obtain the supply and use tables in 2016 valued at 2015 prices (PYP^{16}). This procedure is followed by dividing Table A by Table B in Table 17.3, resulting in Table C (the supply and use tables in 2016 valued at 2015 prices).

- $\mathbf{CYP^{16} / (P^{16}/P^{15}) = P^{16}Q^{16} / (P^{16}/P^{15}) = P^{15}Q^{16} = PYP^{16}}$

That is, the supply and use tables for 2016 valued at 2015 prices.

Step 2: The next step is to divide the supply and use tables in 2016 valued at 2015 prices (PYP^{16}) by the supply and use tables in 2015 valued at 2015 current prices (CYP^{15}). This yields the table of volume links in 2016 relative to 2015 (Table E is derived by dividing Table C by Table D). In Table 17.3, this corresponds to dividing Table C by Table D to derive Table E:

- $\mathbf{PYP^{16} / CYP^{15} = P^{15}Q^{16} / P^{15}Q^{15}}$

That is, the volume links in 2016 relative to 2015 (valued at 2015 prices).

Step 3: The resulting Table E contains the volume links for 2016 over 2015. By subtracting 1 from each link in this table, the real (volume-based) growth rate for each item in 2016 can be obtained.

Table 17.3 Derivation of the supply and use tables in volume terms and the corresponding growth rates

A. Supply and use tables at current prices in 2016 (= $P^{16}Q^{16}$)

Supply table (at current prices in 2016) Use table (at current prices in 2016)

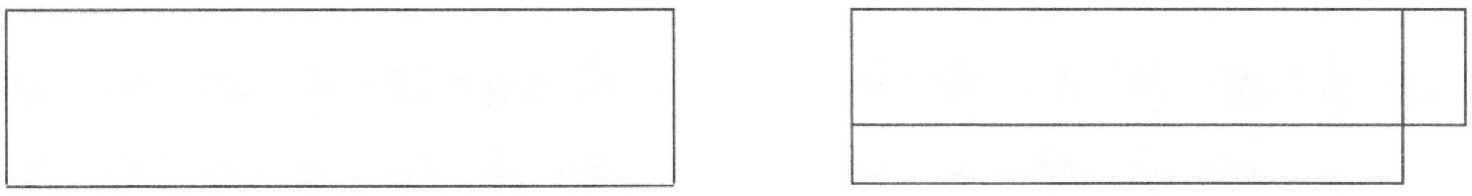

B. Price index matrix in 2016 relative to 2015 (= P^{16}/P^{15})

Price index matrix in the supply table Price index matrix in the use table

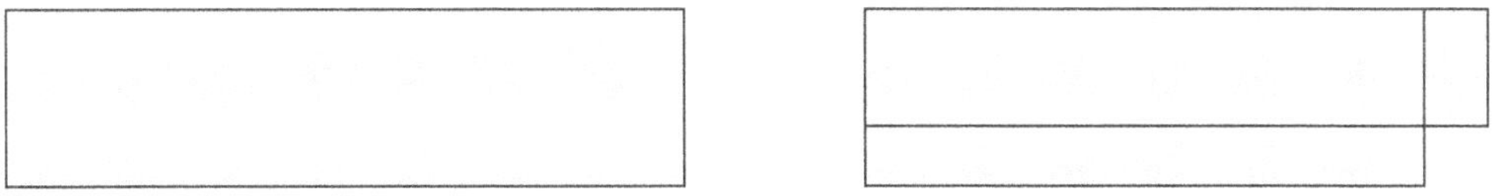

C. Supply and use tables in 2016 valued at 2015 prices (= $P^{15}Q^{16}$)

Supply table (at previous year prices) Use table (at previous prices)

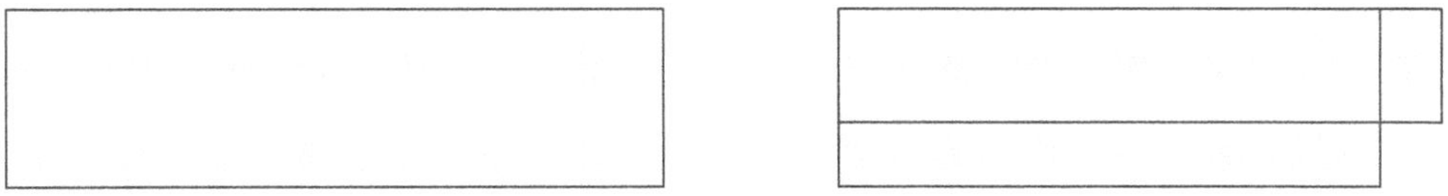

D. Supply and use tables at current prices in 2015 (= $P^{15}Q^{15}$)

Supply table (at current prices in 2015) Use table (at current prices in 2015)

E. Volume link in 2016 relative to 2015 (= $P^{15}Q^{16}/P^{15}Q^{15}$)

Supply table (volume link) Use table (volume link)

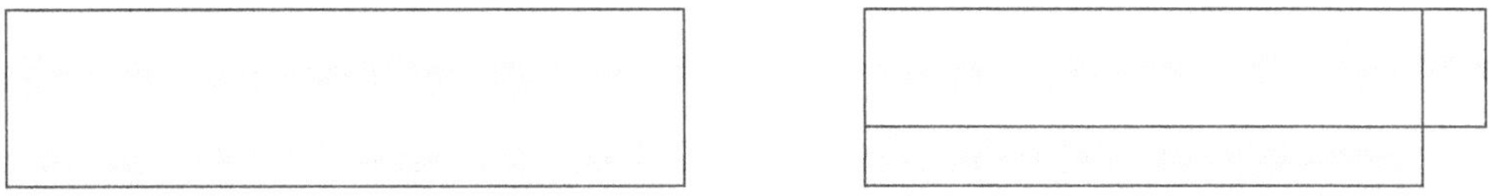

In general, the supply and use tables are compiled first at current prices, and subsequently transformed into tables at constant prices. However, compilation manuals issued by international organizations recommend that the supply and use tables both at current prices and at constant prices be compiled simultaneously while balancing each other. In other words, from the perspective of statistical consistency, it is desirable to establish a system so that the supply and use tables in volume terms are compiled concurrently with those at current prices by integrating the deflation process using appropriate price indices.

Chapter 18. Derivation of aggregate measures of real income

The previous chapter examined methodologies for estimating GDP in volume terms from the production, expenditure, and income distribution perspectives within the national accounts, as well as procedures for compiling the supply and use tables in volume terms. Building upon this volume measure of GDP, this chapter addresses methods for deriving aggregate real income indicators, specifically real gross national income (real GNI) and real gross national disposable income (real GNDI). Two primary approaches can be adopted for deriving aggregate measures of real income from GDP in volume terms: the production-side approach and the expenditure-side approach. Each of these methods is explained in detail below.

18.1 Derivation of real income aggregates from the production side of GDP in volume terms

When compiling aggregate income measures at current prices for the whole economy, gross national income (GNI) is derived directly from GDP, the production-side aggregate measure. However, in the derivation of aggregate income measures in real terms, an intermediate measure called **real gross domestic income** (real GDI) must first be compiled from GDP in volume terms before deriving **real gross national income** (real GNI). Subsequently, real GNI is obtained by adding "net real earned incomes receivable from abroad" (i.e., real earned incomes receivable from abroad minus real earned incomes payable abroad) to real GDI.

Real gross domestic income (real GDI) measures the real purchasing power of the total income generated from the gross domestic product. Real GDI is computed by adding the **trading gains and losses from changes in the terms of trade** arising from trades with foreign countries to GDP in volume terms. In other words, real GDI captures changes in domestic purchasing power due to relative fluctuations in the **terms of trade** (defined as export prices divided by import prices) and incorporates these effects into aggregate real income measures.

The mechanism through which trading gains and losses from changes in the terms of trade occur can be illustrated with the following example. Suppose that South Korea initially exports mobile phones to a Middle Eastern country at a price of $100 per unit and, in exchange, imports oil at the same price of $100. If the export price of mobile phone subsequently rises from $100 to $120 while the import price of oil remains unchanged, South Korea can purchase more oil with the same quantity of exported mobile phones, resulting in an increase of $20 in real purchasing power.

This scenario represents an improvement in the terms of trade (= export prices/import prices) and a corresponding increase in real income, calculated as follows:

Real trading gains = $X/P_m - X/P_x$ = 120/1 – 120/1.2 = $20

where X is exports at current prices, P_m is the import price index, and P_x is the export price index.

Conversely, if the import price of oil increases from $100 to $130 while the export price of mobile phone remains unchanged, South Korea can purchase less oil than before with the same export earnings, resulting in a decrease in real purchasing power by $30. In this case, the real trading loss is calculated as follows:

Real trading losses = $M/P_x - M/P_m$ = 130/1 – 130/1.3 = $30

where M is imports at current prices, P_x is the export price index, and P_m is the import price index.

The net change in real purchasing power due to changes in the terms of trade (20 – 30 = –10) represents trading gains and losses. This simplified numerical example is for illustrative purposes; ideally, both the P_m in X/P_m, which serves as the benchmark deflator for mobile phone exports, and the P_x in M/P_x, which serves as the benchmark deflator for oil imports, should use a price index (P) based on a uniform numeraire. Thus, trading gains and losses from changes in the terms of trade can be formally expressed by the following equation:

(18.1) **Trading gains and losses (T)** $= \frac{X-M}{P} - \left(\frac{X}{P_x} - \frac{M}{P_m}\right)$

where X = exports at current prices, M = imports at current prices, P_x = the price index for exports, P_m = the price index for imports, and P = a deflator based on a uniform numeraire.

P_x, P_m, and P are all equal to 1 in the index reference year. In addition, $\left(\frac{X-M}{P}\right)$ represents the balance of the current account (net exports) deflated by the price index based on a specific numeraire, while the expression within parentheses indicates the real balance of the current account deflated separately by the export price index and the import price index.

Figure 18.1 Example of changes in trading gains and losses due to changes in the terms of trade

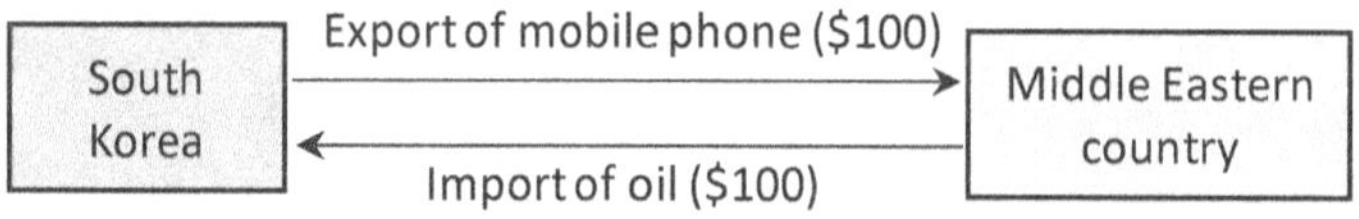

1) If the export price of mobile phone rises: \$100 → \$120

Improvement in the terms of trade ⟹ Purchasing power (real income) increased by \$20

Trading gains due to the change in the terms of trade: (X/P – X/Px) ..... (A)

2) If the import price of oil rises: \$100 → \$130

Deterioration in the terms of trade ⟹ Purchasing power (real income) decreased by \$30

Trading gains due to the change in the terms of trade: – (M/P – M/Pm) ..... (B)

Therefore, **Total trading gains and losses = (A)+(B) = (X - M)/P - (X/Px - M/Pm)**

(where, X: export at current prices, M: import at current prices, Px: export price index, Pm: import price index, P: price index based on a specific numeraire)

The price index of the specific numeraire chosen to measure trading gains and losses may be the export price index or the import price index, but the SNA typically recommends the "average of the export price index and the import price index".

If we assume that $P = \frac{P_x + P_m}{2}$ in equation (18.1) shown above, then trading gains and losses (T) can be transformed into the following:

(18.2) **Trading gains and losses:** $T = \frac{\left(\frac{P_x}{P_m} - 1\right)\left(\frac{X}{P_x} + \frac{M}{P_m}\right)}{\left(\frac{P_x}{P_m} + 1\right)}$

In equation (18.2), if the terms of trade $\left(\frac{P_x}{P_m}\right) > 1$, trading gains and losses (T) become positive (+); conversely, if the terms of trade $\left(\frac{P_x}{P_m}\right) < 1$, trading gains and losses become negative (-).

Based on the above explanation, the formulas for deriving real GDI, real GNI, and real GNDI from GDP in volume terms can be represented as follows:

a) GDP in volume terms

+ trading gains and losses due to changes in the terms of trade

b) = real gross domestic income (real GDI)

+ real net earned incomes receivable from abroad (= real earned incomes receivable from abroad – real earned income payable abroad)

c) = real gross national income (real GNI)

+ real net current transfers receivable from abroad (= real current transfers receivable from abroad – real current transfers payable abroad)

d) = real gross national disposable income (real GNDI)

– depreciation and depletion at constant prices

e) = real net national disposable income (real NNDI)

In the above equations, as the deflator used to convert the items arising from transactions with the rest of the world, namely, earned incomes receivable, earned incomes payable, current transfers receivable and current transfers payable into real terms, the "price index for gross domestic final expenditures" is commonly used. Gross domestic final expenditures refer specifically to the aggregate final expenditures incurred in a domestic economy, and it includes either "final consumption expenditure plus gross capital formation" or equivalently "GDP plus imports minus exports." The rationale for using this particular deflator is that it comprehensively measures domestic purchasing power by reflecting overall price changes within the domestic economy.

Table 18.1 below illustrates the calculation results of South Korea's GDP in volume terms, real GDI and real GNI. GDP in volume terms is the gross value added (at basic prices) plus taxes less subsidies on products by industry, using the chain-linked Laspeyres index method with 2015 as the index reference year. In 2015, the GDP in volume terms is KRW 1,658.0 trillion, and the trading gains and losses due to changes in the terms of trade is "zero" since it is the value in the reference year. Therefore, real GDI equals GDP in volume terms in 2015. It can be seen that the terms of trade deteriorated (-) in the years before 2015 and improved (+) after 2015. The real net earned income receivable from abroad in 2015 is KRW 5.2 trillion, making the real GNI KRW 1,663.2 trillion.

Table 18.1 GDP in volume terms, real GDI and real GNI of South Korea

(Unit: KRW trillion, reference year: 2015)

Item	2013	2014	2015	2016	2017
Agriculture	31.7	33.3	33.2	31.4	32.1
Mining	2.4	2.4	2.1	2.3	2.2
Manufacturing	420.5	433.9	441.1	451.3	468.1
Electricity, gas and water supply	39.5	40.5	41.8	41.3	43.8
Construction	75.3	76.4	81.2	89.1	94.4
Services	866.8	894.0	921.5	948.4	973.1
Gross value added in volume terms (basic prices) (1)	1,436.1	1,480.5	1,520.9	1,563.8	1,613.7
Taxes less subsidies on products (2)	126.6	132.2	137.1	143.1	147.1
GDP in volume terms (3) = (1)+(2)	1,562.7	1,612.7	1,658.0	1,706.9	1,760.8
Trading gains and losses (4)	-60.7	-55.9	-	23.6	25.9
Real GDI (5) = (3)+(4)	1,502.0	1,556.8	1,658.0	1,730.5	1,786.7
Real net earned income from abroad (6)	9.7	7.6	5.2	6.2	7.1
Real GNI (7) = (5)+(6)	1,511.6	1,564.4	1,663.2	1,736.6	1,793.8

18.2 Derivation of real income aggregates from the expenditure side of real GDP

Another method for deriving real income aggregates from GDP in volume terms, as described above, involves an expenditure-side approach. This approach uses GDP in current prices derived from the expenditure perspective to compute various aggregate real income measures, including real gross domestic income (real GDI). The formula for GDP in current prices from the expenditure side is as follows:

- GDP in current prices = final consumption expenditure + gross capital formation + exports – imports = gross domestic final expenditure + exports – imports = gross domestic income (GDI) in current prices

To convert this formula into constant prices, each component is divided by its respective price index as follows:

$$\text{(18.3)} \quad \textbf{GDP at constant prices} = \frac{\textbf{Gross domestic final expenditures}}{\textbf{Deflator for gross domestic final expenditure}} + \frac{\textbf{Exports}}{\textbf{Export price index}} - \frac{\textbf{Imports}}{\textbf{Import price index}}$$

However, real GDI does not simply represent GDP at constant prices. Instead, it measures the total real income generated domestically, which reflects the real purchasing power of the economy. Therefore, equation (18.3) as typically applied for GDP from the expenditure side cannot be directly used. To calculate real GDI, the values of exports and imports, which are transactions with the rest of the world sector, should not be deflated separately by their individual price indices of exports and imports. Instead, a unified deflator that reflects domestic real purchasing power must be used. The equation reflecting this consideration is:

$$(18.4) \qquad \textbf{Real GDI} = \frac{\textbf{Gross domestic final expenditures}}{\textbf{Deflator for gross domestic final expenditure}} + \frac{\textbf{Exports} - \textbf{Imports}}{\textbf{P}}$$

In this formula, P represents a common deflator used to convert both exports and imports at current prices into domestic real purchasing power terms. In the perspective of real GDI, the reason why it is not appropriate to deflate exports and imports individually by their respective price indices, can be explained as follows. For example, if export prices rise faster than import prices, exports in real terms (= current values of export / export price index) will decrease, reducing the overall GDP at constant prices. However, this does not necessarily imply a real decrease in domestic purchasing power. In such cases, it is rational either to deflate exports using the import price index instead of the export price index that is used for the deflation of exports, or to use a common deflator applicable to both exports and imports. Consequently, the difference between real GDI and GDP at constant prices (= equation 18.4 – equation 18.3) can be expressed as follows:

$$(18.5) \ \textbf{Real GDI} - \textbf{GDP at constant prices} = \frac{\textbf{Exports} - \textbf{imports}}{\textbf{P}} - \left(\frac{\textbf{Exports}}{\textbf{Export price index}} - \frac{\textbf{Imports}}{\textbf{Import price index}}\right)$$

Equation (18.5) above measures trading gains and losses arising from changes in the terms of trade (export price index divided by import price index). P can either be the import price index or the average of the export price index and import price index.

Based on this, the process of deriving real GDI from GDP at constant prices using the expenditure-side approach is follows:

a) GDP at constant prices

+ imports at constant prices – exports at constant prices

b) = gross domestic final expenditure at constant prices (= final consumption expenditure at constant prices + gross capital formation at constant prices)

+ real trade balance (deflated using either the import price index or the average of export price index and import price index)

c) = real GDI

The subsequent calculation of real gross national income (real GNI) and real gross national disposable income (real GNDI) follows the same procedures as the production-side approach described earlier. Here, for converting the earned incomes receivable from and payable to the ROW (rest of the world) and the current transfers receivable from and payable to the ROW into real terms, the **deflator for gross domestic final expenditure** is commonly applied. The reason for using this deflator consistently across these international transactions is to maintain coherence by applying the same numeraire to both domestic final expenditures and cross-border inflows and outflows.

18.3 Derivation of real income aggregates by the chain index approach

This section explores the derivation of real income aggregates such as real GDI, real GNI, and real GNDI when GDP in volume terms is calculated using a chain-linked Laspeyres volume index instead of a fixed-weight Laspeyres volume index.

18.3.1 Data required to derive real income aggregates using chain index techniques

To derive real income aggregates using chain index techniques, it is essential first to collect the basic data required for compiling these indices. The necessary data are categorized as follows:

a) CYP data: GDP, earned incomes receivable from and payable to the ROW, current transfers receivable from and payable to the ROW

b) PYP data: GDP, trading gains and losses (exports, imports, export price index, import price index), earned incomes receivable from and payable to the ROW, current transfers receivable from and payable to the ROW

18.3.2 Calculation of real income aggregates on the production side using chain index techniques

Real income aggregates using chain indices are derived based on the CYP and PYP data through the sequential calculation of **chain links, chain indices, chain volume measures** (CVM), following the production-side approach introduced above (Section 18.1). However, to calculate these real income aggregates under the chaining method, it is necessary to assume that the PYP data must be additive in the following way:

- GDP (PYP) + trading gains and losses (PYP) = GDI (PYP)
- GDI (PYP) + earned incomes receivable from the ROW (PYP) – earned incomes payable to

the ROW (PYP) = GNI (PYP)

- GNI (PYP) + current transfers receivable from the ROW (PYP) – current transfers payable to the ROW (PYP) = GNDI (PYP)

Here, trading gains and losses (PYP) is calculated as follows:

$$(18.6) \qquad \textbf{Trading gains and losses (PYP}^t\textbf{)} = \frac{X(CYP^t) - M(CYP^t)}{P^t/_{P^{t-1}}} - [X(PYP^t) - M(PYP^t)]$$

where X and M represent total exports and total imports, respectively, and $(P^t/_{P^{t-1}}) = (P_x^t/P_x^{t-1} + P_m^t/P_m^{t-1})/2$, with P_x^t and P_m^t denoting the export deflator and import deflator in period t.

The procedure to obtain the **chain volume measures** (CVM) of real income aggregates is in the following way. Based on the CYP and PYP data above, chain links, chain indices, and chain volume measures are sequentially derived for real income-related items (GDP, GDI, earned incomes receivable from and payable to abroad, GNI, current transfers receivable from and payable to abroad, GNDI). Since the chain-linked trading gains and losses may be positive or negative, these are obtained as a residual by subtracting the chained GDP from the chained GDI. Similarly, the chained net earned income receivable is calculated by chained earned income receivable less chained earned income payable. In addition, the chained net current transfers receivable are obtained by chained current transfers receivable less chained current transfers payable:

- Trading gains and losses (chained) = GDI (chained) – GDP (chained)
- Net earned incomes receivable (chained) = earned incomes receivable (chained) – earned incomes payable (chained)
- Net current transfers receivable (chained) = current transfers receivable (chained) – current transfers payable (chained)

In the chain-linked volume measures, additivity across constituent items does not hold. Thus, the sum of chain-linked GDI and chain-linked net earned incomes receivable may not equal the actual chain-linked GNI. Similarly, summing chain-linked GNI and chain-linked net current transfers receivable may also result in discrepancies from the actual chain-linked GNDI.

18.3.3 Calculation of real income aggregates on the expenditure side using chain index techniques

When deriving real income aggregates on the expenditure approach using the chain index approach, GDP is measured through the expenditure-side components. However, this may result in statistical discrepancies when they are compared with the aggregates of GDP by the production approach. In this case, an explicit item for "statistical discrepancy" is introduced on the expenditure side to reconcile the difference of the two aggregates.

The derivation of real GNI on the expenditure side basis is expressed as follows:

- Real GNI = gross domestic expenditure (chained) + trading gains and losses (chained) + net earned incomes receivable from abroad (chained) + **statistical discrepancy** = GDP chained) + trading gains and losses (chained) + net earned incomes receivable from abroad (chained)

where, gross domestic expenditure = final consumption expenditure + gross capital formation + exports – imports.

18.3.4 Example of deriving GDP in volume terms and real income aggregates using chain index techniques

This section presents a detailed example of deriving GDP in volume terms and real income aggregates using chain Laspeyres volume indices, based on actual case of South Korea. Table 18.2 below provides the basic data for South Korea from 2014 to 2018 for estimating production-side GDP in volume terms, real GDI and real GNI. It shows data on gross value added (GVA) by industry and income transactions with the rest of the world (CYP and PYP). Based on this dataset, we will derive the links, chain indices, chain volume measures, and chain growth rates for GDP and real income aggregates.

Table 18.2 Basic data for GDP and GNI (South Korea, 2014-2018)

(Unit: KRW trillion)

Item	Gross value added at current prices (CYP)					Gross value added at previous year's prices (PYP)				
	2014	2015	2016	2017	2018	2014	2015	2016	2017	2018
Agriculture	32.1	33.2	32.4	34.0	33.2	33.1	32.1	31.4	33.1	34.0
Mining	2.1	2.1	2.4	2.3	2.1	2.1	1.9	2.3	2.3	2.2
Manufacturing	422.7	441.1	458.8	494.6	505.7	430.3	429.7	451.3	475.9	511.0
Electricity,gas,water	35.7	41.8	44.3	40.0	35.2	30.1	36.8	41.3	47.0	39.3
Construction	72.3	81.2	91.5	101.2	103.3	69.5	76.8	89.1	96.9	98.4
Services	869.7	921.5	963.7	1,006.8	1,057.1	854.7	896.4	948.4	988.8	1,045.4
Gross value added (basic price)	1,434.7	1,520.9	1,593.1	1,679.0	1,736.5	1,419.8	1,473.8	1,563.8	1,644.0	1,730.4
Taxes less subsidies on products	128.3	137.1	147.7	156.7	161.7	129.1	133.1	143.1	151.8	158.7
GDP	1,562.9	1,658.0	1,740.8	1,835.7	1,898.2	1,548.9	1,606.8	1,706.9	1,795.8	1,889.1
Trading gains	-	-	-	-	-	6.7	57.7	23.6	1.6	- 24.3
GDI	1,562.9	1,658.0	1,740.8	1,835.7	1,898.2	1,555.6	1,664.5	1,730.5	1,797.4	1,864.8
Earned incomes receivable from abroad	32.1	28.4	31.9	35.0	40.7	31.9	28.1	31.0	34.1	40.0
Earned incomes payable abroad	24.6	23.2	25.5	27.5	33.1	24.4	23.0	24.8	26.8	32.5
Net earned incomes receivable	7.6	5.2	6.4	7.5	7.6	7.5	5.1	6.2	7.3	7.5
GNI	1,570.5	1,663.2	1,747.1	1,843.2	1,905.8	1,563.1	1,669.7	1,736.6	1,804.7	1,872.3

Based on the chain index approach (using CYP and PYP as input data), the resulting links and chain indices of GDP in volume terms and real income aggregates are shown below (Table 18.3). The calculation method follows Section 16.3.4.2 in Chapter 16. The reference year for the indices is 2015, thus all chain indices equal 1 in 2015.

Table 18.3 Links and chain indices for GDP in volume terms and real income aggregates (South Korea)

(Reference year: 2015)

Item	Link ($L^t = PYP^t/CYP^{t-1}$)					Chain index ($C^t = C^{t-1} \times L^t$)				
	2014	2015	2016	2017	2018	2014	2015	2016	2017	2018
Agriculture	1.051	0.998	0.944	1.023	1.002	1.002	1.000	0.944	0.965	0.966
Mining	1.003	0.908	1.070	0.960	0.926	1.102	1.000	1.070	1.028	0.952
Manufacturing	1.032	1.017	1.023	1.037	1.033	0.983	1.000	1.023	1.061	1.096
Electricity, gas, water	1.025	1.031	0.988	1.062	0.983	0.970	1.000	0.988	1.049	1.032
Construction	1.015	1.062	1.098	1.059	0.972	0.941	1.000	1.098	1.163	1.130
Services	1.031	1.031	1.029	1.026	1.038	0.970	1.000	1.029	1.056	1.097
Gross value added (basic price)	1.031	1.027	1.028	1.032	1.031	0.973	1.000	1.028	1.061	1.093
Taxes less subsidies on products	1.044	1.037	1.044	1.028	1.013	0.964	1.000	1.044	1.073	1.087
GDP	1.032	1.028	1.029	1.032	1.029	0.973	1.000	1.029	1.062	1.093
Trading gains and losses	-	-	-	-	-	-	-	-	-	-
GDI	1.036	1.065	1.044	1.033	1.016	0.939	1.000	1.044	1.078	1.095
Earned incomes receivable from abroad	0.956	0.876	1.091	1.070	1.143	1.141	1.000	1.091	1.168	1.335
Earned incomes payable abroad	1.025	0.937	1.069	1.051	1.181	1.068	1.000	1.069	1.124	1.327
GNI	1.035	1.063	1.044	1.033	1.016	0.941	1.000	1.044	1.079	1.096

Based on the chain indices, the resulting chain volume measures (CVM based on the chain Laspeyres formula) and growth rates for real GDP and real income aggregates are shown in Table 18.4. Note that, as the trading gains and losses can take either positive or negative values, they are not derived directly from chain indices. Instead, they are obtained indirectly by subtracting the chained GDP value from the chained GDI value. Similarly, the chain volume measure for net earned incomes receivable from abroad is derived by subtracting the chained earned incomes payable abroad from the chained earned incomes receivable from abroad.

Table 18.4 GDP in volume terms, real income aggregates, and growth rates by the chain index approach

(Reference year: 2015)

Item	Chain volume measure (KRW trillion)					Growth rate				
	2014	2015	2016	2017	2018	2014	2015	2016	2017	2018
Agriculture	33.3	33.2	31.4	32.1	32.1	0.051	-0.002	-0.056	0.023	0.002
Mining	2.4	2.1	2.3	2.2	2.0	0.003	-0.092	0.070	-0.040	-0.074
Manufacturing	433.9	441.1	451.3	468.1	483.5	0.032	0.017	0.023	0.037	0.033
Electricity, gas, water	40.5	41.8	41.3	43.8	43.1	0.025	0.031	-0.012	0.062	-0.017
Construction	76.4	81.2	89.1	94.4	91.7	0.015	0.062	0.098	0.059	-0.028
Services	894.0	921.5	948.4	973.1	1,010.4	0.031	0.031	0.029	0.026	0.038
Gross value added (basic price)	1,480.5	1,520.9	1,563.8	1,613.7	1,663.1	0.031	0.027	0.028	0.032	0.031
Taxes less subsidies on products	132.2	137.1	143.1	147.1	149.0	0.044	0.037	0.044	0.028	0.013
GDP	1,612.7	1,658.0	1,706.9	1,760.8	1,812.0	0.032	0.028	0.029	0.032	0.029
Trading gains and losses	-55.9	-	23.6	25.9	3.0					
GDI	1,556.8	1,658.0	1,730.5	1,786.7	1,815.0	0.036	0.065	0.044	0.033	0.016
Earned incomes receivable from abroad	32.4	28.4	31.0	33.1	37.9	-0.044	-0.124	0.091	0.070	0.143
Earned incomes payable abroad	24.8	23.2	24.8	26.1	30.8	0.025	-0.063	0.069	0.051	0.181
Net earned incomes receivable	7.6	5.2	6.2	7.1	7.1					
GNI	1,564.4	1,663.2	1,736.6	1,793.8	1,822.2	0.035	0.063	0.044	0.33	0.016

18.4 Calculation of the GDP deflator, GDP growth rate, and sectoral contributions to the GDP growth

The **GDP deflator** is generally calculated from "GDP at current prices/GDP at constant prices." When using a chain index approach, the GDP deflator is computed as follows:

- **GDP deflator = GDP at current prices / GDP chain volume measure = $CYP^{t}_{GDP}/CVM^{t}_{GDP}$**

The GDP deflator serves as an implicit price index of GDP, derived ex post.

The **GDP growth rate** is defined as the period-on-period percentage change in GDP at constant prices valued at the prices of a specific period (price reference period). The GDP growth rate between period (t-1) and period t is expressed as:

GDP growth rate (t-1, t) (%) = (GDP^{t} at constant prices/GDP^{t-1} at constant prices - 1) x 100

When GDP is measured using a chain Laspeyres volume index, the base year prices change annually (i.e., each year uses the previous year's prices as weights). Accordingly, the GDP growth rate is calculated as:

- **GDP growth rate (t-1, t) (%) = [{GDP^{t} at previous year (t-1) prices / GDP^{t-1} at current year prices} – 1] x 100**

In addition, if one wishes to compute the contribution of individual sectors (industries) to overall GDP growth (i.e., **sectoral contributions to GDP growth**), it is expressed in the following formula. This equation assumes that the growth rate is measured by the chain Laspeyres volume index method.

Contribution to the GDP growth$^{t}_{sector\ i}$ = ($PYP^{t}_{sector\ i}$ – $CYP^{t-1}_{sector\ i}$)/CYP^{t-1}_{GDP}

Table 18.5 illustrates the GDP deflator and the sectoral contributions to the overall growth of GDP in South Korea, based on the data of Table 18.2 and 18.4. As the GDP deflator is based on the reference year of 2015, the index is set to 100 for 2015, and reaches 104.8 in 2018.

In 2018, the overall GDP growth rate was 2.91%. Looking at the contributions to GDP growth by industry, the manufacturing industry contributed 0.89%, the construction industry -0.15%, and the service industry 2.10% respectively.

Table 18.5 GDP deflator and sectoral contributions to the GDP growth (South Korea)

Item	2014	2015	2016	2017	2018
GDP deflator	0.9691	1.0000	1.0199	1.0425	1.0476
(Contribution to GDP growth)					
Agriculture	0.0011	-0.0001	-0.0011	0.0004	0.0000
Mining	0.0000	-0.0001	0.0001	-0.0001	-0.0001
Manufacturing	0.0088	0.0045	0.0061	0.0098	0.0089
Electricity, gas and water supply	0.0005	0.0007	-0.0003	0.0016	-0.0004
Construction	0.0007	0.0029	0.0048	0.0031	-0.0015
Services	0.0173	0.0171	0.0163	0.0144	0.0210
Gross value added (basic price)	0.0284	0.0250	0.0258	0.0292	0.0280
Taxes less subsidies on products	0.0036	0.0031	0.0036	0.0024	0.0011
GDP growth rate	0.0320	0.0281	0.0295	0.0316	0.0291

The **percentage contribution to the GDP growth by sector** (or industry) indicates the share (percentage) of each sector's contribution to the real GDP growth when the GDP growth rate is converted to 100. They are calculated by dividing the sector's contribution to the GDP growth by the total GDP growth rate.

Percentage contribution to the GDP growth$^t_{sector\ i}$ = (contribution to the GDP growth$^t_{sector\ i}$ / GDP growth rate^t) x 100

Table 18.6 illustrates the percentage contributions to the GDP growth rate, calculated by converting the values in Table 18.5 into percentage terms. In 2018, the industry that contributed most significantly to the GDP growth was the service industry (72.3%), followed by the manufacturing industry (30.6%).

Table 18.6 Percentage contributions to the GDP growth by industry (South Korea)

Percentage contribution to the GDP growth	2014	2015	2016	2017	2018
Agriculture	0.033	-0.002	-0.038	0.013	0.001
Mining	0.000	-0.004	0.003	-0.002	-0.003
Manufacturing	0.276	0.162	0.208	0.310	0.306
Electricity, gas and water supply	0.015	0.025	-0.010	0.050	-0.013
Construction	0.021	0.103	0.163	0.098	-0.053
Service	0.542	0.608	0.552	0.456	0.723
Gross value added (basic price)	0.887	0.891	0.877	0.925	0.962
Taxes less subsidies on products	0.113	0.109	0.123	0.075	0.038
GDP	1.000	1.000	1.000	1.000	1.000

Chapter 19. Major compilation techniques for quarterly national accounts

The national accounts compilation methods described so far have implicitly assumed annual periods for the source data. However, this chapter addresses several key techniques specifically required for the compilation of quarterly national accounts (QNA), in which the underlying data or short-term indicators typically cover periods of less than one year. Although the general principles for compiling quarterly national accounts are broadly similar to those used in annual national accounts, the use of monthly or quarterly indicators necessitates certain specialized techniques not typically applicable in annual compilations.

To begin with, short-term indicators differ significantly from annual indicators in their nature and characteristics. Understanding these differences is crucial when compiling quarterly accounts. Short-term indicators prioritize timeliness and rapid dissemination, often at the expense of accuracy. Consequently, initial estimates are inherently provisional and subject to frequent revisions as more complete and accurate information becomes available. In the compilation process for quarterly national accounts, compilers may often face situations where desired short-term indicators are either available or incomplete. Therefore, compilers need to strike an appropriate balance between timeliness and accuracy. In such cases, estimates can be made, or suitable proxy indicators may be employed to approximate missing quarterly data. As a result, quarterly aggregates may not initially align precisely with annual totals, necessitating subsequent benchmarking to new annual data when these become available. Moreover, due to the reliance on frequently updated source data, quarterly estimates are subject to continuous revisions. When annual data become finalized, the quarterly series are often benchmarked or adjusted accordingly to ensure consistency with annual accounts.

Quarterly data also inherently exhibit seasonal patterns, reflecting systematic fluctuations associated with specific periods within a calendar year. For example, agricultural production often displays a distinct seasonal pattern, typically characterized by reduced output in the first quarter and increased production in subsequent quarters. Therefore, when measuring quarter-to-quarter growth rates, it is advisable to first remove seasonal effects from the quarterly data, thereby enabling a meaningful and accurate assessment of underlying economic growth.

In this chapter, several methodological approaches are presented to address common issues arising in the compilation of quarterly national accounts. First, the "benchmarking" technique is explained in detail, which aligns quarterly data to the corresponding annual aggregates. Second, the methods for calculating chain-linked volume growth rates within the quarterly national accounts framework are discussed comprehensively. Finally, the chapter provides an overview of seasonal adjustment methods used to eliminate seasonal effects, thereby facilitating reliable quarter-to-quarter growth analysis.

19.1 Benchmarking: Resolving inconsistencies between quarterly and annual data

Benchmarking refers to the technique used in adjusting quarterly data to ensure consistency with updated annual data. When annual benchmarks are revised, quarterly estimates previously compiled bases on preliminary or older benchmarks must be recalibrated to align with the newly available annual totals.

For example, assume that original quarterly data for 2015 were reported as 93.5, 112.8, 123.4 and 137.1, summing to an annual total of 466.8. If new survey information subsequently revises the annual total for 2015 upwards to 493.4, the quarterly figures must then be adjusted accordingly. A straightforward approach to adjusting quarterly data involves applying a uniform ratio, derived as the **benchmark-to-indicator (BI) ratio**, calculated by dividing the revised annual total by the original total. In the above example, the BI ratio is calculated as 1.057 (= 493.4/466.8). Each quarterly figure would then be multiplied by this BI ratio equally (see Table 19.1). In this case, the original quarterly data are termed "Indicator," and the revised annual figure is the "Benchmark." If, for instance, the annual figure for 2016 is revised from the initial estimate of 601.1 to a new figure of 681.2, the BI ratio for that year becomes 1.133 (= 681.2/601.1), and each quarterly figure is similarly adjusted by multiplying by this new BI ratio. This adjustment method is known as the **pro-rata distribution method**.

However, the pro-rata distribution method introduces an issue known as the **step problem**, characterized by an abrupt and artificial break between the fourth quarter of the previous year ($t-1$) and the first quarter of the current year (t). This continuity arises due to the shift in the annual BI ratios between consecutive years. Table 19.1 and 19.2 illustrate this phenomenon clearly. Table 19.1 presents original quarterly data alongside their quarter-to-quarter growth rates ($Q^t/Q^{t-1}-1$), and shows revised annual totals and corresponding BI ratios. Table 19.2 compares adjusted quarterly data derived from the pro-rata distribution method and the "proportional Denton method" (which is described just below), including quarter-to-quarter growth rates. A notable discrepancy can be observed in the first quarter of 2016. While the original quarter-to-quarter growth rate was –5.5%, the rate adjusted by the pro-rata method becomes 1.4%, a significant difference of 6.9 percentage points. This occurs because the annual BI ratio changed from 1.057 in 2015 to 1.133 in 2016. If the BI ratio had remained constant across the two years, say 1.057, the quarter-to-quarter growth rate for the first quarter of 2016 would have been consistent with the original rate of -5.5%.

To address this "step problem," alternative benchmarking techniques, such as the **proportional Denton method**, can be employed. Unlike the simple pro-rata approach, the proportional Denton method distributes adjustments across quarters in a smoother and more proportionate manner, minimizing abrupt changes between periods (refer to Figure 19.1 for visual illustration).

Table 19.1 Benchmark-to-indicator ratios following revised annual data

	Quarterly data (original)	Q^t/Q^{t-1} growth rate (%)	Annual data			
			Year	Original (1)	Revised (2)	BI ratio (2)/(1)
2015. 1	93.5		2015	466.8	493.4	**1.057**
2015. 2	112.8	20.6%				
2015. 3	123.4	9.4%				
2015. 4	137.1	11.1%				
2016. 1	129.6	**-5.5%**	2016	601.1	681.2	**1.133**
2016. 2	147.5	13.8%				
2016. 3	159.3	8.0%				
2016. 4	164.7	3.4%				

Table 19.2 Comparison of Pro-rata and Proportional Denton methods

	Adjusted quarterly data		Q^t/Q^{t-1} growth rate (%)		Quarterly BI ratio	
	Pro-rata	Proportional Denton	Pro-rata	Proportional Denton	Pro-rata	Proportional Denton
2015. 1	98.8	97.2			1.057	1.040
2015. 2	119.2	117.9	20.6%	21.3%	1.057	1.045
2015. 3	130.4	130.5	9.4%	10.7%	1.057	1.058
2015. 4	144.9	147.7	11.1%	13.2%	1.057	1.078
2016. 1	146.9	143.3	**1.4%**	**-3.0%**	1.133	1.106
2016. 2	167.2	166.3	13.8%	16.1%	1.133	1.128
2016. 3	180.5	182.1	8.0%	9.5%	1.133	1.143
2016. 4	186.6	189.5	3.4%	4.1%	1.133	1.151

Figure 19.1 BI ratios and quarter-to-quarter growth rates

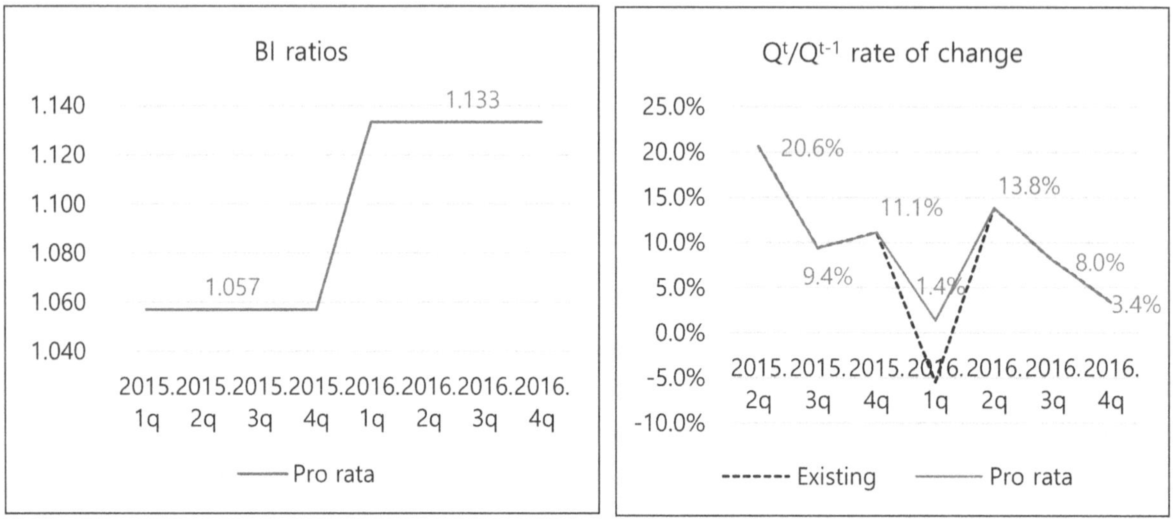

The proportional Denton method resolves the step problem by applying flexible adjustments (smoothing) to the quarterly BI ratios across consecutive years. Instead of applying a uniform BI ratio within each year, this method gradually moderates the changes in BI ratios, ensuring a smoother transition across all years. The blue line in the left-hand panel of Figure 19.2 demonstrates the smoothing of annual BI ratios achieved through this method. Consequently, the right-hand panel of Figure 19.2 shows that quarter-to-quarter growth rates, adjusted by the proportional Denton method (solid blue line), align closely with the original data-based growth rates (dashed line), effectively eliminating large discrepancies such as those observed in the first quarter of 2016.

Figure 19.2 Comparison between Pro-rata and Proportional Denton methods

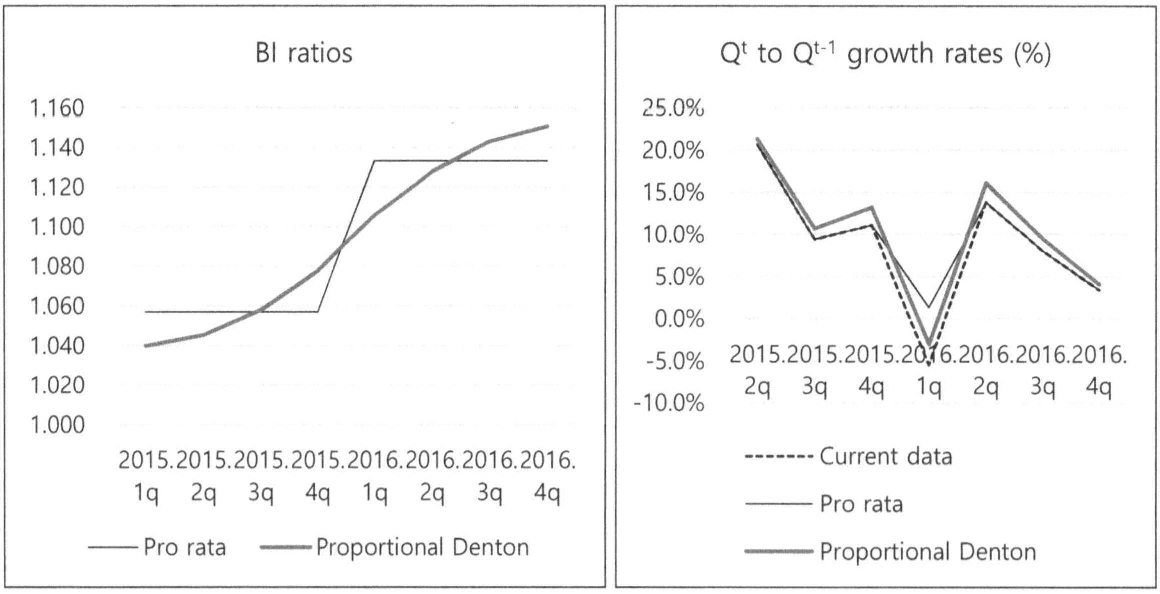

The proportional Denton method is a statistical approach designed to minimize the squared differences between BI ratios of consecutive quarters, thus producing adjusted quarterly data (X^t) that smoothly connect across periods. The method is expressed mathematically as:

$$\textit{Minimize} \ \sum_{t=2}^{4\beta}(BI^t - BI^{t-1})^2 = \textit{Minimize} \ \sum_{t=2}^{4\beta}(\frac{X^t}{I^t} - \frac{X^{t-1}}{I^{t-1}})^2$$

where t represents each quarter, y(1, 2, ⋯ β) represents each year, X^t is the adjusted quarterly value, and I^t is the original quarterly indicator value. Each year's quarterly totals must be equal to the corresponding annual benchmark as expressed by the following constraint:

$$\sum_{y,t=1}^{y,4} X^{y,t} = A^y, \text{(where } A^y \text{ is the annual benchmark for } y\text{)}$$

The original quarterly indicator I^t must always be positive for computational feasibility. If negative values are present, they must be substituted with minimal positive values for calculation purposes. The indicator I^t can represent the same variable as X^t, or any related quarterly measure. For example, if X^t is the quarterly output value, I^t can be the quarterly production quantity.

The proportional Denton method is a benchmarking technique that identifies a set of quarterly benchmark-to-indicator ratios and a corresponding adjusted quarterly time series (X^t) such that the sum of squared differences between the BI ratios of adjacent quarters is minimized. This technique ensures the smoothness of BI ratios across quarters, implying that the ratios are not held constant within a year and that any discontinuities between the fourth quarter of year ($t-1$) and the first quarter of year t are effectively removed. Unlike the simple proportional distribution method, the proportional Denton method is based on a numerical optimization approach and therefore requires specialized software for implementation. For this purpose, the IMF provides an Excel-based add-in called "XLPBM" that enables automatic computation. In addition, Eurostat's statistical software "ECOTRIM" also supports this functionality.

19.2 Compilation of quarterly chain indices

Although the SNA recommends the use of chain indices in the context of annual accounts, quarterly chain indices are also compiled in practice to facilitate the timely detection of business cycle fluctuations. The method for constructing quarterly chain indices differs slightly from that for annual chain indices. (The methodology for compiling quarterly chain Laspeyres volume indices is presented in the Quarterly National Accounts Manual (IMF, 2017).)

Quarterly chain indices can be compiled using three principal approaches, depending on how quarterly values are linked: the annual overlap technique, the one-quarter overlap technique, and the over-the-year technique. This section describes each technique using the chain Laspeyres-type volume index as the reference framework.

19.2.1 Annual overlap technique

The **annual overlap (AO) technique** compares the quarterly averages derived from the previous year's annual values at current prices with the quarterly values of the current year valued at the prices of the previous year. The estimation procedure is as follows:

1. The annual benchmark value for year $(t-1)$ is established by deriving the annual value at current prices for year $(t-1)$.
2. The quarterly average value for year $(t-1)$ is obtained by dividing the annual current price value of year $(t-1)$ by four. This quarterly average is used as a common denominator for the derivation of quarterly links.
3. The quarterly values for year t are derived by valuing each quarter of year t at the annual average prices of year $(t-1)$.
4. Quarterly links (with the previous year = 100) are derived by taking the estimates obtained in Step 3 as the numerator and the quarterly average value obtained in Step 2 as the denominator.

(19.1) $$\boldsymbol{Link_i^t = PYP_i^t / (CYP_{annual}^{t-1} / 4)}$$

where PYP_i^t denotes the value for quarter i of year t, valued at the annual average prices of year $(t-1)$, and CYP_{annual}^{t-1} denotes the annual value at current prices for year $(t-1)$.

If the basic data are available only in the form of current-price values and *price relatives*, rather than volumes and prices, the above quarterly links can be expressed as follows. First, the price relative (PR) is defined as:

$$PR_{(t,i)} \equiv P_i^t / P_{avg}^{t-1},$$

where P_i^t is the price index for quarter i of year t, and P_{avg}^{t-1} is the annual average price index for year $(t-1)$. The numerator of equation (19.1) can then be written as:

$$PYP_i^t = {CYP_i^t}\big/{PR_{(t,i)}} = CYP_i^t \times \frac{1}{P_i^t \big/ P_{avg}^{t-1}}$$

Accordingly, when only current-price values and price relatives are available, the quarterly links under the annual overlap technique can be expressed as:

$$\boldsymbol{Link_i^t = CYP_i^t \frac{1}{P_i^t/P_{avg}^{(t-1)}} \,/\, (CYP_{annual}^{(t-1)}/4)}$$

An empirical illustration of this calculation is provided in Table 19.3, which represents quarterly data for current price values (CYP), price relatives, and values at the previous year's price (PYP) for industry A and industry B during 2015-2018. Based on these data, Table 19.4 presents the calculated quarterly links, the resulting quarterly chain indices (reference year = 2015), and the chain volume measures in accordance with the annual overlap technique. To illustrate the procedure for deriving quarterly links, consider the index for the first quarter of 2016 as an example. In this case, the numerator is the value of the first quarter of 2016 valued at the annual average prices of the previous year (2015). For industry A this amounts to 1,065, and for industry B to 2,779, giving a total of 3,844. The denominator is obtained by dividing the annual value at current prices for 2015 by four. This yields 1,446 for industry A (= 5,783/4), 2,850 for industry B (= 11,398/4), and 4,296 for the total (= 17,182/4). Accordingly, under the annual overlap technique, the links for the first quarter of 2016 is calculated as:

- Industry A: 0.737 (= 1,065/1,446)
- Industry B: 0.975 (= 2,779/2,850)
- Total: 0.895 (= 3,844/4,296)

Applying the same approach to fourth quarter of 2016 yields:

- Industry A: 1.169 (= 1,690/1,446)
- Industry B: 1.070 (= 3,048/2,850)
- Total: 1.103 (= 4,738/4,296)

Meanwhile, the annual link for the total of two industries in 2016 is obtained by dividing the sum of the quarterly values of 2016 expressed at previous-year prices (17,426 = 5,768 + 11,658) by the annual value at current prices for 2015 (17,182), resulting in 1.014.

Table 19.3 Quarterly data on CYP, price relatives, and PYP

Year, quarter	Current-price value (CYP) CYP^t_i			Price relative $(P^t_i / P^{t-1}_{avg} \times 100)$		Price relative (P^t_i / P^t_{avg})		Value at previous year's prices (PYP) $PYP^t_i = CYP^t_i / (P^t_i / P^{t-1}_{avg})$		
	Industry A	Industry B	Total	Industry A	Industry B	Industry A	Industry B	Industry A	Industry B	Total
2015.1	1,093	2,730	3,823	101.86	105.12	98.52	100.38	1,057	2,607	3,664
2015. 2	1,553	2,866	4,419	102.64	105.64	99.28	100.87	1,502	2,737	4,239
2015. 3	1,447	2,847	4,294	103.88	104.02	100.48	99.32	1,400	2,718	4,118
2015. 4	1,690	2,956	4,646	104.64	104.16	101.21	99.46	1,635	2,823	4,457
2015	**5,783**	**11,399**	**17,182**	**103.39**	**104.73**	100.00	100.00	5,594	10,884	16,478
2016. 1	1,095	2,807	3,902	102.34	102.75	99.58	101.72	1,065	2,779	3,844
2016. 2	1,609	2,957	4,566	101.13	101.69	98.40	100.67	1,566	2,927	4,493
2016. 3	1,487	2,933	4,420	103.34	99.73	100.56	98.73	1,447	2,904	4,351
2016. 4	1,737	3,079	4,816	104.07	100.00	101.27	99.00	1,690	3,048	4,738
2016	5,928	11,776	17,704	102.77	101.01	100.00	100.00	**5,768**	**11,658**	**17,426**
2017. 1	1,127	2,922	4,049	100.27	100.38	98.97	99.65	1,112	2,901	4,013
2017. 2	1,586	3,098	4,684	99.44	99.42	98.15	98.70	1,565	3,076	4,641
2017. 3	1,548	3,102	4,650	101.98	100.68	100.66	99.95	1,528	3,080	4,608
2017. 4	1,874	3,254	5,128	102.97	102.33	101.64	101.59	1,850	3,230	5,080
2017	6,135	12,376	18,511	101.31	100.73	100.00	100.00	6,056	12,287	18,342
2018. 1	1,210	3,151	4,361	101.94	101.91	98.74	99.50	1,172	3,077	4,249
2018. 2	1,679	3,369	5,048	100.90	102.40	97.73	99.98	1,626	3,289	4,916
2018. 3	1,622	3,307	4,929	103.97	102.26	100.71	99.85	1,571	3,229	4,800
2018. 4	1,986	3,521	5,507	105.41	103.04	102.10	100.61	1,924	3,438	5,362
2018	6,497	13,348	19,845	103.24	102.42	100.00	100.00	6,293	13,033	19,326

Table 19.4 Quarterly links, chain indices and chain volume measures by Annual overlap technique

Year, quarter	Link $(l^t_i = PYP^t_i / (CYP^{t-1}/4))$			Chain index (Reference year: 2015=1) $(C^t_i = C^{t-1} \times l^t_i)$			Chain volume measure $CVM^t_i = C^t_i \times (CYP^0/4)$		
	Industry A	Industry B	Total	Industry A	Industry B	Total	Industry A	Industry B	Total
2015				**1.000**	**1.000**	**1.000**	**5,783**	**11,399**	**17,182**
2016. 1	0.737	0.975	0.895	0.737	0.975	0.895	1,065	2,779	3,844
2016. 2	1.083	1.027	1.046	1.083	1.027	1.046	1,566	2,927	4,493
2016. 3	1.001	1.019	1.013	1.001	1.019	1.013	1,447	2,904	4,351
2016. 4	1.169	1.070	1.103	1.169	1.070	1.103	1,690	3,048	4,738
2016	0.997	1.023	1.014	0.997	1.023	**1.014**	5,768	11,658	17,426
2017. 1	0.751	0.985	0.907	0.749	1.008	**0.920**	1,082	2,872	3,950
2017. 2	1.056	1.045	1.049	1.054	1.068	1.064	1,523	3,045	4,568
2017. 3	1.031	1.046	1.041	1.028	1.070	1.056	1,487	3,049	4,535
2017. 4	1.248	1.097	1.148	1.245	1.122	**1.164**	1,800	3,198	5,001
2017	1.022	1.043	1.036	1.019	1.067	1.051	5,892	12,163	18,054
2018. 1	0.764	0.994	0.918	0.779	1.061	0.965	1,126	3,024	4,144
2018. 2	1.060	1.063	1.062	1.080	1.134	1.116	1,562	3,233	4,795
2018. 3	1.024	1.044	1.037	1.044	1.114	1.090	1,509	3,173	4,682
2018. 4	1.254	1.111	1.159	1.278	1.186	1.217	1,848	3,379	5,229
2018	1.026	1.053	1.044	1.045	1.124	1.097	6,044	12,809	18,849

Quarterly chain indices are calculated using the following formula:

$$\textbf{Chain index}_i^t = \textbf{chain index}_{annual}^{(t-1)} \times \textbf{link}_i^t$$

Alternatively, this can be expressed as the cumulative product of annual and quarterly link indices starting from the reference year (year 0):

$$\textbf{Chain index}_i^t = \textbf{link}_{annual}^0 \times \textbf{link}_{annual}^1 \times \cdots \times \textbf{link}_{annual}^{(t-1)} \times \textbf{link}_i^t$$

For example, the quarterly chain indices for 2017 are obtained by multiplying the annual chain index of 2016 (1.014 for the total of two industries) by the quarterly links for each quarter of 2017. Hence, the chain index for Q1 2017 is 0.920 (=1.014 × 0.907) and for Q4 2017 it is 1.164 (=1.014 ×1.148). The chain volume measures (CVM) for quarter i of year t, expressed in volume terms, is calculated by multiplying the quarterly chain index by one-fourth of the annual current price value in the reference year (year 0):

$$\textbf{CVM}_i^t = \frac{\textbf{CYP}^0}{4} \times \textbf{Chain index}_i^t$$

For instance, the chain volume measures for Q1 2018 are computed as follows:

- Industry A: 1,126 (= 5,783/4 x 0.779)
- Industry B: 3,024 (= 11,399/4 x 1.061)
- Total: 4,144 (= 17,182/4 x 0.965)

A key advantage of the annual overlap technique is that the arithmetic average of the quarterly chain indices for a given year is equal to the independently derived annual chain index for that year. This ensures internal consistency and accuracy in volume measurement, making the annual overlap technique a preferred method in the compilation of quarterly national accounts.

$$\textbf{Chain index}_{annual}^t = \sum_{i=1}^{4} \textbf{Chain index}_i^t / 4$$

For instance, the arithmetic mean of the quarterly chain indices for the total of two industries in 2018 is 1.097 (= (0.965+1.116+1.090+1.217)/4), which coincides with the independently calculated annual chain index of 1.097 (= 1.051×1.044), as shown in Table 19.4. However, when using the annual overlap technique, there may be a discontinuity between Q4 of year (t – 1) and Q1 of year t due to a sharp shift in index values. To mitigate such discontinuities (often referred to as "step problem"), it is advisable to apply benchmarking techniques that reduces this gap between years.

19.2.2 One-quarter overlap technique

The **one-quarter overlap (QO) technique** derives quarterly links by comparing the value of a specific quarter of the previous year, typically the fourth quarter, valued at that year's annua; weighted average prices, with the estimated values of each quarter of the current year valued at the average prices of the previous year. The estimation procedure is as follows:

1. The value of the fourth quarter of year $(t-1)$, valued at the annual weighted average prices of year $(t-1)$, is calculated. This value is used as the reference denominator for deriving quarterly links under the one-quarter overlap technique.
2. The values of each quarter i of year t are derived by valuing them at the annual weighted average prices of year $(t-1)$ (as in the annual overlap technique).
3. Quarterly links are calculated by taking the value obtained in Step 2 as the numerator and the value obtained in Step 1 as the denominator.

The formula for quarterly links is:

$$\boldsymbol{Link_i^t = PYP_i^t/(CYP_4^{t-1}/\frac{P_4^{t-1}}{P_{average}^{t-1}})} \qquad (19.2)$$

where PYP_i^t denotes the value of quarter i of year t, valued at the annual average prices of year $(t-1)$, and $CYP_4^{t-1}/\frac{P_4^{t-1}}{P_{avg}^{t-1}}$ represents the value of the fourth quarter of year $(t-1)$ at current prices adjusted to the annual weighted average prices of year $(t-1)$ (see the "current-price value" column in table 19.5). Here, P_4^{t-1} denotes the price index for the fourth quarter of year $(t-1)$, and P_{avg}^{t-1} is the annual average price index of year $(t-1)$.

If the basic data are available only in the form of current-price values and price relatives, rather than volumes and prices, the above quarterly links can be expressed as follows. As in the previous case, using the year-over-year price relatives $(\mathrm{P_i^t/P_{average}^{t-1}})$ and the within-year price relatives $\mathrm{P_4^t/P_{average}^t}$, the quarterly links under the one-quarter overlap technique can be written as:

$$\boldsymbol{Link_i^t = CYP_i^t\frac{1}{P_i^t/P_{avg}^{t-1}}/(CYP_4^{t-1}/\frac{P_4^{t-1}}{P_{avg}^{t-1}})}$$

As an illustration, using the same data from Table 19.3 in the same manner as above, the quarterly links for 2018 under the one-quarter overlap technique are derived as follows. First, the value of the total industry for the fourth quarter of 2017 (valued at annual weighted average prices of 2017) is 5,047 (= 1,844 for Industry A + 3,203 for Industry B). The estimated values of the first and fourth quarters of 2018 valued at the annual average prices of the previous year (2017) are 4,279 and 5,301 respectively. Therefore, the links for the first and fourth quarters of 2018 are calculated as follows:

- Link for Q1 2018: 0.842 (= 4,249/5,047)
- Link for Q4 2018: 1.062 (= 5,362/5,047)

The full set of quarterly links, resulting chain indices (with reference year 2015 = 1), and chain volume measures derived from this technique are summarized in Table 19.5.

Table 19.5 Quarterly links, chain indices, and chain volume measures by One-quarter overlap technique

Year, quarter	Current-price value (Adjusted $CYP^t_i = P^t_{avg} Q^t_i$)			Value at previous year's prices ($PYP^t_i = P^{t-1}_{avg} Q^t_i$)			Link ($l^t_i = PYP^t_i$ / Adjusted CYP^{t-1}_4)			Chain index (Reference year: 2015=1) ($C^t_i = C^{t-1}_4 \times l^t_i$)			Chain volume measure ($CVM^t_i = C^t_i \times CYP^0$)		
	A	B	Total	A	B	Total	A	B	Total	A	B	Total	A	B	Total
2015	5,783	11,399	17,182	5,594	10,884	16,478				1.000	1.000	1.000			
2016	5,928	11,776	17,704	5,768	11,658	17,426	0.997	1.023	1.014	0.997	1.023	1.014	5,768	11,658	17,426
2017	6,135	12,376	18,511	6,056	12,287	18,342	1.022	1.043	1.036	1.019	1.067	1.051	5,892	12,163	18,054
2018	6,497	13,348	19,845	6,293	13,033	19,326	1.026	1.053	1.044	1.045	1.124	1.097	6,044	12,809	18,849
2016. 1	1,100	2,760	3,859	1,065	2,779	3,844	0.737	0.975	0.895	0.737	0.975	0.895	1,065	2,779	3,844
2016. 2	1,635	2,937	4,572	1,566	2,927	4,493	1.083	1.027	1.046	1.083	1.027	1.046	1,566	2,927	4,493
2016. 3	1,479	2,971	4,450	1,447	2,904	4,351	1.001	1.019	1.013	1.001	1.019	1.013	1,447	2,904	4,351
2016. 4	1,715	3,110	4,825	1,690	3,048	4,738	1.169	1.070	1.103	1.169	1.070	1.103	1,690	3,048	4,738
2017. 1	1,139	2,932	4,071	1,112	2,901	4,013	0.649	0.933	0.832	0.758	0.998	0.917	1,096	2,843	3,941
2017. 2	1,616	3,139	4,755	1,565	3,076	4,641	0.913	0.989	0.962	1.067	1.058	1.061	1,543	3,014	4,557
2017. 3	1,538	3,103	4,641	1,528	3,080	4,608	0.891	0.990	0.955	1.041	1.059	1.053	1,506	3,018	4,524
2017. 4	1,844	3,203	5,047	1,850	3,230	5,080	1.078	1.039	1.053	1.261	1.111	1.161	1,823	3,166	4,988
2018. 1	1,225	3,167	4,392	1,172	3,077	4,249	0.636	0.961	0.842	0.801	1.067	0.978	1,159	3,041	4,199
2018. 2	1,718	3,370	5,088	1,626	3,289	4,916	0.882	1.027	0.974	1.112	1.141	1.131	1,608	3,251	4,859
2018. 3	1,611	3,312	4,923	1,571	3,229	4,800	0.852	1.008	0.951	1.074	1.120	1.105	1,553	3,192	4,745
2018. 4	1,945	3,500	5,445	1,924	3,438	5,362	1.043	1.073	1.062	1.315	1.192	1.234	1,902	3,398	5,300

Under the one-quarter overlap technique, the quarterly chain index for a given quarter of year t is calculated by multiplying the chain index of the reference quarter (typically the fourth quarter of year $(t-1)$) by the link for the current quarter of t.

$$\textbf{Chain index}^t_i = \textbf{Chain index}^{t-1}_4 \times \textbf{link}^t_i$$

For example, under the one-quarter overlap technique, the chain index for Q1 2018 is 0.978 (= 1.161 × 0.842), and for Q4 2018 it is 1.234 (= 1.161 × 1.062). Alternatively, if the chain index is to be derived cumulatively from the reference year, the links used for the intervening years are those for the fourth quarter of each year, except for the current quarter i of year t. Since quarterly chain indices are not defined for the reference year itself, the quarterly indices for the subsequent year must be computed using the annual overlap technique. For example, the cumulative chain index for the quarter i of year t can be computed as follows:

$$\boldsymbol{Chain\ index_i^t = Chain\ index^0 \times link_4^1 \times \cdots \times link_4^{t-1} \times link_i^t}$$

Therefore, the chain index for the first quarter of 2018, calculated using this approach, is 0.978 (= 1 × 1.103 × 1.053 × 0.842), which is consistent with the result obtained earlier.

Unlike the annual overlap technique, the one-quarter overlap technique does not guarantee that the arithmetic average of the quarterly chain indices equals the independently compiled annual chain index. Similarly, the sum of the quarterly chain volume measures does not necessarily match the independently calculated annual chain volume measures. Therefore, in such cases, benchmarking techniques, as discussed in the previous section, should be applied to align the quarterly chain indices with the annual chain indices.

$$\boldsymbol{Chain\ index_{annual}^t \neq \sum_{i=1}^{4} chain\ index_i^t/4}$$

Since the one-quarter overlap technique constructs each quarterly chain index by linking it to the fourth quarter of the previous year, it avoids the step problem between Q4 of year $(t-1)$ and Q1 of year t. Owing to this characteristic, this technique is widely used in price index statistics to measure the rate of change relative to the end of the previous year.

19.2.3 Over-the-year technique

The **over-the-year technique** compares the value of each quarter of the current year valued at the annual average prices of the previous year (as in the other techniques) with the value of the corresponding quarter of the previous year valued at the annual weighted average prices of that year.

The key distinction between this technique and the one-quarter overlap technique is in the denominator used for deriving the quarterly link. While one-quarterly overlap technique uses the current price value of a specific quarter in the previous year (usually Q4), the over-the-year technique uses the current price value of the same quarter in the previous year, adjusted to annual average prices. The quarterly link under this technique is calculated as follows:

$$Link_i^t = PYP_i^t / (CYP_i^{t-1} / \frac{P_i^{t-1}}{P_{avg}^{t-1}})$$

For example, using the same data in Table 19.3, the quarterly link of the total of two industries for Q1 2018 is calculated as 1.044 (=4,249/4,071), with the value at previous-year prices (4,249) as the numerator and the value for the first quarter of 2017 adjusted to the annual average prices of 2017 (4,071) as the denominator (see the "current-price values" column in table 19.5). Similarly, the link for the second quarter of 2018 is calculated as 1.034 (= 4,916/4,755) (see Table 19.6).

The quarterly chain index is then obtained by multiplying the chain index of the corresponding quarter in the previous year by the link of the same quarter in the current year t.

$$Chain\ index_i^t = Chain\ index_i^{(t-1)} \times Link_i^t$$

For example, the chain index for the total of two industries in the first quarter of 2018 is obtained as 0.971 (=0.931 × 1.044) by multiplying the chain index for the first quarter of 2017 by the link for the first quarter of 2018. Likewise, the chain index for the second quarter of 2018 is derived as 1.098 (=1.062 × 1.034).

As with the annual overlap technique, the over-the-year technique may give rise to a step problem between the fourth quarter of the previous year and the first quarter of the current year.

Table 19.6 Quarterly links, chain indices, and chain volume measures by Over-the-year technique

Year, quarter	Link (I^t_i = PYP^t_i / Adjusted CYP^{t-1}_i)			Chain index (Reference year: 2015=1) ($C^t_i = C^{t-1}_i \times I^t_i$)			Chain volume measure ($CVM^t_i = C^t_i \times CYP^0$)		
	A	B	Total	A	B	Total	A	B	Total
2015				1.000	1.000	1.000			
2016	0.997	1.023	1.014	0.997	1.023	1.014	5,768	11,658	17,426
2017	1.022	1.043	1.036	1.019	1.067	1.051	5,892	12,163	18,054
2018	1.026	1.053	1.044	1.045	1.124	1.097	6,044	12,809	18,849
2016. 1	0.737	0.975	0.895	0.737	0.975	0.895	1,065	2,779	3,844
2016. 2	1.083	1.027	1.046	1.083	1.027	1.046	1,566	2,927	4,493
2016. 3	1.001	1.019	1.013	1.001	1.019	1.013	1,447	2,904	4,351
2016. 4	1.169	1.070	1.103	1.169	1.070	1.103	1,690	3,048	4,738
2017. 1	1.012	1.051	1.040	0.746	1.025	0.931	1,078	2,921	3,998
2017. 2	0.957	1.047	1.015	1.037	1.076	1.062	1,499	3,065	4,561
2017. 3	1.033	1.037	1.036	1.034	1.056	1.049	1,495	3,010	4,505
2017. 4	1.078	1.039	1.053	1.261	1.111	1.161	1,823	3,166	4,988
2018. 1	1.029	1.049	1.044	0.767	1.076	0.971	1,109	3,065	4,173
2018. 2	1.006	1.048	1.034	1.044	1.127	1.098	1,509	3,212	4,715
2018. 3	1.022	1.040	1.034	1.056	1.099	1.085	1,527	3,132	4,659
2018. 4	1.043	1.073	1.062	1.315	1.192	1.234	1,902	3,398	5,300

When estimating the quarterly real GDP using chain-weighting methods, the annual overlap technique is advantageous in that the arithmetic average of the quarterly chain indices for a given year is equal to the annual chain index. However, this approach may result in a step problem between the fourth quarter of the previous year and the first quarter of the current year. In contrast, the one-quarter overlap technique avoids the step problem, but the average of the quarterly chain indices for a given year does not, in general, match the corresponding annual chain index. Although it is not possible to definitely conclude which technique is superior in all cases, in practice the one-quarter overlap technique is often used in price statistics to facilitate comparisons with the end of the previous year. On the other hand, in national accounts, the annual overlap technique is generally preferred for estimating Laspeyres-type volume measures, as it ensures consistency between the quarterly average index and the annual index. The over-the-year technique, by contrast, is not commonly favored in either context.

19.3 Calculation of quarter-to-quarter growth rates using seasonally adjusted data

When quarterly national accounts are compiled based on short-term indicators with durations of less than one year, the source indicators are often affected by seasonal factors that influence production or expenditure patterns. For example, industries such as agricultural are highly seasonal, and their output can vary significantly from quarter to quarter.

Figure 19.3 illustrates the quarterly gross value added of agriculture and electricity industries in South Korea. For the agriculture industry, the value added tends to peak in the fourth quarter and reach its lowest level in the first quarter, displaying a clear seasonal pattern. Conversely, the electricity industry exhibits its highest value added in the third quarter and the lowest in the second quarter. When the underlying quarterly data exhibits such **seasonality**, it becomes necessary to use seasonally adjusted figures (that is, data from which seasonal variations have been removed), in order to accurately assess economic trends and compute quarter-to-quarter growth rates, or to forecast future developments.

Figure 19.3 Quarterly gross value added for the agriculture and electricity industries (South Korea)

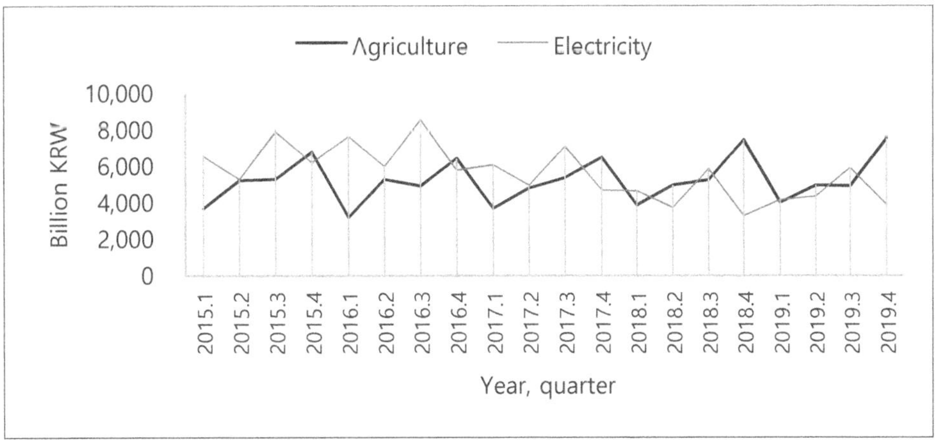

19.3.1 Method for removing seasonality

To eliminate seasonality, that is, recurring intra-annual fluctuations, a commonly used approach involves computing **seasonal factors** for each quarter. This is done by dividing the average value for each quarter (e.g., Q1 across all years) by the overall average for the entire time series. Each original data point in the series is then divided by the corresponding seasonal factor to obtain

seasonally adjusted values. This adjustment effectively removes the seasonal effects embedded in the raw data, providing a clear view of the underlying trend and cyclical movement.

Table 19.7, 19.8 and 19.9 provide illustrative examples of this seasonal adjustment procedure. They demonstrate how seasonal factors are derived from raw quarterly data and applied to generate seasonally adjusted figures.

Table 19.7 Quarterly output of manufacturing industry (Unadjusted, South Korea)

(Unit: Billion KRW)

Year, quarter	Output	Year, quarter	Output	Year, quarter	Output
2005.1	301,755.4	2008.1	358,414.3	2011.1	430,182.5
2005.2	329,929.1	2008.2	386,378.0	2011.2	465,076.7
2005.3	327,636.3	2008.3	378,346.2	2011.3	455,424.9
2005.4	351,886.5	2008.4	380,725.6	2011.4	485,794.0
2006.1	320,330.2	2009.1	347,307.0	2012.1	450,541.7
2006.2	346,755.6	2009.2	385,946.1	2012.2	484,230.4
2006.3	343,855.6	2009.3	390,713.6	2012.3	471,219.6
2006.4	366,993.6	2009.4	414,110.4	2012.4	502,227.3
2007.1	332,279.2	2010.1	396,890.7	2013.1	459,176.1
2007.2	363,023.7	2010.2	432,706.8	2013.2	497,394.5
2007.3	359,567.1	2010.3	424,780.9	2013.3	480,155.5
2007.4	388,564.2	2010.4	452,134.7	2013.4	489,155.5

Calculation of seasonal factors

Quarterly seasonal factors are calculated by dividing the average value for each specific quarter (for example, all first quarters) over the full time series period (in this case, nine years) by the overall average of all 36 quarters. For instance, the average of all first-quarter values during the entire period is: (301,755.4 + 320,330.2 + 332,279.2 + ... + 459,176.1) / 9 = 377,430.8

The overall average for all 36 quarterly observations in the time series is:

(301,755.4 + 329,929.1 + 327,636.3 + ... + 489,155.5) / 36 = 404,461.4

Therefore, the seasonal factor for the first quarter is:

377,430.8 / 404,461.4 = 0.933169

The seasonal factors for each quarter, calculated in the same way, are shown below.

Table 19.8 Seasonal factors by quarter

Quarter	Seasonal factor
Q1	0.933169
Q2	1.014090
Q3	1.000150
Q4	1.052591

Derivation of seasonally adjusted values

Seasonal adjusted quarterly values can be approximated by dividing each original unadjusted quarterly observation by its corresponding seasonal factor. For instance, the seasonally adjusted value for the first quarter of 2005 is 301,755.4/0.933169 = 323,366.3, and the seasonally adjusted value for the second quarter of 2005 is 329,929.1/1.014090 = 325,345.1.

Figure 19.4 presents the comparison between the original adjusted series and the seasonally adjusted series.

Table 19.9 Seasonally adjusted quarterly output in manufacturing (South Korea)

(Unit: Billion KRW)

Year, quarter	Output	Year, quarter	Output	Year, quarter	Output
2005.1	323,366.3	2008.1	384,083.0	2011.1	460,991.0
2005.2	325,345.1	2008.2	381,009.7	2011.2	458,615.0
2005.3	327,587.1	2008.3	378,289.3	2011.3	455,356.4
2005.4	334,305.1	2008.4	361,703.2	2011.4	461,522.1
2006.1	343,271.4	2009.1	372,180.2	2012.1	482,808.3
2006.2	341,937.8	2009.2	380,583.8	2012.2	477,502.5
2006.3	343,803.9	2009.3	390,654.8	2012.3	471,148.8
2006.4	348,657.3	2009.4	393,420.1	2012.4	477,134.3
2007.1	356,076.1	2010.1	425,314.9	2013.1	492,061.1
2007.2	357,979.9	2010.2	426,694.8	2013.2	490,483.7
2007.3	359,513.0	2010.3	424,717.1	2013.3	489,081.9
2007.4	369,150.2	2010.4	429,544.5	2013.4	464,715.6

Figure 19.4 Comparison of original unadjusted and seasonally-adjusted quarterly output in manufacturing

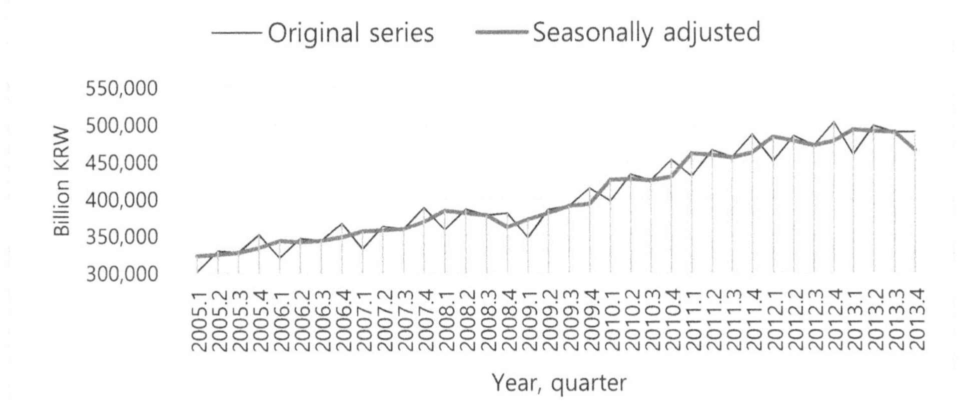

Application of diverse seasonal filters

The seasonal factors discussed above were calculated by applying equal weights (e.g., 1/9) 세 the same quarters across all years in the time series. However, in practice, when compiling quarterly national accounts, seasonal adjustment software such as **X-12-ARIMA** (and equivalently in X-13ARIMA-SEATS) employs a more sophisticated approach. Instead of equal weighting, it uses different weighting schemes that give more weight to observations near the corresponding quarter of the target year.

For instance, when calculating the seasonal factor for the second quarter of year t, equal weights of (1/3, 1/3, 1/3) are assigned to the second quarters of year $(t-1)$, t, and $(t+1)$. This method is referred to as the $S_{3\times1}$ seasonal filter. A **seasonal filter** is a statistical mechanism used in X-12-ARIMA and X-13ARIMA-SEATS to estimate seasonal effects by averaging data from the same quarter in adjacent years with specified weights. This approach can be extended to wider spans. The $S_{3\times3}$ filter, for example, applies weights of (1/9, 2/9, 3/9, 2/9, 1/9) across the corresponding quarter of five years centered on year t. Likewise, the $S_{3\times5}$ filter assigns weights of (1/15, 2/15, 3/15, 3/15, 3/15, 2/15, 1/15) to the seven corresponding quarters. For instance, to calculate the seasonal factor for the second quarter of 2009 using the $S_{3\times3}$ seasonal filter, the weights would be distributed as follows: 1/9 for Q2 2007, 2/9 for Q2 2008, 3/9 for Q2 2009, 2/9 for Q2 2010, and 1/9 for Q2 2011. As a result, the seasonal factor obtained through these filters differ from those computed using uniform weights across all years.

The seasonal filters in X-12-ARIMA allow users to select the number of surrounding years and the distribution of weights. Typically, weights decline as the distance from the target quarter increases. However, this method poses a challenge for calculating seasonal factors for the first and last quarters of a time series. Since there are no preceding or subsequent years for these quarters within the chosen range, alternative filters or adjustment procedures are employed.

Adjustment for calendar effects

In quarterly seasonal adjustment, it is also important to address **calendar effects**, variations in the number of working days between quarters that can influence output and other economic indicators. For example, a quarter with 77 working days (excluding holidays) may yield higher output than a quarter with 75 working days, even if the underlying production capacity is unchanged. If left uncorrected, these differences can distort comparisons across quarters. Therefore, alongside standard seasonal adjustment, it is necessary to apply additional adjustments to remove calendar effects. (This topic is revisited in more detail in section 19.3.3.)

19.3.2 Year-to-year growth rates versus quarter-to-quarter growth rates

When calculating quarterly growth rates, two primary methods are commonly employed. One is the **year-to-year growth rate**, which compares a given quarter to the same quarter in the previous year. The other is the **quarter-to-quarter growth rate**, which is derived after removing seasonal effects though seasonal adjustment and then comparing the current quarter with the immediately preceding one. The year-to-year growth rate, by comparing the same quarters across years, inherently assumes that seasonal patterns are consistent and repeat annually. This assumption implies that some seasonal effects may cancel out, mitigating the influence of seasonality to some extent. However, when comparing the year-to-year growth rate to the seasonally adjusted quarter-to-quarter growth rate, key differences become apparent.

The year-to-year growth rate captures the change from a year ago, not from the most recent quarter. As such, it is not a precise measure of short-term or within-year economic momentum. In contrast, the quarter-to-quarter growth rate based on seasonally adjusted data reflects more immediate and pure short-term changes in economic activity. Therefore, it allows for a more refined interpretation of underlying economic trends and turning points in the business cycle.

Figure 19.5 illustrates the difference between these two methods by presenting both the year-to-year and quarter-to-quarter growth rates of manufacturing output in South Korea. According to the year-to-year basis, the lowest growth rate was observed in the first quarter of 2009 at -3.1%, whereas the lowest growth rate on the quarter-to-quarter basis occurred earlier in the fourth quarter of 2008 at -3.7%. Conversely, the highest growth rate on the year-to-year basis was recorded in the first quarter of 2010 at 14.2%, while on the quarter-to-quarter basis, it peaked earlier in the second quarter of 2009 at 4.1%.

This comparison shows that the quarter-to-quarter rates of change tend to signal turning points in the economic cycle ahead of the year-to-year rates of change. In other words, quarter-to-quarter rates of change are more effective at detecting economic peaks or troughs earlier. As a result, this measure is considered more useful for the timely analysis of business cycle and policy decision-making. For this reason, the seasonally adjusted quarter-to-quarter changes of rate are generally preferred when analyzing short-term growth patterns within a year.

Figure 19.5 Comparison between Year-to-year and Quarter-to-quarter growth rates (Manufacturing output, South Korea)

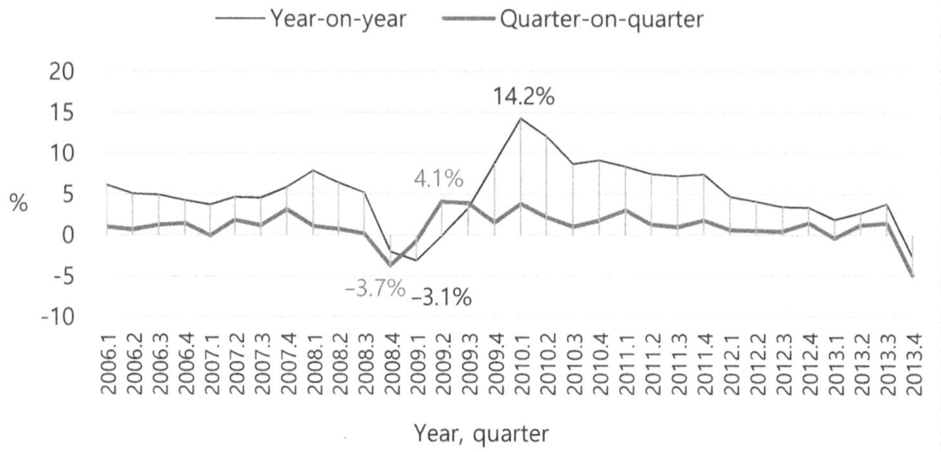

19.3.3 Measurement of calendar effects

The **calendar effect** is an important factor to be considered alongside seasonal adjustment when calculating quarter-to-quarter growth rates. To ensure a meaningful comparison across quarters, growth rates should ideally be measured based on an equal number of working days. For example, if the previous quarter had 75 working days and the current quarter has 77, it is reasonable to expect that the output for the current quarter would naturally increase by the equivalent of two working days. This would result in an upward bias in the measured growth rate. Since such variation resembles seasonal influences, adjusting for differences in working days allows for a more accurate estimation of quarter-to-quarter growth rates.

In order to account for calendar effects with greater precision, several specific factors should be taken into consideration:

- Weekday composition: If productivity is assumed to vary by day (e.g., Monday vs. Saturday), the number of each day type in a given quarter may affect total output. Therefore, adjustments for the weekday composition may be necessary.

- Leap years: In leap years, February has 29 days instead of 28, introducing a one-day difference in the quarterly length. Such discrepancies should be corrected to ensure consistency in comparisons.

- Moving holidays: Holidays such as Easter or Ramadan which occur on different calendar dates each year, can shift production and consumption activity across quarters. These shifts should also be accounted for during adjustment.

19.3.4 Adjustment of outliers

Outliers are unusual or extreme values that deviate significantly from the general pattern of a time series. These irregular observations often arise due to exceptional events or one-off shocks and can distort both model estimation and the seasonal adjustment process. Therefore, it is essential to identify and adjust for outliers prior to the actual seasonal adjustment procedure.

Outliers can be generally be categorized into the following types:

- **Level shifts**: These refer to permanent changes in the level of a time series, typically caused by structural or institutional events (e.g., tax reform or financial crises)
- **Additive outliers or transitory changes**: These are abnormal values observed at specific points in time, resulting from short-lived disturbances. After such events, the time series typically returns to its usual trend.

Modern seasonal adjustment software is equipped with algorithms that automatically detect and adjust for these outliers. Implementing outlier adjustment as a preliminary step helps reduce distortions in the adjustment process and ensures that the underlying structure of the time series is more accurately represented.

19.3.5 Procedures of seasonal adjustment

In quarterly national accounts, seasonal adjustment is essential for improving the accuracy of short-term growth rate estimates and for identifying turning points in the economic cycle. This is accomplished by adjusting for various factors that affect sub-annual time series, including seasonal effects, calendar-related variations, and the presence of outliers. The process for seasonal adjustment of quarterly national accounts follows a procedure that is generally consistent with that applied to other economic indicators. The steps involved are as follows.

(a) Compilation of original quarterly time series data;

(b) Pre-adjustment prior to seasonal adjustment: correction for calendar effects and outliers;

(c) Execution of seasonal adjustment: derivation of seasonally adjusted time series.

Once the original quarterly data series have been compiled, seasonal adjustment is performed using standard software such as X-13ARIMA-SEATS, TRAMO-SEATS, or JDemetra+. The pre-adjustment stage, addressing calendar effects and outliers, is a shared feature across all software platforms. Following this, each software applies its specific methodology to complete the seasonal adjustment. X-13ARIMA-SEATS and JDemetra+ programs are designed to produce and compare results based on both the X-12-ARIMA and TRAMO-SEATS frameworks. X-12-ARIMA performs seasonal adjustment based on seasonal filters, as described previously. In contrast, TRAMO-SEATS adopts a *model-based approach* that estimates and removes seasonal components using statistical parameters.

The following section provides a brief overview of the model-based approach to seasonal adjustment.

19.3.6 Methodology of seasonal adjustment using a model-based approach

This section outlines several technical considerations involved in model-based seasonal adjustment of quarterly data. Three key issues must be addressed in this process:

First, the original time series must be decomposed into its constituent components, such as the underlying trend, seasonal fluctuations, and irregular movements. Second, a decision must be made as to whether seasonal adjustment should be applied at the disaggregated (component) level of the source data or at the aggregated top-level series. Third, the issue of potential inconsistencies between the seasonally adjusted quarterly series and the corresponding annual totals must be addressed, particularly when reconciling the quarterly data with annual benchmarks.

19.3.6.1 Decomposition of the original series

To understand the methodology of model-based seasonal adjustment, one must first consider the standard assumptions regarding the structure of the original unadjusted time series. It is generally assumed that the original data series is composed of the following components: an underlying trend-cycle component, seasonal component, calendar component, and irregular component. This relationship can be expressed as:

$$Y^t = f(T^t, S^t, C^t, I^t)$$

where, Y^t= original time series, T^t= trend-cycle component, S^t= seasonal component, C^t= calendar component, I^t= irregular component.

Two alternative approaches can be taken to model the relationship between the original series and its components: **additive model** and **multiplicative model**. In the additive model, the original series is expressed as the sum of its individual components. This implies that the impact of each component on the original series is additive, meaning that their contributions combine linearly. The multiplicative model, on the other hand, assumes that the original series can be expressed as the product of its individual components. In this model, the influence of each component on the original series is multiplicative.

Additive model: $Y^t = T^t + S^t + C^t + I^t$

Multiplicative model: $Y^t = T^t \times S^t \times C^t \times I^t$

Following seasonal adjustment, the final adjusted series A^t can be expressed as:

(19.3) **Additive model:** $A^t = T^t + I^t = Y^t - (S^t + C^t)$

(19.4) **Multiplicative model:** $A^t = T^t \times I^t = Y^t / (S^t \times C^t)$

where A^t denotes the seasonally adjusted series, which includes only the trend component (T^t) and the irregular component (I^t) after removing the seasonal component (S^t) and the calendar component (C^t). The irregular component (I^t) is not independently estimated but is derived residually as the difference between the adjusted series and the estimated trend component.

In the case of the multiplicative model, a logarithmic transformation can be applied to convert it into an additive form:

Log transformation of the multiplicative mode: $\ln A^t = \ln Y^t - (\ln S^t + \ln C^t)$

Selection criteria between additive and multiplicative models

The choice between the additive and multiplicative modes depends on the characteristics of the underlying original series. If the seasonal fluctuations increase proportionally with the level of the series, the multiplicative model is generally more appropriate. In contrast, if the seasonal variation is relatively independent of the trend cycle and does not vary proportionally with the level of the original series, the additive model is adopted (This model is used even when the series contains negative values). In practice, model selection is based on both visual inspection and formal statistical tests. Empirical experience suggests that the multiplicative model is more frequently used, as many time series exhibit proportional seasonal effects relative to the level of the series.

The following data present the results of seasonal adjustment using X-13ARIMA-SEATS software, based on the quarterly output series of South Korea's food and beverage manufacturing industry and the paper and wood product manufacturing industry. As shown in Table 19.10 and Figure 19.6, the food and beverage sector displays a pattern in which the magnitude of seasonal fluctuations increases in proportion to the upward trend in the series. In contrast, the paper and wood product sector shows a relatively flat trend with stable and consistent seasonal variation across years. Based on these observed patterns and supported by statistical testing, the multiplicative model was selected for the food and beverage series, whereas the additive model was deemed more appropriate for the paper and wood product series.

Table 19.10 Original quarterly output series for Food and beverage manufacturing and Paper and wood manufacturing (South Korea)

(Unit: billion KRW)

Year, quarter	Food & beverage	Paper & wood	Year, quarter	Food & beverage	Paper & wood	Year, quarter	Food & beverage	Paper & wood
2005.1	21,325.6	10,590.3	2008.1	23,026.7	11,701.0	2011.1	27,745.7	11,013.0
2005.2	24,324.6	15,256.9	2008.2	25,534.9	15,768.8	2011.2	30,355.5	15,109.6
2005.3	24,985.5	13,786.0	2008.3	25,868.5	14,978.1	2011.3	30,306.3	15,154.7
2005.4	26,402.1	15,927.4	2008.4	25,437.2	16,929.0	2011.4	32,666.0	17,865.9
2006.1	22,412.8	10,875.5	2009.1	21,883.0	11,853.5	2012.1	30,215.8	11,573.4
2006.2	24,735.7	15,157.4	2009.2	25,345.6	16,301.1	2012.2	32,633.9	15,440.8
2006.3	25,305.0	14,377.5	2009.3	27,024.8	15,350.4	2012.3	33,278.8	15,411.0
2006.4	26,609.5	17,323.3	2009.4	27,718.9	17,811.1	2012.4	35,300.7	17,714.1
2007.1	21,788.6	11,452.4	2010.1	25,550.6	12,073.1	2013.1	30,666.5	11,982.0
2007.2	24,730.7	15,612.6	2010.2	28,284.9	16,336.8	2013.2	33,492.4	16,855.2
2007.3	24,979.8	14,591.8	2010.3	28,517.9	15,323.7	2013.3	34,600.8	16,689.2
2007.4	26,334.9	17,947.1	2010.4	30,315.1	17,616.2	2013.4	34,600.8	16,689.2

Figure 19.6 Quarterly output series for Food and beverage manufacturing and Paper and wood manufacturing (Original series)

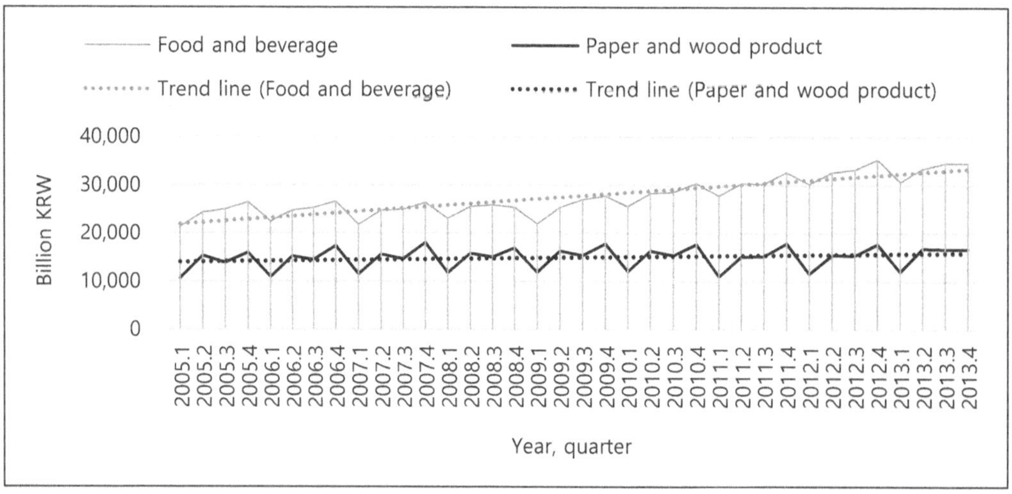

Seasonal adjustment using the multiplicative model

Table 19.11 presents the results of seasonal adjustment for the food and beverage manufacturing industry in South Korea, using the multiplicative model. In this table, the trend-cycle component is expressed in monetary terms (in billion KRW), while the remaining components (namely, irregular, seasonal, and calendar components) are presented in index forms. The figures confirm that the seasonally adjusted values align precisely with those obtained using the multiplicative model formula presented in equation (19.4). For example, in the second quarter of 2005, the seasonally adjusted value (A^t) is 24,124.2 billion KRW, which is equal to the product of the trend-cycle component and the irregular component ($T^t \times I^t$ = 24,191.4 × 0.997221). This value is also consistent with the original series value for the same quarter divided by the seasonal and calendar factors ($Y^t/(S^t \times C^t)$ = 24,324.6 / (1.008306 × 0.999998)).

Table 19.11 Seasonally adjusted data for the food and beverage manufacturing industry (Multiplicative model)

Year, quarter	Seasonally adjusted (billion KRW) (A^t)	Trend cycle (billion KRW) (T^t)	Irregular component (I^t)	Seasonal factor (S^t)	Calendar factor (C^t)
2005.1	23,674.5	24,038.5	0.984859	0.900783	0.999998
2005.2	24,124.2	24,191.4	0.997221	1.008306	0.999998
2005.3	24,388.1	24,381.0	1.000293	1.024495	1.000000
2005.4	24,790.6	24,553.4	1.009662	1.065002	1.000001
2006.1	24,830.0	24,677.5	1.006179	0.902650	1.000002
2006.2	24,538.5	24,712.6	0.992956	1.008035	1.000000
2006.3	24,677.7	24,650.1	1.001117	1.025421	0.999998
2006.4	25,089.7	24,548.6	1.022041	1.060575	1.000000
2007.1	24,009.8	24,492.3	0.980300	0.907483	1.000002
2007.2	24,531.2	24,541.1	0.999597	1.008134	1.000002
2007.3	24,369.0	24,681.1	0.987354	1.025064	1.000000
2007.4	24,964.9	24,851.2	1.004576	1.054875	0.999999
2008.1	25,195.9	24,969.0	1.009084	0.913908	1.000002
2008.2	25,313.5	25,010.1	1.012130	1.008747	0.999999
2008.3	25,302.4	24,989.5	1.012521	1.022373	1.000001
2008.4	24,247.2	24,988.9	0.970319	1.049078	1.000002
2009.1	23,719.3	25,136.2	0.943632	0.922582	1.000000
2009.2	25,112.6	25,476.7	0.985711	1.009276	0.999999
2009.3	26,528.0	25,995.7	1.020475	1.018729	0.999999
2009.4	26,513.9	26,619.4	0.996036	1.045449	1.000001
2010.1	27,511.3	27,275.7	1.008640	0.928731	1.000001
2010.2	28,040.9	27,891.9	1.005341	1.008702	0.999999
2010.3	28,065.9	28,437.9	0.986919	1.016104	1.000001
2010.4	29,038.2	28,960.3	1.002693	1.043972	1.000001
2011.1	29,737.3	29,497.2	1.008139	0.933027	1.000001
2011.2	30,124.0	30,067.6	1.001874	1.007685	1.000001
2011.3	29,886.5	30,683.1	0.974039	1.014046	0.999999
2011.4	31,246.2	31,328.7	0.997366	1.045439	1.000001
2012.1	32,363.9	31,934.9	1.013431	0.933628	0.999999
2012.2	32,413.8	32,468.4	0.998320	1.006790	1.000000
2012.3	32,845.8	32,891.3	0.998617	1.013183	1.000000
2012.4	33,725.7	33,159.5	1.017075	1.046701	1.000000
2013.1	32,853.0	33,281.9	0.987113	0.933445	1.000000
2013.2	33,283.9	33,324.3	0.998789	1.006263	1.000000
2013.3	34,136.8	33,364.1	1.023158	1.013592	1.000001
2013.4	33,030.7	33,436.9	0.987851	1.047535	1.000001

Figure 19.7 presents the seasonal factors for the food and beverage manufacturing industry as derived in the preceding section. These seasonal factors provide insight into the relative magnitude of seasonal fluctuations in production compared to the overall trend. The chart exhibits a clear and consistent quarterly pattern, indicating that the influence of seasonality varies throughout the year. The average seasonal factor in the first quarter is the lowest, at 0.9196, suggesting that the actual output in this quarter typically falls below the annual average level. In contrast, the fourth quarter shows the highest average seasonal factor of 1.0510, implying that the actual output during this quarter tends to exceed the average level for the year.

Figure 19.7 Seasonal factors for the food and beverage manufacturing industry

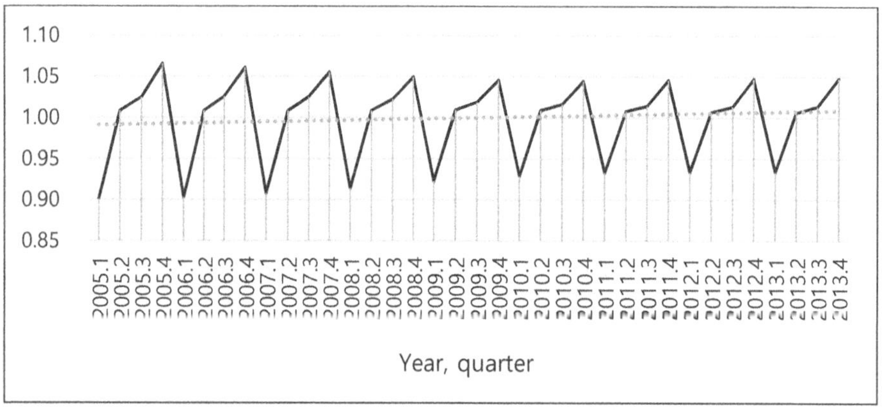

Seasonal adjustment using the additive model

Next, the results of seasonal adjustment for the paper and wood products manufacturing industry using the additive model are examined (Table 19.12). Unlike the multiplicative model, the additive model expresses all components in monetary terms. Applying the formula presented earlier (equation 19.1), the following outcome is obtained. For instance, in the second quarter of 2005, the seasonally adjusted value (A^t) is recorded at 14,697.2 billion KRW. This figure is equal to the sum of the trend-cycle component and the irregular component ($T^t + I^t$ = 13,986.3 + 710.9). It also matches the original series value after removing the seasonal and calendar effects, calculated as $Y^t - (S^t + C^t)$ = 15,256.9 – (875.7 - 316.0).

Table 19.12 Seasonally-adjusted data for the paper and wood manufacturing industry (Additive model)

(Unit: billion KRW)

Year, quarter	Seasonally adjusted (A^t)	Trend-cycle (T^t)	Irregular (I^t)	Seasonal (S^t)	Calendar (C^t)
2005.1	13,940.4	13,928.6	11.8	-3,350.1	0.0
2005.2	14,697.2	13,986.3	710.9	875.7	-316.0
2005.3	14,036.2	14,004.3	31.9	-77.8	-172.5
2005.4	13,341.6	14,174.2	-832.6	2,543.0	42.7
2006.1	14,201.5	14,300.5	-99.0	-3,326.0	0.0
2006.2	14,476.7	14,444.0	32.7	853.1	-172.4
2006.3	14,739.1	14,588.3	150.8	-76.5	-285.2
2006.4	14,621.0	14,724.4	-103.4	2,546.8	155.4
2007.1	14,764.0	14,837.9	-73.9	-3,311.6	0.0
2007.2	15,074.8	14,908.6	166.1	823.0	-285.1
2007.3	14,822.2	14,920.8	104.6	-44.2	-186.2
2007.4	15,017.4	14,907.4	110.0	2,540.6	389.1
2008.1	15,020.8	14,877.4	143.5	-3,319.8	0.0
2008.2	14,500.7	14,856.3	-355.6	787.0	481.0
2008.3	14,519.4	14,867.9	-348.5	16.5	442.2
2008.4	14,964.0	14,929.1	34.9	2,536.9	-571.9
2009.1	15,196.3	15,036.1	160.2	-3,342.8	0.0
2009.2	15,120.1	15,175.0	-54.9	738.8	442.2
2009.3	15,202.1	15,320.6	-118.5	111.8	36.4
2009.4	15,467.8	15,425.4	42.4	2,509.5	-166.2
2010.1	15,461.6	15,449.1	12.5	-3,388.5	0.0
2010.2	15,577.0	15,383.1	193.9	723.3	36.5
2010.3	15,411.6	15,247.0	164.7	228.0	-315.9
2010.4	14,983.4	15,086.8	-103.4	2,446.5	186.3
2011.1	14,473.5	14,952.4	-478.9	-3,460.5	0.0
2011.2	14,673.2	14,879.3	-206.1	752.4	-315.9
2011.3	14,956.7	14,875.8	81.0	370.4	-172.5
2011.4	15,142.8	14,924.2	218.6	2,334.0	389.1
2012.1	15,108.1	15,011.5	96.7	-3,534.7	0.0
2012.2	14,916.5	15,128.8	-212.3	809.4	-285.1
2012.3	15,110.9	15,264.6	-153.7	486.3	-186.2
2012.4	15,428.1	15,396.6	31.5	2,229.6	56.4
2013.1	15,561.4	15,500.7	60.6	-3,579.4	0.0
2013.2	16,186.2	15,567.4	618.8	855.2	-186.2
2013.3	15,650.2	15,577.3	72.9	558.0	481.0
2013.4	15,152.6	15,537.8	-385.2	2,147.4	-610.7

Alongside this seasonally adjusted dataset, it is also important to examine the magnitude and pattern of intra-annual seasonal fluctuation observed in the paper and wood products manufacturing industry. Figure 19.8 presents the seasonal component extracted from the original time series. The seasonal variation in this industry exhibits a distinct and recurrent pattern around the baseline value of zero. In particular, the amplitude of the seasonal effects remains relatively stable across quarters. The first quarter consistently shows the most negative seasonal adjustment value of the year, indicating the lowest production levels due to seasonal factors. In contrast, the fourth quarter records the highest seasonal values, reflecting a peak in production during this quarter. These findings confirm that the paper and wood products industry is subject to a well-defined seasonal production cycle, with predictable and recurring seasonal effects that influence the output each year in a consistent quarterly pattern.

Figure 19.8 Seasonal component (value) in the paper and wood industry

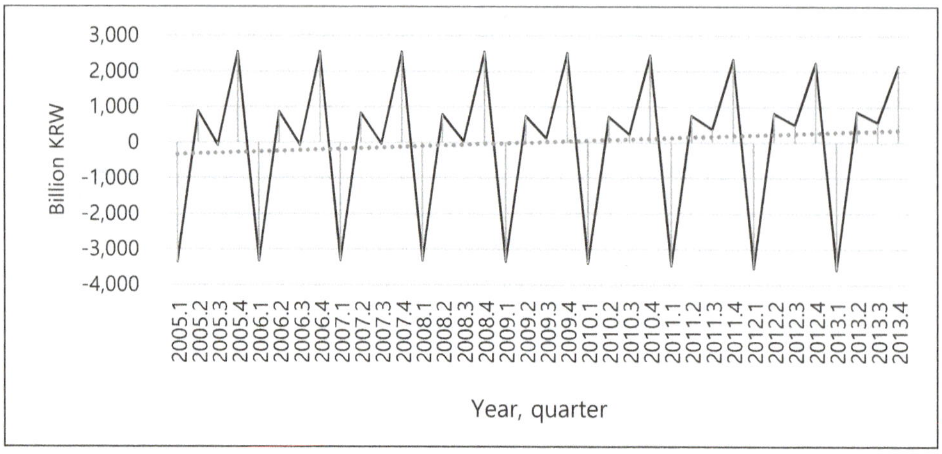

19.3.6.2 Indirect and direct seasonal adjustment

When performing seasonal adjustment, a decision must be made on whether to seasonally adjust the aggregated series or its individual component series, particularly when the time series data consist of both lower-level components and a higher-level aggregate. For instance, in the case of total manufacturing output, two approaches are available:

- **Indirect seasonal adjustment**: Each component series (i.e., the output of individual manufacturing sub-industries) is seasonally adjusted separately, and the adjusted components are then aggregated to form the seasonally adjusted value of the total manufacturing sector. A key advantage of this method is that it preserves additivity between the seasonally adjusted lower-level components and the higher-level aggregate.
- **Direct seasonal adjustment**: The original aggregate series for total manufacturing is directly seasonally adjusted. In this case, additivity is not preserved, meaning that the seasonally adjusted aggregate will not necessarily equal the sum of the seasonally adjusted component series.

Table 19.13 and Figure 19.9 illustrate the results of seasonal adjustment for manufacturing sub-industries, conducted using both approaches based on X-13ARIMA-SEATS software. The table compares the results derived from the indirect method (i.e., aggregation of seasonally adjusted sub-industry series) and the direct method (i.e., seasonal adjustment of the original total manufacturing series). In practice, there is no significant difference between the two methods. For example, in the first quarter of 2006, the seasonally adjusted output of manufacturing obtained via the indirect approach is 339,187.8 billion KRW, while the result from the direct approach is 339,278.6 billion

KRW, implying a negligible difference of approximately 0.0%. Similar patterns are observed in other quarters as well, where the differences between the two methods remain generally small. These results suggest that the choice between indirect and direct seasonal adjustment methods may ultimately depend on the strategic judgment of the statistical compiler.

Table 19.13 Comparison of seasonal adjusted data between indirect versus direct approaches (Manufacturing output, South Korea)

(Unit: billion KRW)

Year, quarter	Indirect (a)	Direct (b)	Difference (a-b)/a	Year, quarter	Indirect (a)	Direct (b)	Difference (a-b)/a	Year, quarter	Indirect (a)	Direct (b)	Difference (a-b)/a
2005.1	320,026.0	319,903.8	0.0%	2008.1	376,963.9	377,311.3	-0.1%	2011.1	450,138.0	450,094.5	0.0%
2005.2	325,572.1	325,064.3	0.2%	2008.2	379,802.8	380,144.2	-0.1%	2011.2	456,079.4	455,991.0	0.0%
2005.3	329,957.2	329,870.1	0.0%	2008.3	380,357.7	381,027.0	-0.2%	2011.3	459,517.9	460,481.8	-0.2%
2005.4	335,640.6	335,818.3	-0.1%	2008.4	367,734.9	366,912.9	0.2%	2011.4	469,690.5	468,875.8	0.2%
2006.1	339,187.8	339,278.6	0.0%	2009.1	363,853.8	364,246.9	-0.1%	2012.1	472,284.9	471,967.9	0.1%
2006.2	342,075.8	341,663.0	0.1%	2009.2	379,046.3	379,146.8	0.0%	2012.2	474,729.0	474,693.0	0.0%
2006.3	346,212.9	346,009.6	0.1%	2009.3	393,537.1	394,017.8	-0.1%	2012.3	475,278.2	476,784.1	-0.3%
2006.4	350,710.8	351,138.6	-0.1%	2009.4	400,328.3	400,074.4	0.1%	2012.4	485,240.6	483,698.6	0.3%
2007.1	351,020.0	350,985.9	0.0%	2010.1	415,759.6	415,446.7	0.1%	2013.1	482,168.8	481,816.8	0.1%
2007.2	358,000.6	357,479.0	0.1%	2010.2	424,601.2	424,580.4	0.0%	2013.2	487,555.4	487,727.7	0.0%
2007.3	361,854.2	361,791.1	0.0%	2010.3	428,553.5	429,031.1	-0.1%	2013.3	492,310.4	494,792.6	-0.5%
2007.4	373,063.8	373,172.0	0.0%	2010.4	437,599.8	436,910.5	0.2%	2013.4	473,386.1	470,452.0	0.6%

Figure 19.9 Seasonally-adjusted data of the direct versus indirect adjustment method (Manufacturing output, South Korea)

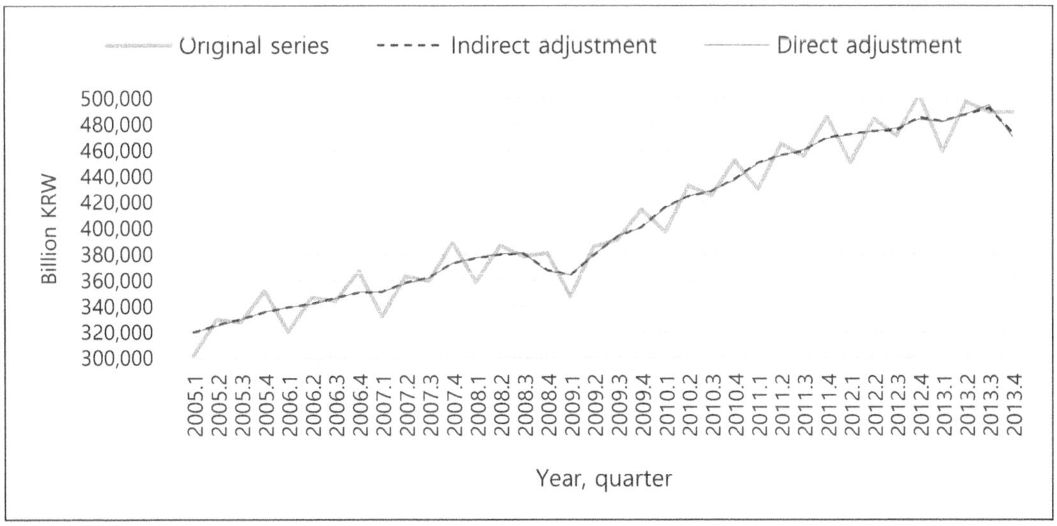

19.3.6.3 Consistency between annual totals of original unadjusted series and seasonally-adjusted data

In general, the annual total derived from quarterly original unadjusted data does not match the annual total obtained from seasonally adjusted quarterly data. This discrepancy arises because various elements (such as seasonal effects and calendar effects) are removed or adjusted during the seasonal adjustment process, which can impact the quarterly figures and lead to a mismatch in the aggregated values. Since seasonal adjustment methods rely on moving averages, data from a given year may be influenced by observations from adjacent years. In addition, when calendar effects (e.g., differences in the number of working days between years) are removed, discrepancies between pre- and post-adjustment annual totals may occur.

In practice, this can be observed by comparing the quarterly output series for manufacturing industry above (Table 19.7 and 19.13), where the annual totals of the original series and the seasonally adjusted series do not coincide. For example, in 2006, the annual total based on the original series is 1,377,935 billion KRW, whereas the seasonally adjusted annual total amounts to 1,378,187.3 billion KRW using the indirect adjustment method, and 1,378,089.8 billion KRW using the direct adjustment method.

Although such differences are inherent to the seasonal adjustment process, the Quarterly National Accounts manual (IMF, 2017, Chapter 7, paragraphs 109-113) allows for an additional adjustment procedure to reconcile the annual total of the seasonally adjusted series with that of the original series, with the aim of minimizing confusion for general user. Accordingly, compilers of quarterly national accounts may undertake post-adjustment reconciliation of annual totals depending on the intended use of the data. This reconciliation can be implemented using features provided in seasonal adjustment software packages. For instance, both X-13ARIMA-SEATS and TRAMO-SEATS offer options that force the annual total of the seasonally adjusted series to match that of the original series. Alternatively, if another method is preferred, the "benchmarking" techniques described earlier in this chapter can be applied. However, when using the proportional benchmarking method, a step problem may arise between the fourth quarter of the previous year and the first quarter of the current year. To mitigate this issue, it is preferrable to use the proportional Denton method, which smooths the transition and preserves coherence. Table 19.14 below provides an example in which the annual totals of the original series and the seasonally adjusted series, previously presented, are reconciled using the proportional Denton method.

Table 19.14 Reconciliation of annual totals between the original and seasonally adjusted series (using the proportional Denton method)

Year, quarter	Indirect	Direct	Year, quarter	Indirect	Direct	Year, quarter	Indirect	Direct
2005.1	320,043.7	320,087.6	2008.1	376,637.5	376,960.0	2011.1	450,282.5	450,291.0
2005.2	325,584.2	325,231.4	2008.2	379,461.7	379,688.4	2011.2	456,337.9	456,237.5
2005.3	329,957.3	329,999.7	2008.3	380,101.3	380,589.2	2011.3	459,837.0	460,764.9
2005.4	335,622.0	335,888.6	2008.4	367,663.7	366,626.5	2011.4	470,020.7	469,184.7
2005 Total	1,311,207.3	1,311,207.3	2008 Total	1,503,864.1	1,503,864.1	2011 Total	1,836,478.1	1,836,478.1
2006.1	339,143.7	339,266.0	2009.1	364,048.5	364,208.7	2012.1	472,563.4	472,285.1
2006.2	342,013.8	341,606.2	2009.2	379,409.5	379,283.7	2012.2	474,944.1	474,994.2
2006.3	346,140.8	345,948.3	2009.3	393,955.5	394,257.9	2012.3	475,417.6	477,044.5
2006.4	350,636.7	351,114.6	2009.4	400,663.6	400,326.8	2012.4	485,293.9	483,895.2
2006 Total	1,377,935.0	1,377,935.0	2009 Total	1,538,077.1	1,538,077.1	2012 Total	1,908,219.0	1,908,219.0
2007.1	350,953.5	351,042.8	2010.1	415,874.3	415,622.2	2013.1	482,121.7	481,920.3
2007.2	357,913.7	357,548.6	2010.2	424,575.4	424,706.6	2013.2	487,431.9	487,762.3
2007.3	361,719.4	361,800.4	2010.3	428,481.8	429,141.4	2013.3	492,134.8	494,780.4
2007.4	372,847.6	373,042.3	2010.4	437,581.6	437,042.9	2013.4	473,193.2	470,418.5
2007 Total	1,443,434.2	1,443,434.2	2010 Total	1,706,513.1	1,706,513.1	2013 Total	1,934,881.6	1,934,881.6

19.3.6.4 Use of software packages for seasonal adjustment

Seasonal adjustment is a process aimed at removing seasonal patterns and adjusting for calendar effects in time series data, in order to accurately measure quarter-to-quarter growth rates, as discussed earlier. To perform this task, a range of specialized computer software packages has been developed and is now widely used in statistical practice. This section provides a brief overview of the main types of software that are practically available for seasonal adjustment. In the past, seasonal adjustment required advanced statistical expertise, making it difficult for general statistical staff to carry out such adjustments. However, with the development and dissemination of more user-friendly software, access to seasonal adjustment tools has significantly improved, allowing even non-specialists to perform seasonal adjustments, provided they have a basic understanding of statistical principles.

Two of the most widely used software tools are X-12-ARIMA, developed by the U.S. Census Bureau, and TRAMO-SEATS, developed by the Bank of Spain. A unified system combining both approaches is available in X-13ARIMA-SEATS. In addition, JDEMETRA+, a platform endorsed by Eurostat and used by many national statistical offices, also integrates both methods. Some countries have developed their own seasonal adjustment tools, such as SABL, STL, and SEASABS. Moreover, in addition to these specialized statistical tools, simpler seasonal adjustment packages are also available as **Excel add-ins**, which further enhance accessibility and allow non-expert users to perform basic seasonal adjustment tasks in a familiar Excel environment. Given the wide array of software options, compilers can choose the most appropriate seasonal adjustment tool depending on the characteristics of the data, the analytical objectives, and the user environment.

Chapter 20. Measurement of capital stock, depreciation, and capital services

This chapter introduces the methodology for deriving the value of fixed asset and depreciation in the balance sheet using the data of gross fixed capital formation. It also delves into the concept of capital stock, which serves as the foundation for these estimation methods. Traditionally, the term **capital stock** was not incorporated into the national accounts framework. However, it has long been used in academics and research institutions for the purpose of measuring productivity and estimating capital income, that is, the return to the services generated by capital. In recognition of its significance, the 2008 SNA introduced the concept of "capital stock" into the national accounts system as a means to measure fixed assets and depreciation more clearly from an economic conceptual perspective, and linkages have been established with the OECD's manuals on Measuring Capital (OECD, 2001, 2009).

This chapter aims to describe the methodology presented in the OECD's Capital Stock Manual, explaining how capital stock and depreciation can be derived from gross fixed capital formation (GFCF) data. The OECD manual sets out the concept and scope of capital stock, but does not explicitly define the scope of its measurement (Measuring Capital, section 5.1 "Concept and scope"). However, if the primary objective of estimating the capital stock is to measure the depreciation for fixed assets employed in production process, the scope of capital stock can be limited to fixed assets within non-financial produced assets, i.e. assets that incur depreciation. In other words, within non-financial assets, non-produced assets, inventories, and valuables are excluded from the measurement of capital stock, as they do not incur depreciation. Although certain non-produced assets, such as land, may contribute to production, this chapter confines the scope of capital stock to fixed assets for the purpose of the discussion.

20.1 Overview of the OECD approach to measuring capital stock

This section provides an overview of the methods presented in the OECD Measuring Capital manual for measuring capital stock and depreciation, and introduces the concept of "productive capital stock" used in the measurement of capital services. More detailed examples of measurement for capital stock and depreciation are set out in sections 20.2 through 20.4.

20.1.1 Procedure for measuring capital stock and depreciation

The OECD manual presents methods for deriving the capital stock of fixed assets using the data of gross fixed capital formation (GFCF). Capital stock is measured in two forms: gross capital stock and net capital stock, the latter being derived by applying an **age-price function** (i.e., a depreciation function such as declining balance/geometric or straight-line). In particular, net capital stock is used to represent the value of fixed assets in the national balance sheet, while depreciation is calculated ex-post from the GFCF time series data together with the age-price function. In addition, the productive capital stock, which is derived by applying an **age-efficiency function** to the GFCF time series data, is used for measuring **capital income** (i.e., the cost of capital services).

Before discussing these concepts in depth, this section first outlines the steps for estimating the capital stock and depreciation from GFCF data. To measure capital stock and depreciation, the first step is to convert all underlying data to constant prices by eliminating price fluctuation factors, and then the above items are calculated according to prescribed formulae. Then, the resulting capital stock and depreciation at constant prices are converted back to current prices.

The figure below (Figure 20.1) shows the process of deriving the gross capital stock and net capital stock of fixed assets from the time series of gross fixed capital formation. Initially, gross fixed capital formation at current prices is converted to gross fixed capital formation at constant prices by dividing it by the appropriate deflator (average of the opening and closing periods) of the corresponding fixed assets. **Gross capital stock** at constant prices is then defined as the cumulative value of GFCF minus the portion that can no longer be used as fixed assets and is therefore retired. This value is obtained by applying a retirement (discard) function to the time series of GFCF. **Net capital stock** at constant prices is defined as the value obtained after deducting not only retirements but also the decline in market value due to physical deterioration and obsolescence. This value is, in practice, obtained by applying to the GFCF time series an age-price function that takes account of the retirement rate. Here, the combination of the retired portion and the decline in market value attributable to deterioration and obsolescence corresponds to **depreciation**. Depreciation at constant prices is obtained by opening net capital stock at constant prices plus GFCF at constant prices during the period minus closing net capital stock at constant prices. The current price measures of net capital stock and depreciation are obtained by multiplying the corresponding constant values by, respectively, the end-of-period deflator (for stocks) and average-of-period deflator (for flows). Finally, productive capital stock at constant prices is derived by applying to the GFCF time series an age-efficiency function that takes account of the retirement rate; to express it at current prices, an end-of-period deflator is applied. The resulting productive capital stock at current prices is used to estimate the value of capital services.

Figure 20.1 Process flow for measuring capital stock and depreciation

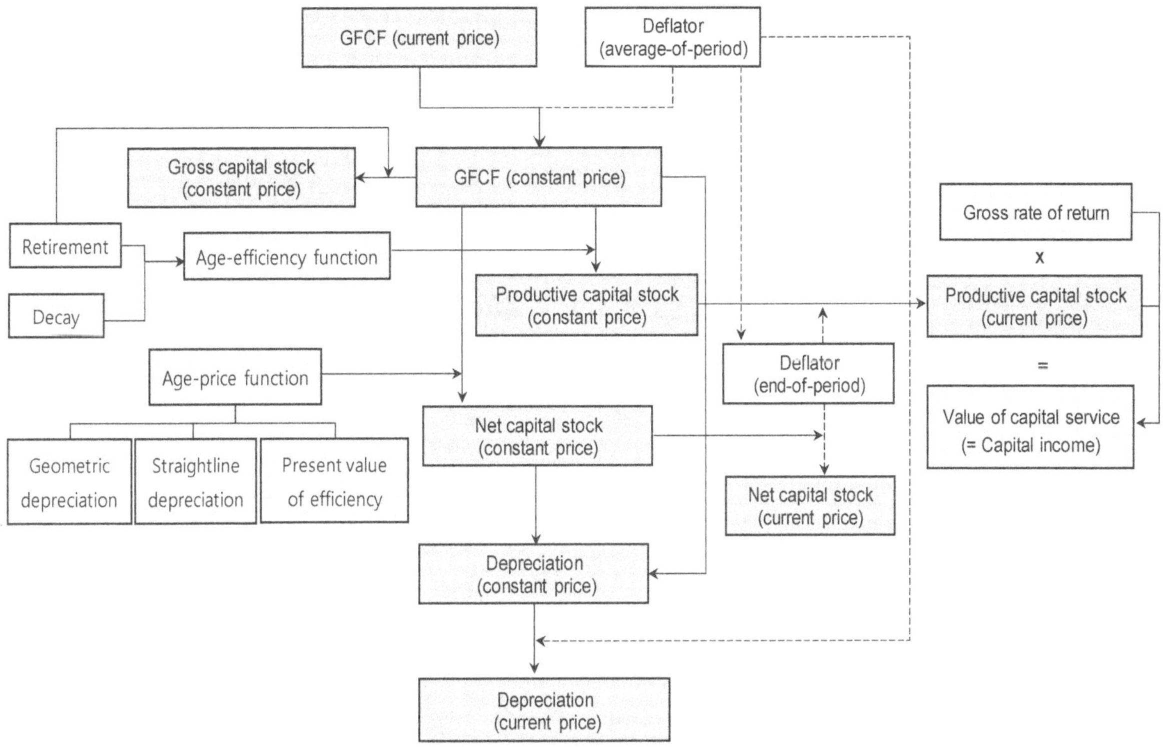

20.1.2 Retirement function, age-efficiency function, and age-price function

In this section, we take a closer look at three concepts used to measure gross capital stock, net capital stock, and productive capital stock: the retirement (discard) function, the age-efficiency function, and the age-price function.

20.1.2.1 Retirement function

When calculating the capital stock of fixed assets on the basis of time series of gross fixed capital formation, it is necessary to allow for the portion that is scrapped or retired (discarded) as fixed assets reach the end of their service lives. **Gross capital stock** is obtained by subtracting from the cumulative gross fixed capital formation up to the current period, the total value of retired assets over that interval. However, individual assets are not retired exactly in accordance with their service lives. They may be retired much earlier than their normal service lives or may continue to be used after their service lives have elapsed. In other words, retirements of individual assets occur most frequently around the average service lives, but they can occur both earlier and later as well.

Therefore, it is assumed that the pattern of retirement of individual assets follows a probability distribution centered on their service lives. The distributional forms used in the literature include the Winfrey distribution, the lognormal distribution, and the Weibull distribution functions. The **Winfrey distribution** can take various forms depending on its shape parameter, including symmetric normal distribution (S-type), left-skewed normal distribution (L-type), and right-skewed normal distribution (R-type); in particular, the symmetric S-type can be further divided into S0 through S6 according to the degree of kurtosis. The lognormal distribution generally shows a left-skewed normal distribution, while the Weibull distribution can take a various types of distribution depending on the parameters of the function.

Figure 20.2 Types of Winfrey curves

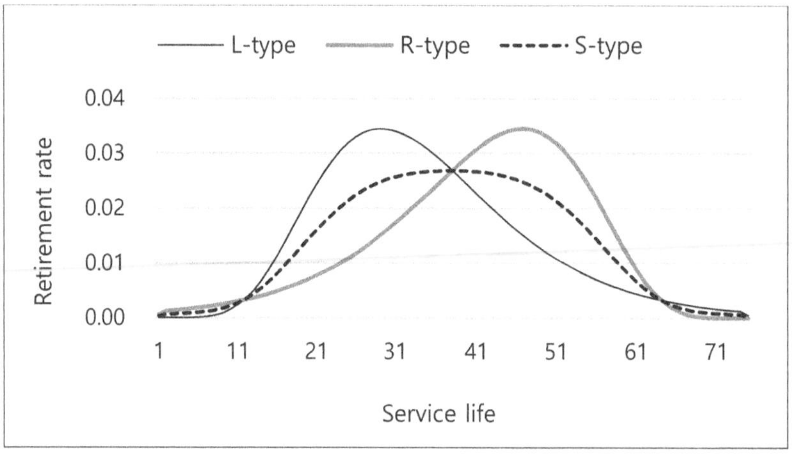

An example of the retirement probability distribution curve (with an average service life of six years) and the corresponding cumulative retirement probability curve is shown in the following figure.

Figure 20.3 Retirement curve and cumulative retirement curve

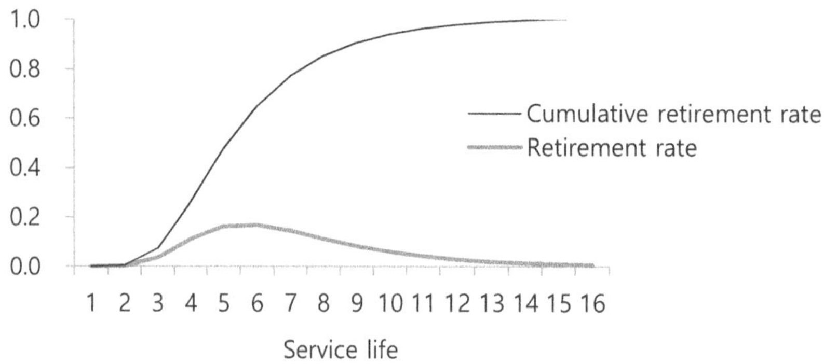

On the other hand, the portion of a fixed asset that remains after retirements by service life is represented by the **survival function** (S^t). That is, the survival function denotes the probability that the asset is still in use at time t, and it can be expressed as one minus the cumulative retirement rate up to that age.

$$\textbf{Survival function: } S^t = 1 - \sum_{i=1}^{t} \text{Retirement rate}^i$$

20.1.2.2 Age-efficiency function and age-price function

This subsection explains how to measure the decline in efficiency of a **single asset** due to deterioration or obsolescence as the asset elapses its service life, and how to measure the resulting decline in the asset's price. The efficiency of an asset is measured differently for a single asset and for a **cohort of assets**. Below, we consider the methods for measuring efficiency for a single asset and for a cohort.

Measurement of the efficiency for a single asset

For a single asset, efficiency gradually declines with age owing to physical deterioration or normal obsolescence. To quantify this decline, an **efficiency parameter** (β) is introduced. The parameter is intended to capture the reduction in the economic efficiency or service potential of a fixed asset as time passes. It typically lies between 0 and 1, for more durable assets and toward 0 for less durable ones. For example, a value of 0.75 is applied for buildings and 0.5 for machinery. The indicator that measures the relative efficiency of a fixed asset over time (age, t) can be expressed as follows:

$$\textbf{Efficiency at age } t \textbf{ for a single asset} = \frac{\text{Service life} - \text{Age } (t)}{\text{Service life} - \beta \times \text{Age } (t)}$$

For instance, for a building with a service life of 30 years (β = 0.75), if it has been used for 10 years, its efficiency is (30 – 10)/(30 – 0.75 × 10) = 0.889. If the same building has been used for 20 years, the value falls to (30 – 20)/(30 – 0.75 × 20) = 0.667. After 30 years of use, the value becomes zero. Thus, as the age approaches the maximum service life, the efficiency of the building declines.

Measurement of the efficiency for a cohort of assets

When measuring the efficiency of a cohort formed by aggregating individual assets, an additional consideration arises compared with the case of a single asset. For an individual building, only the decline in efficiency over time is measured; but for the cohort of buildings as a whole, one must also take into account the probability that individual assets are retired according to their service lives. In other words, at the cohort level, accurate measurement of efficiency requires that both **the declining efficiency of individual assets and the retirement probability distribution of that asset group** be considered simultaneously.

However, it is important to distinguish between the decline in efficiency when a fixed asset is employed in production and the decline in its market value. The former (decline in efficiency as service life elapses) is measured using the **age-efficiency function**, while the latter (decline in market value as age increases) is measured using the **age-price function**. The age-efficiency function is used to measure the actual efficiency delivered by a fixed asset in production, that is, to quantify the value of capital services. The age-price function is used to value the market price of fixed assets for recording on the balance sheet. It should be noted that depreciation reflects the decline in market value, not the decline in efficiency of fixed assets. In general, the decline in the market value of an asset over its service life tends to occur more rapidly than the decline in its efficiency (see Figure 20.4).

Figure 20.4 Comparison of the age-efficiency profile and the age-price profile

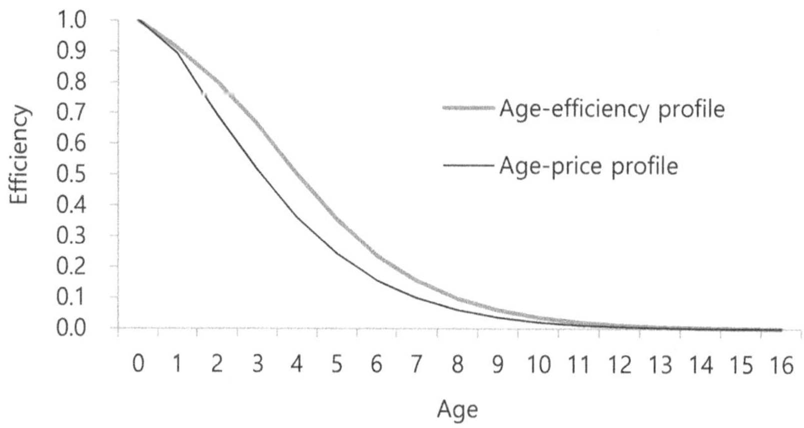

The value of the capital stock measured on the basis of the age-efficiency function is referred to as the **productive capital stock**. The productive capital stock is a concept measured not at the market value of the asset, but on the basis of the efficiency it actually provides. In particular, starting with the 2008 SNA, the concept of measuring the value of services provided by capital stock to production activities was introduced. These services are referred to as **capital services**, and the capital stock data used in the measurement of capital services are those of the productive capital stock. This is based on the rationale that the volume of capital services arises in proportion to the size of the productive capital stock.

In practice, the value of capital services is measured by summing depreciation and net return on capital. This approach is grounded in the notion of opportunity cost, which represents the sum of the decline in asset's value after it has been purchased (depreciation) and the return on investment that would be earned if the asset has been invested elsewhere (net return on capital) (see 20.3.2 for further details).

20.2 Derivation of the age-price function

This section examines the pattern of declining asset prices as assets are retired and depreciated, and shows examples to illustrate the process of deriving the age-price function to measure how asset prices change over time. The age-price function enables the estimation of the residual value of assets and the value of capital stock. This section also examines how the efficiency of assets declines over time by dividing it into a single asset and an asset group (cohort) to derive an age-efficiency function that measures the services provided by the assets. The age-efficiency function is an important tool used for measuring the actual efficiency or service potential of capital, not for valuation aspect.

20.2.1 Declining-balance method and straight-line method

The declining-balance method (geometric depreciation method) assumes that the depreciation of an asset occurs each year at a constant rate. Under this method, the price an asset at time t ($\boldsymbol{P^t}$) is calculated as follows:

$$\boldsymbol{P^t = P^0 \times (1 - \delta)^t}$$

where P^0 is the initial asset price, and δ is the declining-balance depreciation rate. From the above equation, the depreciation rate (δ) can be derived as:

$$\boldsymbol{\delta = 1 - (P^t/P^0)^{\frac{1}{t}}}$$

For example, if the initial acquisition price (P^0) of an asset is set at 1, and the maximum service life (n) of the asset is assumed to be 10 years, the salvage value at the end of service life will be $(1-\delta)^{10}$. The age-price function representing the remaining value of the asset by the age of the asset according to the declining-balance method is illustrated in Table 20.1 below. In practice, the declining-balance generally applies a depreciation rate equal to twice the rate used in the straight-line method (1/service life), which is "2/service life" (commonly referred to as the **double declining balance rate**). Therefore, if the service life is 10 years, the depreciation rate under the declining-balance method is 2/10 (20%), which is twice of 1/10. In this case, the remaining value of the asset in year 5 is $(1-0.2)^5 = 0.328$. The age-price function derived from the declining-balance method is characterized by a steep decline in asset value in the early years, followed by a progressively slower rate of decline over time.

Table 20.1 Age-price table under the declining-balance method

(Initial asset value =1, depreciation rate = 20%)

Age	0	1	2	3	4	5	6	7	8	9	10
Age-price value	1.000	0.800	0.640	0.512	0.410	0.328	0.262	0.210	0.168	0.134	0.107

In contrast, the **straight-line method** assumes that the same absolute amount of depreciation is incurred each year, with the depreciation rate fixed at 1/service life. In this case, the asset price decreases evenly over time, resulting in a decline curve that is gentler and more linear in shape compared with the declining-balance method (see Figure 20.5).

Figure 20.5 Comparison of age-price curves under the declining-balance and straight-line methods

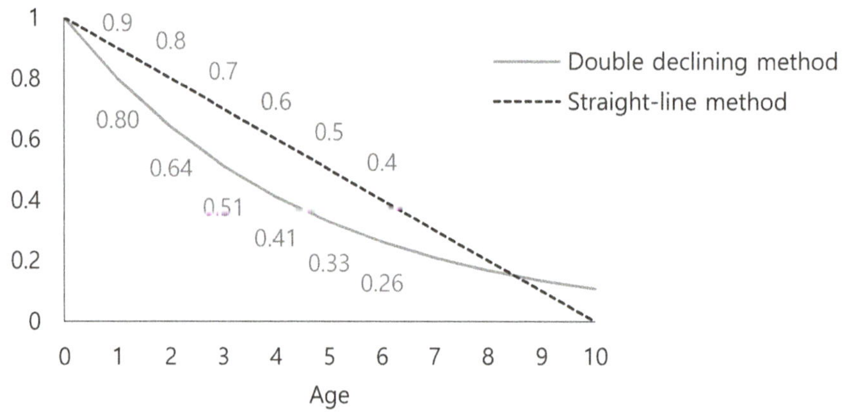

20.2.2 Straight-line method combined with a retirement function

The straight-line method combined with a retirement function is based on the straight-line depreciation of individual assets at each period, but takes into account the rate at which assets within the asset group (cohort) become retired or unusable. Thus, the age-price function derived under this approach is a combination of the straight-line depreciation of individual assets and the retirement distribution of the asset group. For example, suppose that vehicles have a maximum service life of 16 years and that the probability of retirement by asset age within the cohort of vehicles follows the log-normal distribution shown in Figure 20.6.

Figure 20.6 Probability of retirement (Cohort of vehicles)

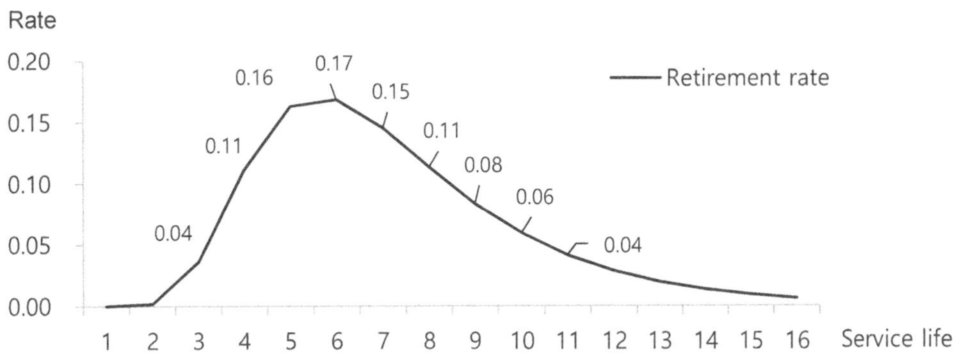

Straight-line depreciation for a single asset

When the straight-line method is applied to an individual vehicle, and the annual depreciation rate is given by "1/service life," the residual value after t years of age is calculated as:

$$\textbf{Residual value} = \textbf{Initial value} \times (\mathbf{1} - \frac{\textbf{age}}{\textbf{service life}})$$

For instance, in Table 20.2, a vehicle with a service life of 7 years will have an accumulated depreciation of 3/7 in year 3, resulting in a residual value of 0.57 (=1 - 3/7). Similarly, a vehicle in year 5 with a service life of 9 would have a residual value of 0.44 (=1 - 5/9).

Age-price function for a cohort of assets

However, for a cohort of vehicles as a whole, the residual value (age-price function) over time (age) is calculated by multiplying the retirement probability for each service life (column 2, grey area) by the residual value of an individual vehicle under straight-line depreciation, and then summing across service lives. This result is illustrated in the second row from the bottom of the table. For example, the residual value of the cohort in year 2 (column 5, shaded blue area) is the sum of the products of the retirement probability for each service life (column 2) and the residual value after two years of straight-line depreciation, i.e.,

$$0.68 = (0.04 \times 0.33) + (0.11 \times 0.50) + (0.16 \times 0.60) \ldots + (0.01 \times 0.88)$$

The bottom row of the table shows depreciation rates for the cohort of asset under the straight-line method, representing the year-to-year depreciation rates. For instance, the depreciation rate for year 2 is 0.19 (= 1 - 0.68/0.84).

Table 20.2 Age-price data under the straight-line method combined with a retirement function (Individual vehicle and a cohort)

Age (→) Service life (↓)	Retirement probability	0	1	2	3	4	5	6	7	8	9	10	11	12	13	14	15	16
1	0.00	1.00																
2	0.00	1.00	0.50															
3	0.04	1.00	0.67	0.33														
4	0.11	1.00	0.75	0.50	0.25													
5	0.16	1.00	0.80	0.60	0.40	0.20												
6	0.17	1.00	0.83	0.67	0.50	0.33	0.17											
7	0.15	1.00	0.86	0.71	0.57	0.43	0.29	0.14										
8	0.11	1.00	0.88	0.75	0.63	0.50	0.38	0.25	0.13									
9	0.08	1.00	0.89	0.78	0.67	0.56	0.44	0.33	0.22	0.11								
10	0.06	1.00	0.90	0.80	0.70	0.60	0.50	0.40	0.30	0.20	0.10							
11	0.04	1.00	0.91	0.82	0.73	0.64	0.55	0.45	0.36	0.27	0.18	0.09						
12	0.03	1.00	0.92	0.83	0.75	0.67	0.58	0.50	0.42	0.33	0.25	0.17	0.08					
13	0.02	1.00	0.92	0.85	0.77	0.69	0.62	0.54	0.46	0.38	0.31	0.23	0.15	0.08				
14	0.01	1.00	0.93	0.86	0.79	0.71	0.64	0.57	0.50	0.43	0.36	0.29	0.21	0.14	0.07			
15	0.01	1.00	0.93	0.87	0.80	0.73	0.67	0.60	0.53	0.47	0.40	0.33	0.27	0.20	0.13	0.07		
16	0.01	1.00	0.94	0.88	0.81	0.75	0.69	0.63	0.56	0.50	0.44	0.38	0.31	0.25	0.19	0.13	0.06	
Residual value	1.00	1.00	0.84	0.68	0.52	0.37	0.25	0.16	0.10	0.06	0.04	0.02	0.01	0.01	0.00	0.00	0.00	0.00
Depreciation rate			0.16	0.19	0.24	0.29	0.33	0.35	0.37	0.38	0.40	0.41	0.43	0.46	0.51	0.59	0.72	1.00

The residual values in this table (second row from the bottom) represent the age-price function for the cohort of vehicles under the straight-line method combined with the retirement function. When depicted graphically, as in Figure 20.7, this curve is characterized by a steep initial decline, similar to the declining-balance method, followed by a more gradual decrease over time.

Figure 20.7 Age-price curve for a cohort of vehicles under the straight-line method combined with a retirement function

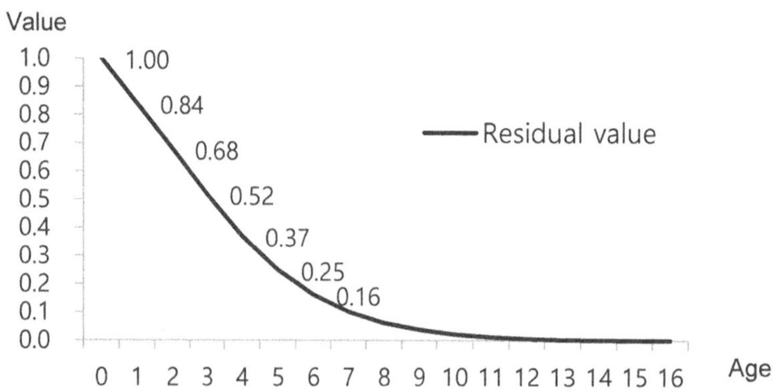

20.2.3 Present value of efficiency method

The present value of efficiency method (PVE method) estimates the residual value of assets by combining the "age-efficiency function" of a cohort of assets with the present value of the annual rental income generated over the service life of that cohort. This approach is based on the principle that, as the years of use (age) of an asset increase, the present value of its future income gradually declines, thereby producing an age-price curve that reflects the decrease in the asset's value over time.

Efficiency of a single asset and its efficiency function

The **efficiency function of an individual asset** is a curve that describes how the service capacity (efficiency) the asset can provide changes with years of age. In general, assets lose efficiency over time, and the pattern of decline may take several forms:

- **Hyperbolic**: Efficiency declines slowly at first, then more sharply as time passes; considered the most common form.
- **Linear**: Efficiency decreases proportionally with the increase in years of age.
- **Geometric**: Efficiency declines rapidly at the outset, with the rate of decrease slowing thereafter; less commonly used to represent efficiency decline.

Figure 20.8 illustrates these different forms of efficiency functions, showing how efficiency decreases with the age of an asset.

Figure 20.8 Forms of the efficiency function for individual assets

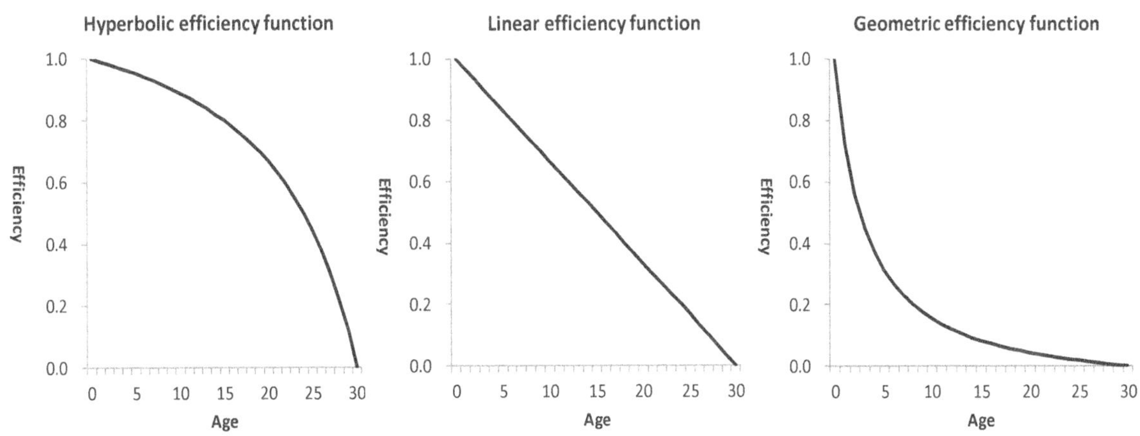

Procedure of the present value of efficiency method

The age-efficiency function under the present value of efficiency method is derived through the following two steps:

1. **Specification of the efficiency function (decay function) for a single asset**: Define a function that represents the decline in efficiency of an assets as its age increase.
2. **Derivation of the age-efficiency function for a cohort of assets**: Apply the retirement probability distribution of the cohort to the efficiency function specified for individual assets, thereby constructing the age-efficiency function for the cohort as a whole.

The following section examines in detail the process for deriving the age-efficiency function using the present value of efficiency method.

20.2.3.1 Efficiency function of a single asset

The efficiency function for a single asset describes how the efficiency of the asset declines over time, given its service life. It reflects the fact that, as the asset age increases, its efficiency gradually decreases. For example, let n denote the service life of the asset (in years), t denote the age of the asset (in years), and β denote the efficiency coefficient representing the rate of efficiency decline respectively. The efficiency function for a single asset is expressed as:

$$\text{Efficiency function for a single asset: } \mathbf{E(n,t)} = \frac{\mathbf{n-t}}{\mathbf{n-\beta t}}$$

The meaning of this equation can be interpreted from two perspectives. First, the efficiency curve shows different patterns depending on the value of the efficiency coefficient β. Figure 20.9 illustrates how the decline in asset efficiency changes with different values of β.

- When β = 1, the asset maintains a constant efficiency throughout its service life, losing it entirely at the end. Assets such as light bulbs, which cease functioning abruptly, belong to this category.
- When 1 > β > 0, efficiency follows a hyperbolic pattern, declining slowly in the early years and more sharply towards the end. This is the typical pattern observed for most asset types such as buildings, structures, and machinery. For example, buildings and structures use β = 0.75, while transport equipment and machinery often use β = 0.5.
- When β = 0, efficiency declines at a constant rate each year, forming a linear pattern.

- When β < 0, efficiency follows a geometric decline, with a step drop in the early years and a slower rate of decrease thereafter.

Therefore, in determining the efficiency coefficient β, one should consider the characteristics of the asset and select the decline pattern that best reflects reality. In most cases, the efficiency of an asset declines in a hyperbolic manner, and thus β generally lies between 0 and 1.

Figure 20.9 Efficiency curves for a single asset by efficiency coefficient (β)

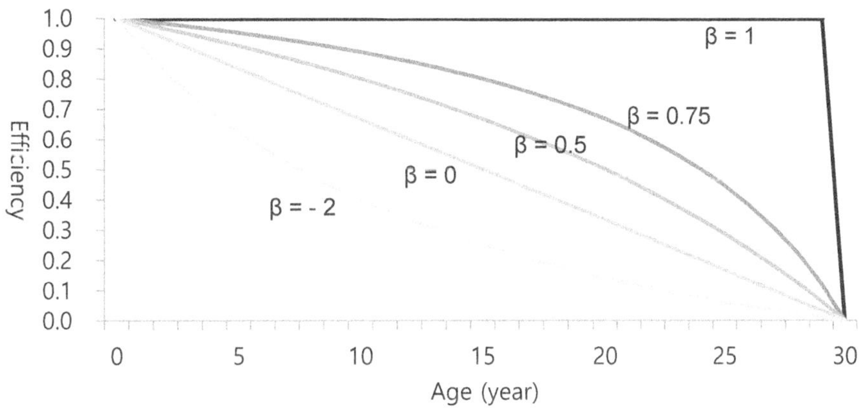

Secondly, the efficiency function for a single asset varies according to its service life. Figure 20.10 presents the efficiency functions by service life for vehicles with an efficiency coefficient of 0.5, an average service life of 8 years, and a maximum service life of 16 years. For example, the efficiency curve for a vehicle with a service life of 8 years is displayed as a dotted line as it ages. The efficiency curve for the maximum service life of 16 years appears as the hyperbolic line on the far-right edge. In this case, the asset has an efficiency of 0.97 after one year of age, and declines to 0.93 after two years of age.

Figure 20.10 Efficiency curves for a single asset by service life

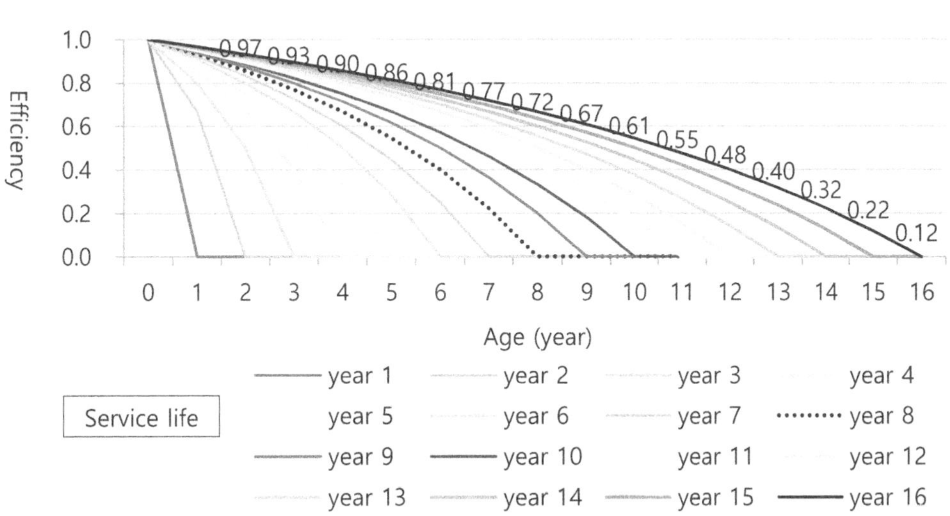

Table 20.3.1 The efficiency function (decay function) for a single asset, compiled in numerical form based on the assumption described above, namely an efficiency coefficient (β) of 0.5, an average service life of 8 years, and a maximum service life of 16 years for vehicles. Column 2 of the table indicates service lives of the vehicle, while the efficiency function of the single asset is displayed from column 3 onward. For example, if an efficiency coefficient (β) of 0.5 is applied to a vehicle, the efficiency in the second year (highlighted in blue) for a vehicle with a service life of 6 years is calculated as $(6-2)/(6-0.5\times2) = 0.80$, and the efficiency in the second year for the vehicle with a service life of 8 years is $(8-2)/(8-0.5\times2) = 0.86$.

Table 20.3 Retirement probability and age-efficiency table under the PVE method

Table 20.3.1: Service life, retirement probability, and efficiency by age for a single asset

Retirement probability	Age(→) Service life (↓)	0	1	2	3	4	5	6	7	8	9	10	11	12	13	14	15	16
0.000	1	1.00	0.00															
0.002	2	1.00	0.67	0.00														
0.036	3	1.00	0.80	0.50	0.00													
0.111	4	1.00	0.86	0.67	0.40	0.00												
0.163	5	1.00	0.89	0.75	0.57	0.33	0.00											
0.168	6	1.00	0.91	0.80	0.67	0.50	0.29	0.00										
0.145	7	1.00	0.92	0.83	0.73	0.60	0.44	0.25	0.00									
0.113	8	1.00	0.93	0.86	0.77	0.67	0.55	0.40	0.22	0.00								
0.083	9	1.00	0.94	0.88	0.80	0.71	0.62	0.50	0.36	0.20	0.00							
0.059	10	1.00	0.95	0.89	0.82	0.75	0.67	0.57	0.46	0.33	0.18	0.00						
0.041	11	1.00	0.95	0.90	0.84	0.78	0.71	0.63	0.53	0.43	0.31	0.17	0.00					
0.028	12	1.00	0.96	0.91	0.86	0.80	0.74	0.67	0.59	0.50	0.40	0.29	0.15	0.00				
0.020	13	1.00	0.96	0.92	0.87	0.82	0.76	0.70	0.63	0.56	0.47	0.38	0.27	0.14	0.00			
0.013	14	1.00	0.96	0.92	0.88	0.83	0.78	0.73	0.67	0.60	0.53	0.44	0.35	0.25	0.13	0.00		
0.009	15	1.00	0.97	0.93	0.89	0.85	0.80	0.75	0.70	0.64	0.57	0.50	0.42	0.33	0.24	0.13	0.00	
0.006	16	1.00	0.97	0.93	0.90	0.86	0.81	0.77	0.72	0.67	0.61	0.55	0.48	0.40	0.32	0.22	0.12	0.00

Table 20.3.2: Age-efficiency function for a cohort

Age-efficiency	1.00	0.91	0.80	0.66	0.50	0.35	0.24	0.15	0.10	0.06	0.04	0.02	0.01	0.01	0.00	0.00	0.00

The first column of this table illustrates the probability of retirement by service life for vehicles. The retirement probability distribution for the asset cohort is modelled in a peaked form. The most commonly used distributions for this purpose are the Winfrey curve, the log-normal distribution, and the Weibull distribution, all of which have bell-shaped probability density functions centered around the mean value. In this example (column 1), a log-normal distribution is applied, which exhibits a left-skewed, asymmetric form (see Figure 20.6 for the corresponding graph).

For example, the probability that a vehicle is retired at a service life of 8 years (indicated by a circle) is 11.3% of all vehicles. In this table, the retirement probability peaks at 16.8% for 6 years of service life, with the probabilities decreasing in both directions away from this peak.

20.2.3.2 Age-efficiency function for a cohort of assets

The age-efficiency function for a cohort of assets, such as vehicles grouped together, is derived by combining the efficiency values for each service life of a single asset with the corresponding retirement probabilities, using the latter as weights. For example, in the case of a cohort of vehicles, the efficiency E^t at asset age t is calculated according to the following steps:

1. **Calculate efficiency values by service life**: For each service life n, apply the following formula:

$$E(n,t) = \frac{n-t}{n-\beta t}$$

where β is the efficiency coefficient, to obtain the efficiency value.

2. **Apply retirement probability weights**: Multiply the efficiency value for each service life n by the retirement probability π^n for that service life (column 1 of Table 20.3.1).

3. **Sum the weighted efficiency values**: For all service lives where $n \geq t$, calculate as:

$$E^t = \sum_{n=t}^{N} E(n,t) \times \pi^n$$

to obtain the efficiency of the cohort at asset age t, where N denotes the maximum service life.

For example, in Table 20.3.1, the efficiency of the cohort of vehicles at age 4 years is calculated by multiplying the values from the formula (n – 4)/(n – 0.5 × 4) (grey column) by the retirement probabilities (column 1) for each service life starting from 4 years, and summing the results. For a service life of 5 years, the calculation is (5 – 4)/(5 – 0.5 × 4) × 0.163; for a service life of 6 years, (6 – 4)/(6 – 0.5 × 4) × 0.168; for a service life of 7 years, (7 – 4)/(7 – 0.5 × 4) × 0.145, and for a service life of 16 years, (16 – 4)/(16 – 0.5 × 4) × 0.006. Summing all these weighted efficiency values yields an efficiency of 0.50 at age 4. Using the same procedure, the efficiency at age 5 is calculated as 0.35, and at age 6 as 0.24, and so on. Linking this sequence of efficiency values produces the age-efficiency function for the cohort of vehicle assets (see Table 20.3.2).

The age-efficiency curve for the cohort of assets as a function of age is shown in Figure 20.11.

Figure 20.11 Age-efficiency curve for a cohort of vehicles

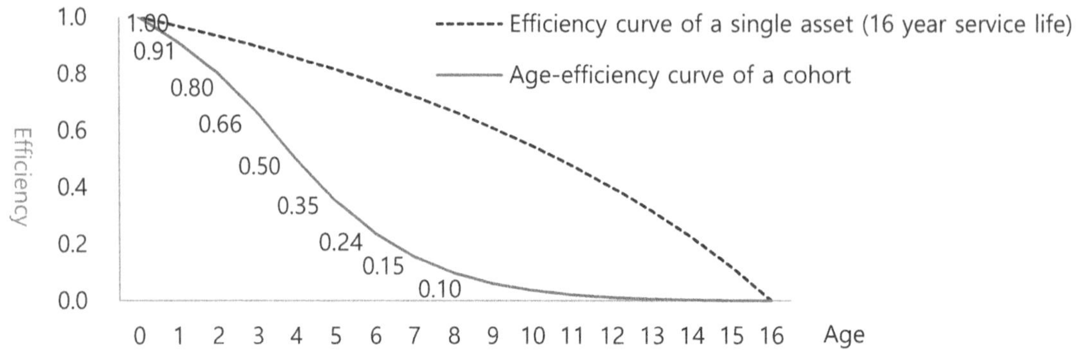

The age-efficiency function for a cohort of assets under the present value of efficiency method is characterized by rapid decline in efficiency in the early years of the age, followed by a progressively slow rate of decline in the later years. Compared with the efficiency function for a single asset, the initial drop is larger and steeper, reflecting the weighted pattern of efficiency decline for the cohort as a whole.

20.2.3.3 Age-price function under the present value of efficiency method

Under the present value of efficiency method, the age-price function is derived on the basis of the age-efficiency function for a cohort of assets. The key feature of this approach is that the residual value is calculated as the residual value is calculated as the weighted sum of the present value of annual rental income from assets, with the weights given by the efficiency values for each corresponding year (as derived from the age-efficiency function of the cohort).

Outline of the calculation procedure

Take, for example, a cohort of vehicles. Table 20.4 illustrates the age-efficiency function for the cohort of vehicle assets with the present values of rental income at each age of the same assets. The rental income in the first year is set to 1. The annual growth rate of rental income is assumed to be 1% (payable at the end of each year), and the discount rate for converting rental income into present value is assumed to be 4% per year. For instance, the present value of the rental income at the beginning of year 4 is calculated as:

$$(1+0.01)^4/(1+0.04) = \text{present value of rental income}$$

Multiplying this rental income by the efficiency value in year 4 (0.5002) yields the efficiency-weighted present value of rental income for year 4:

$$0.5002 \times \frac{(1+0.01)^4}{1+0.04} = 0.501$$

This value is then discounted back for years 3, 2, 1, and 0 as follows:

- Year 3: 0.501/(1+0.04) = 0.481, Year 2: $0.501/(1+0.04)^2$ = 0.463, Year 1: $0.501/(1+0.04)^3$ = 0.445, Year 0: $0.501/(1+0.04)^4$ = 0.4278

From a column-wise perspective in Table 20.4, the present value of rental income for year 11 is calculated as:

- Age 11: $0.0211 \times (1 + 0.01)^{11} / (1 + 0.04)$ = 0.0226, Age 12: 0.0126 / (1 + 0.04) = 0.0121, Age 13: $0.0064 / (1 + 0.04)^2)$ = 0.0060, Age 14: $0.0028 / (1 + 0.04)^3$ = 0.0025, Age 15: $0.0008 / (1 + 0.04)^4$ = 0.0007

Thus, the cumulative sum is: 0.0226 + 0.0121 + 0.0060 + 0.0025 + 0.0007 + 0 = 0.0439

This represents the total present value of remaining rental income from year 11 onwards, and is shown in the third row from the bottom of Table 20.4 (P^n).

Generalizing this calculation for any column yields the following formula:

$$\boldsymbol{P^n = E^n \times \frac{(1+i)^n}{1+r} + E^{n+1} \times \frac{(1+i)^{n+1}}{(1+r)^2} + \cdots + E^N \times \frac{(1+i)^N}{(1+r)^{N-n+1}}}$$

where P^n represents the residual value of the cohort of assets at age n (sum of the present values of the future rental income from years n, n+1, ..., N, each weighted by the efficiency at that year); E^n denotes the efficiency of the cohort of assets at age n; i denotes the growth rate of annual rental income; r denotes the annual discount rate for present value; and N denotes the maximum service life of the cohort (16 years in this example).

Table 20.4 Present value of rental income weighted by age-efficiency for a cohort of vehicle assets and the resulting age-price function

Rental income (→)		1.000	1.010	1.020	1.030	1.041	1.051	1.062	1.072	1.083	1.094	1.105	1.116	1.127	1.138	1.149	1.161	1.17
Efficiency (Cohort)	**Age (n)** / **Beginning of year (→)**	0	1	2	3	4	5	6	7	8	9	10	11	12	13	14	15	16
1.0000	0	0.9615																
0.9110	1	0.8507	0.885															
0.8006	2	0.7260	0.755	0.785														
0.6598	3	0.5811	0.604	0.628	0.654													
0.5002	**4**	**0.4278**	**0.445**	**0.463**	**0.481**	**0.501**												
0.3530	5	0.2932	0.305	0.317	0.330	0.343	0.357											
0.2369	6	0.1911	0.199	0.207	0.215	0.224	0.233	0.242										
0.1536	7	0.1203	0.125	0.130	0.135	0.141	0.146	0.152	0.158									
0.0971	8	0.0739	0.077	0.080	0.083	0.086	0.090	0.094	0.097	0.101								
0.0601	9	0.0444	0.046	0.048	0.050	0.052	0.054	0.056	0.058	0.061	0.063							
0.0362	10	0.0260	0.027	0.028	0.029	0.030	0.032	0.033	0.034	0.036	0.037	0.038						
0.0211	11	0.0147	0.015	0.016	0.017	0.017	0.018	0.019	0.019	0.020	0.021	0.022	**0.0226**					
0.0116	12	0.0079	0.008	0.009	0.009	0.009	0.010	0.010	0.010	0.011	0.011	0.012	**0.0121**	0.0126				
0.0059	13	0.0039	0.004	0.004	0.004	0.005	0.005	0.005	0.005	0.005	0.006	0.006	**0.0060**	0.0062	0.0064			
0.0025	14	0.0016	0.002	0.002	0.002	0.002	0.002	0.002	0.002	0.002	0.002	0.002	**0.0025**	0.0026	0.0027	0.0028		
0.0007	15	0.0004	0.001	0.001	0.001	0.001	0.001	0.001	0.001	0.001	0.001	0.001	**0.0007**	0.0007	0.0007	0.0008	0.0008	
0.0000	16	0.0000	0	0	0	0	0	0	0	0	0	0	**0**	0	0	0	0	0
Sum of present value of rental income (P^n)		4.3246	3.498	2.717	2.009	1.410	0.946	0.613	0.386	0.236	0.141	0.081	**0.0439**	0.0221	0.0099	0.0036	0.001	0
Age-price function (Cohort)		1.000	0.809	0.628	0.465	0.326	0.219	0.142	0.089	0.055	0.033	0.019	**0.010**	0.005	0.002	0.001	0.000	0
Depreciation rate ($1-P^n/P^{n-1}$)			0.191	0.223	0.261	0.298	0.329	0.352	0.370	0.387	0.405	0.427	**0.456**	0.496	0.554	0.639	0.772	1.00

* Note: Growth rate of annual rental income = 0.01. Annual discount rate for present value = 0.04

If, in the above formula, $E^n \times (1+i)^n$ is replace by F^n, the expression can be simplified as follows:

$$\boldsymbol{P^n = F^n/(1+r) + F^{n+1}/(1+r)^2 + \cdots + F^N/(1+r)^{N-n+1} = \sum_{k=0}^{N-n} F^{n+k}/(1+r)^{k+1}}$$

Here, F^n represents the product of the rental income generated at age n (year 11 in this case) and the efficiency of the cohort at that age. P^n is the total present value of the future rental income streams from years n, n+1, ..., N, weighted by the efficiency values. This sum is shown in the third row from the bottom of the table. Dividing the present value of rental income at each age by the present value of rental income at age 0 (4.3246) yields the **age-price function**, which represents the relative value of the cohort of vehicle assets as it ages (second row from the bottom).

- Age-price function for the cohort at age $n = P^n/P^0$, $\quad n = 0,1,2,\ldots,N$

where, P^0 represents the present value of the total expected rental income from age 0 up to the maximum service life (N), weighted by the efficiency of the cohort at each age. P^N represents the present value of the rental income that can be expected at the maximum service life (N), multiplied by the efficiency at each age. In order to derive the age-price function under the Present value of efficiency method, additional information is required on the discount rate (r) for converting income into present value and the growth rate (i) of rental income.

The bottom row of Table 20.4 shows the **depreciation rate** calculated from the age-price function. The depreciation rate ($\boldsymbol{\delta^n}$) is defined as the decline in the value of an asset from one year (n) to the next, expressed as:

$$\boldsymbol{\delta^n = 1 - P^n / P^{n-1}}$$

For example, the depreciation rate in year 1 is 1 – (0.809/1.000) = 0.191, while in year 2, it is 1 – (0.628/0.809) = 0.223.

Comparison of the age-efficiency curve and the age-price curve

When comparing the age-price function for the cohort derived in this table with the age-efficiency function, Figure 20.12 shows that the age-price curve declines more steeply than the age-efficiency curve. This indicates that, in valuing assets, an assessment based on the present value of rental income produces lower values than one based on only on efficiency or productive capacity. The age-price function is used for valuing net capital stock, while the age-efficiency function is applied in valuing productive capital stock.

Figure 20.12 Comparison of the age-efficiency curve and age-price curve

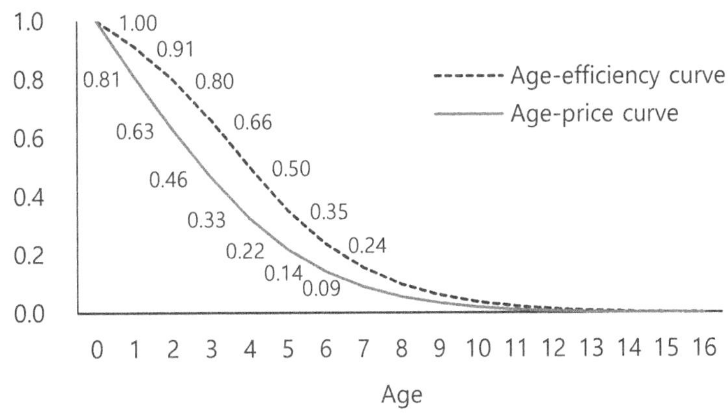

20.3 Estimation of gross capital stock, productive capital stock, and net capital stock

In the preceding section, the methods for deriving the retirement function (or survival function), the age-efficiency function, and the age-price function required for measuring the capital stock of fixed assets were discussed. In this section, these three functions are applied to show how the gross capital stock, the productive capital stock, and the net capital stock of fixed assets can be estimated, and how depreciation is subsequently derived. The derivation process involves converting the time series of gross fixed capital formation into capital stocks by applying the retirement (or survival) function, the age-efficiency function, and the age-price function, respectively. Through this process, gross capital stock, productive capital stock, and net capital stock are calculated, and depreciation can be obtained ex-post.

20.3.1 Estimation of gross capital stock

Gross capital stock of fixed assets (in real terms) is derived from the cumulative sum of fixed assets that remain after retirements or discards, based on the time series of gross fixed capital formation (GFCF). Gross capital stock does not take into account the decline in value due to depreciation; it only reflects the physical retirement or withdrawal of assets. It is therefore a measure of the volume of assets, which was mainly used as an indicator for cross-country comparison of capital productivity before the concept of productive capital stock was introduced.

The method of deriving gross capital stock can be described as follow. For year t, gross capital stock is obtained by summing the values of gross fixed capital formation (in constant prices) in each year, multiplied by the survival rate for the corresponding year. Repeating this process for other years yields the time series of gross capital stock. Gross capital stock can be estimated when applying the straight-line method or the present value of efficiency method. By contrast, it cannot be derived under the declining-balance method, since that method applies only an age-price function and does not make use of a retirement function.

Formally, gross capital stock in year t is expressed as:

- $$\textbf{Gross capital formation}^{\mathbf{t}}_{\mathbf{constant}} = \mathbf{GFCF}^{\mathbf{t}}_{\mathbf{constant}} \times \textbf{survival rate}^{\mathbf{0}} + \mathbf{GFCF}^{\mathbf{t-1}}_{\mathbf{constant}} \times \textbf{survival rate}^{\mathbf{1}} + \ldots + \mathbf{GFCF}^{\mathbf{0}}_{\mathbf{constant}} \times \textbf{survival rate}^{\mathbf{t}} = \textstyle\sum_{\mathbf{k=0}}^{\mathbf{t}}(\mathbf{GFCF}^{\mathbf{t-k}}_{\mathbf{constant}} \times \textbf{survival rate}^{\mathbf{k}})$$

Here, $\text{survival rate}^{\text{k}}$ denotes the probability that an asset with an age of k years is still in service in the given year. By applying this method iteratively, the gross capital stock can be calculated for each year.

Table 20.5 illustrates an example of deriving gross capital stock. The series of gross fixed capital formation is expressed in real terms, i.e., current-price value divided by appropriate deflators. The table uses the same data as in the earlier example for the present value of efficiency method (see Table 20.3), assuming a maximum service life of 16 years for fixed assets and applying the survival function (= 1− cumulative probability of retirement). For example:

- Gross capital stock in 2009: 6,862×1.0000 + 5,995×0.9980 + 6,743×0.9618 + 6,191×0.8505 +... + 6,647×0.0000 = 39,449
- Gross capital stock in 2008: 5,995×1.000 + 6,743×0.998 + 6,191×0.9618 + 6,098×0.8505 + ... + 5,532×0.000 = 39,108

Using the same method, the gross capital stock in 1994 is calculated as 27,123. If the survival function varies from year to year, then the survival rates specific to each year should be applied in the calculation.

Table 20.5 Derivation of gross capital stock (in real terms)

Year	Gross fixed capital formation (real terms, $)	Survival function	Gross capital stock (real terms, $)
2009	6,862	1.0000	39,449
2008	5,995	0.9980	39,108
2007	6,743	0.9618	39,747
2006	6,191	0.8505	39,780
2005	6,098	0.6874	40,449
2004	5,693	0.5190	41,148
2003	6,452	0.3738	42,079
2002	8,056	0.2605	42,103
2001	7,101	0.1772	40,452
2000	6,956	0.1179	39,713
1999	6,768	0.0767	38,951
1998	3,929	0.0482	37,894
1997	8,552	0.0287	39,033
1996	7,861	0.0153	34,915
1995	7,026	0.0062	30,883
1994	6,647	0.0000	27,123
1993	5,532		
1992	5,139		
1991	4,486		
1990	3,711		
1989	2,835		
1988	2,336		
1987	2,196		
1986	1,749		
1985	1,607		
1984	1,562		
1983	1,330		
1982	1,008		
1981	824		
1980	564		
1979	699		

20.3.2 Estimation of productive capital stock and costs of capital services

20.3.2.1 Productive capital stock

Productive capital stock serves as an intermediate step to measure the flows of services provided by capital. The productive capital stock (at constant prices) represents the stock of fixed assets in terms of productive efficiency rather than market value. Its estimation method is as follows.

The productive capital stock in year t (at constant prices) is obtained by summing the annual time series of gross fixed capital formation up to that year (at constant prices), each weighted by the efficiency corresponding to asset age derived from the age-efficiency function of the cohort. For other years, the productive capital stock is derived by repeating the same procedure. This calculation can be expressed as follows.

- $\mathbf{Productive\ capital\ stock^{t}_{constant}} = \mathbf{GFCF^{t}_{constant}} \times \mathbf{efficiency^{0}} + \mathbf{GFCF^{t-1}_{constant}} \times \mathbf{efficiency^{1}} + \ldots + \mathbf{GFCF^{0}_{constant}} \times \mathbf{efficiency^{t}} = \sum_{k=0}^{t}(\mathbf{GFCF^{t-k}_{constant}} \times \mathbf{efficiency^{k}})$

As an example, using the same series of gross fixed capital formation (at constant prices) and the age-efficiency function for a cohort with a maximum service life of 16 years (as given in Table 20.3.2), the productive capital stock can be derived as follows:

- Productive capital stock in 2009:

  6,862×0.911 + 5,995×0.801 + 6,743×0.666 + 6,191×0.500 + ... + 6,647×0.00 = 24,813

- Productive capital stock in 2008:

  5,995×0.911 + 6,743×0.801 + 6,191×0.660 + ... + 5,532×0.00 = 24,374

Using the same procedure, the productive capital stock in 1994 is calculated as 18,893. If the age-efficiency function varies from year to year, the efficiency function applicable to that year should be used.

Table 20.6 Derivation of productive capital stock (at constant prices)

	Gross fixed capital formation (real terms, $)	Age-efficiency function	Productive capital stock (real terms, $)
2009	6,862	0.911	24,813
2008	5,995	0.801	24,374
2007	6,743	0.660	24,805
2006	6,191	0.500	24,607
2005	6,098	0.353	25,048
2004	5,693	0.237	25,687
2003	6,452	0.154	26,766
2002	8,056	0.097	27,093
2001	7,101	0.060	25,755
2000	6,956	0.036	25,226
1999	6,768	0.021	24,800

	Gross fixed capital formation (real terms, $)	Age-efficiency function	Productive capital stock (real terms, $)
1998	3,929	0.012	24,426
1997	8,552	0.006	26,601
1996	7,861	0.003	23,950
1995	7,026	0.001	21,326
1994	6,647	0	18,893
1993	5,532		
1992	5,139		
1991	4,486		
1990	3,711		
1989	2,835		
1988	2,336		
1987	2,196		
1986	1,749		
1985	1,607		
1984	1,562		
1983	1,330		
1982	1,008		
1981	824		
1980	564		
1979	699		

The productive capital stock in year t at current prices is obtained as follows:

- $\textbf{Productive capital stock}^{t}_{\textbf{current}} = \textbf{productive capital stock}^{t}_{\textbf{constant}} \times \textbf{deflator}^{t}_{\textbf{end of period}}$

20.3.2.2 Capital services

As noted earlier, the productive capital stock is used to derive **capital services.** Capital services refer to the monetary valuation of the contribution made to production by capital that is employed in the production process during a given accounting period. They represent the cost of using capital (user cost) incurred in the process of generating value added. In the SNA, the measurement of capital services is based on the cost-of-capital approach, in which capital services are obtained as the sum of depreciation and net return to capital.

Providing capital services means that the assets concerned contribute to production through repeated and continuous use. The assets that generate such services include fixed assets (buildings and structures, machinery and equipment, intellectual property products, and cultivated biological assets) and land (which, although not subject to depreciation, provides a continuous contribution to production). Exhaustible natural resources (such as minerals and petroleum), inventories, and natural biological resources (such as natural forests and fish stocks) do not provide repeated contribution to production in the same manner as fixed assets. In this chapter, the scope of capital stock is limited to produced assets, and capital services stemming from non-produced assets are therefore excluded.

Capital services are assumed to arise in proportion to the size of the productive capital stocks[29]. In this context, capital services have an *ex-ante* interpretation, and therefore may differ from the capital income that is observed *ex-post*.

- $\textbf{Capital serives}^{t} = \textbf{productive capital stock at current prices}^{t} \times \textbf{gross rate of return}^{t}$

The gross rate of return may be specified either as an **exogenous rate**, defined as the sum of the external financing cost and the depreciation rate, minus capital gains, or as an **endogenous rate** based on the actual gross operating surplus realized in the period. The exogenous rate of return is used as a means of estimating an appropriate expected return on capital in advance. By contrast, the endogenous rate of return is consistent with the gross operating surplus (including depreciation) recorded in the national accounts and therefore has an *ex-post* interpretation.

20.3.3 Estimation of net capital stock

The net capital stock of fixed assets, measured in volume terms, is used to capture the market value of the capital held, expressed in real terms. It is derived in the following way. For example, the net capital stock in year t is obtained by multiplying the time series of annual gross fixed capital formation (at constant prices) by the age-price ratios derived from the age-price function of assets, and summing the results. The net capital stock for other years is derived by repeating this procedure. The values of the age-price function are applied according to the depreciation method adopted, such as the declining-balance method, straight-line method, or the present value of efficiency method.

- $$\textbf{Net capital stock}^{t}_{constant} = \textbf{GFCF}^{t}_{constant} \times \textbf{age price ratio}^{0} + \textbf{GFCF}^{t-1}_{constant} \times \textbf{age price ratio}^{1} + \cdots + \textbf{GFCF}^{0}_{constant} \times \textbf{age price ratio}^{t} = \sum_{k=0}^{t}(\textbf{GFCF}^{t-k}_{constant} \times \textbf{age price ratio}^{k})$$

Table 20.7 below provides an illustration of the calculation of the net capital stock (at constant and current prices). It uses the same series of gross fixed capital formation (at constant prices) as in the previous example, together with the age-price function with a maximum service life of 16 years (see Table 20.4 in the present value of efficiency method). For instance:

---

[29] This assumption is a simplified model that does not account for economies of scale and does not allow capital services to vary non-proportionally with the size of the productive capital stock. However, it is used in practice because the data required to measure such effects are difficult to obtain and because the assumption enhances international comparability.

- Net capital stock in 2009: 6,862×0.890 + 5,995×0.628 + 6,743×0.465 + ... + 6,647×0.000 = 18,101
- Net capital stock in 2008: 5,995×0.809 + 6,743×0.628 + 6,191×0.465 + ... + 5,532×0.000 = 17,677

The net capital stock at current price is derived by multiplying the net capital stock at constant prices by the relevant end-of-year deflator (with 2005 annual average = 1.0). This value reflects the market value of fixed assets at that point in time and corresponds to the amounts recorded in the balance sheet.

$$\textbf{Net capital stock}^{t}_{\textbf{current}} = \textbf{net capital stock}^{t}_{\textbf{constant}} \times \textbf{asset deflator}^{t}_{\textbf{end of year}}$$

Table 20.7 Derivation of net capital stock (at constant and current prices)

Year	Gross fixed capital formation (constant, $)	Age-price function	Net capital stock (constant, $)	Deflator (year-end)	Net capital stock (current, $)
2009	6,862	0.809	18,101	1.142	20,680
2008	5,995	0.628	17,677	1.065	18,821
2007	6,743	0.465	18,042	0.982	17,716
2006	6,191	0.326	17,769	0.991	17,612
2005	6,098	0.219	18,038	1.007	18,170
2004	5,693	0.142	18,513	0.948	17,553
2003	6,452	0.089	19,525	0.948	18,502
2002	8,056	0.055	19,978	0.957	19,125
2001	7,101	0.033	18,863	0.881	16,617
2000	6,956	0.019	18,413	0.862	15,870
1999	6,768	0.010	17,995	0.764	13,744
1998	3,929	0.005	17,651	0.699	12,343
1997	8,552	0.002	20,002	0.675	13,508
1996	7,861	0.001	18,058	0.653	11,799
1995	7,026	0.000	16,125	0.606	9,777
1994	6,647	0.000	14,357	0.593	8,510
1993	5,532			0.602	
1992	5,139			0.569	
1991	4,486			0.567	
1990	3,711			0.575	
1989	2,835			0.551	
1988	2,336			0.502	
1987	2,196			0.469	
1986	1,749			0.435	
1985	1,607			0.445	
1984	1,562			0.434	
1983	1,330			0.424	
1982	1,008			0.377	
1981	824			0.352	
1980	564			0.321	
1979	699			0.350	

The estimates presented above are based on the age-price function derived using the present value of efficiency method (Table 20.4). However, the same procedure may also be carried out using age-price functions derived under the declining-balance or straight-line methods.

Estimation of net capital stock using the declining-balance method

Table 20.8 provides an example of calculating the net capital stock by applying an age-price function based on the declining-balance method. Assuming a depreciation rate of 20 percent and an average service life of 12 years for the cohort of asset, the age-price function is derived from the declining-balance formula as $(1-0.2)^{0.5}$, $(1-0.2)^{1.5}$, ... $(1-0.2)^{11.5}$ (see column 5 of the table). For years prior to 1998, no data on gross fixed capital formation are available. Instead, the capital stock is assumed to be given as 17,534. The annual stock balance is then calculated by applying the survival rate (1 − 0.2) successively, yielding values such as 14,027, 11,222, ... , and 1,205 (refer to column 4 of the table). Then, the year-by-year net capital stock can be calculated as follows:

- Net capital stock in 2009: 6,862×0.894 + 5,995×0.716 + 6,743×0.572 + ... 3,929×0.077 + **1,205** = 28,106
- Net capital stock in 2008: 5,995×0.894 + 6,743×0.716 + 6,191×0.572 + ... + 3,929×0.096 + **1,506** =27,461

By the same procedure, the net capital stock in 1998 is obtained as 17,542.

Table 20.8 Derivation of net capital stock using the declining-balance method

Year	Age	Gross fixed capital formation (constant, $)	Capital stock before 1998 ($)	Age-price function	Net capital stock (constant, $)
2009	0.5	6,862	**1,205**	0.894	28,106
2008	1.5	5,995	**1,506**	0.716	27,461
2007	2.5	6,743	1,883	0.572	27,623
2006	3.5	6,191	2,353	0.458	26,990
2005	4.5	6,098	2,942	0.366	26,816
2004	5.5	5,693	3,677	0.293	26,702
2003	6.5	6,452	4,596	0.234	27,013r
2002	7.5	8,056	5,746	0.188	26,553
2001	8.5	7,101	7,182	0.150	24,184
2000	9.5	6,956	8,977	0.120	22,291
1999	10.5	6,768	11,222	0.096	20,087
1998	11.5	3,929	14,027	0.077	**17,542**
Before 1998			17,534		17,534

20.3.4 Comparison of gross, productive, and net capital stock

Based on the data derived using the present value of efficiency method presented in section 20.2.3, the results for gross capital stock, productive capital stock, and net capital stock can be compared as a time series, as illustrated in the graph below. In general, gross capital stock is the highest, as it only accounts for retirements (disposals) of assets. Productive capital stock is lower, as it incorporates the decline in efficiency with age. Net capital stock is the lowest, as it reflects the market value of assets through the age-price function.

Figure 20.13 Comparison of gross, productive, and net capital stock

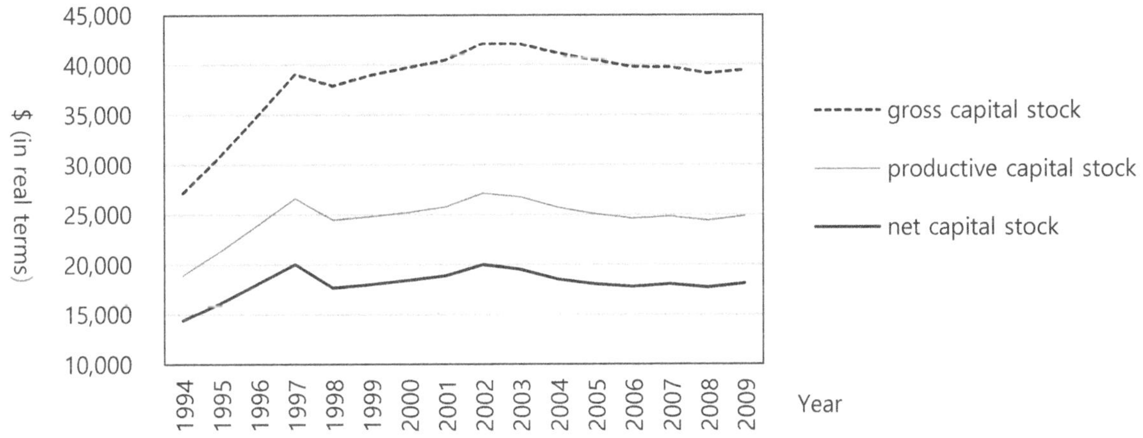

20.4 Derivation of depreciation

Depreciation is an essential component in the national accounts, as it is required for deriving net value-added, net domestic product (NDP), and net national income (NNI). According to the SNA, depreciation is defined as a forward-looking measure that reflects the decline in the value of fixed assets as they are used in production during their remaining service lives, based on the future benefits expected to be derived from them. In other words, the amount of depreciation should be determined with reference to the benefits that the assets are expected to generate over their remaining lifetime.

By contrast, depreciation in business accounting is typically calculated by allocating the historical acquisition cost of a fixed asset over its remaining service life. For this reason, it is not appropriate to use this depreciation directly as depreciation in the national accounts. The SNA therefore recommends that depreciation be estimated separately, and in particular, that it be calculated in conjunction with the *estimation of capital stock*.

This section, following this logic, explains how to calculate depreciation using the data of net capital stock and gross fixed capital formation derived above. When these data are available, depreciation can be obtained at both constant and current prices as follows:

- $\mathbf{Depreciation^{t}_{constant}} = \mathbf{net\ capital\ stock^{t-1}_{constant}} + \mathbf{GFCF^{t}_{constant}} - \mathbf{net\ capital\ stock^{t}_{constant}}$
- $\mathbf{Depreciation^{t}_{current}} = \mathbf{Depreciation^{t}_{constant}} \times \mathbf{deflator^{t}_{average\ of\ period}}$

For example, Table 20.9 shows the results of estimating depreciation using the same dataset cited in the previous example. In the case of 2009, depreciation at constant prices is calculated as 18,906 + 6,862 – 19,378 = 6,390. At current prices, this corresponds to 6,390 x 1.1876 = 7,588.

Table 20.9 Derivation of depreciation (at constant and current prices)

(Unit: $)

Year	Gross fixed capital formation (constant price)	Net capital stock (constant price)	Depreciation (constant price)	Deflator of GFCF (average of period, 2005=1)	Depreciation (current price)
2009	6,862	19,378	**6,390**	1.1876	**7,588**
2008	5,995	18,906	6,392	1.1722	7,493
2007	6,743	19,303	6,431	1.0583	6,806
2006	6,191	18,991	6,474	1.0135	6,561
2005	6,098	19,275	6,612	1.0000	6,612
2004	5,693	19,789	6,813	0.9484	6,461
2003	6,452	20,909	6,967	0.8874	6,183
2002	8,056	21,424	6,838	0.8325	5,692
2001	7,101	20,205	6,611	0.7889	5,215
2000	6,956	19,716	6,500	0.7343	4,773
1999	6,768	19,261	6,398	0.7227	4,623
1998	3,929	18,890	6,571	0.7307	4,802
1997	8,552	21,532	6,470	0.6972	4,511
1996	7,861	19,450	5,788	0.6596	3,817
1995	7,026	17,376	5,133	0.6306	3,237
1994	6,647	15,482	-	0.5917	-

Depreciation and rentals

When a producer purchases machinery and equipment for production, depreciation incurs on the production side, along with the financial cost associated with the acquisition of the asset. By contrast, if the producer rents machinery and equipment instead, **rental payments** are made. Rentals are the payments made to the owner of the asset in return for the right to use the asset for production purposes for a specified period under an operating lease or similar contract. The **rental** can be broken down into the following components:

- Direct costs incurred by the owner of the asset,
- Depreciation accruing over the rental period

- Interest costs associated with the asset.

Among these, the cost of *capital services* corresponds to the sum of depreciation and interest costs. In the input-output framework, when a producer uses leased fixed assets, the lease payments are recorded as intermediate consumption of the producer. In contrast, when the same asset is purchased and used directly in production, the corresponding depreciation and interest costs (excluding FISIM), that is, the cost of capital services, become part of the producers' gross value-added. Hence, the choice of whether to lease or purchase fixed assets will affect the gross value-added ratios of individual industries.

20.5 Summary of methods for measuring capital stocks and depreciation

The following table summarizes the methods for measuring capital stocks by type and depreciation, as discussed in the preceding sections.

Table 20.10 Summary of methods for measuring capital stocks and depreciation

Item	Derivation formula
Gross fixed capital formation (constant prices)	GFCF (current prices) / Deflator for the cohort of assets (average of period)
Retirement function	Winfrey function, lognormal distribution, Weibull function etc.,
Decay function (efficiency function for a single asset)	(Service life – age) / (Service life – β x age)
Age-efficiency function (for a cohort of assets)	∑ (Retirement probability x Efficiency rates for individual asset)
Gross capital stock (constant prices)	∑ (GFCF (constant prices) × Survival rates)
Productive capital stock (constant prices)	∑ (GFCF (constant prices) × Age-efficiency for cohort)
Productive capital stock (current prices)	Productive capital stock (constant prices) × Deflator of the relevant asset group (end of period)
Age-price function (for a cohort of assets)	1) Declining-balance method: Rate of geometric depreciation
	2) Straight-line method: Σ (straight-line depreciation rate × retirement probability)
	3) PVE method: Σ (Age-efficiency × (1+ growth rate of annual rental income)^{t}/(1+ annual discount rate)$^{t-n+1}$)
Net capital stock (constant prices)	∑ (GFCF (constant prices) × Age-price function)
Net capital stock (current prices)	Net capital stock (constant prices) × Deflator for the relevant asset group (end of period)
Depreciation (constant prices)	Beginning net capital stock (constant prices) + GFCF (constant prices) – Closing net capital stock (constant prices)

Item	Derivation formula
Depreciation (current prices)	Depreciation (constant prices) × Deflator for the relevant asset group (average of period)
Capital services (capital income)	Productive capital stock (current prices) × Gross rate of return to capital

Chapter 21. Transformation of the supply and use tables into input-output tables

21.1 Introduction

The primary purpose of compiling supply and use tables (**SUTs**) is to provide the basic data for the production account and, more broadly the sequence of economic accounts. There is, however, another important use: by applying a small set of matrix operations, SUTs can be converted into input-output tables (**IOTs**). The input-output table presents, in matrix form, the input and demand structure by product (or by industry). In most cases, IOTs are derived from SUTs, although a few countries still compile them directly. Manuals published by international organizations, however, recommend deriving input-output tables indirectly from SUTs rather than compiling them directly. The reason for this is that, as the production structure becomes more complex, it is difficult to obtain establishment-level data on the input structure for each individual product, and that the conversion methods based on matrix algebra are both verifiable and more convenient for compiling IOTs.

Unlike SUTs, IOTs can be manipulated explicitly with matrix equations, making it a versatile tool in economic analysis. It can be used to study the cost input structure and output structure of a given economy, as well as to estimate the ripple (multiplier) effects of changes in economic variables. This chapter will explain in detail how to convert SUTs into IOTs.

In general, the **supply table** is prepared on the premise that a single **establishment** (**industry**) may produce multiple products. Therefore, the column for a given industry in the supply table can contain several different products. By contrast, the IOT assumes that an establishment (or industry) produces a single product at a single site and records the input costs associated with that specific product. Therefore, if an establishment produces multiple products, the costs that are incurred must be separated and allocated to each product. In other words, the IOT corresponds to the "use table that would be obtained if the supply table were reconstructed so that products are produced only at the matrix's main diagonal" (i.e., only principal products are recorded on the main diagonal of the supply table).

Within a single establishment, in addition to the principal (or primary) product, there may also be secondary products. For example, a slaughterhouse produces meat as its principal product, but may also produce hides and bones as secondary products. In order to compile an IOT, one must reassign these secondary products to the industries where they are produced as principal products.

Concretely, in the supply table, only the principal product of each industry is retained, and any secondary products are transferred to the industries for which those products are principal. At the same time, in the use table, the input costs and value added incurred in producing those secondary products are moved to the industries that produce them as principal products. As a result of this procedure, the supply table shows that each industry produces only one principal product, and the corresponding amounts appear solely on the main diagonal of the table. **The Input-output table can thus be regarded as the use table adjusted for input costs and value added on the premise that products appear only on the main diagonal of the supply table**.

Types of secondary products

Within a single establishment, secondary products can arise in addition to the principal product. These secondary products may be broadly classified into subsidiary products, joint-products, and by-products.

- **Subsidiary products** are goods or services produced together with the principal product at the same establishment but are not technologically related to the principal product. They are often produced as a way to utilize excess capacity or to generate additional revenue from existing resources. Examples include a manufacturing plant that also operates retail or wholesale sales of its own products, or a retailer that uses its delivery vehicles for transporting its goods and also offers those vehicles for other transport services.

- **Joint-products** are those that are produced simultaneously with the principal product and cannot be considered by-products in terms of the production process or their monetary or quantitative value. They are intended to be produced from the point when raw materials are input and are sold as separate finished products. Examples include diesel, fuel oil, and gasoline obtained in petroleum refining, and cheese, cream, and butter produced in milk processing.

- **By-products** are products that were not intended but arise incidentally alongside the principal product during the production process. Examples include rice bran generated in the milling of harvested rice and whey produced in cheese manufacturing. However, some by-products may be recycled or further processed into other products. Note that among by-products, there are items not classified as products in the product classification such as scrap metal, waste paper, and waste plastics. These can be treated under a separate **residual waste** item for compilation purposes.

Square-matrix structure and the Leontief multiplier

When secondary products are removed from the supply table, only principal products remain; based on this adjusted supply table, the use table is revised and the input-output table (IOT) is compiled. The supply table that results from eliminating secondary products becomes a matrix with the same number of rows and columns, and accordingly the intermediate input quadrant of the IOT also takes the form of a square matrix. The reason for imposing a square structure is that it enables a wide range of analyses using matrix algebra. For example, under the assumption that the cost (input) structure of a product and its demand structure are unchanged, one can predict the ripple effects of a change in demand for a particular product on the whole economy. The key tool for this calculation is the **Leontief multiplier** (**Leontief inverse**).

Let X denote the vector of domestic output, A the matrix of input coefficients for domestic output ($0<A<1$), and Y final demand (final use). Then, the accounting identity for domestic output can be written as

$$AX + Y = X$$

Which can be rearranged to

$$(I - A)\,X = Y$$

and thus

$$X = (I - A)^{-1}\,Y$$

In other words, if final demand increases by ΔY, domestic output changes by

$$\boldsymbol{\Delta X = (I - A)^{-1}\,\Delta Y}$$

Here, the matrix $(I - A)^{-1}$ is known as the **Leontief multiplier** (**Leontief inverse**), which serves the fundamental instrument for analyzing economic effects with an IOT. To make use of this matrix formulation, the IOT must be square, because an inverse matrix can only be calculated in a square matrix structure.

21.2 Converting supply and use tables to input-output tables

The methods for compiling an input-output table (IOT) can be divided into two broad approaches. One, as noted earlier, is to transform IOTs form existing supply and use tables (SUTs); the other is to compile IOTs directly by aggregating and processing primary survey data. Countries that follow the latter approach generally do so because they had a long-standing practice of compiling IOTs before the SUT framework was introduced. In contrast, the UN and Eurostat manuals, assuming that statistical offices can now compile SUTs on a regular basis, recommend transforming IOTs from SUTs. This recommendation reflects the advantages of using a common data foundation, the verifiability of the matrix-based transformation, and the more efficient use of resources. Consistent with this guidance, the present chapter explains the compilation methodology of IOTs **on the basis of the conversion method of IOTs using SUTs**.

21.2.1 Principles for constructing transformation tables

There are two methods for converting the supply and use tables into input-output tables. One method is to compile a **product-by-product table**, which is the conventional IOT format used for product-centered analysis; and the other is to compile an **industry-by-industry table**.

The former converts the structure of the supply and use tables, in which rows are classified by products and columns by industries, into a product-by-product format by rearranging the data recorded in the industry columns into product columns. The latter converts the supply and use tables into an industry-by-industry format by rearranging the data in the product rows into industry rows. The following subsections describe each of these conversion methods in turn.

21.2.1.1 Transformation to a product-by-product input-output table

An input-output table in which both rows and columns consist of products is traditionally the format most widely used for input-output analysis at the product level. The method for compiling a product-by-product input-output table is to retain the products shown in the rows of SUTs and to convert the industries shown in the columns into products.

The transformation process first involves identifying, in the supply table, the multiple products produced by each industry (column) and extracting all outputs other than the principal product (that is, secondary products), which are then reallocated to the columns of the industries that produce those products as principal products. After this reallocation, the supply table is transformed into a diagonal product-by-product matrix in which only principal products are recorded in both rows and columns. In parallel, in the use table, the intermediate inputs and value added attributable to the secondary products in each industry (column) are extracted and reallocated to the columns of the industries that produce those products as principal products. As a result, a product-by-product use table, that is, a **product-by-product input-output table**, is obtained.

Let's illustrate this process with an example in Figure 21.1. Suppose that, in the supply table, agriculture industry produces agricultural products (50); manufacturing industry produces agricultural products (5), manufactured products (100), and services (10); and service industry produces services (70) in the supply table. The treatment in this case is as follows: from the manufacturing industry column, move agricultural products (5, secondary for manufacturing) to the agriculture industry column, and move services (10) to the service industry column. The supply table then becomes a diagonal matrix with agricultural products (55), manufactured products (100), and services (80) on the main diagonal. Correspondingly, in the use table, the intermediate inputs and value added in the manufacturing industry column must be reallocated between the agriculture and service industry columns in line with the amounts transferred in the supply table. There are two possible methods for this adjustment. One method is to **allocate according to the technology of the original producing industry**, whereby, on the basis of the total intermediate consumption and value added of the manufacturing column, a proportion of 5/115 is transferred to the agriculture column and a proportion of 10/115 is transferred to the services column. The other method is to **apply the technology of the receiving industries**, whereby an amount equal to 5/50 of the agriculture column is extracted from the manufacturing column and added to the agriculture column, and an amount equal to 10/70 of the services column is extracted from the manufacturing column and added to the services column. Whichever method is used, provided that the adjustments to intermediate consumption and value added in the use table are consistent with the adjustments made in the supply table, a **product-by-product** input-output table can be ultimately be obtained.

Figure 21.1 Construction of a product-by-product table

Supply table

	Agriculture industry	Manufacturing industry	Service industry	Total supply
Agricultural product	50 ←	(5)		55
Manufactured product		100		100
Services		(10)	→ 70	80
Total	50	115	70	235

⇩

	Agriculture industry	Manufacturing industry	Service industry	Total supply
Agricultural product	55			55
Manufactured product		100		100
Services			80	80
Total	55	100	80	235

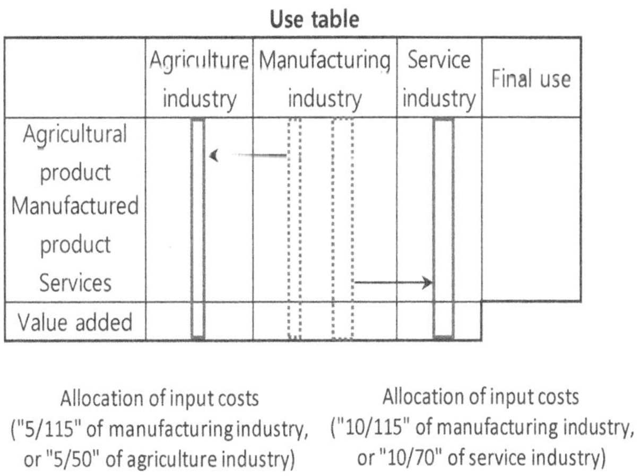

21.2.1.2 Transformation to an industry-by-industry input-output table

A method for compiling an input-output table in which both the rows and columns are classified by industries is to retain the industries shown as columns in the supply and use tables and to convert the products shown in the rows into industries. Under this approach, all products produced by a given industry (rows) are aggregated as that industry's output and allocated to the corresponding industry row. This industry-by-industry input-output table is particularly useful when a single establishment produces both a principal product and secondary products, because it presents those outputs at the industry level.

The conversion procedure first involves, in the supply table, reallocating the secondary products recorded under each industry column to the row of that industry's principal product and adding them to that industry's output. After this reallocation, the supply table is transformed into an industry-by-industry diagonal matrix in which the output of each industry is concentrated in its own industry row. In parallel, in the use table, the amounts of intermediate use and final use recorded in the rows of secondary-products are extracted and reallocated to the principal-product row of the corresponding industry.

In practice there are two alternative methods for carrying out this reallocation. One method is to transfer the amounts to the principal product row of the industry by applying allocation ratios **based on the shares of the original product rows in which the secondary products were recorded**. The other method is to calculate expansion factors **based on the scale of the receiving side (the principal product row)** and to extract corresponding amounts from the secondary product rows and add them to the principal product row.

Whichever of these two allocation rules is applied, as long as the adjustments in the use table are made consistently with the reassignments in the supply table, that result is an **industry-by-industry input-output table**.

To illustrate this process, consider the following example in Figure 21.2. Suppose that, in the supply table, agricultural products are supplied by agriculture industry (50); manufactured products are supplied by agriculture industry (30), manufacturing industry (100), and service industry (20); and services are supplied by service industry (70). In this case, the procedure is to move manufactured products (30) recorded under agriculture industry to the principal product row of agriculture (the agricultural products row), and to move manufactured products (20) recorded under service industry to the principal product row of the services industry (the services row). After this reallocation, the supply table becomes a diagonal matrix with values of 80 in the agriculture row, 100 in the manufacturing row, and 90 in the services row respectively.

Correspondingly, in the use table, the amounts of intermediate use and final use recorded in the manufactured products row must be split and reallocated to the agricultural products row and the services row. One method for doing so is to transfer proportions of 30/150 of that row to the agricultural products row and 20/150 to the services row, based on the total amount recorded in the manufactured products row. The alternative method is to base the reallocation on the scale of the receiving side, by extracting an amount equal to 30/50 of the agricultural products row from the manufactured products row and adding it to the agricultural products row, and extracting an amount equal to 20/70 of the services row from the manufactured products row and adding it to the services row. Once these reallocations have been completed, both the supply table and the use table are aligned on an industry basis, yielding an **industry-by-industry input-output table**.

Figure 21.2 Construction of an industry-by-industry table

Supply table

	Agriculture industry	Manufacturing industry	Service industry	Total supply
Agricultural product	50			50
Manufactured product	30	100	20	150
Services			70	70
Total	80	100	90	270

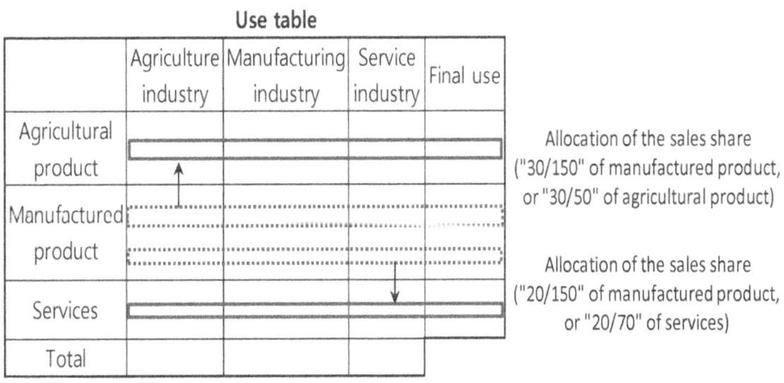

⇩

	Agriculture industry	Manufacturing industry	Service industry	Total supply
Agricultural product	80			80
Manufactured product		100		100
Services			90	90
Total	80	100	90	270

21.2.1.3 Clarifying the terminology of the input-output table

Even when the supply and use tables are transformed, by adjusting columns and rows as describe above, into a product-by-product IOT or an industry-by-industry IOT, the result is not a perfect conversion in the strict, physical-technology sense. For example, what appears to be a conversion of a product-by-industry use table into product-by-product table is, in practice, an adjustment in which the industry columns are re-expressed as product columns under technology assumptions. The defining characteristics of the industry as the production unit do not entirely disappear. Therefore, in a strict sense, the outcome is better described as **product by product-**

adjusted industry rather than a pure product-by-product table. By the same token, when a product-by-industry use table is reshaped into an industry-by-industry table using the fixed sales structure assumption, this does not mean that the characteristics of the product embodied in the rows are eliminated. A more precise term would be **industry-adjusted product by industry**, rather than a pure industry-by-industry table.

Nevertheless, both in practice and in the literature, the traditional terms **product-by-product** and **industry-by-industry** are still used due to their wide spread adoption and ease of understanding (See Box 12.1 in the SUTs and IOTs manual (UN), 2018).

21.2.2 Examples of constructing transformation tables

This example illustrates, with concrete examples based on the supply and use tables, how to transform the data into product by product and industry by industry IOTs.

21.2.2.1 Constructing product-by-product IOTs

Consider the simplified data in Table 21.1. In the supply table, suppose that agriculture industry produces agricultural products (90) as its principal product and manufactured products (10) as secondary products, while manufacturing industry produces manufactured products (300). For this production, the use table assumes that the agriculture industry uses manufactured products (60) as intermediate inputs and generates value added (40); the manufacturing industry uses agricultural products (80) and manufactured products (150) as intermediate inputs, and generates value added (70). The **input coefficient table**, which represents the proportion of intermediate inputs and value-added to the output of each industry computed from the use table, can be shown on the right-hand side of Table 21.1.

Table 21.1 Basic data for the SUT-to-IOT transformation

	Supply table			Use table			
Industry / Product	Agriculture	Manufacturing	Total supply	Agriculture	Manufacturing	Final use	Total use
Agricultural product	90	0	90	0	80	10	90
Manufactured product	10	300	310	60	150	100	310
Value added				40	70		110
Total output	100	300	400	100	300	110	

	Input coefficients of the use table			
Industry / Product	Agriculture (a)	Manufacturing (b)	Final use	Total use
Agricultural product	0.00	0.27		
Manufactured product	0.60	0.50		
Value added	0.40	0.23		
Total output	1.00	1.00		

Reference: Eurostat manual of SUTs and IOTs (2008), Box 11.6

Under the setting of Table 21.1, to obtain a product-by-product IOT, first make the **diagonal structure of the supply table** by allocating every secondary product to the industry that produces it as a principal product. In the above example, manufactured product (10) recorded in the agriculture industry column is a secondary product; move it to the manufacturing industry column, which yields a diagonal supply structure. To maintain consistency, perform a matching adjustment in the use table: transfer from the agriculture column to the manufacturing industry column the portions of intermediate inputs and value-added that correspond to manufactured product (10).

There are two possible ways to allocate these intermediate inputs and value-added in the use table. The first method is to compute the proportion of 10 in the input structure of the manufacturing industry column (that is, "10/300", or "the manufacturing input-coefficient column (b) x 10"), extract this value from the agriculture industry column, and add it to the manufacturing industry column. This method is intuitive but, because one subtracts amounts from the agriculture column based on another industry's structure, it can generate negative entries in the agriculture column during the extraction process. The second method is to compute the proportion of 10 in the input structure of the agriculture industry column (that is, "10/100", or "the agriculture input-coefficient column (a) x 10"), extract this value from the agriculture industry column, and add it to the manufacturing industry column. The former method is called the treatment by the **product technology assumption (PTA)**, and the latter method is called the treatment by the **industry technology assumption (ITA)**.

According to the PTA, the proportion of intermediate inputs and value-added of the secondary products in the use table are calculated from the input structure of the industry that produces these secondary products as principal products (that is, manufacturing industry), regardless of the industry where the secondary products actually occur (agriculture industry), and these amounts are extracted from the industry (that is, agriculture industry) that produces the secondary products and added to the manufacturing industry. On the other hand, according to the ITA, the proportion of intermediate inputs and value-added of the secondary products in the use table are extracted from the input structure of the industry where the secondary products are generated (that is, agriculture industry), and added to the industry (manufacturing industry) where these secondary products are classified as principal product.

The intermediate ("transfer-only") stage and the final, fully adjusted tables under these two assumptions are presented in Table 21.2 (PTA) and Table 21.3 (ITA). In both cases, once the supply table has been made diagonal, the use table is adjusted correspondingly, and the result is a product-by-product input-output table.

Table 21.2 Matrix transformations under the product technology assumption

	Supply table			Use table			
	Agriculture	Manufacturing	Total supply	Agriculture	Manufacturing	Final use	Total use
Agricultural product	0	0	0	-2.7	2.7		0
Manufactured product	-10	10	0	-5	5		0
Value added				-2.3	2.3		0
Total output	-10	10	0	-10	10		

⇩

	Supply table			Use table			
	Agriculture	Manufacturing	Total supply	Agriculture	Manufacturing	Final use	Total use
Agricultural product	90	0	90	-2.7	82.7	10	90
Manufactured product	0	310	310	55	155	100	310
Value added				37.7	72.3		110
Total output	90	310	400	90	310	110	

Table 21.3 Matrix transformations under the industry technology assumption

	Supply table			Use table			
	Agriculture	Manufacturing	Total supply	Agriculture	Manufacturing	Final use	Total use
Agricultural product	0	0	0	0.0	0.0		0
Manufactured product	-10	10	0	-6.0	6.0		0
Value added				-4.0	4.0		0
Total output	-10	10	0	-10	10		

⇩

	Supply table			Use table			
	Agriculture	Manufacturing	Total supply	Agriculture	Manufacturing	Final use	Total use
Agricultural product	90	0	90	0	80	10	90
Manufactured product	0	310	310	54	156	100	310
Value added				36	74		110
Total output	90	310	400	90	310	110	

After these transformations, the **column totals** (industry outputs) are rearranged from industry totals to product totals, and they match the **row totals** by product in both the supply table and the use table (under the usual assumption of no imports in this presentation. In the example, industry outputs of agriculture 100 and manufacturing 300 are rearranged to product outputs of agricultural products 90 and manufactured product 310.

Which assumption, PTA or ITA, is more appropriate depends on the nature of the secondary products. When the secondary product differs substantially in character from the principal product, PTA can be more persuasive. By contrast, for joint-products or by-products that are tightly linked in the same process, ITA may be more realistic. In general, because many analysts view products as having their own characteristic input structures, PTA is often conceptually appealing; however, PTA can produce negative entries in the process of extracting the amounts of intermediate inputs from the industry where the secondary products are produced. On the other hand, ITA does not generate negative entries and can be applied even when the use table is not a square matrix, which makes it attractive in practical implementations.

21.2.2.2 Constructing industry-by-industry IOTs

The process of deriving the industry-by-industry IOTs is also presented with the same figures as in the previous example. To construct this table, it is necessary to derive the **output (distribution) coefficients** instead of the input coefficients from the use table. This table consists of the ratios obtained by dividing, for each product row, intermediate use and final use by that product's total use (row total); in other words, it presents horizontal shares whose row sums equal one. The resulting coefficients show, horizontally, how the product's total use is distributed between intermediate use by industries and final use. For example, in Table 21.4, if the row for agricultural products has shares (0.00, 0.89, 0.11), this means that 0.89 of the row total for agricultural product is allocated to manufacturing industry's intermediate use and 0.11 to final use.

Table 21.4 Basic data for the SUT-to-IOT transformation

	Supply table			Use table			
	Agriculture	Manufacturing	Total supply	Agriculture	Manufacturing	Final use	Total use
Agricultural product	90	0	90	0	80	10	90
Manufactured product	10	300	310	60	150	100	310
Value added				40	70		110
Total output	100	300	400	100	300	110	

Output coefficients of the use table				
	Agriculture	Manufacturing	Final use	Total use
Agricultural product (A)	0.00	0.89	0.11	1.0
Manufactured product (B)	0.19	0.48	0.32	1.0
Value added	0.36	0.64		1.0
Total output				

Under this set-up, manufactured product (10), which is a secondary output in agriculture industry, is added to the agricultural product (90) to create a diagonal matrix for agriculture industry (100) and manufacturing industry (300) in the supply table. To keep the system consistent, the use table must be adjusted in parallel: the amounts of intermediate use and final use, equivalent to manufactured product row (10) must be moved to the agricultural product row. There are two practical ways to compute these transfers.

The first method is to calculate the proportion of 10 from the distribution structure of the agricultural product row which corresponds to the principal product (that is, 10/90, or "row A x 10" in the output coefficients of the use table), and extract these values from the manufactured product row and add them to the agricultural product row. This method may result in negative entries in the manufactured product row since the values calculated from the agricultural product row is subtracted from the manufactured product row (see Table 21.5). The second method is to calculate the proportion of 10 from the distribution structure of manufactured products row that correspond to the secondary product row of agriculture industry (that is, 10/310, or "row B x10" in the output coefficients in the use table), and extract these values from the manufactured product row, and add them to the agricultural product row (see Table 21.6). The former method is called the treatment by the **fixed industry sales structure assumption (FISS)**, and the latter method is called the treatment by the **fixed product sales structure assumption (FPSS)**. Under FISS, the distribution pattern of the receiving row (here, the agricultural product row) is used to determine the transfer. Under FPSS, the distribution pattern of the sending row (the manufactured product row) is used to determine the transfer.

Table 21.5 Matrix transformations under the fixed industry sales structure assumption

	Supply table			Use table			
	Agriculture	Manufacturing	Total supply	Agriculture	Manufacturing	Final use	Total use
Agricultural product	10	0	10	0.0	8.9	1.1	10.0
Manufactured product	-10	0	-10	0.0	-8.9	-1.1	-10.0
Value added							
Total output	0	0	0				

⇩

	Supply table			Use table			
	Agriculture	Manufacturing	Total supply	Agriculture	Manufacturing	Final use	Total use
Agricultural product	100	0	100	0.0	88.9	11.1	100.0
Manufactured product	0	300	300	60.0	141.1	98.9	300.0
Value added				40.0	70.0		110
Total output	100	300	400	100	300	110	

Table 21.6 Matrix transformations under the fixed product sales structure assumption

	Supply table			Use table			
	Agriculture	Manufacturing	Total supply	Agriculture	Manufacturing	Final use	Total use
Agricultural product	10	0	10	1.9	4.8	3.2	10.0
Manufactured product	-10	0	-10	-1.9	-4.8	-3.2	-10.0
Value added							
Total output	0	0	0				

⇩

	Supply table			Use table			
	Agriculture	Manufacturing	Total supply	Agriculture	Manufacturing	Final use	Total use
Agricultural product	100	0	100	1.9	84.8	13.2	100.0
Manufactured product	0	300	300	58.1	145.2	96.8	300.0
Value added				40.0	70.0		110
Total output	100	300	400	100	300	110	

Once the transfers and reallocations are completed, both the supply and use tables display industry-based structures. Consequently, row totals (supply and use totals) are rearranged from product totals to industry totals, while consistency with column totals (industry outputs) is preserved. In this example, agricultural product row changes from 90 to 100, and the manufactured product row from 310 to 300, reflecting the reallocation of the secondary output (manufactured product 10).

21.3 Practical procedures for deriving input-output tables

In the previous section, the principles of deriving input-output tables were explained. However, it would be too cumbersome and time-consuming to apply them step by step through the logical processes. In operational work, the same logic is condensed into matrix formulas that permit a more compact derivation.

As noted earlier, product-by-product IOTs are compiled under one of two technological assumptions: product technology assumption (PTA) and industry technology assumption (ITA). Similarly, industry-by-industry IOTs are compiled under one of two sales structure assumptions: fixed industry sales structure assumption (FISS) and fixed product sales structure assumption (FPSS). This section will delve into the practical derivation method of IOTs using matrix formulas for each of these four assumptions from the supply and use tables, employing concrete examples to illustrate the process. Additionally, a technical approach to eliminate negative cell entries that may arise when applying the product technology assumption. Finally, beyond matrix-based techniques, a brief note is provided on a compilation alternative based on manual adjustments, specifically re-definition process, that can also be used to correct negative cell values.

21.3.1 Compilation of product-by-product IOTs under the product technology assumption

For expositional simplicity, assume a **supply matrix**[30] (hereafter denoted by **S**) with three industries and three products, and a **use matrix** (hereafter denoted by **U**) with corresponding intermediate inputs and value-added, as shown in the shade area of Table 21.7. The supply matrix excludes the imports column, and the use matrix likewise excludes the final use column. The final use column (e) represents net final use (= final use – imports). In these tables, **q** is the column

[30] The supply matrix is represented as the transposed matrix of the "**make matrix**" in the 1968 SNA, notated by "V^T" (the transposed matrix of V).

vector of domestic output by product, and $\mathbf{g}^{\mathbf{T}}$ represents the row vector (i.e., the transpose of the column vector $\mathbf{g}$) of domestic output by industry.

Table 21.7 Basic data of the supply and use tables

Supply table / Supply matrix (S)

	Industry			Total supply (q)
Product	45	20	0	65
	5	150	0	155
	0	0	90	90
Total output (g^T)	50	170	90	310

Use table / Use matrix (U)

	Industry			Total intermediate use	Net final use (e)	Total use (q)
Product	10	13	5	28	37	65
	12	102	26	140	15	155
	6	8	21	35	55	90
Total intermediate input	28	123	52	203	107	310
Value added (y^T)	22	47	38	107		
Total input (g^T)	50	170	90	310		

* Note: Symbols and notations of the supply and use tables follow the 1968 SNA conventions (see Appendix to Chapter 21).

Based on these data, the set of basic matrices in Table 21.8 is first created. In this table, the matrices B, C, C^{-1}, and D are repeatedly used in converting SUTs into IOTs.

- $\mathbf{B} = \mathbf{U}\,\hat{\mathbf{g}}^{-1}$: the input coefficients matrix by industry derived from the use table, which shows share of intermediate inputs and value-added per unit of industry output.
- $\mathbf{C} = \mathbf{S}\,\hat{\mathbf{g}}^{-1}$: the "product-mix matrix" by industry derived from the supply table, which shows the composition of products produced by each industry.
- $\mathbf{C}^{-1} = \hat{\mathbf{g}}\,\mathbf{S}^{-1}$: the inverse of C.
- $\mathbf{D} = \mathbf{S}^{\mathrm{T}}\,\hat{\mathbf{q}}^{-1}$: the "market share matrix" by product derived from the transposed supply table, which shows shares of industries producing each product.

Here, $\hat{\mathrm{g}}$ and $\hat{\mathrm{q}}$ are the diagonal matrices formed from g and q respectively, and $\hat{\mathrm{g}}^{-1}$, $\hat{\mathrm{q}}^{-1}$ are their inverses.

Table 21.8 Building blocks for the SUT-to-IOT transformation

Supply matrix (S)

45	20	0
5	150	0
0	0	90

Use matrix (U)

10	13	5
12	102	26
6	8	21
28	123	52
22	47	38
50	170	90

Final use (e)

37
15
55
107

$\hat{g}$ (Diagonal matrix of g)

50	0	0
0	170	0
0	0	90

$\hat{g}^{-1}$ (Inverse matrix of $\hat{g}$)

0.020	0	0
0	0.006	0
0	0	0.011

S^T (Transposed matrix of S)

45	5	0
20	150	0
0	0	90

$\hat{q}$ (Diagonal matrix of q)

65	0	0
0	155	0
0	0	90

$\hat{q}^{-1}$ (Inverse matrix of $\hat{q}$)

0.0154	0	0
0	0.0065	0
0	0	0.0111

$B = U\hat{g}^{-1}$

0.200	0.076	0.056
0.240	0.600	0.289
0.120	0.047	0.233
0.560	0.724	0.578
0.440	0.276	0.422
1.000	1.000	1.000

$C = S\hat{g}^{-1}$

0.900	0.118	0
0.100	0.882	0
0	0	1

$C^{-1} = \hat{g}\, S^{-1}$

1.128	-0.150	0
-0.128	1.150	0
0	0	1

$D = S^T\hat{q}^{-1}$

0.692	0.032	0
0.308	0.968	0
0	0	1

With these in place, the product-by-product IOT under the product technology assumption is obtained as follows. (Refer to Annex to Chapter 21 for the algebraic derivations.) First, the input coefficients matrix (B) from the use table is multiplied by the inverse of the product-mix matrix (C^{-1}) from the supply table to obtain the **product-based coefficient matrix A** (covering both intermediate inputs and value-added) (equation 21.1). This equation corresponds to the use matrix multiplied by the inverse of the supply matrix.

(21.1) **Coefficient matrix of intermediate inputs and value-added:** $A = B\,C^{-1} = (U\hat{g}^{-1})(\hat{g}S^{-1}) = U\,S^{-1}$

Next, convert these coefficients into values by multiplying by the diagonal matrix ($\hat{q}$) of product totals (domestic supply by product, excluding imports) (equation 21.2).

(21.2) **Value matrix of intermediate inputs and value-added:** $A\,\hat{q} = B\,C^{-1}\,\hat{q} = (U\,S^{-1})\,\hat{q}$

For the final use of the product-by-product IOTs under the product technology assumption, apply the final use vector from the use table without any modifications, since it is already expressed on a product basis (net of imports).

- **Final use in the IOT = e (from the use table)**

Properties and implications

Two features should be noted. First, as seen in equation 21.1, the computation requires the inverse S^{-1}. This implies that the supply matrix (S) must be square (the numbers of products and industries must be equal) for the inverse to be calculated and for the PTA-based product-by-product table to be compiled. Second, the resulting intermediate input matrix can contain negative cell entries. Under the product technology assumption, the intermediate inputs and value-added of secondary products are not directly subtracted from the industry where the secondary products are produced, but are estimated and subtracted from the industry where the secondary products are produced as a principal product. These negative values in the cells are not economically interpretable, so it requires a modification procedure to adjust these negative values to non-negative values.

As a result of applying the above formulas, the product-by-product IOTs based on the product technology assumption is derived as follows in Table 21.9. The left panel presents the input coefficient matrix BC^{-1}; the center panel presents the value matrix $BC^{-1}\hat{q}$ (intermediate input plus value added, in value terms); and the right panel shows the final use vector e. From these blocks one obtains intermediate inputs, value added, and total output by products.

Table 21.9 Derivation of input-output tables under the product technology assumption

Coefficient matrix of inputs (BC^{-1})

	(Product)		
(Product)	0.216	0.058	0.056
	0.194	0.654	0.289
	0.129	0.036	0.233
Total intermediate input	0.539	0.748	0.578
Value added	0.461	0.252	0.422
Total output	1	1	1

Value matrix of inputs ($BC^{-1}\hat{q}$)

	(Product)		
(Product)	14.03	8.97	5.00
	12.61	101.39	26.00
	8.41	5.59	21.00
Total intermediate input	35.04	115.96	52.00
Value added	29.96	39.04	38.00
Total output (q^T)	65	155	90

Final use (e)

Final use	**Total use (q)**
37	65
15	155
55	90
107	310

21.3.2 Compilation of product-by-product IOTs under the industry technology assumption

The process of deriving the input-output table under the industry technology assumption is made in the following way, based on the same data of use matrix (U) and supply matrix (S) introduced in the previous subsection (see Table 21.7 and 21.8). The algebraic derivation of the formula is given in the Annex to Chapter 21. Operationally, proceed as follows. First, multiply the input-coefficient matrix by industry derived from the use table, $B = U\hat{g}^{-1}$ by the market-share matrix by product derived from the transposed supply table, $D = S^{T}\hat{q}^{-1}$. This yields, under the industry technology assumption (ITA), the **product-by-product coefficient matrix A** for intermediate inputs and value-added (equation 21.3):

(21.3) **Coefficient matrix of intermediate inputs and value-added:** $\mathbf{A = BD = (U\hat{g}^{-1})(S^{T}\hat{q}^{-1})}$

Next, the "intermediate input and value-added matrix" of the product-by-product IOTs (in value terms) are derived by multiplying A by the diagonal matrix of total domestic supply by product (imports excluded), $\hat{q}$. Because $D\hat{q} = (S^{T}\hat{q}^{-1})\hat{q} = S^{I}$, the expression simplifies as in equation (21.4):

(21.4) **Value matrix of intermediate inputs and value-added:** $\mathbf{A\hat{q} = BD\hat{q} = (U\hat{g}^{-1})S^{T}}$

For the final use of the product-by-product IOTs under the product technology assumption, use the final use vector from the use table without any modifications, since it is already on a product basis (net of imports).

- **Final use in the IOT = e (from the use table)**

Properties and implications

Two observations follow from this construction. First, the resulting intermediate-input matrix does not generate negative (-) entries. Under the industry technology assumption, the intermediate inputs and value-added associated with secondary products are estimated directly using the technology of the industries where those secondary products are actually produced, and are deducted there, avoiding negative cells. Second, because equations (21.3) and (21.4) do not require S^{-1}, the supply matrix need not be square when deriving the input-output table. However, since the number of industries (columns in S) is often smaller than the number of products (rows), so the derived product-by-product matrix will have a number of columns equal to the number of products, which may exceed the number of industries in the original supply table.

Applying formulas (21.3) and (21.4) yields the product-by-product IOTs based on the industry technology assumption (Table 21.10). The left panel shows the input coefficient matrix BD; the center panel shows the value matrix $BD\hat{q} = (U\hat{g}^{-1})S^T$; and the right panel shows the final use vector e. From these blocks, one obtains intermediate inputs, value added, and total output by products.

Table 21.10 Derivation of input-output tables under the industry technology assumption

Coefficient matrix of inputs (BD)

	(Product)		
(Product)	0.162	0.080	0.056
	0.351	0.588	0.289
	0.098	0.049	0.233
Total intermediate input	0.610	0.718	0.578
Value added	0.390	0.282	0.422
Total output	1	1	1

Value matrix of inputs (BD$\hat{q}$)

	(Product)		
(Product)	10.53	12.47	5.00
	22.80	91.20	26.00
	6.34	7.66	21.00
Total intermediate input	39.67	111.33	52.00
Value added	25.33	43.67	38.00
Total output (q^T)	65	155	90

Final use vector (e)

Final use	Total use (q)
37	65
15	155
55	90
107	310

21.3.3 Compilation of industry-by-industry IOTs under the fixed industry sales structure assumption

Under the fixed industry sales structure assumption, the input-output table is derived, based on the same supply matrix (S) and use matrix (U) data used in the technology assumption (Tables 21.7 and 21.8). The algebraic derivation of the formulas is summarized below (see the Annex to Chapter 21 for details).

Operationally, let $B = U\hat{g}^{-1}$ denote the intermediate input coefficient matrix by industry derived from the use table, $C = S\,\hat{g}^{-1}$ denote the product-mix matrix by industry derived from the supply table, and $C^{-1} = \hat{g}\,S^{-1}$ denote its inverse. The **coefficient matrix of intermediate inputs (A)** of the industry-by-industry IOT under the fixed industry sales structure assumption is derived as follows:

(21.5) **Coefficient matrix of intermediate inputs:** $\mathbf{A = C^{-1} B = (\hat{g}\,S^{-1})(U\hat{g}^{-1})}$

Expressing intermediate inputs in value terms follows by multiplying by $\hat{g}$ (the diagonal matrix of industry outputs). Noting that $U = B\,\hat{g}$,

(21.6) **Value matrix of intermediate inputs (value terms of A):** $\mathbf{A\hat{g} = C^{-1} B\hat{g} = (\hat{g}\,S^{-1})\,U}$

The value-added sector of the industry-by-industry" IOTs is compiled on an industry basis and is therefore taken directly from the use table without modifications:

- **Value-added in the IOT = y^T (from the use table)**

Because the matrix in (21.6) is in a form of industry-by-industry, the final use, which is observed on a product basis in the use table, must be converted to an industry basis. The conversion is made by multiplying the net final use vector (e) of the use table by C^{-1}:

- **Final use in the IOT = C^{-1} e = $(\hat{g}\,S^{-1})$ e**

Properties and implications

Two practical implications deserve emphasis. First, as evident in equation 21.5, computation of C^{-1} requires S^{-1}; hence the supply matrix must be square (same number of industries and products) to derive the input-output table. Consequently, to construct an input-output table based on the fixed industry sales structure assumption, a square-form supply matrix must be constructed, similar to the product technology assumption. Second, the coefficient and value matrices of intermediate inputs obtained under this assumption may contain negative values. This can occur because, when reallocating the shares of secondary product rows to principal product rows using the fixed industry sales structure assumption, deductions are not taken directly from the secondary product rows themselves. In applied work, such negatives are commonly addressed through non-negativity adjustments and targeted redefinition and reallocation.

Applying these relations yields the industry-by-industry results shown in Table 21.11. The left panel presents the coefficient matrix of inputs C^{-1}B; the center panel presents the value matrix of inputs C^{-1} B $\hat{g}$ = $(\hat{g}\ S^{-1})$ U; and the right panel shows the converted final use vector C^{-1} e. Together with value added by industry from the use table, these tables provide intermediate inputs, value added, and total output in the industry-by-industry format.

Table 21.11 Derivation of input-output tables under the fixed industry sales structure assumption

Coefficient matrix of inputs

(C^{-1}B)

	(Industry)		
(Industry)	0.189	-0.004	0.019
	0.251	0.680	0.325
	0.120	0.047	0.233

Value matrix of inputs

(C^{-1}B $\hat{g}$)

	(Industry)		
(Industry)	9.47	-0.68	1.73
	12.53	115.68	29.27
	6.00	8.00	21.00
Value added (y^T)	22	47	38
Total output (g^T)	50	170	90

Final use vector

(C^{-1}e)

Final use	Total use (g)
39.47	50
12.53	170
55.00	90
107.00	310

21.3.4 Compilation of industry-by-industry IOTs under the fixed product sales structure assumption

The process of deriving the input-output table under the fixed product sales structure assumption is as follows based on the same supply matrix (S) and use matrix (U) data (Tables 21.7 and 21.8). The algebraic derivation is summarized here (see the Annex to Chapter 21 for details).

First, form the market share matrix from the transposed supply table ($D = S^T \hat{q}^{-1}$), and the intermediate input coefficient matrix by industry from the use table ($B = U \hat{g}^{-1}$). The coefficient matrix of intermediate inputs (A) for the industry-by-industry IOT under the fixed product sales structure assumption is then obtained as:

(21.7) **Coefficient matrix of intermediate inputs: $A = DB = (S^T \hat{q}^{-1})(U \hat{g}^{-1})$**

To express intermediate inputs in values, multiply by $\hat{g}$ (the diagonal matrix of industry outputs). Noting that $U = B\hat{g}$,

(21.8) **Value matrix of intermediate inputs (value terms of A): $A\hat{g} = DB\hat{g} = (S^T \hat{q}^{-1})U$**

The value-added sector of the industry-by-industry IOT is compiled on an industry basis and is therefore taken directly from the use table without modifications:

- **Value-added in the IOT = y^T (from the use table)**

Because the matrix in (21.8) is in the form of industry-by-industry, final use, which is observed on a product basis in the use table, must be converted to an industry basis. The conversion is made by multiplying the net final use vector (e) of the use table by D:

- **Final use of the IOT = $De = (S^T \hat{q}^{-1})e$**

Properties and implications

Unlike the case of the fixed industry sales structure assumption, the fixed product sales structure assumption does not require the supply matrix S to be square; it can be applied when the supply table is rectangular. However, this does not imply that the resulting IOT is a rectangular matrix: after the transformation, the compiled table is industry-by-industry and therefore square. Second, unlike the case of fixed industry sales structure assumption, negative cell entries do not arise in the derived matrix of intermediate inputs. The reason is that the shares of secondary products reallocated to principal product rows are computed directly from the sales structure of the product row in which the secondary product occurs and are deducted there.

Applying these relations yields the industry-by-industry results in Table 21.12. The left panel shows the coefficient matrix of inputs DB; the center panel shows the value matrix of input $DB\hat{g} = (S^T \hat{q}^{-1})U$; and the right panel shows the converted final use vector De. Combined with value-added from the use table, these tables provide intermediate inputs, value added, and total output in an industry-by-industry framework.

Table 21.12 Derivation of input-output tables under the fixed product sales structure assumption

Coefficient matrix of inputs (DB)

	(Industry)		
(Industry)	0.146	0.072	0.048
	0.294	0.604	0.297
	0.120	0.047	0.233

Value matrix of inputs ($DB\hat{g}$)

	(Industry)		
(Industry)	7.31	12.29	4.30
	14.69	102.71	26.70
	6.00	8.00	21.00
Value added (y^T)	22	47	38
Total output (g^T)	50	170	90

Final use vector (De)

Final use	Total use (g)
26.10	50
25.90	170
55.00	90
107.00	310

21.3.5 Handling negative cell entries in the input-output table under the product technology assumption

When a product by-product IOT is derived under the product technology assumption (PTA), negative entries may appear in the cells associated with secondary products. There are two typical methods to correct this problem. The first is the method proposed by Almon, and the second is a mixed technology approach in which the industry technology assumption (ITA) is applied selectively to the specific cells that would otherwise produce negative values. In practice, these methods are often complemented by arbitrary adjustments, commonly referred to as "redefinition process", undertaken by compilers. The remainder of this subsection discusses practical ways to deal with negative cell entries that arise during the transformation of supply and use tables to input-output tables.

21.3.5.1 Almon method[31]

The method proposed by Almon corrects negative cells by first resetting any negative entry to **zero**, and then redistributing the same magnitude to the most similar item (so that the relevant row or column total is preserved), and finally applying an offsetting adjustment in the corresponding row (or column) to keep value-added unchanged. After these corrections, the use matrix (U) is reconstructed from the adjusted input-output table and the supply table. To illustrate, consider the following supply and use tables.

Table 21.13 Illustrative supply and use tables

Supply table

		Industry				Total
		Agriculture	Manufacturing	Service 1	Service 2	
Product	Agricultural product	50	20	0	0	70
	Manufactured product	10	240	0	0	250
	Service 1	0	0	70	0	70
	Service 2	0	0	0	330	330
Total		60	260	70	330	720

Use table

		Industry				Final use	Total use
		Agriculture	Manufacturing	Service 1	Service 2		
Product	Agricultural product	0	0	0	0	70	70
	Manufactured product	0	0	0	0	250	250
	Service 1	0.5	24.5	0	0	45	70
	Service 2	43.5	76.5	30	5	175	330
Value added		16	159	40	325		540
Total		60	260	70	330	540	

Based on these data, a product-by-product IOT derived under the product technology assumption (PTA) is obtained as follows.

Table 21.14 Derived input-output table

		Product				Final use	Total use
		Agricultural	Manufactured	Service 1	Service 2		
Product	Agricultural product	0	0	0	0	70	70
	Manufactured product	0	0	0	0	250	250
	Service 1	**-0.7**	25.7	0	0	45	70
	Service 2	57.4	62.6	30	5	175	330
Value added		13.3	161.7	40	325		540
Total		70.0	250.0	70	330	540	

[31] Clopper Almon (2000), "Product-to-Product Tables via Product Technology with No Negative Flows."

In this derived input-output table, a negative value (– 0.7) appears in the entry at the service 1 row and the agricultural product column. Therefore, a procedure is taken to set the negative value to zero and reduce the entry of the most similar product (here, 25.7 at the service 1 row and the manufactured product column) by 0.7 so that the row total is maintained. Then, to hold value-added constant and preserve column totals, the same value is adjusted in the entry at the row of service 2. As a result, the following modified input-output table is derived.

Table 21.15 Input-output table adjusted by the Almon procedure

		Product				Final use	Total use
		Agricultural	Manufactured	Service 1	Service 2		
Product	Agricultural product	0	0	0	0	70	70
	Manufactured product	0	0	0	0	250	250
	Service 1	**0.0**	25.0	0	0	45	70
	Service 2	56.7	63.3	30	5	175	330
Value added		13.3	161.7	40	325		540
Total		70.0	250.0	70	330	540	

Finally, using the adjusted input-output coefficient (A) together with the supply matrix (S), reconstruct the new use matrix by U = A S. This yields a revised use table that replaces the original use table as shown below and satisfies non-negativity.

Table 21.16 Reconstructed (adjusted) use table

		Industry				Final use	Total use
		Agriculture	Manufacturing	Service 1	Service 2		
Product	Agricultural product	0	0	0	0	70	70
	Manufactured product	0	0	0	0	250	250
	Service 1	1	24	0	0	45	70
	Service 2	43	77	30	5	175	330
Value added		16	159	40	325		540
Total		60	260	70	330	540	

21.3.5.2 Hybrid (or mixed) technology assumption method

The hybrid technology assumption method for constructing input-output tables involves separating secondary products of different natures into two groups and creating two tables accordingly. It applies the product technology assumption (PTA) and the industry technology assumption (ITA) to each table, respectively. Concretely, the original supply table is split into (i) a table that contains a principal product and subsidiary products only, and (ii) a table that contains joint-products and by-products only. Then, the PTA is applied to the former (a principal product and subsidiary products) and the ITA to the latter (joint-products and by-products). Combining the two resulting matrices yields an input-output table that mitigates manly shortcomings that arise when only one assumption is used.

The following example illustrates the procedure of deriving an input-output table using the supply and use tables by applying the PTA and the ITA separately. Assume that the original supply table and use tables are given as shown in Table 21.17.

Table 21.17 Example of the supply and use tables

Supply table

	Industry A	Industry B	Industry C	Total supply (q)
Product A	155	20	15	190
Product B	40	300	60	400
Product C	5	10	245	260
Total output (g^T)	200	330	320	850

Use table

	Industry A	Industry B	Industry C	Final use	Total use (q)
Product A	37	107	12	34	190
Product B	25	89	18	268	400
Product C	71	20	13	156	260
Value added	67	114	277	458	
Total input (g^T)	200	330	320		

First, identify which entries will be handled by the PTA and which by the ITA. To do this task, start from the transposed matrix (V) of the supply table $V = S^T$ and define a mask matrix (H) to apply the PTA. Cells shaded in light blue in H are those to which the PTA will apply, and the remaining cells will be treated under the ITA.

Transposed supply table ($V = S^T$)

	Product A	Product B	Product C	Total (g)
Industry A	155	40	5	200
Industry B	20	300	10	330
Industry C	15	60	245	320
Total (q^T)	190	400	260	850

A matrix to which the PTA is applied (H)

1	1	0
1	1	0
0	0	1

Using H, split V into two parts:

- $V_1 = V \# H$ (Hadamard, i.e., element-wise product): the part handled under the PTA
- $V_2 = V - V_1$: the residual handled under the ITA.

Transposed supply table for applying the PTA ($V_1 = V \# H$)

	Product A	Product B	Product C	Total (g_1)
Industry A	155	40	0	195
Industry B	20	300	0	320
Industry C	0	0	245	245
Total (q^T_1)	175	340	245	760

Transposed supply table for applying the ITA ($V_2 = V - V_1$)

	Product A	Product B	Product C	Total (g_2)
Industry A	0	0	5	5
Industry B	0	0	10	10
Industry C	15	60	0	75
Total (q^T_2)	15	60	15	90

Then, the input coefficients (A) by the hybrid technology and the resulting input-output table (in value terms) are obtained with the following matrices (see page 50 in the 1968 SNA for the derivation formulas). Let U denote the use matrix (intermediate input quadrant of the use table). Let g be the column vector of output by industry, and q be the column vector of output by product, respectively; $\widehat{g}$ and $\widehat{q}$ denote the diagonal matrices formed from g and q. The unit matrix is I and ι is a unit vector.

$\mathbf{C_1 = V_1^T \widehat{g_1}^{-1}}$	Product-mix coefficient matrix for the PTA part of the supply table
$\mathbf{D_2 = V_2 \widehat{q}^{-1}}$	Market-share coefficient matrix for the ITA part of the supply table
$\mathbf{R = C_1^{-1} (I - \widehat{D_2^T \cdot \iota}) + D_2}$	Transformation matrix with mixed technology
$\mathbf{B = U \widehat{g}^{-1}}$	Input coefficient matrix derived from the use table

Here, C_1 and D_2 must be square matrices to permit inversion (for C_1) and to preserve dimensional consistency. With these definitions, the coefficient matrix of intermediate inputs (A) and the value matrix of intermediate inputs in the input-output table under the hybrid technology assumption are:

- **Coefficient matrix of inputs: A = B R**
- **Value matrix of inputs: $\mathbf{A\widehat{q} = BR\widehat{q}}$**

Here's how the matrices are calculated according to the above expressions and the resulting tables.

Table 21.18 Computational steps and results with the hybrid technology approach

$\widehat{g_1}$

195	0	0
0	320	0
0	0	245

$\widehat{g_1}^{-1}$

0.0051	0	0
0	0.0031	0
0	0	0.0041

$C_1 = V_1^T \cdot \widehat{g_1}^{-1}$

0.7949	0.0625	0
0.2051	0.9375	0
0	0	1.0000

$\widehat{q}$

190	0	0
0	400	0
0	0	260

$\widehat{q}^{-1}$

0.0053	0	0
0	0.0025	0
0	0	0.0038

$D_2 = V_2 \cdot \widehat{q}^{-1}$

0	0	0.0192
0	0	0.0385
0.0789	0.15	0

$(C_1)^{-1}$

1.2801	-0.0853	0
-0.2801	1.0853	0
0	0	1.0000

I

1	0	0
0	1	0
0	0	1

ι

1
1
1

D_2^T

0	0	0.0789
0	0	0.15
0.0192	0.0385	0

$D_2^T \iota$

0.079
0.150
0.058

$\widehat{D_2^T \cdot \iota}$

0.079	0	0
0	0.150	0
0	0	0.058

$I - \widehat{D_2^T \cdot \iota}$

0.921	0	0
0	0.850	0
0	0	0.942

$(C_1)^{-1} (I - \widehat{D_2^T \cdot \iota})$

1.179	-0.073	0
-0.258	0.923	0
0	0	0.942

$R = (C_1)^{-1}(I - \widehat{D_2^T \cdot \iota}) + D_2$

1.179	-0.073	0.019
-0.258	0.923	0.039
0.079	0.15	0.942

Coefficient matrix of inputs (B R)

	Product A	Product B	Product C
Product A	0.1374	0.2913	0.0514
Product B	0.0822	0.2482	0.0658
Product C	0.4061	0.0363	0.0474
Value added	0.3742	0.4242	0.8354
Total input	1.0000	1.0000	1.0000

Input-output table ($\mathbf{B\,R\,\hat{q}}$)

	Product A	Product B	Product C	Final use	Total use (q)
Product A	26.1	116.5	13.4	34	190.0
Product B	15.6	99.3	17.1	268	400.0
Product C	77.2	14.5	12.3	156	260.0
Value added	71.1	169.7	217.2	458	
Total input (q^T)	190.0	400.0	260.0		

For comparison, Table 21.19 reports the results when the same supply and use tables are processed only under the PTA (i.e., without the ITA component). As shown, negative entries arise, reducing interpretability. The hybrid approach therefore serves as a practical alternative, especially when secondary products are highly heterogeneous, because it helps to satisfy non-negativity while respecting the distinct technological characteristics of different kinds of secondary products.

Table 21.19 Input-output table by the PTA only (for comparison)

Coefficient matrix of inputs (B R)

	Product A	Product B	Product C
Product A	0.1503	0.3482	**-0.0455**
Product B	0.0863	0.2910	**-0.0031**
Product C	0.4482	0.0362	0.0167
Value added	0.3152	0.3246	1.0318
Total input	1.0000	1.0000	1.0000

Input-output table ($\mathbf{B\,R\,\hat{q}}$)

	Product A	Product B	Product C	Final use	Total use (q)
Product A	28.6	139.3	**-11.8**	34	190
Product B	16.4	116.4	**-0.8**	268	400
Product C	85.2	14.5	4.4	156	260
Value added	59.9	129.8	268.3	458	
Total input (q^T)	190.0	400.0	260.0		

21.3.5.3 Manual adjustments

Manual adjustment refers to a manual, ex-ante procedure carried out before applying the matrix transformations implied by the technology assumption etc. The idea is to pre-rearrange secondary products in the supply table and, in parallel, to shift the corresponding input shares in the use table. Concretely, secondary products are moved from the industries where they were originally recorded to the industries in which those products are treated as principal products (a **redefinition** step). At the same time, the intermediate inputs and value added used to produce those secondary products are reallocated to the receiving industries (a **reallocation** step). This manual treatment allows heterogenous items, particularly secondary products with input structures that differ markedly from the primary production activities of the origin industry, or that belong to very different industrial classifications, to be sorted out in advance. For example, if a manufacturing enterprise supplies construction or trade services as secondary outputs, those outputs can be reassigned to construction or trade industries, respectively, with the associated intermediate input costs shifted accordingly.

The procedure follows the same logic as the transformations discussed earlier for constructing input-output tables under technology assumptions. By undertaking this ex-ante, manual adjustment, negative input coefficients that might otherwise arise under the product technology assumption (PTA) can often be mitigated or eliminated. After these adjustments, secondary products are relocated to the refined industries, and the supply and use tables are left composed of products that share more homogenous input structures. Applying the technology-based conversion to these cleaned tables generally yields input-output tables that are more internally consistent and easier to interpret.

21.3.6 Pre-adjustments required for transforming SUTs into IOTs

When transforming the supply and use tables (SUTs) into the input-output tables (IOTs) using the methods discussed above, certain pre-adjustments are required to ensure the transformation can be carried out properly. In practice, the SUT often needs to be reshaped toward the target IOT format, and its rows and columns may need to be reorganized so that the matrix formulas used in the conversion are valid. This subsection describes the preparatory steps that should precede the conversion work. These steps are essential to obtain well-adjusted input coefficients and a smooth transformation.

Aligning the supply and use tables at basic prices

For the matrix formulas introduced earlier to hold, it is most coherent to pair the supply table at basic prices with the use table at basic prices. Specifically, the domestic output matrix in the supply table and the intermediate input matrix (quadrant I) in the use table must both be expressed at basic prices to preserve consistency. Since the domestic output matrix in the supply table is compiled only at basic prices, the intermediate input matrix in the use table should likewise be converted to basic prices before applying the matrix transformations.

Harmonizing the ordering of product and industry classifications

SUTs typically employ international standards, e.g., the *Central Product Classification* (CPC) for products and the *International Standard Industrial Classification* (ISIC) for industries. However, these two international classification systems differ not only in item coverage but also in ordering. For example, in ISIC classification (Rev. 5), manufacturing (10–33) is followed by electricity, gas, steam and air conditioning supply (35), whereas in CPC (version 3.0), electricity appears under section 17 and manufactured goods under 21–49, placing electricity before manufactured goods. Such misalignment disrupts the natural correspondence of principal products and principal industries along the main diagonal of the supply table, and can introduce errors or distortions during the IOT conversion. A practical remedy is to reorder rows and columns ex ante, on the basis of product-industry similarity, so that each principal product is aligned on the diagonal with the industry that primarily produces it.

Adjusting the number of product rows and industry columns

The dimensional requirements of the supply table depend on the conversion assumption to be applied:

- **Cases requiring a square matrix**: Under the product technology assumption (for product-by-product IOTs) and the fixed industry sales structure assumption (for industry-by-industry IOTs), the computation uses inverses of supply-derived matrices (e.g., S^{-1}, C^{-1}). Hence, the supply table must be square (same number of product rows and industry columns). Before applying these assumptions, adjust the counts of products and industries, typically by aggregating the side with more categories, so that the supply (and the matched use) matrices are square.
- **Cases allowing a rectangular matrix**: Under the industry technology assumption and the fixed product sales structure assumption, the algebra can be carried out even if the supply table is rectangular. Note, however, that the dimension of the resulting IOT differs: with the industry technology assumption, the resulting table is product-by-product (its dimension matches the number of product rows in the original supply table), whereas with the fixed product sales structure assumption, the result is industry-by-industry (its dimension matches the number of industry columns).

In short, whether an assumption requires a matrix inverse and which target format is intended (product-by-product IOT vs. industry-by-industry IOT) determine the need to reconcile row/column counts prior to conversion.

Redefinition and reallocation

In the supply table, if the secondary product recorded in a given industry is markedly different in nature from the industry's principal product, the input coefficients may be more unstable when the table is converted into an input-output table. In such cases, **redefine** the secondary product by moving it in the supply table to the industry where it is treated as a principal product, and **reallocate** in the use table the corresponding intermediate inputs and value added in the same proportion. Redefinition and reallocation are usually manual and tend to be concentrated in a few industries. Common examples include:

- Housing rental (including owner-occupied dwellings): Classify as an industry of single-product for clarity.
- Distribution margins: For consistent adjustments from purchasers' prices to basic prices, consolidate margins generated outside the trade industries into the trade industry when compiling the output of margins.
- Construction: Given its distinctive input structure (e.g., building materials as intermediate inputs), it is preferable to redefine construction so that it reflects pure construction activities.

These ex-ante adjustments help remove heterogeneous secondary products, reduce the likelihood of negative coefficients under the product technology assumption, and improve the interpretability and stability of the resulting IOT.

Treating direct overseas purchases by residents and domestic purchases by non-residents

SUTs often include two rows that do not appear in IOTs: "Direct overseas purchases by residents" and "domestic purchases by non-residents." These represent expenditures made by travelers and are not captured in the data on final use (household final consumption expenditure and exports) and imports because they are not recorded at customs statistics. To apply the formulas of the matrix transformations, these non-standard rows must be removed by distributing them across the relevant product rows:

- **Direct overseas purchases by residents**: Allocate the expenditures directly to the corresponding imports by product and add them to household final consumption expenditure, thereby removing the separate row.
- **Domestic purchases by non-residents**: Deduct the expenditures from domestic household final consumption expenditure and add them to exports for corresponding products, removing the separate row.

Conceptually, these two items belong to the exports and imports of "travel services" in the balance of payments. They are split out as separate rows only for transparency during the compilation of SUTs. Therefore, in the transformation stage of IOTs, they must be reintegrated into the relevant product expenditures so that the matrix formulas operate cleanly.

21.4 Examples of deriving input-output tables from supply and use tables

This section presents a compact set of worked examples showing how to transform actual supply and use tables into input-output tables. The examples use the supply and use tables of South Korea at basic prices as of 2015, and apply the transformation approaches introduced earlier, the technology assumptions (PTA/ITA) and the sales structure assumptions (FISS/FPSS). The original dataset comprises 32 industries and 33 products. For expositional clarity, these categories are aggregated to five sectors (see Section 22.5 for the aggregation procedure). No redefinition is undertaken during the transformations; consequently, there may be some cross-sector discrepancies, but the overall figures are consistent.

Table 21.20 Supply and use tables (South Korea, at basic prices, 2015, 5-sector)

Supply table (Unit: billion KRW)

	Agriculture	Mining & manufacturing	Electricity, gas & water	Construct ion	Service industries	Total output
Agricultural	61,331	1	0	0	0	61,332
Mining & manufactured	13	1,661,089	12.922	33.386	611.19	1,661,759
Electricity,gas,water	0	29	107,291	0	2,567	109,888
Construction	-	-	0	209,697	0	209,697
Services	40	14,906	728	2,388	1,656,281	1,674,343
Total output	61,384	1,676,025	108,032	212,118	1,659,459	3,717,019

Use table (Unit: billion KRW)

	Agricultur e	Mining, manufacturi ng	Electricity, gas, & water	Construction	Service industries	Total intermediate use	Final use	Imports (-)	Total use (-imports)
Agricultural	3,180	38,903	13	496	11,321	53,913	18,993	11,574	61,332
Mining & manufactured	17,091	919,817	39,283	85,503	198,992	1,260,686	895,132	494,058	1,661,759
Electricity, gas & water	767	39,088	13,925	1,001	33,701	88,483	21,531	126	109,888
Construction	72	1,322	402	159	9,159	11,114	198,643	59	209,697
Services	6,489	228,523	8,551	40,051	452,123	735,737	1,036,220	97,614	1,674,343
Total IC	27,600	1,227,653	62,175	127,209	705,296	2,149,933	2,170,519	603,433	3,717,019
Gross value added[1)]	33,785	448,372	45,858	84,909	954,164	1,567,086			
Total input	61,384	1,676,025	108,032	212,118	1,659,459	3,717,019			

Footnote: 1) includes taxes less subsidies on products

21.4.1 Derivation of a product-by-product IOT under the product technology assumption

Table 21.21 illustrates the result of converting South Korea's supply and use tables (as of 2015, aggregated to five sectors) into a product-by-product input-output table under the product technology assumption. The conversion formula of input-output table uses the following expressions. The input coefficient matrix (shares of intermediate inputs and value added per unit of output) is computed as BC^{-1}. The intermediate inputs and value-added of the monetary IOT are obtained using the formula $BC^{-1}\hat{q}$. The final use vector already on a product basis in the use table, so it is taken directly as e.

Table 21.21 Input coefficients and product-by-product IOT under the PTA

Input coefficients matrix (BC^{-1})

Product \ Product	Agricultural	Mining & manufactured	Electricity, gas, water	Construction	Services
Agricultural	0.05185	0.02336	0.00007	0.00228	0.00683
Mining & manufactured	0.27848	0.55267	0.36525	0.40630	0.11937
Electricity	0.01249	0.02335	0.12965	0.00454	0.02014
Construction	0.00117	0.00075	0.00371	0.00070	0.00552
Services	0.10559	0.13512	0.07783	0.18787	0.27280
Total intermediate input	0.44957	0.73524	0.57652	0.60168	0.42467
Value added	0.55043	0.26476	0.42348	0.39832	0.57533
Total input	1.00000	1.00000	1.00000	1.00000	1.00000

Input-output table

(Intermediate inputs and value-added = $BC^{-1}\hat{q}$, Final use = e) (Unit: billion KRW)

Product \ Product	Agricultural	Mining & manufactured	Electricity, gas, water	Construction	Services	Total intermediate use	Final use	Imports (-)	Total output
Agricultural	3,180	38,817	8	478	11,430	53,913	18,993	11,574	61,332
Mining & manufactured	17,080	918,397	40,137	85,199	199,873	1,260,686	895,132	494,058	1,661,759
Electricity	766	38,800	14,247	953	33,718	88,483	21,531	126	109,888
Construction	72	1,240	408	146	9,248	11,114	198,643	59	209,697
Services	6,476	224,545	8,553	39,395	456,768	735,737	1,036,220	97,614	1,674,343
Total intermediate input	27,573	1,221,799	63,353	126,171	711,037	2,149,933	2,170,519	603,433	3,717,019
Value added	33,759	439,960	46,535	83,526	963,307	1,567,086			
Total input	61,332	1,661,759	109,888	209,697	1,674,343	3,717,019			

21.4.2 Derivation of a product-by-product IOT under the industry technology assumption

Similarly, the results of converting the above supply and use tables of South Korea (as of 2015, 5 sectors) into the product-by-product IOT under the industry technology assumption are shown below (Table 21.22). The transformation applies the following expressions: the input coefficients matrix is BD; the intermediate inputs and value-added of the monetary IOT are $BD\hat{q}$. The final use vector is taken directly from the use table on a product basis, e.

Table 21.22 Input coefficients and product-by-product IOT under the ITA

Input coefficients matrix (BD)

Product \ Product	Agricultural	Mining & manufactured	Electricity, gas, water	Construction	Services
Agricultural	0.05181	0.02321	0.00029	0.00234	0.00696
Mining & manufactured	0.27844	0.54864	0.35798	0.40309	0.12425
Electricity	0.01250	0.02332	0.12633	0.00472	0.02036
Construction	0.00117	0.00079	0.00376	0.00075	0.00547
Services	0.10571	0.13640	0.08369	0.18881	0.27103
Total intermediate input	0.44963	0.73236	0.57205	0.59971	0.42807
Value added	0.55037	0.26764	0.42795	0.40029	0.57193
Total input	1.00000	1.00000	1.00000	1.00000	1.00000

Input-output table

(Intermediate inputs and value-added = $BD\hat{q}$, Final use = e)

(billion KRW)

Product \ Product	Agricultural	Mining & manufactured	Electricity, gas, water	Construction	Services	Total intermediate use	Final use	Imports (-)	Total output
Agricultural	3,177	38,561	32	490	11,653	53,913	18,993	11,574	61,332
Mining & manufactured	17,077	911,715	39,337	84,527	208,030	1,260,686	895,132	494,058	1,661,759
Electricity	766	38,754	13,883	990	34,090	88,483	21,531	126	109,888
Construction	72	1,314	413	157	9,157	11,114	198,643	59	209,697
Services	6,483	226,662	9,196	39,594	453,802	735,737	1,036,220	97,614	1,674,343
Intermediate input	27,576	1,217,006	62,861	125,757	716,732	2,149,933	2,170,519	603,433	3,717,019
Value added	33,755	444,753	47,027	83,940	957,611	1,567,086			
Total input	61,332	1,661,759	109,888	209,697	1,674,343	3,717,019			

21.4.3 Derivation of an industry-by-industry IOT under the fixed industry sales structure

Applying the fixed industry sales structure assumption to South Korea's supply and use tables (as of 2015, 5 sectors) yields the industry-by-industry IOT shown in Table 21.23. The transformation uses these expressions: the input coefficients matrix is $C^{-1}B$; the intermediate inputs of the monetary IOT is $C^{-1}B\hat{g}$; the final use (and imports to be deducted) vector is $C^{-1}e$. Value-added is taken directly from the use table, y^T, since it is defined on an industry basis.

Table 21.23 Input coefficients and industry-by-industry IOT under the FISS

Input coefficients matrix ($C^{-1}B$)

Industry \ Industry	Agriculture	Mining & manufacturing	Electricity, gas & water	Construction	Services
Agriculture	0.05185	0.02323	0.00012	0.00234	0.00683
Mining & manufacturing	0.28089	0.55369	0.36685	0.40664	0.12089
Electricity	0.01242	0.02327	0.12967	0.00446	0.02002
Construction	0.00119	0.00080	0.00376	0.00076	0.00558
Services	0.10328	0.13149	0.07512	0.18551	0.27170
Intermediate input	0.44962	0.73248	0.57552	0.59971	0.42502
Value added	0.55038	0.26752	0.42448	0.40029	0.57498
Total input	1.00000	1.00000	1.00000	1.00000	1.00000

Input-output table

(Intermediate inputs = $C^{-1}B\hat{g}$, Value-added = y^T, Final use = $C^{-1}e$) (Unit: billion KRW)

Industry \ Industry	Agriculture	Mining & manufacturing	Electricity, gas & water	Construction	Services	Total intermediate use	Final use	Imports (-)	Total output
Agriculture	3,183	38,936	13	496	11,331	53,959	19,009	11,584	61,384
Mining & manufacturing	17,242	927,992	39,631	86,257	200,606	1,271,728	902,760	498,463	1,676,025
Electricity	762	38,999	14,008	946	33,228	87,942	20,063	- 27	108,032
Construction	73	1,338	407	161	9,264	11,242	200,937	60	212,118
Services	6,340	220,389	8,115	39,350	450,867	725,061	1,027,750	93,352	1,659,459
Intermediate input	27,600	1,227,653	62,175	127,209	705,296	2,149,933	2,170,519	603,433	3,717,019
Value added	33,785	448,372	45,858	84,909	954,164	1,567,086			
Total input	61,384	1,676,025	108,032	212,118	1,659,459	3,717,019			

21.4.4 Derivation of an industry-by-industry IOT under the fixed product sales structure

Applying the fixed product sales structure assumption to South Korea's supply and use tables (as of 2015, 5 sectors) yields the industry-by-industry IOT shown in Table 21.24. The transformation uses the following expressions: the input coefficients matrix is A = DB; the intermediate inputs of the monetary IOT is $DB\hat{g}$; the final use (and imports to be deducted) vector is De. Value-added is taken directly from the use table, y^T, since it is defined on an industry basis.

Table 21.24 Input coefficients and industry-by-industry IOT under the FPSS

Input coefficients matrix (DB)

Industry \ Industry	Agriculture	Mining & manufacturing	Electricity, gas, water	Construction	Services
Agriculture	0.05181	0.02322	0.00013	0.00234	0.00683
Mining & manufacturing	0.27927	0.54981	0.36421	0.40461	0.12230
Electricity	0.01225	0.02283	0.12589	0.00469	0.01995
Construction	0.00133	0.00099	0.00384	0.00103	0.00591
Services	0.10496	0.13562	0.08145	0.18703	0.27003
Intermediate input	0.44962	0.73248	0.57552	0.59971	0.42502
Value added	0.55038	0.26752	0.42448	0.40029	0.57498
Total input	1.00000	1.00000	1.00000	1.00000	1.00000

Input-output table

(Intermediate inputs = $DB\hat{g}$, Value-added = y^T, Final use = De) (Unit: billion KRW)

Industry \ Industry	Agricultural	Mining & manufacturing	Electricity, gas, water	Construction	Services	Total intermediate use	Final use	Imports (-)	Total output
Agricultural	3,180	38,915	14	497	11,333	53,940	19,025	11,580	61,384
Mining & manufacturing	17,143	921,491	39,347	85,825	202,946	1,266,751	904,002	494,728	1,676,025
Electricity	752	38,271	13,600	996	33,103	86,722	21,480	170	108,032
Construction	82	1,667	415	218	9,807	12,188	200,139	209	212,118
Services	6,443	227,309	8,799	39,674	448,106	730,331	1,025,874	96,746	1,659,459
Intermediate input	27,600	1,227,653	62,175	127,209	705,296	2,149,933	2,170,519	603,433	3,717,019
Value added	33,785	448,372	45,858	84,909	954,164	1,567,086			
Total input	61,384	1,676,025	108,032	212,118	1,659,459	3,717,019			

Annex to Chapter 21: Matrix formulas for transforming SUTs into IOTs under the technology and sales structure assumptions (quoted from the 1968 SNA)

The 1968 SNA presents, in matrix forms, how to derive input-output tables under the product technology and industry technology assumptions as well as under the fixed industry sales structure, and fixed product sales structure assumptions. This annex briefly outlines those derivations. To begin, denote the cells of the supply and use tables with abbreviations as shown in Table 21.25.

Table 21.25 Notations in each cell of the supply and use tables

	Product	Industry	Net final use	Output
Product		U	e	q
Industry	V			g
Value-added		y^T		
Input	q^T	g^T		

In the table above, each abbreviation is explained as follows:

V: Industry-by-product matrix of output (the transpose of the supply table, S^T; imports are excluded).

U: Product-by-industry matrix of intermediate inputs (intermediate input quadrant of the use table)

e: Column vector of net final use (= final use - imports)

y^T: Row vector of value-added (primary inputs)

g: Column vector of domestic output by industry

q: Column vector of domestic output by product

g^T: Transposed vector of g

q^T: Transposed vector of q

With these notations, the following input-output relationship is established.

(1) $\mathbf{q} = \mathbf{U}i + \mathbf{e}$ where i denotes the unit column vector.

(2) $\mathbf{q} = \mathbf{V}^T i$

(3) $\mathbf{g} = \mathbf{V}i$

(4) $\mathbf{U} = \mathbf{B}\hat{\mathbf{g}}$ where **B** is the product-by-industry matrix of "input coefficients" of the use table, and $\hat{\mathbf{g}}$ denotes the diagonal matrix of g.

(5) $\mathbf{V}^T = \mathbf{C}\hat{\mathbf{g}}$ where **C** is the product-by-industry matrix of "product-mix by industry" of the supply table.

(6) $\mathbf{V} = \mathbf{D}\hat{\mathbf{q}}$ where **D** is the industry-by-product matrix of "market share by product" of the transposed supply table.

Here, equation (5) embodies the idea that "each industry produces its products in its own fixed proportions." Also, equation (6) embodies the idea that each product is produced in its own fixed proportions from various industries."

Under these premises, the input coefficients matrix $\boldsymbol{A}$ of the resulting input-output table on the basis of the technology assumption and the sales structure assumption is derived as follows.

Derivation under the assumptions of product technology and fixed industry sales structure

From equations (1), (2), (4), and (5) above, the input-output coefficients can be derived on the basis of the product technology assumption. Initially, the following equation is derived from equations (1) and (4).

(7) $q = Ui + e = Bg + e$

From equations (2) and (5), $q = V^{T}i = C\hat{g}i = Cg$, hence $g = C^{-1}q$. Substituting into equation (7) gives:

(8) $q = Bg + e = BC^{-1}q + e$

Solving for q in equation (8), we get the following equation:

$$q(I - BC^{-1}) = e$$

Therefore, the value of q is obtained as:

(9) $\mathbf{q} = (\boldsymbol{I} - \mathbf{BC}^{-1})^{-1}\mathbf{e}$

where I denotes the unit matrix. If $\boldsymbol{A}$ denotes the input coefficients of the product-by-product IOT, the IO identity is $Aq + e = q$, which can be written as $q(I - A) = e$, and hence $q = (I - A)^{-1}e$. Therefore, comparing this with equation (9) yields:

$$\mathbf{A} = \mathbf{BC}^{-1}$$

From this equation, we can derive the input coefficients matrix under the product technology assumption as follows:

- Intermediate input coefficients of the product-by-product IOT: $A = BC^{-1}$ (intermediate input coefficients of the use table x the inverse of the product-mix matrix of the supply table).

- Value-added coefficients of the product-by-product IOT: value-added coefficients of the use table x the inverse of the product-mix matrix of the supply table

Because C^{-1} is required, both supply and use tables must be square matrices with the same number of rows and columns so that the relevant inverse exists. In addition, applying this formula may generate negative entries in the input coefficients matrix, so non-negativity adjustments are often required (see 21.3.5).

Next, from the previous equations (2) and (5), $g = C^{-1}q$. Substituting q from equation (7) yields:

(10) $\mathbf{g = C^{-1}(Bg + e) = C^{-1}Bg + C^{-1}e}$

Solving equation (10) for g, we get the following equation:

$$\mathbf{g(I - C^{-1}B) = C^{-1}e}$$

Therefore, g is obtained as follows:

(11) $\mathbf{g = (I - C^{-1}B)^{-1}C^{-1}e}$

If $\boldsymbol{A}$ now denotes the input coefficients of the industry-by-industry IOT, then the IO identity is $Ag + C^{-1}e = g$. Here, $C^{-1}e$ represents final use converted to industries (value of net final use by industry). Transforming this equation, we get $g(I - A) = C^{-1}e$ and $g = (I - A)^{-1}C^{-1}e$. Therefore, comparing this with equation (11) gives:

$$\mathbf{A = C^{-1}B}$$

Based on this equation, the input coefficients under the fixed industry sales structure assumption can be derived as follows:

- Intermediate input coefficients of the industry-by-industry IOT: $A = C^{-1}B$ (the inverse of the product-mix matrix of the supply table x intermediate input coefficients of the use table)

Similarly, the supply table and the use table must be square matrices, as the inverse (C^{-1}) of the product-mix matrix of the supply table is required. Moreover, as with PTA, this transformation can produce negative cell entries, so non-negativity adjustments may be needed (see 21.3.5).

Finally, for the industry-by-industry IOT, value added is inherently defined by industry, therefore the value-added coefficients in the IOT are taken directly from the use table:

- Value-added input coefficients of the industry-by-industry IOT: equal to the value-added coefficients from the use table

Derivation under the assumptions of industry technology and fixed product sales structure

From the above formulas (1), (3), (4) and (6), the input coefficients under the industry technology assumption can be derived as follows.

Initially, in equations (1) and (4), the following equation is derived:

(12) $q = Ui + e = Bg + e$

Since $g = Vi$ in equation (3) and $V = D\hat{q}$ in equation (6), we have $g = Dq$.
Substituting this into equation (12) gives:

(13) $q = Bg + e = BDq + e$

Collecting terms in q, we get the following equation:

$$q(I - BD) = e$$

Therefore, the value of q is obtained as:

(14) $\mathbf{q = (\mathit{I} - BD)^{-1}e}$

where I denotes the unit matrix.

If $\boldsymbol{A}$ denotes the product-by-product input coefficients matrix of the resulting IOT, the IO identity is $Aq + e = q$, implying $q = (I - A)^{-1}e$. Comparing this equation with equation (14) yields:

$$\mathbf{A = BD}$$

This formula allows us to derive the input coefficients matrix under the industry technology assumption as follows:

- Intermediate input coefficients of the product-by-product IOT: A = BD (intermediate input coefficients of the use table x market share matrix of the transposed supply table)
- Value-added input coefficients of the product-by-product IOT: Value-added input coefficients of the use table x market share matrix of the transposed supply table

Next, since $g = Dq$ from the previous equations (3) and (6), substituting q from equation (12) into this equation, we get g as follows:

(15) $\mathbf{g = D(Bg + e) = DBg + De}$

Collecting terms in g, we get the following equation:

$$\mathbf{g}(I - \mathbf{D}\,\mathbf{B}) = \mathbf{D}\,\mathbf{e}$$

Therefore, g is obtained as:

(16) $\mathbf{g} = (I - \mathbf{D}\,\mathbf{B})^{-1}\,\mathbf{D}\,\mathbf{e}$

If $\boldsymbol{A}$ denotes input coefficients of the industry-by-industry IOT, the IO identity is $A g + D e = g$. Here, "D e" represents the final use converted to industries (net final use of output by industry). Transforming this equation, we get $g(I - A) = De$, and $g = (I - A)^{-1} De$. Therefore, comparing this with the above equation (16) gives:

$$\mathbf{A} = \mathbf{D}\,\mathbf{B}$$

Based on this formula, the input coefficients under the fixed product sales structure assumption can be derived as follows:

- Intermediate input coefficients of the industry-by-industry IOT: A = D B (market share matrix of the transposed supply table x Intermediate input coefficients of the use table)

In an industry-by-industry table, value added is identical to the industry-based value added in the use table. Accordingly, the value-added coefficients matrix for the industry-by-industry IOT is taken directly from the use table.

- Value-added input coefficients of the industry-by-industry IOT = Value added coefficient matrix from the use table

Summary of transformation formulas

The following table summarizes the formulas used to transform the supply and use tables into the input-output tables.

Table 21.26 Transformation formulas from the supply and use tables into input-output tables

IOT format	Assumption of transformations	Intermediate input coefficients	Value-added coefficients	Final use
Product-by-product	Product technology	$A = BC^{-1}$	Coefficients of the use table x C^{-1}	e
Product-by-product	Industry technology	$A = BD$	Coefficients of the use table x D	e
Industry-by-industry	Fixed industry sales structure	$A = C^{-1}B$	Coefficients of the use table	$C^{-1}e$
Industry-by-industry	Fixed product sales structure	$A = DB$	Coefficients of the use table	De

Where the elements in the formulas are defined as follows.

	Description of notations	Expression
B	Input coefficients of the use table *U* (product-by-industry)	$U\hat{g}^{-1}$
C	Product-mix matrix of the supply table *S* (product-by-industry)	$S\hat{g}^{-1}$
C^{-1}	Inverse of C	$\hat{g}S^{-1}$
D	Market share matrix of the transposed supply table S^T (industry-by-product)	$S^T\hat{q}^{-1}$
e	Vector of net final use (= final use – imports)	

(Here, $\hat{g}$ and $\hat{q}$ denotes the diagonal matrices formed from the industry output vector g and the product output vector q, respectively.)

Chapter 22. Interpretation and application of the input-output table

This chapter aims to provide an in-depth understanding of the nature of input-output tables, which are derived from the transformation of the supply and use tables (SUTs), and how they can be used in the national accounts, most notably for industry-level requirements and multiplier analysis (economic impact analysis). Input-output tables are the core statistical basis for "input-output analysis", which uses matrix formulae to study the inter-industry linkages within an economy and provides structural information that cannot be obtained from accounting aggregates alone. Because input-output analysis necessarily relies on matrix operations, the discussion proceeds on the premise of a basic familiarities with linear algebra.

This chapter is organized as follows. Section 22.1 introduces the basic concepts needed to understand input-output tables. Section 22.2 presents typical applications of input-output analysis. Specifically, it illustrates, using stylized examples, (i) the direct and indirect requirements and multipliers arising from changes in final use in the real economy, and (ii) the input-output price model that traces the pass-through of changes in price-related variables (wages, prices, exchange rates, etc.) to domestic prices. Section 22.3 discusses the assumptions underpinning input-output analysis and the limitations of such analysis. Section 22.4 describes a technical method for updating intermediate input coefficients in interval years other than the benchmark year of the input-output table. Finally, section 22.5 illustrates a practical method for aggregating (consolidating) rows and columns of the input-output table to produce a reduced set of industries or products.

22.1 Basic concepts of the input-output table

An **input-output table** is the form of the use table that is made consistent with a supply arranged so that each column contains a single product (or industry). When the supply table is expressed with one product (or industry) per column, the supply matrix becomes diagonal, that is, non-zero entries appear only on the **main diagonal** (where row and column indices coincide) and all other cells are zero. The use table derived consistently from such a diagonal supply table constitutes the input-out table. Consequently, the intermediate consumption quadrant of the input-output table is **symmetric** in the sense that the numbers of rows and columns coincide.

However, the presentation of the input-output table typically differs from that of the use table. In the use table, the last column shows **total use**, whereas in the input-output table, imports are added as a deduction item, so the last column shows **total output** (= total use - imports). As a result, in the input-output table, total output (rightmost column) and total input (bottom row) coincide, not only for each item but also in the aggregate.

22.1.1 Presentation of imports in the input-output table

As noted above, the input-output table includes a deduction item of "imports". This deduction item can be classified into two versions depending on how the deduction item is presented.

1. **Net-exports column** presentation: This type involves setting up a column of imports and subtracting it from the total use column in the table. In this format, the rest of the world sector is shown as a net exports column (= exports – imports), and the entries for intermediate use and final use are shown inclusive of imports. Adding net exports to domestic final use yields total output in the rightmost column of the table (see Table 22.1). This type is the most common way to present input-output tables adopted by statistical agencies.

Table 22.1 Input-output table with net-exports presentation

	Intermediate use (1)				Domestic final use (2)	Exports (3)	Imports (4)	Net exports (5=3-4)	Total output (1+2+5)
	Agriculture	Manufacturing	Electricity & construction	Services					
Agriculture	60	75	160	32	90	40	57	- 17	400
Manufacturing	85	85	125	65	115	55	30	25	500
Electricity, construction	67	60	95	70	330	15	37	- 22	600
Services	78	130	60	73	125	45	61	- 16	450
Value-added	110	150	160	210					630
Total input	400	500	600	450	660	155	185	- 30	

2. **Domestic/imports split** presentation: This type involves recording domestic output and imports separately. The **main input-output table** shows domestically produced output only, and an additional imports row allocates imports across intermediate use and final use (see Table 22.2). This imports row can, if desired, be compiled in full matrix form as **input table of imports**. In effect, this second type of the input-output table can be seen as a more detailed version of the first type, as it separates the use patterns of domestic output and imported goods.

Table 22.2 Input-output tables distinguishing domestic output and imports

Main input-output table

	Intermediate use (1)				Domestic final use (2)	Exports (3)	Total output (1+2+3)
	Agriculture	Manufacturing	Electricity & construction	Services			
Agriculture	55	61	157	26	61	40	400
Manufacturing	84	81	119	64	99	53	500
Electricity, construction	65	41	92	68	319	15	600
Services	76	108	51	56	115	44	450
Imports	10	59	21	26	66	3	185
Value added	110	150	160	210			630
Total input	400	500	600	450	660	155	

Input table of imports

	Intermediate use (1)				Domestic final use (2)	Exports (3)	Total (1+2+3)
	Agriculture	Manufacturing	Electricity & construction	Services			
Agriculture	5	14	3	6	29	0	57
Manufacturing	1	4	6	1	16	2	30
Electricity, construction	2	19	3	2	11	0	37
Services	2	22	9	17	10	1	61
Total	10	59	21	26	66	3	185

In this chapter, the exposition of input-output tables will, in principle, be based on the first type with an imports column and a deduction from final use. However, when we turn to the empirical measurement of total requirements (multipliers) in input-output analysis, the discussion will be developed entirely using the second type, which separates domestic output and imports.

22.1.2 Basic structure of the input-output table

As shown in Figure 22.1, **quadrant I**, the endogenous submatrix of the input-output table, comprises intermediate uses (horizontally) and intermediate inputs (vertically), which forms a square matrix as "product by product" or "industry by industry". The column of the quadrant I shows the **input structure** for producing a given output (x_j), the values of intermediate goods and services required to produce that output. For example, the column for bread would include values of flour, sugar, yeast, edible oils, electricity, water, rentals, etc. used as intermediate inputs to produce bread. Adding **quadrant III** (**value-added**) to that column yields the total input cost (= intermediate inputs + value-added) used to produce the output. This total input corresponds to the total output.

The row of the quadrant I shows the **distribution structure** of a particular output (x_i) as intermediate use in the production of other products. For instance, in the case of the coal product, the row records the values of coal used as intermediate use in briquettes, thermal power generation, chemical products, and so on. Adding **final use** (**quadrant II**) to this intermediate use row gives **total use** of that output. If the value of imports of that output is subtracted from the value of total use of the same output, it becomes the **total output** which is consistent with the total input in the column of the same output.

Figure 22.1 Basic structure of the input-output table

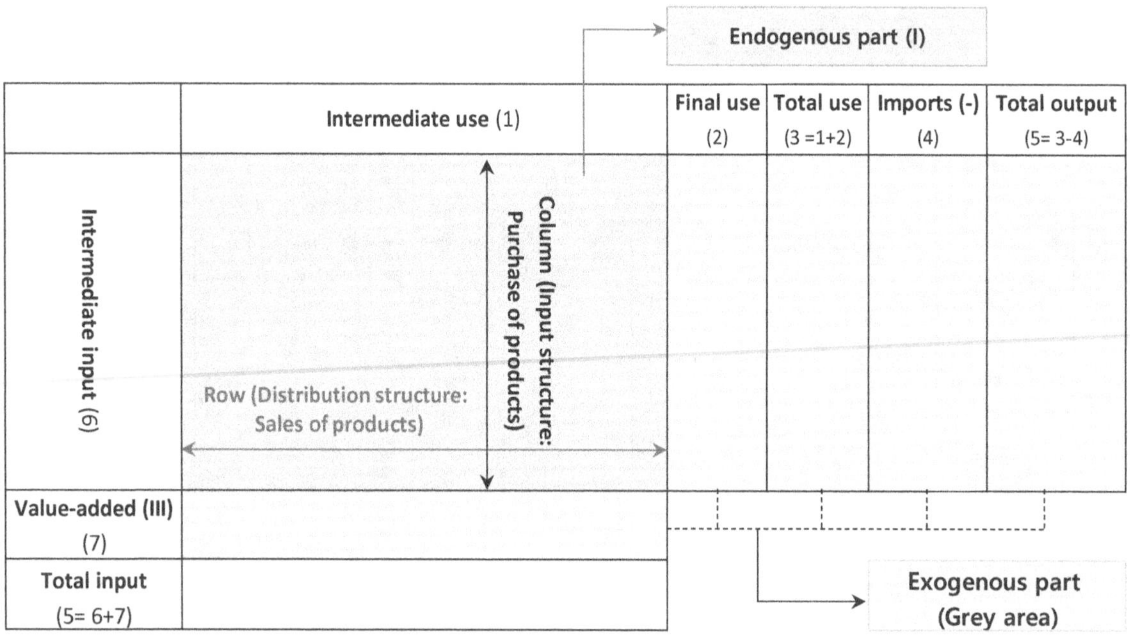

The description of the input-output table above presents a conceptual layout without specifying the price basis of the products. However, in practice, the input-output table (IOT) is compiled by reflecting the types of prices used in the supply and use tables, and it is displayed in the following two types. It is identical to the distinction made in section 22.1.1 between the net-exports presentation and the presentation that separates domestic output and imports. In the first format (**Type I**), products in intermediate use and final use are presented at both basic prices and purchasers' prices, with a bridging row for "taxes less subsidies on products" to connect the two valuations. In the second format (**Type II**), the same row of "taxes less subsidies on products" is included, but the imports column is removed; the imports values embedded in the intermediate use and final use cells are extracted and reallocated to a newly added imports row across intermediate use and final use. Type II is the layout most commonly used for input-output impact (*requirements*) analysis, and it is derived from a supply table at basic prices together with the corresponding use table at basic prices. In this chapter, the input-output analysis will be conducted on the basis of Type II.

Figure 22.2 Layouts of the input-output table reflecting price concepts

Type I

	Intermediate use (1)	Domestic final use (2)	Exports (3)	Total use (4=1+2+3)	**Imports (5)**	Total output at basic prices (6= 4−5)
Intermediate input						
Total intermediate input at basic prices (6)						
Taxes less subsidies on products (7)						
Total intermediate input at purchasers' prices (8=6+7)						
Gross value added (9)						
Total input at basic prices (10= 8+9)						

Type II

	Intermediate use (1)	Domestic final use (2)	Exports (3)	Total output at basic prices (4=1+2+3)
Domestic intermediate input				
Total domestic intermediate input at basic prices (5)				
Imports (6)				
Taxes less subsidies on products (7)				
Total intermediate input at purchasers' prices (8=5+6+7)				
Gross value added (9)				
Total input at basic prices (10= 8+9)				

Various analytical work with input-output tables begins by expressing the structure of intermediate uses or intermediate inputs (quadrant I) in a matrix form and then deriving and utilizing the Leontief inverse from it. If each element in quadrant I is denoted by $\boldsymbol{x_{ij}}$, the matrix formula ($\boldsymbol{X}$) is expressed as follows. Here, the subscript i and j indicate the row and column indices, respectively.

<Notation of quadrant I in the input-output table>

$$\boldsymbol{X} = \begin{bmatrix} x_{11} & \cdots & x_{1n} \\ \vdots & \ddots & \vdots \\ x_{n1} & \cdots & x_{nn} \end{bmatrix}$$

22.1.3 Input coefficients versus output coefficients

To derive the Leontief inverse, the input-output table must first be transformed into a coefficient table. Two kinds of coefficient are used. The first one is a table of **input coefficients**, which standardizes the column-wise input structure by scaling each column so that its total input equals 1. The second one is a table of **output coefficients**, which standardizes the row-wise distribution (use) structure by scaling each row so that its total output equals 1.

For example, given the input-output table as shown in Table 22.3, the input coefficients and output coefficients are displayed as follows.

Table 22.3 Schematic presentation of an input-out table

		Intermediate use							Final use	Imports (-)	Total output
		1	2	3	…	j	…	n			
Intermediate input	1	x_{11}	x_{12}	x_{13}	…	x_{1j}	…	x_{1n}	y_1	m_1	x_1
	2	x_{21}	x_{22}	x_{23}	…	x_{2j}	…	x_{2n}	y_2	m_2	x_2
	3	x_{31}	x_{32}	x_{33}	…	x_{3j}	…	x_{3n}	y_3	m_3	x_3
	⋮	⋮	⋮	⋮		⋮		⋮	⋮	⋮	⋮
	i	x_{i1}	x_{i2}	x_{i3}	…	x_{ij}	…	x_{in}	y_i	m_i	x_i
	⋮	⋮	⋮	⋮		⋮		⋮	⋮	⋮	⋮
	n	x_{n1}	x_{n2}	x_{n3}	…	x_{nj}	…	x_{nn}	y_n	m_n	x_n
Value added		v_1	v_2	v_3	…	v_j	…	v_n			
Total input		x_1	x_2	x_3	…	x_j	…	x_n			

First, the input coefficients (column basis) are obtained by dividing intermediate inputs and gross value-added by the column total input, and are expressed as follows:

Input coefficient in each column cell: $\boldsymbol{a_{ij}} = \frac{x_{ij}}{x_j}, \ \boldsymbol{w_j} = \frac{v_j}{x_j}$

with the column-sum constraint: $\sum_{i=1}^{n} (\boldsymbol{a_{ij}} + \boldsymbol{w_j}) = \sum_{i=1}^{n} (\boldsymbol{x_{ij}/x_j} + \boldsymbol{v_j/x_j}) = \mathbf{1}$

where a_{ij}: coefficient for the intermediate-input cell in row i and column j,

x_{ij}: value for the intermediate-input cell in row i and column j,

x_j: value for total input in column j (= intermediate inputs + gross value added),

v_j : gross value-added in column j

w_j: coefficient for gross value-added in column j (= v_j / x_j),

Next, the output coefficients (row basis) are obtained by dividing the intermediate use and "final use – imports" by the row total (total output), and are expressed as follows:

Output coefficient in each row cell: $b_{ij} = \frac{x_{ij}}{x_i}$, $d_i = (y_i - m_i)/x_i$

with the row-sum constraint: $\sum_{j=1}^{n}(b_{ij} + d_i) = \sum_{j=1}^{n}(x_{ij}/x_i + (y_i - m_i)/x_i) = 1$

where b_{ij} : coefficient for the intermediate-use cell in row i and column j,

x_{ij} : value for the intermediate-use cell in row i and column j,

x_i : value for total output in row i (= intermediate use + final use – imports),

y_i: final use in row i,

m_i : imports in row i

d_i : coefficient for "final use – imports" in row i (= $(y_i - m_i)/x_i$).

Given the same input-output table as in Table 22.1, the input coefficient table and the output coefficient table are computed as in Table 22.4 and Table 22.5, respectively.

Table 22.4 Input coefficient table

	Agriculture	Manufacturing	Electricity and construction	Services
Agriculture	0.150	0.150	0.267	0.071
Manufacturing	0.213	0.170	0.208	0.144
Electricity and construction	0.168	0.120	0.158	0.156
Services	0.195	0.260	0.100	0.162
Total intermediate input	0.725	0.700	0.733	0.533
Value added	0.275	0.300	0.267	0.467
Total input	1.000	1.000	1.000	1.000

Table 22.5 Output coefficient table

	Intermediate use					**Domestic final use**	**Net exports (= exports-imports)**	**Total output**
	Agriculture	Manufacturing	Electricity and construction	Services	Total			
Agriculture	0.150	0.188	0.400	0.080	0.818	0.225	-0.043	1.000
Manufacturing	0.170	0.170	0.250	0.130	0.720	0.230	0.050	1.000
Electricity, construction	0.112	0.100	0.158	0.117	0.487	0.550	-0.037	1.000
Service	0.173	0.289	0.133	0.162	0.758	0.278	-0.036	1.000

22.1.4 Intermediate input ratio and intermediate use ratio

From the input coefficient table in Table 22.4, the **intermediate input ratio** is defined as the share of total intermediate inputs in the column total input. It indicates the proportion of other products used as intermediate inputs in producing a given product and is commonly interpreted as a measure of **backward linkage**. In the table, the electricity and construction sector has the highest intermediate input ratio (0.733), suggesting the strongest reliance on the procurement of intermediate inputs.

Conversely, from the output coefficient table in Table 22.5, the **intermediate use ratio** is defined as the share of total intermediate use in the row total output. It shows how extensively a product is used (sold) as intermediate consumption in the production of other products, that is, the **forward linkage**. In this table, agricultural products record the highest intermediate-use ratio (0.818), indicating that the output of this sector is used most intensively as an input in other sectors' production. (The interpretation and use of forward and backward linkages are further discussed in section 22.2.4.)

22.1.5 The Leontief matrix and the Leontief inverse

The input coefficient table can be used to do various economic impact analyses. For example, when a final use for a product arises or increases, the demand for the intermediate inputs required to support its production rises accordingly. The principal tool for quantifying this is the **Leontief inverse**, which is derived as follows:

Let's assume the following notations. If X denotes domestic output, A (element-wise $0<A<1$) is the input-coefficient matrix describing the input cost structure of the domestic output, and Y is net final use (= final use – imports). Then the domestic output can be expressed as:

$$\mathrm{AX} + \mathrm{Y} = \mathrm{X},$$

and it can be transformed as:

$$(\mathrm{I} - \mathrm{A})\mathrm{X} = \mathrm{Y},$$

therefore, the following formula is derived:

$$\mathbf{X} = (\mathbf{I} - \mathbf{A})^{-1}\mathbf{Y}$$

Hence, if final use increases by $\Delta\mathrm{Y}$, the change in domestic output is $(\mathrm{I} - \mathrm{A})^{-1}\,\Delta\mathrm{Y}$. Here, $(\mathrm{I} - \mathrm{A})$ is called the **Leontief matrix**, and $(\mathrm{I} - \mathrm{A})^{-1}$ is called the **Leontief inverse.** The general form of the Leontief matrix, as shown in the format of the preceding Table 22.3, can be expressed as follows.

Presentation of Leontief matrix

$$\begin{vmatrix} (1-a_{11}) & -a_{12} & -a_{13} & \cdots & -a_{1j} & \cdots & -a_{1n} \\ -a_{21} & (1-a_{22}) & -a_{23} & \cdots & -a_{2j} & \cdots & -a_{2n} \\ -a_{31} & -a_{32} & (1-a_{33}) & \cdots & -a_{3j} & \cdots & -a_{3n} \\ \vdots & \vdots & \vdots & & \vdots & & \vdots \\ -a_{i1} & -a_{i2} & -a_{i3} & \cdots & (1-a_{ij}) & \cdots & -a_{in} \\ \vdots & \vdots & \vdots & & \vdots & & \vdots \\ -a_{n1} & -a_{n2} & -a_{n3} & \cdots & -a_{nj} & \cdots & (1-a_{nn}) \end{vmatrix}$$

Then, let's explain the meaning of this Leontief matrix in another way. If we calculate $(\mathrm{I}-\mathrm{A})$ in the above expression using the input coefficients table in Table 22.4, we obtain the following table.

Table 22.6 Leontief matrix: $(\mathrm{I}-\mathrm{A})$

	Agriculture	Manufactured	Electricity and construction	Services
Agriculture	0.850	-0.150	-0.267	-0.071
Manufactured	-0.213	0.830	-0.208	-0.144
Electricity, construction	-0.168	-0.120	0.842	-0.156
Services	-0.195	-0.260	-0.100	0.838

In this matrix, the diagonal elements are one minus the corresponding intermediate input coefficients, and the off diagonal elements are the intermediate input coefficients with a negative sign. Consequently, the sum of each column equals that column's **value-added coefficient**. For example, the column sum for agriculture products is 0.275, which is equal to one minus the sum of its intermediate input coefficients 0.725.

22.1.6 Requirements

Let's consider the output requirements for domestic production when a final demand arises within an economy. When one unit of final use for a product occurs, there is first a one-unit demand for that product itself. To produce that unit, first-round demands arise for the necessary intermediate inputs. In turn, producing those intermediate inputs generates second-round, third-round, and further successive intermediate demands. This sequence of induced demand is referred to as the **induced requirements**.

For example, using the input-coefficient table in Table 22.4, if one unit of final use occurs in agricultural products, then the first-round intermediate requirements are 0.150 for agricultural products, 0.213 for manufactured products, 0.168 for electricity and construction, and 0.195 for services, respectively. In the next-round, producing those amounts itself requires additional intermediate inputs, and so on. This process repeats continuously, and this series of production-inducing process can be expressed in a matrix form as follows.

Output requirements induced by one unit (value) of final use in agricultural products

$$\begin{vmatrix} 0.150 & 0.150 & 0.267 & 0.071 \\ 0.213 & 0.170 & 0.208 & 0.144 \\ 0.168 & 0.120 & 0.158 & 0.156 \\ 0.195 & 0.260 & 0.100 & 0.162 \end{vmatrix} \times \begin{vmatrix} 1 \\ 0 \\ 0 \\ 0 \end{vmatrix} = \begin{vmatrix} 0.150 \\ 0.213 \\ 0.168 \\ 0.195 \end{vmatrix}$$

$$\begin{vmatrix} 0.150 & 0.150 & 0.267 & 0.071 \\ 0.213 & 0.170 & 0.208 & 0.144 \\ 0.168 & 0.120 & 0.158 & 0.156 \\ 0.195 & 0.260 & 0.100 & 0.162 \end{vmatrix} \times \begin{vmatrix} 0.150 \\ 0.213 \\ 0.168 \\ 0.195 \end{vmatrix} = \begin{vmatrix} 0.113 \\ 0.131 \\ 0.108 \\ 0.133 \end{vmatrix}$$

$$\begin{vmatrix} 0.150 & 0.150 & 0.267 & 0.071 \\ 0.213 & 0.170 & 0.208 & 0.144 \\ 0.168 & 0.120 & 0.158 & 0.156 \\ 0.195 & 0.260 & 0.100 & 0.162 \end{vmatrix} \times \begin{vmatrix} 0.113 \\ 0.131 \\ 0.108 \\ 0.133 \end{vmatrix} = \begin{vmatrix} 0.075 \\ 0.088 \\ 0.073 \\ 0.088 \end{vmatrix}$$

$$\vdots$$

Expressing this process in matrix form, the **total requirements** matrix/vector (Z) for a product equals the sum of the initial one unit of final use (I) and the successive induced rounds (A, A^2, A^3, A^4, ⋯, A^n):

(22.1) $$\mathbf{I + A + A^2 + A^3 + \cdots + A^n = Z}$$

Here, A is the input-coefficient matrix and I is the identity matrix. Equation (22.1) can be obtained by using the standard sum of a geometric series as follows. Multiplying both sides of equation (22.1) by the common ratio A (1> A >0) gives equation (22.2).

(22.2) $$\mathbf{A + A^2 + A^3 + A^4 + \cdots + A^{n+1} = ZA}$$

Subtracting equation (22.2) from equation (22.1) yields:

$$\mathbf{I - A^{n+1} = Z - ZA = Z\,(I - A),}$$

Therefore,

$$\mathbf{Z = (I - A)^{-1}\,(I - A^{n+1})}$$

Here, as n approaches infinity, A^{n+1} becomes zero ($\lim_{n\to\infty} A^{n+1} = 0$), and thus Z = $(I - A)^{-1}$. This is equivalent to the coefficient of equation "X = $(I - A)^{-1}$ Y" derived earlier. In other words, when one unit of final use arises ($\Delta Y=1$), the increase in output requirements, including the initial unit and the additional induced impacts, equals $(I - A)^{-1}$. The matrix $(I - A)^{-1}$ is the Leontief inverse mentioned above and represents so-called the **total requirements table** when assuming a one-unit increase in final demand for domestic output[32]. The results of total requirements table from the example of the previous input-output table are illustrated as follows. (See section 22.2.1 for further explanation on the total requirements.)

Table 22.7 Total requirements: $(I-A)^{-1}$

	Agriculture	Manufactured	Electricity, construction	Services	Total
Agriculture	1.488	0.460	0.623	0.321	2.892
Manufactured	0.608	1.541	0.626	0.433	3.208
Electricity, construction	0.493	0.429	1.497	0.394	2.812
Services	0.594	0.636	0.518	1.450	3.198
Total	3.182	3.066	3.264	2.598	

Example of measuring total requirements

Using the total requirements table $(I - A)^{-1}$, we can measure the requirements induced when final use arises. Suppose one-unit (in value terms) of final use for agricultural product occurs. The total requirements can be measured as:

$$\underset{(I-A)^{-1}}{\begin{vmatrix} 1.488 & 0.460 & 0.623 & 0.321 \\ 0.608 & 1.541 & 0.626 & 0.433 \\ 0.493 & 0.429 & 1.497 & 0.394 \\ 0.594 & 0.636 & 0.518 & 1.450 \end{vmatrix}} \times \underset{\Delta Y}{\begin{vmatrix} 1 \\ 0 \\ 0 \\ 0 \end{vmatrix}} = \underset{\Delta X}{\begin{vmatrix} 1.488 \\ 0.608 \\ 0.493 \\ 0.594 \end{vmatrix}}$$

Each total requirement can be interpreted as the sum of (i) the initial unit of demand (1), (ii) the direct requirement (the first-round input coefficient), and (iii) the indirect requirements (higher-round induced requirements). Thus, for one unit of final use in agricultural products, the total requirement for that sector is 1.488 (= 1 + 0.150 + 0.338); with the agricultural product contributing one unit (1) of final demand, input coefficient of 0.150, and other induced impact of 0.338. For manufactured products, it is 0.608 (input coefficient of 0.213 and other induced impact of 0.395).

[32] In April 2009, the U.S. Bureau of Economic Analysis (BEA) adopted the term **requirements** in place of **multipliers** to avoid conceptual confusion with the term "multipliers" used in macroeconomics as a fiscal stimulus effect.

For electricity and construction, it is 0.493; and for services, it is 0.594. In total, the induced output requirement sums to 3.182 (= 1,488 + 0.608 + 0.493 + 0.594) (Table 22.8).

In practical applications, the induced requirements are calculated by inputting the monetary value instead of a one-unit increase in final use for agricultural products.

Table 22.8 Decomposition of requirements for one unit of final use in agriculture products

	Initial unit (1)	Input coefficient (2)	Other induced requirements (3)	Total requirements (1+2+3)
Agriculture	1	0.150	0.338	1.488
Manufactured	0	0.213	0.395	0.608
Electricity, construction	0	0.168	0.325	0.493
Services	0	0.195	0.399	0.594
Total	1	0.725	1.457	3.182

22.1.7 Ghosh inverse

The Leontief inverse represents the inverse of the Leontief matrix, i.e., $(I - A)^{-1}$, which is derived from the intermediate input coefficients **A** of the input-output table. On the other hand, there is a method of calculating the inverse of (I – B), namely $\mathbf{(I - B)^{-1}}$, based on the output coefficient matrix **B** of the intermediate use part. This is referred to as the **Ghosh inverse**. The Ghosh inverse can be used in measuring the forward linkage effects of each industry, as explained later (see section 22.2.4).

22.2 Applications of input-output analysis

Once the input-output table is compiled, matrix techniques can be applied to this table to quantitively analyze various impacts of economic variables such as production, wages, employment and price changes. This method is known as "input-output analysis technique", which uses the Leontief inverse derived from the input coefficients of the input-output table mentioned earlier as a primary analytical instrument. The main application areas of this input-output analysis can be enumerated as follows.

Measurement of the impact on economic variables by quantity models

- Estimating the impact on domestic output in response to changes in domestic final use, using output multipliers.

- Estimating the impact on imports in response to changes in domestic final use, using import multipliers.
- Estimating the impact on value-added in response to changes in domestic final use, using value-added multipliers.
- Estimating the impact on taxes less subsidies on products in response to changes in domestic final use, using net taxes on products multipliers.
- Estimating the impact on employment (i.e., the number of employed persons) in response to changes in domestic final use, using employment multipliers.
- Estimating the impact on domestic production, imports, and value-added resulting from changes in the production activities of specific industries.
- Estimating the impact on pollutant emissions in response to changes in domestic final use, using emission multipliers.

Measurement of the impact on price variables by price models

- Estimating the impact on domestic prices resulting from the changes in wage rate.
- Estimating the impact on domestic prices resulting from the changes in import prices.
- Estimating the impact on domestic prices resulting from the exchange rate fluctuations.
- Estimating the impact on domestic prices resulting from the changes in the prices of specific domestic products.

All of the above applications share the same analytical framework, an approach centered on the Leontief inverse, and provide a systematic account of the channels and magnitudes through which policy changes or exogenous shocks transmit across the economy.

22.2.1 Derivation and interpretation of the total requirements table

The principal purpose of using the input-output table is to quantify, on the basis of input coefficients, (i) the various total effects on economic variables (in value or quantity terms) and (ii) price effects via price models. The instrument employed for this measurement is the **Leontief inverse** of the input-output table, $(I - A)^{-1}$, which is derived from the production inducement process of intermediate inputs in response to final demand. In this section, using the system of simultaneous equations composed of the coefficients in the row and columns of an actual input-output table, we will specifically explore how to derive these total requirements (coefficients) and how to interpret, in more concrete terms, the requirements associated with each entry.

The input-output table can be displayed as the following system of linear equations:

$$\begin{aligned}
a_{11}x_1 + a_{12}x_2 + \cdots + a_{1n}x_n + y_1 - m_1 &= x_1 \\
a_{21}x_1 + a_{22}x_2 + \cdots + a_{2n}x_n + y_2 - m_2 &= x_2 \\
&\vdots \\
a_{i1}x_1 + a_{i2}x_2 + \cdots + a_{in}x_n + y_i - m_i &= x_i \\
&\vdots \\
a_{n1}x_1 + a_{n2}x_2 + \cdots + a_{nn}x_n + y_n - m_n &= x_n
\end{aligned}$$

where a_{ij} denotes the intermediate input coefficient at the cell where row i and column j intersect ($a_{ij} = x_{ij}/x_j$), x_{ij} is the value of the intermediate input at the cell where row i and column j intersect, x_j is the total output (= total input) in column j, x_i is the total output in row i, y_i is the final use in row i, and m_i is imports in row i, respectively.

To express the above equations in a matrix form, it is as follows:

$$\begin{vmatrix} a_{11} & a_{12} & \cdots & a_{1j} & \cdots & a_{1n} \\ a_{21} & a_{22} & \cdots & a_{2j} & \cdots & a_{2n} \\ \vdots & \vdots & & \vdots & & \vdots \\ a_{i1} & a_{i2} & \cdots & a_{ij} & \cdots & a_{in} \\ \vdots & \vdots & & \vdots & & \vdots \\ a_{n1} & a_{n2} & \cdots & a_{nj} & \cdots & a_{nn} \end{vmatrix} \begin{vmatrix} x_1 \\ x_2 \\ \vdots \\ x_i \\ \vdots \\ x_n \end{vmatrix} + \begin{vmatrix} y_1 \\ y_2 \\ \vdots \\ y_i \\ \vdots \\ y_n \end{vmatrix} - \begin{vmatrix} m_1 \\ m_2 \\ \vdots \\ m_i \\ \vdots \\ m_n \end{vmatrix} = \begin{vmatrix} x_1 \\ x_2 \\ \vdots \\ x_i \\ \vdots \\ x_n \end{vmatrix}$$

$$\mathbf{AX + Y - M = X}$$

where A is the matrix of intermediate input coefficients, X is the column vector of total output, Y is the column vector of final use, and M is the column vector of imports, respectively. Transforming this equation and solving for X gives:

$$\mathrm{X - AX = Y - M}$$

$$(I - \mathrm{A})\mathrm{X} = \mathrm{Y - M}$$

Therefore,

$$\mathbf{X = (\mathit{I} - A)^{-1}(Y - M)},$$

where $(I - \mathrm{A})^{-1}$ is the Leontief inverse (i.e., **total requirements table**). I denotes the identity matrix, whose diagonal elements are all 1 and off-diagonal elements are all 0.

Interpretation of total requirements table

Let's examine the meaning of each element's value, assuming that the intermediate use in the input-output table consists of three products and the Leontief inverse (total requirements table) has been derived as illustrated in the table below (Table 22.9).

Column reading: Let's consider the columns of the total requirements table. In the first column, r_{11} represents the requirement of product A, namely, the one unit of A itself destined for final use plus the direct and indirect requirements for intermediate inputs of product A when final use for the product increases by one unit. r_{21} represents the requirement for intermediate inputs of product B, and r_{31} represents the requirement for intermediate inputs of product C, respectively, in response to an increase in the final use by one-unit of product A. Therefore, the column sum (R_1) indicates total requirements across all products in the economy generated by a one-unit increase in final use of product A. The elements in the second and third columns can be explained in the same way.

Table 22.9 Total requirements table: $(I-A)^{-1}$

	Product A	Product B	Product C	Row sum
Product A	r_{11}	r_{12}	r_{13}	S_1
Product B	r_{21}	r_{22}	r_{23}	S_2
Product C	r_{31}	r_{32}	r_{33}	S_3
Column sum	R_1	R_2	R_3	

This can be explained using the actual data of total requirements table for the three sectors introduced in Table 22.7. Looking at the first column for agricultural products, if the final use for these products increases by one unit, then to meet this demand, 1.488 of agricultural products including one unit of its final use, 0.608 of manufactured products, 0.493 of electricity and construction, and 0.594 of services will be required for intermediate inputs respectively. Therefore, the column sum of 3.182 represents total requirements for products, including the final use itself, when the final use for agricultural products increases by one unit.

Row reading: Next, let's consider the rows of total requirements table in Table 22.9. In the first row, r_{11} represents the one unit of product A itself (for final use) together with the remaining direct and indirect requirements for A when the final use for A increases by one unit. r_{12} represents the requirement for intermediate use of product A when the final use for product B increases by one unit, and r_{13} represents the requirement for intermediate use of product A when final use for product C increases by one unit. Therefore, the row sum of the first row (S_1) indicates total requirements of product A when the final use for each product increases by one unit respectively. The same interpretation applies to the row sums of the second and third rows.

This can be explained using the actual data of total requirements table introduced in Table 22.7. Looking at the second row for manufactured products, when the final use for agricultural products increases by one unit, the requirement for manufactured products is 0.608. When the final use for manufactured products increases by one unit, the requirement (including one unit of final use for manufactured products itself) is 1.541. When the final use for electricity and construction increases by one unit, the requirement for manufactured products is 0.626, and when the final use for services increases by one unit, the requirement for manufactured products is 0.433. Therefore, the row sum of 3.208 represents total requirements for manufactured products when the final use for each product increases by one unit.

Box 22.1 Direct derivation of total requirements table from the SUTs

When final demand for a product arises, the increase in output generated directly and indirectly within the endogenous part (quadrant I) can, in general, be measured using the total requirements table (Leontief inverse) derived from the input-output table. Although the input-output table (IOT) is obtained indirectly from the supply and use tables (SUTs) by imposing several assumptions, one can also derive the total output requirements directly from the SUTs. The method for the direct derivation of total requirements uses the transformation formulae presented in the Annex to Chapter 21 for deriving the IOTs from the SUTs. The specific formulae depend on whether the target symmetric IOT is "product-by-product" or "industry-by-industry," and on which assumption is adopted among the product technology assumption, industry technology assumption, fixed industry sales structure assumption, and fixed product sales structure assumption (see Table 22.10).

For a **product-by-product** symmetric input-output table, the formula for deriving the total requirements table (Leontief inverse) depends on whether the product technology assumption or the industry technology assumption is adopted. The former uses $(I - BC^{-1})^{-1}$, and the latter uses $(I - BD)^{-1}$. For an **industry-by-industry** symmetric input-output table, the formula for deriving total requirements table uses $(I - C^{-1}B)^{-1}$ under the fixed industry sales structure assumption and $(I - DB)^{-1}$ under the fixed product sales structure assumption.

Table 22.10 Deriving total requirements from the SUTs

Symmetric IOT type	Assumption of transformation	Formula for total output requirements
Product-by-product	Product technology	$(I - BC^{-1})^{-1}$
Product-by-product	Industry technology	$(I - BD)^{-1}$
Industry-by-industry	Fixed industry sales structure	$(I - C^{-1}B)^{-1}$
Industry-by-industry	Fixed product sales structure	$(I - DB)^{-1}$

Notations of the above formulas are defined as follows.

Notation	Description	Definition
I	Unit matrix	
B	Input coefficient matrix based on the use table U (product-by-industry)	$\mathrm{B} = U\hat{\mathrm{g}}^{-1}$
C	Product-mix matrix by industry, based on the supply table S (product-by-industry)	$\mathrm{C} = S\hat{\mathrm{g}}^{-1}$
C^{-1}	Inverse matrix of C	$\hat{\mathrm{g}}S^{-1}$
D	Market share matrix by product, based on the transpose of the supply table S (industry-by-product)	$S^{\mathrm{T}}\hat{\mathrm{q}}^{-1}$

Here, $\hat{\mathrm{g}}$ denotes the diagonal matrix of total output by industry, and $\hat{\mathrm{q}}$ denotes the diagonal matrix of total output by product.

Derivation of "Industry-by-product" total requirements

For analytical purposes, one may wish to obtain total requirements from an input-output table laid out with rows = industries and columns = products. In this case, total requirements must be derived on an **industry by product** basis. To apply the basic formulae above, the rows and columns must be transformed to industries and products, respectively. Under the product technology assumption and the fixed industry sales structure assumption, we use the equation $\mathrm{C}^{-1}(\mathrm{I}-\mathrm{B}\mathrm{C}^{-1})^{-1}$ or $(\mathrm{I}-\mathrm{C}^{-1}\mathrm{B})^{-1}\mathrm{C}^{-1}$ (both equations yield the same result). Under the industry technology assumption and the fixed product sales structure assumption, we use the equation $\mathrm{D}(\mathrm{I}-\mathrm{B}\mathrm{D})^{-1}$ or $(\mathrm{I}-\mathrm{D}\mathrm{B})^{-1}\mathrm{D}$ (both equations yield the same result) to measure total requirements.

Table 22.11 Formulas for deriving total requirements of "industry-by-product" tables

Transformation assumption	Formula for total requirements
Production technology	$\mathrm{C}^{-1}(\mathrm{I}-\mathrm{B}\mathrm{C}^{-1})^{-1}$
Industry technology	$\mathrm{D}(\mathrm{I}-\mathrm{B}\mathrm{D})^{-1}$
Fixed industry sales structure	$(\mathrm{I}-\mathrm{C}^{-1}\mathrm{B})^{-1}\mathrm{C}^{-1}$
Fixed product sales structure	$(\mathrm{I}-\mathrm{D}\mathrm{B})^{-1}\mathrm{D}$

22.2.2 Types of total requirements table

As explained earlier, from the basic identity $\mathrm{X} = (\mathrm{I}-\mathrm{A})^{-1}(Y - M)$, once the exogeneous vector $(Y - M)$ is given, multiplying it by the total requirements $(\mathrm{I}-\mathrm{A})^{-1}$ yields total output X. Because the value of output generated varies not only with final use Y but also with imports M, how the imports term is treated is crucial. As mentioned earlier in section 22.1.1, input-output tables are compiled in two alternative layouts depending on how imports are recorded.

First, there is a layout that places imports in a separate column and presents "net exports" as a column (exports minus imports). Second, there is a layout that allocates imports across intermediate and final uses in a separate row, thereby not setting up an imports column. Below, we describe how to derive the requirements under each of these two layouts of input-output tables.

22.2.2.1 Derivation of total requirements table in an IOT with a net-exports column

This type of total requirements table is derived from the identity "$AX+Y-M=X$" as introduced earlier. The total requirements form in this case is $\mathbf{(I-A)^{-1}}$, and given the exogenous vector $(Y-M)$, the value of total output induced by the total requirements is $(I-A)^{-1}(Y-M)$. In this formula, imports M are treated as a separate exogenous term, so a distinct set of imports requirements cannot be identified. The total requirements table obtained in this way are shown earlier in Table 22.7.

In practice, however, imports often move in line with changes in total output (covering domestic intermediate and final uses), rather than behaving like an independent exogenous item of final use. To reflect this, the imports column in the input-output table can be modeled as a fixed proportion m of total output. That is, the original identity is modified to:

$$\mathbf{AX+Y-\hat{m}X=X}$$

By factoring out X from this formula, it can be expressed as $X(I-A+\hat{m})=Y$, leading to the following expression:

$$\mathbf{X=(I-A+\hat{m})^{-1}Y}$$

where $\hat{m}$ is the diagonal matrix of m and represents the ratio of imports to total output (which is called **imports coefficient**). Under this specification, total requirements are $(I-A+\hat{m})^{-1}$, and the imports coefficient $\hat{m}$ are treated as endogenous, as is the intermediate input coefficients A. The imports coefficients and the resulting total requirements computed from this specification are reported in Table 22.12.

Table 22.12 Total requirements table accounting for imports coefficients

Imports coefficient ($\hat{m}$)					Total requirements: $(I-A+\hat{m})^{-1}$			
Agriculture	Manufactures	Electricity and construction	Services		Agriculture	Manufactures	Electricity and construction	Services
0.1425	0	0	0	Agriculture	1.1930	0.3220	0.4493	0.2068
0	0.060	0	0	Manufactures	0.4288	1.3491	0.4717	0.3069
0	0	0.0617	0	Electricity and construction	0.3451	0.3177	1.3134	0.2823
0	0	0	0.1356	Services	0.3890	0.4575	0.3510	1.1798
				Total	2.3559	2.4464	2.5854	1.9758

22.2.2.2 Derivation of total requirements table from the IOT that separates domestic output and imports

In an input-output table where domestic output and imports are recorded separately, the table is split into an input-output table for domestic output (comprising intermediate and final use for domestic output only) and an input table for imports (comprising intermediate and final use for imported products). When deriving total requirements table in this layout, the coefficients for domestically produced products used in intermediate and final uses are distinguished from those for imported products. The matrix structure of this input-output table, which is separately indicated into domestic output and imported products, is represented as follows:

(22.3) **Domestic output:** $\mathbf{A^d X + Y^d = X}$

(22.4) **Imports:** $\mathbf{A^m X + Y^m = M}$

where A^d is the intermediate input coefficients of domestic output, Y^d is the final use of domestic output (including exports), A^m is the intermediate input coefficient of imports, and Y^m is the final use of imports. Rearranging the expression (22.3) in terms of X, we have:

$$(I - A^d)X = Y^d,$$

(22.5) $$\mathbf{X = (I - A^d)^{-1} Y^d}$$

The implication of equation (22.5) is that when the final use for domestic products (Y^d) arises, the multiplier $(I - A^d)^{-1}$ generates domestic output equal to X. In this case, $(I - A^d)^{-1}$ represents total requirements matrix for domestic output. The total requirements table for domestic output derived from the example in Table 22.2 (the IOT that separates domestic output and imports) are shown as follows.

Table 22.13 Total requirement table for domestic output from an IOT that separates domestic output and imports

Total requirements table for domestic output: $(I-A^d)^{-1}$

	Agriculture	Manufactures	Electricity and construction	Services
Agriculture	1.3859	0.3132	0.5251	0.2330
Manufactures	0.5215	1.4123	0.5276	0.3549
Electricity and construction	0.4001	0.2760	1.4008	0.3130
Services	0.4682	0.4432	0.3801	1.3106
Total	2.7757	2.4447	2.8336	2.2115

Furthermore, by substituting equation (22.5) into equation (22.4) in place of X, it can be expressed as follows:

(22.6) $$\mathbf{M = A^m (I - A^d)^{-1} Y^d + Y^m}$$

According to equation (22.6), when the final use for domestic output (Y^d) arises, the value of imports induced by the multiplier $A^m(I-A^d)^{-1}$ is generated by $A^m(I - A^d)^{-1} Y^d$. By adding the final use for imported products (Y^m), the total induced value for imports is derived. In this formulation, $\mathbf{A^m(I - A^d)^{-1}}$ is the **imports requirements** matrix. (For an example of deriving total requirements for domestic output and imports using the input-output table, refer to section 22.2.3.1.)

In practical applications, the analysis of domestic impacts in the input-output uses the requirements matrix $(I - A^d)^{-1}$, which excludes imports from intermediate inputs. The total requirements table that includes imports in intermediate inputs is not suitable for analyzing effects confined to the domestic economy. Accordingly, **in what follows, all analyses of total requirements on economic variables (impact analyses) will be conducted on the basis of the latter inverse matrix** $\mathbf{(I - A^d)^{-1}}$.

22.2.3 Impact analyses based on the quantity model

This section examines the methodology for measuring the total effects of changes in final use on various economic variables by using the Leontief inverse matrix derived from input coefficients of the input-output table, together with illustrative examples of such measurements. Target variables for which total effects can be measured in response to changes in final use include domestic output, imports, value-added, taxes on products, employment, and material emissions.

The standard approach is to compile the input-output table by separating both the intermediate use and final use into domestic output and imports, and then to use the inverse of the resulting input-coefficients matrix. To express this relationship in equations, we refer back to $A^d X + Y^d = X$ (equation 22.3) and $A^m X + Y^m = M$ (equation 22.4), which were derived in section 22.2.2.2. In these equations, X is domestic output, A^d the intermediate input coefficients of domestic output, Y^d the final demand for domestic output, M imports, A^m the intermediate input coefficients of imports, and Y^m the final demand for imports, respectively. In practical compilation, when compiling the table, equation (22.3) is obtained by subtracting equation (22.4) from the combined total input-output table (which includes both equations (22.3) and (22.4)). From these equations, we obtain

$$\mathbf{X = (I-A^d)^{-1} Y^d, \quad M = A^m (I-A^d)^{-1} Y^d + Y^m,}$$

so that $(I - A^d)^{-1}$ is the total requirements for domestic output, and $A^m (I - A^d)^{-1}$ the imports requirements. This framework is used widely to measure how changes in the final use for domestic output affect domestic output and imports, and further, underpin the analysis of price effects discussed in section 22.2.5 (e.g., the impacts of wages, import prices, exchange rates, or price changes of individual product on domestic prices). Accordingly, most applications proceed under this model when quantifying various total effects. The analysis below likewise follows this model.

As basic data, we use the input-output table of South Korea, as shown in the table below (based on the year 2015, with product-by-product of four sector table).

Table 22.14 Example of input-output table (South Korea, 2015, product-by-product)

Total input-output table (Unit: trillion KRW)

	Agriculture	Manufactures	Electricity, construction	Services	Total intermediates (1)	Domestic final use	Exports	Final use (2)	Total use (1+2)	Imports (3)	Total output (basic price) (4=1+2-3)
Agriculture	3.2	38.9	0.5	11.3	53.9	18.3	0.7	19.0	72.9	11.6	61.3
Manufactures	17.1	919.0	125.0	199.6	1,260.7	284.4	610.7	895.1	2,155.8	494.1	1,661.8
Electricity, constr.	0.8	39.8	15.4	43.5	99.6	219.5	0.7	220.2	319.8	0.2	319.6
Services	6.5	223.4	48.9	457.0	735.7	931.4	104.9	1,036.2	1,772.0	97.6	1,674.3
Total (basic price)	27.6	1,221.1	189.8	711.4	2,149.9	1,453.6	717.0	2,170.5	4,320.5	603.4	3,717.0
Net taxes on products	0.6	5.0	7.9	32.7	46.2	90.9	-	90.9	137.1	20.6	116.5
Total IC (purchaser's price)	28.1	1,226.1	197.7	744.2	2,196.1	1,544.5	717.0	2,261.5	4,457.6	624.0	3,833.6
Remuneration of employees	5.2	176.8	75.4	492.8	750.2						
Operating surplus	22.6	140.0	25.5	253.4	441.5						
Depreciation	4.8	114.8	20.0	170.0	309.7						
Net taxes on production	0.6	4.0	1.0	14.0	19.6						
Gross value added	33.2	435.6	121.9	930.2	1,520.9						
Total input (basic price)	61.3	1,661.8	319.6	1,674.3	3,717.0						

Input table for imports (Unit: trillion KRW)

	Agriculture	Manufactures	Electricity, construction	Services	Total intermediates	Domestic final use	Exports	Final use	Total use (3)
Agriculture	0.3	8.1	0.1	0.6	9.1	2.5	0.0	2.5	11.6
Manufactures	1.1	324.1	38.5	31.1	394.9	97.1	2.1	99.2	494.1
Electricity, constr.	0.0	0.0	0.0	0.1	0.1	0.1	0.0	0.1	0.2
Services	0.4	15.9	1.8	44.3	62.5	35.2	0.0	35.2	97.6
Total (basic price)	1.8	348.1	40.4	76.2	466.5	134.8	2.1	136.9	603.4

Input-output table for domestic output (Unit: trillion KRW)

	Agriculture	Manufactures	Electricity, construction	Services	Total intermediates	Domestic final use	Exports	Final use	Total use (4)
Agriculture	2.9	30.8	0.5	10.7	44.8	15.8	0.7	16.5	61.3
Manufactures	16.0	594.9	86.5	168.4	865.8	187.3	608.6	796.0	1,661.8
Electricity, constr.	0.8	39.8	15.4	43.5	99.5	219.4	0.7	220.1	319.6
Services	6.1	207.5	47.1	412.7	673.3	896.2	104.9	1,001.1	1,674.3
Total (basic price)	25.8	873.0	149.4	635.3	1,683.4	1,318.8	714.8	2,033.6	3,717.0

From the above table, the input coefficients tables can be derived as follows (Table 22.15). The procedure begins by deriving the **total input coefficients matrix (A)** by taking the input entries of the total input-output table as the numerator and the "total input" value as the denominator. Similarly, input coefficient tables for imports ($\mathbf{A^m}$) and domestic output ($\mathbf{A^d}$) are prepared by using the total input value as the denominator, while distinguishing between imports and domestic output.

Table 22.15 Input coefficients tables (South Korea, 2015)

Total input coefficients (A)

	Agriculture	Manufactures	Electricity, construction	Services
Agriculture	0.0518	0.0234	0.0016	0.0068
Manufactures	0.2785	0.5530	0.3911	0.1192
Electricity, construction	0.0136	0.0240	0.0481	0.0260
Services	0.1053	0.1344	0.1530	0.2729
Total (basic price)	0.4493	0.7348	0.5939	0.4249
Taxes less subsidies on products	0.0091	0.0030	0.0248	0.0195
Total intermediates (purchaser's price)	0.4584	0.7378	0.6186	0.4445
Gross value added	0.5416	0.2622	0.3814	0.5555
Total input (basic price)	1.0000	1.0000	1.0000	1.0000

Input coefficients for imports ($\mathbf{A^m}$)

	Agriculture	Manufactures	Electricity, construction	Services
Agriculture	0.0053	0.0049	0.0002	0.0004
Manufactures	0.0177	0.1950	0.1206	0.0186
Electricity, construction	0.0000	0.0000	0.0000	0.0000
Services	0.0061	0.0096	0.0058	0.0265
Total (basic price)	0.0291	0.2095	0.1265	0.0455

Input coefficients for domestic output ($\mathbf{A^d}$)

	Agriculture	Manufactures	Electricity, construction	Services
Agriculture	0.0465	0.0185	0.0014	0.0064
Manufactures	0.2608	0.3580	0.2705	0.1006
Electricity, construction	0.0136	0.0240	0.0481	0.0260
Services	0.0992	0.1248	0.1473	0.2465
Total (basic price)	0.4202	0.5254	0.4673	0.3794

Using the above three input coefficient tables, one can analyze various total effects for the domestic economy. For effects associated with changes in final use, we use the Leontief inverse for domestic output, $(I-\mathbf{A^d})^{-1}$. Here, I denotes the identity matrix (one on the main diagonal and zeros elsewhere). To calculate the Leontief inverse, we first construct $(I-\mathbf{A^d})$.

Table 22.16 Leontief matrix for domestic output: $(I-\mathbf{A^d})$

	Agriculture	Manufactures	Electricity, construction	Services
Agriculture	0.9535	-0.0185	-0.0014	-0.0064
Manufactures	-0.2608	0.6420	-0.2705	-0.1006
Electricity, construction	-0.0136	-0.0240	0.9519	-0.0260
Services	-0.0992	-0.1248	-0.1473	0.7535

From this matrix, we derive the inverse $(I - A^d)^{-1}$ as follows. Using this inverse in the subsequent sections, we illustrate examples of applying various impact analyses.

Table 22.17 Leontief inverse matrix for domestic output: $(I - A^d)^{-1}$

	Agriculture	Manufactures	Electricity, construction	Services
Agriculture	1.0597	0.0338	0.0133	0.0140
Manufactures	0.4799	1.6369	0.5031	0.2400
Electricity, construction	0.0334	0.0495	1.0714	0.0438
Services	0.2256	0.2853	0.2945	1.3772
Total	1.7986	2.0056	1.8824	1.6750

22.2.3.1 Total effects on economic variables by changes in final use for domestic output

When quantifying, in value or quantity terms, the total effects on various economic variables resulting from changes in final use, the basic framework is formed as:

$$Z = B(I - A)^{-1} Y$$

where Z is the value (or quantity) of total effects (total requirements) for the variable of interest (e.g., output, imports, value added, employment, pollutant emissions), B is the coefficients matrix (or vector) of that variable, I is the identity matrix, A is the matrix of intermediate input coefficients, and Y is the final use vector, respectively. Based on this equation, hereafter, we will examine the total effects of each economic variable.

Domestic output generated by changes in final use for domestic output

The Leontief inverse matrix for domestic output, $(I - A^d)^{-1}$ is used as the **total requirements matrix for domestic output**. Here, the coefficient B, which corresponds to the coefficient of domestic output, is the identity matrix. Therefore, the amount of domestic output (X) generated by an increase in final use for domestic output (Y^d) is calculated as:

$$X = (I - A^d)^{-1} Y^d$$

Applying this to the four-sector South Korean example above (2015), where the final use for domestic output is 2,033.6 trillion KRW (16.5 for agriculture, 796.0 for manufacturing, 220.1 for electricity and construction, and 1,001.1 for services), the total induced value of domestic output is calculated as follows.

Table 22.18 Total requirements and domestic output generated by changes in final use for domestically produced output

(Unit: trillion KRW)

	Total requirements for domestic output: $(I - A^d)^{-1}$				Final use for domestic output (Y^d)	**Total domestic output generated: $(I - A^d)^{-1} Y^d$**
	Agriculture	Manufactures	Electricity, construction	Services		
Agriculture	1.0597	**0.0338**	0.0133	0.0140	16.5	61.3
Manufactures	0.4799	**1.6369**	0.5031	0.2400	796.0	1,661.8
Electricity, construction	0.0334	**0.0495**	1.0714	0.0438	220.1	319.6
Services	0.2256	**0.2853**	0.2945	1.3772	1,001.1	1,674.3
Total	1.7986	**2.0056**	1.8824	1.6750	2,033.6	3,717.0

From this table, each column sum of the inverse (total requirements for domestic output) shows the increase in total domestic output when the final use of that sector rises by one unit. In this example, the column sums are 1.7986 for agricultures, 2.0056 for manufactures, 1.8824 for electricity and construction, and 1.6750 for services. For instance, a one-unit increase in manufactures' final use induces domestic output of 0.0338 in agriculture, 0.0495 in electricity and construction, 0.2853 in services, and 1.6369 in manufactures itself (including direct and indirect requirements). The column sum of 2.0056 therefore indicates that a one-unit increase in final use for manufactures generates 2.0056 of total domestic output across the economy. Comparing the column sums shows that, per unit of sectoral final use, the domestic-output effect is largest for manufactures (2.0056) and the smallest for services (1.6750).

Given the final use for domestic output (= domestic final use + exports) of 2,033.6 trillion KRW, the total induced values of domestic output are as follows: 61.3 trillion KRW in agriculture, 1,661.8 trillion KRW in manufactures, 319.6 trillion KRW in electricity and construction, and 1,674.3 trillion KRW in services, respectively. Thus, the total induced value of domestic output, including the final use itself (2,033.6 trillion KRW), amounts to 3,717.0 trillion KRW (= 61.3+1,661.8+319.6+1,674.3). This value equals the total output at basic prices and total input at basic prices in the total input-output table shown in Table 22.14, and matches the actual total use in the domestic input-output table (at basic prices). Meanwhile, the **domestic output multiplier** with respect to final use for domestic output is 1.8278 (= 3,717.0/2,033.6).

Imports generated by changes in final use for domestic output

How much imports are generated by changes in final use for domestic output can be measured by the **imports requirements matrix**, $A^m(I-A^d)^{-1}$, which is set out in the previous equation (22.6) (refer to 22.2.2.2). This matrix shows the amount of imports induced when final use for domestic output occurs by one unit. Accordingly, the value of imports generated by final use for domestic output (Y^d) is calculated as $\mathbf{A^m (I - A^d)^{-1} Y^d}$. Adding the final use for imports (Y^m) to this induced value of imports yields total induced imports **M**:

$$\mathbf{M} = \mathbf{A^m (\mathit{I} - A^d)^{-1} Y^d + Y^m}$$

If the same final use for domestic output (Y^d) is applied as in the previous example, the total induced value of imports is computed as follows.

Table 22.19 Imports requirements and total imports generated by changes in final use for domestic output

(Unit: trillion KRW)

	Imports requirements: $A^m (I - A^d)^{-1}$				Final use of domestic output (Y^d)	**Imports generated: $A^m (I - A^d)^{-1} Y^d$**	**Total imports: $A^m (I-A^d)^{-1} Y^d + Y^m$**
	Agriculture	Manufactures	Electricity, construction	Services			
Agriculture	0.0080	0.0083	0.0028	0.0018	16.5	9.1	11.6
Manufactures	0.1206	0.3311	0.2331	0.0779	796.0	394.9	494.1
Electricity, construction	0.0000	0.0000	0.0000	0.0001	220.1	0.1	0.2
Services	0.0172	0.0237	0.0189	0.0391	1,001.1	62.5	97.6
Total	0.1458	0.3632	0.2547	0.1189	2,033.6	466.5	603.4

According to this table, the column sums of the imports requirements by sector show that manufactures have the largest (0.3632), while services have the smallest (0.1189). This indicates that the dependence on imports is higher for manufacturing sector and lower for services sector. Given final use for domestic output of 2,033.6 trillion KRW (= domestic final use plus exports), the imports generated on the domestic economy amounts to 466.5 trillion KRW by the formula $\mathbf{A^m (I - A^d)^{-1} Y^d}$ (9.1 for agriculture, 394.9 for manufactures, 0.1 for electricity and construction, and 62.5 for services). Total imports, which is the sum of this induced imports (466.5 trillion KRW) and final use for imports (Y^m) of 136.9 trillion KRW, equals 603.4 trillion KRW (11.6 trillion KRW for agriculture; 494.1 trillion KRW for manufacturing; 0.2 trillion KRW for electricity and construction; and 97.6 trillion KRW for services). This amount (603.4 trillion KRW) matches the actual total imports in the **input table for imports** in Table 22.14.

Value-added generated by changes in final use for domestic output

The effects of changes in the final use for domestic output on value added are measured as follows. Let V denote the value-added vector and $\hat{A}^v$ the diagonal matrix of value-added input coefficients. Then,

$$\mathbf{V = \hat{A}^v X}$$

where X is the column vector of total outputs. Since $X = (I - A^d)^{-1} Y^d$ in the previous equation (22.5), substituting this equation into $V = \hat{A}^v X$ yields the following equation:

$$\mathbf{V = \hat{A}^v (I - A^d)^{-1} Y^d}$$

Accordingly, the **value-added requirements** for measuring the effects of changes in final use for domestic output are given by $\mathbf{\hat{A}^v (I - A^d)^{-1}}$. This matrix shows the amount of value-added generated when final use for domestic output occurs by one unit. Hence, total value-added induced by an increase in final use for domestic output (Y^d) is obtained from the expression $\mathbf{\hat{A}^v (I - A^d)^{-1} Y^d}$.

The table below reports the results when Y^d is the same as in the previous example.

Table 22.20 Value-added requirements and value-added generated by changes in final use for domestic output

(Unit: trillion KRW)

	Value-added requirements: $\hat{A}^v (I - A^d)^{-1}$				Final use for domestic output (Y^d)	**Total value-added generated: $\hat{A}^v (I - A^d)^{-1} Y^d$**
	Agriculture	Manufactures	Electricity, construction	Services		
Agriculture	0.5739	0.0183	0.0072	0.0076	16.5	33.2
Manufactures	0.1258	0.4291	0.1319	0.0629	796.0	435.6
Electricity, construction	0.0127	0.0189	0.4086	0.0167	220.1	121.9
Services	0.1253	0.1585	0.1636	0.7651	1,001.1	930.2
Total	0.8378	0.6248	0.7113	0.8523	2,033.6	1,520.9

As a result of the final use for domestic output (i.e., domestic final use plus exports) amounting to 2,033.6 trillion KRW, the value-added generated is 33.2 trillion KRW in agriculture, 435.6 trillion KRW in manufactures, 121.9 trillion KRW in electricity and construction, and 930.2 trillion KRW in services, respectively. Therefore, total value-added generated is 1,520.9 trillion KRW (= 33.2+435.6+121.9+930.2), which is consistent with the actual gross value-added reported in Table 22.14. The **value-added multiplier** with respect to final use for domestic output is 0.748 (= 1,520.9/2,033.6).

Taxes less subsidies on products generated by changes in final use for domestic output

The effects on taxes less subsidies on products arising from changes in final use for domestic output can be measured as follows. Let T be the vector of taxes less subsidies on products, $\hat{A}^t$ the diagonal matrix of input coefficients for taxes less subsidies on products, X the column vector of total output, and let T^d and T^m denote the amounts of taxes less subsidies on products embedded in the final use for domestic output and imports, respectively. Then, the matrix for taxes less subsidies on products can be expressed as follows:

$$\text{(22.7)} \qquad \mathbf{T} = \mathbf{\widehat{A}^t X} + \mathbf{T^d} + \mathbf{T^m}$$

From equation (22.5), $X = (I - A^d)^{-1} Y^d$. Substituting this into equation (22.7) yields the following:

$$\mathbf{T} = \mathbf{\widehat{A}^t (I - A^d)^{-1} Y^d} + \mathbf{T^d} + \mathbf{T^m}$$

Thus, when one unit of final use for domestic output occurs, the **requirements for taxes less subsidies on products** is given by the matrix $\mathbf{\widehat{A}^t (I - A^d)^{-1}}$. Given Y^d, the total amount of taxes less subsidies on products is obtained by adding the taxes less subsidies on products embedded in final use ($T^d + T^m$) to the generated amount $\mathbf{\widehat{A}^t (I - A^d)^{-1} Y^d}$. If final use for domestic output occurs at the same amount as in the previous example, the requirements and total values for taxes less subsidies on products can be calculated as follows.

Table 22.21 Requirements and values for "taxes less subsidies on products" generated by changes in final use for domestic output

(Unit: Trillion KRW)

	Taxes less subsidies on products requirements: $\widehat{A}^t (I - A^d)^{-1}$				Final use for domestic output (Y^d)	**Generated taxes less subsidies on products: $\widehat{A}^t (I - A^d)^{-1} Y^d$**	**Total taxes less subsidies on products: $\widehat{A}^t (I - A^d)^{-1} Y^d + (T^d + T^m)$**
	Agriculture	Manufactures	Electricity, construction	Services			
Agriculture	0.0097	0.0003	0.0001	0.0001	16.5	0.6	
Manufactures	0.0014	0.0049	0.0015	0.0007	796.0	5.0	
Electricity, construction	0.0008	0.0012	0.0265	0.0011	220.1	7.9	
Services	0.0044	0.0056	0.0058	0.0269	1,001.1	32.7	
Total	0.0163	0.0120	0.0339	0.0289	2,033.6	46.2	46.2+90.9 = 137.1

From the above table, as a result of the final use for domestic output (2,033.6 trillion KRW), the generated taxes less subsidies on products are 0.6 trillion KRW from agriculture, 5.0 trillion KRW from manufactures, 7.9 trillion KRW from electricity and construction, and 32.7 trillion KRW from services, totaling 46.2 trillion KRW. Adding the taxes less subsides on products embedded in final use (90.9 trillion KRW: domestic output 70.4, imports 20.6) yields the total taxes less subsidies on products of 137.1 trillion KRW. This figure matches the actual total in the "total input-output table" in Table 22.14.

Finally, note that combining the imports requirements $A^m (I - A^d)^{-1}$, the value-added requirements $\widehat{A}^v (I - A^d)^{-1}$, and the requirements for taxes less subsidies on products $\widehat{A}^t (I - A^d)^{-1}$ yields the identity matrix. The reason for this can be explained as follows: In the input coefficients matrix,

$A^d + A^m + \widehat{A}^t + \widehat{A}^v = I$, hence $A^m + \widehat{A}^t + \widehat{A}^v = I - A^d$. Dividing both sides by $(I - A^d)$, we get:

$$(A^m + \widehat{A}^t + \widehat{A}^v)\,(I - A^d)^{-1} = I$$

Thus,

$$\mathbf{A^m (I - A^d)^{-1} + \widehat{A}^t (I - A^d)^{-1} + \widehat{A}^v (I - A^d)^{-1} = I}$$

Employment generated by changes in final use for domestic output

Employment effects measure how many additional persons are employed when final use for domestic output increases. The basic indicator used here is the **employment coefficient**, which shows the number of employed persons per unit of output for each industry (or product). "Employed persons" include both employees in enterprises and the self-employed workers. When the measure is restricted to employees only, it is usually referred to as the **employee coefficient**.

To measure employment generated by changes in final use, an employment coefficient table must first be constructed. The vector of employment coefficients (L^w) can be defined as follows:

- **Employment coefficient (L^w) = Employed persons by sector/output by sector**

Table 22.22 below shows the resulting number of employed persons and employment coefficients for South Korea in 2015, based on the above formula. The output per sector used to calculate the employment coefficients is obtained from the 2015 South Korea's Input-output table (Table 22.14), which was introduced earlier.

Table 22.22 Employed persons and employment coefficients (South Korea, 2015)

	Employed persons (thousand)	Output (Basic price, trillion KRW)	Employment coefficient[1] (thousand/ trillion KRW): (L^w)
Agriculture	1,227.5	61.3	20.01
Manufactures	4,097.5	1,661.8	2.47
Electricity, construction	1,850.7	319.6	5.79
Services	16,946.5	1,674.3	10.12
Total	24,122.2	3,717.0	6.49

Note: 1) Employment coefficient = employed person / value of output

The number of employed persons by industry (or product) can be expressed as "employment coefficient × output", which can be represented in a matrix form as $\mathbf{L} = \widehat{\mathbf{L^w}}\,\mathbf{X}$. Here, L denotes the vector of employed persons by industry (or product), $\widehat{L^w}$ is the diagonal matrix of employment coefficients, and X is the output vector, respectively. Substituting X in this equation with the domestic output requirements formula $X = (I - A^d)^{-1} Y^d$, the equation transforms into the following:

$$\mathbf{L = \widehat{L^w}\,(I - A^d)^{-1}\,Y^d}$$

Thus, the **employment requirements** for measuring the effects of changes in final use for domestic output are $\mathbf{\widehat{L^w}\,(I - A^d)^{-1}}$. This matrix shows the number of persons employed when final use for a given domestically produced output increases by one unit (in value terms). Consequently, the number of employed persons generated by Y^d (final use for domestic output) is expressed by the formula $\mathbf{\widehat{L^w}\,(I - A^d)^{-1}\,Y^d}$.

For example, if Y^d is the same as in the previous example, the total number of employed persons generated is as follows.

Table 22.23 Employment requirements and total employment generated

	Employment requirements (thousand person/ trillion KRW): $\widehat{L^w}\,(I - A^d)^{-1}$				Final use for domestic output (trillion KRW): (Y^d)	**Total employment generated** (thousand person): $\widehat{L^w}(I - A^d)^{-1}\,Y^d$
	Agriculture	Manufactures	Electricity, construction	Services		
Agriculture	21.21	0.68	0.27	0.28	16.5	1,227.5
Manufactures	1.18	4.04	1.24	0.59	796.0	4,097.5
Electricity, construction	0.19	0.29	6.20	0.25	220.1	1,850.7
Services	2.28	2.89	2.98	13.94	1,001.1	16,946.5
Total	24.87	7.89	10.69	15.06	2,033.6	24,122.2

In the table above, if final use for manufactured products increases by 1 trillion KRW, employment generated equals 0.68 thousand in agriculture, 0.29 thousand in electricity and construction, 2.89 thousand in services, and 4.04 thousand within manufactures itself (of which 2.47 is the own employment coefficient and 1.57 arises through inter-industry requirements). The column sum 7.89 (thousand person per trillion KRW) is the total employment effect associated with a one-unit increase in final use for manufactured products.

Moreover, when final use for domestic output (= domestic final use plus exports) amounts to 2,033.6 trillion KRW, the total employment generated is 24,122.2 thousand persons (1,227.5 in agriculture; 4,097.5 in manufactures; 1,850.7 in electricity and construction; and 16,946.5 in services). These totals coincide with the actual numbers of employed persons by sector (see Table 22.22). Hence, the **total employment multiplier** with respect to final use is 11.9 thousand persons per trillion KRW (= 24,122.2 / 2,033.6).

Emissions generated by changes in final use for domestic output

The emission effects measure the total quantities of physical emissions, such as greenhouse gases, waste, energy use, generated within the domestic economy when final use for domestic output increases. If emission coefficients for domestic products are available, the effects of changes in final use can be quantified. The **emission coefficient** (**p**) represents emissions per unit of output of an economy. The **emission requirements** are derived by using the formula $p(I-A^d)^{-1}$, which combines the emission coefficient with the Leontief inverse matrix. This is the total coefficient, interpretable as the sum of the direct emission coefficient p and the indirect component p $[(I-A^d)^{-1}-I]$. Given final use for domestic output Y^d, the emissions generated are:

$$p\,(I-A^d)^{-1}\,Y^d$$

As an illustration, suppose annual emissions of CO_2, waste, and energy by industry are as shown below, then the emission coefficients for each substance (= quantity of emission/ value of output) can be computed as in Table 22.24 and 22.25.

Table 22.24 Source data for physical emissions

(Unit: million Ton)

	Agriculture	Manufactures	Electricity, construction	Services	Total industry (1)	Final consumption (2)	Total emissions (1+2)
CO_2 emission	28.0	256.4	205.7	109.5	599.6	34.7	634.3
Waste emission	0.4	7.8	1.1	3.5	12.8	3.0	15.8
Energy emission (TOE)	2.2	81.0	35.4	16.7	135.3	1.4	136.8

Table 22.25 Emission coefficients by substance (p)

(Unit: million tonnes/trillion KRW)

	Agriculture	Manufactures	Electricity, construction	Services	Total industry
CO_2 coefficient	0.457	0.154	0.644	0.065	0.161
Waste coefficient	0.007	0.005	0.004	0.002	0.003
Energy coefficient	0.035	0.049	0.111	0.010	0.036
Total output (trillion KRW)	61.3	1,661.8	319.6	1,674.3	3,717.0

The resulting emission requirements and total emissions generated are illustrated in Table 22.26. For example, for CO_2, when final use for domestic output increases by one unit, the emission requirements for agriculture is 0.595 (million tonnes/trillion KRW). This figure is the sum of the direct coefficient (0.457) and the indirect coefficient 0.138 (= 0.595 – 0.457). When final use for domestic output (i.e., domestic final use plus exports) occurs as in Table 22.14, CO_2 emissions generated in the industrial sectors amounts to 599.6 million tonnes. Adding the 34.7 million tonnes emitted directly in the final consumption sector yields total emissions of 634.3 million tonnes (= 599.6 +34.7). Applying the same method to waste and energy, the quantities generated in the industrial sector are 12.8 million tonnes of waste and 135.3 million TOE of energy use; including the additions from final consumption, the corresponding totals are 15.8 million tonnes and 136.8 million TOE, respectively.

Table 22.26 Emission requirements and total emissions generated by substance

(Unit: million Tonnes)

	Emission requirements: $p(I-A^d)^{-1}$				Emissions generated (1): $p(I-A^d)^{-1}Y^d$	Total emission generated: (1)+Emissions from final consumption
	Agriculture	Manufactures	Electricity, construction	Services		
CO_2 emission	0.595	0.319	0.792	0.162	599.6	634.3
Waste emission	0.010	0.009	0.007	0.004	12.8	15.8
Energy emission	0.067	0.089	0.147	0.031	135.3	136.8

22.2.3.2 Effects generated by the production activity of a specific industry

In the previous sections, we examined how changes in final use (final demand) for domestic products transmit to various economic variables and quantity variables, using the Leontief inverse from the input-output table. Input-output analysis can be used to measure not only the impact of changes in final use on domestic industries, but also the impact of production activities in a particular industry on other domestic economy. For example, when construction activity or government expenditure increases, we can quantify the impact of output, imports, and value-added generated in other domestic industries. Below, we will discuss how the input-output analysis can be used to measure the economic impact on other industries when the output of one industry changes.

Domestic output generated by the production activity of a specific industry

In the input-output table, the production activity of a specific industry lies in the intermediate input quadrant (endogenous block). Therefore, the effects of changes in that industry's own output cannot be directly identified within this framework. However, if we treat that industry as exogenous (i.e., remove it from the endogenous block and move it to the exogenous block), we can compute how changes in that industry's output affect the others.

The method of treating a specific industry as exogenous involves shifting its row and column out of the endogenous block into the exogenous block. For example, citing the same input-output table as in Table 22.14 above (four industries; domestic and imports distinguished), we aim to measure the impact of the services sector's production on domestic output. Then, extract the services sector' row and column in the intermediate input quadrant and move them to the exogenous block as illustrated in Table 22.27.

Table 22.27 Transfer of the services sector to the exogenous block in the input-output table

		Endogenous			Exogenous		Imports	Total output
		Agriculture	Manufactures	Electricity, construction	Services	Final use		
Domestic	Agriculture	X^d_{11}	X^d_{12}	X^d_{13}	X^d_{14}	F^d_1		X_1
	Manufactures	X^d_{21}	X^d_{22}	X^d_{23}	X^d_{24}	F^d_2		X_2
	Electricity, construction	X^d_{31}	X^d_{32}	X^d_{33}	X^d_{34}	F^d_3		X_3
Imports	Agriculture	X^m_{11}	X^m_{12}	X^m_{13}	X^m_{14}	F^m_1	M_1	
	Manufactures	X^m_{21}	X^m_{22}	X^m_{23}	X^m_{24}	F^m_2	M_2	
	Electricity, construction	X^m_{31}	X^m_{32}	X^m_{33}	X^m_{34}	F^m_3	M_3	
Services		X_{41}	X_{42}	X_{43}	X_{44}	F_4	M_4	X_4
Taxes less subsidies on products		T_1	T_2	T_3	T_4	T_F	T_m	T_d
Value-added		V_1	V_2	V_3	V_4			V
Total input		X_1	X_2	X_3	X_4			

After moving the services sector to the exogenous block, the relationship between the sector and the remaining endogenous sectors (agriculture, manufacturing, and electricity-construction) can be written in matrix form as:

$$\underbrace{\begin{vmatrix} a^d_{11} & a^d_{12} & a^d_{13} \\ a^d_{21} & a^d_{22} & a^d_{23} \\ a^d_{31} & a^d_{32} & a^d_{33} \end{vmatrix}}_{\mathbf{A^d}} \underbrace{\begin{vmatrix} X_1 \\ X_2 \\ X_3 \end{vmatrix}}_{\mathbf{X}} + \underbrace{\begin{vmatrix} a^d_{14} \\ a^d_{24} \\ a^d_{34} \end{vmatrix}}_{\mathbf{A^d_4}} \underbrace{\begin{vmatrix} X_4 \end{vmatrix}}_{\mathbf{X_4}} + \underbrace{\begin{vmatrix} F^d_1 \\ F^d_2 \\ F^d_3 \end{vmatrix}}_{\mathbf{F^d}} = \underbrace{\begin{vmatrix} X_1 \\ X_2 \\ X_3 \end{vmatrix}}_{\mathbf{X}}$$

where a^d_{ij} $(= X^d_{ij}/X_j)$ is the domestic intermediate input coefficient in row i and column j; X^d_{ij} is the domestic intermediate input in that cell; X_j is total input in column j; and F^d is final use for domestic products. This can be expressed in compact form as:

$$\mathbf{A^d X + A^d_4 X_4 + F^d = X}$$

where A^d is the (3 x 3) matrix of domestic intermediate input coefficients among the non-services industries (the endogenous sectors), A^d_4 is the (3 x 1) vector of domestic intermediate input coefficients for services column that has been moved to the exogenous block, and X_4 is total inputs (output) of the services sector. Grouping X on one side, we get:

$$(I - A^d)\, X = A^d_4\, X_4 + F^d$$

From this, the following equation is derived:

(22.8) $$\mathbf{X = (I - A^d)^{-1} (A^d_4 X_4 + F^d)}$$

where $(I - A^d)^{-1}$ denotes the domestic total output requirements for endogenous block excluding services. If we assume there is no final use for domestic output ($F^d = 0$), equation (22.8) becomes as follows:

(22.9) $$\mathbf{X = (I - A^d)^{-1} A^d_4 X_4}$$

In other words, the output generated in the other industries by the services' output (X_4) equals $(I - A^d)^{-1} A^d_4 X_4$, and total induced amount of domestic output is derived by adding the services' own output (X_4) to this amount.

Total domestic output generated by the services' output (X_4): $(I - A^d)^{-1} A^d_4 X_4 + X_4$

Let's now look at an example applying the above equation in practice. By using the same data already cited in Table 22.14, and replacing the products category in this table with industries, the following table is obtained by moving the row and column of the services industry's intermediate inputs to the exogenous side.

Table 22.28 Result of moving the services industry to the exogenous side in the IOT

(Unit: trillion KRW)

	Endogenous			Exogenous		Imports	Total output
	Agriculture	Manufactures	Electricity, construction	Services	Final use (= Domestic final use + exports)		
Domestic	2.9	30.8	0.5	10.7	16.5		61.3
	16.0	594.9	86.5	168.4	796.0		1,661.8
	0.8	39.8	15.4	43.5	220.1		319.6
Imports	0.3	8.1	0.1	0.6	2.5	11.6	
	1.1	324.1	38.5	31.1	99.2	494.1	
	0.0	0.0	0.0	0.1	0.1	0.2	
Services	6.5	223.4	48.9	457.0	1,036.2	97.6	1,674.3
(Domestic)	6.1	207.5	47.1	412.7	1,001.1		1,674.3
(Imports)	0.4	15.9	1.8	44.3	35.2	97.6	
Taxes less subsidies on products	0.6	5.0	7.9	32.7	90.9	20.6	116.5
Value-added	33.2	435.6	121.9	930.2			1,520.9
Total input	61.3	1,661.8	319.6	1,674.3	2,261.5	624.0	

The result of converting the above input-output table into an input coefficient table is as follows.

Table 22.29 Input coefficients table

	Endogenous			Exogenous	
	Agriculture (A_1)	Manufactures (A_2)	Electricity, construction (A_3)	Services (A_4)	Final use (F)
Domestic (A^d)	0.046	0.019	0.001	0.006	
	0.261	0.358	0.271	0.101	
	0.014	0.024	0.048	0.026	
Imports (A^m)	0.005	0.005	0.000	0.000	
	0.018	0.195	0.121	0.019	
	0.000	0.000	0.000	0.000	
Services (domestic) (A^d_4)	0.099	0.125	0.147	0.246	
Services (imports) (A^m_4)	0.006	0.010	0.006	0.026	
Taxes less subsidies on products (A^T)	0.009	0.003	0.025	0.020	
Value-added (A^V)	0.542	0.262	0.381	0.556	
Total input (X)	1.000	1.000	1.000	1.000	

Table 22.30 illustrates the result of measuring how much the services industry's output of 1,674.3 trillion KRW induces the output in other industries. First, the requirements which measure the impact on output in the other industries due to the services' output is $\mathbf{(I-A^d)^{-1} A^d_4}$ (excluding the services' row and column), and the induced output in each industry except services industry is $\mathbf{(I-A^d)^{-1} A^d_4 X_4}$. As a result, total output of other industries generated by the output of services industry (1,674.3 trillion KRW) is 17.0 trillion KRW in agriculture, 291.7 trillion KRW in manufacturing, and 53.3 trillion KRW in electricity and construction, leading to 362.0 trillion KRW in total (=17.0+291.7+53.3). Therefore, total domestic output generated is 2,036.3 trillion KRW, which is the sum of the 362.0 trillion KRW induced in other industries and the 1,674.3 trillion KRW of services industry's own output.

Total domestic output generated by services: $\mathbf{(I-A^d)^{-1} A^d_4 X_4 + X_4}$ = 362.0 + 1,674.3 = 2,036.3

Table 22.30 Domestic output generated by a specific industry (services)

	Output requirements (1): $\mathbf{(I-A^d)^{-1} A^d_4}$	Output in services industry (trillion KRW) (2): (X_4)	**Output generated** (trillion KRW): (3=1x2): **(X)**	**Total generated output** (trillion KRW): $\mathbf{(I-A^d)^{-1} A^d_4 X_4 + X_4}$
Agriculture	0.010		17.0	
Manufactures	0.174		291.7	
Electricity, construction	0.032		53.3	
Total	0.216	1,674.3	362.0	2,036.3

Imports generated by the production activity of a specific industry

The method for quantifying the imports generated by a specific industry's production activity is the same as for domestic output above. Recalling Table 22.27 (the method of transferring to exogenous part in the input-output table), let's examine the formula for deriving the requirements on imports. First, in this table, imports (M) can be written as:

(22.10) $$\mathbf{A^m X + A^m_4 X_4 + F^m = M}$$

where A^m is the input coefficients matrix for imports from the endogenous block excluding services, $\mathbf{A^m_4}$ is the input coefficients vector for services industry that are moved to exogenous block, $\mathbf{X_4}$ is the total output of services sector, and $\mathbf{F^m}$ denotes the final use for imports associated with the services sector. By substituting equation (22.9) for X in equation (22.10), it can be expressed as follows:

(22.11) $$\mathbf{A^m (I - A^d)^{-1} A^d_4 X_4 + A^m_4 X_4 + F^m = M}$$

If we assume there is no final demand for imports ($F^m = 0$) in this expression, this reduces to:

(22.12) $$\mathbf{A^m (I - A^d)^{-1} A^d_4 X_4 + A^m_4 X_4 = M}$$

Here, $A^m (I - A^d)^{-1} A^d_4 X_4$ is the imports induced by the output of services sector (X_4), while $A^m_4 X_4$ is the own direct imports by the services sector.

Let's apply this formula to a practical example. Referring again to the previously cited Table 22.28 and Table 22.29, the following results are derived (Table 22.31): The own imports in the services sector are 44.3, and the induced imports are 65.1, thus total imports generated by the services sector amounts to 109.5 trillion KRW (= 44.3+65.1).

Table 22.31 Imports generated by the production activity of a specific industry (services)

	Imports requirements: $A^m (I - A^d)^{-1} A^d_4$	Output of services industry (trillion KRW): (X_4)	Induced imports (trillion KRW): $A^m (I - A^d)^{-1} A^d_4 X_4$	Total imports generated (trillion KRW): $A^m (I - A^d)^{-1} A^d_4 X_4 + A^m_4 X_4$
Agriculture	0.0009		1.5	
Manufactures	0.0380		63.6	
Electricity, construction	0.0000		0.00	
Total	0.0389	1,674.3	65.1	109.5

Value-added generated by the production activity of a specific industry

The total value-added generated by the production activity of the services sector is calculated as:

Total value-added from the services sector' output (X_4): $A^v(I-A^d)^{-1}A^d_4X_4 + A^v_4X_4$

Here, $A^v(I-A^d)^{-1}A^d_4X_4$ represents the value-added generated in other industries by the output of services sector, while $A^v_4X_4$ denotes the services' own value-added, reflecting the actual value-added of the services sector. If this formula is applied to actual data in Table 22.28 and Table 22.29, the following results are calculated (Table 22.32). With the output of services sector X_4 = 1,674.3 trillion KRW, the own value-added is 930.2 trillion KRW, and the value-added generated in other industries is 106.0 trillion KRW, resulting in total of 1,036.2 trillion KRW.

Table 22.32 Value-added generated by the production activity of a specific industry (services)

Generated in other industries (1)			Own generation (2)	Total
$A^v(I-A^d)^{-1}A^d_4$	X_4 (trillion KRW)	$A^v(I-A^d)^{-1}A^d_4X_4$ (trillion KRW)	$A^v_4X_4$ (trillion KRW)	(1)+(2) (trillion KRW)
0.0633	1,674.3	106.0	930.2	1,036.2

Domestic output generated by the production activity of government services

Most government services' output is imputed to government's final consumption expenditure, whereas government investment is not related to the endogenous part and appears as an exogenous item in final use. Accordingly, to measure the effects on domestic output by the government services' activity, it is necessary to distinguish between these two parts:

- The current production of government services is treated as exogenous (i.e., government sector's row and column are removed from the endogenous block and transferred to exogenous block), and the output effects to other industries are computed as in the case of section 22.2.3.2.
- The government's investment activity, being separate from its current production activity, does not require special adjustments, and the output effects can be directly measured from changes in its own final use (see section 22.2.3.1).

22.2.3.3 Summary of impact analyses in the quantity model

Thus far, we have explained how to derive value- or quantity-based effects (the impact analyses in terms of value or quantity) using the Leontief inverse of the input-output table, and the summary is as follows. If the exogenous (independent) variable is **final use**, the requirements take the generic form of $\mathbf{B\,(I-A^d)^{-1}}$, where B is the coefficient matrix (or vector) for the variable being measured (output, imports, value added, employment, emissions), and $\mathbf{(I-A^d)^{-1}}$ is the domestic Leontief inverse. In addition, if a particular industry belonging to the endogenous block is treated as exogenous in order to measure its effects, that industry's row and column must be moved to the exogenous side, and its total effects are computed (the total generated amount includes the industry's own size).

Table 22.33 Summary of formulas in the quantity model

Measurement target	Exogenous variable	Requirements (coefficient)	Total generated value or quantity[1)]
Impact on domestic output	Final use (Y^d)	$(I-A^d)^{-1}$	$(I-A^d)^{-1}\,Y^d$
Impact on imports	Final use (Y^d)	$A^m\,(I-A^d)^{-1}$	$A^m\,(I-A^d)^{-1}\,Y^d$ + $[Y^m]$
Impact on value-added	Final use (Y^d)	$\widehat{A^v}\,(I-A^d)^{-1}$	$\widehat{A^v}\,(I-A^d)^{-1}\,Y^d$
Impact on taxes less subsides on products	Final use (Y^d)	$\hat{A}^t\,(I-A^d)^{-1}$	$\hat{A}^t(I-A^d)^{-1}\,Y^d + [T^d + T^m]$
Impact on employment	Final use (Y^d)	$\widehat{L^w}((I-A^d)^{-1}$	$\widehat{L^w}(I-A^d)^{-1}Y^d$
Impact on emissions	Final use (Y^d)	$p\,(I-A^d)^{-1}$	$p\,(I-A^d)^{-1}\,Y^d$ + [Emissions from final expenditure]
Impact on domestic output[2)]	Specific industry (X_e)	$(I-A^d)^{-1}\,A^d_e$	$(I-A^d)^{-1}\,A^d_e\,X_e$ + $[X_e]$
Impact on imports[2)]	Specific industry (X_e)	$A^m\,(I-A^d)^{-1}\,A^d_e$	$A^m\,(I-A^d)^{-1}\,A^d_e\,X_e$ + $[A^m_e\,X_e]$
Impact on value-added[2)]	Specific industry (X_e)	$A^v\,(I-A^d)^{-1}\,A^d_e$	$A^v\,(I-A^d)^{-1}\,A^d_e\,X_e$ + $[A^v_e\,X_e]$

Footnote: 1) Items in square brackets [ ] denotes the final use for the target variable itself.

2) X_e, A^d_e, A^m_e, and A^v_e denote, respectively, the output, domestic input coefficients, imports coefficient and value-added input coefficients of the specific industry which is moved to exogenous part.

22.2.4 Measurement of forward and backward linkages using inverse matrices

Earlier, it was mentioned that if the **intermediate input ratio**, which represents the share of other products used as intermediate inputs in the production of a certain product, is higher, the **backward linkage** becomes larger. Likewise, if the **intermediate use ratio**, which indicates the extent to which a product is used as the intermediate use for other products, is higher, the **forward linkage** also becomes larger. (See "Intermediate input ratio and intermediate use ratio" in section 22.1.4.) However, for more precise measurement than these simple ratios, it is often preferable to use indicators based on the Leontief inverse or the Ghosh inverse. The procedure is as follows:

- **Backward linkage**: take the column sum of the Leontief inverse for domestically produced output, $(I - A^d)^{-1}$, and normalize it by dividing by the average of all column sums. (This normalized index is called the influence coefficient.) Values greater than 1 indicate above-average backward linkage; values less than 1 indicate below-average linkage.
- **Forward linkage**: take the row sum of the Ghosh inverse for domestically produced output, $(I - B^d)^{-1}$, and normalize it by dividing by the average of all row sums. (This normalized index is called the sensitivity coefficient.) Values greater than 1 indicate above-average forward linkage; values less than 1 indicate below-average linkage.

If Table 22.17 is cited again as an example, the average of the column sums of the domestic Leontief inverse is 1.840 (= (1.799+2.006+1.882+1.675)/4). Dividing each column sum by this average yields the influence coefficients. In this example, this ratio for manufactured products is 1.090 (= 2.006/1.840), which is the highest among the four sectors.

Table 22.34 Leontief inverse for domestic output and backward linkage

Leontief inverse: $(I - A^d)^{-1}$	Agriculture	Manufactures	Electricity, construction	Services	Average (2)
Agriculture	1.060	0.034	0.013	0.014	
Manufactures	0.480	1.637	0.503	0.240	
Electricity, construction	0.033	0.049	1.071	0.044	
Services	0.226	0.285	0.295	1.377	
Column sum (1)	1.799	2.006	1.882	1.675	1.840
Influence coefficient (1/2)	0.977	1.090	1.023	0.910	

Similarly, for the domestic Ghosh inverse, the average of the row sums is 1.927 (= (2.427+1.993+1.565+1.725)/4). Dividing each row sum by this average yields the sensitivity coefficients. In the example below, this ratio for agricultural products has the highest coefficient, 1.259 (= 2.427/1.927) among all products.

Table 22.35 Ghosh inverse for domestic output and forward linkage

Ghosh inverse: $(I - B^d)^{-1}$	Agriculture	Manufactures	Electricity, construction	Services	Row sum (1)	Sensitivity coefficient (1/2)
Agriculture	1.060	0.917	0.070	0.381	2.427	1.259
Manufactures	0.018	1.637	0.097	0.242	1.993	1.034
Electricity, construction	0.006	0.257	1.071	0.230	1.565	0.812
Services	0.008	0.283	0.056	1.377	1.725	0.895
Average (2)					1.927	

In short, the influence coefficient (backward linkage) is an intuitive index showing (relative to the average) the economy-wide output generated by a one-unit increase in the sector's final use, while the sensitivity coefficient (forward linkage) shows the use generated in other sectors by a one-unit increase in the sector's output.

22.2.5 Impact analyses based on the price model

In the previous subsection, we examined how to analyze the impacts in terms of quantity or value using the Leontief inverse from the input-output table. Here, we apply the same inverse on the price side to explain how a price change in a particular sector transmits to the overall price level.

22.2.5.1 Methodology for impact analyses on the price side

The input coefficients matrix of the input-output table allows us to measure how a price increase in one sector passes through to price in other sectors. The method starts from the identity that, in any column of the input-output table, total input equals the sum of intermediate inputs and value added. That identity can be rewritten by decomposing it into price and quantity components. This contrasts with the quantity model, which used a row identity starting that the sum of intermediate use and final use (net of imports) equals total output.

Decomposition into quantities and prices

The key to the price model in the input-output framework is that the "price" variable can be replaced by the "rate of price change" variable. This can be demonstrated through the development of the following equations. For the sake of explanation, let's assume the following input-output table in quantity terms and unit prices given in Table 22.36. The table is represented by dividing inputs into quantities and prices. For example, the first column consists of the intermediate inputs x_{11}, x_{21}, x_{31} and the value-added x_1^v, all in quantity terms. Multiplying these quantities by the corresponding unit prices p_1, p_2, p_3 and p_1^v, and summing them yields the expenditure amount

$x_1 p_1$ for the output x_1. With this setup, we can trace how a price change in one sector (expressed as a rate of change) affects the economy's prices and expenditures.

Table 22.36 Input-output table in quantity terms and unit prices

		Sector 1	Sector 2	Sector 3	Final use	Unit price
Intermediate input	Sector 1	x_{11}	x_{12}	x_{13}	F_1	p_1
	Sector 2	x_{21}	x_{22}	x_{23}	F_2	p_2
	Sector 3	x_{31}	x_{32}	x_{33}	F_3	p_3
Value-added	Sector 1	x^v_1				p^v_1
	Sector 2		x^v_2			p^v_2
	Sector 3			x^v_3		p^v_3
Output (volume)		x_1	x_2	x_3		

From the above input-output table in quantity terms, the following value (cost) identities can be written for each column:

(22.13) Column of sector 1: $x_1 p_1 = x_{11} p_1 + x_{21} p_2 + x_{31} p_3 + x^v_1 p^v_1$

Column of sector 2: $x_2 p_2 = x_{12} p_1 + x_{22} p_2 + x_{32} p_3 + x^v_2 p^v_2$

Column of sector 3: $x_3 p_3 = x_{13} p_1 + x_{23} p_2 + x_{33} p_3 + x^v_3 p^v_3$

Here, x_j is the output (in quantity terms) in column j; p_i is the unit price of the product in row i; x_{ij} is the intermediate input (in quantity terms) in row i and column j; x^v_j is the value-added (in quantity terms) in column j; and p^v_j is the unit price of value-added in column j (e.g., wage rate).

The system of equations (22.13) above is equivalent to the transposed expression of the column-wise equations in the input-output table. By dividing both sides of each equation by the output of the corresponding column x_j, the following equations are derived:

$$p_1 = (x_{11}/x_1)\, p_1 + (x_{21}/x_1)\, p_2 + (x_{31}/x_1)\, p_3 + (x^v_1/x_1)\, p^v_1,$$

$$p_2 = (x_{12}/x_2)\, p_1 + (x_{22}/x_2)\, p_2 + (x_{32}/x_2)\, p_3 + (x^v_2/x_2)\, p^v_2,$$

$$p_3 = (x_{13}/x_3)\, p_1 + (x_{23}/x_3)\, p_2 + (x_{33}/x_3)\, p_3 + (x^v_3/x_3)\, p^v_3.$$

Introducing time subscripts (base-year prices p^0 and comparison prices p^t), the equation can be rewritten as follows. For convenience, we show only the equation for p^1:

$$p_1^t = (x_{11}/x_1)\, p_1^t + (x_{21}/x_1)\, p_2^t + (x_{31}/x_1)\, p_3^t + (x^v_1/x_1)\, (p^v_1)^t$$

Dividing both sides by the base-year price (p_1^0) gives the following equations:

$$\frac{p_1^t}{p_1^0} = \frac{x_{11}}{x_1}\frac{p_1^t}{p_1^0} + \frac{x_{21}}{x_1}\frac{p_2^t}{p_1^0} + \frac{x_{31}}{x_1}\frac{p_3^t}{p_1^0} + \frac{x_1^v}{x_1}\frac{p^{v}{}_1^t}{p_1^0}$$

$$= \frac{x_{11}\,p_1^0}{x_1\,p_1^0}\frac{p_1^t}{p_1^0} + \frac{x_{21}\,p_2^0}{x_1\,p_2^0}\frac{p_2^t}{p_1^0} + \frac{x_{31}\,p_3^0}{x_1\,p_3^0}\frac{p_3^t}{p_1^0} + \frac{x^v{}_1\,p^{v0}{}_1}{x_1\,p^{v0}{}_1}\frac{p^{vt}{}_1}{p_1^0}$$

$$= \frac{x_{11}\,p_1^0}{x_1\,p_1^0}\frac{p_1^t}{p_1^0} + \frac{x_{21}\,p_2^0}{x_1\,p_1^0}\frac{p_2^t}{p_2^0} + \frac{x_{31}\,p_3^0}{x_1\,p_1^0}\frac{p_3^t}{p_3^0} + \frac{x_1^v\,p^{v0}{}_1}{x_1\,p_1^0}\frac{p^{vt}{}_1}{p^{v0}{}_1}$$

$$= a_{11}\frac{p_1^t}{p_1^0} + a_{21}\frac{p_2^t}{p_2^0} + a_{31}\frac{p_3^t}{p_3^0} + a_1^v\frac{p^{vt}{}_1}{p^{v\,0}{}_1}$$

where a_{ij} denotes the monetary input coefficient in row i and column j at the base year (0). That is, $a_{ij} = x_{ij}\,p_i^0/x_j\,p_j^0$, $a_j^v = x_j^v\,p^{v0}{}_j/x_j\,p_j^0$.

In the above equation, to convert the "price relative" (p_1^t/p_1^0) into the rate of price change, we substitute p_1^t/p_1^0 = $1+\dot{p}_1$, which leads to the following equation:

$$\mathbf{1+\dot{p}_1 = a_{11}(1+\dot{p}_1) + a_{21}(1+\dot{p}_2) + a_{31}(1+\dot{p}_3) + a_1^v(1+\dot{p}^v{}_1)}$$

Since the sum of the monetary input coefficients in a column equals 1 ($a_{11} + a_{21} + a_{31} + a_1^v = 1$), the equation simplifies as follows:

$$\mathbf{\dot{p}_1 = a_{11}\,\dot{p}_1 + a_{21}\,\dot{p}_2 + a_{31}\,\dot{p}_3 + a_1^v\,\dot{p}^v{}_1}$$

Applying the same steps to P_2 and P_3, the following equations are derived:

$$\mathbf{\dot{p}_2 = a_{12}\,\dot{p}_1 + a_{22}\,\dot{p}_2 + a_{32}\,\dot{p}_3 + a_2^v\,\dot{p}^v{}_2}$$

$$\mathbf{\dot{p}_3 = a_{13}\,\dot{p}_1 + a_{23}\,\dot{p}_2 + a_{33}\,\dot{p}_3 + a_3^v\,\dot{p}^v{}_3}$$

Collecting the results of P_1, P_2, and P_3 into matrix form:

(22.14) $$\mathbf{\dot{P} = A^T\dot{P} + \hat{V}\,\dot{P}^v}$$

where $\dot{P}$ is the vector of price change rates for the output x_j, A^T is the transpose of the monetary input coefficient matrix, $\hat{V}$ is the diagonal matrix of value-added coefficients, and $\dot{P}^v$ is the vector of price change rates of value-added (e.g., wage rates).

Solving for $\dot{P}$ gives:

$$\mathbf{(I-A^T)\,\dot{P} = \hat{V}\,\dot{P}^v}$$

Thus, the following equation is derived:

(22.15) $$\mathbf{\dot{P} = (I-A^T)^{-1}\,\hat{V}\,\dot{P}^v}$$

In short, the price model in the input-output analysis can be recast as an input-output model expressed in terms of **rates of price change**. Accordingly, the price model enables one to measure how changes in the unit prices of value-added transmit to product prices via the Leontief-type price multiplier $(I-A^T)^{-1}$.

Price model under the disaggregation of domestic output and imports

If the intermediate inputs in the previous equation (22.14) are disaggregated into domestic output and imports, we can distinguish the effects of price changes in domestic and imports as in equation (22.16):

(22.16) $$\dot{\mathbf{P}}^{\mathbf{d}} = (\mathbf{A}^{\mathbf{d}})^{\mathrm{T}}\dot{\mathbf{P}}^{\mathbf{d}} + (\mathbf{A}^{\mathbf{m}})^{\mathrm{T}}\dot{\mathbf{P}}^{\mathbf{m}} + \hat{\mathbf{V}}\dot{\mathbf{P}}^{\mathbf{v}}$$

where A^d is the matrix of input coefficients for domestic output, A^m is the matrix of input coefficients for imports, $\dot{\mathbf{P}}^{\mathbf{d}}$ is the vector of price change rates for domestic output, and $\dot{\mathbf{P}}^{\mathbf{m}}$ is the vector of price change rates for imports. The equation (22.16) can be expressed in matrix form as follows.

$$\underset{(\mathbf{A}^{\mathbf{d}})^{\mathrm{T}}}{\begin{vmatrix} a^d_{11} & a^d_{21} & a^d_{31} \\ a^d_{12} & a^d_{22} & a^d_{32} \\ a^d_{13} & a^d_{23} & a^d_{33} \end{vmatrix}} \underset{\dot{\mathbf{P}}^{\mathbf{d}}}{\begin{vmatrix} \dot{p}^d_1 \\ \dot{p}^d_2 \\ \dot{p}^d_3 \end{vmatrix}} + \underset{(\mathbf{A}^{\mathbf{m}})^{\mathrm{T}}}{\begin{vmatrix} a^m_{11} & a^m_{21} & a^m_{31} \\ a^m_{12} & a^m_{22} & a^m_{32} \\ a^m_{13} & a^m_{23} & a^m_{33} \end{vmatrix}} \underset{\dot{\mathbf{P}}^{\mathbf{m}}}{\begin{vmatrix} \dot{p}^m_1 \\ \dot{p}^m_2 \\ \dot{p}^m_3 \end{vmatrix}} + \underset{\hat{\mathbf{V}}}{\begin{vmatrix} v_1 & 0 & 0 \\ 0 & v_2 & 0 \\ 0 & 0 & v_3 \end{vmatrix}} \underset{\dot{\mathbf{P}}^{\mathbf{v}}}{\begin{vmatrix} \dot{p}^v_1 \\ \dot{p}^v_2 \\ \dot{p}^v_3 \end{vmatrix}} = \underset{\dot{\mathbf{P}}^{\mathbf{d}}}{\begin{vmatrix} \dot{p}^d_1 \\ \dot{p}^d_2 \\ \dot{p}^d_3 \end{vmatrix}}$$

Solving the equation (22.16) for $\dot{P}^d$, it can be expressed as follows:

$$\dot{\mathbf{P}}^{\mathbf{d}} = [\mathbf{I} - (\mathbf{A}^{\mathbf{d}})^{\mathrm{T}}]^{-1}\,[(\mathbf{A}^{\mathbf{m}})^{\mathrm{T}}\dot{\mathbf{P}}^{\mathbf{m}} + \hat{\mathbf{V}}\dot{\mathbf{P}}^{\mathbf{v}}]$$

If the item of "taxes less subsidies on products" is added to the above equation, it can be expressed as follow:

(22.17) $$\dot{\mathbf{P}}^{\mathbf{d}} = [\mathbf{I} - (\mathbf{A}^{\mathbf{d}})^{\mathrm{T}}]^{-1}\,[(\mathbf{A}^{\mathbf{m}})^{\mathrm{T}}\dot{\mathbf{P}}^{\mathbf{m}} + \hat{\mathbf{T}}\dot{\mathbf{P}}^{\mathbf{t}} + \hat{\mathbf{V}}\dot{\mathbf{P}}^{\mathbf{v}}]$$

where $\hat{T}$ is the diagonal matrix of the input coefficients for taxes less subsidies on products, and $\dot{P}^t$ is the vector of price change rates for taxes less subsidies on products. If we assume that there are no price changes for imports and taxes less subsidies on products ($\dot{P}^m = 0$, $\dot{P}^t = 0$), the following equation is derived:

(22.18) $$\dot{\mathbf{P}}^{\mathbf{d}} = [\mathbf{I} - (\mathbf{A}^{\mathbf{d}})^{\mathrm{T}}]^{-1}\,\hat{\mathbf{V}}\dot{\mathbf{P}}^{\mathbf{v}}$$

where $[I - (A^d)^T]^{-1}\hat{V}$ is the multiplier for domestic prices in response to **unit price changes in value-added** alone. By multiplying this multiplier by the rate of change in the unit price of value-added ($\dot{P}^v$), we can measure total impact on domestic prices due to changes in unit price of value-added.

Here, the input coefficient for value-added can be split into that of remuneration of employees, operating surplus, depreciation, and other taxes on production to decompose their contributions to price effects.

Likewise, assuming no change in unit prices of the taxes less subsidies on products and value-added in equation (22.17) ($\dot{P}^t$ = 0, $\dot{P}^v$ = 0), the rate of price change in domestic output can be expressed as follows:

(22.19) $$\dot{\mathbf{P}}^{d} = [\mathbf{I} - (\mathbf{A}^{d})^{T}]^{-1} (\mathbf{A}^{m})^{T}\, \dot{\mathbf{P}}^{m}$$

where $[I - (A^d)^T]^{-1} (A^m)^T$ is the multiplier of how **changes in import prices** affect domestic prices. By multiplying this multiplier by the rate of change in import prices ($\dot{P}^m$), the impact of price change in imports on domestic prices can be measured.

22.2.5.2 Examples of impact analysis in terms of prices

In this subsection, we apply the price model introduced above to actual figures, illustrating the calculation steps and interpretation. The data are the same as in the earlier example presented in the impact analysis by quantity model (Table 22.14, South Korea 2015). Based on that table, we again present the input coefficients table as follows (Table 22.37).

Table 22.37 Input coefficients table

	Input coefficients for domestic output (A^d)				Input coefficients for imports (A^m)			
	Agriculture	Manufactures	Electricity, construction	Services	Agriculture	Manufactures	Electricity, construction	Services
Agriculture	0.0465	0.0185	0.0014	0.0064	0.0053	0.0049	0.0002	0.0004
Manufactures	0.2608	0.3580	0.2705	0.1006	0.0177	0.1950	0.1206	0.0186
Electricity, construction	0.0136	0.0240	0.0481	0.0260	0.0000	0.0000	0.0000	0.0000
Services	0.0992	0.1248	0.1473	0.2465	0.0061	0.0096	0.0058	0.0265
Gross value added	0.5416	0.2622	0.3814	0.5555				

Based on the above table, we compute the transpose of the intermediate input coefficients for domestic output $(A^d)^T$ and the corresponding Leontief-type price inverse $[I - (A^d)^T]^{-1}$. We also obtain the transpose of the intermediate coefficients for imports $(A^m)^T$ necessary for the analysis of the price model as follows.

Table 22.38 Coefficients table for the price model

Transpose of input coefficients for domestic output: $(A^d)^T$ | Leontief-type price inverse: $[I - (A^d)^T]^{-1}$

	Agriculture	Manufactures	Electricity, construction	Services	Agriculture	Manufactures	Electricity, construction	Services
Agriculture	0.0465	0.2608	0.0136	0.0992	1.0597	0.4799	0.0334	0.2256
Manufactures	0.0185	0.3580	0.0240	0.1248	0.0338	1.6369	0.0495	0.2853
Electricity, construction	0.0014	0.2705	0.0481	0.1473	0.0133	0.5031	1.0714	0.2945
Services	0.0064	0.1006	0.0260	0.2465	0.0140	0.2400	0.0438	1.3772

Transpose of input coefficients for imports: $(A^m)^T$

	Agriculture	Manufactures	Electricity, construction	Services
Agriculture	0.017	0.0140	0.0200	0.0150
Manufactures	0.028	0.0133	0.0356	0.0367
Electricity, construction	0.004	0.0021	0.0385	0.0058
Services	0.012	0.0047	0.1047	0.0291

Based on the table above, we will exercise several types of impact analyses on prices. The equation used in the price model generally takes the following form:

$$\mathbf{Z} = [I - (\mathbf{A}^d)^T]^{-1}\, \mathbf{B}^T\, \dot{\mathbf{P}}^B$$

where Z is the impact of price change rates on domestic output, I is the identity matrix, $(A^d)^T$ is the transpose of the intermediate input coefficients for domestic output, B^T is the transpose of input coefficients matrix for the specific price shock variable (e.g., wages, taxes on products, import prices, etc.), and $\dot{\mathbf{P}}^B$ is the vector of rates of price change for that variable.

Below, using this framework, we will examine three examples that measure the impact of the rate of price changes on domestic output arising from changes in specific price variables: first, the effects of an increase in remuneration of employees (wage rate) within value-added; second, the effects of changes in import prices and the exchange rate; and finally, the effects of price changes in a specific industry's product on the overall domestic prices. As the necessary figures and matrices are summarized in Table 22.37 and 22.38, it suffices in each scenario to specify the corresponding B^T and $\dot{P}^B$ and substitute them into the equation above.

The impact on domestic prices due to changes in wage rate

When wages rise, each industry's cost structure changes, and their effect transmits through the network of intermediate transactions to the prices of other industries. Here we examine how a 10% increase in wage rates affects the prices of other domestic output. To do this, value added must be further disaggregated to isolate remuneration of employees and derive its input coefficients. The following Table 22.39 shows, for each producing sector, the amount of remuneration of employees and the corresponding input coefficients (column-wise shares of wages in total cost).

Table 22.39 Remuneration of employees and its input coefficients

Remuneration of employees (Unit: trillion KRW)

	Agriculture	Manufactures	Electricity, construction	Services
Remuneration of employees	5.2	176.8	75.4	492.8
Gross value added	33.2	435.6	121.9	930.2

Input coefficients for remuneration of employees

	Agriculture	Manufactures	Electricity, construction	Services
Remuneration of employees (V^w)	0.0855	0.1064	0.2359	0.2943
Gross value added	0.5416	0.2622	0.3814	0.5555

The impact of price change due to the increase in wage rate is derived using the previous equation (22.18). In this equation, it is assumed that the prices of all other factors excluding remuneration of employees (other components of value-added, taxes less subsidies on products, and imports) remain constant. As a result, the coefficient (multiplier) to measure the total impact of price changes on domestic sector is derived using the formula $\mathbf{[I-(A^d)^T]^{-1}\hat{V}^w}$, and the effect of domestic price changes is calculated as:

$$\mathbf{\dot{P}^d = [I-(A^d)^T]^{-1}\hat{V}^w\dot{P}^w}$$

where $\dot{P}^d$ is the vector of rates of price changes in domestic output, $\hat{V}^w$ is the diagonal matrix of the input coefficients for remuneration of employees (the wage share in total cost by industry), and $\dot{P}^w$ is the vector of wage-rate changes. If wages are raised by 10% in the electricity and construction sector, the price changes in domestic economy are shown in Table 22.40: 0.08% in the agricultural sector, 0.12% in the manufacturing sector, 2.53% in the electricity and construction sector, and 0.10% in the services sector.

Table 22.40 Multiplier of the wage rate and its impact on domestic prices

	Multiplier of the wage rate on domestic prices: $[I-(A^d)^T]^{-1}\hat{V}^w$				Rate of wage increase (%): $(\dot{P}^w)$	Domestic price changes (%): $[I-(A^d)^T]^{-1}\hat{V}^w\dot{p}^w$
	Agriculture	Manufactures	Electricity, construction	Services		
Agriculture	0.091	0.051	0.008	0.066		0.08
Manufactures	0.003	0.174	0.012	0.084		0.12
Electricity, construction	0.001	0.054	0.253	0.087	10	2.53
Services	0.001	0.026	0.010	0.405		0.10

The impact on domestic prices due to changes in import prices

The impact of changes in import prices on domestic economy's prices is calculated using the previous equation (22.19), under the assumption that unit prices of the taxes less subsidies on products and value-added are unchanged. In that equation, the coefficient (multiplier) of the impact of import prices on domestic prices is derived using $[I-(A^d)^T]^{-1}(A^m)^T$, and the effect of domestic price changes is calculated as:

$$\dot{P}^d = [I-(A^d)^T]^{-1}(A^m)^T\dot{P}^m$$

where $\dot{P}^d$ is the vector of rates of price changes in domestic output, $(A^m)^T$ is the transpose of the input coefficients for imports, and $\dot{P}^m$ is the rate of price changes for imported products. For example, in Table 22.41 below, if the import prices of manufactured products rise by 20%, the resulting impact on domestic prices is as follows: a 2.41% increase in agriculture, a 6.62% increase in manufacturing, a 4.66% increase in electricity and construction, and a 1.56% increase in services sector.

Table 22.41 Multiplier of the import prices and its impact on domestic prices

	Multiplier of import prices on domestic prices: $[I-(A^d)^T]^{-1}(A^m)^T$				Rate of increase in import prices (%): $(\dot{P}^m)$	Domestic price changes (%): $[I-(A^d)^T]^{-1}(A^m)^T\dot{P}^m$
	Agriculture	Manufactures	Electricity, construction	Services		
Agriculture	0.008	0.121	0.000	0.017		2.41
Manufactures	0.008	0.331	0.000	0.024	20	6.62
Electricity, construction	0.003	0.233	0.000	0.019		4.66
Services	0.002	0.078	0.000	0.039		1.56

The impact on domestic prices due to changes in exchange rate

To measure the impact of an exchange rate increase on domestic prices, the same formula used for the impact of import prices on domestic prices are applied. The only difference is that the changes in exchange rate applies uniformly to all imported products. For example, if the exchange rate of imported products rises by 5%, it is assumed that all import prices rise by 5%. As shown in the following table (Table 22.42), the domestic prices caused by the exchange rate increase (5%) rise by 0.73% in agriculture, 1.82% in manufacturing, 1.27% in electricity and construction, and 0.59% in services sector.

Table 22.42 Impact of changes in exchange rates on domestic prices

	Increase in exchange rate (%): ($\dot{P}^m$)	**Domestic price changes (%): $[I-(A^d)^T]^{-1}(A^m)^T\dot{P}^m$**
Agriculture	5	0.73
Manufactures	5	1.82
Electricity, construction	5	1.27
Services	5	0.59

The impact on domestic prices due to simultaneous changes in the exchange rate and import prices

If both the exchange rate and the import prices change simultaneously, for example, the exchange rate rises by 5% and the import price of manufactured products in U.S. dollar terms rises by 20%, how are these effects on domestic prices computed? When the exchange rate and the import price of a particular product move at the same time, total rate of increase in each imported product is given by the product of the two effects. Table 22.43 shows the result of multiplying the diagonal matrices of the exchange-rate increase and the import-price increase: agricultural products rise by 5%, manufactured products by 26%, electricity and construction by 5%, and services by 5%.

Table 22.43 Calculation of total rates of price change when the exchange rate and import prices change simultaneously

$$\underset{\text{Increase in exchange rate (5\%)}}{\begin{vmatrix} 1.05 & 0 & 0 & 0 \\ 0 & 1.05 & 0 & 0 \\ 0 & 0 & 1.05 & 0 \\ 0 & 0 & 0 & 1.05 \end{vmatrix}} \times \underset{\text{Increase in import prices for manufactured products (20\%)}}{\begin{vmatrix} 1 & 0 & 0 & 0 \\ 0 & 1.2 & 0 & 0 \\ 0 & 0 & 1 & 0 \\ 0 & 0 & 0 & 1 \end{vmatrix}} = \underset{\text{Total rate of price change}}{\begin{vmatrix} 1.05 & 0 & 0 & 0 \\ 0 & 1.26 & 0 & 0 \\ 0 & 0 & 1.05 & 0 \\ 0 & 0 & 0 & 1.05 \end{vmatrix}}$$

Using the same domestic price multiplier as above and applying these new increase rates of exchange-rate and import prices, the resulting domestic price changes are shown in Table 22.44: domestic prices rise by 3.26% for agriculture, 8.77% for manufactures, 6.17% for electricity and construction, and 2.23% for services sector.

Table 22.44 Impact of both exchange rate and import prices on domestic prices

	Change in exchange rate and import prices (%)	Change in domestic prices (%): $[I - (A^d)^T]^{-1} (A^m)^T \dot{p}^m$
Agriculture	**5**	3.26
Manufactures	**26**	8.77
Electricity, construction	**5**	6.17
Services	**5**	2.23

The impact on domestic prices due to the change in commodity prices for a specific industry

To measure how a price change in a specific industry's output affects the domestic prices, we use the same price model as above. But we first separate that industry from the endogenous side and treat it as exogenous in the input-output table. Below, we will describe the procedure for moving an industry's price variable to the exogenous side and calculating the resulting price effects on domestic industries.

1) Setting up the system of equations for the price model

If we express equation (22.16) in section 22.2.5.1 as a three-sector system of simultaneous equations, it is as follows:

$$(a^d_{11}\,\dot{p}^d_1 + a^m_{11}\,\dot{p}^m_1) + (a^d_{21}\,\dot{p}^d_2 + a^m_{21}\,\dot{p}^m_2) + (a^d_{31}\,\dot{p}^d_3 + a^m_{31}\,\dot{p}^m_3) + v_1\,\dot{p}^v_1 = \dot{p}^d_1,$$

$$(a^d_{12}\,\dot{p}^d_1 + a^m_{12}\,\dot{p}^m_1) + (a^d_{22}\,\dot{p}^d_2 + a^m_{22}\,\dot{p}^m_2) + (a^d_{32}\,\dot{p}^d_3 + a^m_{32}\,\dot{p}^m_3) + v_2\,\dot{p}^v_2 = \dot{p}^d_2,$$

$$(a^d_{13}\,\dot{p}^d_1 + a^m_{13}\,\dot{p}^m_1) + (a^d_{23}\,\dot{p}^d_2 + a^m_{23}\,\dot{p}^m_2) + (a^d_{33}\,\dot{p}^d_3 + a^m_{33}\,\dot{p}^m_3) + v_3\,\dot{p}^v_3 = \dot{p}^d_3$$

where a^d_{ij} is the input coefficient for domestic output in row i and column j; a^m_{ij} is the input coefficient for imports in row i and column j; $\dot{p}^d_j$ is the rate of price change of domestic output in column j; $\dot{p}^m_j$ is the rate of price change of imports in column j; v_j is the input coefficient for value-added in column j; and $\dot{p}^v_j$ is the rate of the unit price change of value-added in column j.

2) Moving the target sector to the exogenous block

Suppose we wish to measure the price change for sector 2 (manufactures). We separate sector 2 from the endogenous block and move it the right-hand side (the exogenous block) as follows:

$$(a^d_{11}\,\dot{p}^d_1 + a^m_{11}\,\dot{p}^m_1) + (a^d_{31}\,\dot{p}^d_3 + a^m_{31}\,\dot{p}^m_3) + (\boldsymbol{a}^d_{21}\,\dot{\boldsymbol{p}}^d_2 + \boldsymbol{a}^m_{21}\,\dot{\boldsymbol{p}}^m_2) + v_1\,\dot{p}^v_1 = \dot{p}^d_1$$

$$(a^d_{13}\,\dot{p}^d_1 + a^m_{13}\,\dot{p}^m_1) + (a^d_{33}\,\dot{p}^d_3 + a^m_{33}\,\dot{p}^m_3) + (\boldsymbol{a}^d_{23}\,\dot{\boldsymbol{p}}^d_2 + \boldsymbol{a}^m_{23}\,\dot{\boldsymbol{p}}^m_2) + v_3\,\dot{p}^v_3 = \dot{p}^d_3$$

Expressed in matrix form, this becomes:

$$\underset{(\mathbf{A^d})^\mathbf{T}}{\begin{vmatrix} a^d_{11} & a^d_{31} \\ a^d_{13} & a^d_{33} \end{vmatrix}} \underset{\dot{\mathbf{P}}^\mathbf{d}}{\begin{vmatrix} \dot{p}^d_1 \\ \dot{p}^d_3 \end{vmatrix}} + \underset{(\mathbf{A^m})^\mathbf{T}}{\begin{vmatrix} a^m_{11} & a^m_{31} \\ a^m_{13} & a^m_{33} \end{vmatrix}} \underset{\dot{\mathbf{P}}^\mathbf{m}}{\begin{vmatrix} \dot{p}^m_1 \\ \dot{p}^m_3 \end{vmatrix}} + \underset{(\mathbf{A^d_2})^\mathbf{T}}{\begin{vmatrix} \boldsymbol{a}^d_{21} \\ \boldsymbol{a}^d_{23} \end{vmatrix}} \underset{\dot{\mathbf{P}}^\mathbf{d}_2}{\dot{\boldsymbol{p}}^d_2} + \underset{(\mathbf{A^m_2})^\mathbf{T}}{\begin{vmatrix} \boldsymbol{a}^m_{21} \\ \boldsymbol{a}^m_{23} \end{vmatrix}} \underset{\dot{\mathbf{P}}^\mathbf{m}_2}{\dot{\boldsymbol{p}}^m_2} + \underset{\hat{V}\,\dot{\mathbf{P}}^\mathbf{v}}{\begin{vmatrix} v_1\,\dot{p}^v_1 \\ v_3\,\dot{p}^v_3 \end{vmatrix}} = \underset{\dot{\mathbf{P}}^\mathbf{d}}{\begin{vmatrix} \dot{p}^d_1 \\ \dot{p}^d_3 \end{vmatrix}}$$

If we put this in the form of an equation:

(22.20) $$(\mathbf{A^d})^\mathbf{T}\,\dot{\mathbf{P}}^\mathbf{d} + (\mathbf{A^m})^\mathbf{T}\,\dot{\mathbf{P}}^\mathbf{m} + (\mathbf{A^d_2})^\mathbf{T}\,\dot{\mathbf{P}}^\mathbf{d}_2 + (\mathbf{A^m_2})^\mathbf{T}\,\dot{\mathbf{P}}^\mathbf{m}_2 + \hat{V}\,\dot{\mathbf{P}}^\mathbf{v} = \dot{\mathbf{P}}^\mathbf{d}$$

where $(A^d)^T$ and $(A^m)^T$ denote the transposes of input coefficients for the domestic output and imports, excluding the exogenized sector, $(A^d_2)^T$ and $(A^m_2)^T$ are the corresponding transposes for exogenized sector (sector 2 here), and $\hat{V}$ is the diagonal matrix of value-added input coefficients. When equation (22.20) is rearranged by $\dot{\mathbf{P}}^\mathbf{d}$, it is expressed as follows:

(22.21) $$\mathbf{P}^\mathbf{d} = [\mathbf{I} - (\mathbf{A^d})^\mathbf{T}]^{-1}\,[(\mathbf{A^m})^\mathbf{T}\,\dot{\mathbf{P}}^\mathbf{m} + (\mathbf{A^d_2})^\mathbf{T}\,\dot{\mathbf{P}}^\mathbf{d}_2 + (\mathbf{A^m_2})^\mathbf{T}\,\dot{\mathbf{P}}^\mathbf{m}_2 + \hat{V}\,\dot{\mathbf{P}}^\mathbf{v}]$$

In equation (22.21), if import prices and the unit price of value-added do not change ($\dot{P}^m = \dot{P}^m_2 = 0$, $\dot{P}^v = 0$), this simplifies to:

(22.22) $$\dot{\mathbf{P}}^\mathbf{d} = [\mathbf{I} - (\mathbf{A^d})^\mathbf{T}]^{-1}\,(\mathbf{A^d_2})^\mathbf{T}\,\dot{\mathbf{P}}^\mathbf{d}_2$$

The meaning of equation (22.22) is that due to the change in domestic prices of a specific industry (e.g., sector 2) $\dot{P}^d_2$, the impact on domestic prices is given by $[I - (A^d)^T]^{-1}(A^d_2)^T\,\dot{P}^d_2$.

3) Numeric illustration

As a worked example, let us refer again to the input coefficient table in Table 22.37 and examine how a price increase in manufactures (sector 2) impacts on the domestic prices. In Table 22.45 below, A^d denotes the matrix of domestic input coefficients for the sectors other than manufactures (i.e., excluding the sector where the price increase occurs), and $[I - (A^d)^T]^{-1}$ is the Leontief-type price inverse of the transpose of A^d.

Table 22.45 Coefficient table of other sectors excluding manufactures (sector 2)

	A^d			$[I-(A^d)^T]^{-1}$		
	Agriculture	Electricity, construction	Services	Agriculture	Electricity, construction	Services
Agriculture	0.046	0.001	0.006	1.050	0.019	0.142
Electricity, construction	0.014	0.048	0.026	0.003	1.056	0.207
Services	0.099	0.147	0.246	0.009	0.037	1.335

If the price of manufactures (sector 2) rises by 10%, the impact on domestic prices from the above formula is shown in Table 22.46. As a result of multiplying the 10% price increase for manufactures by the multiplier $[I-(A^d)^T]^{-1}(A^d_2)^T$, the impact on domestic prices shows 2.93% for agriculture, 3.07% for electricity and construction, and 1.47% for services.

Table 22.46 Impact on domestic prices due to the price increase (10%) of manufactures

	$(A^d_2)^T$	Multiplier of manufactures on domestic prices: $[I-(A^d)^T]^{-1}(A^d_2)^T$	Price change in manufactures (%): $\dot{P}^d_2$	Increase in domestic prices (%): $[I-(A^d)^T]^{-1}(A^d_2)^T\dot{P}^d_2$
Agriculture	0.261	0.293	**10**	2.93
Electricity, construction	0.271	0.307	**10**	3.07
Services	0.101	0.147	**10**	1.47

22.2.5.3 Summary of impact analyses by the price model

In the above, we explained how to measure the impact on domestic prices resulting from changes in the prices of exogenous variables (wages, import prices, exchange rate, the domestic price of a specific industry) using the price mode derived from the input-output table. To summarize, it is as follows.

Table 22.47 Formulas for impacts on prices

Measurement target	**Exogenous variable**	**Multiplier (price requirements)**	**Impact on domestic prices**
Impact on domestic prices	Rate of wage increase ($\dot{P}^w$)	$[I-(A^d)^T]^{-1}\hat{V}^w$	$[I-(A^d)^T]^{-1}\hat{V}^w\dot{P}^w$
Impact on domestic prices	Import prices, exchange rate ($\dot{P}^m$)	$[I-(A^d)^T]^{-1}(A^m)^T$	$[I-(A^d)^T]^{-1}(A^m)^T\dot{P}^m$
Impact on domestic prices[1)]	(Exogenized) price change of domestic specific sector ($\dot{P}^d_e$)	$[I-(A^d)^T]^{-1}(A^d_e)^T$	$[I-(A^d)^T]^{-1}(A^d_e)^T\dot{P}^d_e$

Footnote: 1) A^d_e and $\dot{P}^d_e$ denote, respectively, the domestic input coefficients of the exogenized sector (e) and that sector's price change (scaler or vector).

22.3 Assumptions and limitations of the input-output analysis

The impact analyses by the quantity and price models introduced above is conducted under the premise that the Leontief inverse and the input coefficients for the economic variables being analyzed from the input-output table remain unchanged. This premise entails the following assumptions.

1. **Fixed-technology assumptions**: The composition of primary inputs (labor and capital) and the composition of intermediate inputs used in production do not change over time; that is, the technical input structure of each product is fixed.
2. **Constant relative prices**: Relative prices among inputs used in production are invariant. If the relative price of input items changes, a substitution effect between inputs may occur, which can lead to a change in the input combinations and consequently a technical change in the input structure.
3. **Linearity and constant returns to scale**: In input-output analysis, no economies of scale are present, and the level of output increases in proportion to the increase in inputs. Hence, the model assumes linear (proportional) relationships and no external economies.
4. **Limits of the price model (supply-side focus)**: The impact analysis in the price model of input-output table attributes price changes solely to supply-side cost factors (e.g., wages, import prices) and does not consider demand-side determinants. Moreover, it measures only the maximum impact of price changes and does not identify the timing (lags) with which the effects of price change materialize.

Given these strong assumptions and constraints, results from input-output analysis are best interpreted as static approximations. It is advisable to use them in conjunction with supplementary indicators or complementary models, taking account of the analysis purpose and data environment.

22.4 Updating intermediate input coefficients in the input-output table

Because an input-output table is compiled from extensive data and involves complex compilation procedures, once it is constructed for a benchmark year, it typically takes a considerable time until the next benchmark year (usually on every five years). Nevertheless, the demand for timelier input-output statistics has been growing, creating the need for annual or quarterly compilation. Yet, each time a fresh input-output table is compiled, collecting directly (through surveys) the necessary data, especially intermediate input data, is inefficient in terms of time and cost. Accordingly, in practice, for **non-benchmark** (intervening) **years**, updated values of intermediate input data can be derived via an adjustment procedure based on previously measured intermediate input coefficients. To perform this adjustment, it is essential to have the following new data except for the detailed cell entries of intermediate input quadrant; namely, (i) column totals of output by product (or industry), (ii) column totals of intermediate input by product (or industry) (from which value-added can be derived), and (iii) row totals of intermediate use by product (or industry) (which are obtained ex post by subtracting from total use once final use has been identified). By combining these new data along with the existing intermediate input coefficients, one can estimate updated intermediate input coefficients. There are several techniques for this estimation, but this section will focus on the most widely used **RAS** method, the bi-proportional balancing technique.

22.4.1 Principle of the RAS method

The RAS method is a procedure used to estimate new intermediate input coefficients for a target year by repeatedly applying row and column adjustments so that the row totals (intermediate use) and column totals (intermediate input) of the updated intermediate-use quadrant match their targets, starting from the benchmark-year coefficients. It is said that RAS originates from the abbreviation of "**R**aking **a**nd **S**caling." This method updates the intermediate input coefficients by first calculating **row adjustment factors** and **column adjustment factors** based on the existing input coefficients in the input-output table, and iteratively modifying these adjustment factors until they converge to "1" (i.e., until the target row and column totals are attained). In practice, a rounding tolerance at a specified decimal place is set, and convergence is deemed achieved when the factors round to 1.

- **Row adjustment factor** represents the target row total (u) divided by the row total obtained by proportionally allocating the existing intermediate-use amounts.
- **Column adjustment factor** represents the target column total (v) divided by the column total obtained by proportionally allocating the existing intermediate-input amounts.

Below, we illustrate the RAS updating procedure for intermediate input coefficients of an input-output table with a simple example. Let us assume that there are an input-output table and its input coefficient table for the benchmark year as in Table 22.48, and we will calculate the intermediate input coefficients for another year based on this.

Table 22.48 Input-output table and input coefficients for the benchmark year (year 0)

Input-output table (year 0)

	Product 1	Product 2	Product 3	Total intermediate use	Final use (– imports)	Total output
Product 1	50	70	25	145	115	260
Product 2	80	130	65	275	155	430
Product 3	35	100	90	225	65	290
Total intermediate input	165	300	180	645	335	980
Value-added	95	130	110	335		
Total input	260	430	290	980		

Input coefficients (year 0)

	Product 1	Product 2	Product 3
Product 1	0.192	0.163	0.086
Product 2	0.308	0.302	0.224
Product 3	0.135	0.233	0.310
Total intermediate input	0.635	0.698	0.621
Value-added	0.365	0.302	0.379
Total input	1	1	1

Now, suppose that the following new data (Table 22.49) is available for a new input-output table in year t. Let's find out how to estimate the detailed amounts of intermediate inputs in the blank area (the shaded area in Table 22.50) of the input-output table for year t.

Table 22.49 New data for year t

	Product 1	Product 2	Product 3	Total
Output (X)	280	480	310	1,070
Intermediate input (v)	180	330	180	690
Intermediate use (u)	185	290	215	690

Table 22.50 Input-output table for year t

	Product 1	Product 2	Product 3	Total intermediate use (u)	Final use (– imports)	Total output (X)
Product 1				**185**	95	**280**
Product 2				**290**	190	**480**
Product 3				**215**	95	**310**
Total intermediate input (v)	**180**	**330**	**180**	690	380	1,070
Value-added	100	150	130	380		
Total input (X)	**280**	**480**	**310**	1,070		

First, apply the input coefficients of year "0" to the new column totals of total input (X) for year t to obtain an initial estimate of the intermediate-input quadrant, as follows. For example, for product 1 in year *t*, multiplying its total input of 280 by the "year 0" intermediate input coefficients for Product 1 (0.192, 0.308, and 0.135) yields 53.85, 86.15, and 37.69, respectively. The same calculation is performed for Product 2 and 3, producing the following results.

Provisional calculation (1st round)

	Product 1	Product 2	Product 3	Row total (intermediate use)	Target row total (u)	Row adjustment factor (1)
Product 1	53.85	78.14	26.72	158.71	185	1.1656
Product 2	86.15	145.12	69.48	300.75	290	0.9642
Product 3	37.69	111.63	96.21	245.53	215	0.8757
Column total (intermediate input)	177.69	334.88	192.41	704.99	690	
Target column total (v)	180	330	180	690		

However, the row totals (intermediate-use totals) obtained for the intermediate use quadrant (158.71, 300.75, and 245.53) do not match the target intermediate use u of 185, 290, 215 in year *t*. Accordingly, each row must be scaled by a row adjustment factor to bring its total to the target. Specifically, multiply the entries in the row for Product 1 (53.85, 78.14, 26.72) by 1.1656 (=185/158.71); those in the row for Product 2 (86.15, 145.12, 69.48) by 0.9642 (=290/300.75); and those in the row for Product 3 (37.69, 111.63, 96.21) by 0.8757 (=215/245.53) to obtain the updated intermediate use amounts, respectively. The adjusted results are as follows.

Provisional calculation (2nd round)

	Product 1	Product 2	Product 3	Row total
Product 1	62.77	91.08	31.15	185.0
Product 2	83.07	139.93	67.00	290.0
Product 3	33.01	97.75	84.25	215.0
Column total	178.85	328.76	182.39	690.0
Target column total (v)	180	330	180	690
Column adjustment factor (1)	1.0065	1.0038	0.9869	

As a result, while the row totals of the intermediate use have been adjusted, the column totals (intermediate-input totals) still do not match the target data (v: 180, 330, 180), so the column values need to be adjusted. Accordingly, multiply each column by its column adjustment factor to bring it to the target column total. Specifically, multiply the intermediate inputs in the column for Product 1 (62.77, 83.07, 33.01) by the column adjustment factor) of 1.0065 (=180/178.85); the intermediate inputs in the column for Product 2 (91.08, 139.93, 97.75) by 1.0038 (=330/328.76); and the intermediate inputs in the column for Product 3 (31.15, 67.00, 84.25) by 0.9869 (=180/182.39), respectively, and derive the revised intermediate input values. The adjusted results are as follows.

Provisional calculation (3rd round)

	Product 1	Product 2	Product 3	Row total	Target row total (u)	Row adjustment factor (2)
Product 1	63.17	91.43	30.74	185.34	185	0.9982
Product 2	83.61	140.46	66.12	290.18	290	0.9994
Product 3	33.22	98.12	83.14	214.48	215	1.0024
Column total	180.0	330.0	180.0	690.0	690	

As a result, while the intermediate-input column totals have been adjusted, the row totals (intermediate-use totals) still do not match the target value (u). We therefore repeat the rows adjustment in the same manner as before. This process of adjusting the values of rows and columns is repeated until both the row adjustment factors and column adjustment factors converge to 1. However, since the adjustment factors will never exactly reach the integer "1," a decision must be made on the decimal place of the digit at which the adjustment factors will be rounded up to "1". In this example, we adopt the rule that any adjustment factor rounded to 1 at the fifth decimal place is treated as 1. After 4 iterations of row adjustments and 3 iterations of column adjustments, the final result was obtained, with the column totals of intermediate input and the row totals of intermediate use approximating the figures for year *t*. This process is illustrated in the tables below.

Provisional calculation (4th round)

	Product 1	Product 2	Product 3	Row total
Product 1	63.06	91.26	30.69	185.0
Product 2	83.56	140.37	66.08	290.0
Product 3	33.30	98.36	83.34	215.0
Column total	179.91	329.98	180.10	690.0
Target column total (v)	180	330	180	690
Column adjustment factor (2)	1.0005	1.0001	0.9994	

Provisional calculation (5th round)

	Product 1	Product 2	Product 3	Row total	Target row total (u)	Row adjustment factor (3)
Product 1	63.09	91.26	30.67	185.02	185	0.9999
Product 2	83.6	140.4	66.0	290.01	290	1.0000
Product 3	33.3	98.4	83.3	214.97	215	1.0001
Column total	180.0	330.0	180.0	690.0	690	

Provisional calculation (6th round)

	Product 1	Product 2	Product 3	Row total
Product 1	63.08	91.26	30.66	185.0
Product 2	83.59	140.37	66.04	290.0
Product 3	33.32	98.37	83.30	215.0
Column total	180.00	330.00	180.00	690.0
Target column total (v)	180	330	180	690
Column adjustment factor (3)	1.0000	1.0000	1.0000	

Provisional calculation (7th round)

	Product 1	Product 2	Product 3	Row total	Target row total (u)	Row adjustment factor (4)
Product 1	63.08	91.26	30.66	185.00	185	1.0000
Product 2	83.60	140.37	66.03	290.00	290	1.0000
Product 3	33.32	98.38	83.30	215.00	215	1.0000
Column total	180.0	330.0	180.0	690.0	690	

Provisional calculation (8th round, Final result)

	Product 1	Product 2	Product 3	Row total
Product 1	63.08	91.26	30.66	185.00
Product 2	83.60	140.37	66.03	290.00
Product 3	33.32	98.38	83.30	215.00
Column total	180.00	330.00	180.00	690.00

Summarizing the iterative results above, they can be compactly expressed in the following matrix notation. First, there were four rounds of row adjustments; and multiplying these four row adjustment factors successively yields a vector R, which is represented as the diagonal matrix $\hat{R}$.

	Row adjustment factor (1)	Row adjustment factor (2)	Row adjustment factor (3)	Row adjustment factor (4)	R: (1)×(2)×(3)×(4)
Row 1	1.1656	0.9982	0.9999	1.0000	1.1634
Row 2	0.9642	0.9994	1.0000	1.0000	0.9636
Row 3	0.8757	1.0024	1.0001	1.0000	0.8779

$\hat{R}$

1.1634	0	0
0	0.9636	0
0	0	0.8779

Similarly, there are three rounds of column adjustments; and multiplying these column adjustment factors successively yields a vector S, which is represented as the diagonal matrix $\hat{S}$.

	Column 1	Column 2	Column 3
Column adjustment factor (1)	1.0065	1.0038	0.9869
Column adjustment factor (2)	1.0005	1.0001	0.9994
Column adjustment factor (3)	1.0000	1.0000	1.0000
S: (1)×(2)×(3)	1.0070	1.0038	0.9863

$\hat{S}$

1.0070	0	0
0	1.0038	0
0	0	0.9863

Then, pre-multiplying the initial benchmark-year coefficient matrix (A^0) by the diagonal matrix of row adjustment factors ($\hat{R}$), and post-multiplying by the diagonal matrix of column adjustment factors ($\hat{S}$) yields the adjusted input coefficients ($\mathbf{A^t}$) for the target year t, under the RAS method as shown in the table below.

Input coefficients matrix for the benchmark year: (A^0)

0.1923	0.1628	0.0862
0.3077	0.3023	0.2241
0.1346	0.2326	0.3103

Input coefficients matrix for the target year: ($A^t = \hat{R}\, A^0\, \hat{S}$)

0.2253	0.1901	0.0989
0.2986	0.2924	0.2130
0.1190	0.2049	0.2687

Accordingly, multiplying this revised input coefficients matrix by the diagonal matrix of total input for each product in year t ($\hat{X}$) yields the intermediate input amounts identical to those from the 8th round (final) above.

$$\overbrace{\begin{vmatrix} 0.2253 & 0.1901 & 0.0989 \\ 0.2986 & 0.2924 & 0.2130 \\ 0.1190 & 0.2049 & 0.2687 \end{vmatrix}}^{A^t = \hat{R}\, A^0\, \hat{S}} \times \overbrace{\begin{vmatrix} 280 & 0 & 0 \\ 0 & 480 & 0 \\ 0 & 0 & 310 \end{vmatrix}}^{\hat{X}} = \begin{vmatrix} 63.08 & 91.26 & 30.66 \\ 83.60 & 140.37 & 66.03 \\ 33.32 & 98.38 & 83.30 \end{vmatrix}$$

In short, by iteratively applying the row and column adjustment factors summarized by $\hat{R}$ and $\hat{S}$, one can derive a set of intermediate input coefficients in year t that simultaneously satisfy the target constraints u and v.

22.4.2 Use of RAS software

If the row totals and column totals (that is, marginal totals) are updated and the values of endogenous block (intermediate consumption quadrant) are to be adjusted or modified using the method described above, it can be easily handled using the already developed software. Packages available to date include **R**, **Python**, **SAS/IML**, **GAMS**, **MATLAB**, and **Stata**, and RAS calculations can also be performed easily via **Excel add-ins**.

When applying the RAS procedure, note that if any individual cell, or a row or column total in the matrix is 0, the scaling adjustment factors cannot be computed, so preliminary adjustments are required. For example, if a particular cell in the intermediate input matrix is zero, replace it with a small positive number (e.g., 10^{-10}) so that the adjustment factors can be computed and the cell value and the corresponding totals are defined (apply the same fix when a row or column total is zero). By contrast, the generalized RAS (**GRAS**), an extension of RAS, can handle tables with mixed signs (positive and negative entries) and thus deals with most issues involving negatives and zeros.

22.5 Aggregation to a higher-level classification using a conversion matrix

In compiling input-output tables, there are cases where detailed industry (or product) groups must be aggregated to produce a more compact table or converted to a higher-level classification. In such cases, the table can be reduced or converted by simple matrix operations using a conversion (aggregation) matrix introduced below. As an example, consider collapsing a 10 x 10 intermediate input matrix to a 4 x 4 matrix. First, create a correspondence table that maps the 10 detailed sectors to 4 higher sectors ("Industry code mapping" on the left-hand side of Table 22.51). Based on this, construct a conversion matrix T of size 10 x 4 for aggregation ("Conversion matrix for aggregation" on the right-hand side of Table 22.51). Each row of T contains a single 1 (indicating the higher-level group to which the detailed item belongs) and zeros elsewhere.

Table 22.51 Industry code mapping and its conversion matrix for aggregation

Industry code mapping

10 sectors of industry	Code No.	4 sectors of industry	Code No.
Agriculture	1	Agriculture	1
Manufacturing	2	Manufacturing	2
Electricity	3	Electricity, construction	3
Construction	4	Electricity, construction	3
Trade services	5	Other services	4
Transportation	6	Other services	4
Food, accommodation	7	Other services	4
Telecom, finance, business	8	Other services	4
Public admin, defense	9	Other services	4
Education, health	10	Other services	4

Conversion matrix for aggregation (T)

Code	1	2	3	4
1	**1**	0	0	0
2	0	**1**	0	0
3	0	0	**1**	0
4	0	0	**1**	0
5	0	0	0	**1**
6	0	0	0	**1**
7	0	0	0	**1**
8	0	0	0	**1**
9	0	0	0	**1**
10	0	0	0	**1**

The matrix equation for converting the 10-sector intermediate input matrix (A_{10}) into the 4-sector intermediate input matrix (A_4) is as follows:

$$\mathbf{A_4} = T^{\mathrm{T}} \mathbf{A_{10}} T$$

where T^{T} is the transpose of the 10 x 4 "conversion matrix for aggregation," and A_{10} is the 10 x 10 intermediate-input coefficient matrix. Right-multiplication by T aggregates columns to the higher-level groups, while left-multiplication by T^{T} aggregates rows to the higher-level groups. As a result, the detailed flows in A_{10} are summed to the four higher-level groups according to the mapping, yielding A_4.

The rationale for deriving this matrix formula follows from the basic properties of summation. If we multiply any matrix by a unit column vector, the vector of its row sums is obtained. For example, multiplying matrix A (3 x 3) by the unit column vector i (3 x 1) produces the row sums of matrix A:

A (3 x 3) × **Unit column vector (i)** = **Row sums of A**

$$\begin{vmatrix} a_{11} & a_{12} & a_{13} \\ a_{21} & a_{22} & a_{23} \\ a_{31} & a_{32} & a_{33} \end{vmatrix} \times \begin{vmatrix} 1 \\ 1 \\ 1 \end{vmatrix} = \begin{vmatrix} a_{11}+ a_{12}+ a_{13} \\ a_{21}+ a_{22}+ a_{23} \\ a_{31}+ a_{32}+ a_{33} \end{vmatrix}$$

Similarly, if we multiply matrix A by the unit row vector i^{T} (1 x 3), the column sums of matrix A will be obtained:

Unit row vector (i^{T}) × **A (3 x 3)** = **Column sums of A**

$$\begin{vmatrix} 1 & 1 & 1 \end{vmatrix} \times \begin{vmatrix} a_{11} & a_{12} & a_{13} \\ a_{21} & a_{22} & a_{23} \\ a_{31} & a_{32} & a_{33} \end{vmatrix} = \begin{vmatrix} a_{11}+a_{21}+a_{31} & a_{12}+a_{22}+a_{32} & a_{13}+a_{23}+a_{33} \end{vmatrix}$$

Therefore, if we multiply the unit row vector i^{T}, matrix A, and the unit column vector i consecutively, the grand total of all entries in matrix A can be obtained:

i^{T} × **A (3 x 3)** × **i**

$$\begin{vmatrix} 1 & 1 & 1 \end{vmatrix} \times \begin{vmatrix} a_{11} & a_{12} & a_{13} \\ a_{21} & a_{22} & a_{23} \\ a_{31} & a_{32} & a_{33} \end{vmatrix} \times \begin{vmatrix} 1 \\ 1 \\ 1 \end{vmatrix} = \sum_{i,j=1}^{3} a_{ij}$$

Using this logic, the desired aggregated matrix can be derived. First, construct a conversion matrix for consolidation T, where entries are "1" for the detailed rows and columns to be merged into each aggregate group and "0" otherwise. Then, by placing the transposed conversion matrix (T^{T}) to the left of matrix A and the conversion matrix (T) to the right of matrix A, and multiplying the three matrices, the reduced matrix at the higher classification level can be obtained.

The following example applies this conversion matrix to aggregate the 10-sector intermediate input table into a 4-sector intermediate input table, based on South Korea's input-output table (2015, basic prices).

Table 22.52 10-sector intermediate input table of South Korea (2015, basic prices)

(Unit: Billion KRW)

	Agriculture	Manufactures	Electricity	Construction	Trade	Transport	Food, accommodation	Telecom, finance, business	Public admi, defense	Education, health	Total intermediate use
Agriculture	3,176	38,910	13	491	114	28	9,085	267	303	1,527	53,913
Manufact.	17,081	919,012	39,673	85,329	15,439	31,575	43,669	45,346	6,584	56,979	1,260,686
Electricity	766	38,750	14,025	926	3,794	2,151	3,411	12,928	1,509	10,225	88,483
Construct.	72	1,097	365	64	257	174	199	7,881	584	420	11,114
Trade	2,239	67,336	938	7,200	10,175	2,412	11,779	14,073	1,291	15,237	132,681
Transport	782	44,201	1,353	1,933	16,804	24,342	818	8,488	2,126	1,966	102,813
Food, accom.	423	10,206	531	766	9,085	1,699	949	14,988	1,842	13,570	54,060
Telecom., finance, business	2,352	92,938	5,978	28,596	50,509	14,732	11,767	162,038	11,546	28,239	408,693
Public adm.	96	-	-	-	-	530	-	-	-	2,131	2,758
Education, health	568	8,695	548	1,063	3,995	3,360	990	9,265	378	5,871	34,733
Total intermediate input	27,554	1,221,143	63,421	126,367	110,172	81,004	82,668	275,273	26,164	136,166	2,149,933

Applying the formula $A_4 = T^T A_{10} T$ to Table 22.52 aggregates the 10-sector matrix to a 4-sector matrix as follows.

Table 22.53 Intermediate input table aggregated to 4 sectors

(Unit: Billion KRW)

	Agriculture	Manufactures	Electricity, construction	Services	Total intermediate use
Agriculture	3,176	38,910	503	11,324	53,913
Manufactures	17,081	919,012	125,002	199,591	1,260,686
Electricity, construction	837	39,847	15,379	43,534	99,596
Services	6,460	223,375	48,905	456,998	735,737
Total intermediate input	27,554	1,221,143	189,788	711,447	2,149,933

In short, by pre- and post-multiplying with the conversion matrix to aggregate columns and rows to higher-level sectors, we can collapse the detailed flows of the original table to the target classification while preserving the intermediate inputs total (2,149,933) before and after aggregation.

References

Allen R.G.D. (1975), Index Numbers in Theory and Practice.

Bank of Korea (2014), Manual of Korean Input-output Table.

Bank of Korea (2014), Korean National Balance Sheet.

Bank of Korea (2020), Korean National Balance Sheet.

Bank of Korea (2020), Korean System of National Accounts.

Bank of Korea, Economic Statistic System (https://ecos.bok.or.kr).

BEA (1990.6), NIPA Personal Consumption Expenditure, Methodology papers.

BEA (2000.1), GDP: One of the Great Inventions of the 20th Century (Survey of Current Business).

BEA (2009.4), Concepts and Methods of the U.S. Input-Output Accounts.

BEA (2022.12), Concepts and Methods of the U.S. National Income and Product Accounts.

Canada Statistics (2000.4), Current price value of changes in inventories of output: Sub-annual and annual totals, Joint ECE/Eurostat/OECD Meeting on National Accounts.

Eurostat (2000), Manual on the Economic Accounts for Agriculture and Forestry (rev. 1.1).

Eurostat (2008), Eurostat Manual of Supply, Use and Input-Output Tables.

Eurostat (2010), European System of Accounts.

Eurostat, European Central Bank (2011), Technical Compilation Guide for Pension Data in National Accounts.

Eurostat (2013), Handbook on Quarterly National Accounts.

Eurostat (2014), Manual on Goods Sent Abroad for Processing.

Eurostat and OECD (2015), Compilation Guide on Land Estimation.

Eurostat (2016), Handbook on Prices and Volume Measures in National Accounts.

Eurostat and OECD (2017), Compilation Guide on Inventories.

Eurostat (2018), Handbook on Seasonal Adjustment.

ILO et al. (2004), Consumer Price Index Manual: Theory and Practice.

IMF (2001), Quarterly National Accounts Manual: Concepts, Data Sources, Compilation.

IMF (2004), Producer Price Index Manual: Theory and Practice.

IMF (2007), The System of Macroeconomic Accounts Statistics: An Overview.

IMF (2009), Balance of Payments and International Investment Position Manual (BPM 6th).

IMF et al. (2009), Export and Import Price Index Manual: Theory and Practice.

IMF (2014), Government Finance Statistics Manual 2014.

IMF (2016), Monetary and Financial Statistics Manual and Compilation Guide.

IMF (2017), Measure up: A Better Way to Calculate GDP, IMF staff discussion note.

IMF (2017), Quarterly National Accounts Manual (pre-publication).

IMF et al. (2020), Consumer Price Index Manual: Concepts and Methods.

Ministry of Data and Statistics, Republic of Korea, Korean Statistical Information Service (https://kosis.kr).

OECD (2001), Measuring Capital: OECD Manual (1st edition).

OECD (2002), Measuring the Non-Observed Economy: A Handbook.

OECD (2009), Measuring Capital: OECD Manual (2nd edition).

OECD (2010), Handbook on Deriving Capital Measures of Intellectual Property Products.

OECD (2015), Frascati Manual.

OECD (2023), Handbook on Compiling Digital Supply and Use Tables

OECD (2025), Measuring natural resources in the national accounts: a compilation guide.

UN (1968), A System of National Accounts.

UN (1986), Handbook of National Accounting, Accounting for Production: Sources and methods.

UN et al. (1993), System of National Accounts.

UN (1999), Handbook of Input-Output Table Compilation and Analysis.

UN (2000), Classification of Expenditure According to Purpose: COFOG, COICOP, COPNI, COPP, (Statistical Paper Series M No. 84).

UN (2000), Links Between Business Accounting and National Accounting.

UN (2002), Use of Macro Accounts in Policy Analysis.

UN (2003), Handbook on Non-Profit Institutions in the System of National Accounts.

UN et al. (2008), System of National Accounts.

UN (2010), International Merchandise Trade Statistics: Concepts and Definitions.

UN et al. (2010), Manual on Statistics of International Trade in Services 2010 (MSITS 2010).

UN (2016), Classification by Broad Economic Categories Rev.5

UN (2017), Handbook on Supply, Use and Input-Output Tables with Extensions and Applications.

UN (2024), International Standard Industrial Classification of All Economic Activities (Revision 5).

UN (2024), Central Product Classification (CPC) Version 3.0

UN et al. (2025), System of National Accounts.

UNECE (2011), The Impact of Globalization on National Accounts.

Viet Vu (2009.12), GDP by Production approach: A general introduction with emphasis on an integrated economic data collection framework.

Viet Vu (2011.5), GDP by Final expenditure approach: An operational guide for using commodity flow approach.

World Bank (2013), Measuring the Real Size of the World Economy: The Framework, Methodology, and Results of the International Comparison Program.

WTO et al. (2023), Handbook on Measuring Digital Trade

Index

accounts in volume terms, 6

accrual basis, 195, 395

accumulation accounts, 5, 200

acquisitions less disposals of valuables, 14, 110, 282

actual final consumption, 94, 97, 100, 229, 235, 340, 342, 348

additivity, 491

adjusted disposable income, 229, 231

adjustment for the change in pension entitlements, 232, 247, 256, 269, 343, 418, 429

age-efficiency function, 578, 588

age-price function, 579, 582, 589

derivation, 580

allocation of earned income account, 214

Almon method, 625

ancillary activities, 36

annual overlap (AO) technique, 547

annuities, 243, 426

backward linkage, 651, 681

balance on goods and services, 353

balance sheets, 6, 200, 324, 328

balancing item, 6, 197, 200, 201, 203, 354

bank interest, 405

basic price, 24, 27, 28

benchmarking, 543

benchmark-to-indicator (BI) ratio, 543

biological resources, non-cultivated, 288

Broad Economic Categories (BEC), 152

calendar effect, 561

capital account, 273

capital external balance, 277

capital flow table, 105

capital services, 579, 596

capital stocks and capital services tables, 7

capital taxes, 16, 22, 226, 227

Capital taxes, 294

capital transfers, 227, 276, 293

central bank, 403

Central Product Classification (CPC), 120

chain index, 488, 520, 535

chain volume measures (CVM), 492, 535

change of ownership, 48, 374

changes in inventories, 59, 106, 281, 399

estimation, 110, 148

types, 106

valuation, 108

changes in net worth, 202, 276, 312, 325

changes in net worth due to nominal holding gains or losses, 316

CIF/FOB adjustment, 29, 51, 73, 134, 375

claims, adjusted, 419

Classification of Functions of Government (COFOG), 98

Classification of Individual Consumption According to Purpose (COICOP), 95

Classification of the Purposes of Non-profit Institutions Serving Households (COPNI), 100

collective consumption expenditure, 97

column totals, 613

computer software, 443

consolidation, 200

constant prices, 472

consumer price indices (CPIs), 522

contracts, leases and licences, 289

Contribution to the GDP growth, 540

corporation, 179

costs of ownership transfer, 86, 102, 280

cross-classification table by industries and institutional sectors (CCIS), 8, 177, 191

crypto assets with a corresponding liability designed to act as a medium of exchange, 304

crypto assets without a corresponding liability, 290

current account, 200, 210

current external balance, 233, 277, 353

current prices, 472

current taxes on income, wealth, etc., 16

current transfers, 225, 227

data and databases, 447

debt securities, 305

declining-balance method, 580

deductible VAT, 20

defined benefits, 253

defined contributions, 253

deflation method, 473

depletion, 117, 291

depletion borne by legal owners, 215

depreciation, 13, 117

definition, 284

derivation, 600
digital products, 457
disposable income, 225
distributable income, 220, 221, 251
distribution margin, 161, 397
definition, 76
distribution margin adjustment, 78
distribution margin table, 162
distribution structure, 122, 647
dividends, 219
domestic output, 47
domestic use table, 160
double deflation method, 506
double-entry accounting, 197
dwelling services, 431
earned income, 214, 215, 237
earned income accounts, 212
e-commerce platforms, 401
economic ownership, 196
efficiency function, 584
employment-related schemes, 244, 256
entrepreneurial income, 224, 240, 251
entrepreneurial income account, 240
equity and investment fund shares, 306
establishment, 35, 38, 177
expenditure approach, 31
expenditure basis versus acquisition basis, 341
export and import price indices (XMPIs), 523
export taxes, 17
exports, 14, 72, 111, 134
extended accounts, 7
factoryless goods production (FGP), 371
farm-gate price, 391
final consumption expenditure, 14, 91, 140
general government, 96
households, 92
NPISHs, 99
financial account, 298
financial assets, classification, 297
financial intermediation services indirectly measured (FISIM), 219, 385, 404
financial statements, 462
financial transactions, 198
FISIM, allocation, 410
fixed industry sales structure assumption (FISS), 615

fixed product sales structure assumption (FPSS), 615
flows, 194
forward linkage, 651, 681
Frascati Manual, 439
free online platforms, 459
free software, 460
GDP deflator, 540
GDP growth rate, 540
GDP in real terms, 518
general government, 181
generation of earned income account, 212
Ghosh inverse, 655
gold accounts, 302
gold bullion, 299, 302
goods and services account, 30, 204
goods sent abroad for processing, 352, 366
government account, 333
government expenditure (or outlay), 335
government revenue, 334
gross capital formation, 13, 515
    types, 101
gross capital stock, 593
gross domestic product, 31, 210, 237
gross fixed capital formation, 13, 278
    estimation, 143
    types, 101
gross national disposable income (GNDI), 226
gross national income (GNI), 216, 237
gross operating surplus, 32, 115
gross system, 21
gross value added, 31, 112, 115
head offices and holding companies, 453
hedonic price index, 499
holding gains and losses, 62
household expenditure survey, 140
household survey method, 93
household unincorporated enterprises, 93, 185
hybrid technology assumption method, 626
import duties, 17
import taxes, 17
imports, 13, 29, 47, 134
imports distribution survey, 168
imports use table, 160
imputation, 248

income approach, 33
income on equity, 237, 240
income transfers other than transfers in kind account, 225
income, concept, 236
index numbers, 475
individual consumption expenditure, 97
industry, 36
industry technology assumption (ITA), 612
input coefficient table, 611
input coefficients, 649
input cost survey, 122, 136
input VAT, 19
input-output table, 605, 644
  industry-by-industry, 609
  product-by-product, 607
institutional sector, 37, 179
institutional sectoring, 190
institutional sectors, 5, 35
institutional unit, 35, 36, 178
intellectual property products, 146
interest, 219
intermediate consumption, 13, 88
  estimation, 136
  types, 89
  valuation, 89
international accounts, 349
international investment position (IIP), 386
International Standard Industrial Classification (ISIC), 120
inventory valuation adjustment, 63
investment income, 237
investment income disbursements, 252
invoiced VAT, 20
labour market tables, 6
land, 286
land improvements, 279
Laspeyres and Paasche indices, 481
Leontief inverse, 651, 656, 666
Leontief matrix, 651, 665
Leontief multiplier, 606
life insurance, 242, 417
loans, 304
make matrix, 616
manual adjustment, 629
margin service, 76, 397
marginal totals, 128
market and non-market output, mixed

production, 65
market output, 39, 58
merchanting, 351, 360, 363
military equipment, 451
mineral and energy resources, 286
mineral exploration and evaluation, 450
monetary gold, 302
natural resources, 285
net capital stock, 597
net domestic product, 31
net lending/net borrowing, 354
net lending/net borrowing, 276
net operating balance, 335
net system, 21
netting, 199
neutral holding gains and losses, 322
nominal holding gains and losses, 317
non-deductible VAT, 20
non-financial assets, classification, 273
non-life insurance, 243, 417
non-life insurance technical reserves, 307
non-margin service, 76, 397
non-market output, 39, 64
non-produced assets, 273, 285
non-profit institutions, 181
non-profit institutions serving households (NPISHs), 190, 345
notional resident unit, 184, 257
one-quarter overlap (QO) technique, 551
operating surplus and mixed income, 115
other changes in assets and liabilities account, 311
other changes in the volume of assets and liabilities account, 311
other flows, 194
other import taxes, 17
other subsidies on production, 23, 114
other taxes on production, 114
other taxes on products, 17
output, 12, 38, 57
estimation, 130
output coefficients, 614, 649
output for own final use, 40, 67
output VAT, 19
output, gross, 61
output, usable, 61
over-the-year technique, 553
own-account production, 67
own-account software, 147

partitioning of a transaction, 257
pay-as-you-go basis, 427
pension contributions, net, 429
pension entitlements, 307
pension schemes, 246
present value of efficiency method, 584, 585
price index, 477
price index, Lowe, 477
price model for input-output analysis, 685
price relatives, 478
primary products, 35
produced assets, 273
producer price indices (PPIs), 523
producer's price, 25
product balance, 30
product balance identity, 28, 129
product basis and trader basis, 134
product flow method, 94
product technology assumption (PTA), 612
production, 10
production account, 210
production approach, 31
production boundary, 10
production units, 176
productive capital stock, 579, 595
property income, 218, 237
proportional Denton method, 544
pro-rata distribution method, 543
provisions for calls under standardized guarantees, 307
public sector, 186
purchased goodwill and marketing assets, 290
purchaser's price, 25
quadruple-entry accounting, 197
RAS method, 695
real GNI, expenditure side, 537
real gross domestic income (real GDI), 529
real gross national income (real GNI), 529
real holding gains and losses, 323
real terms, 473
reallocation, 629, 631
redefinition, 629, 631
reference period, 475
reference period, index, 480
reference period, weight, 480
reference rate, 404

reinvested earnings on foreign direct investment, 221, 250

reinvestment of earnings, 308

remuneration of employees, 32, 112

rent, 218, 223, 237

rental, 601

requirements, 652

requirements matrix

- domestic output, 666
- emission, 673
- employment, 672
- imports, 667
- taxes less subsidies, 670
- value added, 669

requirements, imports, 663

requirements, total, 653

research and development (R&D), 435

residence, 33

resource lease, 285

resource rent, 116, 224

rest of the world, 202

rest of the world account, 200, 390

retail sales method, 94

retained earnings, 241

retirement function, 576

revaluation account, 316

row totals, 613

saving, 232

savings ratio, 233

seasonal adjustment, 562

- additive and multiplicative model, 564
- Indirect and direct adjustment, 569

seasonal factors, 557

seasonal filter, 559

seasonality, 556

secondary products, 35, 605

sequence of economic accounts, 200

SNA interest, 405

social accounting matrix (SAM), 295

social assistance benefits in cash, 262

social benefits, 226, 246

- types, 263

social contributions, 246, 258

social contributions, actual, 259

social contributions, imputed, 259

social contributions, net, 226, 259

social insurance schemes, 244

social security schemes, 244, 256
social transfers in kind, 230, 239
social transfers in kind account, 229
special drawing rights (SDRs), 303
split-asset approach, 224, 287
stablecoins with a claim on the issuer, 305
standardized guarantee schemes, 429
statistical discrepancy, 355
step problem, 543
stocks, 194
straight-line method, 581
subsidies on products, 23, 66, 85
sum of costs method, 36, 147, 339
super dividends, 220
superlative indices, 485
supply and use tables, 8, 45
    balancing procedure, 125
    compilation by product flow method, 152
    compilation of non-benchmark years, 149
    example, 174
supply table, example, 86
taxes and subsidies, 15
taxes less subsidies on products,
    extraction, 164
taxes on production and imports, 16
taxes on products, 16, 84
thematic and extended accounts, 4
Törnqvist price index, 485
total requirements table, 656
    types, 660
total supply, 11, 28
total use, 11, 29
trading gains and losses from changes in the terms of trade, 529
transactions, 194
transfer income, 239
transferable deposits, 304
transport cost, 79, 82
transport margin, 79, 81
    definition, 79
    extraction, 163
transport margin adjustment, 82
travel agency industry, 455
undistributed income, 251
unincorporated enterprises, 183
unit value index, 503
usable output, 392

use of adjusted disposable income account, 234

use of disposable income account, 232

use of income accounts, 232

use table, 48, 55

components, 88

example, 118

use table at basic prices, 158, 166

value added tax, 17

value index, 476

VAT-exempt entities, 20

VAT-exempt goods or services, 165

volume and quantity, 502

volume index, 476

volume terms, 472

Winfrey distribution, 577

withdrawal of income from a quasi-corporation, 220

Young index, 480

zero-rated goods, 165

About the Author

Yong-Gil CHO is a national accounts expert with decades of experience in the development, compilation, and analysis of national accounts statistics. He has held positions in both national and international organizations, including secondments to the **U.S. Bureau of Economic Analysis** (2001–2002) and the **OECD Statistics Directorate** (2003–2006), where he further strengthened his expertise and contributed to advancing national accounting methodologies and frameworks.

As a consultant to the **Asian Development Bank** (2017–2018), he played a key role in supporting the compilation of Myanmar's national accounts, working closely with national statistical authorities to establish robust and internationally consistent accounting frameworks. He has also made significant methodological contributions during his career at the **Bank of Korea**, particularly in the areas of national accounts compilation and statistical development.

His work reflects a strong commitment to both the theoretical foundations and practical implementation of national accounts. Drawing on extensive hands-on experience, he has contributed to improving compilation practices and strengthening statistical capacity. This handbook reflects his longstanding dedication to supporting national accounts compilers and providing practical guidance for the implementation of internationally recommended standards.

www.ingramcontent.com/pod-product-compliance
Lightning Source LLC
LaVergne TN
LVHW060214210926
848481LV00009B/2743
* 9 7 9 1 1 9 9 0 8 2 1 0 6 *